"Value-packed, accurate, and comprehensive..."

—Los Angeles Times

"Unbeatable..."

—The Washington Post

Let's Go
MEXICO

is the best book for anyone traveling on a budget. Here's why:

■ **No other guidebook has as many budget listings.**

Take Mexico City, for example. We found 11 places to stay for under $15 a night. We tell you how to get there the cheapest way, whether by bus, plane, or bike, and where to get an inexpensive and satisfying meal once you've arrived. We give hundreds of money-saving tips that anyone can use, plus invaluable advice on discounts and deals for students, children, families, and senior travelers.

■ Let's Go **researchers have to make it on their own.**

Our Harvard-Radcliffe researcher-writers travel on budgets as tight as your own—no expense accounts, no free hotel rooms.

■ Let's Go **is completely revised each year.**

We don't just update the prices, we go back to the place. If a charming café has become an overpriced tourist trap, we'll replace the listing with a new and better one.

■ **No other guidebook includes all this:**

Honest, engaging coverage of both the cities and the countryside; up-to-the-minute prices, directions, addresses, phone numbers, and opening hours; in-depth essays on local culture, history, and politics; comprehensive listings on transportation between and within regions and cities; straight advice on work and study, budget accommodations, sights, nightlife, and food; detailed city and regional maps; and much more.

■ Let's Go **is for anyone who wants to see Mexico, Belize, Guatemala, Costa Rica, and Nicaragua on a budget.**

Books by Let's Go, Inc.

EUROPE

Let's Go: Europe

Let's Go: Austria

Let's Go: Britain & Ireland

Let's Go: France

Let's Go: Germany & Switzerland

Let's Go: Greece & Turkey

Let's Go: Ireland

Let's Go: Italy

Let's Go: London

Let's Go: Paris

Let's Go: Rome

Let's Go: Spain & Portugal

NORTH & CENTRAL AMERICA

Let's Go: USA & Canada

Let's Go: Alaska & The Pacific Northwest

Let's Go: California & Hawaii

Let's Go: New York City

Let's Go: Washington, D.C.

Let's Go: Mexico

MIDDLE EAST & ASIA

Let's Go: Israel & Egypt

Let's Go: Thailand

Let's Go

The Budget Guide to

MEXICO 1994

Michael Kai Ng
Editor

Sarthak Das
Assistant Editor

Written by
Let's Go, Inc.
A subsidiary of
Harvard Student Agencies, Inc.

St. Martin's Press ■ New York

HELPING LET'S GO

If you have suggestions or corrections, or just want to share your discoveries, drop us a line. We read every piece of correspondence, whether a 10-page letter, a velveteen Elvis postcard, or, as in one case, a collage. All suggestions are passed along to our researcher-writers. Please note that mail received after May 5, 1994 will probably be too late for the 1995 book, but will be retained for the following edition. Address mail to:

Let's Go: Mexico
Let's Go, Inc.
1 Story Street
Cambridge, MA 02138
USA

In addition to the invaluable travel advice our readers share with us, many are kind enough to offer their services as researchers or editors. Unfortunately, the charter of Let's Go, Inc. and Harvard Student Agencies, Inc. enables us to employ only currently enrolled Harvard students.

Distributed outside the U.S. and Canada by Pan Macmillan Ltd.

ISBN: 0-312-09853-7

First edition
10 9 8 7 6 5 4 3 2 1

Let's Go: **Mexico** is written by the Publishing Division of Let's Go, Inc., 1 Story Street, Cambridge, MA 02138.

Printed in the U.S.A. on recycled paper with biodegradable soy ink.

Editor — Michael Kai Ng
Assistant Editor — Sarthak Das
Managing Editor — Jonathan Taylor
Publishing Director — Mark N. Templeton
Production Manager — Edward Owen
Office Coordinator — Susan P. Krause
Assistant General Manager — Anne E. Chisholm

Researcher-Writers

Costa Rica; near Oaxaca; Chiapas and Tabasco states — Gabriela Carrión

Yucatán Peninsula; Belize — Sarah Dry

Guanajuato, Querétaro, San Luis Potosí, Zacatecas, Nayarit, Jalisco, and Michoacán states — Nadia Herman

Baja California; northwest Mexico — Allen Hutcheson

Northeast Mexico; northern Veracruz state; Puebla; Pachuca; Tula; Cuernavaca; Taxco; Mexico City, D.F. — Plamen Russev

Nicaragua; southern Veracruz state; Tlaxcala; Cholula; Oaxaca state (except near Oaxaca) — David J.C. Shafer

Sales Group Manager — Swati Y. Rao
Sales Group Assistant Manager — Paul Kyong Hwan Kim
Sales Group Representatives — Jonathan N. Adolph, Wendy A. Gribb, Ashley Hubka, Carolyn B. Rendell, Tara E. Walpert

President — Martín E. Escobari
General Manager — Richard M. Olken

Acknowledgments

An entire summer of shifting fonts and, as one of our researchers wrote, "adjusting the price of pork tortas in Tijuana," has left just enough creative juices puddled at the bottom of our crania to eke out this final and wholly inadequate note of gratitude to all those who have helped us in our endeavor. First and foremost, thanks goes to the researcher-writers, underappreciated and underpaid. This book is theirs. Fortunately for us, **Gabriela Carrión** stuck out in the interviewing process. Her sensual descriptions of Costa Rica and cultural insights in southern Mexico have been invaluable contributions to this book. **Sarah Dry** weathered the commercialism of Cancún, waded through the flooded streets of Mérida, and peeked under every Mayan stone on the entire Yucatán Peninsula. After suffering the almost-unbearable heat for weeks, she rewarded herself with a Red Stripe or two on the Belizian Cayes, and rewarded us with action-packed copybatches. **Nadia Herman** turned in a solid performance in the Guadalajara region, surviving a hurricane and Puerto Vallarta.

Allen Hutcheson wrote in Chihuahua (¡Ay!), "I have great respect for anyone who can write anything besides the straight facts on the road." The man should then have a tremendous amount of self-respect—his perfectly deadpan humor kept us rolling at every turn of the page. **Plamen Russev** sent back volumes, undaunted by Mexico City and its environs. His detailed research set the standard for thoroughness for the entire series. Weeks into his original itinerary, **David Shafer** volunteered to venture down to Nicaragua, new territory uncharted by *Let's Go.* With minimal preparation and only a few supplies, David produced an incredibly complete and complex section. Only the Corn Islands eluded him, casting doubt on their existence.

The eleventh *avatar* of Vishnu and our mentor, Jonathan Taylor, cannot be thanked enough for his tireless efforts. His late nights, intelligent commentary, and seamless coordination have won our unending respect. Ed's patience with our computer ineptitude ran as deep as the *Barrancas del Cobre.* Thanks, too, to the JT group's toleration of our music, humor, and early deadline. The work of many others around the office and around the world are contained in these pages: Sue Krause, Sidney Chen, Anna More and roommates, World Teach, Ileana Ricci, Leda Nemor, sales group, and the residents of San Blas.

I would like to thank Sarthak Das for keeping my mind healthy while erasing ",000" over and over again. You have an amazing gift of insight that I know will never be wasted. I would also like to thank my entire family, Andy, Vania, Min Ji, Chris, Kevin, Charlie, Tasha, Bunchai, Min Yung, Mary, Barry, Mom, and Dad; my summer roomates (esp. Ashley for the daily report); Kochi, Stipe, Mikane, the Krush, WCSR, and Garen; and Marina for extending the reaches of understanding. Finally, thanks to the whole *Let's Go* crew for a thoroughly entertaining spring and summer.

— MKN

Before anyone else, I would first like to thank Mike Ng for tolerating my ignorance about Mexico, my trip to Cancún, and my distracting chatter. Your great candor and openness has produced not only a great book but also a friendship. and your love for others and desire to give have earned my deep respect. I would also like to thank my school-year roommates. Thank you Maitri for your ability to listen. Thanks Sujatha for understanding me for two summers now—I know you'll succeed in the Bay area and beyond, besides you'll have baba and a ghanoush. Thanks also to my sister Sarba and dog PeeWee. Finally, I thank most of all my parents for instilling me with my love of travel, supporting me, and allowing me the opportunity to see so much already. This book is dedicated to you Ma and Baba, I love you both very much indeed!

— SD

Contents

Maps

About Let's Go

Back in 1960, a few students at Harvard got together to produce a 20-page pamphlet offering a collection of tips on budget travel in Europe. For three years, Harvard Student Agencies, a student-run nonprofit corporation, had been doing a brisk business booking charter flights to Europe; this modest, mimeographed packet was offered to passengers as an extra. The following year, students traveling to Europe researched the first full-fledged edition of *Let's Go: Europe*, a pocket-sized book featuring advice on shoestring travel, irreverent write-ups of sights, and a decidedly youthful slant.

Throughout the 60s, the guides reflected the times: one section of the 1968 *Let's Go: Europe* talked about "Street Singing in Europe on No Dollars a Day." During the 70s, *Let's Go* gradually became a large-scale operation, adding regional European guides and expanding coverage into North Africa and Asia. The 80s saw the arrival of *Let's Go: USA & Canada* and *Let's Go: Mexico*, as well as regional North American guides; in the 90s we introduced five in-depth city guides to Paris, London, Rome, New York, and Washington, DC.

This year we're proud to announce three new guides: *Let's Go: Austria* (including Prague and Budapest), *Let's Go: Ireland*, and *Let's Go: Thailand* (including Honolulu, Tokyo, and Singapore), bringing our total number of titles up to twenty.

We've seen a lot in thirty-four years. *Let's Go: Europe* is now the world's #1 best selling international guide, translated into seven languages. And our guides are still researched, written, and produced entirely by students who know first-hand how to see the world on the cheap.

Every spring, we recruit nearly 100 researchers and an editorial team of 50 to write our books anew. Come summertime, after several months of training, researchers hit the road for seven weeks of exploration, from Bangkok to Budapest, Anchorage to Ankara. With pen and notebook in hand, a few changes of underwear stuffed in our backpacks, and a budget as tight as yours, we visit every *pensione*, *palapa*, pizzeria, café, club, campground, or castle we can find to make sure you'll get the most out of *your* trip.

We've put the best of our discoveries into the book you're now holding. A brand-new edition of each guide hits the shelves every year, only months after it was researched, so you know you're getting the most reliable, up-to-date, and comprehensive information available. And even as you read this, work on next year's editions is well underway.

At *Let's Go*, we think of budget travel not only as a means of cutting down on costs, but as a way of breaking down a few walls as well. Living cheap and simple on the road brings you closer to the real people and places you've been saving up to visit. This book will ease your anxieties and answer your questions about the basics—to help *you* get off the beaten track and explore. We encourage you to put *Let's Go* away now and then and strike out on your own. As any seasoned traveler will tell you, the best discoveries are often those you make yourself. If you find something worth sharing, drop us a line and let us know. We're at Let's Go, Inc., 1 Story Street, Cambridge, MA, 02138, USA.

Happy travels!

How To Use This Book

The purpose of this book is not to hold your hand, but rather to facilitate your independent exploration of Mexico, Belize, Costa Rica, Guatemala, and Nicaragua. In place of planned itineraries, you will find the nitty-gritty information you need to develop your own. Our researchers have been crawling over every inch of the region for over a decade, discovering the best bargains and improving the listings contained here so that you, the budget traveler, can experience these countries from your own perspective, and hopefully refine that perspective.

The first pages of this book are dedicated to the **Essentials** section. This section contains sections on **Planning Your Trip, Getting There, Traveling in Mexico,** and **Life and Times.** The Essentials section gives information on general information which pertains to travel in the entire region covered by this book, not just a specific area. "Planning Your Trip" includes sections on **Climate, Useful Organizations, Documents and Formalities** (including information on visas and passports), **Customs, Money, Packing, Safety and Security, Health, Insurance, Alternatives to Tourism, Keeping in Touch** and subsections regarding **Women and Travel, Older Travelers, Travelers with Disabilities,** and **Bisexual, Gay, and Lesbian Travelers.** "Getting There" covers various modes of transportation to Mexico with listings of discount ticket agents. "Traveling in Mexico" is an overview of Mexico **By Plane, By Train, By Bus, By Car** and **By Thumb,** and a preview of coming attractions in **Accommodations,** including **Hotels, Hostels,** and **Camping.** "Life and Times" takes a brief look at Mexico's history and culture. Belize, Costa Rica, Guatemala and Nicaragua each have a similar introductory section with information specific to that country; for more general travel information refer back to the Mexico Essentials section.

This Mexico section of this book is organized geographically, beginning with Mexico City and then moving southeast from Baja California, through Northwest Mexico, Northeast Mexico, Central Mexico, El Bajío, Southern Mexico, to the Yucatán Peninsula. Coverage of Belize, Guatemala, Costa Rica, and Nicaragua follows in that order. This book also contains a glossary and an appendix on language.

Each city or town is further divided. The introduction, meant to convey a sense of the city, its culture, and its history, is followed by **Orientation,** which describes the geography and layout of the city. Orientation is often integrated into **Practical Information,** which also lists essential schedules, offices, addresses, and phone numbers. **Accommodations, Food, Sights,** and **Entertainment** are, or should be, self-explanatory. The listings we feel are the best bargains, that is, the most for the money, are given first. Food listings are weighted towards restaurants which are difficult to locate or unusual, like vegetarian restaurants, since no one in Mexico needs a guidebook to find a cheap *típico* taco stand.

A NOTE TO OUR READERS

The information for this book is gathered by *Let's Go*'s researchers during the late spring and summer months. Each listing is derived from the assigned researcher's opinion based upon his or her visit at a particular time. The opinions are expressed in a candid and forthright manner. Other travelers might disagree. Those traveling at a different time may have different experiences since prices, dates, hours, and conditions are always subject to change. You are urged to check beforehand to avoid inconvenience and surprises. Travel always involves a certain degree of risk, especially in low-cost areas. When traveling, especially on a budget, you should always take particular care to ensure your safety.

Essentials

PLANNING YOUR TRIP

CLIMATE

The Tropic of Cancer bisects Mexico into a temperate north and tropical south, but the climate varies considerably even within these belts. For each of the geographic divisions used in this book, very general climate conditions hold true. **Northwest Mexico,** including Baja California, is the driest area of the country, but still offers a unique array of desert flora and fauna, while the **Northeast** is a bit more temperate. Pleasant beaches are scattered on the **Gulf Coast** although they do not compare with the beauty of those elsewhere in Mexico. The central region north of Mexico City, known as the **Bajío,** and **South Central Mexico** both experience the cooler climates of the highlands as well as coastal warmth. Natural beauty extends from world-famous beaches to inland forests. Lush, green jungles obscure ruins of the ancient civilizations of the **Yucatán Peninsula.**

The rainy season lasts from May until October (with a hurricane season in the south Aug.-Oct.). The southern half of the country averages over 100 in. per year (75% of that during the rainy season), so a summer vacation is likely to be on the damp side. Exhaustive statistics on climate are available in a chart compiled by the International Association for Medical Assistance to Travelers (IAMAT) (see Health below).

USEFUL ORGANIZATIONS

Government Agencies

Embassy of Mexico, 1911 Pennsylvania Ave. NW, Washington, DC 20006 (tel. (202) 728-1600); in the **U.K.,** 42 Hertford St., Mayfair, London W1 (tel. 071 499-85-86, fax 071 495-40-35); in **Canada,** 130 Albert St. #1800, Ottawa, Ont. K1P 5G4 (tel. (613) 233-8988); in **Australia,** 14 Perth Ave., Yarralumla, 2600 Canberra (tel. (+61 6) 273-3905 or 273-3947, fax 273-1190).

Consulate of Mexico, 1019 19th St. NW, #810, Washington, DC 20036 (tel. (202) 736-1000); in **Canada,** 60 Bloor St. W #203, Toronto, Ont. M4W 3B8 (tel. (416) 922-2718); in the **U.K.,** 8 Halkin St., London SW1 X7DW (tel. (+44 71) 235-63-93); in **Australia,** 135-153 New South Head Rd., Edgecliff, Sydney 2027 NSW (tel. (+61 2 326-1311 or 326-1292, fax +61 2 327-1110).

Mexican Government Tourism Office (Secretaría de Turismo or **SECTUR):** In the **U.S.,** 405 Park Ave. #1402, New York, NY 10022 (tel. (212) 838-2949 or 755-4756; fax 753-2874; 24-hr. information tel. (800) 262-8900); 10100 Santa Monica Blvd. #224, Los Angeles, CA 90067 (tel. (310) 203-8191, fax 203-8316); 128 Aragon Ave., Coral Gable, FL 33134 (tel. (305) 443-9160, fax 443-1186); 70 E. Lake St. #1413, Chicago, Illinois 60601-5977 (tel. (312) 606-9015, fax 606-9012); 2707 N. Loop W. #450, Houston, TX 77008 (tel. (713) 880-5153, fax 880-1833); 1911 Pennsylvania Ave., Washington, DC 20036 (tel. (202) 728-1750, fax 728-1758); in **Canada,** 2 Floor St. W #1801, Toronto, Ont. M4W 3E2 (tel. (416) 925-0704, fax 925-6061) or 1 Place Ville Marie, #2409, Montreal, Qc. H3B 3M9 (tel. (514) 871-1052, fax 871-3825), 1610-999 West Hastings Ave., Vanvcouver, B.C. V6C 2W2; in **Germany**, Wiessenhuttenplatz 26, D 6000 Frankfurt Am Main 1 (tel. (4969) 25-3413, 25-3541, fax 25-3755); in **Japan**, 2-15-1 Nagata-Cho., Chiyoda-Ku, Tokyo 100 (tel. (813) 580-2962, fax 581-5539); in the **U.K.,** 60/61 Trafal-

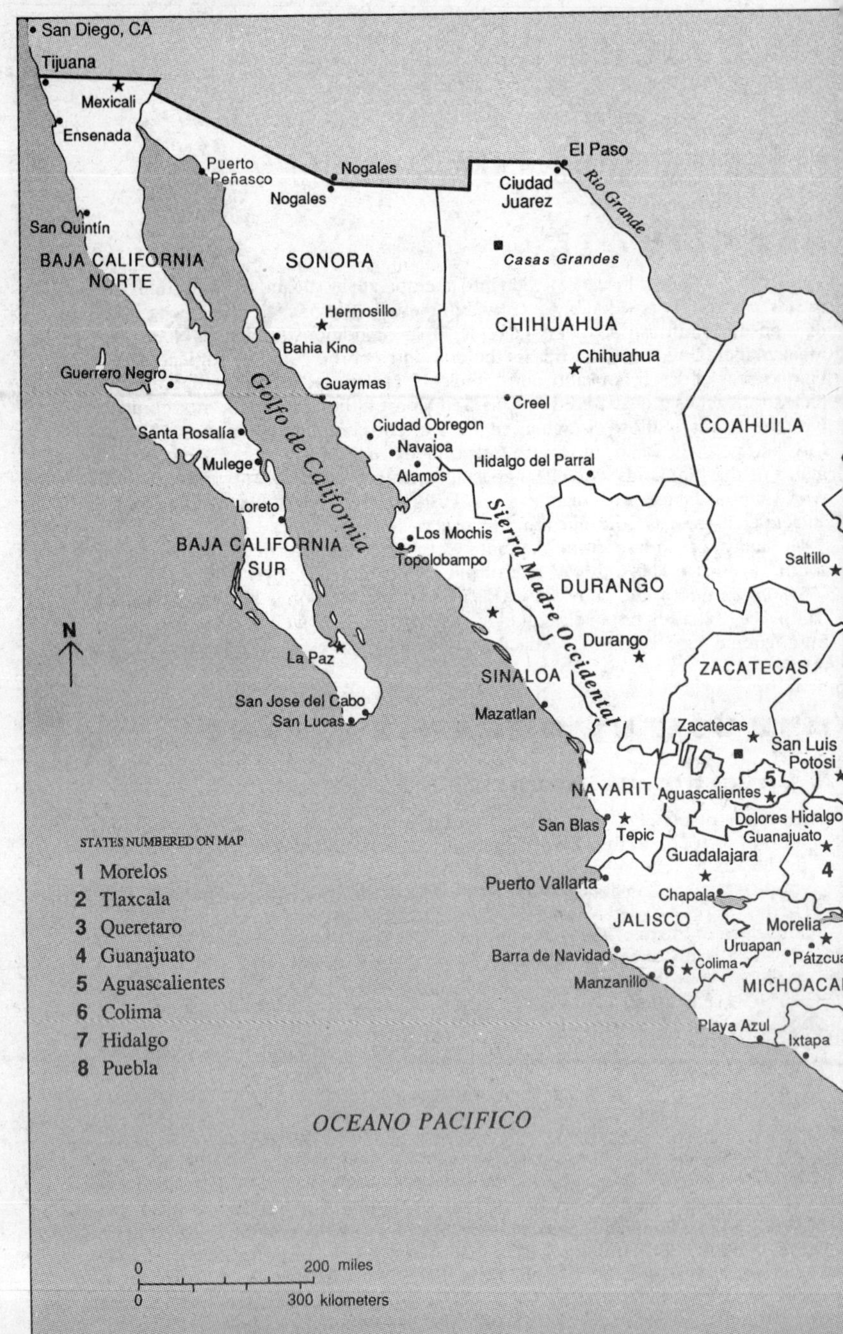
San Diego, CA
Tijuana
Mexicali
Ensenada
Puerto Peñasco
Nogales
Nogales
El Paso
Ciudad Juarez
Rio Grande
San Quintín
BAJA CALIFORNIA NORTE
SONORA
Casas Grandes
Hermosillo
CHIHUAHUA
Bahia Kino
Chihuahua
Guerrero Negro
Guaymas
Creel
Golfo de California
COAHUILA
Santa Rosalía
Ciudad Obregon
Navajoa
Mulege
Alamos
Hidalgo del Parral
Loreto
Los Mochis
Sierra Madre Occidental
BAJA CALIFORNIA SUR
Topolobampo
Saltillo
DURANGO
La Paz
Durango
SINALOA
ZACATECAS
San Jose del Cabo
San Lucas
Mazatlan
Zacatecas
San Luis Potosi
5
NAYARIT
Aguascalientes
Dolores Hidalgo
San Blas
Tepic
Guanajuato
Guadalajara
4
Puerto Vallarta
Chapala
JALISCO
Morelia
Uruapan
Barra de Navidad
6
Colima
Manzanillo
MICHOACA
Playa Azul
Ixtapa
STATES NUMBERED ON MAP
1 Morelos
2 Tlaxcala
3 Queretaro
4 Guanajuato
5 Aguascalientes
6 Colima
7 Hidalgo
8 Puebla
OCEANO PACIFICO
0
200 miles
0
300 kilometers
N

Mexico
UNITED STATES OF AMERICA
Piedras Negras
Laredo
Nuevo Laredo
McAllen
Brownsville
Reynosa
Matamoros
Monterrey
Golfo de Mexico
NUEVO LEON
Sierra Madre Oriental
TAMAULIPAS
Tampico
SAN LUIS POTOSI
Isla Mujeres
Cancun
Mérida
Valladolid
YUCATAN
Chichen Itza
Isla Cozumel
Cobá
Uxmal
Campeche
San Miguel de Allende
7
Queretaro
3
Chicomoztoc
Pachuca
Tuxpan
Papantla
VERACRUZ
CAMPECHE
QUINTANA ROO
Mexico City
2
Tlaxcala
Jalapa
Chetumal
Toluca
8
Puebla
Veracruz
San Andrés Tuxtla
TABASCO
Escarcega
Cuernavaca
1
Taxco
Tehuacan
Catemaco
Villahermosa
Belize City
GUERRERO
Tuxtepec
Palenque
Tikal
Belmopan
Chilpancingo
OAXACA
Oaxaca
Mitla
San Cristobal de las Casas
Bonampak
BELIZE
Tuxtla Gutierrez
Acapulco
CHIAPAS
Comitan
Tehuantepec
Tonalá
Ciudad Cuauhtémoc
GUATEMALA
Puerto Escondido
Puerto Angel
HONDURAS
Tapachula
Guatemala City
Tegucigalpa
Antigua
San Salvador
EL SALVADOR

gar Sq., London WC2N 5DS (tel. (+44 71) 839 3177). Provides maps, information and tourist cards. Check your phone book for local offices. Also operates a 24-hr. hotline out of Mexico City (tel. (5) 250-01-23) for complaints, emergencies and less urgent information.

■ Travel Organizations

Council on International Educational Exchange (CIEE), 205 E. 42nd St., New York, NY 10017 (tel. (212) 661-1414; for charter flights (800) 223-7402, in New York (212) 661-1450). CIEE offers information on budget travel as well as educational, volunteer, and work opportunities around the world. CIEE also offers dicount fares on major airlines and issues ISICs (International Student Identity Cards) and International Youth Cards (for non-students under the age of 26). They publish *Work, Study, and Travel Abroad: The Whole World Handbook* ($10.95, postage $1) and *Volunteer! The Comprehensive Guide to Voluntary Service in the U.S. and Abroad* ($6.95, postage $1). Students should pick up the annual *Student Travel Catalog* for free at any CIEE office or send for one ($1 for postage and handling). Operates 56 **Council Travel** offices throughout the U.S., including those listed below and branches in Providence, RI; Amherst and Cambridge, MA; Berkeley, La Jolla, and Long Beach, CA. **Boston,** 729 Boylston St. #201, MA 02116 (617-266-1926). **Chicago,** 1153 N. Dearborn St., IL 60610 (312-951-0585). **Dallas,** 6923 Snider Plaza, B, TX 75205 (214-363-9941). **Los Angeles,** 1093 Broxton Ave. #220, CA 90024 (310-208-3551). **Portland,** 715 S.W. Morrison #600, OR 97205 (503-228-1900). **San Diego,** 953 Garnet Ave., CA 94108 (619-270-6401). **San Francisco,** 919 Irving St. #102, CA 94122 (415-566-6222). **Seattle,** 1314 N.E. 43rd St. #210, WA 98105 (206-632-2448).

STA Travel: In U.S., 17 E. 45th St., New York, NY 10017 (tel. (800) 777-0112 or (212) 986-9470). Operates 10 offices in the U.S. and over 100 worldwide. Offers discount airfares for travelers under 26 and full-time students under 32; sells ISICs, HI memberships, and Eurail passes. **Boston,** 273 Newbury St., MA 02116 (617-266-6014). **Los Angeles,** 7202 Melrose Ave., CA 90046 (213-934-8722). **New York,** 48 E. 11th St., NY 10003 (212-477-7166). **Philadelphia,** University City Travel, 3730 Walnut St., PA 19104 (215-382-2928). **San Francisco,** 51 Grant Ave., CA 94108 (415-391-8407). In **Great Britain,** 86 Old Brompton Rd., London SW7 3LQ and 117 Euston Rd., London NW1 2SX England (tel. (071) 937 9921 for European travel; (071) 937 9971 for North American; (071) 937 9962 for long haul travel; (071) 937 1733 for round the world travel). **In Australia,** 220 Faraday St., Melbourne, Victoria 3053 (tel. (03) 347 69 11). In **New Zealand,** 10 High St., Auckland (tel. (09) 309 9995).

Travel CUTS (Canadian Universities Travel Service), 187 College St., Toronto, Ont. M5T 1P7 (tel. (416) 979-2406). 35 offices throughout Canada. In Britain, 295-A Regent St., London W1R 7Y4 (tel. (071) 637-3161). Offers discounted flights with special student fares. Sells the ISIC, FIYTO, and HI hostel cards, and discount travel passes. The *Student Traveler* is available at all offices and campuses across Canada.

International Student Exchange Flights (ISE Flights), 5010 E. Shea Blvd., #A104, Scottsdale, AZ 85254 (tel. (602) 951-1177). Budget student flights, travelers' checks, and travel guides.

Campus Travel, 52 Grosvenor Gardens, London SW1W 0AG (tel. (071) 730 8832, fax (071) 730 5739). Offers special student and youth fares on travel by plane, train, boat and bus, as well as flexible airline tickets; discount and ID cards for youths; special insurance for students and those under 35; and maps and guides.

London Student Travel, 52 Grosvenor Gardens, London WC1 (tel. (071) 730 3402).

USIT Ltd., Aston Quay, O'Connell Bridge, Dublin 2 (tel. (01) 679 8833, fax (01) 677 8843).

Laughing Heart Adventures, P.O. Box 660, Willow Creek, CA 95573 (tel. (800) 541-1256 or (916) 629-3516). Offers 7-21 day packages in Baja, Barrancas del Cobre, and Belize. Trips range from backpacking and canoeing to whale-watching

to barrier reef snorkeling off Belize. Fees run US$80-150 per day and include meals, transportation, gear and accommodations.

Servicio Educativo de Turismo de los Estudiantes y la Juventud de México (SETEJ), Hamburgo 301, Col. Juárez, 06600 México D.F. (tel. (5) 211-07-43 or 211-66-36). Sells ISIC and FIYTO cards. Arranges group tours with Mexican students. Has information about hostels and budget hotels. Offers language courses and helps with domestic and international flights. See Accommodations below for hostel information.

■ Transportation Services

American Automobile Association (AAA), 1000 AAA Dr., Box 75, Heathrow, FL 32746-5063 (tel. (407) 444-7000). Sells road maps and travel guides. American Express traveler's checks commission-free for members. Issues Mexican auto insurance (see Getting There: By Car below). No routing service for Mexico.

Asociación Mexicana Automovilística, A.C. (AMA), Av. Orizaba 7, México, D.F. 06700 (tel. (5) 511-62-85). Write for up-to-date road maps and information about car travel in Mexico.

Asociación Nacional Automovilística (ANA), Oficinas ANA, José María Iglesias 59, México, D.F. 06470 (tel. (5) 705-05-01 or 705-10-01); emergency services Lerdo 361, Entre San Timor y Manuel González, México, D.F. 06470 (tel. (5) 597-42-83 or 597-19-62).

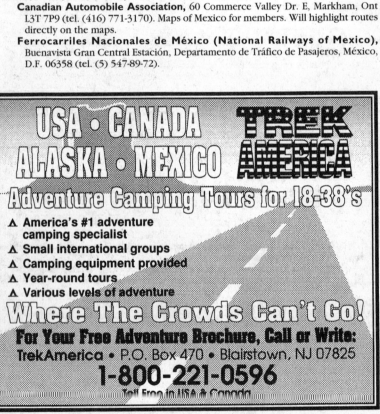

Canadian Automobile Association, 60 Commerce Valley Dr. E, Markham, Ont L3T 7P9 (tel. (416) 771-3170). Maps of Mexico for members. Will highlight routes directly on the maps.

Ferrocarriles Nacionales de México (National Railways of Mexico), Buenavista Gran Central Estación, Departamento de Tráfico de Pasajeros, México, D.F. 06358 (tel. (5) 547-89-72).

■ Publications

Adventures in Mexico (AIM), Apdo. 31-70, Guadalajara, Jalisco, 45050 México. Newsletter on retirement and travel in Mexico. Endearing approach to the country's quirks. Annual subscription (6 issues) costs US$16 or CDN$19. Personal checks accepted. Back issues, most of which are devoted to a single city or region, available for US$2 each.

Animal and Plant Health Inspection Service, 6505 Belcrest Rd., #G110, Hyattsville, MD 20782 (tel. (301) 436-8413). Gives information on the U.S. agriculture quarantine on certain food, plant and animal products. Write for free *Traveler's Tips* pamphlet.

Forsyth Travel Library, P.O. Box 2975, Shawnee Mission, KS 66201 (tel. (800) 367-7984). Mail-order maps and travel guides for Mexico. Write for a free newsletter and catalogue.

Wide World Books and Maps, 1911 N. 45th St., Seattle, WA 98103 (tel. (206) 634-3453). Open Mon.-Fri. 10am-7pm, Sat. 10am-6pm, Sun. noon-5pm. Wide selection of books about Mexico as well as hard to find maps of the country.

Hippocrene Books, Inc., 171 Madison Ave., New York, NY 10016 (tel. (212) 685-4371; orders (718) 454-2360, fax (718) 454-1391). Publishes travel reference books, travel guides, maps, and foreign language dictionaries. Free catalog.

Gateway Books, 13 Bedford Cove, San Rafael, CA 94901 (tel. (415) 454-5215, fax 454-1901). Publishes comprehensive *RV Travel in Mexico* (US$9.95) as well as guides to seasonal and retirement living in Latin America, like *Choose Mexico: Retire on $600 a Month* (US$10.95).

Hunter Publishing, 300 Raritan Center Parkway, Edison, NJ 08818 (tel. (908) 225-1900, fax 417-0482). Sells the exhaustive *Bicycling Mexico* (US$16.95 plus $2.50 shipping).

John Muir Publications, P.O. Box 613, Santa Fe, NM 87504 (tel. (800) 888-7504 or (505) 982-4078, fax 988-1680). Publishes the *Shopper's Guide to Mexico* (US$9.95) on the subject of folk art, the *People's Guide to Mexico* (US$17.95), which includes Belize and Guatemala, and the *People's Guide to RV Camping in Mexico* (US$13.95). Add US$3.75 shipping for one book, 50¢ for each additional book.

México Desconocido, Monte Pelvoux 110-104, Lomas de Chapultepec, México, D.F. 11000 (tel. (5) 202-65-85 or 259-09-39, fax 540-17-71). Monthly travel magazine in Spanish and English describing little-known areas and customs of Mexico. Write for information.

Superintendent of Documents, Washington, DC 20402 (tel. (202) 783-3238). Publishes *Your Trip Abroad* (US$1), *Safe Trip Abroad* (US$1), *Health Information for International Travel* (US$5), *Tips for Travelers to Mexico* (US$1) and *Tips for Travelers to Central and South America* (US$1). To order the latter two, call the Citizens Emergency Hotline at (202) 647-5225.

Travelling Books, P.O. Box 77114, Seattle, WA 98177 (tel. (206) 367-5848). Wide selection of handbooks and maps for Mexico, Guatemala, Belize and Costa Rica.

Wide World Books and Maps, 1911 N. 45th St., Seattle, WA 98103 (tel. (206) 634-3453). Wide selection of books about Mexico and hard-to-find maps of the country.

■■■ DOCUMENTS AND FORMALITIES

■ Tourist Cards

All foreigners in Mexico must carry a **tourist card (FMT,** Spanish for *folleto de migración turística*). Although cards are available at Mexican embassies, consulates and tourist offices (see Useful Addresses), most people pick them up when they cross the border or when they check in at the airline ticket counter for their flight into Mexico. On the FMT, you must indicate your intended destination and expected length of stay. If your financial condition looks suspect, you will be asked to prove that you have a return ticket. Finally, proof of citizenship is a necessity. Travelers from outside North America must present a passport. U.S. and Canadian citizens can obtain a tourist card with an original birth certificate or naturalization papers, plus some type of photo ID. But be forewarned: traveling in Mexico without a passport is asking for trouble. A passport carries much more authority with local officials than does a birth certificate. U.S. and Canadian citizens spending no more than three days in Mexico, if they remain in the duty-free border towns or ports, do not need tourist cards but still must carry proof of citizenship.

Tourist cards are valid for 90 or 180 days. Try to get a card that will be valid longer than your projected stay. It is easier to obtain a 180-day tourist card at the border than to extend a 90-day card or validate an expired card (which requires that you leave the country temporarily). If you do need an extension, visit a local office of the Delegación de Servicios Migratorios several weeks before your card expires. (They also take care of lost cards.) You must get a new FMT every time you re-enter the country even if your old one has not expired.

While in Mexico, you are required by law to carry your tourist card at all times. Make a photocopy and keep it in a separate place. Although it won't replace a lost or stolen tourist card, a copy should facilitate replacement. If you do lose your card, expect at least two hours of delay and bureaucratic inconvenience while immigration verifies your record of entrance.

■ Passports

As a precaution in case your passport is lost or stolen, be sure *before you leave* to photocopy the page of your passport that contains your photograph and identifying information. Especially important is your passport number. Carry this photocopy in a safe place apart from your passport, perhaps with a traveling companion, and leave another copy at home. Better yet, carry a photocopy of all the pages of the passport, including all visa stamps, apart from your actual passport, and leave a duplicate copy with a relative or friend. These measures will help prove your citizenship and facilitate the issuing of a new passport. Consulates also recommend that you carry an expired passport or an *official* copy of your birth certificate in a part of your baggage separate from other documents. You can request a duplicate birth certificate from the Bureau of Vital Records and Statistics in your state or province of birth.

Losing your passport can be a nightmare. It may take weeks to process a replacement, and your new passport may be valid only for a limited time. In addition, any visas stamped in your old passport will be irretrievably lost. If it is lost or stolen, however, immediately notify the local police and the nearest embassy or consulate of your home government. To expedite the replacement of your passport, you will need to know *all the information that you had previously recorded and photocopied* and to show identification and proof of citizenship. Some consulates can issue new passports within two days if you give them proof of citizenship. In an emergency, ask for immediate temporary traveling papers that will permit you to return to your home country.

Remember that your passport is a public document that belongs to your nation's government. You may have to surrender your passport to a foreign government official; if you don't get it back in a reasonable time, inform the nearest mission of your home country.

Applying for a passport is complicated, so make sure your questions are answered in advance; you don't want to wait two hours in a passport office just to be told you'll have to return tomorrow because your application is insufficient.

U.S. citizens may apply for a passport, valid for 10 years (5 yrs. if under 18) at any one of several thousand federal or state **courthouses** or **post offices** authorized to accept passport applications, or at any of the 13 **U.S. Passport Agencies.** Parents must apply in person for children under age 13. You must apply in person if this is your first passport, if you are under age 18, or if your current passport is more than 12 years old or was issued before your 18th birthday.

For a U.S. passport, you must submit the following along with a completed application form: (1) proof of U.S. Citizenship (either a certified birth certificate, naturalization papers, or a previous passport); (2) identification bearing your signature and either your photo or a personal description and (3) two identical, recent passport-size (2 in. by 2 in.) photographs with a white or off-white background taken within the past six months. Bring these items and $65 (under 18 $40) in check or money order. Passport Agencies accept cash in the exact amount. Write your date of birth on the check, and photocopy the data page for your personal records. You can **renew** your passport by mail (or in person) for $55.

Processing usually takes three to four weeks, perhaps fewer from a Passport Agency, more in spring and summer. Passports are processed according to the departure date indicated on the application form. *File your application as early as possible.* If you fail to indicate a departure date, the agency will assume you are not planning any immediate travel. Your passport will be mailed to you. You may pay for express mail return of your passport. Passport agencies offer **rush service:** if you have proof that you are departing within five working days (e.g. an airplane ticket), a Passport Agency will issue a passport while you wait.

Abroad, a U.S. embassy or consulate can usually issue new passports, given proof of citizenship. For more information, contact the U.S. Passport Information's helpful 24-hour recorded message (tel. (202) 647-0518) or call the recorded message of the passport agency nearest you.

Canadian application forms in English and French are available at all passport offices, post offices, and most travel agencies. Along with the application form, a citizen must provide: (1) citizenship documentation (as an old passport does *not* suffice as proof); (2) two identical passport-size photographs less than one year old that indicate the photographer, the studio address, and the date the photos were taken; and (3) a $35 fee. Both photographs must be signed by the applicant, and the application form and one of the photographs must be certified by a guarantor (someone who has known the applicant for two years and whose profession falls into one of the categories listed in the application form). Citizens may apply in person at any one of 29 regional Passport Offices across Canada. Citizens who reside in the U.S. can contact a Canadian diplomatic mission; those outside Canada and the U.S. should contact the nearest embassy or consulate. You can apply by mail by sending a completed application form with appropriate documentation and the $35 fee to Passport Office, External Affairs, Ottawa, Ontario, K1A OG3.

The processing time is approximately five business days for in-person applications and three weeks for mailed ones. Applicants over age 16 should file form A. Citizens under 16 who travel with a parent should use Form B and may be included on the parent's passport. Keep in mind that some countries require that a child carry his or her own passport whether traveling with a parent or not. A passport is valid for 5 years and is not renewable. If a passport is lost abroad, Canadians must be able to prove citizenship with another document.

For additional **information,** call the 24-hour number (tel. (800) 567-6868, in Metro Toronto 973-3251, Montreal, 283-2152). Refer to the booklet *Bon Voyage, But...* for further help and a list of Canadian embassies and consulates abroad. It is available free of charge from any passport office or from: Info-Export (BPTE), External Affairs, Ottawa, ON, K1A OG2, Canada.

British citizens can obtain either a full passport or a more restricted Visitor's Passport. For a **full passport** valid for 10 years (5 yrs. if under 16), apply in person or by mail to the London Passport Office or by mail to a passport office located in Liverpool, Newport, Peterborough, Glasgow, and Belfast. Along with a completed application, you must submit: 1) a birth certificate and marriage certificate (if applicable); 2) two identical, recent photos signed by a guarantor (a professional who is not a relative who has known you for two years); and 3) the £18 fee. Children under 16 may be included on a parent's passport. Processing usually takes four to six weeks. The London office offers same-day walk-in rush service; arrive early.

Irish citizens can apply for a passport by mail to one of the following two passport offices: Department of Foreign Affairs, Passport Office, Setanta Centre, Molesworth St., Dublin 2 (tel. (01) 6711633), or Passport Office, 1A South Mall, Cork (tel. (021) 272 525). You can obtain an application form at a local Garda station or request one from a passport office. First-time applicants should send their long-form birth certificate and two identical photographs. To renew, citizens should send the old passport (after photocopying it) and two photos. Passports cost £45 and are valid for 10 years. Citizens younger than 18 and older than 65 can request a 3 year passport that costs £10.

Australian citizens must apply for a passport in person at a local post office, a passport office, or an Australian diplomatic mission overseas. An appointment may be necessary at all three. A parent may file an application for a child who is under 18 and unmarried. Along with your application, you must submit: 1) proof of citizenship (such as an expired passport, a birth certificate, or a citizen's certificate from the Immigration service); 2) proof of your present name; 3) two identical, signed photographs (45mm by 35mm) less than six months old; 4) other forms of ID (such as a driver's license, credit card, rate notice, etc.) Application fees are adjusted every three months; call the toll-free information service for current details (tel. 13 12 32).

A **visa** is an endorsement or stamp placed in your passport. Visas are not necessary for U.S., Canadian, or British citizens unless they will be in Mexico for more than six months. Holders of European Community passports need only their **permanent resident cards ("green cards").** Australians and New Zealanders, however, do need visas, regardless of the length of stay. Businesspeople, missionaries and students who expect to earn a diploma in Mexico also must obtain a visa. Applications require a valid passport, six frontal photos and five profile photos. Consulates claim to have 24-hr. visa service if you apply in person; by mail, however, they may take weeks.

■ Student and Youth Identification

It's hardly worth your while to buy a student ID card to use in Mexico; foreign students are only rarely entitled to special discounts on accommodations, long-distance bus and train fares, and admission to archaeological sites, theatrical performances and museums. Where a student rate is advertised, a current university ID card is generally sufficient proof of student status.

Still, you might consider spending your hard-earned money on an **International Student Identity Card (ISIC),** available at many student travel offices (see Useful Addresses: Travel Organizations, above). It provides access to CIEE student airfares and includes repatriation insurance of US$3000, US$3000 of accident-related coverage, and US$100 per day for up to 60 days of in-hospital illness (if issued in the U.S., this insurance covers only foreign travel). To get an ISIC, you must supply dated proof of student status and a 1½ by 2 in. photo with your name printed on the back. The card costs US$15 and is valid for 16 months, from September 1 of one year until the end of the following year. You cannot purchase a new card in January unless you were in school during the fall semester.

If you are ineligible for the ISIC but are under 26, you can take advantage of the **International Youth Card,** issued by the **Federation of International Youth Travel Organizations (FIYTO),** which entitles you to some price reductions in Mexico. To get the card, you must submit proof of birthdate, a passport-sized photo with your name printed on the back, and US$10 (with insurance $15). The card is offered by most of the travel organizations listed above.

Once in Mexico, those under 26 may purchase a **SETEJ card,** which provides discounts in hostels, hotels, restaurants and museums. (See Useful Addresses: Travel Organizations and Mexico City: Practical Information for addresses.) Even if you don't have student identification, never hesitate to ask about youth discounts, and carry proof of age with you.

■ Driver's License and Vehicle Permits

An international driver's license is not necessary for driving in Mexico; any valid driver's license is acceptable. You will, however, need a Mexican **vehicle permit,** issued as you cross the border. Requirements for these permits have changed rapidly in the past year and become progressively stricter; contact a Mexican consulate or tourist office for the most up-to-date information. As of April 1993 you had to be able to prove ownership of your vehicle. Bring the title with you or, if the car is rented or not fully paid for, a notarized letter from the bank or other owner authorizing you to take the vehicle into Mexico. Having a credit card (AmEx, MC, or Visa) makes the process easiest—you can charge the US$10 fee. You will have to sign an affidavit stating you won't sell the car or let someone else drive it and then leave a photocopy of your proof of ownership, driver's license and credit card. You will receive a multiple-entry permit good for a maximum of six months. Without a credit card, you must post a bond based on the value of the vehicle as determined by the Mexican government. Fees and requirements vary at different border crossings, but the bond could be for as much as 50% of the Blue Book value of the vehicle, and non-refundable processing charges average 1-2% of the bond value with an $80 minimum. Regulations change frequently; the Mexican government has a hotline for info at tel. (800) 446-8277. To extend a vehicle permit beyond its original expiration date, contact the temporary importation department of Mexican customs. Permits are not required within the **Free Zone** (see Getting There: By Car below).

Resist the temptation to abandon, sell or give away your car in Mexico. Once you enter the country with a car, your tourist card will be marked such that you will not be allowed to collect the bond or to leave without the vehicle. Even if your car disintegrates somewhere in Mexico, you must get permission to leave without it; permission can be obtained (for a fee) at either the federal registry of automobiles in Mexico City or a local office of the treasury department. If you have received permission to leave your broken-down car behind in Mexico, you have up to 45 days after the expiration of your vehicle permit to reclaim the car before the Mexican government disposes of it.

A vehicle permit is valid only for the person to whom it was issued unless another driver is approved by the federal registry. Violation of this law can result in confiscation of the vehicle or heavy fines. Furthermore, only legitimate drivers may purchase car-ferry tickets.

■ Fishing Licenses

If you plan to fish in Mexico, you will need a license. The fee is US$7.50 per week, US$10 per month, or US$20 per year. Licenses are available in port cities at any Mexican **Oficina de Pesca.**

■■■ CUSTOMS

■ Entering Mexico

A clean, neat appearance will help upon your arrival. Don't pass out *mordidas* (bribes; literally, "little bites"). These days they are often inappropriate and may do more harm than good. *Do not* attempt to bring drugs into Mexico.

Entering Mexico overland, you'll first see the border guards. They will direct travelers to the immigration office, where a new batch of officials will issue a tourist card to those who don't have one already and a car permit to auto drivers. Customs officials will then inspect luggage and stamp papers. If there is anything amiss when you arrive at the immigration checkpoint 22km into the interior, you'll have to turn back.

Entering Mexico by air is somewhat easier. Agents process forms and examine luggage right in the airport. Because air passengers are rarely penniless, immigration officials are less strict than at the border. If your papers are out of order at any official location, however, count on a long wait. Keep some form of picture ID with you at all times, since customs officials stop buses all over Mexico, not just at the border.

Each visitor may enter with up to 110 pounds of luggage (140 lb. on Mexicana Airlines). Adults may carry 50 cigars, 200 cigarettes and 250 grams of tobacco with them. One camera and one 8mm motion picture camera, with 12 rolls of film for each, are also allowed. To use flashes or a tripod at archaeological sites, you must get permits (for personal use, flashes and tripods not permitted; for videos, 25 peso permit required, other permits available) from the Instituto Nacional de Antropología e Historia, Director de Asuntos Jurídicos, Cordoba No. 45, 2o piso, Col. Roma, México, D.F. 06700 (tel. (5) 511-08-44).

A dog or cat may accompany you into the country if the little critter has proof of vaccination for rabies, hepatitis, pip and leptospirosis, and a health certificate issued by a veterinarian less than 72 hours before entry and stamped by a local office of the U.S. Department of Agriculture and a Mexican consulate. The consulate pet visa fee is US$20. Keep in mind that animals will be unwelcome at most hotels.

■ Leaving Mexico

Crossing the border can take five minutes or five hours; the better your paperwork, the shorter your ordeal with customs should be. When reentering your home country, you must declare all articles acquired abroad and pay a duty on those which exceed your country's customs allowance. To establish value when you return home, keep receipts for items purchased abroad. Since you pay no duty on goods brought from home, record the serial numbers of any expensive items (cameras, computers, radios, etc.) you are taking on vacation before you leave. Check with your country's customs office to see if it has a special form for registering these valuables and turn in your list to the airport customs office before you depart.

Most countries object to the importation of firearms, explosives, ammunition, obscene literature and films, fireworks and lottery tickets. Do not try to take drugs out of Mexico. To avoid problems when carrying prescription drugs, label bottles clearly and have the prescription or a doctor's certificate ready to show the customs officer.

Crossing the border (on your return) with live animals is usually prohibited. For information on wildlife and wildlife products, contact TRAFFIC USA, World Wildlife Fund, 1250 24th St. NW, Washington, DC 20037 (tel. (202) 293-4800), or the Animal and Plant Health Inspection Service (see Useful Addresses: Publications).

United States citizens returning home may bring $400 worth of accompanying goods duty-free and must pay a 10% tax on the next $1000. You must declare all purchases, so remember to have sales slips ready. Goods are considered duty-free if they are for personal or household use (this includes gifts) and cannot include more than 100 cigars, 200 cigarettes (1 carton), and one liter of wine or liquor. You must be over 21 to bring liquor into the U.S. To be eligible for the duty-free allowance, you must have remained abroad for at least 48 hours and cannot have used this exemption or any part of it within the preceding 30 days.

You can mail unsolicited gifts duty-free if they are worth less than $50, though you may not mail liquor, tobacco, or perfume. Officials occasionally spot check parcels, so mark the price and nature of the gift and the words "Unsolicited Gift" on the package. If you send back a non-gift parcel or a gift worth more than $50, the Postal Service will collect a duty for its value plus a handling charge to deliver it. If you mail home personal goods of U.S. origin, you can avoid duty charges by marking the package "American goods returned." For more information, consult the brochure

Know Before You Go, available from R. Woods, Consumer Information Center, Pueblo, CO 81009 (item 477Y). You can direct other questions to the U.S. Customs Service, P.O. Box 7407, Washington, DC 20004 (tel. (202) 927-6724). Foreign nationals living in the U.S. are subject to different regulations; refer the leaflet *Customs Hints for Visitors (Nonresidents).*

Canadian citizens who remain abroad for at least one week may bring back up to CDN$300 worth of goods duty-free once every calendar year; goods that exceed the allowance will be taxed at 20%. You are permitted to ship goods home under this exemption as long as you declare them when you arrive. Citizens over the legal age (which varies by province) may import in-person (not through the mail) up to 200 cigarettes, 50 cigars, 400g loose tobacco, 1.14L wine or alcohol, and 355ml beer; the value of these products is included in the CDN$300 allowance. For more information, contact External Affairs, Communications Branch, Mackenzie Ave., Ottawa, Ontario, K1A 0I5 (tel. (613) 957 0275).

British citizens are allowed an exemption of up to £36 of goods purchased outside the EC, including not more than 200 cigarettes, 100 cigarillos, 50 cigars, or 250g of tobacco; and no more than 2L of still table wine plus 1L of alcohol over 22% volume. You must be over 17 to import liquor or tobacco. For more information about U.K. customs, contact Her Majesty's Customs and Excise, Custom House, Heathrow Airport North, Hounslow, Middlesex, TW6 2LA (tel. (081) 750-1603, fax 081 750 1549). HM Customs & Excise Notice 1 explains the allowances for people traveling to the U.K. both from within and without the European Community.

Australian citizens may import AUS$400 (under 18 AUS$200) of goods duty-free, including 250 cigarettes, 250g tobacco, and 1L alcohol. You must be over 18 to import either. For information, contact the nearest Australian consulate.

MONEY

The prices given in the book were accurate in the summer of 1993, when the book was researched.

As of January 1993 new currency was introduced by the Mexican Treasury Department in an effort to stabilize the currency. The new bills are worth 1000 times the old peso. In some areas, prices may be listed in the old peso or both old and new peso as the old peso is gradually removed from circulation. Travelers should be particularly careful to know which currency to purchase, carry, and spend to avoid the potential for confusion. *All prices in this book are listed in new pesos; simply multiply by 1000 to derive the price in old pesos.* If you find that *Let's Go* prcies are consistently high or low by a certain amount, use that figure to anticipate other recent changes.

US$1 = 3.115 pesos	**1 peso = US$0.32**
CDN$1 = 2.41 pesos	**1 peso= CDN$0.41**
UK£1 = 4.638 pesos	**1 peso = UK£0.21**
AUS$1 = 2.116 pesos	**1 peso = AUS$0.47**
NZ$1 = 1.705 pesos	**1 peso = NZ$0.58**

Currency and Exchange

Be sure to buy approximately US$50 worth of pesos before leaving home, especially if you will arrive in the afternoon or on a weekend, including the equivalent of US$1 in change. This will save you time at the airport and help you avoid the predicament of having no cash after bank hours. The symbol for pesos is the same as for U.S. dollars (although an "S" with *two* bars is always a dollar-sign). The common abbreviation **"M.N."** (*Moneda Nacional*) also stands for the peso.

Changing money in Mexico can be inconvenient. Some banks won't exchange until noon, when the daily peso quotes come out, and then stay open only until

MONEY

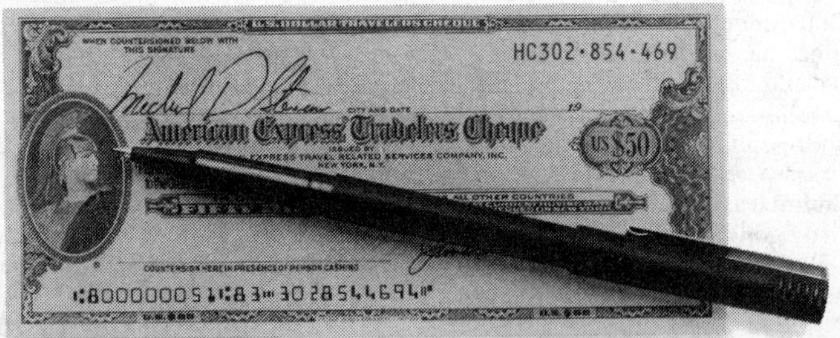
HC302·854·469
American Express Travelers Cheque
US$50

AMERICAN EXPRESS
Travelers Cheques

1:30pm. You can switch U.S. dollars for pesos anywhere, but some banks refuse to deal with other foreign currencies. **Banks** use the official exchange rates, but they sometimes extract a flat commission as well. Therefore, the more money you change at one time, the less you will lose in the transaction. The lineup of national banks in Mexico includes **Bánamex, Bancomer, Comermex** and **Serfin.**

Casas de cambio (currency exchange booths) may offer better exchange rates than banks and are usually open as long as the stores near which they do business. In most towns, the exchange rates at restaurants and hotels are extremely unfavorable; avoid them unless it's an emergency.

■ Traveler's Checks

If money makes your world go round, then a pickpocket could bring the world to a screeching halt. Traveler's checks will take the sting out of theft, but there are places (especially in northern Mexico) accustomed to the real, green dollar that will not accept any substitute. To avoid problems when cashing your checks, always have your passport with you (not just the number); it often means the difference between apologetic refusal and grudging acceptance. Carry traveler's checks in busy towns and cities, but stick to cash, risky though it may be, when traveling through the less touristed spots.

Many banks and companies sell traveler's checks, usually for the face value of the checks plus a 1-2% commission. Bank of America WorldMoney traveler's checks are sold commission-free in California, and AAA supplies American Express traveler's checks to its members *sans* commission. Even if you don't have a card, holding AmEx Cheques allows you to use their offices to receive mail.

The following toll-free numbers provide information about purchasing traveler's checks and obtaining refunds:

American Express: In the **U.S.** and **Canada,** tel. (800) 221-7282; in the **U.K.,** tel. (0800) 52-13-13; in **Australia,** tel. (008) 25-1902; in **Australia, New Zealand** and **South Pacific,** tel. (02) 886-0689; from elsewhere, call U.S. collect tel. (801) 964-6665 for referral to offices in individual countries. AmEx traveler's cheques are the most widely recoginzed worldwide and easiest to replace if lost or stolen—just call the information number or the AmEx Travel office nearest you. AmEx offices cash their own cheques commission-free (except where prohibited by national government) and sell cheques which can be signed by either of two people traveling together ("Cheque for Two"). Cheques available in seven currencies. American Automobile Association memebers can obtain AmEx traveler's cheques commission-free at AAA offices.

Barclays Bank: In the **U.S.** or **Canada,** tel. (800) 221-2426; in the **U.K.,** tel. (202) 67-12-12; from elsewhere, call New York collect tel. (212) 858-8500. Associated with Visa. Checks available in four currencies. Commission 1%. Representative banks in many locations throughout Mexico.

Citicorp: In the **U.S.** and **Canada,** tel. (800) 645-6556; from elsewhere; in London (071) 982-4040; from abroad call collect (813) 623-1709. Commission 1-1½%, four currencies available. Checkholders are automatically enrolled in Travel Assist Hotline (tel. (800) 523-1199) for 45 days after purchase.

MasterCard: In the **U.S.** and **Canada,** tel. (800) 223-9920; elsewhere, call New York collect (609) 987-7300. Checks available in 11 currencies. MasterCard itself charges no commission, but depending on the bank where you purchase the checks, you may have to pay 1-2%.

Thomas Cook: Thomas Cook and Mastercard have formed a partership whereby Thomas Cook distributes checks with both logos in US dollars and ten other currencies. Call (800) 223-7373 for refunds in the U.S., (800) 223-4030 for orders. From elsewhere call collect (212) 974-5696. Some Thomas Cook Currency Services offices (located in major cities around the globe) do not charge any fee for purchase of checks while some charge a 1-2% commission.

Visa: In **U.S.** and **Canada,** tel. (800) 227-6811; from the **U.K.,** call collect tel. (+44 71) 937 8091; elsewhere, call New York collect tel. (212) 858-8500. Checks in 13 currencies. No commission through Visa but individual banks might charge 1%.

Each agency refunds lost or stolen traveler's checks, but expect hassles if you lose track of them. When buying checks, get a list of refund centers. To expedite the refund process, separate your check receipts and keep them in a safe place. Record check numbers as you cash them to help identify exactly which checks might be missing. As an additional precaution, leave a list of the numbers with someone at home. Even with the check numbers in hand, you will probably find that getting a refund involves hours of waiting and spools of red tape.

It's best to buy most of your checks in small denominations (US$20) to minimize your losses at times when you need cash fast and can't avoid a bad exchange rate. Don't keep all your money in the same place: split it up among pockets and bags, or better yet, use a money belt. If possible, purchase checks in U.S. dollars, since many *casas de cambio* refuse to change other currencies.

■ Credit Cards and Cash Cards

Most of the banks that cash traveler's checks will make cash advances on a credit card as well. Be prepared to flash your passport. Major credit cards—**Visa, MasterCard,** and **American Express**—can prove invaluable in a financial emergency. Not only are they accepted by many Mexican businesses, especially in tourist areas, but they can also work in some **automated teller machines (ATMs).** And if you lose your airline ticket, you can charge a new one.

All major credit card companies have some form of worldwide lost card protection service, and most offer a variety of additional travel services to cardholders—make sure to inquire before you leave home. Students and other travelers who may have difficulty procuring a credit card should know that family members can sometimes obtain a joint-account card. American Express will issue an extra green card for US$30 per year or an extra gold card for US$35 (bills go to the main cardholder). Visa also issues extra cards on accounts, but the fee varies. For more information contact your local bank. They can also give you ATM locations throughout the U.S. and Mexico; also call tel. (800) 4-CIRRUS (424-7787) for current ATM availability information. Foreign ATM machines often have keypads with numbers only. If you remember your ATM password by letters only, be sure to jot down its numeric equivalent before leaving the U.S.

Some Mexican ATM machines have been known to withdraw money from an account without issuing any money. If you attempt to withdraw money and are turned down, be sure to keep any record of the transaction and write down the time, location and amount of the transaction, and check this against bank statements.

■ Sending Money

Sending money to Mexico requires a somewhat existential leap of faith. The cheapest way to receive emergency money is to have it sent through a large commercial bank that has associated banks within Mexico. The sender must either have an account with the bank or bring in cash or a money order, and some banks cable money only for regular customers. The sender can specify whether the money is to be disbursed in pesos or U.S. dollars. The service costs US$25-80, depending on the amount sent. Cabled money should arrive in one to three days if the sender can furnish exact information (i.e. recipient's passport number and the Mexican bank's name and address); otherwise, there will be significant delays. To pick up money, you must show some form of positive identification, such as a passport. The sender will receive no confirmation that the money has reached you.

Western Union (tel. (800) 325-6000) offers a convenient service for cabling money. Visa or MasterCard holders can call (800) 225-5227, recite their card number, and send any amount of money that the sender's credit limit can sustain. If the sender has no credit card, he or she must go in person to one of Western Union's offices with cash—no money orders accepted, and cashier's checks are not always accepted. The money will arrive at the central telegram office or post office of the designated city, where the recipient can obtain it upon presentation of suitable identification. If you are in a major Mexican city, the money should arrive within 24 hrs. In a smaller city, it could take 48 hrs., and if you are out on a donkey trail somewhere, the time frame is indefinite. The money will arrive in pesos and will be held for 30 days. If no one picks it up, it will be returned to the sender minus the transaction cost. Cabling costs run up to US$48 for sending as much as US$1000.

Sending money through **American Express** (in U.S., tel. (800) 543-4080; in Canada, tel. (800) 933-3278) costs about as much as using a bank, and the sender need not have an American Express card. Money will arrive immediately at any of the 41 international offices in Mexico, or in three to five days at other designated offices, where it will be held until further notice. Money is disbursed in traveler's checks (U.S. dollars) to the international offices and in peso form to other locations. It costs between US$15 and $35 to send to one of the international offices. When sending money to Mexico with a credit card, you are limited to US$1000 per day.

Finally, if you are a U.S. citizen and suddenly find yourself in an extreme emergency, you can have money sent via the State Department's Citizen Emergency Center (tel. (202) 647-5225, open Mon.-Fri. 8:15am-10pm, Sat. 9am-3pm; after hours call tel. (202) 647-4000). The center will need to know the sender's name and address, the recipient's name, and the reason for sending the money. The quickest way to get the money (preferably less than US$500) to the State Department is to cable it through Western Union or else to drop off cash, certified check, bank draft, or money order at the center itself. It takes longer to send the money through your own bank. Once they receive it, the State Department will cable the money, for a fee of US$15, to the nearest embassy or consulate, which will then release the cash according to the sender's instructions. The money should arrive within 24 hrs. If you want to, you can send a short telegraphic message along with the money. The center's address is: Bureau of Consular Affairs, CA/PA #5807, U.S. Dept. of State, Washington, DC 20520.

■■■ PACKING

Pack light. That means you.

Set out everything you'll need, and then take half of that plus more money. One *New York Times* correspondent recommends that you "take no more than you can carry for half a mile at a dead run." This advice may be extreme (unless you expect to be pursued by *federales*), but the gist is clear.

Decide whether a light suitcase, shoulder bag, backpack or shoebox is best for the kind of traveling you'll be doing. A **convertible pack** could spare you this difficult decision. If you will be staying in one city or town for a while, a light suitcase ought to suffice. Those striving for the more casual, unobtrusive look should take a large **shoulder bag** that closes securely. If you will be riding a lot of buses or covering a lot of ground by foot, a **backpack** may be the best choice. An internal-frame model is less bulky and can't be broken as easily by baggage handlers. For hiking, an external frame lifts weight off the back and distributes it more evenly, allows for some ventilation, and is more pleasant to carry over uneven terrain; internal frames mold to the back better, keep a lower center of gravity, and are more comfortable for long-distance hiking on the level. If you're taking a sleeping bag, keep in mind that you can strap it onto the outside of an **external frame,** while you usually must allow room for bedding inside an internal frame pack. A pack that loads from the front rather than the top saves you from having to grope at the bottom for hidden items, but the greater stress on a larger zipper area makes this a weaker design. Packs with several compartments are convenient, but outside zippers and flaps make easy targets for pickpockets. When choosing a backpack, consider how much more cumbersome it will be with 50 pounds of gear stuffed inside. Decent packs start at about US$120.

In addition to your main bag, bring a smaller day-pack for sightseeing or carry-on; it is a good idea to keep some of your valuables with you. A small **purse, neck pouch,** or **moneybelt** helps guard your money, passport and other important articles. Moneybelts are available at most camping supply stores and through the Forsyth Travel Library (see Useful Organizations: Publications).

Shorts, on either sex, are appropriate only at the beach and in the more cosmopolitan parts of Mexico.

Many Mexican cities have no public places to do **laundry.** One solution is to give your clothes to the hotel cleaning person, who is often more-than-eager to earn some extra money and will do a much better job than a washing machine would. Make sure that whomever you approach is a permanent employee of the hotel and establish a price in advance. Another possibility is to carry a mild laundry soap and do laundry by hand in hotel sinks. A soft squash ball will magically serve as a plug where there are usually none.

Footwear is not the place to cut costs. Comfortable walking shoes or a good pair of running shoes is essential. Save your sandals and other non-utilitarian shoes for short walks and evenings out. If you plan to hike or climb over pyramids and ruins, bring a pair of sturdy hiking shoes. Most toiletries such as aspirin and razor blades are available in Mexican pharmacies, but some items—tampons, prescription drugs and contraceptives—are best brought from home. Even when these items are available over the counter, their ingredients may differ from the same-named product in the U.S. Cities sometimes carry U.S. brands of saline solution for contact lens wearers, but no stores stock comparable cleaners. Toilet paper is often elusive; always carry some for those out-of-the way places and cheap hotels.

If your Spanish is not fluent, buy a good Spanish-English dictionary before you leave, because language dictionaries are scarce and expensive in Mexico. A compass may actually come in handy for orienting yourself in new places and for following the directions in *Let's Go* listings. You should also bring film and batteries from home, since the quality and variety of such goods are poorer in Mexico.

■■■ SAFETY AND SECURITY

Contrary to what you've probably heard about *bandidos*, squalor and other perils, Mexico is relatively safe, although large cities (especially Mexico City) demand extra caution. After dark, keep away from bus and train stations, subways and public parks. Shun empty train compartments; many travelers avoid the theft-ridden Mexican train system altogether. When on foot, stay out of trouble by sticking to busy, well-lit streets, and conducting yourself as the local people do. Act as if you know exactly where you are going: an obviously bewildered bodybuilder is more likely to be harassed than a stern and confident 98-lb. weakling. Ask the manager of your hotel or hostel for advice on specific areas. In small, cheap and dark accommodations, check to make sure your door locks to guard against unwanted visitors and thieves. Rural areas may seem blissfully free of the dangers of the city, but make sure that in your quest for isolation you do not stray too far from help.

To protect belongings, buy small luggage locks and keep your bags locked when storing them in your hotel room or in a bus or train station. When traveling, it's best never to let possessions out of your sight; even checking baggage on trains and buses poses a risk. Keep your money and valuables near you at all times: under the pillow at night and in the bathroom while you shower. A **money belt** is probably the best idea. A **neck pouch**, although less accessible, is equally safe. In city crowds and especially on public transportation, pickpockets are amazingly deft at their craft. Hold your bags tightly. *Ladrones* have been known to surgically remove valuables by slitting the underside of bags as unsuspecting travelers hold on to them. Fanny packs worn loosely outside clothing scream "steal me!" to thieves. If you must keep money in a pocket, place it in the front pocket with your hand over it. Make two photocopies of all important documents; keep one copy with you (separated from the original) and leave one with someone at home.

■ Drinking and Drugs

Drinking in Mexico is not for amateurs; bars and *cantinas* are strongholds of Mexican *machismo*. When someone calls you *amigo* and orders you a beer, bow out quickly unless you want to match him glass for glass in a challenge that could last several days.

You are also likely to be offered marijuana, which is potent and inexpensive in Mexico. Note that a minimum 10-year jail sentence awaits anyone found guilty of possessing more than a token amount of any drug, and that Mexican law does not distinguish between marijuana and other narcotics. Even if you aren't convicted, arrest and trial might just ruin your day. Derived from Roman and Napoleonic law, the Mexican judicial process does *not* assume that you are innocent until proven guilty, and it is not uncommon to be detained for a year before a verdict is even reached. Foreigners and suspected drug traffickers are not released on bail. Furthermore, there is little your consulate can do to help you out (except inform your relatives and bring care packages to you in jail), even if it wants to. Bearing all this in mind, many opt for the less risky alternative: they drink themselves under the table in thousands of Mexican bars and the only sentence they face will be tomorrow morning's *cruda*.

Finally, don't even think about bringing drugs back into the U.S. Customs agents and their perceptive K-9s are not to be taken lightly. Every few weeks they auction off the cars they've confiscated from unsuccessful smugglers. On the northern highways, especially along the Pacific coast, expect to be stopped repeatedly by burly, humorless troopers looking for contraband. That innocent-looking hitchhiker you were kind enough to pick up may be a drug peddler with a stash of illegal substances. If the police catch it in your car, the drug possession charges will extend to you, and your car may be confiscated. For the free pamphlet *Travel Warning on Drugs Abroad,* send a self-addressed, stamped envelope to the Bureau of Consular Affairs, Public Affairs #5807, Dept. of State, Washington, DC 20520 (tel. (202) 647-1488).

■■■ HEALTH

Before you can say "pass the *jalapeños*," a long-anticipated vacation can turn into an unpleasant study of the wonders of the Mexican health care system. Keep your body and, more importantly, everything you put into it, clean; don't cut out nutritious food in favor of junk just to save money. Stop short of physical overexertion, drink lots of replenishing fluids like juice and purified water, and stay away from too many dehydrating caffeinated sodas.

Take a look at your **immunization records** before you go. **Typhoid** inoculations are good for three years, tetanus for 10. Although visitors to Mexico (unless from an area infected with yellow fever) do not need to carry vaccination certificates, gamma globulin shots that protect against **hepatitis** are recommended for back-country travel in Chiapas and the Yucatán. **Malaria** still exists in some rural parts of southern Mexico and is most prevalent on the southwest coast. Doctors frequently prescribe a chloroquine regimen and mosquito repellent with DEET. Ask your doctor or check the malaria chart published by IAMAT to find out if you will be traveling in a high-risk area (see below for address). **Dengue** has also been reported in Mexico and is just one more reason to arm yourself against dive-bombing mosquitoes. *Health Information for International Travel* (US$5) is available from the Superintendent of Documents (see Useful Addresses: Publications, above).

Anyone with a chronic condition requiring medication on a regular basis should see a doctor before leaving. People with allergies should find out if their conditions are likely to be aggravated in the regions they plan to visit. Obtain a full supply of any necessary medication before your trip, since matching your prescription to a foreign equivalent is not always easy, safe or possible. Always carry up-to-date, legible prescriptions and/or a statement from your doctor, especially if you use insulin, a syringe, or any narcotic drug. Distribute medicines among your bags to minimize potential loss. You may also want to write out a brief medical record (half a page or so) and keep it with your passport in case you need a doctor and are unable to communicate.

Those with medical conditions that cannot be immediately recognized (e.g. diabetes, allergies to antibiotics, epilepsy, heart conditions) should obtain a steel **Medic Alert identification tag** (US$35), which identifies the disease and gives a toll-free number to call for more information. Contact Medic Alert Foundation International, P.O. Box 1009, Turlock, CA 95381 (tel. (800) 432-5378).

One of the greatest health threats to travelers in Mexico is the water. The Mexican government now advises its own citizens to boil their water before drinking it. **Traveler's diarrhea,** known in Mexico as *turista*, is the dastardly consequence of ignoring this advice. *Turista* often lasts two or three days; symptoms include cramps, nausea, vomiting, chills and a fever as high as 103°F (39°C). Consult a doctor if symptoms persist. To avoid *turista,* never drink unbottled water. Do not brush your teeth with or even rinse the brush in running water. During showers or baths, keep your mouth closed. Do not eat uncooked vegetables, including lettuce. If you go to a bar, avoid the clever disguise of impure water—the ice-cube. Beware of food from markets or street vendors that may have been washed in dirty water or fried in rancid cooking oil. Peel all fruits and vegetables before eating them, and beware of watermelon, which is often injected with impure water. Don't forget mother's advice; always wash your hands before eating. Watch out for open bottles of hot sauce sitting on tables in restaurants. Also beware of ice or frozen treats that may have been made with bad water. A golden rule in Mexico: boil it, peel it, cook it, or forget it.

Be sure to drink plenty of liquids—much more than you're accustomed to drinking. Heat and high altitudes will dehydrate you more swiftly than you expect, and you can avoid many health problems if you drink enough fluid to keep your urine clear. Buy bottled water, boil tap water, use water purification tablets (available in U.S. drugstores), or obtain a small water filter. Many restaurants and hotels offer *agua purificada*. Alcoholic beverages are dehydrating, as are coffee, strong tea and caffeinated sodas.

When you absolutely must eat questionable food, many douse it with lime juice and wash it down with a beer to kill bacteria. Lots of garlic may do the trick and keep away vampires to boot.

Since *turista* is such a common problem, many travelers bring along over-the-counter remedies (like Pepto-Bismol). Another possible tactic is to flush out your system by drinking lots of fruit juice and pure water. Rest and let the heinous disease run its course. Locals try 8 oz. of fruit juice, ½ tsp. of honey or sugar and a pinch of salt in one glass, and 8 oz. of water with ¼ tsp. of baking soda in another glass. They then alternate sips from each glass, downing several per day.

In addition, don't eat mangos, chiles or anything greasy while you're sick. Do eat bananas, toast, rice and especially papaya. Heavy doses of *té de manzanilla* (chamomile tea), *caldo de pollo* (chicken soup) and ginger ale could improve the outlook for a diarrhea-free future.

The sun seems to shine more forcefully in Mexico than on the rest of the world especially in the high altitudes of the interior. Take sunscreen and a wide-brimmed hat; use them even on overcast days. Common sense goes a long way in preventing

heat prostration and **sunstroke:** relax in hot weather, and drink lots of fluids. Symptoms of heat prostration include pallor, chills, clamminess, dizziness, blurred vision and a lowered pulse rate. In general, if you're out in the midday sun and start feeling awful, get inside, drink something non-alcoholic and lie down. Sunstroke (which can occur without direct exposure to the sun) is much more serious. The victim will be flushed and feverish, won't be sweating, and must be cooled off with wet towels and taken to a doctor as soon as possible.

Contact lens wearers should bring an adequate supply of cleaning solutions and lubricating drops from home. Mexican equivalents will be hard to find and could irritate your eyes. If you disinfect with a heat system, pack voltage and outlet adapters or switch to cold sterilization. Also bring an extra pair of glasses or a copy of the prescription, or leave either with a friend who can send it along in an emergency.

Local pharmacists can give shots and dispense other remedies for mild illnesses. A sterile, disposable needle is crucial. In every town, at least one *farmacia*, called the *farmacia de la guardia*, remains on duty 24 hrs. Wherever possible, *Let's Go* lists a pharmacy open for extended hours if not 24 hrs. If not listed, you can ask a policeman or cab driver where the pharmacy is. If the door is locked, knock loudly; someone is probably sleeping inside.

All travelers should be concerned about **Acquired Immune Deficiency Syndrome (AIDS),** transmitted through the exchange of body fluids with an infected individual (HIV-positive). Remember that there is no assurance that someone is not infected: HIV tests only show antibodies after a six-month lapse. Do not have sex without using a condom or share intravenous needles with anyone. Those travelers who are HIV-positive or have AIDS should thoroughly check on possible immigration restrictions in the country which they wish to visit. The Center for Disease Control's **AIDS Hotline** provides information on AIDS in the U.S. and can refer you to other organizations with information on Mexico (tel. (800) 342-2437; Spanish (800) 344-7432; TTD (800) 243-7889). Call the **U.S. State Department** for country-specific restrictions for HIV-positive travelers (tel. (202) 647-1488, fax (202) 637-3000; modem-users may consult the electronic bulletin board at (202) 647-9225; or write the Bureau of Consular Affairs, Rm. 5807, Dept. of State, Washington D.C. 20520). The **World Health Organization** provides written material on AIDS internationally (tel. (202) 862-3200).

Reliable **contraception** may be difficult to come by when traveling. Women on the pill should bring enough to allow for possible loss or extended stays. Although **condoms** are increasingly available and used throughout the world to prevent AIDS and unwanted pregnancies, you might want to stock up up on your favorite national brand before you go as quality varies in other countries.

Abortion is illegal in Mexico and permitted only in cases when the mother's life is in danger. The **National Abortion Federation's hotline** (tel. (800) 772-9100, Mon.-Fri. 9:30am-5:30pm) refers its callers to U.S. clinics that perform abortions. Its personnel can direct you to organizations which provide information on abortion in other countries.

For additional information before you go, you may wish to contact the **International Association for Medical Assistance to Travelers (IAMAT).** IAMAT provides several brochures on health for travelers, an ID card, a chart detailing advisable immunizations for 200 countries, and a worldwide directory of English-speaking physicians who have had medical training in Europe or North America. Membership to the organization is free (although donations are welcome) and doctors are on call 24 hrs. a day for IAMAT members. Contact chapters in the U.S., 417 Center St., Lewiston, NY, 14092, (tel. (716) 754-4883); in **Canada**, 40 Regal Rd., Guelph, Ontario, N1K 1B5 (tel. (519) 836-0102), and 1287 St. Clair Ave. West, Toronto, M6E 1B8 (tel. (416) 652-0137); in **New Zealand,** P.O. Box 5049, 438 Pananui Rd., Christchurch 5 (tel. (03) 352-9053, fax (03) 352-4360).

Complete health information travelers is available from a variety of published sources. Consult your local bookstore for books on staying healthy at home or on the road or write the **Superintendent of Documents,** U.S. Government Printing Office, Washington D.C. 20402 (tel. (202) 783-3238). $5 will get you their publication *Health Information for International Travel* detailing immunization requirements and other health precuations for travelers.

■■■ INSURANCE

Beware of unnecessary coverage—your current policies might well extend to many travel-related accidents. **Medical insurance** (especially university policies) often cover costs incurred abroad. **Medicare's** foreign travel coverage is limited and is valid only in Canada and Mexico. Canadians are protected by their home province's health insurance plan: check with the provincial Ministry of Health or Health Plan Headquarters. Your **homeowners' insurance** (or your family's coverage) often covers theft during travel.

Buying an **ISIC,** International Teacher ID or Student Card in the U.S. provides some insurance (see Documents and Formalities below). **CIEE** offers the inexpensive Trip-Safe plan with options covering medical treatment and hospitalization, accidents, baggage loss, and even charter flights missed due to illness; **STA** offers a more expensive, more comprehensive plan. American Express cardholders receive automatic car-rental and flight insurance on purchases made with the card. (For addresses for CIEE and STA, see Useful Organizations—Budget Travel Services.)

Remember that insurance companies usually require a copy of the police report for thefts, or evidence of having paid medical expenses (doctor's statements, receipts) before they will honor a claim and may have time limits on filing for reimbursement. Have all documents written in English to avoid possible translating fees. Always carry policy numbers and proof of insurance. Note that some of the plans listed below offer cash advances or guaranteed bills. Check with each insurance carrier for specific restrictions. If your coverage doesn't include on-the-spot payments or cash transferrals, budget for emergencies.

Access America, Inc., 6600 West Broad St., P.O. Box 11188, Richmond, VA, 23230 (tel. (800) 284-8300). Covers trip cancellation/interruption, on-the-spot hospital admittance costs, emergency medical evacuation. 24-hr. hotline.

ARM Coverage, Inc./Carefree Travel Insurance, P.O. Box 310, Mineola, NY, 11501 (tel. (800) 323-3149 or (516) 294-0220). Offers two comprehensive packages including coverage for trip delay, accident and sickness, medical, baggage loss, bag delay, accidental death and dismemberment, travel supplier insolvency. Trip cancellation/interruption may be purchased separately at a rate of $5.50 per $100 of coverage. 24-hr. hotline.

Globalcare Travel Insurance, 220 Broadway, Lynnfield, MA, 01940 (tel. (800) 821-2488, fax (617) 592-7720). Complete medical, legal, emergency, and travel-related services. On-the-spot payments and special student programs.

Travelers Aid International, 918 16th St., NW, Washington C 20006 (tel. (202) 659-9468, fax (202) 659-2910). Provides help for theft, car failure, illness, and other "mobility-related problems." No fee, but you are expected to reimburse the organization for expenses.

Travel Assistance International, 1133 15th St., NW, Washington DC 20005 (tel. (202) 821-2828, fax (202) 331-1609). Provides on-the-spot medical coverage ranging from US$15,000 to US$90,000 and unlimited medical evacuation insurance, 24-hr. emergency multilingual assistance hotline and worldwide local presence. Optional coverages such as trip cancellation/interruption, baggage and accidental death and dismemberment insurance are also offered. Short-term and long-term plans available.

■■■ ALTERNATIVES TO TOURISM

■ Work

Despite recent immigration legislation imposing heavy penalties on employers of illegal aliens, Mexican workers continue to pour over the border into the U.S., where most live in poverty. This should give you a sense of the job market in Mexico. Just as the U.S. spends billions of dollars every year to safeguard jobs for its own citizens, the Mexican government isn't about to give up precious jobs to traveling *gringos* when many of its own people are unemployed. It used to be that only 10% of the employees of foreign firms located in Mexico could have non-Mexican citizenship; now, as "development" has become a priority, the limit depends on the sector. Hotels, for instance, are often eager to hire English-speaking personnel for prestige and the convenience of their patrons, and are allowed as many legal work permits as they wish. It is no longer the case that to get a job you must have some specialized skill that cannot be found in Mexico; but attitudes are in flux, and you might still be unwelcome even as an English teacher. If you manage to secure a position with a Mexican business, your employer must get you a work permit. It is possible, but illegal, to work without a permit. You risk deportation if caught.

CIEE (see Useful Addresses, Travel Organizations) publishes *Work, Study, Travel Abroad: The Whole World Handbook* (US$12.95 plus $1.50 shipping), *Volunteer! The Comprehensive Guide to Voluntary Service in the U.S. and Abroad* (US$8.95 plus $1.50 shipping) and *Going Places: The High School Student's Guide to Study, Travel, and Adventure Abroad* (US$13.95 plus $1.50 shipping). **Peterson's,** P.O. Box 2123, Princeton, NJ 08543 (tel. (800) 338-3282), publishes the *Directory of Overseas Summer Jobs* (US$14.95, $4.75 shipping) with 50,000 openings worldwide, volunteer and paid. **Vacation Work Publications**, 9 Park End St., Oxford, England OX1 1HJ (tel. (+44 865) 24-19- 78) publishes *The International Directory of Voluntary Work* (£8.95) and *The Directory of Work and Study in Developing Countries* (£7 plus £2 shipping, £1 if within England).

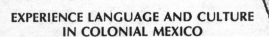

If you have your heart set on extended work in Mexico, contact:

American Friends Service Committee, 1501 Cherry St., Philadelphia, PA 19102 (tel. (215) 241-7295). Runs volunteer work camps in Mexican villages for 18- to 26-year-olds. Work has included construction, gardening, reforestation, health and nutrition, and education. Programs run each summer from late June to early August (participation fee US$700). Fluency in Spanish required. Limited financial aid available. Address inquiries to the Personnel Dept.

Archaeological Institute of America, 675 Commonwealth Ave., Boston, MA 02215 (tel. (617) 353-9361, fax 353-6550). Lists field projects in the *Archaeological Fieldwork Opportunities Bulletin* which is available in Jan. for the following summer (US$10.50, $8.50 for members, plus $3.00 shipping). Sometimes nothing, sometimes one or two sites in Mexico. *Bulletin* also available directly from Kendall/Hunt Publishing Co. (tel. (800) 338-5578).

■ Study

Studying in Mexico is one of the best ways to learn Spanish while broadening your knowledge of Hispanic culture. The *Teenager's Guide to Study, Travel, and Adventure Abroad* (US$9.95 plus $1 postage) is available from CIEE (see Useful Addresses, Travel Organizations) or bookstores, as are the work/study guides listed above. **UNIPUB,** 4611-F Assembly Dr., Lanham, MD 20706-4391 (in U.S., tel. (800) 274-4888; in Canada, (800) 233-0504) distributes UNESCO's unwieldy but fascinating book *Study Abroad* (US$24 plus $2.50 shipping). Programs which take place in Mexico are described in Spanish. The **Institute of International Education (IIE),** 809 United Nations Pl., New York, NY 10017-3580 (tel. (212) 984-5412 for info only; also 883-8200; fax for orders 984-5452) publishes *Academic Year Abroad* (US$39.95 plus $3 shipping) and *Vacation Study Abroad* (US$31.95 plus $3 shipping), which have information on courses, costs and accommodations for programs in Mexico. Together with CIEE and the National Association for Foreign Student Affairs, IIE publishes *Basic Facts on Study Abroad* (free). IIE also operates the **Inter-**

national Education Information Center at the UN Plaza address (open Mon.-Fri. 10am-4pm), but can't provide assistance by phone or letter.

If you're already proficient in Spanish, consider enrolling in the regular programs of a Mexican university—but don't expect to receive credit at your home institution. The **Universidad de las Américas,** Apdo. 100, Santa Catarina Martír, Cholula, Puebla 72820 (tel. (22) 47-00-00, ext. 1108) is the only Mexican university accredited in the U.S.

For general information on studying at Mexican universities, contact the Secretaría de Relaciones Exteriores, Homero 213, 3r piso, México, D.F.

Many U.S. universities offer students the opportunity to study in Mexico for a semester or a year, and some Mexican universities organize programs specifically designed for foreign students. The **Universidad Nacional Autónoma de México (UNAM)** has a school in Mexico City for foreign students that operates semester, intensive and summer programs in Spanish, as well as in art, history, literature and Chicano studies. The program is open to both undergraduates and graduates. The school also has a campus in Taxco, a colonial mining town located on the road between Mexico City and Acapulco. Write to: UNAM, Centro de Enseñanza para Extranjeros, Apdo. 70-391, Ciudad Universitaria, Delegación Coyoacán, México, D.F. 04510 (tel. (5) 550-51-72, fax 548-99-39).

Less intensive programs are offered in Guadalajara and San Miguel de Allende; for more information, see Academic Institutions under those cities. Cuernavaca is the home of a number of language schools. Enrollment is often by the week, and students are usually housed with families in the area. For more information, see a copy of IIE's *Vacation Study Abroad.*

Finally, the Experiment in International Living's **School for International Training (SIT),** College Semester Abroad Admissions, Kipling Rd., P.O. Box 676, Brattleboro, VT 05302 (tel. (800) 451-4465 or (802) 257-7751) runs summer and semester programs in Mexico that include cross-cultural orientation, intensive language, homestay and field study. Summer programs cost US$1600-5200, semester US$6600-10,500, but the Pell Grant, Stafford Loan and PLUS/SLS Loan can apply to

SIT tuition. Some home institutions will provide additional aid and often accept SIT transfer credits. If you are over 14, speak Spanish fluently and have lived in Mexico, you can apply to lead programs for the **Experiment in International Living,** which pays leaders' expenses as well as an honorarium.

■■■ KEEPING IN TOUCH

The modes of communication in Mexico vary greatly in efficiency. The most reliable way to send a message—or money—is by wire; the least reliable is by surface mail.

■ Mail

Mexican mail service can be slow, but it is fairly dependable. Airmail often reaches the U.S. in as few as six days, but can just as easily take a month or more. It takes even longer (at least two weeks) to Europe and other destinations, since it is usually routed through U.S. surface mail. Official estimates average 40 days by boat, but in reality may take months. The set-rate postage for all light mail including postcards, letters and parcels weighing between 20 and 100g is about 1.50 pesos to North American countries, more to other locations. Printed matter receives a cheaper rate than regular mail if it is open for inspection and secured, if necessary, only by string or cord. Anything important should be sent registered mail for an additional charge of several hundred pesos, or else duplicates should be sent. Never deposit anything important in the black holes Mexicans call mailboxes. *La estampilla* or *el timbre* is "stamp" in Spanish, and *la carta* is "letter."

You can have letters sent to you in Mexico through **Lista de Correos,** a letter-holding service similar to General Delivery in the U.S. When picking up mail sent to you via *Lista de Correos,* look for a list posted in the post office. Check it carefully for any possible misspellings or confusions. If there is no list posted, ask the attendant *¿Está la lista de hoy?* (Is today's list here?). If it is, give your name. Letters and packages will be held no more than 15 days and sometimes fewer. If you

have friends or family in Mexico, using their address may be preferable. Hotels where you have reserved a room will usually hold mail for you. **American Express offices** will also hold mail for 30 days before returning it; just write "Client's Mail" on the envelope. Call American Express customer service at (800) 528-4800 for more information and ask for the free *Directory of Traveler Service Offices*.

Mail sent to *Lista de Correos* should be addressed to a first and last name only, capitalizing and underlining the name under which the item should be filed alphabetically. Keep names as simple as possible. Because Mexican *apellidos* (paternal last names) fall in the middle of the written name, confusion arises for foreigners with more than a simple first and last name, or in the case of mail addressed to more than one person. A letter could be filed under any misspelled permutation of the recipient's names. If possible, go through the *Lista de Correos* yourself. If not, watch the person who does and ask for the mail under both your first and your last name, just to make sure. Address letters as follows:

Plamen RUSSEV
a/c Lista de Correos
Tampico [city], Veracruz [state]
12345 [postal code, if you know it], MEXICO

The letter should also be marked *Favor de retener hasta la llegada* ("Please hold until arrival").

To send letters from Mexico, it is wise to use the Spanish abbreviations or names for countries (EEUU or EUA for the U.S.). Write *Por Avión* on all postcards and letters not otherwise marked, unless you don't mind it arriving sometime in the next millennium.

Regulations for mailing parcels are confusing and vary from state to state. While it is often possible to send packages from smaller towns, post offices in large cities (especially ports or trade centers such as Mérida and Acapulco) provide more reliable service. Mailing a package involves locating a box, tape, string, wrapping paper and the correct forms to be stamped and signed by the appropriate officials. Before attempting to send anything, go to the post office and carefully note the size and weight limitations, necessary documentation, addresses and hours of the customs and trade offices in the city, and whether the box should be brought open or sealed. There is a fairly standard size limitation for boxes of 40cm by 60cm. After the contents have been inspected at the post office and at customs, you can wrap your package (usually on the post office floor). All packages are reopened and inspected by customs at the border, so closing the box with string rather than tape is recommended.

In some cases, customs and the post office are under the same roof. In others, the two lie at opposite ends of town and have conflicting schedules. In general, in order to send packages you must provide the following: tourist card data (number, duration of validity, date of issue, place of issue), list of contents including estimated value and nature of the package ("Gift" works best), address and return address. It is customary for those mailing parcels to use their home address, or at least some address in the same country as the parcel's destination, as a return address to ensure eventual delivery.

In a trade office, you may need to show receipts for each item purchased in Mexico. Postal officials usually record the information from the customs form on the front of the package as well. Should it prove impossible or too frustrating to send items by regular mail, look into the alternatives. From the larger cities, airlines will take parcels to the U.S. for enormous fees. Well-established *artesanía* stores often provide a mailing service for their customers. You can sometimes persuade them to include in the package items not bought in the store. Not only will the package be wrapped and addressed professionally, but connections with the post office can often ease processing and delivery. Finally, if you are following a fairly rigid itinerary, use trains, buses and domestic airlines to send packages to points within Mexico (for example, to the airport from which you plan to leave the country). Always double check the requirements of each method and have packages held at the other end long enough to guarantee that parcel and owner meet again.

■ Telephones

When trying to reach Mexico from another country, patience is the key to success. If you are calling Mexican information, don't be surprised if the phone is not answered right away. To reach Mexico from the U.S., dial 011-52, then the city code (5 for Mexico City), and then the phone number.

Patience is also crucial when you're placing a call within Mexico. Half of the public phones are out of service, and the other half take rare low-denomination coins or LADATEL phone cards.

Getting lines to foreign countries is very difficult. Many public phones don't have access to international lines. If you speak Spanish fluently and can't reach the international operator, call the national operator, who will connect you (sometimes even a local operator can help). The term for a collect call is a *llamada por cobrar* or *llamada con cobro revertido*. Calling from hotels is usually faster.

Calling abroad from Mexico is extremely expensive thanks to taxes and surcharges. Long-distance charges vary from city to city, but calls to the U.S. usually set you back about 8 pesos per minute. Call collect if you can; not only is it cheaper (about half the price of direct), but you will avoid the enormous surcharges that hotel switchboards impose if you call direct. Remember, however, that there can be a fee of 1-5 pesos for collect calls that are not accepted, depending on where you place the call. Using a U.S. operator to call collect or with a calling card will let you pay U.S. rates (around $5-6 per min. depending on distance between cities).

LADATEL phones, increasingly prevalent, take coins or LADATEL phone cards. International calls using these phones are cheaper (2 pesos for 1 min. to Cambridge, MA) and involve less waiting than any of the alternatives. LADATEL **phone cards,** available at Teléfonos Mexicanos offices and various stores, eliminate the need for coins. Without them, the challenge is to find enough coins of large denominations, because these phones take no more than 10 coins at a time and some calls require a minimum initial deposit. When dialing, use the station-to-station prefixes. The blue

push-button phones do direct dial while the orange old-fashioned ones do not. Dial 95-800-462-4240 from most phones to reach the **AT&T USADirect operator**.

To reach the English-speaking international operator on a plain old phone, dial 09 and wait until the operator answers (sometimes immediately, but be prepared to wait 30min. or more). For direct calls, dial 01; national operator 02; local assistance 04; for bilingual (Spanish and English) emergency operators 06. To make long-distance phone calls within Mexico, dial 91 plus the telephone code and number (station to station), or 92 plus the telephone code and number (person to person). The prefixes for calling the U.S. or Canada are 95 for station to station and 96 for person to person; for all other countries the prefixes are 98 and 99, respectively. For international phone information, call tel. (800) 874-4000 in the U.S.

■■■ SPECIFIC CONCERNS

■ Women And Travel

"She is an undifferentiated manifestation of life, a channel for the universal appetite," wrote Octavio Paz, Mexican literary great, describing the Mexican view of woman. Women traveling in Mexico and Central America will find that attitudes like that described by Paz can profoundly influence their travel experience. Female *Let's Go* researchers report that as solo travelers they develop an entirely different mindset and perspective because of the daily confrontation with this ethos.

If you look like an *extranjera* (foreigner), you will find it difficult to remain alone except when locked in your hotel room. Persistent men will insist on joining you; walking down the street, you will hear whistles and propositions (called *piropos* in Mexico). If you're fair-skinned, "*güera, güera, güera*" will follow you everywhere. The best response to this is no response and no eye contact, because any kind of answer could be interpreted as a come-on. An obnoxious reply might only prolong the encounter. Should a situation become threatening, however, do not hesitate to lash out. In real emergencies, scream for help. Don't consider yourself safe just because people in uniform are around.

Awareness of Mexican social standards can also prevent unpleasant and dangerous confrontations. Women wearing shorts (opt for a light skirt even in big resort towns), halter tops, or not wearing bras, will most likely attract unwanted attention. *Cantinas* are all-male institutions; the only women who ever enter are working, either as servers or as prostitutes.

Northern Mexico is less congenial to women travelers than anywhere else in Mexico; Oaxaca, Chiapas, and the Yucatán are the most congenial. If you are traveling with a male friend, it may help to pose as a couple. This will assuage any misgivings hotel proprietors have about letting you share rooms and may serve to chill the blood of your Mexican admirer.

Remember, too, that as often as foreign women are stereotyped by Mexican men, Mexican men are stereotyped by foreigners. A man who offers to give you a lift or show you the sights may be acting innocently, but if you feel uncomfortable, politely refuse.

A series of recent travelogues by women outline their sojourns; check a good library or bookstore for these and other books: *Wander Women,* a travel and adventure networking organization for women over 40, publishes a quarterly newsletter. For a sample copy send US$1 to Wander Women, 136 Grand Ave. #237, West Covina, CA 91791; *Nothing to Declare: Memoirs of a Woman Traveling Alone* (Penguin Books; US$9) and *Wall to Wall: From Beijing to Berlin by Rail* (Penguin Books; US$10) by Mary Morris; *Women Going Places* (Inland; US$14); *One Dry Season* (Knopf) by Caroline Alexander; *Tracks* (Pantheon) by Robin Davidson; *The Road Through Miyama* (Random House/Vintage) by Leila Philips, and anything by Isak Dinesen, especially *Out of Africa* (Random House). For additional tips and suggestions, consult *The Handbook for Women Travelers* (£7.99) by Maggie and

Gemma Moss, published by Piatkus Books, 5 Windmill St., London W1P 1HT England (tel. +44 (071) 6310710).

■ Older Travelers And Senior Citizens

The need or wish to travel inexpensively knows no age limits. Older travelers can often travel on a shoestring budget by taking advantage of the numerous discounts available to them. Many youth hostels welcome seniors, and transportation costs and entrance fees to tourist attractions are often lower. National chapters of HI/IYHF (see Useful Addresses: Travel Organizations) sell HI/IYHF cards to those over 54 for US$15. Although a card isn't required in Mexican hostels, it does lower the rates.

Senior travelers should bring a medical record that includes an update on conditions and prescriptions; the name, phone number and address of a regular doctor; and a summary of their recent medical history. Find out if you have insurance that will cover costs you may incur in Mexico.

Travel Tips for Older Americans (US$1) provides information on passports, health and currency for those traveling abroad. Write to the Superintendent of Documents (see Useful Addresses above). The *International Health Guide for Senior Travelers* (US$5.95 plus US$1 postage) is available from Pilot Books, 103 Cooper St., Babylon, NY 11702 (tel. (516) 422-2225).

For more information, write to a Mexican Government Tourism Office (see Useful Addresses: Government Organizations). The following organizations and publications can also be helpful:

American Association of Retired Persons (AARP), Special Services Dept., 601 E St. NW, Washington, DC 20049 (tel. (800) 927-0111 or (202) 434-2277). US$8 annual membership fee. People over 49 receive benefits including group travel programs, discounts on lodging, car and RV rental, and sight-seeing.

Elderhostel, 75 Federal St., 3rd floor, Boston, MA 02110 (tel. (617) 426-7788). Educational workshops at over 1500 locations internationally for those over 59 and those over 49 who have a spouse or companion over 59. U.S. university-sponsored programs in Mexico. Options include Mexican history, folk art and archaeology. US$1500-5000 covers room, board, tuition and extracurricular activities for 1-4 weeks. Registration is an ongoing process, and no membership dues are required. Scholarships available. Free catalogue upon written request.

National Council of Senior Citizens, 1331 F St. NW, Washington, DC 20004 (tel. (202) 347-8800). Membership is open to all ages and costs US$12 per year or US$150 for a lifetime. Hotel and auto rental discounts, newsletter, discount travel agency and supplemental Medicare insurance for those over 64.

Gateway Books, P.O. Box 10244, San Rafael, CA 94912. Publishes Gene and Adele Malott's *Get Up and Go: A Guide for the Mature Traveler* (US$10.95, postage US$1.90). Offers recommendations and general hints for the budget-concious senior. Call (800) 669-0773 for orders.

■ Traveling With Children

Children under 18 need consent from both parents to enter Mexico. One parent must have a decree of sole custody or notarized, written permission from the other parent to bring the fruit of their union into the country. Check with the nearest Mexican consulate for more information.

If a child accompanies you to Mexico, special circumstances may arise. The new atmosphere, climate and diet may be unsettling at first, but most children adapt more quickly than their parents do. If you bring a baby, make sure to carry a piece of mosquito netting large enough to cover a cradle or stroller.

For general information concerning children on the road, consult *Travel with Children* (US$10.95 plus $1.50 postage), chock-full of user-friendly tips and international anecdotes, from Lonely Planet Publications, 155 Filbert St., Oakland, CA 94607-2538 (tel. (800) 275-0122 or (510) 893-8555, fax (510) 893-8563) or P.O. Box 617, Hawthorn, Victoria 3122, Australia; *Sharing Nature with Children* (US$7.95) from Wilderness Press, 2440 Bancroft Way, Berkeley, CA 94704 (tel. (800) 443-7227 or (510) 843-8080); and/or *Backpacking with Babies and Small Children* (US$8.95), also from Wilderness Press.

■ Travelers With Disabilities

Mexico is becoming increasingly accessible to travelers with disabilities, especially in popular resorts such as Acapulco and Cancún. Money talks—the more you are willing to spend, the less difficult it is to find accessible facilities. Most public and long-distance modes of transportation and most of the non-luxury hotels don't accommodate wheelchairs. Public bathrooms are almost all inaccessible, as are many historic buildings and museums. Still, with some advance planning, an affordable Mexican vacation is not impossible.

Air travel in general is gradually becoming less restrictive. Give prior notice of your needs to the airline, which may require a traveling companion or doctor's letter allowing you to fly. Cruises are a costly alternative to flying. When you choose a cruise line, ask about ramps, doorways and special services. Most ships also require a doctor's permission.

If you intend to bring a seeing-eye dog to Mexico, you must have a veterinarian's certificate of health stamped at a Mexican consulate (see Customs—Entering Mexico for pet fee).

The following organizations provide useful information and can help plan your vacation:

American Foundation for the Blind, 15 W. 16th St., New York, NY 10011 (tel. (212) 620-2147). ID cards (US$10); write for an application, or call the Product Center at (800) 829-0500. Also call this number to order AFB catalogs in braile, print, or on cassette or disk.

Disability Press, Ltd., Applemarket House, 17 Union St., Kingston-upon-Thames, Surrey KT1 1RP, England (tel.+44 (081) 549 6399). Publishes the *Disabled Traveler's International Phrasebook,* including French, German, Italian, Spanish, Portuguese, Swedish, and Dutch phrases (£1.75). Supplements in Norwegian, Hungarian and Serbo-Croatian (60p each).

The Guided Tour, Inc. Elkins park house, Suite 114B, 7900 Old York Road, Elkins Park, PA 19117-2348. (tel. (215) 782-1370 or (800) 738-5843) Year-round travel programs for persons with developmental and physical challenges as well as those geared to the needs of persons requiring renal dialysis. Trips and vacations planned both domestically and internationally. Call or write for a free brochure.

Mobility International, USA (MIUSA), P.O. Box 3551, Eugene, OR 97403 (tel. (503) 343-1284 voice and TDD). International headquarters in Britain, 228 Borough High St., London SE1 1JX (tel. +44 (071) 403 5688). Contacts in 30 countries. Information on travel programs, international work camps, accommodations, access guides, and organized tours. Membership costs US$20 per year, newsletter US$10. Sells updated and expanded *A World of Options: A Guide to International Educational Exchange, Community Service, and Travel for Persons with Disabilities* (US$14 for members, US$16 for non-members, postpaid).

Twin Peaks Press, P.O. Box 129, Vancouver, WA 98666 (tel. (800) 637-2256) publishes three books for disabled travelers: *Wheelchair Vagabond* (US$14.95), *Directory for Travel Agencies for the Disabled* (US$19.95), and *Travel for the Disabled* (US$19.95). Add US$2 shipping for the first book, $1 each additional book.

Further sources of information are *The Disabled Traveler's International Phrasebook* (£1.75), which includes Spanish, from Disability Press, Ltd., Applemarket

House, 17 Union St., Kingston-upon-Thames, Surrey, KT1 1RP England (tel. (+44 81) 549-63-99) and *Access to the World* (US$16.95) from Facts on File, Inc., 460 Park Ave. S, New York, NY 10016-7382 (tel. (800) 322-8755 or (212) 683-2244, fax (212) 213-4578).

■ Bisexual, Gay, And Lesbian Travelers

In Mexico, the legal age for consensual homosexual intercourse is 18. Police often ignore the legal status of homosexual activity and Mexicans generally disapprove of public displays of gay affection, but there is a gay rights movement in Mexico and discreet homosexuality is tolerated in most areas.

Giovanni's Room, 345 S. 12th St., Philadelphia, PA 19107 (tel. (215) 923-2960) is an international feminist, lesbian, and gay bookstore and mail-order house with resources and information for tourists.

Ferrari Publications, P.O. Box 37887, Phoenix, AZ 85069 (tel. (602) 863-2408). Publishes *Ferrari's Places of Interest* (US$14.95), *Ferrari's Places for Men* (US$13.95), *Ferrari's Places for Women* (US$12), and *Inn Places: USA and Worldwide Gay Accommodations* (US$14.95). Also available from Giovanni's Room (see below).

Spartacus International Gay Guide, (US$29.95). Order from 100 East Biddle St., Baltimore, MD 21202 (tel. (410) 727-5677) or c/o Bruno Lützowstraße, P.O. Box 301345, D-1000 Berlin 30, Germany (tel. +49 (30) 25 49 82 00); also available from Giovanni's Room (see above) and from Renaissance House, P.O. Box 292, Village Station, New York, NY 10014 (tel. (212) 674-0120). Extensive list of gay bars, restaurants, hotels, bookstores and hotlines throughout the world. Very specifically for men.

Women Going Places, a new women's travel and resource guide emphasizing women-owned enterprises. Geared towards lesbians, but offers advice appropriate for all women. US$14. Available from Inland Book Company, P.O. Box 120261, East Haven, CT 06512 (tel. (203) 467-4257).

Wherever possible, *Let's Go* lists gay and lesbian information lines, centers, bookstores and nightclubs in specific towns and cities.

■ Travelers On Special Diets

Keeping **kosher** in Mexico is a breeze with the *Jewish Travel Guide* (US$10.75 plus $1.50 postage) from **Jewish Chronicle Publications,** 25 Furnival St., London EC4A 1JT, England (tel. (+44 1) 405-92-52). In the U.S., write or call **Sepher-Hermon Press,** 1265 46th St., Brooklyn, NY 11219 (tel. (718) 972-9010).

Vegetarians can obtain information and possibly the slightly out of date *Vegetarian Travel Guide* (US$16 plus $3 shipping) from the **North American Vegetarian Society,** P.O. Box 72, Dolgeville, NY 13329 (tel. (518) 568-7970) or from the **Vegetarian Society of the U.K.,** Parkdale, Dunham Rd., Altrincham, Cheshire WA14 4QG, England (tel. (+44 61) 928-07-03).

For diabetic concerns, see Health.

GETTING THERE

■ By Plane

About 450 flights leave for Mexico from the U.S. each week. A little research can pay off with discounts or cheaper flights. A travel agent is often a good source of information on scheduled flights and fares, and student travel organizations provide leads on airfare discounts (see Useful Addresses, Travel Organizations). If you're coming from Europe, it's cheapest to fly first to a U.S. city, then connect to Mexico City or some other Mexican airport.

Round-trip airfares to Mexico City, in particular those from the U.S., have remained relatively low: in the summer of 1993, round-trip for students from New York cost about US$368. Getting to less central areas from the U.S. often entails flying to Mexico City and transferring. A travel agent can arrange routings within Mexico in advance. The following cities serve as good bases for travel to outlying areas if you are flying into Mexico City: Mérida for the Yucatán, Puerto Vallarta or Guadalajara for Jalisco and Colima, Tuxtla Gutiérrez for Chiapas.

Mexicana (tel. (800) 531-7921) and **Aeroméxico** (tel. (800) 237-6639) are the two major national airlines, covering most of Mexico; regional airlines also provide service in many areas. Though more expensive than land travel, flying in Mexico is very inexpensive compared to air-travel costs in the U.S. and other countries. Mexicana gives occasional discounts that make flying even more attractive. If the alternative is an interminable bus ride through completely rustic territory, a flight may be worth the extra pesos.

Confirm reservations 72 hours in advance for your flight and be aware of the **departure tax** levied at Mexican international airports (US$11.50). Bring pesos with you to the airport in order to avoid losing money in a last-minute currency exchange. Regardless of the airline, expect delays of a few hours.

Many airlines sell package deals that include accommodations and car rental. These deals sacrifice flexibility and may end up including too many expensive extras for the budget traveler; it is advisable to use them only if you are planning a one- to two-week vacation during peak tourist season (around Christmas or during Spring Break), when especially cheap packages are available. You usually have to book well in advance and may receive no refund should you cancel.

The availability of standby flights is declining on many airlines, but if you can find them, their advantage is flexibility. The disadvantage is that during peak season, flying standby can randomize your vacation more than you would like—the number of available seats is established only minutes before departure. Call individual carriers for availability and prices. Tickets are usually sold at the airport on the day of departure. Some travel agents can issue standby tickets, but may hesitate to do so.

More expensive than standby, **Advanced Purchase Excursion (APEX)** fares provide confirmed reservations and permit arrival and departure from different cities. Reservations must be made 21 days in advance, and stays are limited from one week to three months. Changing APEX reservations results in a penalty of US$50-$100, depending on the airline and the type of change.

Couriers are sometimes needed; in return for surrendering luggage space, travelers who agree to serve as couriers receive a considerable discount (50-80%) on the airfare. **Now Voyager,** 74 Varick St. #307, New York, NY 10013 (tel. (213) 432-1616) and **Halbart Express,** 147-05 176th St., Jamaica, NY 11434 (tel. (718) 656-8189), among other firms, mediate such transactions. The *Courier Air Travel Handbook* (US$10.70) explains step-by-step how to work with courier companies. For a copy, contact **Thunderbird Press,** 5930-10 W. Greenway Blvd., #112H, Glendale, AZ 85306 (tel. (800) 345-0096 or (602) 843-6716, fax (602) 978-7836). **Travel Unlimited,** P.O. Box 1058, Allston, MA 02134-1058, publishes comprehensive, monthly newsletters detailing all possible options for international travel on air couriers. Couriers do not advertise, so this is an invaluable resource (1-year subscription US$25, US$35 outside U.S.).

Discount clearing houses also offer savings on charter flights, commercial flights, tour packages, and cruises. These clubs make unsold tickets available from three weeks up to a few days before departure. Annual dues run US$30-50, but the fares offered can be extremely cheap, often less than US$160 each way. Places to investigate include:

Last Minute Travel Club, 1249 Boylston St., Boston, MA 02215 (tel. (800) 527-8646 or (617) 267-9800). No membership fee. Hotline for customers.

Last Minute Travel Connection, 601 Skokie Blvd. #224, Northbrook, IL 60062 (tel. (708) 498-9216, fax 498-5856). Provides information about bargains on air fares, hotels, package tours, cruises and condominiums. Services include registration service, plus bargain listings subscriptions ($40 per month, $200 per week) and 900 number for current travel bargains: tel. (900) 446-8292, $1 per minute (demonstration at tel. (708) 498-3883). Booklet *How to Save Money on Last Minute Travel* available.

Sunline Express, 607 Market St., San Francisco, CA 94105 (tel. (800) SUN-LINE (786-5463) or (415) 541-7800). Specializes in flights to Mexico and South America.

Travel Avenue, 180 N Desplaines St., Chicago, IL 60606 (tel. (800) 333-3335). Discount of 5-16% on international flights, with a US$25 surcharge.

Travelers' Advantage, 49 Music Sq. W, Nashville, TN 37203 (tel. (800) 548-1116). Primarily for U.S. travelers flying round-trip from the U.S.

■ By Bus or Train

Greyhound serves El Paso, Laredo and Brownsville, TX, and Calexico and San Diego, CA. Smaller lines serve these cities plus Eagle Pass, TX, and Nogales, AZ. Buses tend not to cross the border, but at each of these stops you can pick up Mexican bus lines on the other side. Tres Estrellas de Oro, Estrella Blanca, and Transportes Del Norte provide service from the border.

By train, you can take Amtrak to El Paso (US$279 round-trip from New York), walk across the border to Ciudad Juárez and from there use Mexican National Railways trains—or other forms of transportation—to reach points within Mexico. Amtrak also serves San Diego (US$339 round-trip from New York). The San Diego Trolley (information recording tel. (619) 231-8549) marked "San Ysidro" will take you down to the Mexican border for US$1.50. Once in Tijuana you must take a bus to Mexico City, since there is no train service (although trains do serve Mexicali). It is also possible to travel by Amtrak to San Antonio (US$279 round-trip from New York) and take a bus from there to the border towns.

■ By Car

Entrance by car into Mexico is not complicated as long as you keep your vehicle within the *Zona Libre* (Free Zone). The *Zona Libre* extends from the U.S. border 22km into Mexico; it also includes all of Baja California. You will encounter checkpoints as soon as you reach the end of the *Zona Libre* (see Planning Your Trip: Documents and Formalities: Driver's License and Vehicle Permits for details on bringing your car farther into Mexico).

There are 16 entry cities along the U.S.-Mexico border, in California, Arizona, New Mexico and Texas. AAA endorses only three (Laredo, Reynosa, and Matamoros). The main highways into Mexico are Route 1, which leads from Tijuana to the southern tip of Baja California Sur (1680km); Route 15, from Nogales, AZ, to Mexico City (2320km); Route 49, from El Paso, TX, to Mexico City (1800km); Route 57, from Eagle Pass, TX, to Mexico City (1264km); and Route 85 from Laredo or Brownsville, TX, to Mexico City (1176km).

On the U.S. side of the border, several **auto clubs** provide routing services and protection against breakdowns. Find out if your auto club is affiliated with Mexican auto clubs through international motoring agreements; if so, you may receive limited travel services and information from the **Asociación Mexicana Automovilística (AMA)** and the **Asociación Nacional Automovilística (ANA)** (see Useful Addresses: Transportation Services). Both the AMA and the ANA sell road maps. The Mexican consulate or nearest tourist office provides free road maps. **Guía Roji** publishes excellent maps; write them at Governador José Moran 31, Delegación M.

Hidalgo, San Miguel, Chapultepec, 11850 México, D.F. (tel. (5) 515-03-84 or 515-79-63, fax 277-23-07).

If you choose to drive to a border town and then continue by plane, train, or bus, consider storing your car in one of several garages along the U.S. side of the border to avoid permit and insurance hassles.

All non-Mexican **car insurance** is invalid in Mexico, no matter what your policy says. Make sure you arrange to have your car insured in Mexico if you plan to drive it there. **Sanborn's,** Home Office, P.O. Box 310, McAllen, TX 78502 (tel. (512) 686-3601, fax 686-0732) offers insurance with all the trimmings, including road maps, newsletters, a ride board and "Mexico Mike" in Dept. N at the McAllen address (write him for up-to-date, priceless information on driving in Mexico). Remember that if you are in an accident, the police might hold you in jail until everything is sorted out and all claims are settled. If you can prove your ability to pay or can get an adjuster to come out, they will release you.

TRAVELING IN MEXICO

■■■ USEFUL ORGANIZATIONS

Embassies and **consulates** provide a variety of services for citizens away from home. They can refer you to an English-speaking doctor or lawyer, help you replace a lost tourist card, and wire family or friends if you need money and have no other means of obtaining it. They cannot, however, cash checks, act as a postal service, get you out of trouble, supply counsel, or interfere in any way with the legal process in Mexico. Once in jail, you're on your own. (For a list of embassies, see Mexico City Practical Information below.)

Mexico does not want for tourist offices. Branches of the **Mexican Government Tourism Office (Secretaría de Turismo** or **SECTUR)** are located in the capital city of each state and wherever else tourists gather. The address in Mexico City is Av. Presidente Mazaryk 172, Col. Polanco, México, D.F. 11570 (tel. (5) 250-85-55).

■■■ GETTING AROUND

■ By Plane

Flying within Mexico is more expensive than taking a bus or train, but it is considerably cheaper than comparable flights between U.S. cities. In the summer of 1993, you could fly from Huatulco to Oaxaca for US$53.80, from Guadalajara to Manzanillo for $48.50, or from La Paz to Mexico City for US$208.90. Check with Mexican airlines for special rates (see telephone numbers in Getting There: By Plane). Always double-check ticket prices and departure times listed in *Let's Go*, as they were accurate at the time the book was researched in the summer of 1993.

■ By Train

The 15,000 miles of railroad in Mexico are all government-owned, with most lines operating under the name of **Ferrocarriles Nacionales de Mexico** (National Railways of Mexico). Trains run from the border at Nogales, Piedras Negras, Nuevo Laredo, Matamoros, Mexicali and Juárez. The train system is not as extensive nor as punctual as the bus system. Even when they are on time, trains can take twice as long as buses to reach their destination. Riding the rails is best for leisurely travel in very picturesque areas. (The 12-hr. sleeper from Guadalajara to Mexico City is reputed to be pure joy.)

Train fares are generally less expensive than buses, but there is a great risk of theft (of either money or suitcases); the small amount you might save over bus travel could rapidly become a major loss. Pickpockets make their living by boarding first class or other trains at major stops (those which last more than 10min.) and brushing past unwary foreigners. Make sure your luggage is locked and your valuables are with you and inaccessible to prying hands.

There are several train options: *rápido* trains, which cost more than *locales*, cut travel time in half by chugging past smaller towns without stopping. *Rápido* trains are almost always cleaner and more comfortable. *Primera clase* (first class) or, better yet, *primera clase especial* (comparable to "business" or "ambassador" class), cost significantly more than *segunda clase* (second class), but you get cleanliness and comfort for your money. *Segunda clase* may be the cheapest form of transportation in the world (about US$3 for the ride from Guadalajara to Mexico City, as compared to US$7 for a first-class ticket), and according to some travelers it's the only way to see the "real" Mexico. But the "real" Mexico respects only the most intrepid and experienced of budget travelers: those who can stand for 20 hours in a hot, dirty, crowded car, with pickpockets and animals for company, and a hole cut in the floor for a toilet.

Mexico by Rail, P.O. Box 3508, Laredo, TX 78044 (tel. (800) 228-3225 or (512) 727-3814) can reserve first-class railway tickets for travelers. Make arrangements two to three weeks in advance, and the company will mail the tickets to your home.

Another option for arranging train reservations is to write or call the appropriate railroad officer in Mexico. Expect this to take about 30 days, and do so only when you plan to travel on the major routes. Less-traveled stations may misplace such advance orders and may not even sell tickets at all.

■ By Bus

If you have any qualms about being without your own set of wheels in Mexico, the extensive, astoundingly cheap bus service should lay them to rest. A first-class ticket from Tijuana all the way to Mexico City costs US$55. First-class buses are relatively comfortable and efficient; they occasionally even have bathrooms and functioning air-conditioners (ask at the ticket window). Second- and third-class buses, which are only slightly cheaper than first class, are often overcrowded, hot, and uncomfortable. However, they are full of life (human and chicken alike), run more frequently and have food service—at the numerous stops, vendors jump on the bus to sell snacks.

When you buy your ticket the agent will ask where you want to sit. At night, the right side of the bus won't face the constant glare of oncoming headlights. During the day, the shady side of the bus will be a lot cooler (the left when going south, the right when heading north). Mexicans usually refuse to open the windows when the bus is moving.

Buses are either *de local* or *de paso*. *De local* originate at the station from which you leave. Buy your ticket a day (or at least a few hours) in advance because only a few *de locales* leave per day. Once you get on the bus, guard your ticket stub as you may be asked to show it at a later stop.

De paso buses originate elsewhere and pass through your station. First-class *de pasos* sell only as many tickets as there are available seats—when the bus arrives, the driver disembarks to give this information to the ticket seller. When these tickets go on sale, forget civility, chivalry and any ism which might possibly stand between you and a ticket, or plan to spend the greater portion of your vacation in bus stations. Second-class *de paso* buses sell tickets based on the number of people with assigned seats who have gotten off the bus. This system does not, unfortunately, take into account the people and packages jammed into the aisle. You may find someone (or something) already in your assigned seat when you reach it; in this case, enlist the bus driver's help. Hold your ground and try to keep calm. It is proper to offer to hold someone's heavy equipment (such as children or chickens), but if

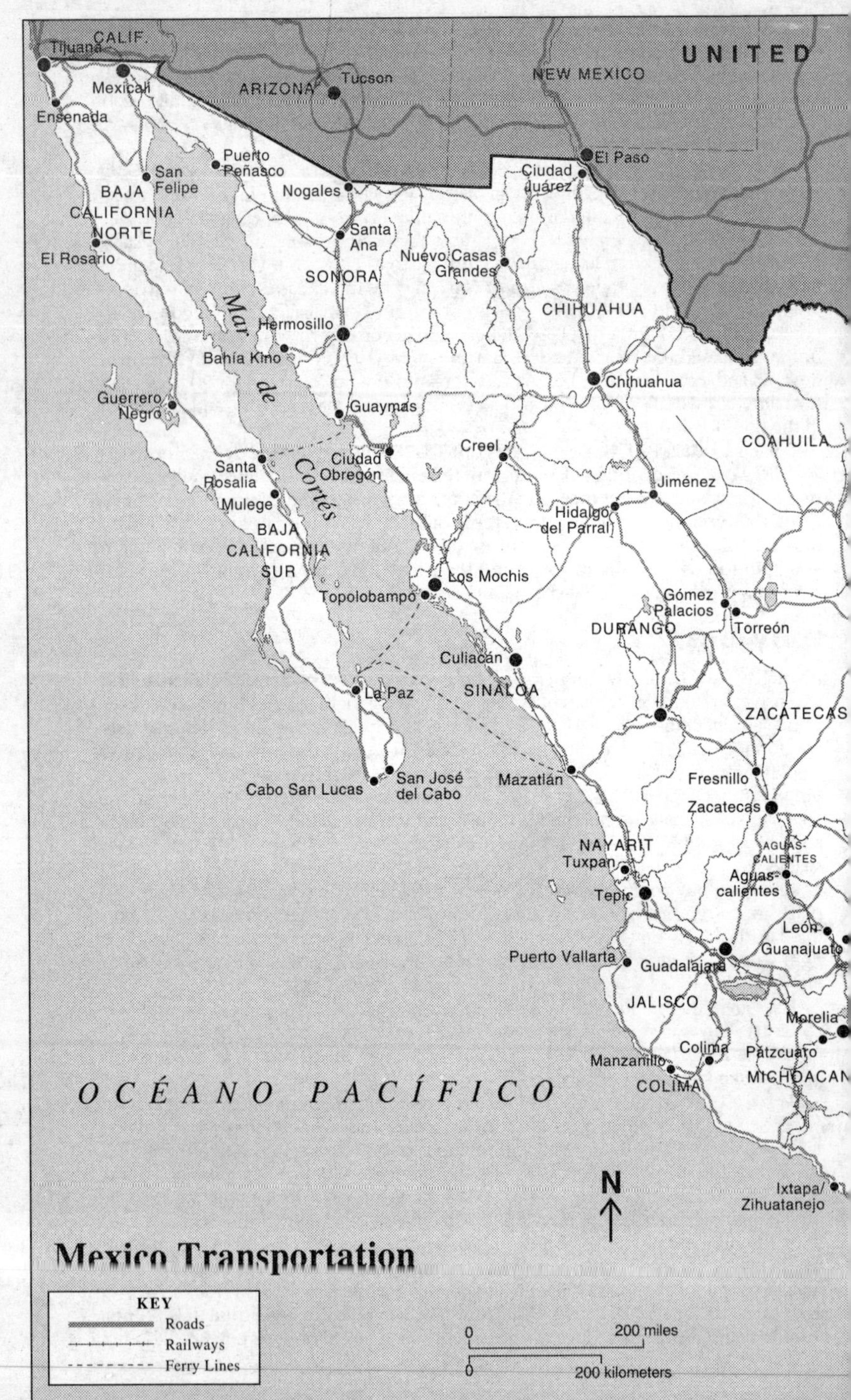

Mexico Transportation

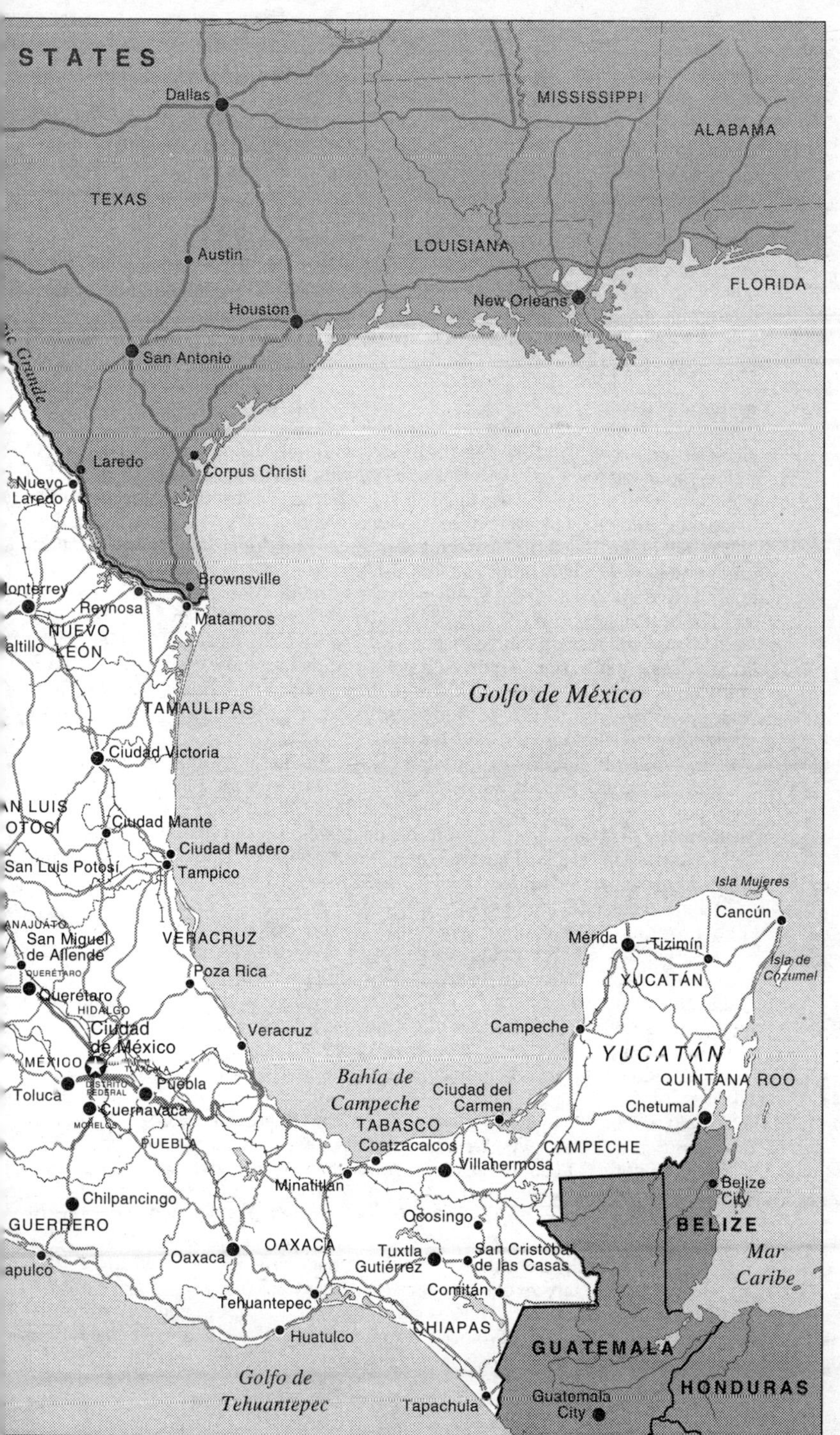
STATES
Dallas
MISSISSIPPI
ALABAMA
TEXAS
Austin
LOUISIANA
Houston
New Orleans
FLORIDA
San Antonio
Laredo
Corpus Christi
Nuevo Laredo
Brownsville
Reynosa
Matamoros
NUEVO LEÓN
TAMAULIPAS
Golfo de México
Ciudad Victoria
Ciudad Mante
Ciudad Madero
San Luis Potosí
Tampico
Isla Mujeres
Cancún
Mérida
Tizimín
San Miguel de Allende
VERACRUZ
Isla de Cozumel
Poza Rica
YUCATÁN
Querétaro
HIDALGO
Ciudad de México
Veracruz
Campeche
YUCATÁN
MÉXICO
Bahía de Campeche
QUINTANA ROO
Toluca
Puebla
Ciudad del Carmen
Chetumal
Cuernavaca
TABASCO
MORELOS
PUEBLA
Coatzacalcos
CAMPECHE
Villahermosa
Minatitlán
Belize City
Chilpancingo
Ocosingo
GUERRERO
BELIZE
OAXACA
Tuxtla Gutiérrez
San Cristóbal de las Casas
Mar Caribe
Oaxaca
Comitán
Tehuantepec
CHIAPAS
Huatulco
GUATEMALA
Golfo de Tehuantepec
HONDURAS
Tapachula
Guatemala City

you feel the urge to give up your seat to someone who looks more in need of a rest than you, just envision how much you'll need it in ten hours.

Though prices are now reasonably stable, the schedules fluctuate constantly; check at the station before making travel plans.

Offering an alternative to traditional bus travel, **Green Tortoise (G.T.)** maintains a fleet of old diesel coaches with foam mattresses, sofa seats, and dinettes, and their self-proclaimed mission is to go where no bus has gone before. G.T. trips roam all over the Mexican mainland, the Baja, and Belize for two to five weeks at a time. Prices average about US$250 per week and include use of the bus at night for sleeping as well as tours of the pertinent regions. Travelers pitch in about US$5.50 a day for communal meals. If a tour isn't full, passengers can abort the program at any point and only pay for the portion they have traveled. During summer months, tours may fill up four to six weeks in advance, so book ahead. Call or write Green Tortoise, P.O. Box 24459, San Francisco, CA 94124 (tel. (800) 227-4766, in CA (415) 821-0803).

■ By Car

Mexican roads vary from smooth turnpikes (with tolls that cost more than gas) to rutted, mountain roads used by trucks for bombing runs. Mexican drivers are just as disparate: some believe that driving over 40km per hour constitutes dangerous folly, while others employ folly as their navigational credo.

The maximum speed on Mexican highways is 100km per hour (62mph) unless otherwise posted. Speed limits can be frustratingly low. In most small towns, you'll come across speed bumps. Usually one slows traffic on each side of town, and another perches right in the middle. Roadwork is continually in progress across Mexico; you will regularly drive by construction workers making utterly incomprehensible but codified signals, at which point you should slow down until you figure out what is going on. One particularly confusing signal looks like a plea for you to back up. In fact, it is a request to move forward. In general, take it easy until you master the sign language of Mexican roads.

Be especially careful driving during the rainy season (May-Oct.), when roads are often in poor condition and landslides are common. At night, pedestrians and livestock pop up on the roadway at the darndest times. This doesn't seem to bother the locals, many of whom drive without headlights. If you can help it, don't drive at night. (And whatever you do, never spend the night on the side of the road.) When approaching a one-lane bridge, labeled *puente angosto* or *solo carril*, the first driver to flash headlights has the right of way.

Exercise particular caution when driving along: Highway 15 in the state of Sinaloa; Highway 2 in the vicinity of Carborca, Sonora; Highway 57 between Matehuala and San Luis Potosí; the highway between Palomares and Tuxtepec, Oaxaca; and Highway 40. A number of assaults have occurred on these stretches of pavement. Check with local authorities or the nearest U.S. consulate to update the situation and to identify other areas of potential danger. When driving on roads near the capital, watch out for fog. A sign warning *Maneje despacio* (Drive slow) should be taken seriously.

To help reduce the heinous pollution in Mexico City, tourist traffic in the metropolis is restricted (see Mexico City: Transportation Within Mexico City for details.)

In Baja California, if you want to leave your car and go somewhere by public transportation for a few days, you must pay to park in an authorized lot; otherwise, the car will be towed or confiscated. The Motor Vehicle Office will tell you where to leave your car legally.

When parking in the rest of the country, someone may help you pull into a space. A rhythmic tap-tap, tap-tap on your back bumper means that you still have room to back up. A sharp, sudden tap means stop. When you return to your car and someone informs you that they have been watching it while you were gone, hand them some change. If a group of kids approaches, pay only one of them.

When asking for directions, don't take your high school Spanish for granted. The word you probably learned for "road"—*camino*—means "path" away from the cities. You'll want to stick to *carreteras* (highways).

PEMEX (Petroleos Mexicanos) sells two types of gas: Nova (regular) and Extra (unleaded). Nova (*no va* in Spanish means "doesn't go") is appropriately named, and one whiff of a Nova-burning car will make you realize why emissions controls are so important. Unless your car is old, rugged, and satisfied with low-quality leaded gas, driving it through Mexico is not the brightest idea. Unleaded gas, no longer as hard to get as in years past, is making its presence felt in Mexico. You will find it throughout the Baja as well as in Guadalajara, Monterrey, Mexico City, most border towns, and all major metropolitan areas. But beware: even if you do find a silver Extra pump, it may be filled with Nova gasoline. The Mexican government has introduced two new types of gas, Nova Plus and Extra Plus, but the gasoline situation remains unpredictable. Mechanically inclined drivers might want to order a "test" pipe from a specialty parts house to replace the catalytic converter so the car can process Nova upon its arrival in Mexico.

Both Nova and Extra are extremely cheap by all but Saudi Arabian standards. Don't get overcharged: know how much gas you'll need before you pull in and make sure the register is rung back to zero before pumping begins. PEMEX accepts cash only. When you pull into a PEMEX station to check the tires, remember that pumps in Mexico are calibrated in kilograms (1kg = 2.2 lb.).

The heat, bumpy roads, and fair-to-middling gas may well take a toll on your car. Mexican mechanics are good and charge very reasonable rates, but if they've never seen your model, reconcile yourself to a lengthy stay. Oil is scarce, and parts are available only for those models that Mexicans drive; all the various VWs are in plentiful supply, especially the Beetle (known as the *Vochito*), as are Datsun/Nissans and 1970s Detroit boat-cars. No matter what kind of car you sport, bring spare oil, spark plugs, fan belts and air and fuel filters—these should take care of all but the biggest problems.

If you break down on one of the major highways sometime between dawn and sunset, pull off the road, raise the hood, and wait for an *Angel Verde* (Green Angel) to come to the rescue. **Green Angels** are the Mexican Government Tourism Office's innovation—emergency trucks dispatched by radio, staffed by English-speaking mechanics and equipped for common repair jobs and minor medical problems (radio communications office at tel. (5) 250-48-17). Your green saviors may take a while to show up, but the service (except for parts, gas and oil) is free. They go everywhere but the Distrito Federal.

If you get into a car accident realize that as soon as the police arrive, they will detain everybody until they have figured out what happened, no matter who's to blame, an immense, and unnecessary legal mess. An insurance policy, which demonstrates your ability to pay, will spring you from jail. You may also become liable by coming to the aid of someone hurt in an accident. Leave the area before the police arrive or risk paying a heavy price for your good Samaritanism.

■ By Thumb

Let's Go urges you to use common sense if you decide to hitch, and to seriously consider all possible risks before you make that decision. The information listed below and throughout the book is not intended to recommend hithchiking; *Let's Go* does not recommend hitchhiking as a means of transportation.

You'll see plenty of Mexicans and *gringos* standing by the side of the road with thumbs pointed skyward. Accepting rides from strangers is potentially dangerous, and caution and knowledge can go a long way. If your Spanish or tolerance for local customs is weak, the ordeal may take more out of you than would the extra pesos for a bus.

The Mexicans who pick up tourists are often friendly, often offering meals, tours, or other extras, but equally often suspicion is warranted. Those who hitch find out where the driver is going before they get in, and think twice if he or she opens the door quickly and offers to drive anywhere. Do not accept a ride if any cause for concern arises; make an excuse and wait for another car to come along. Women should not hitchhike alone. Never accept a ride without sizing up the driver. On many highways (the Mexico City-Acapulco road, for example), *bandidos* are common.

Before getting in, make sure the passenger window or door opens from inside. If there are several people in the car, do not sit in the middle. Assume a quick-exit position, which rules out the back seat of a two-door car. Keep backpacks and other baggage where they are easily accessible—don't let the driver store them in the trunk. If you have trouble getting out for any reason, affecting the pose of someone about to vomit works wonders.

Every city and every road has a best and worst spot for hitchhiking. Hitchers reccomend stretches near a major intersection where many cars converge or PEMEX stations. They also reccomend that hitchers should be cautious when standing on the shoulders of highways, since they are not considered off-limits to drivers, and that they should bring along something to drink and some sort of protection from the sun and rain. Furthermore, it is said that those who appear neat and travel light, have a better chance of getting a ride.

Some drivers may ask for payment for the ride, especially in areas where no alternative form of public transportation exists, or when riding in a pickup truck. Truck drivers often earn extra revenue by taking on passengers. As with a taxi, riders should always ask what a ride in a truck will cost before getting in; it may seem expensive, it is usually based on expenses. Those in the know say that cargo trucks are easy to hitch with, but women are often prohibited from riding in trucks by many companies who feel that a nearby female presence would distract the driver.

■■■ ACCOMMODATIONS

■ Hotels

Though hotels in Mexico include some of the world's most overpriced, the majority are shockingly affordable. All hotels, ranging from luxury resorts in Cancún to dumps in Monterrey, are controlled by the government's **Secretaría de Turismo (SecTur).** SecTur ensures that hotels of similar quality charge similar prices and requires that all hotels display the official tariff sheet. You should always ask to see this sheet if you doubt the quoted price; make sure it is up-to-date. Although hotel prices are regulated, proprietors are not prohibited from charging *less* than the official rate. If the hotel looks like it hasn't seen a customer in several days, a little bargaining may work wonders, especially if you offer to stay a number of days. For a room with one bed, request *un cuarto con una cama*. If bedding down with a fellow way-farer, ask for one *con dos camas* (with two beds).

Usually located within a block or two of the *zócalo* (central plaza), the cheapest hotels (US$4-7) rarely provide private bathrooms or other amenities. Slightly higher-priced hotels (US$9-15) usually reside in the same district but are much better equipped, including rooms with private bathrooms. Before accepting any room, ask to see it—the proprietor should comply gladly. Always ask if the price, no matter how low it seems, includes any meals. Tourists often are so surprised at low hotel prices that unwittingly they forgo meals for which they have paid.

If the hotels listed in *Let's Go* are full or don't appeal to you, ask cab drivers or vendors in the market for a good recommendation. Also, hotel people in one town are often a good source for hotel leads in the next town on your itinerary. For the bare-bones budget traveler, the hammock is the way to go. If you plan to travel on a shoe-string, buy one. Most towns in Mexico are dotted with *palapas*. For a small fee, these open-air restaurants double as places to hang your hat and hammock when the sun goes down. In small *yucateco* towns, locals often let travelers use hammock hooks for a pittance.

Hotels in Mexico often lock their doors at night, and small-town establishments may do so surprisingly early. A locked door doesn't necessarily mean "closed for the night," as someone usually is on duty. By arriving early in small towns or calling ahead if you can't avoid arriving late, and by checking with the hotel desk before going out for a late night on the town, you'll help dispel the Mexican myth of the obnoxious foreigner. If, however, you must choose between angering the hotel guard and sharing the gutter with the drunks and the rats, knock to raise the dead.

Reservations are not absolutely necessary (except during Christmas, Semana Santa, and other festivals), but if you're exhausted upon arrival, they make life much easier. You can just about always find a bed somewhere, but without reservations you may waste money and time.

■ Hostels

Mexican hostels are often run-down, far from town, and no cheaper than local hotels (US$2-10 per night, with meals an additional US$8 per day). The only people who should consider hostelling are younger travelers who want the security and discipline of an orderly establishment with regular meals and nighttime supervision. Their ban on alcohol, smoking restrictions, and limited hours (most are open from 7-9am and 5-10pm) also deter many budget travelers.

Most Mexican hostels will give you a bed even if you don't have a hostel card. They may, however, charge you more for it. If you plan to stay in hostels regularly, get a Hostelling International (HI, formerly International Youth Hostel Federation, IYHF) card (see Useful Addresses: Travel Organizations). For more information, write the Agencia Nacional de Turismo Juvenil, Glorieta del Metro Insurgentes, Local CC-11, Col. Juárez, 06600 México, D.F. (tel. (5) 525-26-99, 525-29-16, 533-12-91, or 525-29-74) for information.

The two Mexican hostel chains, **Consejo Nacional de Recursos para la Atención de la Juventud (CREA)** and **Servicio Educativo de Turismo de los Estudiantes y la Juventud de México (SETEJ)** have their own hostel cards. CREA is the HI-affiliated, government-subsidized hostel chain. SETEJ is internationally subsidized and, in general, the more run-down of the two, though there are exceptions (notably, Acapulco).

For **youth hostel brochures,** write: Asociación Mexicana de Albergues de la Juventud, AC, Av. Francisco 1 Madero No. 6, Despachos 314 y 315, Delegación Cuauhtémoc, 06000 México, D.F., or Red Nacional de Albergues Turísticos, Oxtopulco N. 40, Col. Oxtopulco Universidad, 04310 México, D.F.

For information about the **YMCA** in Mexico, call or write Y's Way International, 224 E. 47th St., New York, NY 10017 (tel. (212) 308-2899).

■ Camping

For the budget travel experience par excellence, try camping in Mexico—it eliminates hotel costs, and if you bring fishing gear to the beach, it can also save you money on food. Campers accustomed to prim and proper campgrounds will be taken aback, however. Mexican national parks often exist only in theory; many are indistinguishable from the surrounding cities. Trails, campgrounds and rangers are strictly *norteamericano* concepts.

Privately owned **trailer parks** are relatively common on major highways—look for signs with a picture of a trailer, or the words *Parque de Trailer*, *Campamento*, or *Remolques*). These places may or may not allow campers to pitch tents. Don't set up camp next to a well-traveled road, or screeching brakes and the shattering glass of your car may shake you from that peaceful slumber.

The best guide for campers is *The People's Guide to RV Camping in Mexico*, which is an expanded version of the camping section in *The People's Guide to Mexico* (both from John Muir; see Useful Addresses: Publications). The **Sierra Club Bookstore,** 730 Polk St., San Francisco, CA 94109 (tel. (415) 776-2211) offers *Adventuring Along the Gulf of Mexico* (US$10.95 plus $3 shipping, 10% discount for members). For adventure narratives or *Mexico's Volcanoes, A Climbing Guide* (US$12.95), which contains maps, photos, and a bilingual mountaineering glossary, write or call **Mountaineers Books,** 1011 SW Klickitat Way, #107, Seattle, WA 98134 (tel. (800) 553-4453, fax (206) 223-6306). **Wilderness Press,** (see address in Planning Your Trip: Additional Concerns: Traveling With Children) disseminates general backpacking information and publishes outdoor guides such as the *Baja Adventure Book* (US$19.95) and *Adventure Travel in Latin America* (US$12.95), which includes Mexico.

For information on hostel-affiliated campgrounds, write to Agencia Nacional de Turismo Juvenil (see Hostels).

LIFE AND TIMES

■ History

Indigenous Civilizations

Human history in Mexico began 30,000-40,000 years ago, with the migration from Asia of the people a disoriented Columbus would later call "Indians." During the first epoch of *indígena* history, known as the Archaic Period (5000-1500 BC), nomads began to shift their means of subsistence. As animal populations thinned out, roaming hunters turned to a more sedentary, agricultural existence. Their main crop, *maíz* (corn), remains a staple of the Mexican diet.

The **Olmecs** formed what is believed to be Mexico's first settled society around 1200BC, in the lowlands of today's Veracruz and Tabasco. The dominant culture during the Pre-Classical Period (1500BC-300 AD), the Olmecs built the cities now known as La Venta, San Lorenzo and Tres Zapotes. Their original inhabitants revered the jaguar, wrote in hieroglyphics and sculpted giant stone figures. San Lorenzo was violently destroyed around 900 BC, and La Venta suffered a similar fate before another four centuries had elapsed. While the Olmecs perished, many of their cultural achievements were transmitted to other Mesoamerican peoples, notably the **Maya.**

The genius of the Maya stands in the remains of their ancient cities: Palenque, Chichén Itzá, Uxmal, Tulum, Bonampak. During the first 300 years of the Mexican Classic Period (300-900 AD), the Maya came to rival and often better contemporary Europe in engineering, mathematics, astronomy, and calendrical calculations. Their architecture and artwork are similarly fabulous.

Around 900 AD, however, the Mayan empire mysteriously collapsed; widespread peasant revolts are one proposed culprit. A Mayan renaissance occurred in the northern Yucatán after 1200 AD, but with a new influence from the west—Teotihuacán culture, as elaborated by the **Toltecs**. Parallel Maya/Toltec legends tell how Quetzalcóatl (The Feathered Serpent), a great Toltec king, broke away from the Toltec empire and made his way to the Yucatán with his people; the myths predict his eventual return.

The Toltec empire dominated most of central Mexico during the Post-Classic Period (900-1540 AD). Its warlike subjects practiced human sacrifice and, like the Olmecs, placed the jaguar at the center of their iconography. The cultural hegemony of the Toltecs was such that their decline in the 12th century AD has been compared, in catastrophic significance, to the fall of the Roman Empire. The Aztecs, also known as the Tenochca or the Mexica, came into contact with the Toltecs from their mythical homeland in northwestern Mexico; the perished Toltec culture would provide the framework for the Aztec civilization, next to forge an empire. Their dominance would crumble only with the Spanish Conquest. After the fall of the Toltecs, they wandered hither and thither from the end of the 12th century until 1325, when at the southwestern border of Lake Texcoco they beheld an eagle with a serpent in its talons. This would be the site of their legendary floating city **Tenochtitlán.**

The Aztecs practiced a religion derived from their Toltec predecessors; they worshipped a supreme being, the aggregate force of numerous deities. The chief Aztec deity was the war-like Huitzilopochtli, the personification of the sun. According to legend, he perished red and sated every evening only to be reborn anemic the following dawn, craving the blood of human victims. In contrast to this solar vampire, Quetzalcóatl, the god of the air, instructed the natives in the use of metals, in agriculture, and in the art of government. He was thought to have been light-skinned with dark hair and a long flowing beard. When Cortés arrived, he was mistaken for this beloved Aztec deity by an insecure and mystical emperor Moctezuma II—an error which would prove costly.

The Aztecs practiced human sacrifice on a large scale. In the yearly offering to Tezcatlipoca, the god of honor, the most attractive youth in the land was selected to live like a king for eleven months and then, stripped of his lavish accoutrements, to part with his heart at the hands of the head-priest and master of ceremonies.

The Aztecs built Mexico's largest *indígena* empire; their penchant for sanguinary expansion helped secure a dominion stretching from the Atlantic to the Pacific and all the way to Guatemala and Nicaragua. The beauty and architectural sophistication of the island city Tenochtitlán, connected to the mainland by a network of canals and causeways, led Western chroniclers to compare it to the fabulous cities of their chivalric romance tales and to dub it the Venice of the New World. *Chinampas*, or "floating gardens," enabled the Aztecs to cultivate the swamp efficiently. Tenochtitlán developed into one of the world's largest cities.

Conquest and Colonization

In 1519, the Spanish arrived on the east coast of Mexico, in what is now the state of Tabasco, prepared to carry out a campaign that would become the tragic foundation of the Mexican nation. Where Cortés passed, history ended and began over again.

His men disembarked from what natives saw as "floating castles" and were carrying "fire-breathing" weapons. They were lavished with gold and other gifts by awed local chieftains. Mexican natives may have believed Cortés to be the returning Quetzalcóatl, who had departed from his devotees after mysteriously incurring the wrath of the gods. Dressed in his snakeskin wizard suit, Quetzalcóatl had embarked on an ocean voyage declaring that he and his descendants would one day return. This myth of a future return would ultimately accelerate the Spanish victory. Moctezuma II felt bound to receive the explorers as gods. He presented them with the ancient treasures of the errant deity.

Pushing on toward Tenochtitlán, the *conquistadores* capitalized on the Aztec empire's lack of cohesion. Defeated inhabitants of a domain held together by sheer force, conquered tribes hated their Aztec overlords. With the help of an Aztec mistress and interpreter known to the Spanish as Doña Marina (or Malinche), Cortés recruited armies of disaffected *indígenas*. By November, the Spanish had reached Tenochtitlán. An initial period of peaceful, if tense, relations quickly soured, and Cortés was driven from the city in a rout. An incredible string of coincidences and luck let Cortés regroup quickly, and two years later, on August 13, 1521, the Aztec capital fell for good. The Spanish erected a cathedral atop the rubble of the temple to the Aztec war-god, ironically dedicating it to their own patron of war, Santiago. Modern-day Mexico City sprawls over the ruins of Tenochtitlán.

Cortés became the first governor-general of the vanquished Aztec empire, renaming it *Nueva España*. As the conquistadors searched for gold to mine and missionaries searched for *indígenas* to convert, the colony expanded northward and southward, but power remained concentrated. The ruling class of New Spain—a few bureaucrats, landowners, and religious officials—lived comfortably while the *encomienda* system made virtual slaves out of the native population who worked the estates and mines. Two-thirds of the *indígena* population died of European diseases.

Meanwhile, the Catholic church was amassing real estate and capital. Religious and economic exploitation were the girders of Spanish-dominated Mexico. Economic disparity gave birth to political tension, and the 18th century saw the decline of Spanish colonial rule. As the peasants struggled under the brunt of imperialism, absentee rule heated the revolutionary kettle. *Criollos*—those of Spanish blood born in the New World—particularly resented the privileges of the displaced Spanish aristocracy, or *peninsulares*. Approximately 300 years after Hernán Cortés won the Aztec empire for the monarch of Spain, Mexico began to reconsider its allegiance to the mother country.

Sporadic rebellion took place during the first few years of the 19th century. Mexico celebrates its independence on September 16 to commemorate the 1810 uprising known as *El Grito de Dolores* (The Cry of Dolores), when **Padre Miguel Hidalgo y Costilla** roused the villagers of Dolores with a cry for racial equality, land reform and—in a bid for moderate support—an end to the rule of those Spanish who had acquiesced to the conqueror Napoleon. The revolt gained in violence and momentum as it approached Mexico City but subsided before reaching the capital. Hidalgo ordered a retreat but was captured and shot in July of 1811.

The cause was then taken up by **José Maria Morelos y Pavón,** a parish priest committed less to social justice and more to outright independence than Hidalgo had been. Rebellion swept through southern Mexico but lost much of its effectiveness after Morelos was executed in December of 1815. Only scattered bands of insurgents remained.

Mexican independence finally came about by default. Ferdinand had regained the Spanish crown but in 1820 was pressured into approving the Constitution of Cádiz, a document too liberal to suit the rich *criollos* and *peninsulares* of Mexico. **Agustín de Iturbide,** the general who had led the Spanish against Hidalgo and Morelos, suddenly joined forces with the rebels in hopes of maintaining the precarious status quo. Their combined Army of Three Guarantees declared the fight for independence, union, and Roman Catholicism; shortly thereafter the viceroy of New Spain signed the Treaty of Córdoba. By August 24, 1821, Mexico was officially a nation.

Independence

Iturbide reigned as Emperor Agustín of Mexico for about a year, until discontented military groups persuaded him to abdicate. A constitutional convention proclaimed the Republic of Mexico in 1823. For the next 50 years, the landed gentry, the military, and the church pursued contradictory interests in the public domain. Mexico had no experience with self-government, and a capricious economy contributed to the political instability. The national debt grew enormous. If military salaries were not paid in full, officers would simply seize control of the state and negotiate new international loans at ever-higher interest. Mexico was independent, but socio-economic conditions did not reflect the change. The *criollo* elite took over right where their predecessors had left off, while most *indígenas* and mestizos continued to live in abject poverty.

Political power swung back and forth between conservative and liberal factions for decades after the establishment of the Republic, but the spotlight singled out one man. Of the 50 governments that cluttered the first 30 years of Mexico's independence, fully 11 were headed by **General Antonio López de Santa Ana.** Corruption, greed, and a touch of the bizarre marked Santa Ana's tenure.

Santa Ana is best known, however, for having presided over the dismemberment of the new nation. The Mexican-American War began in 1836 as a border dispute between Mexico and the Republic of Texas, but when the U.S. annexed Texas in 1845, Mexico found itself up against a more formidable adversary. Despite the protests of Abraham Lincoln and other pacifist politicians, President James K. Polk claimed everything north of the Río Grande for the U.S. In pursuit of Santa Ana, Generals Zachary Taylor and Winfield Scott closed in on Mexico City from the north and east. Young cadets, the *Niños Héroes* (Boy Heroes), valiantly fought off U.S. troops from their military school in Chapultepec Castle, then, wrapped in the Mexican flag, dashed themselves to their deaths when all hope was lost. The war ended in 1847 when the capital fell. Under the terms of the Treaty of Guadalupe-Hidalgo, the U.S. paid US$15 million for Texas, New Mexico and California. Five years later, Santa Ana sold off Arizona as well. Mexico lost half of its territory and most of its pride in the war, and the U.S. inherited states rich with Mexican culture.

Reform

The uniquely "Mexican" self-consciousness that had evolved since independence was shaken by the ease of the U.S. victory. Reforms had to be instituted for Mexico to remain autonomous. **Benito Juárez,** an expatriate *indígena* lawyer, wrote the Constitution of 1857 in New Orleans. He and his fellow liberals called for a clean break with colonialism and for the separation of church and state. In 1860, after a short civil war between the liberals (supported by U.S. President James Buchanan) and the ruling conservatives, Juárez became president of Mexico. Ironically, Mexico's first *indígena* president would exhibit little concern for the native population, which was actually worse off than it had been under the paternalism of the Spanish crown.

Three years later, the country was once again in foreign hands. Under the pretext of enforcing debt payment, the French invaded and conquered Mexico, which was an integral part of the "Latin League" envisioned by Napoleon III. Austrian **Duke Maximilian von Habsburg** became the new emperor of Mexico but did not prove equal to the job. The second empire collapsed when the French withdrew their support in order to counter a Prussian threat across the ocean. Maximilian was executed in 1867, and Juárez resumed office until a heart attack in 1872.

Mexico began to modernize under Juárez, but it was **General Porfirio Díaz** who truly ushered Mexico into the industrial age. Díaz took power through a military coup in 1876, and his dictatorship (known as the *Porfiriato*) lasted until 1911. A scientific positivist, Díaz demanded order and progress at the cost of liberty. His administrative method was simply stated: *pan o palo* (bread or the stick). The press was censored, the congress stultified, elections rigged, and resistance crushed. The economy stabilized, but the country's resources were controlled entirely by a handful of wealthy Mexicans and foreign investors. None of the material prosperity trickled down to workers, peasants, or *indígenas*. Díaz retained control of Mexico for so long possibly because his reign brought peace and progress (of a sort) to a country which had known little of either since independence. Though Díaz did not actually abolish the reforms instituted by Juárez, by the early 1900s, a majority of Mexicans opposed the oppressive *Porfiriato*.

Revolution

Díaz's announcement in 1908 that he would not run for office in the next "election" touched off a frenzy of political activity as the *anti-reeleccionistas* campaigned for their candidate **Francisco Madero,** a wealthy landowner. A sham election returned Díaz to the presidency, and in June of 1910, Madero was arrested. Although he escaped in October, imprisonment turned out to be a step on the road to Madero's martyrdom. Opposition to the *Porfiriato* coalesced around him. From exile in San Antonio, Madero declared November 20 to be the day that Mexicans would rise in arms. Begun as a contest for executive power, the revolution ballooned into an economic and social struggle over who would mold the face of modern Mexico.

Díaz did not fare well over the next year. He resigned in 1911 and Madero was elected president. The notorious leaders of the revolution—**Emiliano Zapata, Pancho Villa,** and **Venustiano Carranza**—bickered and plotted as Madero pursued a moderate course. Rebellions plagued Madero's administration until the day he was murdered. His successor, **Victoriano Huerta,** came from the ranks of his own army.

The years that followed were characterized by political chaos and infighting among former revolutionary allies. When the dust cleared, the moderate Carranza, who had been endorsed by the U.S., governed Mexico under a somewhat radical constitution that he was disinclined to enforce. This Constitution of 1917 nominally guaranteed free secular education, restored land to peasants, limited property accumulation, instituted a 48-hour work week and a minimum wage, and established equal rights for women and workers. The Constitution derived its anti-clericalism from Juárez's 1857 document. It prevented the church from owning land, including temples of worship, and banned priests from wearing cassocks in public. Religious publications were prohibited from commenting on political matters. This civil attack on the church stemmed from the dominance of religion in earlier Mexican politics.

One out of every eight Mexicans was killed during the revolution, and very few were left unaffected by the violence. Zapata and many other Mexicans were dissatisfied with the sluggish progress of reform under Carranza and continued to fight, but by 1920 they had all been bought off or murdered. A brief series of dictators carried Mexico to new dimensions of repression.

Post-Revolutionary Mexico

Champions of radical reform came into power once again when **Lázaro Cárdenas** was elected president in 1934. His government started to fulfill some of the promises of the Constitution of 1917, seizing 49 million acres of land from private owners and distributing it among *ejidos* (communal cooperative farms). He strengthened the labor movement and nationalized the oil companies that had been controlled by foreign countries since the *Porfiriato*, in a crucial step toward economic independence that was widely protested by U.S. oil interests.

The modern feminist movement in Mexico took off during Cárdenas's administration. The United Front for Women's Rights, organized in 1935, had 50,000 members by 1940. Mexican women finally won the right to vote in 1955.

The administrations following that of Cárdenas were conservative and business-oriented. The economy boomed, but most urban and rural workers still suffered from low wages and underemployment. Wary of uprisings, the government began to buy off both workers and landowners with subsidies on everything from tortillas to gasoline. As population growth began to accelerate, the economy weakened and Mexico had to turn to foreign nations for loans again.

In the early 1960s, President **Adolfo López Mateos** further damaged the budget by spending billions of pesos setting up various social welfare programs and redistributing land. Mexico's one-party system received increasing criticism, but the **Institutional Revolutionary Party (PRI)** retained tight control over Mexican politics. Student unrest and worker dissatisfaction in these years culminated in 1968 at Mexico City's Tlatelolco Plaza, where police killed an estimated 300 to 400 peaceful demonstrators just 10 days before the Olympic Games were to open.

Protest subsided in the following years, but other problems have marred more recent administrations, among them large budget deficits, high unemployment, burgeoning population, lagging agricultural production, high inflation, rapid devaluation of the peso, and persistent corruption. Enormous economic disparity has persisted, despite the influx of petrodollars from oil exports.

Under President **Miguel de la Madrid Hurtado,** elected in 1982, the economy rebounded slightly, but, under pressure from the International Monetary Fund, the administration initiated an austerity program to curtail the country's 150% inflation and US$104 billion foreign debt. Between January and October of 1988, the rate of inflation fell drastically, but the economy's growth rate remained at zero during de la Madrid's six-year term.

Current Politics

"The era of one-party rule in Mexico is over," declared PRI presidential candidate **Carlos Salinas de Gortari** during the tense week following the 1988 presidential elections. Salinas officially (and conveniently) received 50.4% of the vote when the final contested results were announced, but many interpreted his remarks and the election itself as a fresh start for Mexican politics.

From 1929 to 1988, Mexico's ruling party did not lose a single presidential, senatorial, or gubernatorial race. In the few local elections that it did lose, the PRI often installed its own candidates anyway. Through a combination of patronage, fraud and ineffectual opposition, the party ran Mexico like a political machine. But in the 1982 election, the murmurs of dissent were heard, and the right-of-center **National Action Party (PAN)** won 14% of the vote, most of it in the northern states. In 1983, the PRI experimented with fraud-free elections, and the PAN picked up three mayorships in the state of Chihuahua alone.

In October of 1989, PRI and PAN voted together for the first time in favor of electoral reform, and the government launched investigations into other kinds of political corruption. The PAN finally broke the PRI stranglehold on national office in the same year, when the first non-PRI state governor was elected in Baja California Norte. Chihuahua followed suit in 1992, electing a PAN governor by a large (and officially acknowledged) margin, even amid charges of pro-PRI fraud.

When Salinas, a Harvard graduate, began his six-year term as president on December 1, 1988, he had to confront high unemployment, a US$105 billion foreign debt, the domestic production and transport of drugs, and a skeptical nation. Salinas instituted wage and price controls to keep inflation down, then boosted his popularity with several prominent arrests of a union boss, a fraudulent businessman, and a drug trafficker.

On February 4, 1990, representatives of the Mexican government and its 450 foreign commercial creditors signed a debt reduction agreement designed to ease the U.S. banking crisis and deflect outlandishly high interest payments. This reprieve, along with Salinas's austerity program, has led to growing foreign investment and steady growth (3% a year) in Mexico's gross domestic product. Inflation has stuck at 16-22%, however, and unemployment remains near 20%. Reduced or not, foreign debt has continued to suck capital out of the country, and a blossoming trade deficit is squeezing out small and medium businesses as foreign franchises move in.

The fate of these smaller firms was at the center of the controversial North American Free Trade Agreement (NAFTA), concluded August 12, 1992. When approved by the legislatures of the U.S., Canada and Mexico, the treaty will eliminate the tariffs, quotas, and subsidies that have protected Mexican industry and agriculture since the 1940s. It will also open up Mexican banking, insurance and securities industries to U.S. and Canadian competition by the year 2000. U.S. unions oppose the pact because they fear the loss of factories and jobs to low-wage competition in Mexico, where workers earn one-tenth as much as U.S. union labor. *Maquiladora* plants, the North American-owned assembly and automotive-sector factories, have already begun to both squeeze Mexican-owned smaller businesses and wreak havoc on the environment and health conditions in the towns which surround them.

In 1991, PRI technocrats dismantled the *ejido* system, which ostensibly guaranteed communal land rights for rural *campesinos.* With this constitutional reform and other changes, including rapid privitization, an agrarian culture thousands of years old is being phased out to pave the way for industrialism. Traditional support systems are lost in urbanization while government safety nets are eliminated, all part of an economic streamlining backed by the U.S. and international lenders. The costs of this structural adjustment program (centered around NAFTA) have yet to be determined, but fall heavily on the lower classes in the meantime, while the benefits loom on the long-term horizon.

■ The Arts

Literature

The literary tradition in Mexico begins with the *indígenas*, but little of their literature escaped the fervor of early Spanish missionaries' bonfires. The oral tradition has bequeathed upon the modern student many examples of Aztec poetry, however, which sound surprisingly contemporary and exhibit considerable artistic self-consciousness. Miguel León Portilla's *Visión de los vencidos* (The Vision of the Conquered, translated in *The Broken Spears*) is a fascinating collection of the *indígena* prose and poetry that did survive to show the other side of the Conquest. The best European account of contact is the remarkable prose work *Verdadera historia de la conquista de Nueva España* (The True History of the Conquest of New Spain) by Bernal Díaz de Castillo, a soldier under Cortés who took pride in the American experience without glorifying it excessively.

Colonial Mexico produced more poetry than prose, leading one 16th-century dramatist to observe that there were "more poets than dung" in New Spain. Most merely imitated the latest European styles. One notable exception came on the scene in the 17th century; **Sor Juana Inés de la Cruz,** an early feminist who became a nun in order to make time for intellectual pursuits, wrote such poems as "Hombres Necios" (Silly Men) and "Primero Sueño" (First Dream). "Primero Sueño," a mystical visionary poem, is considered a masterpiece of the Golden Age on both sides of the Atlantic.

During the 18th century, the Inquisition vied with the French Enlightenment to distract Mexican writers from anything that could be described as innovative. In 1816, **José Fernández de Lizardi,** a prominent Mexican journalist, wrote the first Latin American novel: *El Periquillo Sarmiento* (The Itching Parrot). With the

Spanish-American Modernists of the later 19th century, poetry reached an affective level it had not even approached since Sor Juana.

As discontent spread in the early 20th century, the group called **Anteneo de la Juventud** dissolved genres in the name of socio-political revolution. For the most part, however, intellectuals kept their distance from the revolutionary arena. After the fact, many witnesses took up their pens. **Mariano Azuela's** *Los de abajo* (The Lowly Ones) conveys extreme disillusionment in a rural dialect. Other novels of this period include *El águila y la serpiente* (The Eagle and the Serpent) by **Martín Luis Guzmán** and *El resplandor* (Sunburst) by **Mauricio Magdaleno. Juan Rulfo's** *Pedro Páramo*, set in rural Jalisco, blurs the line between life and death and between past and present in relating one man's allegoric search for his father and is seen as the beginning of magical realistic boom which would later hit the continent.

Mexican literature in the post-revolutionary era is marked by a frustrated desire to forge a national tradition from the vestiges of pre-colonial culture. **Octavio Paz,** in such works as *El laberinto de la soledad* (The Labyrinth of Solitude), draws on Marxism, Romanticism and post-Modernism to explore the making and unmaking of a national archetype. Paz, like his more famous successor **Carlos Fuentes,** concerns himself with stuff of myth and legend in an effort to come to terms with Spanish cultural dominance. Fuentes, Mexico's most celebrated author and one-time Harvard professor, published his first novel, *La región más transparente*, in 1958. His latest novel, *Cristóbal nonato* (Christopher Unborn), chronicles the lengthy search for a god-head who will accurately and unproblematically personify the true spirit of the Mexican people.

Since the "boom," Mexican literature has become even more pluralistic and serves an ever-growing pool of readers. Western prototypes retain their fascination for writers and readers alike, as is evidenced by the wildly popular work of **Gustavo Sainz** and **José Agustín,** the instigators of *literatura de la onda* ("hip" literature). On the other hand, **Luis Spota,** one of Mexico's most widely read authors, restricts himself to Mexican themes and boasts, as a result, international anonymity.

Art and Architecture

Early *indígena* art, like Western art, was devoted to the sacred. The colonial period favored stilted European imitation, but the revolution instilled a sense of nationalism and resuscitated native styles, now informed by modern themes.

Fortunately, this revival is well-supplied with *indígena* prototypes. The Olmecs carved altars and monumental heads out of stone. In western Mexico, the Tarascan people embellished funereal accessories with motifs from daily life. Mayan sculptors excelled at well-proportioned nudes, and the Aztecs imbued enormous figures with both strength and grace.

Much of Mexico's pictorial tradition, however, is attached to buildings. Mayan architecture was richly ornamented in relief, but the Aztecs were the greatest in this field. The monuments and pyramids at **Teotihuacán** put Egypt's stolid emphasis on engineering to shame. Architecture became the province of the church once the Spaniards arrived, and some native flourishes on the portals and altars notwithstanding, Old World structures were essentially transplanted onto Mexican soil. Ever since, Mexican architecture has struggled to keep up with European styles and thus has neglected to forge its own character. The closest thing to a Mexican architectural movement, though technically imported from Spain, was the **Churrigueresque**—baroque carried to an extreme.

During the *Porfiriato*, the **National Academy of San Carlos,** established in 1785, dominated the artistic community. Most Mexican artists rejected the Spanish influence of the 17th and 18th centuries by producing down-to-earth portrayals of *indígena* life. Among these artists was **Dr. Atl** (Gerardo Murillo), whose pseudonym is the Nahuatl word for water.

As the Revolution reduced their land to shambles, Mexican painters developed an unapologetic national style. This success was made possible by José Vasconcelos's

Ministry of Education program, which commissioned murals for public buildings and sent artists into the countryside to teach and participate in rural life.

The Mexican **mural,** unequivocally nationalistic in its current form, ironically dates back to the early days of the conquest when Catholic evangelists, fighting the language barrier, used allegorical murals to impart the rudiments of Christian iconography. Among the famous muralists to have worked in the formative years of the revolution, **Diego Rivera** has achieved the most renown. His murals at the Detroit Institute of Arts and the Rockefeller Center in New York City exposed his political themes—land reform and Marxism—to a wide audience and embroiled him in international controversy. The two other prominent muralists of the 1920s and 1930s, **David Alfaro Siqueiros** and **José Clemente Orozco**, also had disciples outside Mexico. The formally innovative Siqueiros could not resist a curved surface. Orozco focused on the violence and brutality of the Revolution, but was less explicitly political than his colleagues. In his work, the mythic dimension of human history and existence prevails.

The therapeutic role of art receives its most eloquent testimony, however, in the life and work of **Frida Kahlo** (1907-54). Partially paralyzed in a traumatic bus accident at the age of 18, Kahlo married Diego Rivera and was welcomed by Andre Breton into the Surrealist fold of the 1930s. Her paintings and self-portraits are icons of pain: red smudges on the frame of *A Few Small Nips* project the bed-ridden, writhing body from the canvas out into the world. The Museo Frida Kahlo is in her childhood home, Coyoacán, a part of Mexico City.

Film

Mexican film-making began in 1917 and reached its peak in the 1940s. Ex-actor Emilio Fernández won the *Palme D'Or* at the 1943 Cannes Film Festival for his *María Candelaria* and two years later directed *La Perla*, an adaptation of John Steinbeck's novel. Together with legendary cinematographer Gabriel Figueroa, who had studied in Hollywood, Fernández forged the classic image of Mexico: polychrome skies, ornate architecture, and interiors geometricized by beams of light. Thereafter the Mexican film industry went into decline. Poorly financed film-makers suffered in competition with the U.S. and fell back on low-budget pop formulas. Most recently, the magical realism of *Como Agua para Chocolate* ("Like Water for Chocolate") by Esquível Laura, provides a surreal and beautiful portrait through its fantastical romance set in northern Mexico.

Music

Experts know that music played an important role in pre-Conquest *indígena* daily life—but little more. Dancing was a central religious ritual. High-pitched, thin voices were cultivated for their associations with metallic gold and the roar of the jaguar.

The Spanish introduced their own instruments, lyrics and rhythms to Mexico. Music contributed to the conversion of the native population to Christianity and thus contributed materially to the Conquest. The arrival of African slaves and contact with the Caribbean added another musical strain, especially in the Gulf region. In this fertile atmosphere, percussion and syncopation formed the basis for *marimba* music.

Just as music had been used to subdue them, Mexicans used music to regain their autonomy. The *jarabe* exhibition dance was frequently banned during Mexico's last years as a colony and rallied would-be dancers behind the cause. The *corrido*, a narrative ballad, played a similar role during the Revolution, when insurgents sang news to each other to boost morale.

Apart from José Cuervo and the sombrero, the most persistent emblems of Mexico are the *mariachis*, who started out as ragtag groups of farmers singing at country gatherings in Guadalajara. Along with the hat dance—another Guadalajara product—the *mariachi* craze swept across the country. By the 1920s, many were touring Mexico, and as radio became a greater social force in Mexico, *mariachi* music adapted to the times.

■ Food and Drink

Mexicans wait until between 2 and 4pm for the *comida*, the largest meal of the day, often an elaborate banquet of several courses. *Comida corrida* or *corriente*, served at most Mexican restaurants, is a multi-course *à la carte* meal. *Cena* (dinner) is a light meal served after 8pm.

Mexican cuisine is the product of an *indígena* heritage enriched by Spanish and, to a lesser degree, French practices. The enormous variety of Mexican dishes is due in part to the wide range of herbs and spices native to Mexico—including over 60 types of chile peppers. Contrary to stereotype, not all Mexican food is hot. Often *salsas picantes* (hot sauces) are served on the side, so whether to scorch your palate or not is your decision.

Corn is the staple of Mexican existence, and it appears most frequently in tortilla form. An Aztec creation, the **tortilla** is a soft, thin patty, served at nearly every meal. Wrap anything on your plate—meat, cheese, beans—in a tortilla to make a **burrito**. **Enchiladas** are tortillas dipped in sauce, filled and fried. **Tostadas** are fried tortillas topped with vegetables, meat, and cheese. **Tamales,** made out of a ground-corn dough, are fried in corn husks and have the consistency of thick dumplings. Beans will appear on your table almost as often as tortillas. **Frijoles fritos** (refried beans) are a popular variety.

Avoid overdosing on tacos and try some other Mexican dishes. Pork dishes include **chuletas** (pork chops), **carnitas** (bits of pig meat), and **chicharrones** (fried pig skins). **Barbacoa** is lamb that has been covered with *maguey* leaves and buried beneath a fire. **Pollo** (chicken) is also common; don't miss out on **pollo con mole. Mole,** one of Mexico's most interesting culinary creations, is a sauce combining over 30 ingredients, including chiles and chocolate (which, along with vanilla, was introduced to the rest of the world by Mexico).

At restaurants, always find out the price of a meal before you order. Many of the smaller eateries don't have a list of prices and might overcharge if you do not ask in advance. Tips run 15% or so.

Strict vegetarians and those keeping kosher may have difficulty outside of Guadalajara and Mexico City. Many Mexican foods, including tamales, some tortillas and many bean dishes, contain lard. (See Specific Concerns: Travelers on Special Diets in Essentials.)

You can sample a tremendous variety of **aguas frescas** (fruit drinks) in Mexico. Beware of *aguas* made with unpurified water. **Licuados** (made with fruit and milk) are less likely to be contaminated. **Mezcal** is distilled from the *maguey* plant: tequila is a famous *mezcal* from Tequila, Jalisco. If you get a chance to sample *pulque*, the fermented juice of the *maguey*, don't hesitate—it was the sacred drink of the Aztec nobility.

México City

"City" is not the word for it: the 522 square miles of urban settlement that line the Valley of Mexico make up far more than one city. The high-efficiency bustle of the executive areas on *Reforma*, the impoverished neighborhoods on the northern outskirts, the commercial coagulation of the *Centro*, and the wealthy southern ultra-suburbs of Coyoacán and San Ángel cohabitate in the omnipresent smog. Shantytowns sprawl out bereft of public support, themselves as large as cities; a sleek slab of bars and boutiques rises up above the city in the tallest tower in the Republic. Mexico City is a breeding ground for staggering statistics: 2000 new residents and 700 million gallons of water go in every day; 12,000 tons of air pollution come out.

With the simultaneous rising and falling of *indígena* and colonial civilizations, this phoenix-like metropolis contains a plurality of cities, and no one can decide upon a single significance for any single structure. The massive Templo Mayor is simultaneously a paean to the magnificent Aztec empire of which it was once the capital, and a memorial of the carnal sacrifices the Aztecs staged for the sake of their hungry god Huitzilopochtli. The awe and faith inspired by the grand Catedral Metropolitana struggle eternally with bitter resentment at the economic and cultural imperialism of those who forced the indigenous peoples to build it. A few blocks away stands the Palacio de Bellas Artes, a glorious symbol of modern Mexico built by the Porfiriato dictatorship that also sapped the money of a direly struggling nation. Less than a mile to the west, the Monument to the Revolution, originally intended by Díaz as the spectacular seat of his regime's legislature, reaffirms the democratic freedom of a "new" Mexico, transmogrified by ten long years of bloody battle.

Mexicans call this oxymoronic conglomeration **el D.F.,** short for *Distrito Federal* (Federal District), or simply *México*. It's the second largest population center in the world with more than 20 million people in over 220 *colonias* (neighborhoods). Virtually the entire federal bureaucracy inhabits the Distrito Federal, including the Ministry of the Navy (2240m above sea level). The principal national collections of art, ethnography, and archaeology are also found here; the gargantuan Museo Nacional de Antropología is reason enough for a visit. The Aztec Templo Mayor, prostrated though it is on the altar of the majestic Catedral Metropolitana, still inspires awe. Spectacular mosaics and murals by Rivera, Orozco, Siqueiros, and Tamayo twist and shout on the walls of the city.

While more people are arriving (to live in the narrowest apartment building in the world and to pray in the smallest church), Mexico City's denizens are uncomfortably aware of bad tidings to come. The 1985 quake cast citizens as extras in a geological nightmare that is not necessarily over. As water shortages become increasingly serious, citizens curse the topography of their metropolis: landlocked and ringed by mountains, it lets neither water in nor sewage out. Mexico City's infamous demographic crisis becomes daily more difficult to ignore. Within a decade Mexico City will merge with Puebla, Cuernavaca, Tlaxcala, Pachuca, and Querétaro to form a sprawling megalopolis of 35 million. As formerly food-producing rural migrants flock to the shantytowns on the city's edge and the city expands to engulf their abandoned plots, the prospect of feeding everyone becomes decreasingly realistic.

One-quarter of Mexico's population lives in the D.F., and one-quarter of those are employed as *comerciantes*, the independent vendors which crowd the streets. Both the commerce and life of the city are unabashedly displayed as such—Mexico City has neither the space nor the desire to hide its history, culture, and manic vitality. Even art takes on this massive and external character in the immense and awesome murals which celebrate Mexican life. Here, no one buries the ruined triumphs and fiascoes of the past, nor apologizes for the excesses of the present.

ORIENTATION

■■■ GETTING THERE

Don't worry—all roads really do lead to Mexico City. The many temples of transport include the Benito Juárez International Airport, four main bus stations, a train station, and a network of freeways. Airports and stations in Mexico City nearly always have tourist information booths equipped with free or cheap maps and some sort of referral service to lead you into the *Centro*.

■ By Air

Flying into Mexico City from abroad entails the usual customs and immigration procedures. Tourist cards are distributed on the plane and stamped at the airport. If you fly out of the the D.F. always have about 12-15 pesos or the equivalent in dollars for the airport tax.

The **Benito Juárez International Airport** lies 6.5km east of the *zócalo*, the formal center of the city. Blvd. Capitán Juan Sarabío heads northeast to the airport from Blvd. Puerto Aéreo, one of the major roads circling the city. Airport facilities include: **INFOTUR,** *Sala* A (tel. 571-16-63 or 762-67-73) and *Sala* E (tel. 784-85-53 or 784-89-69), open daily 9am-9pm daily, with information and free maps of the city and the metro; a booth operated by the **Instituto Nacional de Antropología y Historia,** which distributes information about archaeological sites and museums throughout the country (*Sala* A, open Mon.-Sat. 8am-10pm, Sun. 8am-3pm); a **map-and-book store** with novels in Spanish and English (*Sala* C, open Mon.-Sat. 7am-9:30pm, Sun. 8am-8pm); a **pharmacy** (*Sala* C, open daily 6am-10pm); **Banamex, Banco Internaciona,** and **Bancomer** with branches in different *salas* for international currency and traveler's check exchange; **ATMs** in *Salas* A and B; *casas de cambio* (*Salas* B, D, and E), open 6am-10pm; **lockers** (10 pesos per 24 hrs.; 15-44 pesos for larger bags), next to the snack bar in *Sala* A; **post office** (*Sala* A, open for full service Mon.-Fri. 8am-7pm, Sat.-Sun. 9am-5pm); **telegram office** (*Sala* A; open Mon.-Fri. 9am-8pm, Sat.-Sun. 9am-noon). Some magazine booths sell phonecards for the **LADATELs** around the airport; some phones take international credit cards. **Restaurants** and **cafeterias** are open 24 hrs. **Car rental** desks are in *Sala* E (see Getting Around below).

¡Bienvenidos a México! Transportation into the city is uncomplicated. The *venta de boletos* desks in *Sala* A or E will sell you, at an authorized going rate, a ticket presentable to any white and yellow taxi labeled *transporte terrestre* waiting outside. The price is set by which zone of the city you're traveling to (35 pesos to the center, more after hours). Ask to see the map. *Don't* pay cash for a ride from the airport, unless you're willing to pay heavily for the convenience. Call 784-48-11 or 571-36-00 (24 hrs.) to get a taxi back to the airport from the city.

The airport subway station, **Terminal Aérea** (Line 5), located at the junction of Capitán Juan Sarabío and Blvd. Puerto Aéreo, is only a five-minute walk from *Sala* A. The subway is dirt cheap (.40 pesos) but prohibitively inconvenient; no luggage larger than a small suitcase is allowed. If you choose to sneak through the turnstile with your pack, it may be impossible to maneuver through the swarming crowds in the station. Guarding your bags and dealing with fellow passengers irritated by your ungainliness may prove difficult on the crowded trains. Still, the Metro is by far the most convenient and fastest transportation; just avoid the rush hours (see Getting Around below). If returning to the airport by Metro, remember that the airport stop is Terminal Aérea, *not* Aeropuerto.

Travelers driving to *el Centro* should take Blvd. Puerto Aéreo north to Eje 2 Nte. (see Circuito Interior and Ejes Viales under Getting Around below), then Eje 2 Nte.

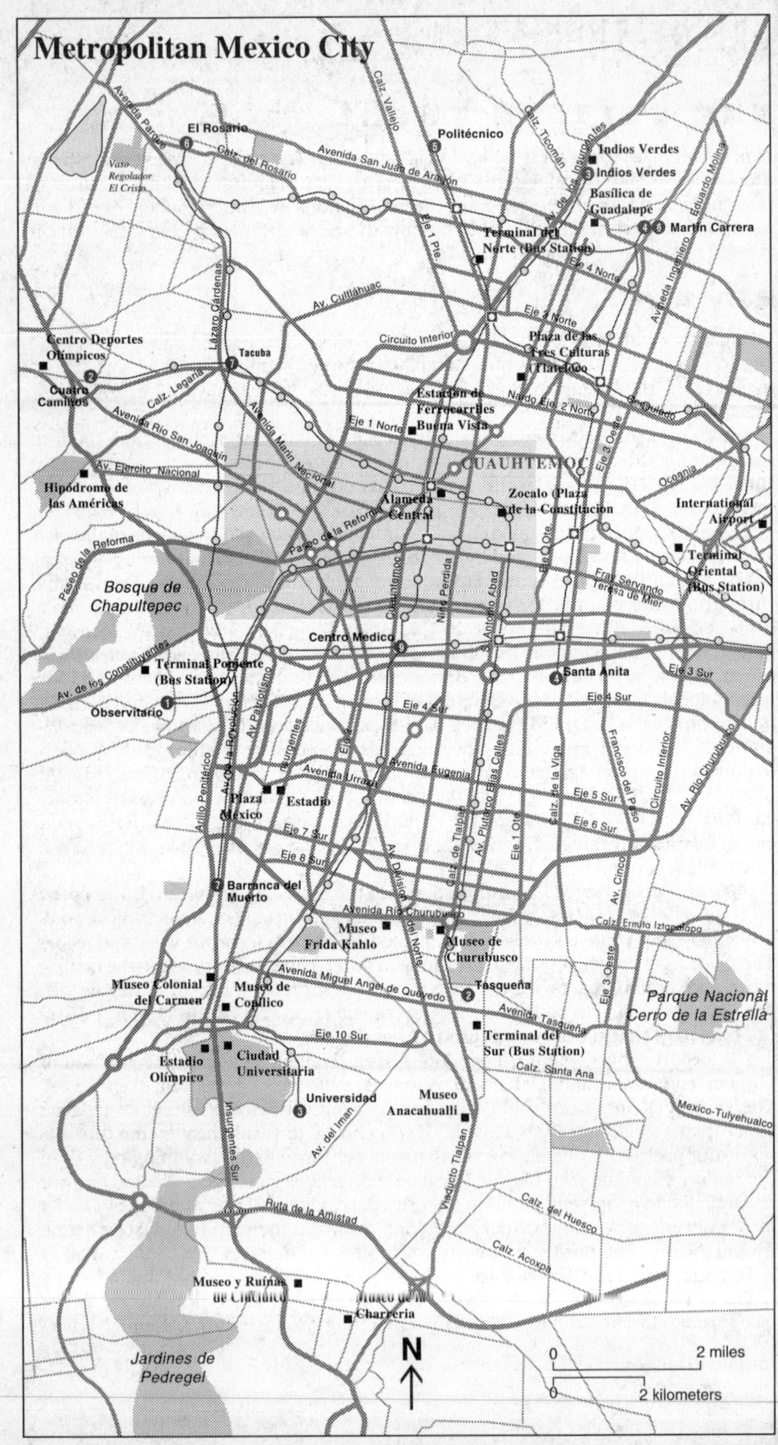
Metropolitan Mexico City
El Rosario
Politécnico
Indios Verdes
Indios Verdes
Basílica de Guadalupe
Martín Carrera
Terminal del Norte (Bus Station)
Vaso Regolador El Cristo
Centro Deportes Olímpicos
Cuatro Caminos
Tacuba
Plaza de las Tres Culturas (Tlatelolco)
Estacion de Ferrocarriles Buena Vista
CUAUHTEMOC
Hipódromo de las Américas
Alameda Central
Zocalo (Plaza de la Constitucion)
International Airport
Terminal Oriental (Bus Station)
Bosque de Chapultepec
Centro Medico
Terminal Poniente (Bus Station)
Observitario
Santa Anita
Plaza México
Estadio
Barranca del Muerto
Museo Frida Kahlo
Museo de Churubusco
Museo Colonial del Carmen
Museo de Copilico
Tasqueña
Parque Nacional Cerro de la Estrella
Terminal del Sur (Bus Station)
Estadio Olímpico
Ciudad Universitaria
Universidad
Museo Anacahualli
Museo y Ruínas de Cuicuilco
Charreria
Jardines de Pedregel
N
0
2 miles
0
2 kilometers

west to Paseo de la Reforma. A left turn here leads southwest to Juárez or, farther down, to Insurgentes.

Benito Juárez International Airport: Tel. 571-36-00 or 571-34-69, for information on domestic flights dial ext. 2303 or 2258, international ext. 2288.

Domestic Flights: Flight schedules and prices change frequently and seasonally. Prices are roughly the same from airline to airline. There are usually no discounts for students, but always ask about *tarifas promocionales* (some of which may be available to students only) that can save you up to 50% on flights. **Aeroméxico,** Paseo de la Reforma 445 (tel. 207-82-33 for reservations, 762-40-22 for information), close to Mississippi. Also at Reforma 80 (566-1078). Open Mon.-Fri. 9am-6:15pm, Sat. 9am-6pm. At the airport (*Sala* A, tel. 571-18-55), open daily 5am-10pm. Flight information: 762-40-22. Reservations: 228-99-10. (Both daily 6am-10pm.) The following information is incomplete and changes frequently. Prices given are one-way coach fare; round-trip is approximately double. To: Acapulco (9 per day, 254 pesos), Aguascalientes (4 per day, 245 pesos), Cancún (4 per day, 567 pesos), Chihuahua (4 per day, 574 pesos), Guadalajara (13 per day, 229 pesos), Ixtapa-Zihuatanejo (2 per day, 352 pesos), La Paz (3 per day, 807 pesos), Los Mochis (8:30am, 663 pesos), Durango (3 per day, 390 pesos), Hermosillo (6 per day, 655 pesos), Hualtco (1:36pm, 373 pesos), Ciudad Obrégon (2 per day, 735 pesos), Manzanillo (4 per day, 370 pesos), Mazatlán (4 per day, 428 pesos), Mérida (4 per day, 547 pesos), Oaxaca (2 per day, 229 pesos), Puerto Vallarta (4 per day, 437 pesos), Tapachula (2 per day, 388 pesos), Villahermosa (2 per day, 527 pesos). **Mexicana,** Amberes and Reforma 312 (tel. 511-04-24), in the Zona Rosa ; Also Reforma 51 (tel. 592-17-71). Open Mon.-Fri. 9am-6pm. At airport (*Sala* B, tel. 227-22-61) and for reservations 325-09-90. Open daily 6am-10:30pm. Again, prices given are one-way coach. To: Acapulco (5 per day, 217 pesos), Cancún (5 per day, 516 pesos), Cozumel (2 per day, 516 pesos), Guadalajara (11 per day, 241 pesos), Hermosillo (7:35am, 196 pesos), Ixtapa/Zihuatanejo (2 per day, 299 pesos), Los Cabos (10:55am, 559 pesos), Manzanillo (7:50am, 336 pesos), Mazatlán (7:45am or 2:20pm, 439 pesos), Mérida (3 per day, 496 pesos), Monterrey (5 per day, 301 pesos), Puerto Vallarta (3 per day, 396 pesos), Tijuana (5 per day, 683 pesos), Villahermosa (3 per day, 447 pesos), Zacatecas (6:15pm, 241 pesos).

International Flights: Air Canada, Hamburgo 108, 5th floor (tel. 511-20-94); **Air France,** Reforma 404, 15th floor (tel. 627-60-60, 566-00-66), at airport (tel. 571-54-43); **American,** Reforma 300, 1st floor (tel. 399-92-22 or 533-54-46), at airport (tel. 571-34-71); **British Airways,** Escobedo 752, 3rd floor (tel. 525-91-33); **Canadian,** Reforma 390-1402 (tel. 208-16-54); **Continental,** Andrés Bello 45 (tel. 208-34-34), at airport (tel. 571-36-65); **United,** Hamburgo 213, ground floor (tel. 627-02-22); **Delta,** Reforma 381 (tel. 202-16-08), at airport (tel. 571-32-37); **KLM,** Reforma 735, 7th floor (tel. 202-44-44), and at airport (tel. 571-32-46); **Lufthansa,** Reforma 239 (tel. 202-88-66), at airport (tel. 571-27-13); **Swissair,** Hamburgo 213, ground floor (tel. 533-63-63).

■ By Train

The train station **Estación Buenavista** (tel. 547-10-97, open daily 6am-10pm), north of the *Alameda* at the corner of Insurgentes and Mosqueta, inconveniently far from the nearest Metro station, Revolución (Line 2). Taxis leave from the parking lot on the Mosqueta side of the Guerrero station. Be sure to check the meter and the official fare chart in the cab before you pay, as abuses are par for the course.

An **information booth** (tel. 547-10-97 or 547-10-84) in the middle of the train station's main lobby provides schedule and price information. (Open daily 6am-9:30pm.) The station also has a 24-hr. restaurant and a *paquetería* (storage room) for luggage (open daily 6:30am-9pm, 4 pesos per item per day). There are four classes: *primera especial* (reserved, without bed), *dormitorio camarin* (reserved with two separate beds per compartment), *alcoba* (reserved, with bunk bed), *primera general* (unreserved). Though you can buy tickets for first class one month in advance, tickets for anytime other than Semana Santa are usually available up to 1hr. before departure. All trains, regardless of the class, tend to be excruciatingly slow, except for those to Guadalajara, Veracruz, Monterrey (without 2nd class service), and Piedras Negras. Other immensely popular routes from the D.F. to Oaxaca, Yucatán, Ciudad, Juárez, and Nuevo Laredo. Get train information in English from the **Gerencia de Trafico de Pasajeros** in the main station lobby (tel. 547-86-55, fax 547-89-72), open Mon.-Fri. 9am-3pm.

Deluxe 1st-class reserved service: Service daily to: Guadalajara (8:30pm, 12hrs., 71 pesos), Veracruz (9:15pm, 10hrs., 47 pesos), San Luis Potosí (9pm, 8hrs., or 6am, 6hrs.; both 47 pesos), Saltillo (9am, 5hrs., or 6pm, 12hrs.; both 88 pesos), Monterrey (6pm, 14hrs., 100 pesos), Querétaro (7am, 9am, and 8pm, 3½hrs., 27 pesos), Aguascalientes (8pm, 10½hrs., 66 pesos), San Miguel de Allende (9am, 5½hrs., 35 pesos), Oaxaca (7pm, 14hrs., 68 pesos).

2nd-class service: Service daily to: Guadalajara (8:30pm, 12hrs., 18.30 pesos), Oaxaca (7pm, 14hrs., 17.35 pesos), Veracruz (7:45am, 11hrs., or 9:15pm, 10hrs.; both 13 pesos), Querétaro (9am, 4hrs., or 8pm, 3½hrs.; both 7.35 pesos), Aguascalientes (8pm, 10hrs., 17.50 pesos), Zacatecas (8pm, 13½hrs., 20.95 pesos), Chihuahua (8pm, 29½hrs., 48.20 pesos), Ciudad Juárez (8pm, 35 hrs., 58.90 pesos), San Miguel Allende (9am, 5½hrs., 9.65 pesos), San Luis Potosí (9am, 8hrs., 15.05 pesos), Monterrey (9am, 17hrs., 30 pesos), Nuevo Laredo (9am, 22½hrs., 37.95 pesos).

■ By Bus

Mexico City's four main bus stations correspond to the points of the compass. **Central de Autobuses del Norte** (North Station) serves the Bajío, northern Veracruz, Jalisco, and most of northern Mexico; **Central de Autobuses del Poniente** (South Station) launches buses to the states of Morelos and Guerrero; **Terminal de Autobuses de Pasajeros de Oriente (TAPO)** (East Station) runs to Puebla, southern Veracruz, Oaxaca, Chiapas and the Yucatán Peninsula; and the **Terminal Central de Autobuses del Sur** (West Station) serves the states of México and Michoacán.

All stations are served by the Metro and offer an official 24-hr. taxi service that charges fixed rates for a ride to any point in the city (rates set by zones) or adjacent parts of Mexico state. Buy your ticket inside to avoid a ripoff, but be wary of being charged for an extra zone—consult the often nonexistent zone map. *Peseros* (a.k.a. *colectivos*) also serve the four stations. The following listings are by no means comprehensive; given the extensive network, it is possible to go almost anywhere at any time. All ticket sales are final and all seats reserved.

Central de Autobuses del Norte

On Cien Metros (tel. 587-15-52), Metro station Autobuses del Norte (Line 5). 24-hr. restaurant, post office, telegrams office, *casa de cambio,* luggage storage room (small 8 pesos, big 16 pesos per 24 hrs.). More companies than those listed below operate out of this terminal/zoo. They appear in the order they appear from waiting room 1 to 8.

Estrella Blanca (tel. 587-12-19). 1st class to: León (13 per day, 44 pesos), Guanajajuato (14 per day, 45 pesos), Guadalajara (36 per day, 69-82 pesos), Aguascalientes (34 per day, 57-67 pesos), San Luis Potosí (24 daily, 46 pesos), Ciudad Juárez (6 per day, 160 pesos), Poza Rica (24 per day, 33 pesos), Chihuahua (6 per day, 127 pesos), Durango (5 per day, 98 pesos).

Primera Plus (tel. 587-52-22). 1st class to: Gudalajara (34 per day, 77 pesos,; Aguascalientes (12 per day, 62 pesos), León (38 per day, 50 pesos), Irapuato (16 per day, 43 pesos), Manzanillo (13 per day, 35 pesos).

ETN (tel. 368-11-88). 1st class to: Moreila (5 per day, 55 pesos), Querétaro (36 per day, 40 pesos, San Luis Potosí (18 per day, 70 pesos).

Transportes del Norte (tel. 587-54-80). 1st class to: Nuevo Laredo (14 per day, 128 pesos), Monterrey (every 1hr., 100 pesos), Saltillo (9 per day, 92 pesos); Matamoros (6 per day, 112 pesos), San Luis Potosí (11 per day, 46 pesos), Ciudad Juárez (11 per day, 197 pesos), Chihuahua (11 per day, 157 pesos).

Autobuses Blancos (tel. 587-53-23). To: Tijuana (4 per day, 292 pesos), Mexicali (4 per day, 294 pesos), Hermosillo, (4 per day, 220 pesos), Culiacán (4 per day, 146 pesos), Los Mochis (4 per day, 167 pesos), Tampico (7 per day, 69 pesos).

Autobuses del Oriente (ADO) (tel. 567-62-47). To: Tampico (6 per day, 65 pesos), Tuxpan (12 per day, 38 pesos), Tulancingo (12 per day, 17 pesos), and many more.

Tres Estrellas de Oro (tel. 587-57-77). 1st class to: Mazatlán (9 per day, 114 pesos), Los Mochis (10 per day, 167 pesos), Tepic (8 per day, 87 pesos), Tijuana (8 per day, 287 pesos), Mexicali (8 per day, 289 pesos).

Transportes México-Pachuca (tel. 577-74-39). To Pachuca every 5min., 5:45am-11pm, less frequent after 9pm (10 pesos).

Flecha Amarilla, primarily 2nd-class service to Querétaro, Guanajuato, and Jalisco.

Terminal de Autobuses de Pasajeros de Oriente (TAPO)

General Ignacio Zaragoza 200 (tel. 762-59-77), Metro station San Lázaro (Line 1). The finest of bus stations. TAPO services include a 24-hr. restaurant and pharmacy, a branch of the federal tourist office, and lockers (10 pesos). Taxi ticket stand and tourist information booth near the entrance to the Metro station.

ADO (tel. 542-71-92). 1st class to: Puebla (every 15min., 2hrs., 16-20 pesos), Oaxaca (23 per day, 15hrs., 60 pesos), Cancún (3 per day, 27hrs., 194 pesos), Jalapa (9 per day, 5hrs., 39 pesos), Mérida (5 per day, 24hrs., 175 pesos), Palenque (2 per day, 14hrs., 111 pesos), Veracruz (14 per day, 7hrs., 52 pesos), San Andrés Tuxtla (5 per day, 15hrs., 64 pesos), Villahermosa (20 per day, 12hrs., 106 pesos), Campeche (6 per day, 22hrs., 156 pesos), Poza Rica (3 per day, 4½hrs., 32 pesos), Tampico (10pm, 15hrs., 67 pesos), Tuxtla Gutíerrez (2 per day, 13 hrs., 128 pesos), Tuxtepec (5 per day, 11hrs., 59 pesos).

Autobuses Unidos (AU) (tel. 542-42-10). To: Cordoba (37 per day, 35 pesos), Jalapa (32 per day, 32 pesos), Oaxaca (13 per day, 50 pesos), Orizaba (39 per day, 32 pesos), San Andrés Tuxtla (4 per day, 57 pesos), Tuxtepec (9 per day, 48 pesos), Villahermosa (3 per day, 85 pesos), Veracruz (37 per day, 41 pesos).

Autobuses Cristóbal Colón (tel. 542-72-63). 1st class to: San Cristóbal de las Casas (4 per day, 17hrs., 125 pesos), Tuxtla Gutiérrez (6 per day, 116 pesos), Tonalá (3 per day, 105 pesos), Tapachula (6 per day, 116 pesos), Oaxaca (8 per day, 56 pesos).

Estrella Roja (tel. 522-72-00), to Puebla every 5min. between 6am and 9:30pm, daily (2hrs., 18 pesos).

Autotransportes Mexico-Texcoco (tel. 542-20-09). To Tlaxcala (2hrs., 17 pesos), plus many others.

Terminal de Autobuses de Poniente

Av. Sur 122 (tel. 271-00-38), Metro station Observatorio (Line 1). Take a left as you exit the metro station, a market-covered bridge leads to the terminal. Operates mainly second-class routes, mostly slow indirect service. 24-hr. station services include: restaurant, long distance *caseta*, luggage storage (5 pesos for 24 hrs.). Pharmacy (open daily 7am-10pm); post and telegram offices (Mon.-Fri. 8am-5pm, Sat. 8am-1pm). Foodstands, shops, and newpaper stands.

Turismos México-Toluca (tel. 271-14-33). To Toluca (every 5min. 6am-10:30pm, 1½hrs., 9 pesos). Altacomulco (every 15min., 6am-8pm, 2hrs., 14 pesos), El Oro (every 30min., 6:10am-8:10pm, 2hrs., 15 pesos).

Herradura de Plata (tel. 271-03-35). To Morelia (16 per day, 4hrs., 31 pesos), Patzuacaro (11 per day, 5½hrs., 40 pesos).

Autobuses de Occidente (tel. 231-01-00), To: Zamora (13 per day, 40 pesos), Moreila (every 20min., 29 pesos), Patzuacuaro (every 20min, 16 pesos).

Terminal de Autobuses del Sur (Taxqueña)

Taxqueña 1320 (tel. 549-02-57), Metro station Taxqueña (Line 2). Telegrams office (Mon.-Fri. 9am-8pm, Sat. 9am-noon), long-distance *caseta* (daily 7am-9:30pm). LADATELs, tourist agency for hotel reservations in Mexico City, Acapulco, and Mazatlan (daily 7am-9:30pm). 24-hr. cafeteria and pharamacy. Lockers (small 12 pesos, 24 hrs., big 16 pesos, 24 hrs.).

Pullman de Morelos (tel. 549-35-05). 1st class to Cuernavaca (every 5min., 5:30am-10:45pm, 1¼hrs., 12-18 pesos), Topoztlán (20 per day, 1½hrs., 10 pesos).

Estrella de Oro (tel. 549-85-20). 1st class to: Taxco (5 per day, 55 pesos), Acapulco (10 per day, 7hrs., 55 pesos; 8 per day 65 pesos), Ixtapa (4 per day, 90 pesos), Zihuatanejo (7 per day, 90 pesos).

Turi-Star (tel. 689-80-00). 1st class to Iguala (9 per day, 29 pesos), Chilapaucingo (13 per day, 50 pesos), Acapulco (30 per day, 75 pesos).

Estrella Blanca (tel. 689-80-00). 1st class to Cuernavaca (32 per day, 15 pesos).

■ By Car

Several major highways lead into the Federal District from elsewhere and intersect with the Circuito Interior, the highway that rings the city, at which point they continue under assumed names. **Route 57,** from Querétaro and Tepotzotlán, becomes Manuel Ávila Camacho just outside the Circuito. **Route 15,** from Toluca, turns into Reforma as it enters the city. **Route 95,** from Cuernavaca and Acapulco, becomes Insurgentes, which plugs into the Circuito on the south side. **Route 150,** from Puebla and Texcoco, becomes Ignacio Zaragoza, which connects to the Circuito on the east side. **Route 85,** from Pachuca, Teotihuacán, and Texcoco, becomes Insurgentes in the city.

■■■ GEOGRAPHY

Circuito Interior and Ejes Viales

The **Circuito Interior** is a roughly rectangular artery made up of several smaller, connected highways. **Boulevard Puerto Aéreo** forms the upper east side of the box, running north from the airport. As it bends left at the northeast corner of the box and heads west it becomes **Avenida Río Consulado.** Río Consulado turns south and becomes **Calzada Melchor Ocampo.** Ocampo heads south until it intersects Paseo de la Reforma at Bosque de Chapultepec, after which it continues as **Avenida Vasconcelos.** From Vasconcelos, two roads run to the southwest corner of the Circuito, **Av. Patriotismo** and **Av. Revolución,** either of which could be considered the Circuito at this point. At that point they turn into Av. Río Mixcoac, which becomes **Avenida Río Churubusco,** running east-west. Río Churubusco is the longest and sneakiest of the highways that constitute the Circuito; it continues east, turns north for a while, heads east again, then turns north once more to connect with Blvd. Puerto Aéreo south of the airport to complete the Circuito.

Aside from the large thoroughfares—Insurgentes, Reforma, and Miguel Alemán—a system of **Ejes Viales** (axis roads) conducts the majority of traffic within the Circuito. *Ejes* run one way (except for the bus lanes, which go against traffic). Running east-west, Eje 1 Nte. and Eje 2 Nte. are north of the *zócalo,* while Ejes 2 through 8 Sur run south of it. The numbers increase heading away from the *zócalo.* **Eje Central Lázaro Cárdenas** runs north-south and bisects the box formed by the Circuito. East of it and parallel lie Ejes 1 through 3 Ote., which veer off to the northwest; west of it are Ejes 1 through 3 Pte. Using the Ejes along with the Circuito you can theoretically reach any general area of the city without much delay. The Guía Roji street atlas (40 pesos), entitled *Ciudad de México,* is available at many newsstands, bookstores, and at the airport.

City Center

Huge as Mexico City is, almost everything of interest to visitors lies within the northern half of the area circumscribed by the Circuito Interior. Moreover, many attractions are within easy reach of **Paseo de la Reforma,** the broad thoroughfare that runs southwest-northeast, or **Av. Insurgentes,** the boulevard running roughly north-south through the city; these streets constitute the heart of the Federal District. The **Bosque de Chapultepec,** home to the principal museums of the city, marks the southwestern limit of most tourists' wanderings. From Chapultepec, Reforma proceeds northeast, punctuated by *glorietas* (traffic circles), each with a distinguishing monument in the center, with which one can orient oneself along Reforma's great length. Moving up Reforma from Chapultepec, the *Zona Rosa* area is followed by *Buenavista* (near the Monumento a la Revolucíon), then the *Alameda* and the *Centro* just before the *zócalo*.

The accommodations and food listings for Mexico City are divided according to the four areas which are of most interest to tourists. The area termed the **Centro** contains most of the historic sights and museums, extensive budget accommodations, and lively inexpensive restaurants. This area is bounded by Cárdenas to the west, Uruguay to the south, Correo Mayoto the east, and Rep. de Peru to the north. The area called the **Alameda** contains budget accommodations and many restaurants, and is bounded by Bucareli to the west, Arcos de Belén to the south, Cárdenas to the east and Violeta to the north. The **Monumento a la Revolución Buenavista** area, like the *Alameda*, contains many inexpensive hotels and eateries. It's bounded by Insurgentes Norte to the west, Reforma to the south and east, and Mosqueta to the north. The **Zona Rosa** (Pink Zone) is the capital's most affluent commercial district. It's the neighborhood contained within Reforma to the north and west, Av. Chapultepec to the south, and Insurgentes to the east.

Unlike the streets themselves, names in Mexico City are systematic. **Streets** in a given area generally carry names that are generically related. For example, streets in the *Zona Rosa* are all named after European cities, while the streets directly across Reforma are named after large rivers of the world. North of Chapultepec, streets are named after famous people. One point to remember when looking for street numbers is that they start from zero at the end of the street nearest the main post office (on *Parque Alameda*'s northeast corner) and continue to the border of the next *colonia* (neighborhood), where the street name changes and the addresses start at zero again. Note that different neighborhoods can use the same street name; the 300 Benito Juárez streets in the Mexico City area attest to this tradition of redundancy.

Outlying Districts

Mexico City reaches outward from the *Centro* roughly 20km to the south, 10km to the north, 10km to the west, and 8km to the east. Year after year, the city's boundaries extend hungrily into neighboring cities. Because of the central location of most sights, few travelers venture past the Bosque de Chapultepec on the west, Tlatelolco on the north, the *zócalo* on the east side of the *Centro*, or south past San Ángel and the university. The major southern thoroughfare is Insurgentes Sur, which extends to the southern limit of the city. Metro Line 3 parallels Insurgentes on Cuauhtémoc and then Universidad, ending at Ciudad Universitaria, well before the city's edge. Most sights to the south, including San Ángel, Coyoacán, Ciudad Universitaria and the Pyramid of Cuicuilco, lie near or along Insurgentes. Metro Line 2 runs east of Line 3 and is closer to Xochimilco, one of the few southern sights not along Insurgentes.

Also beyond reach by Metro are the ruins at Teotihuacán, Tenayuca, Acatitlán and the small town of Tepotzlán, all north of the Distrito Federal boundary. These are best reached by bus from the northern station.

GEOGRAPHY

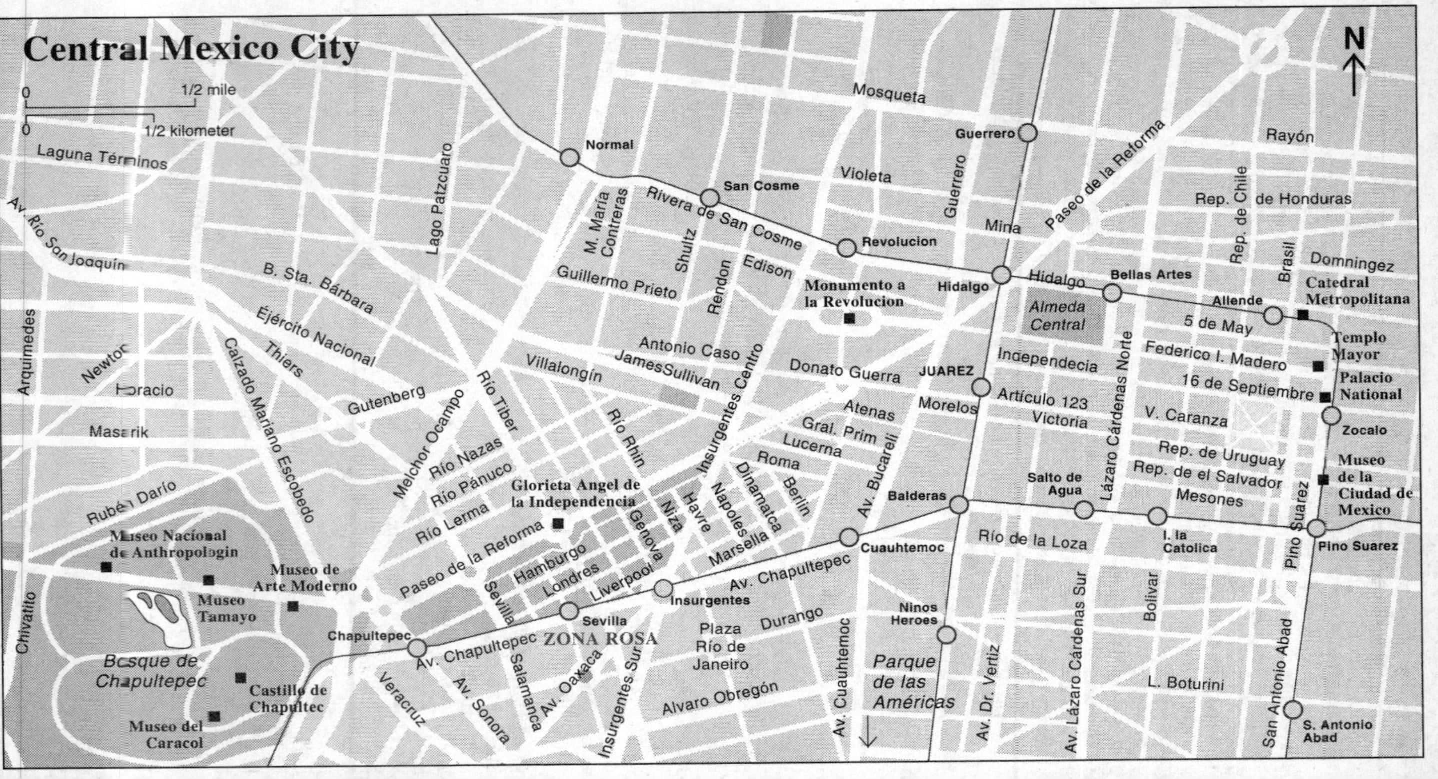
Central Mexico City
0 1/2 mile
0 1/2 kilometer
N
Laguna Términos
Av. Río San Joaquín
Arquimedes
Newton
Horacio
Masarik
Rubén Darío
Chivatito
Museo Nacional de Anthropologin
Museo de Arte Moderno
Museo Tamayo
Bosque de Chapultepec
Castillo de Chapultec
Museo del Caracol
Lago Patzcuaro
B. Sta. Bárbara
Ejército Nacional
Thiers
Calzado Mariano Escobedo
Gutenberg
Melchor Ocampo
Río Tiber
Río Nazas
Río Pánuco
Río Lerma
Paseo de la Reforma
Chapultepec
Veracruz
Av. Sonora
Salamanca
Av. Oaxaca
Av. Chapultepec
ZONA ROSA
Normal
M. María Contreras
Guillermo Prieto
San Cosme
Rivera de San Cosme
Shultz
Rendon
Edison
Villalongín
Antonio Caso
JamesSullivan
Insurgentes Centro
Río Rhin
Glorieta Angel de la Independencia
Hamburgo
Londres
Sevilla
Liverpool
Genova
Niza
Havre
Napoles
Dinamatca
Berlin
Marsella
Insurgentes
Insurgentes Sur
Plaza Río de Janeiro
Durango
Alvaro Obregón
Mosqueta
Violeta
Revolucion
Monumento a la Revolucion
Donato Guerra
Atenas
Gral. Prim
Lucerna
Roma
Av. Bucareli
Cuauhtemoc
Av. Cuauhtemoc
Parque de las Américas
Ninos Heroes
Guerrero
Mina
Hidalgo
JUAREZ
Morelos
Balderas
Paseo de la Reforma
Bellas Artes
Almeda Central
Independecia
Artículo 123
Victoria
Lázaro Cárdenas Norte
Salto de Agua
Río de la Loza
Av. Dr. Vertiz
Av. Lázaro Cárdenas Sur
Rayón
Rep. de Chile
Rep. de Honduras
Brasil
Domningez
Catedral Metropolitana
Allende
5 de May
Federico I. Madero
16 de Septiembre
Templo Mayor
Palacio National
Zocalo
V. Caranza
Rep. de Uruguay
Rep. de el Salvador
Mesones
Museo de la Ciudad de Mexico
I. la Catolica
Bolivar
L. Boturini
Pino Suarez
San Antonio Abad
S. Antonio Abad

■■■ TRANSPORTATION WITHIN MEXICO CITY

The main obstacle to spatial shifts in Mexico City is congestion. Walking sometimes proves as fast as the various other means of surface transportation, which include the municipal gray with green and blue buses (.40 pesos), the thousands of minibuses (white and green) known as *peseros, colectivos, or camiones* (.50–1.50 pesos), and the considerably more expensive but omnipresent taxis. The **Metro** is usually the fastest and most efficient but also inhumanly crowded at peak commuting hours. Most transportation depots in Mexico City are large, clean, well-lit, well-policed, and well-marked. Public transportation—whether by bus, Metro, or *pesero*—is easy to use and economical.

Travelers who plan to make frequent use of the Metro and bus systems should purchase an *abono de ahorro de transporte* (13.30 pesos) at a subway ticket window. *Abonos* (each is a pair of cards), available at all subway stations, Lotería Nacional stands, and Conasupo markets, entitles the bearer to unlimited use of the Metro (the blue card) and public city buses (the purple card) for 15 days following the purchase date. *Abonos* are sold at the beginning and in the middle of every month.

■ By Metro

The Metro always amazes—trains come quickly and regularly, the fare is insanely cheap, the crowds enormous and bizarre, the ride smooth, the service extensive, and the stations immaculate and marmoreal. Built in the late 1960s, the Metro transports 5 million people daily. Its tracks and stations are in continual pursuit of Mexico City's ever-expanding perimeter.

The .40-peso fare includes transfers. Gates operate by inserting a magnetically coded ticket, which must be bought at the booths marked *taquilla*. Transfer gates are marked *correspondencia* and exits are marked *salida*; passing through the turnstiles leaves you outside the station, and you must pay again to re-enter. If you have an *abono*, be sure to enter only through the blue turnstiles. If you use a white turnstile your ticket will be swallowed. Color-coded subway guides are available at the tourist office or at a Metro information booths.

Metro tickets are sold in booths at every station. For lines 1, 2, and 3, the first train runs Monday through Friday at 5am, Saturday at 6am, and Sunday at 7am. For lines 4-9, the first train runs Monday through Friday at 6am, Sunday at 7am. For all lines the last train runs at 12:30am from Sunday through Friday, and on Saturday as late as 1:30am. Try to avoid using the Metro from 7:30 to 9am and 7 to 9pm on weekdays, as well as the lunch break from 2-4pm; huge crowds during these hours attract pickpockets. Cars at either end of the train tend to be slightly less crowded, *ergo* safer and less uncomfortable.

Directions are stated in terms of the station at the end of a given line. Each of the two *andenes* (platforms) has signs indicating the terminus toward which trains are heading. (For example, if you are on Line 3 between Indios Verdes and Universidad, you can go "Dirección Indios Verdes" or "Dirección Universidad.")

Theft occurs frequently on the Metro when it's crowded (and it almost invariably is). Carry bags in front of you or on your lap; simply closing the bag does little good, because thieves have used razors to slit the bag open from the bottom. Subway thieves often work in pairs—one will distract you while the other pulls your wallet. Rear pockets are easy to pick; front pockets are safer, empty pockets are best. If you ride with a backpack on your back, the small pocket will invariably be violated. Non-Mexicans run a higher risk of being robbed, so it is always wise to avoid the outer trappings of tourist status while on the Metro.

Women riding the Metro often have the horrible experience of being groped in a crowd. Do not be afraid to call attention to the offender. During rush hours, many lines have cars reserved for women and children. Use them. They are usually located at the front of the train; often you will see women and children gathering on a separate part of the platform reserved for their car. The safest place in a crowded car is with your back against the wall keeping your backpack (if you have one) in front of you. Don't, however, feel rude when you must push, shove, and trample to exit the car. It is not unheard of to miss stops due to inability to get to the door.

Because of overcrowding, large bags, parcels, or suitcases are not allowed on the Metro. People slip bags past the gate, but you may regret it if you try. On a crowded train, your luggage will make fellow passengers uncomfortable and make you an immobile duck for thieves.

Some Metro stops serve as their own sights. Pino Suárez has a small Aztec building inside the stop, and La Raza houses the science tunnel with space pictures and a huge glow-in-the-dark star map.

For Metro and bus information, contact **COVITUR (Comisión de Vialidad y Transporte Urbano del D.F.),** Public Relations, Universidad 800 on the 14th floor, at the corner of Félix Cuervas just outside the Zapata Metro station (tel. 688-89-55 or 211-90-09), or ask at any information booth. For complaints about the Metro dial 709-11-33, ext. 5009 or 5010. If you lose something on the Metro, call the **Oficina de Objetos Extraviados** (tel. 709-11-33, ext. 3365), located in the Fray Servando station (Line 4). Keep hope alive, but keep expectations modest.

Overall, the Metro is by far the cleanest, fastest, and safest means of transportation in Mexico City. Almost all the restaurants, clubs, and museums of interest to the budget traveler can be reached most easily on the Metro.

■ By Bus

The public bus system extends much farther than the Metro; however, there is no published information about routes and schedules available to the tourist, so unless you stick to the major thoroughfares you might find it difficult to navigate the city by bus. Also, although you do get to see the city above ground, buses are usually slower than the Metro, particularly in the morning and evening rush hours. Buses are tastefully brown and yellow or blue and gray and cost .40 pesos; have change ready when you board. They run daily from 5am to midnight, but are scarce after 10pm. They pass bus stops every 20-30 minutes.

Buses are required to stop only at the bus stops along Ejes Viales and the following major streets: Reforma, Insurgentes, Calzada de Tlalpan, and Viaducto Miguel Alemán. Anywhere, flag the driver by holding out your arm and pointing at the street in front of you. To get off the bus, press the button above the exit door at the rear of the bus. If you don't hear a buzz, bang once on the wall or bark *¡Bajo!* to let the driver know you want out.

In an effort to meet the growing demand for efficient transportation, the city is slowly incorporating "Express" buses into the system. These swift steeds stop only on major avenues such as Insurgentes, Reforma, and Mazaryk. Like the Metro, buses are crowded and seats are hot items. The popular buses along Paseo de la Reforma are notorious for robbery and are plagued by organized gangs of businesslike thieves. Leave your valuables at the hotel; don't keep money in your pockets; carry your bag in front of you; or best yet, avoid this route altogether.

■ By Pesero (Minibus)

Peseros, a.k.a. *colectivos*, *combis*, or *micros*, are white and green minibuses, often with a "Magna Sin" gasoline logo on the side. Priced economically between cabs and buses, they cruise the streets on set routes. Though, like buses, no printed information is available, the destinations are either painted on or posted on the front window. To hail a *pesero*, wave your hand or hold out as many fingers as there are people in your group. Drivers will honk (horns are often rigged to play an annoying melody) at virtually every pedestrian to signal availability.

The fare varies according to distance, averaging .80-1 peso for cross-city routes, 1.50 for over 17km. Pay when you get on and tell the driver your destination, which often prevents a missed stop. Some *peseros* run only until midnight, but the major routes—on Reforma, between Chapultepec and San Ángel, and along Insurgentes run 24 hrs. The fare is 20% higher between 10pm and 6am. Central City routes are indicated by Metro stops, while suburban *peseros* may also have numbers.

Other well-traveled *pesero* routes include: Metro Hidalgo to Ciudad Universitaria (via Reforma, Bucareli, and Av. Cuauhtémoc); La Villa to Chapultepec (via Reforma); Reforma to Auditorio (via Reforma and Juárez); *zócalo* to Chapultepec (via 5 de Mayo and Reforma); San Ángel to Izazaga (via 5 de Mayo and Reforma); Bolívar to Ciudad Universitaria/Coyoacán (via Bolívar in the *Centro*); and San Ángel to Metro Insurgentes (via Av. de la Paz and Insurgentes Sur). Many depart from Chapultepec Metro station to San Ángel, La Merced, and the airport. Be sure you know exactly where you're going when boarding the *pesero* and clearly state your destination to the driver.

■ By Taxi

Cabs constantly cruise the major avenues, offering a quick, private alternative to the public systems. Meters don't show prices but a reference number for the driver's price conversion table. Ask to see it before you pay, to insure that the price you're given matches the meter number. Hotel cabs and *turismo* taxis have no meters and charge up to three times more than regular taxis; green VW bugs are the cheapest but must be hailed; larger, orange taxis have digital meters that require no conversion. At night, all meters tend to be *descompuesto* (broken). Make sure the taxi meter is in clear view so that you can see the numbers turn as you travel. *Insist* on setting the price beforehand so you aren't at the driver's mercy when you reach your destination. Tips are unnecessary unless the cabdriver grants you a special service (helps carry your luggage, gives you a previously agreed-to tour, etc.).

At the airport and at all bus terminals, purchase a taxi ticket for a set fee (according to destination) at a registered booth. In the rare instance that no taxi is in sight, call **Servi-taxi** (tel. 516-60-20) or **Taxi Radio Mexicana** (tel. 574-45-96). VW bug taxis should display the driver's photo, credentials, and license over the glove compartment. Taxis commonly prey on the easy tourist victim. At the airport or bus terminals, try to consult a zone map before buying your ticket and always count your change. On the street, ask a local what the fare should be and insist on paying that and no more, there'll always be a driver who will accept.

■ By Car

Be forewarned that driving is the craziest and least economical way to get around the Federal District. Central Mexico City is encircled by a number of connected highways that together make up the **Circuito Interior.** This system allows motorists to get as close as possible to their destination before hitting the gridlocked streets of the center. Unfortunately, the Circuito itself is frequently jammed, especially during rush hour (Mon.-Fri. 7-9am and 6-9pm).

Mexico City's drivers are notoriously evil; they became so partly because highway engineers did not design the roads with drivers in mind. Highway dividers are often absent, stop signs are planted midstream, and red lights are routinely defied. The fast, efficient and cost-free *Ángeles Verdes* do *not* serve the Distrito Federal, where even angels fear to tread. If your car should break down within city boundaries, call **Asociación Automovilística Mexicana** (tel. 519-34-36) and request assistance. Wait for them beside your car, with the hood raised. If you leave your car alone, kiss it goodbye before you go.

Parking within the city is seldom a problem: parking lots are everywhere (approx. 1-8 pesos per hr., depending on the location and condition of the lot). Street parking in Mexico City is rare, and vandalism is extremely common. Never leave anything valuable inside the car. Police will remove your license plate if you park illegally; should this happen, wait near your car with some cash in your pocket until they return. If anything else was missing and you suspect the police were tampering with your car, report it to LOCATEL (tel. 658-11-11).

All vehicles, even those of non-Mexican registration, must follow Mexico City's anti-smog regulations. Depending on the last digit of the license plate, cars are forbidden from driving one day a week, according to this schedule Monday final digits 5 or 6; Tuesday: 7 or 8; Wednesday: 3 or 4; Thursday: 1 or 2; Friday: 9 or 0. Restrictions apply from 5am-10pm, and penalties for violations are stiff. (No limitations on weekends and between 10pm and 5am daily.)

Car rental rates are exorbitant, driving a hassle and the entire process draining. Requirements to rent vary, but all require the renter to be at least 21 yrs. old but some require the renter to be 26, have a major credit card and show a passport or tourist card,) Any driver's license is valid in Mexico. Prices for rentals tend to be similar; try the *Zona Rosa* or *Sala* E in the airport. **Auto Renta Facil** Río Lerma 157 (tel. 511-76-41), near Río Tiber, rents VW sedans for 71 pesos per day, plus .55 pesos per km, plus 22 pesos insurance; or 186 pesos per day with free mileage. Renter must be 26 yrs. old. (Open Mon.-Sat. 9am-8pm.) **Dollar** Av. Chapultepec 322 (tel. 207-38-38), in the Col. Roma, has similar rates. Renter must be 25. (Open daily 7am-8pm.) **Budget** Hamburgo 71 (tel. 533-04-50), in the *Zona Rosa,* charges 95 pesos, plus .75 pesos per km. (Open Mon.-Fri. 7am-9pm, Sat. 8am-6pm.)

SAFETY

Like all large cities, Mexico City presents safety problems to the traveler. Misconceptions about the magnitude of these problems can easily prevent an enjoyable visit, however. In general, the downtown area, where most sights and accommodations are located, tends to be safer, although the backstreets near Buenavista and the *Alameda* are significantly less so. Try to avoid carrying large amounts of cash and use a money belt or similar security device. Ignore strangers who seem even slightly suspicious, no matter how friendly their chatter or smile may seem. Never follow a vendor or shoeshiner out of the public view.

Women are, unfortunately, at higher risk of attack. Avoid being alone, especially at night or in a lonely area. Light hair and North American-style shorts will attract undesirable stares and propositions. A loud clear *¡Déjame!* (DEH-ha-meh) will make your intentions clear.

Transportation presents its own safety concerns (see Getting Around for more info). Mexico City's drivers are notoriously aggressive and often ignore traffic signals. Insist on seeing a taxi driver's photo license. Locals warn of late-night (1am on) attacks by *bandidos* posing as policemen.

Sidewalk vendors hawk scrumptious-looking food at enticing prices, but a cheap taco may force frequent trips to the *baño* down the road. Remember, too, what everyone back home said and don't drink the water. The city's notoriously smoggy air may cause problems for contact lens wearers and people with allergies. *The News* publishes a detailed smog report daily.

Overall, common sense rules. A rewarding trip can be easily stifled by hyper-caution and worry. Be careful, but don't spend your time in one of the world's greatest cities under a blanket locked in your hotel room.

PRACTICAL INFORMATION

Federal Tourist Office: Infotur Amberes 54 (tel. 525-93-80 through -84), at Londres in the *Zona Rosa*. Most employees speak some English and are well informed. Metro and city maps available. Standardized price list of mid-range tourist hotels in major Mexican cities. Solves all riddles in person or by phone. Open daily 9am-9pm. During the same hours, the office operates information booths in *Salas* A (tel. 571-16-63 or 762-67-73) and E (tel. 784-85-53 or 784-89-69) at the airport, and at the TAPO bus station.

Ministry of Tourism: Presidente Masaryk 172 (tel. 250-85-55), at Hegel in Col. Polanco. From line 7, 1 block down Arqímeded and left onto Masaryk. The huge selection of maps and brochures on every place in Mexico may run low. All sorts of tourist information but a somewhat bewildered staff. Best for hotel reservations throughout the Republic. Open Mon.-Fri. 8am-8pm (24-hr. phone lines).

Department of Tourist Security: Presidente Masaryk 172 (tel. 250-01-51 or 250-04-93), in Col. Polanco. Calls answered by employees of the Ministry of Tourism, who will respond to complaints, suspected abuses, emergencies, and questions. Report all problems with tourist establishments here. Some English. A very good place to start after a mishap. Open 24 hrs. for phone calls; staffed 8am-8pm.

Legal Advice: Supervisión General de Servicios a la Comunidad, Florencia 20 (tel. 625-87-61), in the *Zona Rosa*, nearest the Metro Insurgentes (line 1). 24-hr. **hotline** (tel. 625-86-68). If you are the victim of a robbery or accident and need legal advice. Some employees speak English.

Tourist Card Information: Secretaría de Gobernación, Dirección General de Servicios Migratorios, Av. Chapultepec 284, 5th floor; Col. Juárez, Line 1, Insurgentes (tel. 626-72-00 or 206-05-06). Open Mon.-Fri. 8am-2pm.

Accommodations Service: Hoteles Asociados, Airport *Sala* E (tel. 571-59-02 or 571-63-82). Up-to-date information on prices and locations of Mexico City hotels. Give 'em a price range and an area, they'll get you a reservation, free of charge. If you want budget lodgings, be sure to ask for rock-bottom prices. English spoken.

Embassies: Will replace lost passports, issue visas, and provide legal assistance and sympathy. Visa processing can take up to 24 hrs.; bring plenty of ID. **Australia,** Jaime Balmes 11 (tel. 395-99-88), between Ejército Nacional and Homero. Open Mon.-Fri. 8am-2pm. **Belize,** Thiers 152-B (tel. 203-56-42). Open Mon.-Fri. 9am-1pm. **Canada,** Schiller 529 (tel. 724-79-00), behind the Museum of Anthro. Open Mon.-Fri. 8:30am-2pm. **Costa Rica,** Río Po 113 (tel. 525-77-66), between Río Lerma and Río Pánnco, behind the U.S. embassy. Open Mon.-Fri. 9:30am-4:30pm. **Denmark,** Tres Picos 52 (tel. 255-34-05), between Hegel and Lamartines. Open Mon.-Thurs. 8:30am-3:30pm, Fri. 8:30am-12:30pm. **France,** Havre 15 (tel. 533-13-60), between Hamburgo and Reforma. Open Mon.-Fri. 8:30am-1:30pm. For visas, consulate at Alejandro Dumas 16 (tel. 281-04-47), close to the corner of Campos Eliseos. Open Mon.-Fri. 9am-noon. **Germany,** Byron 737 (tel. 545-66-55). Open Mon.-Fri. 9am-12:30pm. **Guatemala,** 1025 Av. Explanada (tel. 545-75-20). Open Mon.-Fri. 9am-12:30pm. **Honduras,** Alfonso Reyes 220 (tel. 211-57-47), between Saltillo and Ometusco. Open Mon.-Fri. 10am-2pm. **Japan,** Paseo de la Reforma 395, 2nd floor (tel. 211-00-28). Open Mon.-Fri. 9:30am-1:30pm and 3:30-6pm. **Netherlands,** Montes Urales Sur 635; 2nd floor (tel. 202-82-67), before Petroleos Mexicanos. Open Mon.-Fri. 9am-2pm. **New Zealand,** Homero 229 (tel. 250-59-99), on the 8th floor. Open Mon.-Thurs. 8:30am-1:30pm and 3-5pm, Fri. 8:30am-2pm only. **Nicaragua,** Payo de Rivera 120 (tel. 520-24-49), between Virreyes and Monte Atos. Open Mon.-Fri. 10am-2pm. **Norway,** Av. Virreyes 1460 (tel. 540-34-86), between Apalachis and Montes Auberne. Open Mon.-Fri. 9am-2pm. **Panama,** Campos Eliseos 111 (tel. 250-42-29), between Hegel and Lope de Vega. Open Mon.-Fri. 8:30am-2:30pm. **Sweden,** Avila Camacho 1 (tel. 540-63-93), at Plaza Comermex. Open Mon.-Fri.10am-noon. **U.K.,** Río Lerma 71 (tel. 207-20-89), at Cuauhtémoc. Consulate open Mon.-Fri. 8:30am-3:30pm. Visa office open Mon.-Fri. 9am-2pm. **U.S.,** Reforma 305 (tel. 211-00-42), at Glorieta Ángel de la Independencia. Open Mon.-Fri. 8:30am-12:45pm for passports and visas, Mon.-Fri. 8:30am-5:30pm for general business. Call after hours and on weekends for emergencies only.

Currency Exchange: All banks offer the same exchange rate and usually charge commissions. Exchange hours for all 9am-1:30pm, but the wait may be considerable. The nation-wide **ATM** network, **Red Cajeros Compartidos** takes MC and Visa for cash advances, any many work with other U.S. system cards. Scores of ATMs are located along Reforma, in the Zona Rosa and Polanco, and in the Centro. Lost or stolen cards can be reported 24 hrs. to 227-27-77. **Citibank,** Reforma 390 (tel. 211-30-30; 24 hrs.), and **Bank of America,** Reforma 116, 10th-12th floors (tel. 591-00-11), can also help in an emergency. *Casas de cambio* keep longer hours than banks, give better exchange rates, and most are openon Saturday . They are concentrated along Reforma and in the *Zona Rosa*. Most in the *Zona Rosa* can change a number of non-U.S. currencies. The downtown area, where most sights, restaurants, and accommodations are located, has *casas de cambio* within a short distance of everything. Call the **Asociación Mexicana de Casas de Cambio** (tel. 264-08-84 or 264-08-41) to locate an exchange bureau near you. In the *Centro*: **Casa de Cambio Euromex,** Venustiano Carranza 64, 3rd floor (tel. 518-41-99); **Casa de Cambio Velasco Sucesores,** Gante 12, local B (tel. 521-50-28). Near the *Alameda*: **Casa de Cambio Plus,** Juárez 38 (tel. 510-22-88), on the southeast corner of the *Alameda Central*. Open Mon.-Fri. 9am-4pm, Sat. 10am-2pm. *Reforma,* closer to Buenavista and Revolución: **Casa de Cambio Catorce,** Reforma 51 (tel. 705-14-94).

American Express: Reforma 234 (tel. 207-72-82), at Havre in the *Zona Rosa*. Will cash personal checks and accept mail for customers only. Money can be wired here. Report lost credit cards to the branch at Patriotismo 635 (tel. 326-26-66), lost traveler's checks to either branch. Open Mon.-Fri. 9am-6pm, Sat. 9am-1pm. In case of a lost **Visa** card, call 625-21-88.

Central Post Office: Lázaro Cárdenas (tel. 521-73-94), at Tacuba across from Bellas Artes. Open for stamps, regular mail, and *Lista de Correos* Mon.-Fri. 8am-11pm, Sat. 9am-1pm, for registered mail Mon.-Fri. 9am-5pm, Sat. 9am-1pm. Postal museum upstairs. **Postal code:** 06002.

Telephones: For direct long-distance calls, long-distance *casetas* at: Airport *Sala* D (open daily 6am-8:30pm); Buenavista train station (open Mon.-Fri. 9am-9pm, Sat.-Sun. 9am-2pm); or Central Camionera del Norte (open daily 8am-9pm). Also, look for **LADATEL** phones at the airport, bus stations, Metro stations, VIPs Restaurant and on the street in the *Zona Rosa* or *centro* district to make collect calls to the U.S. (See Mexico Essentials: Keeping in Touch: Telephones.) Special phones in the airport take major credit cards. **Telephone code:** 5.

Telegrams: Tacuba 8 (tel. 510-03-94), at the Museo Nacional de Arte in the right wing of the building, behind the central post office. Domestic and international service. From the U.S., send through Western Union to **México Central Telégrafos.** Open Mon.-Fri. 8am-mdnight, Sat. 9am-12:45pm. To send telegrams by phone call 709-8500 national, 709-8625 international.

Courier Services: Estafeta Mensajería y Paquetería, Praga 31 (tel. 208-50-47, 24-hr. service at 325-91-00), at Hamburgo in the *Zona Rosa*. International parcel delivery. Open Mon.-Fri. 9am-5:30pm. **DHL,** Reforma 30 (tel. 562-57-00, 24-hr. service at 227-02-99), also at Insurgentes Sur 859 (tel. 592-60-11), in Col. Nápoles. **Federal Express,** Estocolmo 4 (tel. 228-99-04). Send before 3:30pm for overnight service. Also at Leibnitz and Víctor Hugo (tel. 251-41-40) in the Col. Anzures. Open Mon.-Fri. 8am-7pm.

English Bookstores: American Bookstore, Madero 25 (tel. 512-72-84), in the *Centro* with an extensive selection of fiction, guides and a matchless Latin American history and politics section. Also a branch at Revolución 1570 (tel. 661-1916) in San Ángel. Both branches open Mon.-Sat. 10am-7pm. **Portico de la Ciudad de Mexico,** Central 124 (tel. 510-96-83), at Carranza. Sells English and Spanish Mexican history books and guides to archaeological sites. Open Mon.-Sat. 10am-7pm. For magazines and newspapers in Spanish, English, French, and German try **La Casa de la Prensa Internacional,** Florencia 57 in the *Zona Rosa*. Open Mon.-Sat. 8am-9pm. The **Museo Nacional de Antropología** has a wide selection of archaeological guides in English (see Sights). The English-language newspaper, *The News*, is sold at most newsstands.

Ben Franklin Library: Londres 16 (tel. 211 00 42), at Berlin, 2 blocks southeast of the Cuauhtémoc monument. 75% of the books are in English, including a large variety of newspapers and periodicals. Open Tues.-Thurs. 10am-3pm, Mon. and Fri. 3-7:30pm.

Cultural and Arts Information: Palacio Nacional de Bellas Artes, Juárez and Eje Central (tel. 709-31-11 or 512-36-33), for information and reservations for all Bellas Artes events.

Laundromats: Near the monument to the Revolución: **Lavandería Automática,** Edison 91. Wash 9 pesos per 5 lb., dry 9 pesos. Full service 9 pesos extra. Soap 3 pesos. Open Mon.-Fri. 10am-7pm, Sat. 10am-6pm. In the *Zona Rosa*: **Lavanderet,** Chapultepec 463 (tel. 514-01-06), at Toledo. 9 pesos to wash, 9 pesos to dry. Full service 20 pesos. Open Mon.-Sat. 9am-7pm. Most hotels have laundry service or can tell you where to find the nearest facility.

Supermarket: Most supermarkets are away from the city center at residential Metro stops. **Bodega,** Serapio Rendón 117, just south of Antonio Caso. Open Mon.-Sat. 8am-9pm, Sun. 9am-8pm. **Aurrera,** 5 blocks north of Puente de Alvaro on Insurgentes. Open daily 9am-9pm. **Commercial Mexicana,** at Corregidora and Correo Mayor, on the coutheast side of the Palacio Nacional in the *centro.* Open daily 8am-8pm.

Rape Crisis: Hospital de Traumatología de Balbuena, Cecilio Robelo 103 (tel. 552-16-02 or 764-03-39), near Calle Sur, east of *Alameda*. **Hospital de la Mujer**, (tel. 541 46 61). Also call 06 or LOCATEL.

Gay, Lesbian, and Bisexual Information: Colectivo Sol. Address inquiries care of Apdo. 13-320 Av. México 13, D.F. 03500. A mainly political group that offers information on upcoming political and social events.

Sexually Transmitted Disease Information: Secretaría de Salud (tel. 277-63-11), open Mon.-Fri. 8am-2pm and 3:30-7pm, Sat. 9am-1pm.

AIDS Hotline: TELSIDA/CONASIDA, Florencia 8 (tel. 207-41-43 or 207-40-83), Col. Roma, Metro Cuauhtémoc. Information and help center

LOCATEL: (tel. 658-11-11.) City's official lost-and-found hotline. Call if your car (or friend) is missing. Also information and directions in cases of medical emergencies and information about sports events, etc.

Red Cross: Ejército Nacional 1032 (tel. 557-57-58 or 557-57-57), in the Col. Polanco. Open 24 hrs. Fastest and most efficient ambulance service.

Pharmacies: VYR, San Jerónimo 630 (tel. 595-59-83 or 595-59-98), near Periférico Sur shopping center. Open 24 hrs. More convenient during the day might be **Farmacia El Fénix,** Isabel La Católica 15 (tel. 585-04-55), at 5 de Mayo. Open Mon.-Sat. 9am-10pm. Well-stocked, but will take Spanish prescriptions only. All big markets have well-stocked pharmacy counters.

Medical Care: The **U.S. Embassy** (see above) has a list of doctors in the city, with their specialties, addresses, telephone numbers and languages spoken. **Dirección General de Servicios Médicos** (tel. 518-51-00) has information on all city hospitals, (Open Mon.-Fri. 9am-6pm.) Free emergency medical assistance is available at **Procuraduría General de Justicia del D.F.** Florencia 20 (tel. 625-87-61), in the *Zona Rosa*. For tourists, the **American British Cowdray (ABC) Hospital,** Calle Sur 136 (tel. 227-50-00) at Observatorio, Col. Las Américas. No U.S. health plans valid, but all major credit cards accepted. 24 hrs. **Torre Medica,** José Maria Iglesias 21 (tel. 546-24-80); Metro Revolución. Near Monumento de la Revolución.

Emergency Shelter: Casa de Protección Social (tel. 530-47-62 or 530-85-36).

Police: Secretaría General de Protección y Vialidad (tel. 768-80-44). Dial 08 for the Policia Judicial to report assaults, robberies, crashes, abandoned vehicles, or other emergencies.

ACCOMMODATIONS

Rooms abound in the *Centro* (between *Alameda* and the *zócalo*) and the *Alameda Central*, and are sprinkled throughout the area surrounding the Monumento a la Revolución on the Pl. de la República. Mexico City offers high-quality budget accommodations relative to other large cities in the country. Rooms costing 40-50 pesos and up for one bed and 60-70 pesos and up for two beds should be clean, have carpeting, a TV, and a telephone (with free local calls), or you're getting the high, hard one. Most budget hotels charge according to the number of beds needed and not per person; beds tend to be large enough for two people. If you can deal, this is a potential source of substantial savings.

Avoid the filthier sections of the *Alameda*, and any area which makes you feel uncomfortable—there's plenty more from which to choose. Don't be put off by the mid- to high-priced hotels around Insurgentes Sur and Reforma, just northeast of the *Zona Rosa* tourist belt; they are still inexpensive by U.S. standards. Also stay away anyplace where the hotel, not the parking lot, is marked "Hotel Garage." These rooms are frequented by businessfolk "working late at the office;" the hourly charge is sky-high. Always ask to look at a room before you accept it; they are most likely to be free after check-out time (between noon and 2pm). Hotels whose prices are above 55 pesos per single and 70 pesos per double usually accept MC and Visa. AmEx is less common.

For hostel information, call Villa Deportiva Juvenil (tel. 525-26-99), which operates the city's lone hostel on the Plaza de la Independencia, near the *Zona Rosa* (18 per night). They can't guarantee you a spot and often fill up with visiting sports teams competing in the city.

■ Centro

Situated between the *zócalo* and *Alameda Central*, this *colonia* is the historic colonial heart of Mexico City. Its hotels are reasonably priced and feel fairly safe, though the throngs disappear as they head home for the night, leaving the streets relatively empty. Nonetheless, the *Centro* remains the most exciting place to stay and the best base from which to explore the traditional core of one of the world's largest cities. Along with the action, however, comes noise and congestion. If you are in town for a lengthy stay, consider moving west to the *Buenavista* or *Alameda* areas to escape the roar of the stampede.

Many of the hotels listed are north of Madero and 5 de Mayo, the parallel east-west streets that connect the *Alameda* with the *zócalo*, and east of Lázaro Cárdenas, the north-south Eje Central that runs one block east of *Alameda*. Metro stations Bellas Artes and Allende (both Line 2) serve these hotels. The hotels on 5 de Mayo, Isabel la Católica, and Uruguay are better served by the *zócalo* and Isabel la Católica stations. All the listings in this area except Hotel Rioja accept MasterCard and Visa.

Hotel Antillas, Belisario Domínguez 34 (tel. 526-56-74), near Allende. A wonderfully restored and maintained colonial building. Half of the lobby is dedicated to a small restaurant, which shares the polished wooden beams and iron chandeliers which give the foyer a historic feel. Comfortable rooms with good bathrooms come with TV, phone, drinking wate,r and carpet—ask to see the room beforehand. Singles 60 pesos. Doubles 75 pesos.

Hotel La Marina, Allende 30 (tel. 518-24-45), B. Dominquez. Mid-sized rooms try to match orange and brown furniture with inadequately azure-blue seascapes. Phone, color TV, central radio, and nice bathrooms. An even better deal than Antillas. Singles 45 pesos. Doubles 70 pesos.

Hotel Congreso, Allende 18 (tel. 510-44-46), between Répubica de Cuba and Donceles. A darkish hotel, surprisingly quiet for the area, but all amenities are right (TV, phone, radio, carpet). Smallish rooms seductively combine orange and crimson colors. Singles 45 pesos. Doubles 60 pesos.

Hotel Atlanta, Domníquez Belisario 31 (tel. 518-12-00), across from Hotel Antillas. Rooms are a bit more worn than those in the above 3 hotels, but offer TV, phone, radio, and good bathrooms. Heavy curtains let in little light but also keep noise out. Singles 45 pesos. 1-bed doubles 50 pesos, 2 beds 70 pesos.

Hotel Florida, Belisario Domínguez 57 (tel. 521-77-64). Nice but small, dark rooms with hideously mismatched brown rugs and red bedcovers make you feel like you really are in Florida. All rooms have TV, radio, and phone. Immaculate bathrooms. 5 floors of smallish rooms overlook a clean, marbled courtyard. Free bottled water at main desk. A good value. Singles 40 pesos. Doubles 65 pesos.

Hotel Monte Carlo, Uruguay 69. Metro Isabel la Católica, Metro Allende: equally far away. Very spacious courtyard, beautifully tiled in brown. The outstanding collection of world currencies at reception desk once paid for solid rooms with radio, phone, and *agua purificada*. Good bathrooms. Singles 50 pesos. Doubles 55 pesos for 1 bed, 70 pesos for 2 beds.

Hotel Principal, Bolivar 29 (tel. 521-13-33), Metro Allende, between Madero and 16 de Septiembre. Spacious rooms dominated by almost equally sized wardrobes. TV, phones, meager lighting, and decent bathrooms. Singles 50 pesos. Doubles 60 pesos.

Hotel Isabel, Isabel la Católica 63 (tel. 518-12-13), between El Salvador and Uruguay across from the old Biblioteca Nacional. A sprawling old-fashioned hotel that is a refreshing alternative to its boring modern counterparts. Step into the vast, wood-panelled lobby (complete with coat of arms) through the huge wooden doors with carved lion's heads. The hotel's character continues in the darkish worn rooms with contain shiny brass beds, dark wood dressers and great bathrooms. Singles 60 pesos. Doubles 75 pesos.

Hotel Rioja, 5 de Mayo 45 (tel. 521-83-33). Not particularly comfortable, but a good location and the rooms are as close to free as you'll find. Noisy—room doors open onto inner patio, designed to magnify every stray street sound. Bare lightbulbs illuminate clean mid-sized rooms. Singles 35 pesos. Doubles 40 pesos. Top floor rooms have no private bathrooms (singles 26 pesos, doubles 30 pesos) but offer a somewhat romantic view of the surrounding rooftops.

■ Alameda Central

The long-expected construction of Metro line 8 should have finished by the fall of 1993 thus ending the constant noise and omnipresent dust in the area and a two-year suppression of prices. Prices will probably increase more rapidly in this area than in others. The *Alameda* is probably the least safe of the three areas listed; women in particular will feel more secure in the *Centro, Buenavista,* and *Zona Rosa* areas.

Hotel Hidalgo, Santa Veracruz 37 (tel. 521-87-71), at the 2 de Abril walkway, behind Bellas Artes Metro station. The stalwart exterior, one of the few to survive the 1985 earthquakes, is a paragon of the concrete jungle, a cinder-block stalwart amidst new construction. Fortunately, the interior is better: a modern lively lobby, flawless wood trim, new-looking furniture and decently-lit rooms that afford city views. Restaurant in the lobby. Parking available. Singles 70 pesos. Doubles 85 pesos. Triples 100 pesos.

Hotel Manolo, Luis Moya 111 (tel. 521-77-09), just north of Arcos de Belén; an arrow across the street points the way. Big rooms require a map; landmarks include the enormous bed, color TV, radio and phone. The 4 wild patterns on the carpet, bedspread, curtains, and wallpaper may give you vertigo. Tiled bathrooms with out-of-place bidet. Dire thirsts slaked in the lobby, which is amply stocked with soda and bottled water. Singles and doubles 70 pesos.

Hotel Conde, Pescaditos 15 (tel. 521-10-84), at Revillagigedo. Exit the Metro at Juárez, follow Artículo 123 to Revillagigedo, then take a right and walk 3 blocks. A big white building with a sterilized central lobby. Phone, TV, and blue-tiled bathrooms fit for nobility. Priced lower than its rivals in the area. Lots of parking space in back. Singles 60 pesos. 1 bed doubles 75 pesos, with 2 beds 85 pesos.

Hotel Cosmos, Lázaro Cárdenas 12 (tel. 512-26-31), just south of Madero. Shabby lobby, and the good-sized rooms with TV and phone are worth the meager asking price. An old-fashioned elevator with exposed shaft. Singles and 1-bed doubles 45 pesos. 2-bed doubles 75 pesos. 3-bed triples 100 pesos.

■ Near the Monumento a la Revolución/ Buenavista

Accommodations in the Monumento a la Revolución area offer more peace and quiet than do those in the *Centro* or the *Alameda*, for two main reasons: there are few historical sites here of interest to tourists, and not many people have moved back since the area was heavily damaged in the 1985 quake. These older and less centrally located hotels charge less than their counterparts in the *Alameda* and *Centro*. As a result, budget travelers tend to congregate here, particularly in the hotels on Mariscal and Edison. Metro Revolución and Metro Hidalgo serve those hotels south of Puente de Alvarado/Hidalgo; while Metro Guerrero serves those to the north near the train station.

Hotel Royalty, Jesus Terán 21 (tel. 566-92-55), just block towards the Monumento a la Revolución along Av. de la Népublica, to the left. The tiger-design of the carpet makes the rooms darkish, but they're all clean, comfortable, have ancient phones, TVs, and excellent bathrooms. Exceptional for the price. Singles and doubles 40 pesos.

Hotel Londres, Pl. Buenavista 5 (tel. 705-09-10), off Buenavista, 3 blocks south of the train station, 2 blocks north of Puente de Alvarado. Step out of the smoggy exterior and into a cool courtyard with chilly blue tile, a splashing fountain, and lush greenery. Nothing fancy in the rooms, but clean with bright bedspreads. A deal and a half at 40 pesos for singles and doubles.

Hotel Atoyac, Guerreo 161 (tel. 526-9917), between Degollado Mosqueto, 2 blocks to your left as you exit the train station onto Mosqueto. Excellent conditions for the low asking price. Reasonably large rooms with TVs, wall-to-wall carpeting, and clean, bright bathrooms. Often full; try to get a room after 3pm. Singles and doubles 35 pesos.

Hotel Estaciones, Berual Díaz 17 (tel. 566-68-55), off Puente de Alvarado, 1½ blocks west from Metro Revolucíon. not to be confused with the bland white building next door with same conditions but higher prices. Exceedingly colorful bedcovers are the only bright spot in the dark rooms with TVs. Paint peeling in the area's biggest bathrooms, but still avery good value at 40 pesos for singles or doubles.

Casa de Los Amigos, Ignacio Mariscal 132 (tel. 705-05-21 or 705-06-46), across from Gran Hotel Texas. Originally home to José Clemente Orozco, the House of Friends (Quakers) is a cultural and refugee center and temporary boardinghouse for people working for peace and international justice in Central America. Beds are given to casual travelers on a space-available basis. Not a hostel but a place with its own character, international atmosphere, and reasonable requirements. The staff will give you an information sheet when you arrive so that you understand the purpose of the *casa* and agree to respect their cooperative atmosphere. Friendly, helpful, English-speaking proprietors. Kitchen facilities. Meditation room was once Orozco's art studio. Will hold mail. 2-day minimum stay, 15-day max. stay. Be in by 10pm or pay a 10-peso deposit for a key. Storage fee .80 pesos. Breakfast of yogurt and granola 6 pesos. Dorm room 24 pesos. Private room (when available) 28-60 pesos.

Hotel Oxford, Ignacio Mariscal 67 (tel. 566-05-00), at Alcázar, next to the small park. Fresh flowers in the entry welcome you to this stellar budget option. An elegant winding staircase leads to carpeted rooms blessed by round wood tables, large color TV with several English channels. Drinking water. The only slight drawback: a newspaper distribution center on the street below that cranks up noisily at the crack of dawn. Singles 50-55 pesos. Doubles 75 pesos.

Hotel Carlton, Ignacio Mariscal 32 (tel. 566-29-11), between Alcázar and Arizpe, across from the park. Notoriously good value has attracted budget travelers from afar. A bit more worn than more expensive options, but the friendly management, location, and mid-sized carpeted rooms with TV outweigh this small indiscretion. Restaurant and lively bar attached. Singles 50 pesos. Doubles 60 pesos.

Hotel Yale, Mosqueta 200 (tel. 591-14-88), between Zaragoza and Guerrero, to the left of the train station (if you exit). The rooms in this unfortunately-named hotel are well-maintained and have the works (TV, radio, thick carpet, and *agua purificada*), yet continue to be rated second-best by *U.S. News and World Report*. Those that face the inner courtyard are darker but have the calming whisper of the small water fountain. 50 pesos for both singles and doubles.

Hotel Detroit, Zaragoza 55 (tel. 566-07-55), at Mina in Col. Guerrero. Guerrero runs parallel to Zaragoza. The lobby and halls are run down, with peeling plaster, linoleum floors, and only religious paraphernalia to add luster. Rooms have fake wood floors that are kept clean, curtains with molecular orbit patterns, spotless sheets and tightly made beds. The dimly lit neighborhood is not a place to hang out for an extended period of time. Singles 35 pesos. Doubles 70 pesos.

Hotel Parador Washington, Dinamara 42 (tel. 566-8648), at the corner with Londres, on Plaza Jirge Washington, close to the *Zona Rosa:* Upscale locale without the impossible prices. Winding hallways lend to classy sitting rooms. Bright bedrooms with large beds. Color scheme attempts to reconcile orange and green. Prices very acceptable for the area. Singles 70 pesos. Doubles 80 pesos.

FOOD

The teeming masses which inhabit Mexico City demand an unparalleled quantity and diversity of edibles, a demand readily met by the apparently equal number of stores, stands, restaurants, and vendors. The wide range of choices is matched only by the disparity in cleanliness; as always, no matter how delicious that beef tongue in vinegar dressing looks, inspect it as carefully as possible before popping it into your mouth.

The food in Mexico City is often cheaper than in many other parts of the country, and there are some definite local favorites: *huevos* (eggs) and *pan dulce* (sweet bread) for breakfast, *quesadillas* (fried tortillas with cheese) or *tortas de pierna* (pork sandwiches) for lunch, and *pollo con mole poblano* (chicken with *mole* sauce) or enchiladas for dinner. There are many natural products stores throughout the city, and a surprisingly high representation of vegetarian restaurants (see listings below).

Creativity is the key to enjoying Mexico City's edible diversity. *Panaderías* make mounds of bread daily and sell it at ridiculously low prices. A bag full of breakfast often costs only a few pesos. Overcome aversions and be sure to at least sample the street fare. The options fall into five basic categories: fast and inexpensive *taquerías*, slightly more formal *cafeterías*, more pricy and decorous Mexican restaurants, locally popular and inflated North-Americanized diners, and expensive international fare. In addition, U.S. fast-food chains mass-produce predictable fare for the timid palate. **VIP's** offers 60 commercialized Denny's-like eateries throughout the D.F. If you're preparing your own food, **Conasupos** supermarkets throughout the city stock almost anything you could need; if you can't find what you want there, head to **La Merced** (the market).

Soda is sold at every corner. *Agua mineral* means mineral water; *sidral* is a great carbonated apple drink; and *refrescos* are your standard soda pops. Cans and bottles are customarily recycled here, and patrons pay extra for the privilege of keeping them. Avoid a deposit, however, by imitating the locals and taking your drink in a plastic bag *(bolsa)* with straw *(popote)*, to go.

■ Centro

This area offers the most variety and lowest prices around. Bustling *cafeterías* dish out three meals a day. Portions are usually large, and many small counters offer fruit plates and drinks. *Comidas corridas*, even the vegetarian variety, are in copious supply. Cheap eats can be picked up from the many small *taquerías* or street vendors.

Café Tacuba, Tacuba 28 (tel. 518-49-50), at Allende Metro stop. Authentic Mexican cuisine in a colorful setting. Elaborately painted arches, tiled floors and murals depicting dated scenes of the colonial aristocracy. A bastion of serenity in the heart of downtown since 1912. Beef tongue with vinegar dressing 25 pesos. *Pollo tacuba* 25 pesos. MC, Visa accepted. Open daily 8:30am-11:30pm.

Restaurante El Vegetariano, Filomeno Mata 13 (tel. 510-01-13), between 5 de Mayo and Madero. Crammed with happy and healthy people all walking the meatless path. Nutritious *comida corrida* includes choices of fruit or vegetable salad, soup, entree, and fruit-based dessert (20 pesos). Try the *croquetas de elote* with papaya sauce. All kinds of whole-wheat pastries sold at the register. MC, Visa accepted. Other locations include Matriz Madero 56 altos and San Javier Sorondo 367 y 369. Open Mon.-Sat. 8am-8pm.

Restaurant Danubio, Uruguay 3, just east of Lázaro Cárdenas. Classy, old-fashioned, and popular seafood place with its own coat-of-arms; curtained windows shelter the diners inside. Famous artsy types have left their scribbling on the walls framed. Pricey entrees big enough to feed 2—stick to the 5-course *comida corrida* 30 pesos, Sun. 35 pesos. Open daily 1-10pm for a la carte.

Café La Blanca, 5 de Mayo 40 (tel. 510-03-99). A popular, conveniently located cafeteria with snappy service and fair-sized portions. A high ceiling over 2 circular counters and numerous tables. The bilingual menu offers an immense selection and the staff is warm and friendly towards foreigners as they hustle to serve delicious, although predictable, dishes. Green, red, or sweet corn tamales 7-9 pesos for an order of 2. Inexpensive *antojito* entrees run 10 pesos. The menu offers daily suggestions ranging in price from 14-20 pesos. Open daily 7am-11:30pm.

Super Frutas-La Casa de Ensaladas, Uruguay 52, just west of Isabel la Católica. Simple, open-air fruit shop daubed in bright orange, yellow, and green. Specializes in tasty old and new takes on fruit drinks, desserts, and more. Papaya, melon, banana, alfalfa, celery, carrot, and other *licuados*, *aguas*, juices, single flavor or combined (3-7 pesos). Self-serve bins of fruits and veggies. Salads (7 pesos) and *tortas* (3-6 pesos) are also served. Open Mon.-Sat. 7:30am-7:30pm.

Café París, 5 de Mayo 10 (tel. 521-54-56), at Filomeno Mata. Eurocentrism meets the diner. Clean and comfortable with A/C. A mile-long counter faces a mirrored wall—great for spying on activity behind you. Soft music to set the mood while you dine in a private booth. Great homemade hot biscuits in the morning (1 peso). Breakfast 10 pesos. Daily menu 4 dishes and coffee 16 pesos. Open daily 8am-midnight.

Pastelería La Ideal, 16 de Septiembre 14, just east of Cárdenas. Mexico City does everything on a large scale, and this bakery is no exception. ¼-block-long baking factory, composed of 4 huge sections with a fountain in the center. One section is for plain bread, one for cakes and pies, one with hundreds of pastries, and a 2nd level full of elaborate wedding cakes weighing as much as 70kg. Crowds battle in the afternoon over the steaming bread brought straight out of the oven on baking racks. Open daily 7am-10pm.

■ Zona Rosa

The myth: only moneyed tourists eat in the *Zona Rosa*. The fact: many area eateries cater chiefly to clerks from the scores of surrounding office buildings. However, the city's most expensive restaurants, from all types of international cuisine to traditional Mexican cooking, are located in the *Zona Rosa*. Check out the open-air ambience and consult the prominently displayed menus before choosing a restaurant. Prices vary widely, and it's almost always possible to find a cheap meal, though the street vendors which are crammed into every other inch of Mexican sidewalk are sparse. If you're more interested in the *Zona Rosa's* slick party atmosphere than in filling your stomach, skip dinner and settle for a drawn-out evening appetizer. But hey, this is Mexico, and a very good meal won't run you more than 35 pesos in all.

La Luna, Oslo 11, in the tiny walkway between Niza and Copenhagne. Peaceful and relaxed atmosphere in a bustling zone. Bright and clean small restaurant with whitewashed walls decorated with a tasteful but stylistically chaotic selection of graphics, lithographs, photos, etc. Fresh flowers on the tables and friendly family service. Very popular among experienced *Zona Rosa* inhabitants, who come here for the tasty 4-course daily menu for 10 pesos. Open daily 7am-3am, with plenty of beer flowing after 10pm.

La Bonne Cuisine, Lourdes after Insurgentes. Despite the pretentious name, an inexpensive and very popular lunch spot. The bread is the only French here. Walls plastered with posters of Marilyn Monroe. Daily 15-peso special, 9-12-peso entrees. Pay at the cashier. Open Mon.-Sat. 1-6pm.

Fonda Don Lucas, Lourdes 178-C (tel. 511-20-67), after the crossing with Florencia. A *jovenes-ejecutivos* filled restaurant, with mirrored walls adding to the checkered ambience. Come early for more space and faster service. The *economica* menu costs 12 pesos and the *especial* 14 pesos. Both include 3 dishes, free water, and dessert. Beer 3.50 pesos. *Refresco* 1.50 pesos. Open Mon.-Fri. 1-5pm.

Restaurant Jacarandas, Genova 44 (tel. 514-18-13), in a plaza off the east side of the street. In the heart of the *Zona Rosa*, a respite from the pricey international cuisine in a cozy nook off the main street. Join the crowd of locals that jams the inside and outside tables at this popular lunch spot. 5-course daily menu 15 pesos. MC, Visa accepted. Open Mon.-Fri. noon-6pm.

La Oficina, Hamburgo 45, near Insurgentes. Small family-run place like millions around the Republic, but an oddity in the *Zona Rosa*. Breakfasts of coffee, eggs and ham for 8 pesos, *comida corrida* 8 pesos.

Tacos el Caminero, Río Lerma 138 (tel. 514-56-15), between Tíber and Danubio across Reforma from the *Zona Rosa*. Not far from the U.S. consulate. An authentic taco restaurant, with grill-style specialties for meat-lovers. The small windowless restaurant has only counter eating space and an immense corner grill, but is popular at all hours featuring 13 types of tacos. Steak, sausage and pork chop tacos with delicious hot sauces. 6 tacos 16 pesos, 9 tacos 18 pesos. MC, Visa accepted. Open Mon.-Thurs. noon-midnight, Fri.-Sat. noon-1am, Sun. noon-11pm. An identical *taquería* at Iganacio Ramirez 17.

Parri, Hamburgo 154 (tel. 207-93-19), between Florencia and Amberes. The lack of originality in the plain yet typical decor is compensated for by the grilling process. House-recipe chicken is beheaded then barbecued on massive grill as hungry crowds watch. Eat in or take out. ¼-chicken with burrito, guacamole, and black beans 15 pesos. MC, Visa accepted. Open Mon.-Thurs. 8am-3am, Fri.-Sat. 8am-3pm, Sun. 8am-midnight.

■ Alameda Central

In spite of the inevitable construction work (or perhaps because of the construction workers' hearty appetites), you'll find plenty of good, cheap food in the *Alameda*.

Café La Habana, Bucareli and Morelos (tel. 535-26-20), south of the monument to the revolution. A sign proclaims it home to the best coffee in Mexico City. No need to buy a cup to sample—the whole place is permeated with the delicious aroma. Relaxed atmosphere with couples and groups chatting into the evening makes a great place to sip java and chow down. Fun-to-watch old-fashioned coffee bean roaster/grinder in the front window. Coffee sells by the kg. *Asada Habana* 33 pesos. *Quesadillas sincronizadas* 15 pesos. Open Mon.-Sat. 8am-11pm.

Fonda Santa Anita, Humboldt 48 (tel. 518-46-09), near Juárez. Pan-chromatic restaurant serving Mexican food only. The walls and ceilings fetishize Mexican village life. Flying birds and pigs spiral up the columns. World record for friendly service. Claims to have served its food at 5 World's Fairs. AmEx, MC, Visa accepted. Soups 6.50 pesos. Enchiladas 11 pesos. Meat dishes 25 pesos. Open Mon.-Fri. noon-10pm, Sat.-Sun. 1:30-9pm.

Humboldt 34, Humboldt 34 (tel. 521-22-93), near Juárez. Eclectic but bland mixture of old and new. Wood paneling and leather chairs face off with Aztec and electric guitars. Courteous service. Local families and executives dig the chicken entrees. Bottled music always playing, and late afternoons and evenings may find a small band groovin' in the corner. Full bar. 3 daily menus 13-17 pesos. MC, Visa accepted. Open Mon.-Sat. noon-3am.

Taquería Tlaquepaque, Independencia 4 (tel. 521-30-82), just west of Cárdenas. A popular *taquería* with more sit-down space than the average street *comedor*. Grab tacos to go from the outside grill or a sit a spell and watch the cooks do their thing. All orders of meaty taco delights 3 for 5.50 pesos. Open daily 9am-3am.

Grand Chose, Luis Moya 62 (tel. 521-05-53). Lacks the polish and size of some more expensive restaurants, but a true budget find. Solid *comida corrida* a deal at 9.50 pesos. Breakfasts for 6-9 pesos. Open 7am-6pm.

■ Near the Monumento a la Revolución

Though they lack the variety and innovation of the *Alameda*, *Centro*, or *Zona Rosa*, restaurants in this area serve hefty portions for low prices. Few will tease the taste buds, but almost all will fill your stomach.

Restaurant Mansión, Antonio Caso 31 (tel. 566-61-16), toward Colón from Revolución, just west of Vallarta. Surround yourself with the trappings of luxury—elaborately carved ceilings, huge chandeliers, red velvet curtains, and replicas of Greek masterpieces—while you enjoy a well-cooked afternoon meal, all for scandalously low prices. *Comida corrida* 8-12 pesos. Open Mon.-Fri. 1-6:30pm.

La Taberna, Arriaga at Ignacio Mariscal, next to Hotel Pennsylvania. Below street level, this small, always-packed pizzeria also serves Mexican food. Wood walls, low ceiling, and minimal space make for a cozy, quiet atmosphere. For the best value, order your pizza as part of the *comidas corrida* (soup, starter, pizza and dessert 12.50-23 pesos). MC, Visa accepted. Open Mon.-Sat. 1-10pm.

Xin Guang Zhou, Insugentes Centro 62-B. Pretentious-looking small restaurants with dark mirrors on two of the walls and a trivially colorful photo-wall paper of a forest. The daily menu (8 pesos) is, unfortunately, either entirely Mexican or Chinese, thus limiting the possibility of exotic combinations. An occasional English-subtitled Taiwanese movie. Open daily 8am-11pm.

Restaurant Samy's, Ignacio Mariscal 42 (tel. 591-11-00). A cool hideaway restaurant with orange seats and flower pots livening up the walls. A modest selection of wines is proudly displayed on a wooden shelf around a central column. A good sized 5-item daily menu 13 pesos. Open Mon.-Fri. 8am-6pm.

Restaurant Regis, Edison 57-B (tel. 592-01-78). Decoratively bankrupt. Convenient if you are staying near Mariscal or Edison. The service can be slow. Good-sized *comida corrida* 13 pesos. *Bistek a la plancha* 15 pesos. MC, Visa accepted. Open daily 7am-11pm.

Café Gran Premio, Antonio Caso 72 (tel. 535-09-34), between Insurgentes Norte and Serapio Rendón, under the big coffee cup sign. A great place for connoisseurs to come for coffee and a pastry. Javarama. *Americanos* 4 pesos. *Café con leche* or cappuccino 3.80 pesos, hot chocolate 4 pesos. Open Mon.-Sat. 8am-8pm.

■ Near Chapultepec

In Mexico City's western corner, south of Chapultepec and west of Chapultepec Park, great food greets you in restaurants that provide their own scenery. One is built around a greenhouse, another with maniacal roving *mariachis*, and yet another that is devoutly macrobiotic, reserving half of its dining room to floor seating (remember to sit lotus-style). This area is a fun place to eat, a getaway from the more standardized central eateries. All restaurants are within walking distance of the Sevilla Metro station (Cozumel is right around the corner from the Sevilla exit) and from the museums in Chapultepec park.

Las Palomas Fonda, Cozumel 37 (tel. 553-79-72), in Col. Roma just north of Durango. As if the *mariachis* and vocalists were not entertaining enough, the food is delicious and the prices are reasonable. The exterior dining room is built into a greenhouse, with exotic plants and flowers draped over the tables and hand-painted chairs. Try the *carne asada* (broiled steak) with salad and potatoes (24 pesos). Open Mon.-Fri. 1:30-11pm, Sat.-Sun. 1:30-5pm.

Centro Macrobiótico Tao, Cozumel 76 (tel. 211-46-41), in Col. Roma south of Colima on the east side of the street. No steak and potatoes here. A display case holds stacks of holistic diet books. The dining room features music, bamboo screens, and floor seating at miniature tables with miniature placemats. The front room is an adjoining store that sells miso, lentils, ginger, oats, eastern spices, tofu and honey. Vegetarian *comida corrida* of soup, whole wheat bread, spiced rice, various vegetables, and chef's specialty (19 pesos), served to the mystic rhythm of the funky background music. Open daily 1:30-4:30pm. Store open 10am-6pm.

El Mesón de la Mancha, Puebla 326 (tel. 286-87-64), at Cozumel. Great food and service at a virtuous price. Popular on weekday afternoons with the dapper business crowd, but a haven for solitude for the weekend museum visitor. Occasional live *mariachis*, non-stop Mexican pop, and a big-screen TV to entertain. Complete meals 12-18 pesos; breakfast specials 7 pesos. AmEx, MC, Visa accepted. Open Mon.-Fri. 8am-10pm, Sat. 8am-6pm.

Casa de Nutrición and Cafetería Yug, Puebla 326-6 (tel. 553-38-72), at Cozumel in Col. Roma next door to El Mesón de la Mancha. A multi-faceted store and wholesome restaurant filled with granola, soy products, incense, vitamins, health manuals, and healing crystals. Books on alternative medicine, martial arts, astrology, magic, and discovering your inner self. The place to go if your vitamin supply has dwindled. Reasonably priced lunches or afternoon snacks. Veggie burgers 9 pesos. MC, Visa accepted. Open Mon.-Sat. 10am-8pm.

■ Coyoacán

The southern suburb of Coyoacán attracts students, young couples, and literati to its complement of elegant restaurants. Coyoacán is the birthplace of many Mexican politicians and presidents, and its restaurants play to that upper-level clientele. Outdoor cafés and ice-cream shops fill the colonial buildings which line the cobbled streets. You will find lots of menu items you don't usually see in downtown Mexico City: if you crave brie, cheesecake, or pesto, spend the afternoon in these 'burbs.

Café El Parnaso, Carrillo Puerto 2, at Jardín Centenario across from the cathedral. A beautiful outdoor café, book and record store, and art gallery. Come and brush elbows with Coyoacán's budding intelligentsia. Great for a cup of coffee and a view of the Pl. Hidalgo gardens. Inhale mocha cake, cheesecake with strawberries, or carrot cake 6 pesos. All kinds of pies 6 pesos, coffees 3-6 pesos, and a few sandwiches and salads (8-10 pesos). Open daily 9am-9:30pm.

Restaurante los Balcones, Allende 15-A (tel. 554-79-61), on the northeast corner of the park, above the Farmacia Coyoacán. Great pizza served in a classy dark wood interior decorated with lush greenery. 3 balconies overlook the Pl. Hidalgo for people watching. The pizza is priced to move at 14-16 pesos—try the Hawaiian (16 pesos). Open 8am-11pm.

El Murral, Allende 2 (tel. 554-02-98), across the street from Los Balcones. A surprisingly large restaurant with a glass roof with a tree growing through an opening for a more quaint ambience. Very nicely tiled and creatively decorated. Fresh hot tortillas prepared on the spot. Daily menu 34 pesos. Open 7:30am-8:30pm.

Restaurant El Guarache, Jardín Centenario 14, the green awning next to El Parnaso. The outdoor setting of El Parnaso for the hungry traveler. Mexican food at typically rising Mexican prices. *Pollo a la mexicana* 17.50 pesos. *Guarache verde o rojo* 15.50 pesos. Open daily 9am-10pm.

La Casa de los Tacos, Carrillo Puerto 23, 1 block south of Parque Hidalgo. This *taquería's* no converted garage operation. Upscale decor and a long list of tacos (2.50-15 pesos per order). A superstitious bunch runs this thriving taco business: garlic, horseshoes, and old knives and daggers dot the walls. Open daily 9am-midnight.

■ San Ángel

Especially on Saturdays, when crowds are drawn to the decidedly upscale Bazaar Sábado, both the chic restaurants and *típico* taco stands of San Ángel manage to pack 'em in. If snazzy dining is your thing, then the restaurants on the Plaza San Jacinto won't disappoint, but your wallet will feel plenty lighter afterwards.

Restaurante Hasti Bhawan, Pl. San Jacinto 9. Hindustani atmosphere inside a beautiful colonial building with impressive elephant-shaped planters. Featuring *pakora* and *samosa* appetizers and *lassi*, a thick Indian yogurt drink (5 pesos). Curry dishes and other entrees run 20-40 pesos. Sit at the exquisitely tiled green booth shaded by straw umbrellas. Live jazz Fridays and Saturdays 9pm-midnight. Open Tues.-Thurs. noon-11pm, Fri.-Sat. 1pm-midnight, Sun. noon-6pm.

El Rincón de La Lechuza, Miguel Angel de Quevedo 34 (tel. 661-59-11), to your left as you walk from Metro M.A. Quevedo to the Parque de la Bombilla. Joyfully crowded and very popular. Clay owls dot the walls surrounded by a bright yellow interior. Tacos 5.50-12.50 pesos. *Especiales* casseroles prepared with imported meat from New Zealand 18-26 pesos. Open Mon.-Thurs. 1pm-1am, Fri.-Sat. 1pm-2am, Sun. 1pm-midnight.

SIGHTS

It would be impossible to see everything in Mexico City in a month. You'll need a week to come away with anything resembling a well-rounded picture of the city. If you desire a chaperone, **Promoción Social del Centro Historic,** Chile 8 (tel. 510-25-41, ext. 1499), sponsors free walking tours in English, a different one each Sunday. Call for this week's destination and meeting spot. The **Sindicato Nacional de Guías Turísticos** (tel. 535-77-87), Virginia Fabregas, in Col. San Rafael dispatches licensed guides who cover special sights by foot or by car.

■■■ CENTRO

The heart of Mexico City, the **Centro,** could easily take weeks to explore. From the grand **Palacio Nacional** and the enormous **Catedral Metropolitana** to the **Monte Nacional de Piedad** (National Pawn Shop) and **Museo de la Ciudad de México,** the area is the cradle of much of the nation's culture. Like all of Mexico, the Centro contains history dating back thousands of years. A sometimes uneasy truce has been struck, allowing the ruins of Aztec pyramids to lie peaceably beside the cathedral which usurped its glory and the Palacio Nacional from which the modern state of Mexico is run.

The sights described in this section are divided into those east, north and south of the *zócalo*. To get there by Metro, take Line 2 to the Zócalo station. The station's entrance sits on the east side of the square, in front of the Palacio Nacional. The Catedral Metropolitana lies to the north, the Federal District offices to the south and the Suprema Corte de Justicia to the southeast. For an intelligently annotated checklist of every sight in the *Centro*, get a copy of the *Historic Center of the City of Mexico* from the map's publisher, SAC BE, Apdo. 22-315, 14000 México, D.F. *The Official Guide to Mexico City's Historic Center,* available in the shops of the Museum of Anthropology, Palacio de Bellas Artes, and major Spanish-English language bookstores (35-45 pesos) is another excellent and detailed source of information.

The Zócalo

The principal square of Mexico City, officially named the **Plaza de la Constitución,** is more widely known by its adopted title, the *zócalo*. Now surrounded by imposing colonial monuments, the square was originally the nucleus of the Aztec capital **Tenochtitlán.** The conquistadors razed Tenochtitlán, then built the seat of New Spain on top of the ruins, using stones from the destroyed city to construct Spanish churches and government buildings. To the southwest of the Templo Mayor (the Aztecs' principal place of worship, which they called Teocalli) was the Aztec marketplace and major square. Cortés paved this expanse with stones from the main pyramid, calling it *Plaza de Armas* or *Plaza Real*. He also assigned the plaza its perimeter (the dimensions of 240m on each side persist to this day), but it has since gone through many transformations. In 1692 it went up in flames, and in 1790 it was leveled and reorganized after a Moorish design, with many fountains because the Moors held water sacred. In the re-building process, two very important archaeological objects were unearthed: the statue of Coatlicue (deity of life and death) and "Piedra del Sol ("Stone of the Sun", the Aztec calendar). This second stone spent nearly a century leaning quietly against the cathedral's west side before the old Museo Nacional claimed it in 1885.

The square became the Plaza de la Constitución in 1812 when the representative assembly of the viceroyalty adopted the liberal Constitución de Cádiz here to protest Napoleon Bonaparte's occupation of Spain. This act of rebellion gave direction to the turmoil that eventually led to Mexico's independence. In 1843, the dictator Santa Ana destroyed the Mercado del Parián and ordered that a monument to independence be constructed in the center of the square. Only the *zócalo* (pedestal) was in place when the project was abandoned. The citizens of Mexico began to refer to the square as *el zócalo*, which has become the generic name for the central plazas in nearly all of the Republic's cities and towns. In 1952, Mexico City's *zócalo* was flattened into its present form.

Today, devoid of both merchants and fountains, the *zócalo* is instead filled with protesting groups, *artesanías*, street artists, indigeneous dancers and gaping tourists. Above this esoteric mix of life, the Mexican flag looms large. The flag is lowered daily at 6pm with militaristic and somewhat adolescent pomp, a hollow attempt to match the grandeur of the surrounding *zócalo's* 700 year history.

East of the Zócalo

Palacio Nacional

During his reign, Moctezuma II built a new palace, called the "New Houses," just south of the Teocalli. The Spaniards obliterated the palace, and in 1529 the King of Spain granted the land to Hernán Cortés, who proceeded to erect a new house of his own there. Architects Rodrigo de Pontecillas and Juan Rodríguez designed the building and *indígena* slave laborers built it using the stones from Moctezuma's palace. In 1562, the King of Spain bought back this house and the property from Don Martín Cortés (son of the conquistador) and made it the palace of the king's viceroys. The palace was destroyed during the Riot of 1692 and rebuilt a year later with stones from the original building. Subsequent modifications have given the building a Baroque character, although vestiges of earlier styles remain. The first two stories of the present palace date from the 1692 riot. In 1927, President Plutarco Calles ordered the construction of a third story to beautify the remains of the old palace. On the eastern patio are traces of the botanical gardens once cultivated by Emperor Maximilian's wife. The central patio hosted the first Mexican bullfight, in honor of Cortés's famous return from present day Honduras to resume leadership of the capital. For a time bullfights were staged here every Friday afternoon to entertain viceroys of the palace.

Now called the **Palacio Nacional de México** (tel. 512-20-60), the building occupies the entire east side of the *zócalo*, bounded on the north and south, respectively, by Moneda and Corregidora. Chief executive center of the Republic, the Palacio houses the federal treasury boys and g-men, as well as monumental murals, historical rooms and a museum in honor of Benito Juárez. Connected to the palace is the Museo de Las Culturas (see next section), once Emperor Maximilian's national mint.

It took Diego Rivera from 1929 to 1951 to sketch and paint the **frescoes** on the Palacio's western and northern walls. *Mexico Through the Centuries*, one of his most famous works, is on the west wall of the Palacio at the top of the grand staircase. The mural is divided into five smaller scenes, each depicting an event in the social evolution of Mexico. To the left and right of this grand central mural are two other of Rivera's most famous works. Covering the southern portion of the palace's western wall, *La Lucha de las Clases* (The Class Struggle). The mural depicts Mexican *campesinos* next to workers from around the world. Opposite it on the northern wall is a work entitled *La Leyenda de Quetzalcóatl*, which illustrates the life of the legendary Toltec priest-king who fled from his kingdom, conquered the Mayan people and ruled over the Yucatán Peninsula. The murals on the second floor of the palace on the north and east wall delve even further into Mexico's ancient history. On the east wall, *El Desembarco en Veracruz* graphically depicts the injustices of the slave trade. Three murals relate the achievements of the great Tarascan, Zapotec and Totonac civilizations, and three others show the evolution of corn, the harvesting of cacao, and the all-important *maguey* (a plant used in making tequila) industry. *La Gran Tenochtitlán* is dominated by the Mercado de Tlatelolco and filled out with the Temple of Tlatelolco, the center of Tenochtitlán, and the volcanoes Popocatépetl (Smoking Mountain) and Iztaccíhuatl (Sleeping Woman). Guides and postcards of the murals are sold at the base of the central staircase (10 pesos), but are sometimes unavailable.

The Palacio also contains the **Bell of Dolores,** which was brought to the capital in 1896 from Dolores Hidalgo in Guanajuato state. It can be seen from outside the Palacio, at the top of the baroque façade. Padre Miguel Hidalgo de Dolores rang this bell on September 16, 1810, calling the people of Mexico to fight for their independence. Every year on that date it rings in memory of the occasion, and the Mexican President repeats the words once shouted by the father of independence. (Palacio open daily 8am-6pm. Guided tours Mon.-Fri. 10am-4pm. Free.)

The museum dedicated to Mexico's most revered President, Benito Juárez, is in the room in which he died on the Palacio's second floor. At the entrance to the **Museo Recinto Homenaje a Benito Juárez** (tel. 522-56-46), on the first floor, is a statue of Juárez that is supposedly cast from the bronze of enemy ammunition used in the War of Reform. The museum contains furniture from Juárez's house, some personal belongings and, best of all, a death mask cast before his body had even cooled. In the back room is Juárez's personal library, which houses more than 3000 documents from the reform years. To reach the museum, enter through the northern door of the palace, or walk north through the palace's central court. (Open Tues.-Fri. 9am-7:30pm. Free.)

Other Sights

La Merced, Circunvalación at Anaya east of the *zócalo*, or at Metro Merced on Line 2 (turn left out of the subway's eastern exit), is the largest food market of its kind in the world. Farmers from all over Mexico sell their goods here. The fruit section alone covers a large fraction of the 600 square blocks. Here you'll find fruits of every sort imaginable—papayas, home-grown lichee nuts, *mameyes* from Tabasco, mangos, nine different kinds of *plátanos,* hot tamales and two full blocks of assorted chiles. Exotic indigenous foods such as fried turtles, steamed chicken intestines, *charales*—corn husks stuffed with shiners—and steamed crayfish abound. Die of happiness among infamous displays of *dulces* (candies) that stretch for five blocks; each vendor's stall displays over 300 kinds. The market is well worth a visit if only to get an idea of the diversity of Mexican food. The crowds picking through the pile of scraps and throwaways in the back, however, testify to the economic challenges Mexico still faces.

Near the beehive-like market blocks, on the corner of Manzanares and Circunvalación, sits the faintly bizarre smallest church in the world, **El Señor de la Humildad,** measuring a mere six yards by nine yards and seating a maximum of 20. (Open daily 9am-8pm.) On the corner of Calle de la Santísima and Zapata is an elaborate Rococo church, the exquisite **Templo de la Santísima,** finished in 1783, one of the most important examples in the city of the ornamental Churrigueresque style. Figures on the façade were intended to appear as if constructed of ivory, wood and cloth. The interior is unimpressive as the original decorations are long gone. Don't come here after dusk; the temple is lit but not well-patrolled. (Open daily 7am-1pm and 5-8pm.)

North of the Zócalo

Catedral Metropolitana

The conquest of Aztec religion by the forces of Christianity is perhaps more astonishing than Cortés's military triumph over Moctezuma's warriors. Mexico, once a land devoted to Quetzalcóatl, Tlaloc and Huitzilopochtli, became a New World stronghold of Christianity. In 1524, Cortés had Mexico's first cathedral built on the northwest corner of the *zócalo*, recycling stones from the temples of Tenochtitlán. Until 1552, this was the main church in Mexico and apparently the one the Franciscans used before building their own convent and church near the present site of the Torre Latinoamericana. In 1530, another cathedral went up on the site of the Templo Mayor and remained there until 1624. In 1544, the Spanish began construction of the **Catedral Metropolitana** (tel. 521-76-37), the massive structure on the north side of the *zócalo*. The 109m-long and 54m-wide cruciform cathedral encompasses the architectural styles of three centuries. Between 1544 and 1573, architect Claudio Arciniega directed the construction of the cathedral, modeling it after the one in Sevilla, Spain (Arciniega also designed America's first true cathedral in Santo Domingo). Dedicated in the middle of the 17th century, the Catedral Metropolitana wasn't finished until 1813. In that year, Manuel Tolsá completed the great central dome, the façade and the statues of Faith, Hope and Charity which crown the clock tower. There is an office on the far east side of the cathedral which can answer your questions (open Mon.-Fri. 9am-6:30pm, Sat. 9am-2pm. Cathedral open daily 8:30am-8pm; the schedule for mass is posted on the door furthest west).

The cathedral has several attached **annexes**. The main annex, with its door to the left of the cathedral, holds the **Altar de Perdón** (Forgiveness), a replica of a Churrigueresque altarpiece built by Jerónimo de Balbás between 1731 and 1736 and destroyed by fire in 1967. The cedar interior of the choir gallery, constructed in 1695 by Juan de Rojas, is decorated with an elegant grille of gold, silver and bronze. Juan Correa's murals of the coronation of the Virgin, St. Michael's slaying of the dragon and the triumphant entrance of Jesus into Jerusalem cover the sacristy's walls. Cristóbal de Villalpando painted the two other grand murals in this section, *La Immaculada Concepción* and *El Triunfo de la Iglesia*. Of the cathedral's many altars, one of the most magnificent is Balbás's Churrigueresque **Altar de los Reyes** (Kings), dedicated to those kings who were also saints.

The Spanish introduced the Aztecs to what Roman Catholics refer to as the communion of saints. In the annex holding the Altar de Perdón, there are 14 *capillas* (chapels) dedicated to those saints. Two chapels near the entrance honor Mexico's patron, the Virgin of Guadalupe. Legend holds that she appeared on a mountain before a poor peasant named Diego, entreating him to have a church built in her honor at that site. In order to convince the Mexican bishop of his vision, Diego laid a sheet full of fresh roses cut during the cold of December in front of the bishop. Both in awe, they watched the Virgin's portrait emerge on the sheet. The church was built, and today's paintings depict that first impression on the sheet.

The eastern annex holds the **Sagrario Metropolitano** (sanctuary). The Sagrario holds six chapels, with one main and two lateral altars. The Sagrario Metropolitano, designed by the great Churrigueresque architect Lorenzo Rodríguez, was built between 1749 and 1768 and its façades have since been copied in thousands of Mexican churches. Left of center are statues of the 12 apostles; to the right, the 12 prophets. In the center, above the door, are two statues, St. John and, above him, St. Joseph. Elaborate reliefs decorate the whole façade, and the Virtues crown the structure.

Unfortunately, the splendor of the cathedral is occluded by the green support structures constucted to stem the sinking of the temple into the ground.

Templo Mayor (Teocalli)

North of the *zócalo*'s northeast corner, a pool of water laps at a brass model of the Aztec capital, Tenochtitlán. At the center of this city was a great religious square surrounded by walls, each side 0.5km long. After wandering for hundreds of years, driven by the hummingbird god Huitzilopochtli, this was the first place that the Aztecs could call home. Legend has it that the high priest Tenoch saw an eagle perched on a cactus, which he took as a sign that the people from Aztlán had found their home. The Templo Mayor, or Teocalli, was built on the spot where Tenoch saw the eagle, now the corner of Seminario and República de Guatemala, a few meters north of the brass model. Teocalli is the major excavated archaeological site in Mexico City.

On February 28, 1978, workers digging east of the cathedral struck an immovable rock. They eventually unearthed an eight-ton Aztec stone on which had been carved the dismembered figure of the moon goddess Coyolxauqui, sister of Huitzilopochtli. The stone identified the area as the site of Teocalli, earlier believed to be buried under the Catedral Metropolitana to the southwest.

According to Aztec legend, Coatlicue, the terrible goddess of earth and death (whose monolithic statue now sits in the Museo Nacional de Antropología), became pregnant while sweeping out the temple. Her daughter Coyolxauqui grew jealous of her and plotted with her 400 brothers to kill their mother. When they reached her, however, they discovered that Huitzilopochtli had already been born, full-grown. He beheaded his sister; his brothers he turned into the planets and stars. The stone that the diggers found served in ancient times as part of the base of a great pyramid. At the pyramid's summit were two temples, one dedicated to the war god Huitzilopochtli and one dedicated to the rain god Tlaloc. Moctezuma I, who ruled the Aztec kingdom from 1440-1468, and his ruthless bloodthirsty half-brother Tlacaelel popularized the practice of ritual human sacrifice to the almighty Huitzilopochtli. Having become the head god, the hummingbird god Huitzilopochtli constantly demanded warm, beating human hearts. As sacrifice and a more than a touch of cannibalism rose to the rate of 10,000-20,000 victims per year, the supply of local victims ran low and Moctezuma I and Tlacaelel brilliantly devised the "Flower Wars." These practices were ceremonial battles where the Aztecs coerced their rival neighbors into giving them sacrificial victims in order to avoid a full-scale Aztec attack. (See Essentials: Life and Times for the broader picture.)

When the conquistadors arrived, Teocalli measured 103m by 79.5m at the base and was 61m high. Moctezuma II led Cortés on the grand tour of the temple, proudly pointing out the caked walls and sacrificial stones. Unfortunately the Castillian wasn't as impressed as Moctezuma had originally hoped. Instead of singing praises for the bloody empire, Cortés requested that Moctezuma clear a small place in the temple for an altar to the Virgin Mary. Moctezuma's violent refusal marked the pair's first major disagreement and paved the way for the Aztec's road to destruction.

Today the ruins lie gaping just east of the cathedral and north of the Palacio Nacional. That the huge site appears at first to be no more than the foundation of a demolished modern complex adds to the feeling of ancient grandeur once you are inside exploring the ruins. The excavated ruins reveal five layers of pyramids, built one on top of the other as the Aztec empire grew. Signs along the paths help explain which layer belongs to which temple. Over 7000 artifacts, including sculpture, jewelry and pottery, have been found amidst the ruins. Many of the pieces have been traced to distant societies dominated by the long arm of the Aztec empire. The extraordinary **Museo del Templo Mayor,** now part of the archaeological complex, houses this unique collection. This museum is a requisite for visitors even on a whirlwind tour of Mexico City. The exhibit is divided into eight *salas* (halls): antecedents and the settling of the Aztecs at the site of Tenochtitlán, war and sacrifice, tribute and commerce, Huitzilopochtli, Tlaloc, *faunas*, religion and the fall of Tenochtitlán. The museum was designed to imitate the layout of the original temple, and is constructed so that the artifacts found in the excavation are accompanied by excerpts from the ancient Aztec texts which describe them. Highlights of this exhibit are a scale model of Tenochtitlán at the height of its power, along with the stone of Coyolxauqui and the *Tzompantli* (skull rack), a platform where the freshly picked skulls of sacrificial victims were proudly displayed to the public and the gods above. Along with the silent and decapitated ruins adjacent to it, the museum bears witness to the glories of México-Tenochtitlán and makes the arrogant pride of their *cantares mexicanos* more understandable: "Oh giver of life! Bear it in mind, oh princes. Forget it not. Who can siege Tenochtitlán? Who can disturb the foundations of the sky? With our arrows, with our shields, the city exists. México-Tenochtitlán persists! Proud of herself rises the city of México-Tenochtitlán. No one fears death in combat here. This is our glory. This is your mandate."

(Museums and ruins open Tues.-Sun. 9am-5pm. Guided tours in Spanish free, in English 10 pesos per person. Admission 13 pesos. Sun. Free.)

Iglesia de Santo Domingo

The Iglesia de Santo Domingo, on the corner of Brasil and Venezuela, four blocks north of the *zócalo's* northwest corner, was founded by 12 Dominicans who arrived in 1526, three years after the first 12 Franciscans came from Spain. Within a year, five of the Dominicans had died and the other seven had fallen very ill. In 1527 all but three of the remaining friars returned to Spain. Among the three who stayed behind was Domingo de Bentanzos who founded the Convento de Santo Domingo in Mexico City as well as many more in the provinces of Guatemala. The first church, completed in 1590, was destroyed in a flood; by 1736 the present church was completed. The baroque edifice, considered one of the most beautiful in Mexico City, was built at a cost of 200,000 pesos, an enormous sum at the time. Its highlight, the façade, features the intertwined arms of Santo Domingo and St. Francis, as well as statues of the two saints. Also depicted is Diego holding up the impression of the Virgin of Guadalupe, with the Mexican bishop looking on in awe. There is an exegetical office to the left of the altar. (Office open Mon.-Fri. 10am-2pm and 4-6pm. Church open daily 7:30am-8pm.)

South of the Zócalo

In 1691, a heavy rainfall destroyed the wheat crop, causing a famine among the working classes the following year. The viceroy, Count de Gálvez, initiated rationing, but when rumors of nearly exhausted grain supplies spread, a group of *indígenas* was sent to investigate. De Gálvez turned them away, bringing on the Riot of 1692, the most violent Mexico has ever seen. Several buildings were burned, including part of the palace and much of the Casas del Cabildo, which had sheltered the city government offices and archives. These are now located in the two buildings that compose the offices of the **Departamento del Distrito Federal** (tel. 518-11-00). The older one, on the southwest end of the *zócalo*, was built according to the same plan as the pre-riot structure; on the exterior of this building are tiled mosaic shields that chronicle scenes from the history of Mexico. The newer building, on the southeast end of the *zócalo*, was built between 1940 and 1948, 400 years after its twin. Fortunately, Don Carlos de Sigüenza y Góngora saved the building's archives, currently located in the Archivo Nacional. Now most of the buildings are administrative.

Suprema Corte de Justicia

The Suprema Corte de Justicia, built in 1929, stands on the corner of Pino Suárez and Corregidora, on the spot where the southern half of Moctezuma's royal palace once stood. After the palace was leveled, Spanish colonists turned the area into a garbage dump. Cortés claimed the property, had it cleared and designated it the site of city festivities, including a maypole dance, in which men suspended by ropes swung in circles from a pole. Four rather ferocious Orozco murals cover the second-floor walls of the present day Supreme Court. On the west wall hangs *Riquezas Nacionales*, in which a giant tiger, representing the national conscience, defends the mineral riches of the Republic. The mural on the east wall, *El Trabajo* (Work), symbolizes Article 123 of the Mexican Constitution, which guarantees workers' rights. The two remaining murals are called *La Justicia*. The one on the north wall shows a bolt of fire taking human form; the apparition wields a huge axe, with which it threatens a group of masked evil-doers. On the south wall, Justice sleeps on a pedestal, holding a sword and the law. (Open Mon.-Fri. 9am-2pm.)

Museo de la Ciudad de México

The Museo de la Ciudad de México, Pino Suárez 30 (tel. 542-04-87), at República de El Salvador, three blocks south of the *zócalo*'s southeast corner, is dedicated to the founders of Mexico City, and houses maps, photographs, lithographs and murals charting their lives and achievements. The exhibits start on the ground floor and progress chronologically, illustrating the progression of pre-Conquest development in the Valley of Mexico as you move counter-clockwise around the central courtyard. The first showcases depict the geological formation of the Valley of Mexico and Lake Texcoco. Other rooms detail the rise of the Aztec empire in the 15th and 16th centuries, with models of Tenochtitlán and diagrams of its social structure. The upstairs exhibit again progresses counterclockwise, this time chronicling the evolution of "New Spain" from the 16th century to the usurpations, betrayals and victories of the Revolution of 1910. The final exhibit of the museum is the south wing of the second story which portrays contemporary Mexico City, featuring the construction of the Metro and a gigantic model of the Torre Latinoamericana. A photo of the modern city center fills an entire wall, successfully communicating the immensity of this metropolis. Though the dark building is somewhat gloomy, it contributes to the historical feel of the museum, an appropriate place to display the city's artifacts.

In contrast to the Templo Mayor Museum and its archaeological view of Aztec culture, the Museo de la Ciudad offers an historical account of Mexican culture and provides a broad background for most of your other sight-seeing, making it an ideal first stop in your quest to understand the significance of the city's treasures. (Open Tues.-Sun.10am-6pm. Free.)

Other Sights

Across the street from the cathedral's west side on Calle Monte de Piedad is the **Monte Nacional de Piedad** (tel. 521-19-46), or the National Pawn Shop. This building holds a state-controlled flea market at which dealers sell mostly high-quality jewelry at reasonable prices. (Market open Mon.-Fri. 10am-5pm, Sat. 10am-3pm.)

Calle Corregidora, the street between the Suprema Corte and Palacio Nacional, skirts part of an **ancient canal system** that once connected the Aztec capital to the *pueblos* around Xochimilco. The construction of this intricate and efficient transport system was key in the Aztec's rise to power in the valley. After the conquest of Tenochtitlán, Cortés ordered that the remains of the buildings be dumped into the canals. The Spanish, who had animals for transport, had no use for the canal system. Today, both sides of the ancient canal system are paved as a pedestrian thoroughfare and the canal itself is covered by shrubs and small flower bushes.

Founded in 1603, the **Templo de Porta Coeli** (tel. 542-02-25), across Calle Carranza from the Suprema Corte's southern end, was among the first institutions to inculcate Catholicism to young Spaniards and *indígena* Mexicans. The temple houses a replica of the original **Cristo Negro** (Black Christ), now at the Catedral Metropolitana. (Open Mon.-Sat. 9am-6pm, Sun. 9am-1pm.) **Calle Carranza,** was known for a long time after the Conquest as *Celada* (trap or ambush): during the fighting that led to the conquest of the city, the Aztecs killed many Spaniards by setting ingenious snares in this area.

Southwest of the *zócalo*, at the corner of 5 de Febrero and 16 de Septiembre, is the famous **Gran Hotel de la Ciudad de México.** Visit at midday to see the light shine through the Tiffany stained-glass ceiling with three flower-shaped central domes. Every detail is pure art nouveau; even the parakeets live in elaborate brass cages with stained glass ceilings. Directly above Restaurante El Malecón, Carranza 9, is the skinniest apartment building in the world. Its four stories measure 11m high and only 3m wide.

■■■ ALAMEDA

A large park in the middle of downtown Mexico City, *Alameda Central* is a symbol of the city's glory seen in the light of its history of bloody conquest. Many of the city's historical landmarks are located in the surrounding area, known simply as *Alameda*. Because many bus and Metro routes criss-cross the area, *Alameda* is a superb base for budget travelers.

There are two Metro stations near the park: the Hidalgo station (Lines 2 and 3) is at the intersection of Hidalgo and Paseo de la Reforma, just one block west of the park's northwest corner, and the Bellas Artes station (Line 2) is one block east of the park's northeast corner, between the park and Bellas Artes itself. Maps of the area are available at the tourist office (see Practical Information).

At the corner of Arranza and Puente del Alvarado, three blocks north of the Monumento a la Revolución, the **Museo San Carlos** houses an old art school and an impressive collection of 16th through 19th-century paintings from the European schools. (Open Tues.-Sun. 10am-5pm. Admission 10 pesos, free Sun.)

Alameda Central

Although *Parque Alameda* has existed for hundreds of years, it is only in this century that it became open to the public. It is an icon of the city, as Diego Rivera recognized in his mural of the *Alameda* (see below). All elements of society congregate around it.

While the expansive *zócalo* may serve as the city's centerpiece and the Bosque de Chapultepec as its cultural center-playground, the *Alameda* serves as a microcosm of life in Mexico City. Under the shadow of the grand Palacio de Bellas Artes (see below), rock groups jam and vendors perform skits to hawk their wares. Mime groups, all too willing to poke fun at anyone showing signs of *gringo* background, draw victims from the crowds which relax in the grassy patches that were once the exclusive domain of the rich and powerful. Protesters camping out in makeshift huts mix amiably with the hordes of young couples seeking a quiet moment alone.

Palacio de Bellas Artes

This palace, located at Juárez and Eje Central, at the northeast corner of *Alameda Central* (tel. 709-31-11 ext. 133), is but one result of the progressive "capitalization" plan established during the *Porfiriato*, Porfirio Díaz's dictatorship (1876-1911). Apart from its role as a repository of great works by 20th-century Mexican artists, the Palacio de Bellas Artes, facing the eastern end of *Alameda*, is a fascinating artifact of Díaz's time and the subsequent revolution. Construction began in 1904 under the Italian architect Boari, who promised a fantastically innovative building. The Italian extravaganza was intended to serve as a symbol of national progress and as a theater for Mexico's upper class. Soon after construction began, however, the theater started to sink into the city's soft ground. (It has sunk 5m to date; the sinking is not widely held to be part of the symbolism.) By the time activity was resumed in 1932, Boari was dead and the new government decided to open the Palacio de Bellas Artes instead of a theater. The job was finished in 1934, and the museum finally opened in 1946. In completing the building, the second architect, Federico Mariscal, respected Boari's exterior design but dramatically altered the interior.

Mariscal's art deco interior strikingly contrasts with the conservative exterior. This style, made popular in Paris at the 1925 decorative arts exposition, is characterized by sharp angles, geometric forms and imaginative lighting. The majority of the museum's collection is 19th-century Mexican art, featuring José María Velasco, Eugenio Langesio, Julio Ruelasa and Joaquín Clausell. Most people, however, come to the palace to see the walls of the second and third floors, painted by the most celebrated Mexican muralists of the 20th century. That the murals' aggressive imagery clashes with the industrial decor is tribute to the vitality the artists' talents lend to the building's grandeur.

The Palacio displays a collection of the frescoes of David Alfaro Siqueiros (1896-1974), the 20th-century Mexican muralist, Stalinist, nationalist, and the would-be assassin of Leon Trotsky. Siqueiros experimented with lighting, colors and surfaces, but he is best known as a *típico* muralist. Look for his work on the third floor of the Palacio. Like his contemporary Diego Rivera, Siqueiros's favorite themes were class struggle and social injustice, and he flaunted, like his contemporary, a cavalier disregard for topical subtlety. Two examples of the latter are his *Caín en los Estados Unidos*, an attack on racism in the U.S., and *Nacimiento del Fascismo*. Many of his paintings are layered with masonite, lending them a three-dimensional effect. A good example of this technique is *Explosión en la Ciudad*, in which the smoke from an explosion seems to stream toward the viewer. On the east wall hang of the third floor murals by José Clemente Orozco depicting the tension between natural human characteristics and industrialization.

If you have time for only one mural, see the one by Diego Rivera on the west wall of the third floor. Intended for a North American audience, the original was to be painted in New York City's Rockefeller Center with Rockefeller's chosen theme: "Man at Crossroads Looking with Hope and High Vision to the Choosing of a New and Better Future." Rivera was prohibited from finishing the mural, however, when Rockefeller noticed Lenin in the foreground. When an angry Rivera petitioned the Mexican government to allow him to duplicate the work, he was given this space in the Palacio. This second, more vehement rendering includes an unflattering portrayal of John D. Rockefeller, Sr. (Open daily 10am-8pm.)

On the fourth floor of the palace is the **Museo Nacional de Arquitectura** (National Museum of Architecture). The exhibit is of early sketches and blueprints for the most architecturally complex and distinctive buildings in Mexico City, including the *Teatro Nacional*, the monument to the Revolution, and the Hotel Del Prado. There is a bookstore on the first floor of the museum that sells numerous books about the history of art and Mexican artists, as well as guides to museums in Mexico City. (Palacio de Bellas Artes open Tues.-Sun 10am-6pm. Free, though some traveling exhibits charge 5 pesos admission, free for students and teachers with ID.) The **Ballet Folklórico de México** performs regional and historical dances in the **Palacio de Bellas Artes** and the **Teatro Ferrocarrilero** (Revolución Metro stop). Their two companies, one resident and one traveling, are known the world over for their choreographic and theatrical skill. (Performances Wed. at 9pm, Sun. at 9:30am and 9pm. Tickets 80-110 pesos, sold 3 or 4 days in advance at Bellas Artes but usually available, Mon.-Sat. 11am-3pm and 5-7pm, Sun. 10:30am-1pm and 4-7pm. Tel. 529-17-01.) Travel agencies snatch up lots of tickets during Christmas, *Semana Santa*, and summer; check first at Bellas Artes, then try along Reforma or in the *Zona Rosa*. These performances are the only way to see the wonderful crystal curtain designed by Gerardo Murelli, one of Mexico's greatest painters. It consists of almost one million pieces of multi-colored crystal which, when illuminated from behind, represent the Valley of Mexico in twilight.

Museo Nacional de Arte

The Museo Nacional de Arte, Tacuba 8 (tel. 512-32-24 or 512-16-84), half a block east of the Palacio's north side, is even more representative of the Díaz era than is the Palacio de Bellas Artes. It was intended to house the Secretary of Communications, the brainchild of Porfirio Díaz. The architect, Silvio Conti, designed its pre-Cambrian façade and paid particular attention to the central staircase: its beautifully sculpted baroque handrails and lampposts and ornate blue and gold ceilings were crafted by artists in Florence and shipped to Mexico. The design leaves the museum with an empty feel, and footsteps echo through the lonely galleries.

Unlike the Palacio de Bellas Artes, this museum contains works from the stylistic and ideological schools of every era in Mexican history. The galleries are divided by style and era. The works of the second floor include some by Doctor Atl ("water" in Nahuatl), the great precursor of Mexican muralism. He is best known for his volcano paintings, but *La Nube* (the cloud) is unique among his works in its use of sprightlier blues, yellows and greens. Other works on the second floor include paintings by Orozco, Ramón, Cano Manilla (renowned for his use of color to celebrate *indígena* life) and José María Velasco, whose paintings include several panoramic landscapes of the Valley of Mexico. The upper floors exhibit art from New Spain, religious art, and cartoon and newspaper art. Special temporary exhibits occupy the rear of the ground floor. (Museo Nacional de Arte open Tues.-Sun. 10am-5:30pm. Admission 10 pesos, free Sunday.)

In front of the building is a brilliant bronze equestrian statue, *El Caballito.* At the close of the 18th century, the viceroy of Mexico commissioned Neoclassical sculptor Don Manuel Tolsá to cast this monument in honor of Carlos IV de Borbón, King of Spain. Between 1824 and 1852, the monument had to be hidden at the University of Mexico because of strong anti-Spanish sentiment.

At Tacuba 5, across the street from the Museo Nacional, stands the original **Palacio de Minería** (Palace of Mining, tel. 521-40-20), also built by Tolsá in the late 18th century. It is thought to be one of the best examples of Neoclassical architecture in the country. In 1867 it became the **Escuela Nacional de Ingeniería,** probably the first technical school in the Americas. (Open daily 7am-8pm. Free.)

Near Alameda Central

José Martí was a poet-intellectual and leader of the Cuban independence movement in the late 19th century. He dreamt of a united and free Latin America with Mexico a leader in the region, and repeatedly warned of the dangers of North American imperialism. A poem Martí wrote for Mexico is inscribed on the wall of the **Centro Cultural José Martí,** Dr. Mora 2 (tel. 521-21-15), at Hidalgo on *Alameda's* west end. The center contains books by Martí and other anti-interventionists, and sponsors a program of musical performances, poetry readings and art exhibits. The major visual attraction at the center is an immense mural covering two walls with Martí as the centerpiece and the people of Latin America behind. A tally sheet in the corner of the mural records the Spanish, British, French and U.S. foreign interventions into Latin American countries from 1800 to 1969. (Mexico has the most—with a grand total of 284). The program is posted just outside the center and advertised in *Tiempo Libre*, which can be found at any newsstand. McCarthyites may find the blaring (and largely ignored) Communist propaganda outside annoyingly proletarian but therapeutic. (Open Mon.-Fri. 9am-9pm, Sat. 9am-2pm. Free, of course)

The **Pinacoteca Virreinal de San Diego,** Dr. Mora 7 (tel. 510-27-93), next door to Centro Cultural José Martí, was once a large monastery inhabited by the order of San Diego. The building was originally constructed in the Baroque style, but Neoclassical elements were added in the 19th century. Now the monastery's large rooms with high, decorated ceilings and wooden floors contain an extensive collection of baroque and Mannerist paintings, generally of religious themes. (Open Tues.-Sun. 9am-5pm. Admission 5 pesos.)

The **Museo de la Alameda,** (tel. 521-10-16) on Calzada Colón and Balderas, facing the small park at the west end of the *Alameda*, holds Diego Rivera's *Sueño de un Tarde Dominical en la Alameda Central* (Dream of a Sunday afternoon at the *Alameda Central*), the only item in the museum's permanent collection. Originally commissioned by the Hotel del Prado in 1946, the painting depicts the dreams of different (but in some way fundamentally equal) classes of people parading about the *Alameda* on a Sunday afternoon at the turn of the century. Rivera finished the masterpiece in 1948, but when the Hotel Del Prado proudly hung the just-finished work, a national controversy ensued over the figure of Ignacio Ramírez, who is shown holding up a pad of paper that reads "God does not exist," an excerpt from a speech he gave in 1836. The archbishop of Mexico refused to bless the hotel, and on June 4th at dawn, more than 100 pro-God students broke into the hotel, erased the "does not exist" fragment from the original phrase and damaged the face of the young Diego Rivera in the center of the mural. Newspapers ran headlines about the incident for days, and Rivera later "chose" to change the slogan. On the wall of the museum is a 15-page letter from Frida Kahlo to President Miguel Alemán expressing her outrage at the defacement of her husband's work.

The Hotel del Prado partially collapsed during the 1985 quake, and the mural was moved to the museum, constructed solely to hold this piece. An entire wall chronicles the engineering feat involved in moving a national treasure. The key in front of the mural points out the portrayal of historical figures woven into the crowd: Frida Kahlo, José Martí and a chubby young Rivera, among others. (Museum open daily 10am-2pm and 3-5pm. 3 pesos. Free Sundays and for students and teachers.)

The **Torre Latinoamericana** (Latin American Tower), 181m and 42 stories high, touches the sky over the corner of Lázaro Cárdenas and Madero (the continuation of Juárez), one block east of *Alameda Central's* southeast corner. From the top of the tallest building in Mexico, you can often see the entire city and the mountains surrounding it. (Top-floor observatory open daily 10am-11pm. Admission 10 pesos.) If you are interested in seeing the natural order inverted, visit the 38th floor of the tower which holds "the highest **aquarium** in the world," probably the most fish you will ever see at 2358m above sea level for a mere 8 pesos. (Open daily 10am-11pm.) On the 41st floor, the Miralto bar, separate from the observatory and aquarium, charges prices almost as high as the tower itself for food and drinks—try stalling here for a free view only one story from the top.

La Iglesia de San Francisco (built in 1716) rests in the shadow of the Torre Latinoamericana just to the east on Madero. It was once a vast Franciscan complex that included several churches, a school and a hospital. Two fragments of the original cloisters can be seen at Gante 5, on the east side of the church, and Lázaro Cárdenas 8, behind a vacant lot. The Franciscans were the first order to arrive in Mexico; among the 12 initial monks were some of the greatest linguists, ethnographers and chroniclers of indigenous custom and belief in the annals of Mexican history. The church is open daily 7am to 8:45pm, but avoid visiting Saturday morning and afternoon and all day Sunday during mass hours. Questions are answered in the office in the central nave (open Mon.-Fri. 9am-1pm and 5-7pm, Sat 9am-1pm).

Across the street from San Francisco shimmers the **Casa de Azulejos,** an early 17th-century building covered with *azulejos* (blue and white tiles) from Puebla, now a property of Sanborn's. To be able to afford even a token few of these tiles was a mark of considerable status. This mansion was festooned by an insulted son who set out to prove his worth to his father. There is an Orozco mural on the staircase wall, but you have to pass through Sanborn's restaurant to view it (open daily 7:30am-10pm).

Palacio Iturbide, at Madero 17 between Bolívar and Gante (tel. 521-57-97), one-and-a-half blocks east of Lázaro Cárdenas and near the Iglesia de San Francisco, is a grand 18th-century palace with an impressive colonnaded courtyard. The Count of San Mateo Valparaíso lived here, but in 1821 Emperor Agustín de Iturbide took over the residence. Bánamex took over the building from the Emperor, but there is a gallery on the ground floor with exhibits that change every three months. (Open daily 9am-2pm and 4-6pm.)

Just north of the *Alameda* is the new **Museo Franz Mayer,** Hidalgo 45 (tel. 518-22-65), at Pl. de Santa Veracruz. Formerly the Hospital de San Juan de Dios, the building has been expertly restored and now houses an extensive collection of colonial furniture and other applied arts. (Open Tues.-Sun. 10am-5pm. Admission 5 pesos, 1 peso for students with ID. Free Sun. Spanish tours for 3 pesos, and English or Spanish brochures for .40 pesos.)

Next door to the Franz Mayer museum in the pink building at Hidalgo 39 (tel. 521-22-24), is the **Museo Nacional de la Estampa.** This museum holds the National Institute of Fine Arts's graphic arts and engraving collection, tracing the art of printmaking from pre-Hispanic seals to contemporary engravers, and also displays an extensive exhibit on the method of printmaking, the techniques and tools used to create the intricate and colorful prints. The highlight of the museum is the work of the acclaimed José Guadalupe Posada: skeletons dancing, singing and generally carousing. (Open Tues.-Sun. 10am-6pm. Admission 8 pesos, free Sun.)

The **Mercado de Artesanías de la Ciudadela** is a huge, tourist-patronized crafts market spreading southwest from the corner of Balderas and Ayuntamiento. Even further west, at the Plaza de la República under the **Monumento a la Revolución,** is the **Museo Nacional de la Revolución** (tel. 546-21-15). Díaz originally planned the site as the seat of Congress, but as the revolutionary fighting entered the city streets, progress was halted, and the dome was left only half-way completed. It wasn't until the 1930s that the monument and space below were finally dedicated to the memory of the revolution. Today flag poles of each of the 32 Mexican states line the pathway to this marmoreal dome. The hardest job in the city may be that of the workers who must keep the copper dome polished, a virtually perpetual task.

A star-shaped opening in the ground below the monument provides a preview to the subterranean museum. Just inside the main door, a quote endeavors to capture the revolutionary spirit. From there the exhibit powers into a chronological history of the revolutionary movement, from Porfirio Díaz's dictatorship to the creation of Mexico's current constitution in 1917. The exhibits are mostly 3-D dioramas of scenes and events from this period, created with props, video and life-size cut-outs of important figures. The best scene is probably the revolutionary camp, with clothing, bags and supplies slung up against a photo backdrop of a revolutionary base hidden deep in the hills. (Museum open Tues.-Sun. 9am-5pm. Free.)

■■■ BOSQUE DE CHAPULTEPEC

Literally "Forest of Grasshoppers," this is the area where the Aztecs, new and unwelcome arrivals to the Valley of Mexico, first settled, ending their centuries of wandering by becoming a vassal state to the then all-powerful Tepanecas. Lying on the western side of the city's center, this area is now an enormous park. With its manifold museums, hiking paths and modern sports facilities, it could easily consume several days of your stay. Mexico's most famous museum, the **Museo Nacional de Antropología,** sits among the hills of the park.

All the museums listed are in Old Chapultepec, the eastern half of the park, which fans out to the east of the *Zona Rosa*. Take the Metro to Auditorio (Line 7) or to Chapultepec (Line 1) to reach the park. The Auditorio stop is closer to the zoo; the Chapultepec stop is directly in front of the **Niños Héroes** monument, closer to most of the museums and much more convenient.

Visit the Bosque on Sunday, when families flock here for cheap entertainment. Musical spectacles enliven the park, and voices fill the air promoting foods and trinkets. Best of all, most of the museums in the area and the zoo are free on Sundays. (Open daily 5am-5pm.)

Museo Nacional de Antropología

Some journey to Mexico just to consult this massive mega-museum, located at Paseo de la Reforma and Gandhi (tel. 553-62-66). It is 4km of Mexico's finest archaeological and ethnographic treasures and the yardstick by which all other Mexican museums are measured.

Constructed of volcanic rock, wood and marble, the museum opened in 1964. Pedro Ramírez Vásquez and his team of 42 engineers and 52 architects designed and built the structure in 18 months; meanwhile, archaeologists, buyers and 20 teams of ethnographers scrambled to enlarge the museum's collection. After the huge stone image of the rain-god Tlaloc greets you outside, 23 exhibition halls await on two floors surrounding a spacious central courtyard. Poetry from ancient texts and epics graces the entrances from the main courtyard. In the center of the courtyard, a stout column covered with symbolic sculptures supports a vast, water-spouting aluminum pavilion.

You'll need about three days to do homage to the entire museum. Though after a few hours even the most hardy of visitors may suffer from pottery overload, there is more than enough to fascinate anyone from the dilettante to the Ph.D. candidate. Archaeological *salas* (halls), each devoted to a specific culture or region, occupy the ground floor. On the northern side of the ground floor, galleries display chronologically ordered artifacts of cultures that have dominated the Valley of Mexico. The Oaxacan, Mayan, Gulf Coast, Northern and Western displays are on the southern side. Upper-level rooms contain modern ethnographic displays and lie directly above the rooms devoted to the corresponding ancient culture. All the ethnographic halls of the museum have more or less the same agenda: displaying the cultural accoutrements of the peoples now living in Mexico. Large shelters were built by indigenous people commissioned to duplicate their buildings in the museum.

The museum also contains a **restaurant** (open Tues.-Sun. 9am-6pm) and a large **bookshop** that sells English guides to archaeological sites around the country as well as histories and ethnographies of Mexico's indigenous populations (some of these guides are not available at the sites themselves, so plan ahead). (Museum open Tues.-Sat. 9am-7pm, Sun. 9am-6pm. Admission 13 pesos, free Sun.) To reach the museum, take bus #55 or #76 southwest on Reforma and signal the driver to let you off at the second stop after entering the park. On the Metro, take Line 1 to the Auditorio station; the museum is just down Reforma. For a more scenic route, take Line 1 to Chapultepec station. Outside stands the **Monumento a los Niños Héroes,** six black monoliths dedicated to the young cadets of the 19th-century military academy (then at Castillo de Chapultepec). In 1847, during the last major battle of the war with the U.S., the *Niños Héroes* fought the invading army of General Winfield Scott. Refusing to surrender, the last six boys wrapped themselves in the Mexican flag and threw themselves from the castle wall. Behind the monument, Avenida Gran cuts through the park. Walk west on this street and take the second right on Gandhi. A five-minute stroll north takes you to Reforma and the museum.

Museo Tamayo and Museo de Arte Moderno

Just to the east of the Museo Nacional de Antropología is the **Museo Tamayo de Arte Contemporáneo Internacional** (tel. 286-65-19), on the corner of Reforma and Gandhi. The Mexican government created the nine halls of the museum after Rufino and Olga Tamayo donated their international collection to the Mexican people. Rufino Tamayo, born in 1889 in the city of Oaxaca, was considered un-Mexican during the nationalist era following the Revolution of 1910. Only recently has he been included in the distinguished group of Rivera, Siqueiros and Orozco, rounding out the "Big Four" of modern Mexican art. The museum, opened in 1981, has important works by Max Ernst, de Kooning and the Surrealists Joan Miró and Masson. Other highlights include a few paintings by Pablo Picasso, Torres García, Mathías Goeritz and mainly Tamayo himself. Architects Gonzalo de León and Abraham Zabludovsky designed the building with non-converging lines and planes; the idea was to create a feeling of openness. (Open Tues.-Sun. 10am-5:45pm. Admission 10 pesos. Free Sun and for students and teachers with ID. Call to arrange guided tours.)

The **Museo de Arte Moderno,** at Reforma and Gandhi (tel. 553-62-11), north of the Monumento a los Niños Héroes, houses an impressive collection of contemporary paintings by Mexican artists such as Siqueiros, José Luis Cuevas, Rivera and Velasco. The museum is linked to the smaller circular Galería Fernando Camboa by an outdoor sculpture garden. (Enter the museum on Reforma. Open Tues.-Sun. 10am-6pm. Admission 10 pesos, free Sun.)

Museo Nacional de Historia

Inside the Castillo de Chapultepec, on top of the hill behind the Monumento a los Niños Héroes waits the Museo Nacional de Historia (tel. 553-72-02). This hill has seen its share of action, beginning in 1521 when after the Conquest Hernán Cortés claimed the hill and built a fortress here. Later the King of Spain snapped it up as a wildlife preserve. It then became the official viceroy's residence, then the last bastion against U.S. invaders, and then, redecorated, the palace of Emperor Maximilian and his successors as Mexican head of state. By 1940 the hill had had enough and became the Museo Nacional de Historia.

The intention of the museum is to pick up where the anthropology museum left off, starting at the lower floor of the building where artifacts, murals and documents narrate the history of Mexico from before the time of the Conquest. The galleries contain displays on Mexican economic and social structure during the war for independence, the *Porfiriato* and the Revolution. The upper level exhibits Mexican art, dress and culture from the viceroyalty until the 20th century. The section of the museum termed the *Alcázar* models the offices, homes and belongings of the presidents who lived in the castle. The rooms entered from outside the castle exhibit carriages used by Maximilian (the elaborate ones) and Juárez (the basic black ones). *Sala* 5 contains a Juan O'Gorman mural depicting the revolution, from the cruelties of the aristocracy to the triumph of the constitution as the background moves from night into day. *Sala* 13's walls are completely covered by Siqueiros's *Del Porfirismo a la Revolución*. The skyscrapers abutting the museum afford a view surpassed only by the Torre Latinoamericana. (Open Tues.-Sun. 9am-5pm, tickets sold until 4pm. Admission 13 pesos. Free Sun., but all 2nd-floor *salas* are closed. Video 10 pesos. Camera 5 pesos.)

Museo del Caracol

The **Museo Galería de la Lucha del Pueblo Mexicano por su Libertad** (the Museum of the Struggle of the Mexican People for Liberty, tel. 553-62-85), on the southern side of Chapultepec hill, can be reached by way of the road leading to the castle/museum, to the right as the path turns straight to meet the castle. Designed by Pedro Vásquez, this museum is often listed as **Galería de Historia** or even more commonly as **Museo del Caracol** (Conch) because of its spiral design. The gallery consists of 12 halls dedicated to the greatest hits of Mexican history from the early 19th to the early 20th century. From the start of your downward spiral, the gist of the museum's message is clear: foreign intervention has made Mexico's fight for its liberty an uphill battle. Documented events in the exhibit include the execution of Javier Mina, the compassion of Nicolás Bravo, the executions of Hidalgo and Morelos, the flight of Benito Juárez, the execution of Maximilian, the railroad-building of the dictator Díaz, the strike and massacre at Cananea and the battles of Villa, Zapata and Obregón. The museum's exhibits consist of fading dioramas and non-riveting historical artifacts. Visitors unfamiliar with the major events in Mexican history will be bewildered by the Spanish-only explanations. The staircase leads to a beautiful round skylit hall, the sides of which form the inner wall of the spiral you have been ascending. Also inside is a copy of the Constitution of 1917 in Venustiano Carranza's hand. (Open Tues.-Sat. 9am-5pm, Sun. 10am-4pm. Admission 7 pesos, free Sun.)

Elsewhere in Chapultepec

Twenty-five days before his death in January of 1974, the handy David Alfaro Siqueiros donated his house and studio to the people of Mexico. In compliance with his will, the government created the **Museo Sala de Arte Público David Alfaro Siqueiros,** Tres Picos 29 (tel. 531-33-94), at Hegel just outside the park. Walk north from the Museo Nacional de Antropología to Rubén Darío; west about one block until you come to Hegel; and north on Hegel for one block—the museum is on your left. Fifteen thousand murals, lithographs, photographs, drawings and documents of Siqueiros's life and thoughts fill the galleries. Before his death in 1974, Siqueiros cleared out the garage and garden of his house to make room for *Maternity*, the monstrous work that now covers the walls and parts of the ceiling and floor of the main room. Even if you are not a die-hard Siqueiros fan, come to see the products of a lifetime of prolific work together in the place it was created. Call before visiting to arrange a guided tour in English or Spanish. (Open Mon.-Fri. 10am-2pm and 5-7pm, Sat. 10am-2pm. Admission 3 pesos, students with ID 1.50 pesos. Free Sun.)

West of the Siqueiros museum along Rubén Darío, at the intersection with Reforma, lies the **Jardín Escultórico,** a park containing realist and symbolist statues. To the south and east of the sculpture garden, at Reforma and Av. Heróico Colegio Militar, flourishes the **Jardín Botánico,** a botanical garden whose lake contains a variety of fish. (Open daily 9am-5pm. Free.) Those tired of murals'n'churches make a swim for **Parque Zoológico de Chapultepec,** just east of the Jardín Botánico. The first zoos in the Americas were established in this region. The emperor of Texcoco, Netzahualcóyotl, kept animals; Cortés founded bird sanctuaries and aquariums in Ixtapalpa; and Moctezuma II had a zoo that the Spaniards rudely destroyed to build the Iglesia de San Francisco. Today, the zoo's most noteworthy residents are the rare panda bears, a gift from the People's Republic of China in 1975. Also worth seeing are the *Xoloitzcuintles*, bald Mexican dogs of pre-Conquest origin. The name means "dogs of Xolotl," and they were said to guide people in their passage to Xolotl, the god of death. Though the zoo's collection is quite impressive, animal lovers may shed a tear for the proud beasts restricted to humble habitats, and subjected to the D.F. smog. (Zoo open Wed.-Sun. 9am-4:45pm. Free.)

■■■ TLATELOLCO

Recent archaeological digs have proven that the pre-Hispanic city Tlatelolco ("Mound of Sand" in Nahuatl) existed much earlier than the great Aztec capital of Tenochtitlán. The first king of Tlatelolco, Teutlehuac, began his rule in 1375. He and his warriors distinguished themselves in battle, conquering enemy territory near Tepeyac on the outskirts of Tenochtitlán. The Aztecs, living on an island in the central part of Lake Texcoco, realized by the middle of the 15th century that the rulers of Tlatelolco, built on the northern part of the same lake, were threatening their political and military power.

By 1463, the Tlatelolco king, Moquihuix, had built his city into a busy trading center coveted by the Aztec ruler, Axayacatl. Tension mounted over territorial and fishing boundaries, and soon Moquihuix learned that the Aztecs were preparing to attack his city. Even forewarned, Moquihuix couldn't handle the Aztec war machine, and Tlatelolco was absorbed into the huge empire. Ironically, it was here that the Aztec nation made its own last stand against Cortés, and here that it lived in poverty soon after.

Today, a state low-income housing project surrounds the early 17th-century church that stands on the grounds of Tlatelolco's ancient temple. Three cultures—ancient Aztec, colonial Spanish and modern mestizo—have left their mark on this square, giving rise to the name **Plaza de las Tres Culturas,** at the corner of Lázaro Cárdenas and Ricardo Flores Magón, 13 blocks north of the Palacio de Bellas Artes. This plaza has had an extremely bloody history, starting with its defense by Cuauhtémoc in August of 1521. A plaque in the southwest corner of the plaza states philosophically: "On August 13, 1521, although heroically defended by Cuauhtémoc, Tlatelolco fell to Hernán Cortés. It wasn't a triumph or a defeat, but the birth of the mestizo city that is the México of today."

More than 400 years later, this plaza was the site of the famous Tlatelolco Massacre of October 2, 1968. An innocent rivalry between two secondary schools that led to fighting in the streets. With the 1968 summer Olympic games in Mexico City just a few short months away, the government thought it necessary to quell any disturbance violently. Protests followed, tying into the more general dissatisfaction of workers and students with Mateos and the PRI's economic policies, until government soldiers occupied the city universities in September. On October 2, after a cancelled protest march, students and families gathered in the Plaza de Las Tres Culturas for a peaceful protest rally. Towards the end of the rally, government troops descended on the plaza ruthlessly, shooting and killing hundreds of protesters.

In the plaza, parts of the **Pyramid of Tlatelolco** and its ceremonial square remain. Enter from the southwest corner, in front of the Iglesia de Santiago, and walk alongside the ruins, down a steel and concrete path which overlooks the eight building stages of the main pyramid. By the time of the Conquest, the base of the pyramid extended from what is now Insurgentes to the current site of Iglesia de Santiago. The pyramid was second in importance to the great Teocalli of the Aztec capital, and its summit reached nearly as high as the modern skyscraper just to the south (the **Relaciones Exteriores** building). During the Spanish blockade of Tenochtitlán, the Aztecs heaved the freshly sacrificed bodies of Cortés's forces down the temple steps, within sight of the conquistadors camped to the west at Tacuba. Aztec priests would collect the leftover body parts at the foot of the steps; food was scarce during the siege and all meat was valuable. Today the walls are reconstructed and are surrounded by a well-tended lawn. Though the massive glory of the site has dwindled into the past, the well-kept remnants provide a striking foreground for the colonial church and modern buildings which complete the promised three cultures.

On the east side of the plaza stands the **Iglesia de Santiago,** an enormous, fortress-like church named after the patron saint of Spain, without whose help the Spaniards believed the Conquest could not have succeeded. The church was built in 1609 to replace an earlier structure of 1543. Before this, only a small altar and a cemetery were used to administer the sacraments to converted *indígenas*. Continue past the church for two blocks to get to the **Museo de Siqueiros,** the white building housing a lone three-dimensional mural. (Open Tues.-Sun. 9am-5pm. Free.)

To get to Tlatelolco take the Metro to the Tlatelolco station and exit through the González *salida*. From the exit turn right on González, walk three long blocks east until you reach Cárdenas, turn right and walk one block south until you see the plaza on your left. Be careful as traffic along Cárdenas is insane and buses run against the general flow.

■■■ LA BASÍLICA DE GUADALUPE

In 1531, the Virgin Mary appeared to Juan Diego, an early convert, on the hill where Aztecs worshiped the mother of their gods. The Virgin asked him to petition Fray Zumárraga to build a church on the spot. The petition was granted when, during an audience with the bishop, an image of the Virgin appeared on Diego's mantle. Our Lady of Guadalupe has since been the patron of Mexico, an icon of the religious culture of the nation. The image is found everywhere, from roadside shrines to the windshields of buses. Today the mantle can be seen in **La Basílica de Guadalupe** north of the city center in Col. Gustavo A. Madero. The new Basílica is an immense, aggressively modern structure, yet another city monument built by the venerated Pedro Ramírez Vásquez in the 1970s. The Basílica draws crowds of thousands daily to the Virgin's miraculous likeness and people flock around the central altar and impressive organ to catch a glimpse of Diego's holy cloak. (Basílica open daily 5am-9pm.)

Next to the new Basílica is the old Basílica, built at the end of the 17th century. Today the old Basílica houses the **Museo de la Basílica de Guadalupe,** Pl. Hidalgo 1 (tel. 577-60-22), in the Villa de Guadalupe. The colonial paintings dedicated to the virgin pale beside the intensely emotional collection of *retablos* or *exvotos*, small paintings made by citizens to express their faith in the Virgin of Guadalupe. (Museum open Tues.-Sun. 10am-6pm. Admission .50 pesos.)

Behind the Basílica, winding steps lead up the side of a small hill, past lush gardens, crowds of the faithful and cascading waterfalls. A small chapel dedicated to the Virgin of Guadalupe surmounts the hill. The bronze and polished wood interior of the chapel depicts the apparitions witnessed by Juan Diego. Descending the other side of the hill, and past the spouting gargoyles bearing a surprising resemblance to Quetzalcóatl, statues of Juan Diego and of other *indígena* faithful kneel before a gleaming Virgin white-doused with the spray from a rushing waterfall. On the other side of the hill, another waterfall drenches a bed of flowers. At the foot of the waterfall, a superhuman statue of Juan Diego kneels before the Virgin offering her gifts.

Authorized and unauthorized vendors both inside and outside of the Basílica grounds hawk enough religious paraphernalia to satiate even the most devout. You'd be wise, however, to heed the signs and ignore those inside selling stamps and other allegedly consecrated doo-dads.

To get to the Villa de Guadalupe, take the Metro to La Villa (Line 6), walk two blocks north on Calzada de Guadalupe and two blocks west on Zumarroga. Alternatively, take the Metro to Basílica (Line 3) and walk about 0.5km east straight down Montier to the plaza.

■■■ COYOACÁN

The Toltecs founded Coyoacán ("Place of the Coyotes" in Nahuatl) between the 10th and 12th centuries. Hernán Cortés later established the seat of the colonial government here, until he decided that Tenochtitlán would be more appropriate. After the fall of Tlatelolco, Cortés had Cuauhtémoc tortured here, in the hope that he would reveal the hiding place of the legendary Aztec treasure. This community of conquistadors and their heirs holed up in *haciendas* and remained independent of the metropolis to the north for quite some time.

South-southwest of the center, Coyoacán is Mexico City's most pleasant and attractive suburb, worth visiting for its astonishing museums or simply for a walk through peaceful **Plaza Hidalgo** or **Placita de la Conchita.** If you come to Coyoacán for a visit from downtown Mexico City, your racing pulse will be soothed by the difference in atmosphere. Life in this suburb, especially on the weekends, progresses at a much slower pace. Many people spend the afternoon just chilling with the sculpted hedges of the **Jardín Centenario** or Pl. Hidalgo. Because of the close proximity of the **Universidad Nacional Autónoma de México (UNAM)** to the west, the suburb makes an ideal student residence and social center. Coyoacán is centered on the Pl. Hidalgo, which is just east of the Jardín Centenario. The two parks are split by Calle Cabrillo Puerto which runs north-south just west of the church.

Near the plaza's northeast corner is a bronze statue of Don Miguel Hidalgo, the first spokesperson for Mexican independence. The **Casa de Cortés** (tel. 544-78-22), the one-story, reddish structure at the north end of the plaza, which is now the Palacio Municipal of Coyoacán, was once the administrative building of the conquistador himself in the early colonial period. On the porch sits the coat of arms given to Coyoacán by the King of Spain, and inside are murals by local hero Diego Rivera showing scenes from the Conquest. Public access to the building is sporadic. (Open Mon.-Fri. 9am-9pm.)

South of the plaza, beyond the Hidalgo statue, is the 16th-century **Parroquia de San Juan Bautista,** bordered by Pl. Hidalgo on the north and Jardín Centenario on the west. The church interior is elaborately decorated with gold and bronze. Enter south of the church's main door. (Open Tues.-Sat. 5:30am-8:30pm, Mon. 5:30am-7:30pm.) A few blocks southeast of Pl. Hidalgo, facing the Placita de la Conchita and marked by the gardened plaza at the end of Higuera, is the famous **Casa Colorada,** Higuera 57, which Cortés built for La Malinche, his Aztec lover. When Cortés's wife arrived from Spain, she stayed here briefly with her husband, but soon disappeared without a trace. It is believed that Cortés murdered his spouse because of his passion for La Malinche, although he later gave her away as loot to one of his conquistador cronies. The **Museo Nacional de Culturas Populares,** Hidalgo 289 (tel. 658-12-65), has temporary exhibits on the history of popular culture in Mexico. (Museum open Tues.-Sat. 10am-6pm, Sun. 10am-5pm. Free.)

After Leon Trotsky was expelled from the Soviet Union by Stalin in 1927, he wandered in exile until Mexico's President Lázaro Cárdenas granted him political asylum at the suggestion of Diego Rivera, a friend of the Russian revolutionary. Trotsky arrived in Mexico in 1937 with his wife Natalia Sedova and settled into the house that is now the **Museo y Casa de Leon Trotsky** (tel. 658-87-32), Viena 45, 7 blocks north of Pl. Hidalgo's northeast corner up Allende, then three blocks east on Viena to the corner of Morelos. The entrance is around back at Río Churubusco 410.

The house was heavily fortified; bullet holes riddle many parts of the house from an attack on Trotsky's life led by the brilliant muralist David Alfaro Siqueiros on May 24, 1940. Trotsky and Sedova survived the attack, but Siqueiros's group abducted Trotsky's secretary, Robert Sheldon Harte, whose body was found a few days later on the road to Toluca. A marble plaque just inside the entrance to the house is dedicated to Harte. A monument in the center of the garden holds Trotsky's and Sedova's ashes. Trotsky died on August 20, 1940, stabbed through the skull with an ice pick by Ramón Mercader, a Stalinist agent.

Everything in the house has been left as it was when Trotsky lived. The rooms are very simple, almost stark, decorated only by Mexican rugs. Notice that the library is filled with books in Spanish, English and Russian, and that a book about Stalin is open on Trotsky's desk, in the study where he was assassinated. The rooms display many of the couple's belongings, including a turn-of-the-century Russian dictionary and the complete works of Lenin, Marx and Engels. In the guardhouse outside is a detailed chronology of Trotsky's life, along with a photo exhibit illustrating his childhood and youth in Russia and his old age walking, fishing and gardening in Mexico. There is also a touching letter from Natalia Sedov-Trotsky (his wife) to President Cárdenas, dated a month after Trotsky's death, thanking him for his kindness in allowing them to enter Mexico. (Museum open Tues.-Sun. 10am-5pm. Admission 10 pesos, students with ID 5 pesos. Free Sun.)

One of Coyoacán's truly affecting sights is the **Museo Frida Kahlo,** Londres 247 (tel. 554-59-99), at Allende five blocks north of Pl. Hidalgo's northeast corner, in the blue and brown building. The museum is the dark blue house at the northeast corner of the intersection. Works by Rivera, Orozco, Duchamp and Klee hang in this well-restored colonial house, the birthplace and home of one of Mexico's most artistically talented citizens, Frida Kahlo (1907-1954). Having suffered a debilitating accident as a young woman, Kahlo was confined to a wheelchair and bed for most of her life. While married to Diego Rivera, she began painting and became a celebrated artist. Her chronic health problems, together with a devotion to an adulterous husband, inspired the fantastic and shocking subject matter of her works. During Rivera's absences she became emotionally attached to Leon Trotsky, but after a personal and political break between Rivera and Trotsky, a bust of Stalin replaced the pictures of Trotsky that she once hung in her home. Her wheelchair, crutches and the cast that covered her entire upper torso are still in the house. The cast is covered with patterns and figures painted by Kahlo and her husband. Display cases also show the couple's personal possessions and a death mask of Kahlo along with her ashes wrapped up in the clothes she died in. As testament to Kahlo's ardent support for *indígena* culture, the rooms contain pottery, ceramics, cookware and other provincial decorations. She died at the age of 42, in the upper-story studio that Rivera built for her. (Open Tues.-Sun. 10am–6pm. Admission 10 pesos, students 5 pesos.)

To the northeast of the Pl. Hidalgo once stood a pyramid dedicated to the Aztec war god Huitzilopochtli. Over time, the name degenerated from *Ocholopocho* to *Ochorobusco* to *Churubusco*, and the convent there got called the **Convento de Nuestra Señora de Los Ángeles de Churubusco,** at 20 de Agosto and General Anaya. Built in 1524 over the ruins of the Aztec pyramid, it was originally a Franciscan convent, dedicated to Santa María de los Ángeles. The Franciscans soon abandoned it, and in 1580 the Diegans moved in. The present church was built in 1668. On August 20, 1847, General Manuel Rincón, Pedro Anaya and 800 Mexicans halted 8000 advancing U.S. soldiers here. When the U.S. General Twiggs asked General Anaya to turn over the remaining munitions, Anaya responded, "If we had munitions you would not be here."

Still guarding the convent's main entrance are two of the original seven cannon that defended the convent during the 1847 invasion. Two more cannon and a monument to Anaya flank the western side of the structure. Inside, a beautiful old garden grows, with indecipherable inscriptions and dedications on some of its walls. (Convent open Mon.-Fri. 7am-10pm, Sat. noon-2pm and 6-8:30pm, Sun. 8am-2pm and 5:30-8pm.)

Mexico has been invaded more than 100 times, most often by the U.S. Inside the Convento de Churubusco is a museum dedicated to the history of the invasions, the **Museo Nacional de Las Intervenciones** (tel. 604-06-99). The museum's halls cover four eras, from the late 18th century to 1917. There are also a few halls dedicated to exhibits on North American expansionism and cruelty to *indígenas*, U.S. slavery and its significance for Mexico, and European imperialism. The walls of the museum are decorated with religious paintings from the convent and lists of the interventions and the related historical circumstances. Displays in the halls recount the social, economic and political circumstances that encouraged other nations to intrude. (Museum open Tues.-Sun. 9am-6pm. Admission 10 pesos.)

To get to the convent and museum from Coyoacán, walk four blocks down Hidalgo and then follow Anaya as it branches left, four blocks farther to the convent grounds. If you are coming straight from the Metro, it is far easier to get off at the General Anaya stop (Line 2) and walk two blocks west on 20 de Agosto.

Atop a hill, the **Museo Anahuacalli,** Calle Museo (tel. 677-29-84), is an ominous moated palace. Designed by the ubiquitous Diego Rivera with Aztec, Mayan and Riveran architectural styles in mind, Museo Anahuacalli houses the artist's huge collection of pre-Conquest art. Anahuacalli commands one of the best views in Mexico, comparable to those of the Torre Latinoamericana and Castillo de Chapultepec. (Open Tues.-Sun. 10am-2pm and 3-6pm.) To reach the museum from Pl. Hidalgo or Churubusco, go by *pesero* 5km south on Av. División del Nte. to Calle Museo.

To reach Coyoacán from downtown, take the Metro directly to the Coyoacán station (Line 3). *Pesero* "Coyoacán" at the station stops within two blocks of Pl. Hidalgo. One can also walk; it's a pleasant route. You might want to ask the driver to point out the stop as it is not visible immediately. Turn right onto Museo and soon you'll reach the place.

■■■ SAN ÁNGEL

South of Mexico City is the wealthy, thoroughly suburban community of San Ángel, dotted with exquisite colonial homes and churches whose layouts lend themselves to strolling. To reach the area, 10km south of the *Centro* along Insurgentes, take the Metro to the M.A. Quevedo station (Line 3). Turn left out of the Metro station and left at the intersection, then head west on Quevedo for three blocks to the lush **Parque de la Bombilla,** at the intersection of Insurgentes and Miguel Angel de Quevedo. The centerpiece of this lovely park is the two-tiered circular concrete **Monumento al General Alvaro Obregón,** at Insurgentes Sur, between Arenal and Abasolo. Obregón was one of the four leaders of the revolution united against Huerta, the usurper who seized power and executed Madero in 1913. Obregón became allied with Venustiano Carranza and helped to construct the 1917 constitution. With Carranza's death in 1920, Obregón became the first president of the post-revolutionary era. Reliefs at the entrance to the monument represent peace, agriculture, industry and the people in arms. The inscription on the far wall of the chamber reads, "I die blessing the revolution." In the main hall of the monument is a statue of the one-armed Obregón and a plaque that reads "in place of your sacrifice." (Open daily 7am-3pm. Free.)

For a quiet walking tour of San Angel's quaint residential backstreets, return east on MiguelAngel de Quevedo and then south on Chimalistac. On the east side of the park, you will come to the lovely 16th-century **Plaza** and **Iglesia de San Sebastián Chimalistac,** between the streets of Abasolo and Federico Gamboa. Continuing east along Gamboa, you will come to Paseo del Río (which becomes Río Magdalena further south), a winding road running north-south along an old riverbed. South on Río Magdalena, you'll see the bridges that still span the dry bed. At the third bridge, make a right and walk along the cobblestoned Calle Carmen for a clear view of some of the nicer colonial homes; many of the streets are shaded with trees and decorated with running fountains. Carmen leads directly back to the Insurgentes Sur, on the other side of Parque de la Bombilla.

Walking two blocks along La Paz, the street that runs through *Parque de la Bombilla*'s southwest corner and crosses Insurgentes, you'll come to an intersection. To the south are the three tiled domes of **Iglesia del Carmen,** Revolución at La Paz. Designed and built between 1615 and 1617 by Fray Andrés de San Miguel of the Carmelite order, the church and adjacent ex-convent are decorated with tiles and paintings. An outstanding statue of *Christ the Nazarene* is located in the Capilla del Señor Contreras. (Open daily 7am-1pm and 4:30-9pm.) The ex-convent, now the **Museo del Carmen** (tel. 616-11-77), displays colonial art. The main tourist attraction is the mummy collection. Descend into the coffin's crypt to see these grotesque cadavers, which have more shock value than actual historical significance. Monastic and aristocratic mummies headline. (Museum open Tues.-Sun. 10am-5pm. Admission 7 pesos. Free for students with ID.)

The Pl. del Carmen is across the street and west of the church. One block up Madero is the Pl. de San Jacinto, at San Francisco, Benito Juárez and Frontera. Every Saturday, the plaza fills up with ritzy shoppers scoping pricey arts and crafts at the **Bazaar Sábado.** Although most pieces are beyond the budget travelers' economic grasp, there are plenty of bargains and shady places to relax. The plaza also contains the **Casa de Risco,** and is one block east of the **Iglesia de San Jacinto.** The Casa de Risco, Plaza San Jacinto 15 (tel. 548-23-29), is a well-preserved 17th-century house donated by Isidro Fabela which holds his collection of 14th-18th-century European art. The whitewashed inner courtyard contains an exquisitely tiled fountain made out of pieces of bowls and plates (called *riscos*) that were collected from around the world. If you continue from the plaza one block west on Juárez, you'll reach the **Iglesia de San Jacinto.** Sit in the tranquil garden of this 16th-century church after a walk around the cobblestone streets of the area and take in its ancient orange façade and beautifully carved wooden doors. This neighborhood, the oldest in San Angel, contains many swanky modern mansions as well. (Church open daily 8am-8pm.)

Three blocks north on Revolución from the intersection of La Paz and Madero resides the **Museo Carrillo Gil,** Revolución 1608 (tel. 548-74-67), a modern building housing the contemporary art collection of the late Mr. Carrillo Gil. The museum/gallery contains paintings by Rivera, Siqueiros, Carrillo Gil and a whole floor of Orozcos. Some of the early Riveras on the first floor are interesting contrasts to his later work. (Open Tues.-Sun. 10am-6pm. Admission 3 pesos. Sun. Free.)

Shopping is one of the most popular activities in San ángel. An decent **FONART** (government-run Mexican crafts store) is at La Paz 37. (Open Mon.-Sat. 10am-7pm.) The much richer **Caretta,** another crafts store, is just a few shops down the street at Insurgentes Sur 2105 on the corner of La Paz. (Open Mon.-Sat. 10am-7pm.)

■■■ CIUDAD UNIVERSITARIA

The **Universidad Nacional Autónoma de México** (National Autonomous University—UNAM) is Mexico's largest public university, boasting an enrollment that has now far surpassed the 300,000 mark. Immediately after the new colonial regime was established, the religious orders that arrived in Mexico built elementary and secondary schools to indoctrinate the new converts and Spanish youth. After petitions were made to the king of Spain, the first university was established in 1553 in the building at the corner of the present streets Moneda and Seminario, just off the *zócalo*. As the university grew, classes were moved to the building that now houses the Monte de Piedad, on the west side of the *zócalo*, and then to a building at the east end of the Pl. del Volador, where the Suprema Corte now stands. Today's ultra-modern buildings belie its status as one of the three oldest universities in the Americas, older than Harvard, even, and way, way older than UC Berkeley.

The university now fulfills Mexico's constitutional guarantee of universal education. The sacred power of this right was evidenced by the student strikes which shut down the school in the summer of 1992, in response to proposals to raise tuition from a virtually non-existent 200 pesos to 2,000 pesos (20 pesos new money) per anum.

The **Estadio Olímpico 1968** is located on the west side of Insurgentes Sur, just past the entrance into Ciudad Universitaria. The stadium was built in the 1950s, designed to resemble a volcano with a huge crater—an appropriate motif since lava coats the ground on which it is built. Several small volcanoes lurk in the surrounding area. The stadium is one of the most beautiful monuments in the city. The impressive mosaic that covers it was made by the indefatigable Rivera using large colored rocks, and it depicts a man and a woman holding high two torches, symbolic of the 1968 Olympics held in the stadium.

Although the university's architecture is impressive, most visitors come to see the various murals which meditate upon subjects appropriate to their venue. From Insurgentes, head east from the stadium; west of the Jardín Central's southern half, the university's administrative building is distinguished by a 3-D Siqueiros mosaic on the south wall, which shows students studying at desks supported by society. One of the world's largest mosaics, the work of Juan O'Gorman, wraps around the university library, a windowless box next to the rectory tower. A pre-Hispanic eagle and Aztec warriors peer out from the side facing the philosophy department. The side facing the esplanade shows the arrival of the Spanish and their first encounter with the natives; the opposite side depicts a huge atom and its whirling components, a symbol of scientific and academic progress in modern Mexico.

Facing the Siqueiros mural is the **Museo Universidad de Ciencias y Arte,** central esplanade of the Ciudad Universitaria (tel. 548-99-53). This museum hosts temporary exhibits on contemporary issues and art. It is staffed by the students of the university. (Open Tues.-Fri. 10am-2pm and 4-7pm, Sat.-Sun. 11am-6pm. Admission 5 pesos, 2.50 pesos for students with ID.)

South of the university on Insurgentes is a sculpture park known as the **Espacio Escultórico,** just west of the Biblioteca y Hemeroteca Nacional. Out of a huge lava bed and surrounding cave formations rises a pan-chromatic collection of Herculean sculptures constructed in the early 1980s of metal, cement and wood. The artists wanted to revive through modern techniques the traditions of monumental architecture in pre-Conquest ceremonial centers and plazas. The Espacio Escultórico is optimally visited during the day, since it is located on the outskirts of the campus in a secluded area. From the center of the university, take bus #17 or #130 ("San Fernando") from the stadium and get off at the first designated stop (at the yellow pedestrian overpass).

To get to Ciudad Universitaria, take the C.U. Metro (Line 3) to Universidad. Free shuttle service, though limited timewise and irregular after classes end, is available to all campus areas. From Metro Universitaria, take line #1 to both the stadium and esplanade/museum areas. Alternatively, take the Metro to Copilco (Line 3) and follow the collegiate crowd the short distance to campus. Take the first left as you exit the station and walk two blocks, crossing Av. Copilco. Turn right at the dead end and then left to reach the edge of campus, the Paseo de las Facultades. A right on this main street will lead eventually to the junction with Insurgentes near the Estadio Olímpico.

Near the end of the pre-Classic Period, the tiny volcano **Xitle** erupted, leaving an eight-square-km area covered with several meters of lava rock, inadvertently preserving one of the first pyramids constructed in the Valley of Mexico and forming the **Cuicuilco Archaeological Zone** (tel. 553-22-63) on the southeast corner of the intersection of Insurgentes Sur and Anillo Periférico. Take bus #130 ("San Fernando Huipulco") to the entrance on the west side of Insurgentes Sur, south of the Periférico. The **Pyramid of Cuicuilco,** which means "Place of the Many-Colored Jasper," was built between 600 and 200 BC, when ceremonial centers began to spring up in Mesoamerica and priests gained extraordinary powers. Measuring 125m across at its base and 20m in height, Cuicuilco consists of five layers, with an altar to the god of fire at the summit. The lava rock around the base has been removed, allowing visitors to walk along it and up to the altar, from where, on less smoggy days, you can see Xitle to the south and Popocatépetl to the east. (Zone open daily 9am-4pm. Free.) Next to the pyramid is a small museum with exhibits on volcanology, the geology and ecology of the area, and the eruption of Xitle, as well as pieces of pottery and ceramics found near the pyramid and in the mounds surrounding it. The museum focuses on the general characteristics of the pre-Classic period, tracing the origin and development of ceremonial centers and the increases in pyramid-size. Other exhibits show the lifestyle, adornments, technology and burial practices of the inhabitants of Cuicuilco before the eruption. The three-room museum takes about 15 minutes to meander through. (Open Tues.-Sun. 9am-4pm. Free.)

Pick up a copy of the leaflet **Cartelera,** listing all scheduled events for the month (some of also appear in Tiempo Libre) during your visit at the Centro Cultural Universitario, a bus stop further south along Insurgentes Sur, at another yellow pedestrian crossing. This pleasant, modern complex houses the **Teatro Juan Ruíz de Alacón** (tel. 662-71-66), a few concert halls—biggest is **Nizahualcóyotl** (tel. 622-70-21) and movie theaters—**Salas José Revueltas** and **Julío Braucho** (tel. 665-28-50). many of the performances and movies are excellent and you can get a 50% discount with a student ID.

■■■ XOCHIMILCO

Centuries ago, the Aztecs cultivated floating gardens to feed the inhabitants of Tenochtitlán, a tradition which is celebrated daily in a vastly different form in the southern district of Xochimilco. The multi-colored *chalupa* boats which crowd the maze of canals ferry passengers past a floating market offering food, flowers and music, celebrating Mexico City's aquatic past. Especially on Sunday, the busiest day, hordes of city dwellers and tourists relax in the hand-poled *chalupas*, listening to the water-borne *mariachis* and munching tacos from floating taco bars, which tie up pirate-style to the passenger boats.

The keyword for almost anything you do in Xochimilco is bargaining. From the markets to the boats, this is the only way to get around in this overly-popular tourist spot. Be aware that if you come earlier, you'll find a much emptier (thus much less fun) Xochimilco, with far less boats and ridiculously higher prices. In the summer of 1993 a private boat with a capacity of 6 people should have charged 30 pesos per hour and 20 people 50 pesos per hour according to the offical diagram which also sets the price for almost everything else. The boat owners, however, will try to blow these prices up to 200 pesos per hour. Merely wait for more people to arrive and begin bargaining. The *colectivo* boats cost only 2 pesos per person and are much more colorful and authentic. They run on weekends only starting around noon.

The posted standardized rates also price *mariachis* per song at 25 pesos. To get to Xochimilco, take the Metro to Taxqueña (Line 2) and then *pesero* #26 , #36, or any bus marked "Xochimilco" that leaves from platform "L" outside the Metro station (45min., .80 pesos). Tour guides often wait near the fruit market to escort foreign travelers to the boats. To reach the docks, walk down Nuevo León, past the tremendous **Iglesia de San Bernandino de Cera,** then turn right on Violeta and left on Embarcadero, the next block.

If you wish to stay in this area, a clean and new hotel, **Hotel Xochimilco,** Netzahualcoyotl 7 (tel. 676-08-00) at the corner of Morelos, is one block south of the central market. The rooms are clean and carpeted, with TVs. (Singles and 1 bed doubles 50 pesos, 2 bed doubles 90 pesos.) For more information, call the Director of Tourism at 676-08-10. (Open Mon.-Fri. 9am-9pm, Sat.-Sun. 10am-5pm.)

ENTERTAINMENT

Wearied of the disco neon-scape that swings into view nightly in burgs all over the Republic? Fear no more. The chameleon that is Mexico City entertainment can turn all shades of the spectrum. Be it the Ballet Folklórico at Bellas Artes, an old film by Emilio Fernández at an art cinema, a bullfight in the Pl. México, or blues in a smoke-filled bar, the city has something for everyone and more than enough for anyone.

For current listings of performances and show times, pick up a copy of *The News*, an English-language daily, or look for the weekly issue of *Tiempo Libre* (Free Time), each for 3 pesos at most corner newsstands and is published every Thursday. *The News* has film and theater listings; *Tiempo Libre* also covers galleries, restaurants, dances, museums and most cultural events. *La Jornada* (1.50 pesos), one of the best national newspapers, lists art films showing in less well-known locations such as the university. *Macho Tips*, available at newstands along Reforma, publishes information on gay events in the city. The *Mexico City Daily Bulletin*, a potpourri of news and information on tourist sights, with a helpful map of Mexico City, is available free at the City Tourism Office and all over the *Zona Rosa*.

■■■ BARS AND CLUBS

Bars with dimly lit interiors, no windows, or swinging doors are called *cantinas*; women are not welcome in these bastions of *machismo*. At large nightclubs that make some attempt at respectability, dates of the opposite sex are sometimes prerequisites for admission. Cover charges range from 5 to 50 pesos, but women are sometimes admitted free. Those places without a cover often have minimum consumption requirements and high drink prices. Be aware that Mexican-made drinks, from Kahlúa to *sangría*, are considerably cheaper than imported ones. Watch out for ice-cubes—avoid at all costs these secret agents of *turista*.

The *Zona Rosa* offers the most variety for your entertainment peso. Tourists and Mexicans alike flood the streets in the evenings, often dressed to the hilt and set to have a good time. Bars and discos clog the streets, each attempting to outdo the others in flashiness and decibel output. Although the *Alameda* and other areas also have some places to dance, discos in more run-down parts of town can get seedy. Women venturing out alone should be aware that they will most likely be approached by a gaggle of men offering drinks, dances, dates and their first-born.

For safety, the *Zona Rosa* offers the best lighting and least lonely streets, which are a problem in other areas. Taxis run all night, as do *peseros* on the major routes (see Getting Around above). Try to avoid going out at night alone, however, and the bigger the group, the safer.

■ Zona Rosa—Bars

There is a drinking establishment everywhere you look in the *Zona Rosa*. Taverns here are generally expensive and high-class, but the expense may include live performers and tasty *botanas* (appetizers). *Zona Rosa* bars cater to all ages and tastes, from teeny-bopper to elderly intellectual. Many feature live music or beamed-in video entertainment. The variety of style here may make up for the dominance of male-only cantinas in the rest of the country. Women will probably feel safe at this area's establishments, though the pick-up scene never ceases.

Yarda's Bar, Niza 39 (tel. 514-57-22), not to be confused with Yarda's restaurant on the corner. Big screen entertainment and happening party atmosphere maintain a touch of class with starched white tablecloths, black leather furniture and absence of tacky neon. Half-pitcher of beer 20 pesos. Mixed drinks 15 pesos. Cover Fri.-Sat. 25 pesos. Open Mon.-Sat. 5pm-midnight.

Keops, Hamburgo 146 (tel. 528-57-51). Restaurant by day, intimate bar with live performers playing classic rock by night. Responsive sit-down crowd in dark but social atmosphere. Cocktails 9 pesos. Cover 25 pesos. Restaurant service daily 1-7pm. Nightclub action Tues.-Sat. 8pm-3am.

Liverpool Pub, Hamburgo 111 (tel. 207-23-36). 3 generations of British royalty smile from the entrance while an enormous Union Jack billows down from the ceiling. Beatlemaniacal interior. Live bands rock nightly, mostly to '50s and '60s U.S. favorites but with a sprinkling of Spanish tunes. More sedate, mostly late-20s crowd, but all ages represented. Drinks average 15 pesos. Cover 30 pesos. Open Tues.-Sat. 6:30pm-3am.

Harry's Bar and Grill, Liverpool 155 (tel. 208-63-55), enter on Amberes. Near-beer signs and framed menus from famous bars and *cantinas* all over Mexico. A packrat's paradise; collections of cigarette packs, beer bottles, liquor bottles, business cards and old trumpets line the walls. An extremely lively and popular establishment both for eating and swigging beers. International clientele kicks back and watches the game o' the day on central TV sets. Mini *batanas* 13-26 pesos. Open Mon.-Sat. 1pm-1am.

El Chato, Londres 117. A 3-in-1 bonanza. This elegant and quiet restaurant wines and dines until late in the evening. Mingle with quaint antique typewriters and old-fashioned rifles. Many a loner stares despondently into many a drink. Don't miss the informal jazz-piano bar with Sinatra sound-alikes an arm's reach away. Frequented by famous Mexican actors, politicians, and businessfolk. No glitz, no booming beat, but the almost-thirtysomething clientele likes it that way. A great place to wind down and to imbibe quality beer out of steins (8 pesos). Cocktails 13 pesos, imports 16 pesos. Open Mon.-Sat. 1pm-1am.

El Taller, Florencia 37-A (tel. 533-49-70), in the basement. You might miss the small entrance to this underground bar. Well known, classic hangout for blue-collar gay men. Private, conservative barroom attracts an older, quieter crowd. Drinks, snacks and small paperback bookstand available in the afternoon; dancing during the evening. Male revue Wed. at midnight. Tues. lectures are well-attended. Cover 20 pesos with 1 drink, Fri.-Sat. 35 pesos. Open Tues.-Sun. 9pm-4am.

Salón de Té Auseba, Hamburgo 159-B (tel. 511-37-69), near Florencia. Comfortable tea-room pushes calories on a quiet, older, upper-class clientele. A glass case in front shows off the delicious pastries, cakes, pies, tarts and scones. An alternative for the teetotaler. Teas 5.50 pesos. Try the *manzana en chemise*, an apple tart (8 pesos). Open Mon.-Sat. 9am-10pm, Sun. 11am-10:30pm.

Bar Orsis, Niza 22 (tel. 208-49-54). A younger crowd tosses back beer (12 pesos) while sitting on high barstools and rocking with the live *super grupos*. Cover 20 pesos Thurs.-Sat., free Sun.-Wed. Open daily 7pm-3am.

■ Zona Rosa—Discos

The *Zona Rosa* can claim some of the nation's best discos and highest cover charges. Without a doubt, *the* place to party on a weekend night. High covers and long lines are sure signs of a disco phenom, but the same crowds overflow into less crowded and cheaper clubs. The sidewalk recruiters will try to lure in groups, especially those with high female to male ratios, and may even cut you a deal.

Rock Stock Bar & Disco, Reforma 258, at Niza. Chic disco, very popular with young Mexicans. Often packed; non-famous single men will have difficulty getting in. After a brief examination by the metal detector, enter through rotating air-lock style doors and follow street signs upstairs. You enter into a huge open attic room with fluorescently painted railings, scaffolding and metal cages. A black light shines on the painted floors and walls decorated with handprints, footprints and graffiti art. Free barrels of chips and popcorn. Central band hammers out rock tunes as the young, hip crowd mingles freely. Drinks 12 pesos. Cover 85 pesos. Women get in free on Thurs. Open Thurs. 8pm-1am, Fri.-Sat. 8am-3am.

Boots Bar and Disco, Niza 45 (tel. 514-46-08). Mirrors, a disco ball, black light bulbs and a large-screen TV provide more sensory input, as if the lights, dancing and music weren't enough. Casual crowd both dancing and hanging out at tables. Drinks 15-20 pesos. The best part: no cover Tues.-Thurs. On Fri.-Sat., cover is 20 pesos. Open Tues.-Sun. 8pm-2am.

Celebration, Florencia 56. A busy disco rigged up with speakers heard 'round the world, cranking out the modern rock dance tunes. Stylish set models the latest fashions sold in the *Zona Rosa*'s designer outlets. Admission includes *barra nacional* (open bar, national brands). Cover 80 pesos. Open daily 7pm-3am.

Melódica, Florencia 56 (tel. 523-22-42), just south of Londres. "A new concept in Mexican bars." Probably the first karaoke in Mexico: a TV screen flashes song lyrics while you sing over the bar's sound system, which leaks out into the street within earshot of unfortunate passers by. Neon pink and purple trim. Drinks 10-30 pesos. Cover 20 pesos. Open Mon.-Sat. 7pm-2am.

■ Alameda Central—Bars And Discos

Nightspots here lack the luster and glitter of those in the *Zona Rosa*; fortunately the prices reflect it. An evening here may well be worthwhile, but the surrounding neighborhoods may be dangerous. Caution is advised, especially late at night when streets are deserted. Be sure to check out nearby **Garibaldi Plaza** (see below). Taxis are somewhat sparse in this area.

Zotano's, 20 Revillagigedo (tel. 518-40-37), at Independencia. Quaint subterranean dance club with peppy performers playing *salsa*, *mambo* and rock. The red-lights-and-tinfoil decor suggests the inside of a broiler. *Refrescos* 3 pesos, cocktails 8 pesos. Cover a mere 5 pesos. Open Mon.-Sat. 8pm-4am.

El Miralto, Torre Latinoamericana, Madero at Lázaro Cárdenas. Atop the tallest building in Mexico. Mixed drink prices steep (over 10 pesos), but worth the expense for the best view in the city, especially at night. You'll need an extra drink when you see what you've been breathing all day. Open Mon.-Sat. 1pm-1am, Sun. 2-10pm.

Hostería del Bohemico, Hidalgo 107 (tel. 512-83-28), just west of Reforma. A romantic coffee haven with music, singing and poetry. Seating is on the outdoor terraces of both levels and all 4 sides of a lush 2-tiered courtyard with a central burbling fountain. The slice-of-a-tree tables and chairs lit by old-fashioned lanterns make for intimate conversations above the guitar-accompanied *canciones* in the background. No cover, but coffees, cakes and ice creams run high at 11.50 pesos each. Open daily 5-11pm.

■ Centro—Bars

A few of the bars here are popular among the adult, administrative set, and some have as long and distinguished a history as the buildings that stand over them. Explore, but bear in mind that by midnight the *Centro* streets are completely deserted and potentially dangerous. The following bars spill over into the *Alameda* area, but are distinguished by their clientele and atmosphere.

La Opera, 5 de Mayo 10, just west of Filomeno Mata. A real class act. Restaurant service daily, but evenings are crowded by couples and groups chatting and downing cocktails. Baroque gold-wrought ceiling, mirrored walls, a grandfather clock, and carved dark wood booths. Suit-and-tie crowd sips martinis, but a significant tourist minority tones down the formality. Drinks 10.50-13 pesos. Open daily 1pm-midnight.

Bar de los Azulejos, Casa de los Azulejos on Madero 14 (tel. 518-66-76), 2nd floor. Small bar tucked away in a corner of Sanborn's. Spiral staircase, leather chairs, dimmed lights and red-coated waiters lend a touch of class appropriate for the historic building. Food available from the downstairs restaurant. Mixed drinks, including frozen margaritas, 10-16 pesos. 50% off domestic wines and liquors from 2-3pm and 6-7pm. Open daily 7am-11pm.

Humboldt 34, Humboldt 34 (tel. 521-22-93), near Juárez. Intimate club with wood paneling and leather chairs. Polished brass Aztec calendar prominent on wall, but the electric guitars on center stage keep the place looking modern. Live performances nightly. Open Mon.-Sat. 9pm-3am.

■ Garibaldi Plaza

Garibaldi Plaza hosts some of Mexico City's gaudiest and seediest nightlife. On weekend nights, roving *mariachi* bands compete for pesos along with other regional *ranchera* groups, and will play your favorite tune for 20-50 pesos. Tourists, locals, prostitutes, pickpockets, musicians, food vendors and other flavors of humanity mingle, a significant portion reeling from the liquor sold by the plastic cupful. Big nightclubs, each with their own *mariachi*, do their best to lure the crowds. Though they advertise no cover and no minimum charge, the per-drink price is jaw-droppingly high.

Beware of the many pickpockets and purse-snatchers who target tourists here. The plaza is at the intersection of Lázaro Cárdenas and República de Honduras, north of Reforma. Walk 7 blocks north of the Bellas Artes Metro station. The best time to visit Garibaldi is between 8pm and 2am on weekends, but it's also the least safe then. Prostitutes turn tricks here, and the neighboring streets and small *cantinas* can be dangerous at night. Women and lone travelers should take particular caution.

■■■ SHOPPING

Whereas most Mexican cities have one central market, Mexico City has one central market for every retail good. Rumor has it that *La Merced* moves as much money every day as the entire city of Monterrey. These markets are relatively cheap, since the city usually pays the overhead. Every *colonia* has its own market, but all the major marketplaces are in the center of town. The following are the more important market areas.

La Merced, Circunvalación at Anaya, east of the *zócalo*. Merced Metro stop (Line 2). Primarily food, shipped from all over the country. Huge selection of fresh produce at rock bottom prices. Open daily 8am-7pm. (See Sights: *Centro*.)

Sonora, Teresa de Mier and Cabaña, 2 blocks south of Merced. If you want to turn your significant other into a toad, head for Sonora. Specializes in witchcraft, medicinal teas and spices, ceramic pottery, figurines and ceremonial figures. *The* place to replenish your supply of: lucky cow's feet, shrunken heads, eagle claws, aphrodisiacs, black salt (for nosey neighbors), talismans to ward off evil eye, poison antidotes, powdered skull (for the domination of one's enemies), amber, patchouli incense, energy pills, courage powder, lucky bath oil (for success in business), black candle figurines and dead butterflies, among other things. Tell them your problem, they'll give you a panacea for it. Outside the market are cagefulls of birds, spiders, dogs, ducks and turtles. Rare species sometimes appear. All for sale, but remember that Mexican pets are turned away at the U.S. border. A great place to pick up a cheap and distinctive souvenir of your Mexican travels. Open daily 8am-7pm.

Tepito, between Metro stops Revolución and San Cosme, accessible by a *pesero* called "Tepito" along Reforma. Blocks of outdoor clothing stalls and indoor shoe racks—you've never seen more shoes in one place. Tepito is the national clearinghouse for gray-market imports from the U.S. and South Asia, everything from counterfeit watches to refrigerators. Neat-o police raids occur daily. Watch your wallet. Open daily 9am-9pm.

San Juan, Pl. El Buen Tono, 4 blocks south of *Alameda Central*, 2 blocks west of Lázaro Cárdenas. Bounded by Ayuntamiento, Aranda, Pugibet and Dolores. The painted footprints will lead you in. Targets the tourist money. An incredible variety of baskets, furniture, blankets, traditional clothing, keychains, t-shirts, dolls, sombreros, wall hangings and fake parrots. Open Mon.-Sat. 9am-7pm, Sun. 9am-4pm.

La Lagunilla, Comonfort at Rayón, east of the intersection of Lázaro Cárdenas and Reforma. 2 large yellow buildings on either side of the street. Although famous for its historic Sunday market specializing in antiques and old books, the market has metamorphosed into a daily vending site for practical goods. Open daily 8am-7pm.

Buenavista, Aldana 187, at Degollado in Col. Guerrero. Giant blue and pink crafts warehouse. Like San Juan, it is geared almost exclusively to the tourist. Flyers advertise over 90,000 typical Mexican articles under one roof. Merchandise ranges from stuffed bulls' heads to "genuine" obsidian blades, to videos about traditional Mexico. If you're lucky the man at the door will give you a mini-*sarape* good for a free *refresco* inside. Open Mon.-Sat. 9am-6pm, Sun. 9am-2pm.

Bazaar Sábado, Pl. San Jacinto 11, in San Ángel. Sat. only, as the name suggests, and a good excuse to voyage out to San Ángel. Highest quality folk crafts: dolls, paintings, rugs, papier-mâché, jewelry and much more. A great place to browse—but bring lots of cash if you plan to buy. Slightly cheaper bazaar in the plaza just outside. Open Sat. 10am-7pm.

FONART, one of the government crafts stores selling regional crafts from all over Mexico. No bargaining allowed, but deals are good anyway. Giant tapestries, Oaxacan rugs, silver jewelry, ponchos, glassware, pottery, masks, colorful embroidery, papier-mâché dolls and folk art. There's a FONART near you: Patriotismo 691; Juárez 89; Insurgentes 1630 Sur; Londres 6 at the Museo de Cera; Londres 136, in San Ángel at Av. de La Paz 37; and Ciudad Satélite on Manuel Izaguirre 10. Open Mon.-Sat. 10am-7pm.

Museo Nacional de Artes del Instituto Nacional Indigenista, Juárez 44, across from the *Alameda*. A shop as well as a museum. A map on the wall shows the typical regional crafts from all areas of Mexico. The store stocks most of those crafts and a lot of jewelry. The museum part is a gallery with contemporary artists' work. Open Mon.-Fri. 9am-6pm, Sat.-Sun. 10am-6pm.

■■■ SPORTS

Whether consumed by bullfighting, soccer, jai alai or horse racing, Mexican fans consider their *deportes* to be art forms and are less fans than connoisseurs—albeit rowdy ones.

Plaza México, Insurgentes Sur (tel. 563-39-59). Accessible by the Metro station San Antonio (Line 7). Mexico's principal bullring. Bullfights begin Sun. at 4pm. Professionals fight only Dec.-April; *novilladas* (novices) replace *matadores* in off-season. Stadium capacity: 50,000 fans. Tickets are 10-60 pesos, depending on proximity to the ring and shady or sunny side. Bring sunglasses and a hat. Binoculars come in handy.

Aztec Stadium, SA-Tlalpan 3465 (tel. 677-71-98). Take shuttle train or *pesero* directly from the Tasqueña Metro station (Line 2). The Azteca is the greatest of the many large stadiums where professional soccer—the national sport—is played. Read the sports pages of any newspaper for information on games. The season runs Oct.-July.

Frontón México (tel. 546-14-69), Pl. de la República, 3 blocks south of the Revolución Metro station (Line 2). Watch and bet on jai alai, a rapid-action game played with a little ball and curious curved wicker *cestas*. A dressy occasion; men wear coats and ties, women dresses or skirts. Games usually take place Tues.-Thurs. and Sat.-Sun. Box office opens at 6:30pm. Admission 20 pesos. Betting (not required) starts at 1 peso.

Hipódromo de las Américas, Av. ávila Camacho. Take a *pesero* labeled "Hipódromo" west along Reforma, or bus #17 from Metro Tacuba—the beautiful horsetrack is on the outskirts of the city. Races Thurs. and Sat.-Sun. at 2:15pm. Admission free unless you sit in the upper level, where purchase of food and drink is obligatory.

NEAR MEXICO CITY

■■■ TEOTIHUACÁN

While Europeans lived in caves eating nuts and berries and the group that would one day found Tenochtitlán wandered haplessly, a great civilization flourished in the Valley of Mexico. Little is known about the people who founded Teotihuacán around 200BC; their consummately organized, theocratic society lasted nearly 1000 years and then vanished as mysteriously as it had appeared. Today we speculate that the city's boundaries grew to exceed its capacity to function. Teotihuacán had no means of moving supplies in from outside the valley, and its inhabitants hadn't yet invented the wheel. There is evidence of severe malnutrition and conflagrations in the wreckage of the city. In 850 AD, when the Toltecs founded Tula, not a single citizen walked the paths of that once enormous urban complex. When the Aztecs founded Tenochtitlán in 1325, Teotihuacán, 50km northeast of their capital, lay in ruins. The Aztecs adopted the area as ceremonial grounds and attributed its huge structures to giants who inhabited the world during the era of the first sun. Believing that the lords buried in this hallowed place had become gods, the Aztecs called the area Teotihuacán, meaning "Place of the Gods."

The ruined city's latest incarnation is the most-visited archaeological site in the Republic. The archaeological zone, more commonly referred to as *Las Pirámides*, covers a vast area. The ceremonial center, a 13-square-km expanse, was built along a 2km stretch now called **Calle de los Muertos** (Road of the Dead) after the countless human skeletons that were discovered alongside it. The road leads from the Pyramid of the Moon to the Temple of Quetzalcóatl. Since the Teotihuacanos planned their community around the four cardinal points, Calle de los Muertos runs nearly north-south. The main structure, the Pyramid of the Sun, is on the east side and is squared with the point on the horizon where the sun sets at summer solstice. On the north end of Calle de los Muertos are the Plaza and Pyramid of the Moon. The Palace and Temple of Quetzalcóatl stand on the east side of the southern end.

The best way to wander the ruins is on a general south-to-north vector. Start your visit on the west side of the southern end of the Calle de los Muertos, where a small museum struggles to explicate this civilization. Displays compare the size of the ancient city with various present-day cities, illustrate the architecture and technology of the pyramids, describe the social, religious and economic organization of the society, and exhibit *indígena* art. Although all the pieces you see are replicas (the originals are at the Museo Nacional de Antropología in Mexico City), the museum is a good introduction to the zone. Much of what is known about the area was learned through records kept by the contemporary civilizations in Cholula, Oaxaca, the Yucatán and northern Mexico, all of which traded with Teotihuacán.

As you exit the museum, directly across the Calle de los Muertos is the **Temple of Quetzalcóatl,** once a giant walled-in stadium sheltering a group of ancient temples. Its four flanking platforms served as grounds for priestly ceremonies and dances. The central plaza houses an altar upon which the centennial sacrifice of the "New Fire" was celebrated. Although the temple has lately suffered tremendous erosion from the gods of rain and wind, on the east side of the pyramid you can still make out fierce serpent heads of Quetzalcóatl and traces of the red paint that originally decorated it.

Continuing north along the Calle de los Muertos, you will cross what was once the San Juan river. On the west side of the street are the remains of two temples that were built in two phases, 200-400AD and 400-750AD. Further to the north and east is the **Pyramid of the Sun,** the single most tremendous structure in the ceremonial area. Second in size only to the pyramid at Cholula in Puebla, its base measures 222m by 225m—dimensions comparable to those of Cheops in Egypt. The pyramid rises 63m today, but the grand temple that once crowned its summit is missing. The miniature temple that now stands atop the pyramid once served Tonacatecutli, the god of sun and spiritual warmth. The grueling climb to the top of the pyramid (don't worry, the platforms of the multi-tiered pyramid make convenient rest stops) pays off with a view of the entire site and surrounding valley.

Between the Pyramid of the Sun and the Pyramid of the Moon on the west side of the street is the **Palace of Quetzalpaploti** (the *quetzal* butterfly). This columned structure was the residence of the elites who staked out the area next to the ceremonial space and far from the residential complexes of the common folk. There are bird motifs and geometric patterns carved into the columns. Behind the palace of Quetzalpaploti is the **Palacio de los Jaguars.** Although the palace is entirely restored, complete with fluorescent lights and plastic handrails, some of the original frescoes remain, with red, green, yellow and white symbols that represent birds, maize and water.

At the northern end of the Calle de los Muertos is the stunning **Pyramid of the Moon.** Although it appears to equal the height of the Pyramid of the Sun, it is in fact much shorter, but built on higher ground. The view from the summit down the Calle de los Muertos hints at the magnitude of Teotihuacán.

If you still have the energy, there are two other areas, signless and unmarked, to visit off the Calle de los Muertos on the outskirts of the excavated site. On the northeast side of the Pyramid of the Sun near entrance #4 is the **Tepantitla Palace,** which has some of the best-preserved frescoes on the site. You can still make out priests with elaborate headdresses and representations of Tlaloc, the god of rain. On the southeast border of the site are the palaces of **Atetelco, Zacuala** and **Tetitla,** mostly mazes of what once were elaborate palaces, but now contain only the vestiges of eagle and jaguar frescoes.

Be sure to bring plenty of water, a hat and sunglasses on your jaunt. Vendors do sell water if you run out. You may want to buy a written guide here at the site (25 pesos) or at the Museo de Antropología in Mexico City. Expect to spend about an hour at the museum and another three to four hours walking as many miles exploring the ruins. (Site open daily 8am-5pm. Admission 13 pesos. Free parking.)

An unusual place for a meal is **La Gruta** (The Cave), which is east of the Pyramid of the Sun, near Tepantitla Palace. As the name suggests, the restaurant is in an immense cave, with delicate rainbow-painted tables and chairs. The setting provides a respite from the arid heat; strains of Vivaldi surround the patrons. (Hamburgers 15 pesos, full meals 25 pesos. Open daily 11am-6pm.)

To contact the Teotihuacán offices, dial 601-88 or 600-52 (from Mexico City add the prefix 91-595). Direct **bus service** from Mexico City to the pyramids is available from Autobuses Teotihuacán (every 15 min. 5am-6pm, 1hr., 6 pesos) located in the Terminal de Autobuses del Norte at Sala 0. The same bus line runs from Tepexpan should you come from Texcoco or Chiconcuac. The last bus back from the pyramids to Mexico City leaves the main entrance at 6pm. A few miles before reaching

Teotihuacán, the bus passes just to the right of the town of Acolmán, founded shortly after the Conquest by the Franciscans. The majestic lines of the ex-monastery of Acolmán rise to the sky, breaking the monotony of the corn fields. Even at a distance, the architectural solemnity of this early religious settlement is evident. If you want to stop at the ex-monastery on your way back to Mexico City, take the Indios Verdes bus from the main entrance and get off at Acolmán.

■■■ TEPOTZOTLÁN

On the highway from Mexico City to Tula and Querétaro, the town of Tepotzotlán is a feasible and enjoyable daytrip from Mexico City. The Monastery and Church of Tepotzotlán contain inspirational religious art in the Museo del Virreinato (viceroyalty), attached to the church. For those itching to escape the city, Tepotzotlán offers a view of small-town life and atmosphere. Its proximity to the city makes it popular with tourists, a fact reflected in the steep prices in the town's restaurants and market.

In 16th-century Tepotzotlán the Jesuits established a convent for ambitious indígenas to study language, art, theology and mathematics. An *indígena* convert, Martín Maldonado, donated the land to the missionaries in 1582. Construction of the buildings continued until the end of the following century, and the huge bell in the tower was added in 1762. To the rear of the **Iglesia de San Francisco Javier** is the **Capilla de la Virgen de Loreto.** Behind it, the ridiculously ornate **Camarín de la Virgen** (altar room) is fitted with a mirror so that visitors can see the decorations on the dome that crowns it.

After the expulsion of the Jesuits in 1767, the church and buildings became a reform school for priests. Early in this century, they were returned to the Jesuits, and in 1964, the whole complex went secular as the **Museo del Virreinato** (tel. 207-91-37). Although the actual collection, illustrating the history of the Conquest and formation of New Spain, is somewhat sparse, the exhibit contains many valuable treasures from the colonial period. Jesuit imagery predominates in the monastery's halls. St. Ignatius stares at you from every other altar, and St. Francis Xavier is only slightly less ubiquitous. The **Iglesia de San Francisco Xavier** is a Churrigueresque masterpiece. Paintings hang between the arches of the ex-convent, and other galleries contain sculptures, exhibits of locks from the glorious viceregal era and other artifacts. Be sure not to miss the concealed entrance to the upper floor near the exit. The hall contains mostly paintings of unhappy-looking priests and nuns, but also has a map of Mexico City from 1793 and a balcony with a great view of the surrounding area. The monastery's orchard, acres of greenery, is soothing, particularly for those coming from Mexico City. (Open Tues.-Sun. 11am-5:45pm. Admission 13 pesos, free Sun.)

The plaza outside the church is packed with immaculate eateries alongside a few hotels. Tepotzotlán's best lodgings are in the **Posada Familiar** (tel. 876-05-20), at the center of the *zócalo*. Although the rooms are smallish, they contain sturdy wood furniture, tiled floors and handsome wood beamed ceilings. (Singles 40 pesos. Doubles 60 pesos.) The **Hostería del Convento de Tepotzotlán** (tel. 525-02-43), next to the museum, serves Mexican food atop cheery pink and yellow tables in a flower-filled side courtyard of the monastery. (Soups 9.50 pesos. Entrees 20 pesos. Open daily 1-6pm.) Adjoined to the Posada is the **Restaurant/Bar Pepe** which serves delicious *antojitos* in a music-filled outdoor setting. (*Comida corrida* 21 pesos.) *Mariachis* wander the plaza and will play for a hefty sum while you eat.

To get to Tepotzotlán, take the Metro to Cuatro Caminos (Line 2), then the yellow bus from *salida* H. Buses run from 6am-10:30pm, leaving approximately every 20 min. (2.30 pesos). To get back, catch a bus on Juárez up the street from the church to any of a number of Metro stations.

Baja California

Peeled away from the mainland geological ages ago by earthquakes, Baja California is a 40,000 square mile desert peninsula between the Sea of Cortés on the east and the Pacific Ocean on the west. Spurred by advances in oceanic transportation and economic developments at home, Menán Cortés, and later the Spanish Jesuit missionaries, came to conquer, control, and convert the cave-dwelling indigenous people of Baja in the late 16th and 17th centuries. Many of the missions, like San Felipe and San Jose del Cabo, still lend names and churches to Baja towns.

Nowadays, Californians from Burbank to Berkeley form the solid stream of tourists flowing into Baja to surf, fish, and drink to their hearts' content. The lower prices and lower drinking age, as well as the warm climate, fine beaches, and productive fisheries, are more accessible than ever due to the construction of the Transpeninsular Highway, institution of ferry service, and improvement of toll roads in the north.

Large, usually pink, resort hotels and condominium complexes are sprouting to house human torrents, but they have a ways to go before filling Baja California. A secluded beach is never far away, especially if you have a car, and the central mountains in particualar are far from being overpopulated.

GETTING AROUND

BY LAND

The completion of the Transpeninsular Highway has made it quicker to travel the peninsula by **car,** but driving through Baja is still far from easy. The road was not designed for high-speed driving; often you'll be safely cruising along at 60mph and suddenly careen into a hidden, poorly banked, rutted curve that can only be taken at 30mph.

The *Angeles Verdes* (Green Angels) pass along Route 1 twice per day (for details see Mexico Essentials: Once There: Transportation: By Car). Remember that extra gas (unleaded) may be in short supply along this highway, so don't pass a PEMEX station without filling your tank. All of Baja is in the *Zona Libre* (Free Zone), so strict vehicle permits are not required. If you will be driving in Baja for more than 72 hours, you merely need to get a free permit by showing vehicle title and proof of registration.

All major towns in Baja are served by **bus.** The gruelling 25-hour bus trip from Tijuana to La Paz costs 168 pesos, whence you may zip directly to the mainland by **ferry** for as little as 51 pesos. If you plan to navigate the peninsula by bus, be forewarned that almost all *camiones* between Ensenada and La Paz are *de paso*. This means you have to leave at inconvenient times, fight to procure a ticket and then probably stand the whole way. A much better idea is to buy a reserved seat in Tijuana, Ensenada, La Paz, or the Cabos, and traverse the peninsula in one shot while seated. Unfortunately you'll miss the fantastic Mulegé-Loreto beaches.

Anyway you cut it, Baja beaches and other points of interest off the main highway are often inaccessible on public transportation; buses don't stop at coastal spots between Tijuana and San Quintín. Near Mulegé, Loreto, La Paz and the Cabos (capes) on Baja's southern tip, travelers tied to the bus system can make a short walk from the main road to some of the beaches. Many find that the best way to see Baja is to hitchhike. Baja has but one well-traveled main-drag. Some tourists may not stop for thumbers, but many oblige if caught at a pit stop—PEMEX stations are thick with rides. Mexicans, however, are much more amenable to thumbers. Getting a lift still largely relies upon old-fashioned luck and appearance. Remember, hitchhiking is unpredictable and potentially hazardous; use common sense and don't hesitate to turn down a ride if something doesn't feel right. *Let's Go* does not recommend hitching.

BY SEA

Ferry service was instituted in the mid-'60s as a means of supplying Baja with food and supplies, not as a means of tourist transportation. Boats have come to serve *viajeros*, and passenger vehicles may take up any space left over after the top-priority commercial vehicles. For those who plan to take a car, the best advice is to make reservations one month in advance, either through a travel agent or with the ferry office directly. (See La Paz: Practical Information for details.)

There are three different ferry routes: Santa Rosalía to Guaymas (7hrs.), La Paz to Topolobampo/Los Mochis (9hrs.) and La Paz to Mazatlán (16hrs.). The La Paz to Topolobampo/Los Mochis route provides direct access to the train from Los Mochis through the Barrancas del Cobre (Copper Canyon).

Ferry tickets are generally expensive, even for *turista* class berths—two to a cabin with a sink (bathrooms and showers down the hall). It's extremely difficult to find tickets for *turista* (75 pesos) and *cabina* class (113 pesos, bathroom in the room), and snagging an *especial* berth (a real hotel room, 138 pesos) is as likely as stumbling upon a snowball in the central Baja desert; there are only two such suites on each ferry. This leaves the bottom-of-the-line *salón* ticket (38 pesos), which entitles you to a bus-style seat. If, as is likely, you find yourself traveling *salón* at night, ditch the seats and stake out a spot on the floor early on—just spread out your sleeping bag and snooze. As always, take appropriate security measures. For prices, check the transportation listings for each of the towns. For further ferry information call the State Tourist Department (tel. 2-11-99, 2-79-75, fax 2-77-22).

Always bring food on ferry trips; boat restaurants are prohibitively expensive.

BY AIR

Air travel can save you time, but it is not cheap. A flight from La Paz to Los Mochis takes 20 minutes (223 pesos); the flight between Tijuana and La Paz takes one and a half hours (558 pesos). **Aeroméxico, Mexicana,** and **Aerocalifornia** all have regular daily service from Tijuana to Los Mochis, Guadalajara, La Paz, the Cabos, and Mexico City.

BAJA CALIFORNIA NORTE

■■■ TIJUANA

Like it or not, Tijuana *is* Mexico and (as many *norteamericanos* and other guide books are reluctant to admit) it is *also* the United States in its rawest, most bleakly industrial sense. It's hard to know which of the two largest industries which created this Mexican border city the U.S. should feel prouder of—the tons of day-glo tourist garbage that adorns hundreds of market stalls along Av. Revolución or the thousands of stinking pools of day-glo factory waste that adorn the streets and backyards of the over 2 million people (and 500,000 stray dogs) who call Tijuana home. Sound appealing? Prepare yourself. It's hard to say whether it's the city's certain raunchy charm, its cheap beer, or a perverse celebration of *yanqui imperialismo* which attracts tourists like flies. No matter what the reason, however, no one can leave the same as they came—especially if they take an educational detour from the well-worn tourist paths and into the labyrinthine streets of the *colonia* shantytowns which spread out from the city's center.

Banners boldly proclaim Avenida Revolución the "Most Visited Street in the World," and when you see the crowds, you'll find that boast easy to swallow. If shopping for that which is small and purely ornamental is your passion, Tijuana is your long-lost homeland. There are enough black-velvet portraits of Jesus and Elvis for sale here to start your own gallery back home. Don't despair, however, authenticity (or near authenticity) can be found, but it is often slightly pricier than the flourescent striped sarapes—check the smaller stalls on the side streets off Av. Revolución. As for nightlife, what you see is what you get: every weekend, swarms of Berkeley types join U.S. Marines stationed in San Diego and abandon themselves to the pulsating waves of music at the numerous flashy discos, drowning their PC woes and military consciences in drink and dancing till dawn.

If you feel that Tijuana is good at what it's famous for, there's a reason—it's been the United States' number one cheap vacation and party-zone (rivalling, significantly enough, Havanna for that title) every since prohibition in the 1920s. First settled by the Cochimie, Tijuana made it onto the map in 1829, when Don Santiago Argüello received the title to the Rancho de Tía Juana (Aunt Jane's Ranch). After the 1848 Mexican-American War, the ranch became the new border, and its name was amalgamated. Since World War II, industry has changed the desert horizon, attracting over 1 million people in the past ten years—whole towns from Southern Mexico and still more hopefuls from D.F.'s own destitute slums. Other Mexicans come here to study at the Ibero-American University, one of the finest in northern Mexico or to buy discounted foreign goods.

Despite the common North American perception that Tijuana is simply a springboard for undocumented emigration to the States, many Mexicans have no desire to risk being shot by border patrol or xenophobic right-wing San Diegans and have come simply to work. Still, you may see a poetic irony and a metaphor for economic and political power relations in the two crowds that line up to cross the border every evening at dusk. North American partiers cross confidently, smugly assured of their right, documentation in hand. Stand at the border, off the highway, at this time and you will see the other crossing. Except for the few Mexicans with enough in the bank to assure the U.S. that they will return, most run as *pollitos* (in the absence of a river, Tijuana's name for *mojados*—the wetbacks of El Paso/Juárez), sometimes paying *coyotes* hundreds to safely carry them across.

Warnings: as at all border towns, crime is rampant and can surface in surprising ways. Above all, do not attempt to carry drugs across the border as the German shepherds will not be amused. Indeed, don't even think of buying or using in Mexico—although notoriously cheaper and more lax than the U.S., Mexico also loves a rich American bribe against the threat of a night in the Tijuana jail. If you are a resident alien of the United States or simply have a Latino surname you may receive a lot of hassling from immigration upon your return. This is a deplorable result of racism and you must make up your own mind as to how to react. The most pragmatic manner is to answer as straighforwardly as possible any questions the border patrol might ask (they have been known to ask things such as "who won the Civil War" and other "prove-it" puzzles).

ORIENTATION AND PRACTICAL INFORMATION

Getting to Tijuana from San Diego is easy: take the **San Diego Trolley** marked "San Ysidro" from downtown (US$1.75), or park and join it anywhere along its south-bound route. It lets you off right at the border. Long customs inspection lines when returning can be a hassle on busy days. Bring proper ID for readmission to the U.S. Kindly leave any fruits, vegetables and firearms behind. Driving across the border may seem appealing at first, but the hassles of obtaining Mexican insurance, not to mention parking, make this a bad idea for a day trip. You must buy insurance—or face the possibility of having your car confiscated in the event of an accident. It's a much better idea to leave your car in a parking lot on the U.S. side and join the throngs of people walking across. Parking rates start at US$3 per day and increase closer to the international line.

If you arrive at the central **bus station,** avoid the cab drivers' high rates and head for the public bus (1.10 pesos). When you exit the terminal, just turn to your left, walk to the end of the building and hop a bus marked "Centro Linea." After a half-hour ride, it will let you off on **Calle 3** and any of the central Avenidas, most notably **Revolución**. *Calles* run east-west in sequential numerical order; *avenidas* run north-south.

Tourist Office: Av. Revolución y Calle 1 (tel. 88-05-55). English-speaking staff can help you find any store or bar you desire. Open Sun.-Thurs. 9am-7pm, Fri.-Sat. 9am-9pm.

State Attorney for the Protection of the Tourist: Jesús Montañez Roman and staff take seriously any problems tourists may encounter. Don't hesitate. Same address as tourist office (above). Answering machine operates after hours.

Customs Office: At the international border (tel. 83-13-90).

Consulates: U.S., Tapachula Sur 96 (tel. 81-74-00), in Col. Hipódromo, adjacent to the Agua Caliente racetrack southeast of town. Open Mon.-Fri. 8am-4:30pm. **Canada,** German Gedovius 5-202 (tel. 84-04-61), Zona del Rio.

Currency Exchange: Banks along Constitución change at the same rate. **Bánamex,** at Calle 4 open Mon.-Fri. 9am-5pm. *Casas de cambio* abound and offer better rates.

Post Office: Negrete at Calle 11 (tel. 84-79-50). *Lista de Correos.* Open Mon.-Fri. 8am-7pm, Sat.-Sun. 9am-1pm. **Postal code:** 22000.

Telephones: Farmacia Mayo, Calle 1 and Mutualismo (tel. 85-97-07). No collect calls. Local calls .50 pesos. Open daily 8am-midnight. Street pay phones are unreliable and operators are few and far between. Long distance is cheaper from the U.S. **Telephone code:** 66.

Telegrams: To the right of the post office. Open Mon.-Fri. 8am-5:30pm, Sat.-Sun. 8am-1pm.

Bus Station: (Tel. 26-11-46). Tijuana is a major transportation hub so buses leave frequently from huge terminal. Served by **Transportes Norte de Sonora** with buses to: Mexico City (271 pesos), Guadalajara (218 pesos), Mazatlán (173 pesos) and all points in between. **Auto Transportes de Baja California** specializes in Baja routes. To: Ensenada (15 pesos), Guerrero Negro (82 pesos), and La Paz (168 pesos). Other carriers include **Transportes del Pacífico, Tres Estrellas de Oro** and **Greyhound** (to San Diego US$4 and points as far as Yakima, WA US$195). Greyhound also leaves San Ysidro from the station one block past the end of the trolley line (LA US$12). **Mini-buses** to Rosarito (3 pesos) leave from Madero and Calle 1 in front of Farmacia Long's TJ.

Car Insurance: If you'll be driving in Mexico, spend US$5 per day in San Ysidro to get insurance. There are several drive-through insurance vendors just before the border at Sycamore and Primero who distribute a free booklet with maps and travel tips. (For more details, see Baja California: Getting Around: By Land.)

Red Cross: In an emergency dial 132.

Pharmacy: Farmacia Mayo, Calle 1 at Mutualismo (tel. 85-09-22). Open daily 8am-midnight.

Hospital: Hospital General, Av. Padre Kino, *Zona Río* (tel. 84-09-22).

Police: Constitución at Calle 8. In case of emergency dial 134. For other matters, dial 89-05-15. There's always a bilingual officer at the station.

ACCOMMODATIONS

Tijuana's budget hotels are trapped in the vortex of the town, off Revolución and Calle 1. Prices are monstrous by Mexican standards, and hotels offer little in the luxury department. There's no escaping the blaring music and blaring drinkers since most places are near or above the local *cantinas*. Hotels fill up quickly on weekends, so make reservations and expect to dish out extra *dinero*.

Hotel El Jalisciense, Calle 1 #1715 (tel. 85-34-91), between Niños Héroes and Martínez. Has all the necessities for a romantic evening: soft couches in the hall, large wood paddles on the keys, and *agua purificada* for after a workout. Bedrooms with private bath drenched in pink. Single 50 pesos. Doubles 60 pesos.

Hotel La Posada, Calle 1 #1956 (tel. 85-54-33), across from the tourist office. Cave-like entrance on the street leads back to numerous rooms. Tiny rooms have comfortable beds and hot water, but bed time could be a struggle since the hotel is flanked by two *cantinas*. Singles 45 pesos. Doubles 60 pesos.

Hotel Perla de Occidente, Mutualismo 528 (tel. 85-13-58), between Calles 1 and 2. The healthy hike from the center of "action" makes this a haven from bounding noise. Friendly staff will allow you to see a number of comfortable rooms with a variety of different features. Immaculate private baths. Singles 50 pesos. Triples 70 pesos.

Hotel Las Palmas, Calle 1 #1637, between Mutualismo and Martínez. The cheapest spot around serves up about what you pay out. Freshly made beds and clean towels included. Communal bathrooms located around the central jungle/garden. Singles and doubles 30 pesos.

Motel Díaz, Revolución 375 (tel. 85-71-48), next to Hotel Plaza de Oro. Welcome to CandyLand—a playful pastel color scheme and fresh mint-green doors. Impressive matching bedspreads and curtains. Singles 75 pesos. Doubles 110 pesos.

FOOD

The less expensive *típico* restaurants line Constitución and streets leading from glitzy Revolución to Constitución. Taco vendors set up their carts and stands along Calle 1. Tasty tacos (3 for US$1) can be scarfed while standing in the midday sun. Deep fried *churros*, a heart-stopping snack, cost 1.50 pesos. As always, use your head when choosing what to eat; some vendors are not scrupulous about how long they hold on to stock. If you'd rather not gamble with your health on the street, bar munchies are cheap, filling and generally fresh. Almost all of the *gringo* franchise eateries, including Jack-in-the-Box and Denny's, are conspicuously located on Revolución. Big-name joints serve the same *antojitos* as the small guys at inflated prices.

Los Panchos Taco Shop, Revolución at Calle 3 (tel. 85-72-77). Orange plastic booths are packed with hungry locals chowing on cheap Mexican favorites. Tortillas freshly rolled on the premises. Breakfast served too. *Quesadillas* US$1.50, *tortas* US$2.85 and 2 eggs with ham US$2.50. Open daily 8am-midnight.

Restaurant Nelson, Revolución and Calle 1 (tel. 85-67-50), under Hotel Nelson. Smack in the center of action with enough windows to get a view of it all. Filling meals served up on country-heart place mats. Burger with fries 6.50 pesos, beef *tostadas* 10 pesos, hot cakes with ham 7.50 pesos. Open daily 7am-11pm.

Chico Pollo, Niños Héroes and Calle 1. May seem like another club by a blaring Mexican disco, but in fact it's an open-air restaurant. As the name implies, they specialize in roasted chicken. Whole bird with rice, beans, salad and tortillas 16 pesos. ¼ chicken with all the above 5 pesos. Open daily 9am-9pm.

El Pipirin Antojitos, Constitución between Calles 2 and 3 (tel. 88-16-02). Load up your tacos with a counterful of condiments. Seating under the orange arches and easy street service too. *Flautas gigantes* 7 pesos, *super quesadilla* 12 pesos. Open daily 9am-10pm.

Tía Juana Tilly's, at Revolución and Calle 7, buttressing the Jai Alai Palace. The original and vaguely legendary; black and white photos on the walls tell the story how the bar—now with the restaurant, dance floor and outside patio—has been generating high-action, high-price atmosphere since 1947. All national drinks US$3, beer US$1.75. Bring a healthy appetite for all-you-can-eat tacos (US$5) Fri.-Sun. 11am-4pm. Bar entices Fri.-Sun. 6pm-close with national drinks US$1. Dancing starts around 9pm.

ENTERTAINMENT

Fun in TJ revolves around clubs or money and its concomitant vices—shopping, drinking and gambling. For mild, inexpensive diversion, try snacking and people-watching while strolling down **Revolución.** When your feet get tired, relax in **Teniente Guerrero Park,** Avenidas F and G, off Díaz Mirón. It's one of the more pleasant parts of Tijuana and only a few blocks from Revolución. Tijuana is also a great place to get your car re-upholstered—really. Animal lovers should avert their eyes from the donkeys painted as zebras, adorned with gaudy sombreros and used as picture backdrops.

The cultish game of **jai-alai** is played every night at 8pm in the **Frontón Palacio,** Revolución at Calle 7, a building decorated more like a palace than a sports center. Two two-player teams use arm-baskets to catch and throw a Brazilian ball of rubber and yarn encased in goatskin at speeds reaching 180 mph. All employees are bilingual, and the gambling is carried out in greenbacks. Seating costs from US$3-15, depending on view. Games every night but Wednesday, 8pm-1:30am.

More betting can be done at **Agua Caliente Racetrack** (tel. 81-78-11), also called the **Hipódromo**. Enormous crowds pack the stands for both greyhound and horse racing. (Races daily 7:45pm and 11pm, plus Mon., Wed., Fri.-Sun. 2pm and 5pm.) The track's enclosed **Turf Club** (tel. 86-39-48) has comfortable seating and a restaurant; grandstand admission (nearly 11,000 seats) is free.

Tijuana has two bullrings, **El Toreo de Tijuana,** downtown, and **Plaza Monumental,** 3km east on Agua Caliente. The former presents *corridas* (bullfights) on chosen Sundays at 4pm from early May to late September; the latter is more modern, employs famous *matadores* and hosts fights from early August to mid-September. Tickets are sometimes sold at a booth on Revolución, between Calles 3 and 4 (tel. 85-22-10), but always at the gate. Admission ranges from US$5-22, depending on the seat.

When you finally get tired of all these sports, the **Tijuana Centro Cultural,** on Paseo de los Héroes at Mina (tel. 84-11-11), awaits as "your window to all of Mexico." The architecture alone is reason enough to visit. The center includes the **Space Theater,** a 180-degree giant screen auditorium that shows a film on Mexican culture and history, *People of the Sun*, daily at 2pm (US$4.50). The museum continues the education in Mexican tradition with an impressive chronological and geographical exhibition of Mexico. (Open daily 11am-7pm. Admission US$1, free with movie admission.) A performance center (**Sala de Espectáculos**) and open-air theater (**Caracol al Aire Libre**) host visiting cultural attractions, including the **Ballet Folklórico,** *mariachis*, and various drama performances.

All of this is fine and dandy but if you're here to party, a brief stroll down Revolución at dusk will get you bombarded by thumping music and abrasive club promoters all hawking basically the same thing (2-for-1 margaritas, starting from an inflated price). Although a few sleazy strip joints stud the strand, most clubs scream out for old-fashioned boozin' and *bailando*, and they get it. All Tijuana clubs check IDs (18 plus), with varying criteria for what's acceptable.

Freeday, Revolución 605 (tel. 80-27-05) at Calle 2. With a small dance floor and rock music, this club stands mostly as a place for drinking. From Sun.-Thurs. beer (US$0.99) and 2-for-1 national drinks (US$2.50). No cover. Open Sun.-Thurs. noon-2am, Fri.-Sat. noon-4am. Credit cards accepted.

Tequila Sunrise, Revolución 918 (tel. 88-37-13). An enormous 2-story monster, with terrace and sand-filled volleyball court. Plenty of disco strutting. No promotions. US$2 cover Fri.-Sun. Beer US$1.55. Open Mon.-Thurs. 5pm-2am, Fri.-Sun. 11am-2am.

Tilly's 5th Avenue, Revolución and Calle 5 (tel. 85-72-45). Wooden dance floor in the center resembles a boxing ring, and C&C Music Factory and Marky Mark pump from the speakers. Beer US$1.75, margaritas US$3. Cover Fri.-Sat. US$5. Open Mon.-Thurs. 11am-2am, Fri.-Sun. 11am-4am.

Scandal, Revolución at Calle 6 (tel. 85-82-15). Slamming music in a completely metallic room that resembles the trash compactor from *Star Wars*. Tropical drinks (US$2.50) come 2-for-1. Open Sun.-Thurs. 1:30pm-midnight, Fri.-Sat. 1:30pm-3am.

Margarita's Village, Revolución at Calle 3 (tel. 85-73-62). Forget dancing—drinking is the favorite pastime here. All mixed drinks 2-for-1 and never a cover. Open Sun.-Thurs. 10am-2am, Fri.-Sat. 10am-3am.

■■■ ROSARITO

This town is a string of hotels, restaurants and shops that line the toll-free Route 1 about 27km south of Tijuana. Now growing into a happening time-share spot, Rosarito evolved from ranches owned by the well-endowed Machaca family. It can be a quiet, laid-back place to relax during the weekdays, but it's close enough to the border that come Friday, the Californians descend with the sole intention of escaping to drunken revelry. Sand beaches and cool sea breezes welcome those escaping from the concrete mayhem of the noisy northern neighbor.

Practical Information Everything in Rosarito is on the main street, **Boulevard Juárez,** which is a section of the generally north-south highway. Street numbers are non-sequential; almost everything listed is near the purple Ortega's Restaurant in Oceana Plaza.

To get to Rosarito from Tijuana, board a **mini-bus** (3 pesos) in front of Farmacia Long's TJ at Calle 1 and Negrete, two blocks toward the border from the tourist office. Yellow *taxis de ruta* (3 pesos per person, extra for baggage) leave from Madero between Calles 5 and 6; they guarantee snug seating and make the trip 15 minutes faster than the buses. To return back to Tijuana, once again the surest way is a *taxi de ruta*, which can be flagged down along Juárez or taken from the starting point in front of the Rosarito Beach Hotel. Getting to Ensenada is more of an adventure, because you're at the mercy of buses passing by the Rosarito toll booth (*caseta de cobro*) on Route 1. To get there, take a regular taxi to the *caseta de cobro* (1.50 pesos). Buses pass by frequently (about every ½hr.) but with standing room only (15 pesos).

The **tourist office,** on Juárez at Acacias (tel. 2-02-00), has all the brochures you'll need and lawyers for the protection of tourists. (Open Mon.-Sat. 9am-7pm, Sun. 10am-6pm.) **Bánamex,** Juárez at Cipres (tel. 2-15-56), exchanges currency Mon.-Fri. from 9am-1pm. On weekends, you'll have to go to a *casa de cambio*, which charges a commission. The **post office** is on Acacias (tel. 2-13-55) directly behind the tourist office. (Open Mon.-Fri. 9am-1pm and 3-6pm, Sat. 9am-1pm.) The **postal code** is 22710. **Farmacia Hidalgo,** on Juárez at Acacias (tel. 2-05-57), offers long distance service (no collect calls) daily from 10am-10pm. The **telephone code** is 661. One door down on Juárez, **Lavamática Moderna** (wash 4 pesos, dry 1 peso) is open Mon.-Sat. 8am-8pm and Sun. 9am-6pm. **Calimax Supermarket,** at the north end of Juárez next to Quinta del Mar Resort (tel. 2-15-69) is open daily 7am-10pm. For the **Red Cross,** dial 132. The **police** are located next to the tourist office (tel. 2-11-21); in an **emergency,** dial 134.

Accommodations and Food Nice, cheap accommodations don't exist in Rosarito; even the budget spots sap the wallet. **Rosarito Beach Rental Cabins,** on Lázaro Cárdenas, provide the cheapest beds in the area though the management may be hard to find. Small cabins house cubicle rooms with bunk beds and half baths. Its location, the dirt road on the corner behind Calimax, two blocks from the ocean, is easily identified by the Disney castle spires. (Singles without bath US$5, with shower US$10. Doubles without bath US$8, with shower US$12; US$38 per week.) Three blocks inland from Juárez on the same street is the **Hotel Palmas Quintero** (tel. 2-13-59). Family couch in the clean, large rooms can sleep an extra person. (Singles and doubles US$20.) **Hotel Villanueva,** on Juárez 97 (tel. 2-00-54) across from the tourist office, offers less quality but an excellent location close to the beaches and bar. (Singles and doubles US$17.)

Food is one of Rosarito's strengths, with fresh produce from the fields just south and seafood caught in the bountiful seas. For an economical seafood dinner, go to **Vince's Restaurant,** on Juárez (tel. 2-12-53) next to Hotel Villanueva. Toast the succulent lobster (25 pesos) and shrimp cocktail (15 pesos) with a good stiff drink. The casual atmosphere is enhanced by sturdy plastic plates and vacationers in swimwear. (Open daily 8am-10pm.) Fresh Mexican tacos and the like are served up with spicy salsa in the midday heat at **Tacos Sonora,** on Juárez 306. Fish tacos or *quesadillas* 3 pesos. (Open Mon.-Fri. 7am-10pm, Sat.-Sun. 7am-noon.) Sit down to a staggeringly cheap breakfast (Mon.-Fri. 7am-noon) at **Ortega's Ocean Plaza,** Juárez 1001 in an offensive purple building. A variety of dishes, including cactus omelette (US$1.99) and an all-you-can-eat Mexican buffet (Sat.-Sun. 8am-1pm, US$3.95). Restaurant open Sun.-Thurs. 7am-10pm, Fri.-Sat. 7am-11pm.

Entertainment People don't come to Rosarito to change the world. They come to dance and drink. They live the dream at **Papas and Beer** (tel. 2-04-44), one block north of the Rosarito Beach Hotel and two blocks toward the sea on Calle de Nogal. Open-air dance floor, bar and sand volleyball court are packed and writhing on weekends. Beer is 7 pesos and mixed drinks 9-15 pesos. Cover charge US$4 on Saturday and Sunday. If you're going to drink, the trick is to buy a 40oz. Corona at a liquor store (US$1) and drink it beforehand. (Open daily noon-3am.) Even the most gray-haired will be carded for the 18-year age requirement.

For those who have somehow misplanned their trip and are stuck in Rosarito beyond the weekend, the Rosarito Beach Hotel hosts, unintentionally, great *gringo*-watching. They also have a large-screen cable TV in their lobby. For cheap curios and Guatemalan backpacks, avoid street shops and bargain at the open air market behind Tacos Sonora. Plenty of selection at flexible prices.

■■■ MEXICALI

A couple clubs, a couple restaurants, and the train south. Border town Mexicali is a bulky industrial brute, disinclined to welcome tourists. Unless you have a definite reason to come here, stay away. Mexicali supports a few good restaurants and some active nightspots, but chances are you'll be bored out of your gourd within a few hours. For one brief annual moment in mid-October, during Mexicali's **Fiesta del Sol,** bands, skits, a parade and countless street vendors entertain the crowds.

Practical Information Far from the ordinary route between the U.S. and Mexico, Mexicali can still serve as a jumping-off point for travelers heading south; a train runs via Mazatlán to Guadalajara and Mexico City. The city lies on the California border 189km inland from Tijuana, with Calexico and the Imperial Valley immediately to the north. Because of its valley location, it suffers extreme temperatures; the winter months are chilly, and *normal* summer temperatures are 38-43°C (100-110°F).

Both the bus and train stations are near the intersection of **Mateos,** the main boulevard leading away from the border, and **Independencia,** about 4km south of the border. **Autotransportes de Baja California** buses flee to Tijuana (every hr., 24 pesos) and Ensenada (40 pesos). **Transportes Norte de Sonora** covers routes on the mainland south to Mexico City (265 pesos), Hermosillo (68 pesos) and Mazatlán (163 pesos). **Tres Estrellas de Oro** goes the same places with slightly higher rates. **Golden State** has four buses per day directly to Los Angeles (US$27). To get to the border, take the urban bus marked "Centro" (1.10 pesos) outside the bus terminal, just across the foot bridge. Ride past the mammoth new mall to downtown, then walk down Mateos until the border crossing. **Tourist cards** are readily available at the Federal Immigration office *en la línea* (at the border).

Two **trains** leave daily—the *estrella* (fast) is air-conditioned, serves food and, theoretically, goes twice as fast as the grubby *burro* (slow). *Estrella* leaves daily and promptly sometime in the morning (10-ish) and goes as far as Guadalajara, stopping at major cities; tickets are on sale only from 9am-noon. The *estrella* is often booked far in advance. The *burro*, on the other hand, only sells tickets on the day of departure (5:30-9pm), so tickets are usually available. It departs in the late evening and tools along at 50km/hr. The only difference between the first and the second class on the *burro* is that the first-class tickets have assigned seats. To get to the **train station**, turn off Mateos opposite Denny's onto Ferrocarrilero. Take the first right and it's on the right. To Guadalajara US$75 *estrella,* US$17 *burro.*

Tourist information is available at **El Comité de Turismo y Convenciones** (tel. 57-23-76), at Mateos and Compresora 3km from the border. (Open Mon.-Fri. 8:30am-6pm.) **Currency** can be exchanged in any of the banks along Madero. (Open Mon.-Fri. 9am-1:30pm). The **post office,** at Madero 491, is open Mon.-Fri. 8am-6pm, Sat. 8am-3pm and posts a Lista de Correos daily. The **postal code** is 21101. **Telegrams** are in the same building. (Open Mon.-Fri. 8am-4pm, Sat. 8am-1pm.) **LATADEL** magic international telephones are dispersed throughout the city; one is in the post office and one is in front of Hotel Imperial. The **telephone code** is 65. **Farmacia Patty,** México and Obregón (tel. 57-75-38), is open 24 hrs. In a medical emergency, dial the **Red Cross** (tel. 132), and for other problems contact the **police** (tel. 134).

Accommodations and Food A night in Mexicali will cost you dearly. Alternatively, for about US$25 you can find excellent budget accommodations on the Calexico side of the border. Deep wooden panelling and dim chandelier give the eerie feeling that Elvis *does* live south of the border and here at **Hotel Plaza,** Madero 366 (tel. 52-97-57). Everything is kept tidy, but the TVs can be fuzzy. Range of rooms starting at 55 pesos for a single. Doubles 80 pesos. 24-hr. restaurant downstairs. **Hotel México,** Av. Lerdo 476 (tel. 54-06-69) boasts nondescript rooms in the middle of the *cantina* scene that supply cranking A/C and TV diversion. Sinks are conveniently placed in the middle of the bedrooms. Singles 60 pesos. Doubles 80 pesos. Think of your eventual destinations while at **Hotel Imperial,** Madero 222 (tel. 53-67-33). Don't worry about the unnaturally off-green towels and sink wobbling on 1 leg; just sit on the brown bed and blast the color TV. Noon check-out. Singles 75 pesos. Doubles 95 pesos. 5 peso key deposit.

With Mexicali's large Chinese population, you can count on every restaurant in the *centro*, including those with Mexican surnames, to offer big plates of chow mein and the like. **Café Yin Tun,** Morelos 379 (tel. 52-88-86), has good A/C and Christmas colors all year long. The *comida corrida* and pork chop suey each go for 12 pesos. (Open daily 9pm-midnight.) **Restaurant Buendía,** Altamirano 263 (tel. 52-69-25), specializes in Chinese cuisine, but chefs are happy to whip up authentic *antojitos* anytime. (8-vegetable stir-fry 14.50 pesos. Beef tacos or pork chops 9.50 pesos. Open daily 7am-9pm.) For a fast-food joint with quick service and plastic booths, try **Tortas de Charo,** on Mateos three blocks from the border. *Tortas*, any style, are 5 pesos. (Open daily 8am-9pm.)

You will notice there is no **entertainment** section.

■■■ SAN FELIPE

San Felipe's position on the map would seem to place it too far away from the action on the Pacific coast to be bothered with. The number of *gringo* RV parks lining the desert beaches (200 and counting) definitely shatters that myth. The town was christened San Felipe de Jesús in 1721 but was largely ignored due to its isolation from the western populace. One hundred years later, a U.S. firm began harvesting tons of seafood from the deserted shores of Bahía San Felipe. Finally, in the 1950s northern snowbirds claimed the desert resort as a regular hangout, bringing handfuls of greenbacks and a new industry—tourism—to the area. These sandy beaches have satisfied many a romantic evening.

The **malecón** follows the municipal beach in the center of town. It tends to be crowded and a bit untidy, but its location close to the markets and bars is key in the sweltering 100°F temperature. The *malecón* is also home to the local fishermen, who gladly take vacationers on fishing excursions near Isla San Felipe and the recently planted artificial reefs. Wooden motor-powered boats launch at about 7am for a half-day of angling and seal-watching near the rocks of the *isla* (US$25 per person). **Playa Punta Estrella,** 3km south of town, and **Playa Norte,** several blocks north of the center, offer some relief from the beach congestion and plenty of yellow sand. Take some time to visit the **Shrine of the Virgin Guadalupe** at the top of the *cerritos* near the lighthouse. After a scorching hike, you'll be rewarded with a spectacular view of San Felipe and the blue bay.

Practical Information Located 198km south of Mexicali, San Felipe is a lone town at the end of sizzling-hot Route 5. **Los arcos** are immediately recognizable when entering the village; **Chetumal** is the street continuing straight from the arches toward the sea. All tourist concerns, including hotels, restaurants, banks, etc., cluster on **Mar de Cortés,** one block form the beach. The new **bus terminal** is off on Mar Caribe, a 15-minute walk from the center of action. To get to the main drag from there, walk north on Mar Caribe to the first street, Manzanillo, then hang a right toward the blue water. The extremely helpful English-speaking staff at the **tourist office,** Mar de Cortés at Manzanillo (tel. 7-11-55), knows tons about the town and surrounding areas, and is a **tourist protection center.** (Open Mon.-Fri. 8am-7pm, Sat. 9am-3pm, Sun. 10am-2pm.) **Bancomer,** Mar de Cortés Nte. near Rockodile Bar (tel. 7-10-90) **exchanges currency** from 9am-11pm. The **post office** is on Mar Blanco between Chetumal and Ensenada (tel. 7-13-30), 4 blocks inland from Cortés. (Open Mon.-Fri. 9am-3pm, Sat. 9am-1pm. **Postal code:** 21850.) **Telegrams** can be sent from the office on Mar Bermejo between Peurto Peñasco and Zihunatejo (tel. 7-11-12) in a yellow building. (Open Mon.-Fri. 8am-2pm.) The **Farmacia San Angelín,** Chetumal at Mar de Cortés (tel. 7-10-43), has *casetas* for **long distance calls.** (Open daily 9am-9:30pm. **Telephone code:** 657.) The **bus station** on Mar Caribe Sur (tel. 7-15-16) is served by **Autotransportes Baja California** and **Transportes Norte de Sonora,** which run daily buses to Ensenada (2 per day, 28 pesos) and Mexicali (4 per day, 22 pesos). Gas up at **PEMEX,** Mar Caribe Sur, next to the new bus terminal. Help available with the **Red Cross,** (tel. 7-15-44). In an emergency dial 132. **Farmacia San Angelín,** Mar de Cortés at Chetumal (tel. 7-10-43), is open daily 9am-9:30pm.For **medical services,** go to the **Clínica de S.S.A** on Mar Bermejo Sur (tel. 7-15-21), behind the **police station,** which is on Mar Blanco Sur (tel. 7-13-50), just south of Chetumal.

Accommodations There are two types of accommodations in San Felipe: those with walls and A/C, and those without. Travelers who prefer the former will end up paying *mucho dinero* for mediocre rooms. A number of independently-owned hotels fill San Felipe, the cheapest among them being **Motel El Pescador,** Mar de Cortés at Chetumal. This motor lodging crammed in between the curio shops has icy A/C and private bathrooms. (Singles 80 pesos. Doubles 100 pesos.) The other cheap option is to rent a room in a private residence. **Casa Morada,** on Manzanillo one block behind the tourist office, is easily located by its purple facade. Cluttered with garage-sale-type furniture, the house offers complete use of kitchen and dining room. Inquire within for Jose. (1 bed with A/C US$20, 2 beds with A/C and bath US$30.)

As any Californian with an RV can tell you, San Felipe is well-known for its trailer parks. The most famous and least seasonal is **Ruben's,** out toward the end of Av. Golfo de California in Playa Norte (tel. 7-14-42). Individual parking spaces are topped with two-story open-air bungalows. Spots easily accommodate a simple car-load of folks with sleeping bags or RVs that need full hook-ups. (US$15 per vehicle, up to two people, US$20 beachfront, US$2 for every extra person.) Smack in the middle of town on Mar de Cortés, **Campo San Felipe** (tel. 7-10-12) lures campers with the fabulous beachfront location and groomed, desert garden entrance. Thatched-roof overhangs shelter each fully-loaded trailer slip. (Spaces go for US$11-16.)

Food and Entertainment Mar de Cortés is crammed with a variety of restaurants advertising air-conditioned relief from the blistering heat. Just one block over along the *malecón*, *ostionerías* and fish *taquerías* serve up fresh seafood, hot sauces and crackers for fewer clams. **Restaurant Ruben's,** at Ruben's campground (tel. 7-14-42), is a natural prodigy of its parent's success. The sheer turnover of *norteamericanos* guarantees hot, fresh meals anytime of the day. Shrimp and steak kabob 16 pesos, *antojitos* 13 pesos. (Open daily 7am-11pm.) A less touristed eatery in the center on Mar de Cortés at Acapulco is **Restaurant Petunia.** Vinyl booths and slick plastic placemats add to the homey decor. Scrumptious burritos 12 pesos. Roast beef with guacamole 18 pesos, a whole fried fish 12.50 pesos. (Open daily 7:30am-10pm.)

Restaurant/bars for the weekend warriors in San Felipe abound up and down the main drag. The seasoned veterans nurse drinks all day long at **Bar Miramar,** Mar de Cortés 315 (tel. 7-11-92). The place looks like a *cantina* from the 60s, but the patrons come for company, not glitz. (Beer US$1.25, margaritas US$2. Open daily 10am-2am.) Younger folks usually head a few doors down to **Rockodile,** on the *malecón* at Acapulco (tel. 7-12-19). The new kid on the block tries to imitate the phenomenon of its sister restaurants/bars/discos on the west coast with fluorescent paint, a weirdo name and plenty of t-shirts and caps. (Happy hour daily 10am-4pm and all day Wed. Otherwise beer US$2, jumbo piña colada US$2.75. Open daily 10am-2am. Closed Mon.-Thurs. in winter.)

■■■ ENSENADA

The secret is out—beachless Ensenada is fast becoming the top weekend hot spot south of the border. The masses of Californians that arrive every Friday night have *gringo*-ized the town to an extreme degree; everyone speaks English, down to salespeople pitching tacos, and the store clerks need calculators if you try to buy something with pesos. Still, Ensenada is less brash than its insatiable cousin to the north, and becomes quite pleasant Monday morning when the *gringos* go home and the cool sea breeze kicks in.

The drive from Tijuana to Ensenada is beautiful if you take the Ensenada Cuota (toll road), which costs 7 pesos. The *libre* (free road) is atrocious, poorly maintained, dangerous and about as scenic as a municipal garbage dump. Along the toll road you'll enjoy sparkling ocean vistas, large sand dunes, stark cliffs, and broad mesas. Drive in the right lane only; the left is strictly for passing and the law is enforced. Also, drive only in daytime as there are no streetlights.

Orientation and Practical Information Ensenada is 108km south of Tijuana on Route 1. **Buses** from Tijuana arrive at the main terminal, at Calle 11 and Riveroll, every half hour 7am-10pm and every hour 11pm-1am. Turn right as you come out the door of the bus station (tel. 8-67-70) and 10 blocks will take you to **Mateos** (also called First), the main tourist drag. Five blocks to the left along Mateos you'll find inexpensive motels. **Juárez** (Calle 5) runs parallel to Mateos, while **Espinoza** is perpendicular. The **tourist office,** at Blvd. Castero and Gatelum (tel. 8-24-11) dispenses brochures from expensive hotels, some town maps, and Baja travel material. (Open Mon.-Fri. 9am-7pm, Sat.-Sun. 9am-2pm.) The **Chamber of Commerce,** Mateos 693 (tel. 8-37-70), at Macheros, is closer to the center of town, with brochures, city maps and more helpful English-speaking staff. (Open Mon.-Fri. 8:30am-2pm and 4-6:30pm.) The **customs office** is on Reyersow 1 block up from Uribe (tel. 4-08-97). (Open Mon.-Fri. 8am-3pm.) Banks clump along Av. Juárez, for **currency exchange,** but few will exchange traveler's checks. **Bancomer,** on Juárez at Ruíz (tel. 8-11-08), is the best choice. All open Mon.-Fri. 9am-1:30pm. **Casas de cambio** all over but charge hefty commission and are closed Sun. The **post office** is on Mateos at Floresta (tel. 6-10-88), 1 block past the *arroyo*. (*Lista de Correos*. Open Mon.-Fri. 8am-7pm, Sat.-Sun. 9am-1pm. **Postal code:** 22800.) 2 types of **phones** line Juárez and Mateos. Orange are touchtone and have operator assistance (collect calls 09). Gray phones only accept pesos or credit cards, allowing direct international calling. **Telephone code:** 617. **Blanca,** Cortés at Reforma (tel. 6-26-48) is a frighteningly large laundromat. Hike out Mateos 8 blocks past the *arroyo* to Soto, then turn left, and go a few more blocks to the Limón shopping center. For medical care, contact the **Red Cross,** on Blvd. de Jesús Clark at Flores (tel. 4-45-85). In an **emergency,** dial 132. **Farmacia Del Sol,** Cortés at Reforma (tel. 6-37-75), in the Limón shopping center, is open 24 hrs. **Hospital General,** Carretera Transpeninsular km111 (tel. 6-78-00), is also open 24 hrs. **Police** are available at Calle 9 at Espinoza (tel. 6-24-25).

Accommodations The rooms in Ensenada are expensive when compared to points farther south, but they include ample features that the cheaper spots lack. Leftover motor hotels from the '60s boast the works in each room (kitchens, couches, etc.). Economical hotels line Mateos between Espinoza and Riveroll, while luxury lodgings are on the water closer to the center of town. Most rooms lie about a 20-minute hike from the beaches and a good 10 minutes from the club scene. Although most owners quote prices in greenbacks, they also accept the national currency. **Motel Coronado,** Mateos at the *arroyo* (tel. 6-14-16). Homely yellow facade welcomes guests to humongous rooms that reach back to the good ol' days when value equalled size. (Singles 50 pesos. Doubles 70 pesos.) **Motel Pancho,** Alvarado at Calle 2 (tel. 8-23-44), 1 block off Mateos, has big rooms with yellow walls and beds with ultra-thin white sheets. Huge, clean bathrooms. Closest location to the bar scene. Wooden bed stands are marked by all of those who spent a cheap night before you. Clean, large bathrooms. (Singles US$17. Doubles US$25.) **Hotel Rosita,** Gastelum between Calles 3 and 4 (tel. 8-16-25) is also close to the bars. The rooms are dark and have holes in the floor, but what is important is that the beds hold people and the toilet flushes. (Single (for 1 or 2 people) 20 pesos with communal bath, 30 pesos with private bath. Doubles 35 pesos with bath and 2 or 3 people.)

Food The cheapest restaurants are along Juárez and Espinoza; those on Mateos and near the water jazz up the surroundings and prices for *los turistas*. At **Asadero Chispa,** on Mateos, at Guadalupe, fresh condiments crowding the counter top the tastiest grilled tacos in Baja California. Seats are rarely found at lunchtime. Scrumptious burritos made with whole beans and beef strips on one-ft.-wide tortillas, 9 pesos. Tacos 3.50 pesos. (Open Tues.-Sun.11am-11pm.) **Cafetería Monique Colonial,** Calle 9 and Espinoza (tel. 6-40-41), is popular with locals for its cheap, middle-of-the-line food. Fish filet 16 pesos, steak 17 pesos, yogurt with granola 9 pesos. (Open Mon.-Sat. 6am-10pm, Sun. 6am-3pm.) Add to the hundreds of business cards that fill the walls of **Restaurant Corralito,** Mateos 627 (tel. 8-23-70). White wrought-iron pushcart in center overflows with salad and sauces. Variety of *tortas* 6 pesos, create-your-own Mexican combo 15 pesos, *licuados* 7 pesos. (Open 24 hrs.) Chefs at **Las Parrillas,** Espinoza at Calle 6 (tel. 6-17-28), grill up fresh meat cutlets on the flaming pit as locals watch in anticipation. Squeeze onto a counter stool and prepare yourself for *super antojitos*. Tacos or tostadas 3 pesos and juicy double burger 10 pesos. (Open daily 8am-11:45pm.)

Sights and Entertainment Seeing Ensenada requires more than a quick cruise down Mateos. Climb the **Chapultepec Hills** for a view of the entire city. The steep road leading to the top of the hill begins at the foot of Calle 2. Any number of dirt paths also wind over the nearby hills, which afford a pleasant ocean view. Watch out for broken glass and pack sunscreen and refreshments.

The English-language *Baja Times* is full of bureaucratic propaganda and upcoming event announcements. Enormous quantities of curios are for sale along **Mateos** and **Blvd. Costero;** people spend days in these stores. Also on Costero, known to the locals simply as Boulevard, shuffle through piles of fresh fish and buckets of shellfish, and dine at one of the fish taco stands.

The mild, dry climate of Northern Baja's Pacific coast has made it Mexico's prime grape-growing area. **Bodegas de Santo Tomás,** Miramar 66 (tel. 67-82-509) has produced wine since 1888. Today, they distill over 500,000 cases of wine every year, including rosé and champagne. Tours (US$2) are conducted thrice daily, complete with complimentary wine tasting and an assortment of breads and cheeses.

Most of the popular hangouts along Mateos are members of that common hybrid species, the restaurant/bar/disco. In most, food and drink are served only until 8pm or so, when they turn into full-fledged dance clubs. On the weekends, almost every place has a good number of *norteamericanos* and locals in the festive mood, but during the week only the most popular thrive.

Better known than Ensenada itself is **Hussong's Cantina,** on Ruíz between Mateos and Calle 2 (tel. 8-32-10). It strives to offer all the authentic features of the traditional Mexican watering-hole. (Beer 5 pesos, tequila 10 pesos.) When you tire of the pencil drawings and continuous stream of *mariachi* musicians, cross the street to **Papas and Beer** (tel. 4-01-45). This high-tech music emporium is more popular with the twentysomething crowd, who swill huge margaritas (10 pesos) and spend corresponding amounts of cash. Every Thursday night has a theme with plenty of dancing after 10pm. Cover is US$5 Thursday through Saturday if you arrive after 9pm. (Open daily noon-3am.)

■ Near Ensenada

Since the town's beaches suffer from their proximity to a major fishing port, visitors to Ensenada concentrate on shopping, eating and partying. About 11km north lies **Playa San Miguel.** About 8km to the south are **Playas Santa María** and **Estero.** All are sandy and clean, but the seething crowds might drive you over the edge. Farther south you'll find passable beaches; try **San Quintín,** two hours south of town by car. Locals make their way to the Bahía San Quintín for three reasons: the cool climate, the lack of tourists and the large clam population close to the **Molino Viejo,** near El Presidente 6km south of the city of San Quintín. **Rosario,** another modest beach town, lies 58km south of San Quintín on the Transpeninsular Highway.

La Bufadora, the largest geyser on the Pacific coast, is 30km south of Ensenada. On a good day, the "Blowhole" shoots water 40m into the air. Share the spectacle with the local sea lions. **Agua Caliente** hot springs are 35km east on Route 3. **San Carlos** hot springs, accessed by a dirt road 16km south of town, are not especially clean; both are hot.

BAJA CALIFORNIA SUR

■■■ GUERRERO NEGRO

Twenty degrees cooler than the bleak Desierto de Vizcaíno to the southeast, Guerrero Negro (Black Warrior) will earn a soft spot in the hearts of heat-weary northbound travelers who don't mind wind and lots of gray. Situated about halfway between Tijuana and La Paz, Guerrero Negro is the place to spend a cool night if you'd like to break up the killer 25 hour trans-Baja bus trip. If you're heading south, stock up on cold drinks; several hundred miles of sweltering terrain await you.

Guerrero Negro was founded about 40 years ago, when a North American company began a salt export business. Some excitement is generated between December and early March, when thousands of gray whales make the annual 6000-mile swim from the Bering Sea to the lagoons here to reproduce.

Commune with the whales in the **Parque Natural de las Ballenas Grises,** on the **Laguna Ojo de Liebre,** formerly a deep-water port facility of the salt company.

In the early morning, whales swim right up to the docks, and during the rest of the day you can ascend a tall observation tower to view the 100-odd whales. No public transportation is available to the park. To get there head south on Rte. 1 toward Santa Rosalía for 8 to 15km. A sign points out the 30km dirt road to the *laguna*. Mario Rueda, the administrator of the park, sometimes leads whale-watching tours in early January and February.

For tours of about 10 people, get in touch with **Agencia de Viajes** on Carretera Transpeninsular near the Pemex (tel. 7-10-56, fax 7-07-88). Tours run US$30 per person, including transportation, snacks, a bilingual guide, and beers. (Open Mon.-Fri. 9am-1pm and 3-7pm, Sat. 9am-1pm.)

Unfortunately, when the whales leave for the summer, the pace in Guerrero Negro flatlines once again. Five motor lodges line the access road for those travelers in need of a bed in the middle of the long transpeninsular haul. Nothing special—rooms go for expensive rates, and no one accepts credit cards. The cheapest place in town, **Motel Las Dunas** (tel. 7-00-57), Carretera Transpeninsular below the water tank, has immaculate rooms comparable to more expensive spots. Warm, courteous staff helps in every way possible, but they can't shut down the noisy factory churning right outside your window. (Key deposit10 pesos . Singles 35 pesos, doubles 42 pesos.) To pay the price for color TV, move on to **Motel San Ignacio,** Carretera Transpeninsular, 200m north of the bus station; second floor rooms afford a view of the salt flats across the highway. (Singles 66 pesos, doubles 77 pesos.)

Many aspects of Guerrero Negro are difficult to swallow; its food is no exception. **Restaurant Bar Lupita,** on Carretera Transpeninsular (tel. 7-02-05), near the Union 76 ball and Motel Brisa Salina, is Guerrero Negro's attempt at elegance; miniature wooden tables and chairs with full place settings clump in a small dining area. Chicken enchiladas 13 pesos. *Quesadillas* 13 pesos. (Open daily 7am-11pm.) Across the road, **Cocina Económica Letty** occupies a new building with big new furniture and TV provides entertainment. Fish 12 pesos, enchiladas and the like 10 pesos. (Open Mon.-Sat. 6:30am-10pm.)

Guerrero Negro is for the traveler, scattered along 3km of the **Carretera Transpeninsular.** The highway runs from the bus station at the south end to the riverbed and salt plant, where it turns. The road that continues into Guerrreo Negro is Avenida Baja California, which jogs to the left at the park and church. Change money at **Bánamex,** Av. Baja California (tel. 7-05-55), just across the small bridge in front of the salt plant. (Open Mon.-Fri. 9am-4pm.) The **post office** (tel. 7-03-44) is off Baja California across from the Lion's Club, two blocks past the church. (Open Mon.-Fri. 9am-1pm and 3-6pm.) The **postal code** is 23940. **Telephones** are in **Farmacia San Martín,** on Carretera Transpeninsular (tel. 7-01-11), 100m north of the clinic. (Open Mon.-Sat. 8am-10pm, Sun. 9am-4pm.) An **IMSS Clinic** is on Carretera Transpeninsular ½km north of the water tower (tel. 7-04-33). The **police** are in the Delegación Municipal on Carretera Transpeninsular, just before the salt plant (tel. 7-02-22).

Buses leave from one of the first buildings from the highway on the access road (tel. 7-06-11). *De paso* service goes north and south six to seven times daily. *De local* buses go to Tijuana at 7:30pm (82 pesos), La Paz at 4pm (86 pesos), San Quintín (52 pesos), Santa Rosalía (26 pesos), and Mexicali (100 pesos).

■■■ SAN IGNACIO

More than any other stop on the arid Baja Peninsula, San Ignacio, between Guerrero Negro and Santa Rosalía on the Transpeninsular Highway, is a veritable tropical oasis. The sight of forest green, of leafy date palms, and of flowering bushes in the middle of the blistering desert seems to be only a cruel illusion, the mind playing games after miles of dry sand. But in fact, inhabitants have dammed up an underground water source to form a murky lake used for everything from local orchards to swimming. The locals pioneer a fishing industry on the Pacific coast, some 70km from home.

The colonial colossus towering over the wild vegetation looks like it was built there by accident. Nonetheless, Mexican Jesuits founded the **Mission of San Ignacio** in 1728 and decorated the temple with gold ornaments and original paintings. A visit here and a relaxing nap under the cool, shady palms are the only things to do in town. A winding road canopied by sweet date palms leads from the Transpeninsular Highway to the *zócalo*. Abundant **trailer parks** and **camping** spots line this 2km stretch of road. The town is smaller than you would believe; hence, it lacks services and activities for tourists. A **market, Bancomer,** and the **post office** all surround the plaza, as does the mission.

■■■ MULEGÉ

Veteran beachcombers claim that heaven on earth is the 48km arc of rocky outcrops and shimmering beaches in Southern Baja known as the Bahía de la Concepción, which neighbors Mulegé. Millions of shells in the area will keep you busy for days and vastly expand your collection. Grown sport fishers weep at the variety and sheer size of the specimens caught here, and divers fall under the spell of Mulegé's underwater sights. Located 136km north of Loreto on Rte. 1, Mulegé proper is just a base, to be abandoned during the day for the marvelous beaches to the south.

Practical Information Shortly after leaving the highway, the road into Mulegé forks. To the left is Moctezuma, to the right Martinez which merges into Morelos after the plaza. Zaragoza crosses both and leads to the plaza one block from Martinez. The Hotel Las Casitas, Madero 50 (tel. 3-00-19) serves as the unofficial **tourist office**, with plenty of information regarding beaches, camping, and fishing. Ask for Javier to get to the real nitty-gritty. The **post office** is on the north side of the plaza. (Open Mon.-Fri. 8am-3pm, Sat. 8am-noon. **Postal code:** 23900.) Minisuper Padilla, on Zaragoza at General San Martín, 1 block north of plaza has **phones** for international calls. (Open Mon.-Sat. 9am-1pm and 3-8pm, Sun. 9am-1pm.) A public phone is located in the plaza. (**Telephone code:** 685.) The **bus station** is but a sheltered blue bench at the turnoff to Mulegé from Rte. 1. All buses are *de paso*, roughly translatable as "inevitably arrives late and full." Southbound and northbound buses depart 4 times per day. Buses trail to La Paz and Loreto down under and north to Santa Rosalía, Guerrero Negro, and Tijuana. Southbound buses generally pass in the morning, northbound in the evening, after 4pm. A lucky few catch rides here. **Lavamática Claudia** (tel. 3-00-57), on Moctezuma beside Hotel Terraza is the town laundromat. (Wash 6 pesos, dry 2.50 pesos, soap 1.50 pesos. Open Mon.-Sat. 8am-6pm.) **Farmacia Mulegé** (tel. 3-00-23), is on Zaragoza near General San Martín. (Open daily 8am-9pm.) **Centro de Salud B,** Madero 28 (tel. 3-02-98), also referred to as the ISSTE clinic or the Puesto Periférico, serves medical emergencies. (Open 24 hrs.) **Police,** or **Delegación Municipal de Seguridad y Tránsito,** Madero 30 (tel. 3-02-48), are next to the hospital.

Accommodations and Food A number of economical hotels pile up in the center of town, but they are quite a distance from the beaches. Many find that the best deal for those with a sleeping bag is on the shore. Bargaining might be helpful at any of the several *casas de huéspedes* in town. On hot nights, rooms at **Casa De Huéspedes Mañuelita,** on Moctezuma around the corner from Zaragoza (tel. 3-01-75), relieve the traveler with table fans and private showers if the fans don't quite do the trick. All rooms look onto a cluttered courtyard with thriving grapevines. Campers who just need to use the bathroom and shower pay 6 pesos. (Singles 25 pesos. Doubles 35 pesos.) Suites at **Hotel Rosita,** Madero 2 (tel. 3-02-70), just east of the plaza, are so enormous you could invite the in-laws and still have fun.

Two bedrooms, bath, sitting room, kitchen, all furnished with A/C. Bring your own utensils. (Singles 60 pesos. Quads 80 pesos.) **Hotel Terazas,** on Zaragoza 2 blocks north of the plaza (tel. 3-00-09), is a pleasant establishment with every modern convenience except the boob tube. Restaurant and bar inside lobby. (All rooms without A/C cost 60 pesos, rooms with A/C 75 pesos. AAA membership discounts.) **Casa de Huéspedes Nachita** is on Moctezuma 50m down the left branch of the fork as you enter Mulegé (tel. 3-01-40). Spartan rooms include free fans on request. Bathrooms and shower centrally located in the dirt courtyard. (Singles 30 pesos. Triples 45 pesos.)

Grocery stores equipped to feed nomadic beach bums are plentiful (one is on the plaza), and a few unremarkable restaurants cluster near the bus station. **El Candil Restaurant,** north of the plaza on Zaragoza, serves guests Mon.-Sat. from 7am to 11pm. Dine on sizzling steak for 20 pesos, chicken *a la mexicana* for 15 pesos, or shrimp on the stone floor patio under flowering vines and bushes. For the best seafood in town, try **La Almeja** (tel. 3-01-84), at the end of Morelos near the lighthouse. The floor is the beach, and should you find a bone in your garlic fish (16 pesos) you can spit it into the Sea of Cortés. (Open daily 8am-10pm.) The hike down whets the appetite and rides can usually be begged for the trip back to town. **Restaurant Bar Los Equipales,** on Moctezuma next to Casa Mañuelita's (tel. 3-03-30), boasts a second-story terrace with wicker furniture. Almost all breakfast items for 10.50 pesos, barbecue chicken 20 pesos, shrimp cocktail 20 pesos. (Open daily 8am-10pm.)

At night, most *norteamericanos* in the area meet at the bar of the **Hotel Las Casitas** for drinking and dancing with no cover. The last watering hole to close each night is the bar at the **Hotel Vieja Hacienda,** on the plaza.

Sights Pre-Colombian cave paintings are located four hours by car from Mulegé, in the **Cuevas de San Borjita.** Unfortunately, the caves are located on a private estate called San Bartasar Ranchero (tel. 3-03-56), so you must pay the owner to catch a view. Narciso Villavisecio organizes trips to the caves and will provide explanations (in Spanish) of what you see. If you have transportation to the ranch, then a group tour costs US$25, but if you need a ride from Mulegé, the price soars to US$100. For more information, inquire at the unofficial tourist office at the Hotel La Casita. They have pictures of the cave paintings on view free of charge—a cheaper alternative.

In town, Mulegé's **mission** sits on a hill to the west, down a lane shaded by bananas and palms and past the bridge south of the *zócalo*. The mission is not a museum; services are still held every Sunday. And for those who can't make it to Bahía de la Concepción, two beaches lie only 2km from the center of town. **El Faro** is at the very end of Madero long after it becomes a dirt road; reach the public beach by following the Mulegé River to its finish at the Sea of Cortés. Neither spot, with well-trodden black sand and light waves, can compare to the beaches 18 km south. Watch out for jellyfish, especially in early summer.

■ Near Mulegé: Santa Rosalía

The wooden houses, general stores, and saloons along Santa Rosalía's streets recall the town's previous incarnation as the base for a 19th century French copper operation that mined the surrounding hills. The spectacular prefabricated cast-iron **Iglesia Santa Bárbara,** at Obregón and Calle 1, truly makes the town shine. Designed by Gustave Eiffel (of Tower fame) and installed in the 1890s, this church was one of four destined for missions in Africa before the company that commissioned them forgot to pick up their order. French mining *concessionaires* spotted the iron church at the 1889 *Exhibition Universal de Paris* and decided Santa Rosalía couldn't do without it.

The town's only other draw is as the home to the northernmost **ferry** connecting Baja to the mainland. The boat leaves Santa Rosalía only two times per week, on

Wednesday and Sunday at 8am from the **Sematur** terminal on Rte. 1 (tel. 2-00-13), just south of town. Tickets go on sale the day before the departure date, and those with cars must purchase their spot a day in advance. (Office open Tues., Wed., Fri., and Sun. 9am-5pm. *Salón* 38 pesos, *turista* 76 pesos.) Statistics concerning departure days and times, prices and office hours are in constant flux, so be sure to call the office or talk to a travel agent to confirm the schedule. The ferry dock is across the street about 200m from the bus station. To get from the ferry to Obregón, Santa Rosalía's main strip, turn right as you leave the ferry compound; Obregón is your second left.

Those travelers looking for fun in the sun and abundant water sports would do better to make tracks out of this port down to the heavenly beaches further south.

■■■ MULEGÉ TO LORETO

There's nothing like a swim in the bath-warm waters of the Sea of Cortés followed by a bask in the soft sand or under a *palapa*, and maybe a beer provided by the friendly *norteamericano* RVer up the beach. Forget the northern beaches—the Bahía de la Concepción shines the brightest in Baja. Cactus-studded hills drop straight to white sand beaches and warm transluscent waters. Lying 16km south of Mulegé, the beaches of Bahía de la Concepción are studded with campers and RVs that enjoy the surrounding area as if it were a personal paradise. Many nomadic travelers hitch from Mulegé to the beaches: RVs shuttle to and from the coast frequently, and local produce trucks often carry more than fresh fruits; they shuttle beachseekers down the Transpeninsular Highway towards the bay.

Here's the lineup. **Playa Punta Arena,** 16km south of Mulegé, is one of the most attractive beaches in the area. Connected to the highway by a 2km rutted dirt road barely passable by car, this stretch of sand is distant enough from the traffic that the roar of the waves drowns out the noise from muffler-less trucks. A dozen palm-frond *palapas* line the beach (hammock hookups US$4 per night), with sand-flush toilets behind them. The Paleolithic people who once inhabited the caves on the hillside south of the beach left behind millions of discarded shells; the biggest cave is of some interest to sightseers for its collection of stones worn smooth from grinding.

The next beach down is **Playa Santispac,** whose tranquil shores are overrun with RVs. Tent-pitching is also permitted; a man comes around once per day to collect the US$3-4 camping fee. Yachts and sailboats bob in the harbor at Santispac, making it the liveliest of the beaches on the bay. Santispac is directly on the highway; those hitching will find it more convenient than Punta Arena. **Playas Burro, Los Cocos,** and **Escondido** cling to the neighboring southern coast and also have *palapas*. Batting cleanup is **Playa El Coyote,** perhaps the most dazzling beach, with *palapas* and a restaurant across the street called **Estrella del Mar.** Part of this beach has been privatized by RV settlers; the better beach and *palapas* are down on the southern end.

Fifteen km farther down the road, at primitive **Playa Resquesón,** a beautiful spit of sand broadens into a wide beach. The next beach south, small and undeveloped except for a lone toilet, is the last beach before the highway climbs into the mountains separating Mulegé from Loreto.

All of these main beaches are marked from the main highway. Those with cars, dune buggies, motorized tricycles, or other similar blessings can undoubtedly find more remote options. Divers rave about this area; it teems with underwater life, including gigantic sea turtles. **Mulegé Divers,** Madero 45 (tel. 3-01-34), down the street from Hotel Las Casitas, rents scuba equipment and conducts boat excursions. The day-long scuba-diving trip, including guide and equipment, costs US$50 per person; the snorkeling trip costs US$25 per person including mask, fins, and snorkel. Make reservations one day in advance.

■■■ LORETO

Founded by Jesuit missionaries in 1697, Loreto became the first capital of the Californias and the first link in a chain of missions along the west coast. Not more than 130 years later, a dastardly combination of hurricanes and earthquakes wiped out the town and its mission in 1829. Recent construction has beautifully restored **Our Lady of Loreto Mission,** but the town still pines for its former glory. From the hills just south of town, you can see a maze of roads and sidewalks, palm trees, sprinklers and street lights, but no buildings. Years ago, the Mexican government began to lay the foundations for a major resort, but funds were diverted to other projects. Loreto thus remains a simple town, despite its three luxury hotels. Most of the foreigners in town are middle-aged *norteamericanos* who come to fish the spectacular waters off Loreto's coast. **Tourist information** is in the travel agency on Hidalgo one block from shore. (Open Mon.-Sat. 9am-1pm and 3-7pm.)

The new sidewalk with benches along the water is a popular place for an evening stroll. The **Museo de las Misiones,** which recounts the complete history of the European arrival in and subsequent conquest of Baja California in pictures, artifacts and words, is located next to the reconstructed Mission Loreto, one block west of the plaza. Here you can also receive information on the various other missions scattered throughout the peninsula. (Open Mon.-Fri. 9am-5pm. Admission 5 pesos.)

Budget accommodations in Loreto perished with the missions. The most economical hotel in town is **Hotel San Martín,** two blocks north of the *zócalo*, on Juárez (tel. 5-04-42). The rooms seem to be filled with whatever random furniture there happened to be around the day the place was built. (Singles and doubles 36 pesos. Bargaining may work) A number of pricey restaurant-bars have popped up around the docks, proving supply meets demand. **Café Olé,** north of the *zócalo* on Madero (tel. 5-04-96), offers cheap, quick meals for those travelers passing through. Dine on *chile relleno* (13 pesos) and a banana split (13 pesos). (Open Mon.-Sat. 7am-10pm, Sun. 7am-2pm.)

The principle street in Loreto is **Salvatierra**, which connects *Carretera Transpeninsular* to the Gulf. Hidalgo forks off when Salvatierra becomes a walking only zone, and Francisco Madero crosses Salvatierra two blocks up from the waters and passes directly in front of the *zócalo*. The **bus terminal** (tel. 5-07-67) is on Salvatierra just off the highway, about 2km from Madero. *De paso* buses run north to Loreto and Santa Rosalía and south to La Paz a few times daily. PEMEX **gas stations** stare at the terminal across the street.

You can exchange currency at **Bancomer,** on Madero across from the *zócalo* (tel. 3-03-15, open Mon.-Fri. 8:30am-1pm). International collect **calls** (6 pesos) can be made at the *caseta* on the *zócalo* (open Mon.-Sat. 8am-1pm and 5pm-9pm, Sun 10am-2pm and 5pm-9pm). Loreto's **telephone code** is 683. The **post office** (tel. 5-06-47), off Salvatierra near the bus station, behind the Red Cross, is open Mon.-Fri. 9am-1pm and 3-6pm, Sat. 9am-1pm. The **postal code** is 23880. Stock up for the day at **Supermarket El Pescador,** on Salvatierra and Independencia (tel. 5-00-60, open daily 7am-10pm). The **Centro de Salud,** on Salvatierra 1km from the bus terminal (tel. 5-00-39), is open 24 hrs. Finally, in an emergency, the **police** (tel. 5-00-35) are on the plaza in the building with the sign proclaiming "Capital Histórica de las Californias."

North of Loreto, the road passes the gorgeous **Bahía de la Concepción** on its way to Mulegé. South of Loreto, the road winds away from the coast into rugged mountains and the **Planicie Magdalena,** an intensively irrigated and cultivated plain. The striking white stripes on the first hillside beyond town consist of millions of shells, the refuse left by the region's Paleolithic inhabitants. This whole area is strewn with clam, conch, oyster, and scallop shells. Some caves on the hillside, inhabited as recently as 300 years ago, contain shells and polished stone.

■■■ LA PAZ

For most of the 454 years since Hernán Cortés founded it, La Paz has been a quiet fishing village beloved for its extraordinary off-shore pearls. Cut off from the rest of the world and accessible only by sea, La Paz's iridescent treasure became a frequent target for pirate raids. John Steinbeck set *The Pearl* in La Paz, depicting it as a tiny, unworldly fishing village glittering with small semi-precious orbs. In the 1940s, La Paz's oysters mysteriously sickened and died, wiping out the pearl industry. With the institution of the Baja ferries and the completion of the Transpeninsular Highway in the '60s, however, tourists and new industries discovered La Paz. As night approaches, locals and *viajeros* alike flock to the beach to cruise the strip and watch exquisite sunsets.

ORIENTATION

La Paz overlooks the **Bahía de la Paz,** on the Baja's east coast, 222km north of Cabo San Lucas and 1496km southeast of Tijuana, on the Transpeninsular Highway (Rte. 1). Ferry is by far the cheapest way to get from La Paz to the mainland, but for those with a car procuring a ticket is nearly impossible; ferries carry mostly commercial trucks and the few slots for other vehicles sell out far in advance.

Sematur Company (tel. 5-46-66), 5 de Mayo and Prieto, operates the ferry from La Paz to Topolobampo and Mazatlán (open daily 7am-1pm). In order to secure a place to the mainland, be sure to get there early to get a prime spot in line. Acquiring a *salón* ticket should be no problem on the day of departure, but for other classes, call ahead to make reservations. In all cases, tickets may only be bought on the day of departure (for more about ferries see Baja California: Getting Around). The ferry dock is a 17km hike from the center of town in Pichilingue; don't fret, **buses** run down Obregón hourly from 8am to 6pm, except 3pm, for 3 pesos. To the dock, catch the bus at the downtown terminal on Obregón between Independencia and 5 de Mayo.

During holidays, ferry demand is great. In order to get a vehicle on the ferry you will need—at a minimum—proof of Mexican insurance, car registration and a tourist card; oh, and two photocopies of each. Travelers themselves will at least need a tourist card. Try to procure all of this paper work at the border when entering Mexico (see Planning Your Trip: Documents and Formalities: Driver's License and Vehicle Permits for details on bringing your car farther into Mexico). If not, **Servicios Migratorios** can set you up in La Paz, on Obregón between Allende and Juárez (tel. 2-04-29; open Mon.-Fri. 8am-3pm.) The tricky part is that all of the paper work must be in place before you purchase the ticket; otherwise Sematur will deny you a spot, reservations or not.

Maps of La Paz depict perfect rectilinear blocks around a tiny enclave of disorder on the waterfront. The main streets for travelers are **Obregón,** which follows the waterfront, and **16 de Septiembre,** which runs south (they intersect at the tourist office). On some maps, the stretch of Obregón near the tourist office is called **Malecón.** La Paz can be confusing: on a peninsula, the waterfront faces the bay to the northwest, and street names are very similar.

The municipal bus system in La Paz serves the city sporadically. In general, city buses run daily from 6am to 10pm every half hour (1 peso). Flag them down anywhere, or wait by the stop at Degollado (which runs parallel to 16 de Septiembre and Revolución), next to the market.

PRACTICAL INFORMATION

Tourist Office: Obregón at 16 de Septiembre (tel. 2-59-39), in a pavilion on the water. Excellent city maps and information about Baja Sur, especially Los Cabos. English-speaking staff. Open Mon.-Fri. 8am-8pm.

Currency Exchange: Bancomer, 16 de Septiembre, ½ block from the waterfront. Other banks scattered in small downtown area. All open Mon.-Fri. 8:30am-1pm.

Immigration Office: Servicios Migratorios (tel. 2-04-29), on 2140 Obregón between Allende and Juárez. You must stop here for a tourist card and a stamp on your car permit if you entered Mexico via Baja and are mainland-bound. Open Mon.-Fri. 8am-3pm. After hours, you can go to their outpost in the airport outside of town (tel. 2-18-29; open 7am-7pm).

Post Office: Revolución at Constitución (tel. 2-03-88). Open Mon.-Fri. 8am-7pm, Sat.-Sun. 9am-12:30pm. **Postal code:** 23000.

American Express: Obregón 1570 (tel. 2-83-00), in the Hotel Perla. Open Mon.-Fri. 9am-2pm and 4-6pm, Sat. 9am-2pm. La Paz and Esquerro (tel. 2-83-00, fax 5-52-72), behind the Hotel Perla. Open Mon.-Fri. 9am-2pm and 4-6pm. Sat 9am-2pm.

Telephones: *Caseta* located on Obregón between Muelle and Degollado (tel. 2-12-33). International collect calls 6 pesos. Open daily 8am-10pm. Otherwise, touch-tone public phones on streets and in post office. **Telephone code:** 112.

Telegrams: Upstairs from post office (tel. 2-03-22). Fax service also. Mon.-Fri. 8am-7pm, Sat. 8-11am.

Airport: West of La Paz. Accessible only by 30 peso taxis. Served by **Aeroméxico,** (tel. 2-00-91), **Aerocalifornia** and **Lineas del Noroeste.** Flights to: Los Mochis (223 pesos), Tijuana (558 pesos), Mexico City (874 pesos), and Los Angeles (US$190).

Bus Station: Independencia at Jalisco, about 25 blocks south of downtown. Municipal bus "Central Camionera" (1 peso) runs between the terminal and the public market at Degollado and Revolución, but these are infrequent (every hr. 6am-8pm),and the hike is long, so consider taking a taxi (8 pesos). **Tres Estrellas de Oro, Autotransportes Águila**, and **Norte de Sonora** operate out of the terminal. Buses leave several times daily from La Paz to Tijuana (150 pesos). To: Loreto (40 pesos), Mulegé (50 pesos), and Cabo San Lucas (28 pesos). Also, **mini-bus station** at Obregón and Independencia runs buses to Pichilingue and surrounding beaches (3 pesos) and to Cabo San Lucas (28 pesos).

Ferries: Sematur Company, at 5 de Mayo and Prieto (tel. 5-46-66). To Mazatlán (Sun.-Fri. at 3pm, 16hrs., *salón* 57 pesos, *turista* 76 pesos, cars up to 5m long 417 pesos, motorcycles 95 pesos) and Topolobampo (daily at 8pm except for unfixed "cargo only" days—call for precise info—8hrs., *salón* 38 pesos, *turista* 76 pesos, *cabina* 114 pesos). Open Mon.-Fri. 7am-1pm, Sat.-Sun. 8am-1pm for ticket sales, Mon.-Fri. 4-6pm for reservations. Boats leave Sun.-Fri. at 3pm.

Bookstores/Libraries: Biblioteca de las Californias, at 5 de Mayo and Madero. Books about Baja. **Librería Contempo,** Arreola 2B just off the waterfront, has a section of English-language books, magazines and newspapers. Open daily 9am-9pm.

Laundromat: Lavamática, 5 de Mayo at Rubio (tel. 2-10-01), across the street from the stadium. Wash 4 pesos, 5-min. dry .40 pesos. Open Mon.-Sat. 7am-9pm, Sun. 8am-3pm.

Red Cross: (tel. 2-11-11), 1901 Reforma between Isabel la Católica and Félix Ortega.

Pharmacy: Farmacia Baja California, Independencia at Madero (tel. 2-02-40), facing the plaza. 24 hr.

Hospital: Salvatierra, Bravo at Verdad (tel. 2-14-96).

Police: Colima at México (tel. 2-20-20). Open 24 hrs. In **emergency**, dial 06.

ACCOMMODATIONS

Hotels in La Paz seem to be competing with each other for the cluttered artistic look; a student of Mexican folk art could skip the Museo Antrolpologico and tour the lobbies of these hotels instead. There is a **CREA** youth hostel (tel. 2-46-15) in the youth center of Forjatero near the Technical University, but its distance from the *centro* makes rooms in the hotels a safer, more convenient, and perhaps even cheaper option, considering the La Paz bus and taxi system.

Pensión California Casa de Huéspedes, Degollado at Madero (tel. 2-28-96). Bungalows rooms with concrete floors and beds on concrete slabs. Pleasant sitting area in courtyard, especially if you like small children. Bring your own blanket. Singles 25 pesos. Doubles 38 pesos.

Hostería del Convento, Madero 85 (tel. 2-35-08), almost at Degollado. Eerily similar to the Pensíon around the corner. Rooms are arranged in an open-air maze that is lined with old maps of Baja and Mexico, but alas, no map of the hotel. Light blue rooms and ceiling fans provide comfort from the sticky heat. Private baths. Singles 25 pesos. Doubles 38 pesos.

Hotel Posada San Miguel, B. Domínguez 151 (tel. 2-18-02), just off 16 de Septiembre. Lodgings with fountained courtyards, tiled arches, and wrought-iron scroll work on windows and railings. Cubical rooms with sinks next to large comfortable beds. Singles 30 pesos. Doubles 40 pesos.

Hotel Yeneka, Madero 1520 (tel. 5-46-88). Motel doubles as a museum with a host of eccentric items: a 1916 model T-Ford and a pet hawk. All Tarzan-hut rooms remodeled in matching twig furniture. Singles 48 pesos. Doubles 58 pesos. No to credit cards, yes to traveler's checks.

Hotel San Carlos, 16 de Septiembre at Revolución (tel. 2-04-44). Wide white corridors glowing with fluorescent lighting give the air of an asylum. Bedrooms with grubby pink walls, tile floor, and a fan. Singles and doubles 33 pesos.

FOOD

On the waterfront you'll find decor, menus and prices geared toward peso-spewing tourists. Move inland a few blocks and food prices begin to drop zeros at the end. The **public market,** at Degollado and Revolución, offers a selection of fruits, veggies and fresh fish.

Restaurant El Mexicano, 16 de Septiembre at Serdán (tel. 2-89-65). Bright, striped *mexicano* blankets on the tables accompany good service. Authentic *antojitos* cooked to order. Loaded tostadas 7.50 pesos, fried fish 10 pesos. Open daily (except every other Mon.) 9am-9pm.

Restaurante El Quinto Sol, B. Domínguez at Independencia (tel. 2-16-92). Stands proud as one of the few vegetarian joints in western Mexico. Menu includes sausage *á la soybean*, as well as esoteric and relaxant juices. Half of the eatery doubles as a health food store with plenty of dried fruits and vitamins. Avocado and cheese sandwich 8 pesos. Yogurt smoothie with fruits 18 pesos. Open Mon.-Sat. 7am-10pm.

Rosticería California, Serdán between Degollado and Ocampo (tel. 2-51-18). Everybody and their *hermano* comes here for finger-licking roasted cluckers. Plenty of seating with attentive waiters, or take it to go. Don't miss the exotic live peacocks in the back. Whole chicken including fries 27 pesos, ½ chicken 15 pesos. Open Sun.-Fri. 8am-6pm.

Antojitos de Sinaloa, on 16 de Septiembre between Revolución and Serdán. Enjoy cheap Mexican favorites from the English-Spanish menu scrawled on the wall. Scrumptious tostadas and *gorditas* 10 pesos. Eggs 7 pesos. Open daily 7am-10pm.

Café Olimpia, on 16 de Septiembre, across from Antojitos de Sinaloa. Customers hop on loud orange stools to devour a quickly fried up meal and slurp on frosty *licuados* (3.50 pesos). *Flautas* 9 pesos. Gigantic Mexican-style Egg McMuffin 7 pesos. Open daily 7:30am-11pm.

SIGHTS AND ENTERTAINMENT

Beaches in La Paz and much of eastern Baja are not your usual long, curving expanses of wave-washed sand. Instead, they snuggle into small coves sandwiched between cactus-studded hills and calm, transparent water; this is a prime windsurfing zone.

The best beach near La Paz is **Playa Tecolote** (Owl Beach), 25km northeast of town. A quiet extension of the Sea of Cortés laps against this gorgeous stretch of gleaming white sand, backed up by tall, craggy mountains. Even though there are no bathrooms, Tecolote is terrific for **camping**. You may need to drive here; buses run only during peak seasons—spring break, July, and August. Plenty of other beaches are easily accessible by taking the "Pichilingue" **bus** up the coast (station on Obregón and Independencia, 3 pesos). Be forewarned that the bus only runs back to La Paz until 6pm, so don't be caught stranded. The bus goes as far as the ferry dock, at which point you need to walk 2km further on the dirt road to **Playa de Pichilingue.** This beach is a favorite among the teen set, who dig its eatery and public bathrooms. Along the same bus route lies **Playa El Coronel** near La Concha Hotel. Because of its proximity to downtown, visitors and locals alike flock to its shores on weekends. These are all a hefty hike or a short ride away. Closer to town, there's fine swimming in the placid waters near the tourist office with plenty of eateries and hotels nearby in case the mean sun wears you out. But the farther you venture from La Paz, the better and more secluded it gets.

The fun in La Paz doesn't stop at the beach for those who want to venture out onto the water. Nautilius, on Martinez at Obregón, rents snorkelling equipment for US$25 per day. (Open Mon.-Fri. 9am-2:30pm, 4:30-9pm, Sat.-Sun. 9am-3pm.) **Baja Diving and Service,** Independencia 107-B (tel. 2-18-26), just north of B. Domínguez, organizes daily scuba and snorkeling trips to nearby reefs, wrecks, and islands, where you can mingle with hammer heads, manta rays, giant turtles, and other exotica. (Scuba adventure US$70 per day, snorkeling trips US$40 per day, including equipment and lunch.)

If you tire of the ocean and wish to escape the blistering sun, take a break at the **Museo Antropológico,** 5 de Mayo and Altamirano (tel. 2-01-62), which displays local art and reproductions of pre-Conquest cave paintings, as well as exhibits on the Baja's pre-Conquest past. (Open Mon.-Fri. 11am-6pm. Free.)

On the south side of Constitución Square (the main plaza) soars the **Misión de Nuestra Señora de la Paz** (Our Lady of La Paz Mission), on Revolución between Independencia and 5 de Mayo. This cathedral was founded by Jesuit missionaries in 1720.

Every Sunday evening, La Paz denizens attend concerts under the enormous kiosk on the plaza east of the tourist office. Called "Sunday in the Park with Tecate," these weekly parties are popular with both Mexicans and *gringos*. If you decide to stroll down the pier to stargaze afterward, keep an eye out for missing floorboards.

■■■ TODOS SANTOS

For now, Todos Santos is one of the few towns on the southern Baja coast which is easily accessible by bus, offers budget accomodations, and is for the most part unmutilated by the hand of *norteamericano* resort development. Yet another in the string of towns founded by Jesuit missionaries in the 17th century, Todos Santos was more recently a major producer and exporter of sugar cane. The ruins of old sugar mills are reminders of that boom period, which ended with a decrease in the water level. But another boom is on the horizon in Todos Santos. A large resort hotel, complete with yacht basin and water park, is being planned for the land near Playa Los Lobos. Until its completion, however, the cool Pacific breezes and excellent surf make Todos Santos a welcome relief from the desert heat and tourist excess.

Practical Information Todos Santos's two main streets, **Colegio Militar** (part of the Carretera Transpeninsular) and **Juárez**, which passes beside the church, run parallel to each other. León crosses these at the church and plaza, and three blocks down the highway, Degollado marks the end of the downtown.

The **bus station** is Pilar's taco stand, at the corner of Zaragoza and Colegio Militar, one block from the spotlight. *De paso* buses run south to the Cabos (15 pesos) and north to La Paz (12 pesos) several times daily. Change dollars and traveler's checks at the other end of town at the **Bancomer** on Juárez one block past Topete (open Mon.-Fri. 8:30am-1pm). **Long distance calls** can be made from the *caseta* at the bus station (9am-7pm) or the public phone at the Pememex on Degollado. The **tele-**

phone code is 114. The *Lista de Correos* is posted at the **post office,** on Colegio Militar, on the northbound side of León. (**Postal code:** 23300; open Mon.-Fri. 8am-1pm and 3-5pm.) **Isstotiendas,** the market on Juárez between Morelos and Zaragoza, is open daily 8am-8pm. Next door, **Farmacia Todos Santos** (tel. 5-00-30) offers 24-hr. emergency service. The **police** are at tel. 4-101-22.

Accommodations and Food The **Hotel California** (tel. 4-00-02) at Juárez and Morelos, has a swimming pool, gift shop, view of the church, and good-sized, clean rooms with ceiling fans, all for only 35 pesos for a single, 42 pesos for a double. Visa and MC accepted. If the Hotel California is full, or if you want to prove your mettle on some of the most uncomfortable furniture in the world, go across the street to **Departamentos Gabi,** where the sign just reads "Motel." Rooms come with fan, TV, and furniture. (Singles 50 pesos, doubles 60 pesos.) **El Molino** trailer park, off Degollado at the Pemex corner, offers tired RVers and Airstreamers a 10 peso full hook-up, a book shelf, and coin-operated washing machines.

Food is not hard to find. Several *loncherías* line Colegio Militar near the bus station, offering triple tacos and the like for 9 pesos. Restaurant-bar **Los Fuentes** (tel. 4-02-57), at the stoplight corner, has pleasant fountains and good food: fried fish with rice and salad 20 pesos, breakfast about 12 pesos. English spoken and clean public bathrooms, too. (Open daily 7am-9pm.)

Sights Action in Todos Santos revolves around the **farm** and the **beach.** Most tourists will probably prefer the beach, though the farms are more accessible. The closest beach to town (2km) is **La Posa.** To get there, go up Juárez and turn left on Topete. Follow that as it winds around and across the valley, and comes to a white building that says "Do not pass." Pass that, and you're on the beach. The more popular **Playa Los Lobos** is 3 or 4 km down the dirt road by El Molino trailer park. Turn left at the stadium. **Los Cerritos,** known far and wide for its surf, is 10km south of town on the highway, then a couple more on a dirt road. Rock climbers, hikers, and hunters enjoy **La Laguna de la Sierra,** a beautiful lake on top of a mountain, accessible by dirt road (2hrs. by car) from the other side of town.

LOS CABOS

The towns of **Cabo San Lucas** and **San José del Cabo** comprise the southwestern part of the governmental district of Los Cabos, which includes a significant portion of the coast on the southeastern tip of Baja California. The *vía larga* section of Route 1 passes through this area, but winds through the mountains rather than along the coast. Bus service (Frailes del Sur line) is expanding in this region, but many roads still need improvement. To get to Cabo Pulmo and some of the best diving and snorkelling in the hemisphere, for instance, it is necessary to drive or hitchike 40 or 50km from Las Cuevas or Santa Ribera.

The real tourist draws to the Cabos are the towns of Cabo San Lucas and San José del Cabo. Here luxury hotels intercede between the desert and the ocean, and (sport-fishing, sunbathing, sightseeing, gift-buying, jetskiing) *norteamericanos* congregate by the thousands.

■■■ SAN JOSÉ DEL CABO

This is much more of a town and less of a resort than Cabo San Lucas, but the tourists are taking over. Golf courses and huge hotels separate San José del Cabo from the beach, and institutions like the post office and police station are being pushed out of their traditional locations in the *centro* by tourist information centers and gift shops.

In some ways, this budding resort atmosphere can be kind to budget travelers. Promoters for new hotels and time-shares will snap up anyone who looks like they may have a credit card and offer free boat trips, transportation, even free lunch. Just be sure no strings are attached.

Practical Information The **Transpeninsular Highway** on the west and **Avenida Mijares** on the east connect the town with San José's broad sweep of beautiful beach 2km away. The town is not hard to figure out; the cathedral and the *zócalo* are conspicuous landmarks on Zaragoza. One street over runs **Doblado.** Maps are free at the tourist information center on Zaragoza at Mijares.

Change all your money for new pesos at **Banca Serfín** on Zaragoza between 9:30am and noon. The **tourist information center** is next to the *zócalo* on Zaragoza; many important establishments have flyers there. International collect calls cost 3 pesos at the **caseta** outside the front entrance of the cathedral. (Open Mon.-Fri. 8am-2pm.) The new telephone area code is 114. The **post office** is on Mijar toward the beach. Mail letters or check the *Lista de Correos.* (Open Mon.-Fri. 8am-6pm, Sat. 9am-1pm.) The **postal code** is 23400.

San José del Cabo is such a whirring, buzzing metropolis that it needs two **bus stations**. The **Aguila terminal** launches buses to La Paz (3hrs., 28 pesos) and Cabo San Lucas (40min., 5 pesos). To get to town, walk all the way down González to Mijares to Zaragoza. The **Frailes terminal** (tel. 2-19-06) operates buses to Cabo San Lucas (5 pesos) from 6am-8pm, and has some service up the *vía larga* to La Ribera. The Frailes terminal is just outside the *centro* on Doblado, about a 10-min. walk from Mijares.

Buy groceries at the **Almacen** on Mijares at Zaragoza (tel. 2-09-12). (Open Mon.-Fri. 8am-8pm, Sat.-Sun. 8am-12:30pm.) **Farmacía Profesor Aurora** (tel. 226-11) is up on Green at Dobaldo, across from the Jardín de Niños. (Open daily 9am-2pm and 3-9pm.) The **Red Cross** is always ready at 2-08-84 and the **police** respond to 2-03-61.

Accommodations and Food As prices rise with the approach of the monster resorts, spots on the beach look more and more appealing. Many random rooms are for rent for about 30 pesos a day; look for signs, especially on Obregón. **Hotel Ceci,** Zaragoza 22 (tel. 2-00-5), 1½ blocks up from Mijares, offers comfortable beds with bright, white sheets and standing fans, and is the only real budget hotel in town. (Singles 44 pesos, doubles 50 pesos.) **Hotel San José Inn,** Obregón at Guerrero (tel. 0-11-52), outclasses the Ceci by offering newer, cleaner rooms with ceiling fans, some with a balcony. (Singles 60 pesos, doubles 75 pesos. Additional children 15 pesos.) **Trailer Park Brisa del Mar,** just off the highway to San Lucas when it reaches the coast, provides beach campers, communal bathrooms, and a bar with TV. (Full hook-up US$2 plus tax, US$5 for tent.)

Budget restaurants in San José del Cabo are being pushed out by real estate offices and fancy tourist eateries, leaving few options in between taco stands and filet mignon. **Cafetería Rosy,** on Zaragoza past Banca Serfín, cooks up delicious Mexican seafood dishes and serves them with a smile. Garlic fish 19 pesos. *Quesadillas* 10 pesos. (Open Mon.-Sat. 8am-10pm.) **Cafetería Arco Iris,** Morelos at Zaragoza (tel. 2-17-60), has small orange stools at a little counter. Tacos and *sincronizadas* 10 pesos each. (Open daily 8am-9:30pm.) **Panadería Princesa,** on Zaragoza past Green, sells rolls and muffins for a quick breakfast.

Sights and Entertainment The most popular beach in town is **Costa Azul,** on Palmilla Pt. 1km south of the Brisa del Mar trailer park. It has three- to five-foot waves and four different breaks of great interest to veteran surfers. Many hitch or persuade the bus driver to let them off there; those who do should ask first in order to avoid being driven all the way to Cabo San Lucas. A 15-minute walk down Mijares will lead you to perfectly good beaches much closer to town. The newest luxury hotels line the sand at some spots, but there's plenty of natural, clean coast line in between the artificial structures.

The **Killer Hook Surf Shop,** on Hidalgo between Doblado and Zaragoza (tel. 2-24-30), rents anything you need for a good time around here (snorkel gear US$8, fishing pole US$10, surf board US$15, bike US$11 for 24 hrs.). They also repair surfboard and dispense tips. (Open Mon.-Sat. 9am-1pm and 4-8pm.)

At night, the **Eclipse** on Mijares (tel. 2-16-94), one block down from Dobaldo jams rock music beneath flashing lights and a disco ball. (Never a cover. Margaritas 10 pesos, free Thurs.10-11pm. Happy hour Tues.-Wed. 7-9pm. Open Tues.-Sun. 7pm-3am.) The newest disco, **Bones,** next to the Hotel Presidente, offers a heavily strobe-lit dance floor to sweat out the beer calories. (Open Tues.-Sun. 7pm-2am.)

■■■ CABO SAN LUCAS

Cabo San Lucas is the first of the two Cabos on the *vía corta* bus route from La Paz. Until recently a peaceful fishing village, Cabo San Lucas is fast becoming one of the largest resorts in all of Mexico. For now, the town is haunted more by the skeletons of future pleasure domes than by hotels already completed. Due to the small size of the native population (about 3000), investors import young souls from the mainland to power the service economy. If you had planned to practice your rusty high school Spanish here, think again; waiters at the popular restaurants and bars receive daily English classes in addition to their weekly paychecks. Despite all of this fervor, Cabo San Lucas has yet to develop extensive facilities for the budget traveler. Prices at most eating establishments are high, even by US standards.

Budget travelers would do best to visit Cabo San Lucas only for the day or to camp out on the beach and treat the town solely as one big supermarket; buy your Neutrogena and make tracks for San José del Cabo.

Practical Information The **bus station,** served by **Tres Estrellas de Oro** and **Agulla,** is located on the corner of Zaragoza and 16 de Septiembre. Buses run daily until 9pm to San José (5 pesos) and La Paz (28 pesos), with one per day to Tijuana (165 pesos). To get to the center of action, take Zaragoza down toward the water 2 blocks to Cárdenas. City maps are handed out in bushels at one of the trillion info booths through the town. **Banca Serfín,** at Cárdenas and Zaragoza, and **Bánamex,** at Cárdenas and Hidalgo, exchange cash and traveler's checks Mon.-Fri. 8:30am-1pm. Most hotels and restaurants will gladly exchange dollars at lower rates. The **long-distance caseta** at Cárdenas and Hidalgo charges 3 pesos for international collect calls (Mon.-Sun. 8am-10pm). The **telephone code** is 114. The local supermarket, **Almacenes Grupo Castro,** at Morelos at Revolucíon (tel. 3-05-66), is open daily 9am-11pm. Finally, in case of an emergency, dial the **police** (tel. 3-02-96) or the **Red Cross** (tel. 3-11-14).

Accommodations and Food Multi-million dollar resorts with every service imaginable dominate San Lucas's coast line; for that same reason, simple, cheap beds are seriously lacking. In any case, make reservations early for the winter vacation period and be prepared to shell out more *dinero* than you would during the slower summer months. **CREA Youth Hostel (HI)** (tel. 3-01-48), is a 10-min. walk down Morelos from Cárdenas to Av. de la Juventud, then turn right and 5 min. to the large Instituto Sur Californiano building. Excitement over the cheapest beds in town is certainly dampened by the inconvenient location and hot hike to the beach. (Dorm bunk with communal bath 16 pesos, singles with private bath 25 pesos, doubles with bath 34 pesos.) **Hotel Dos Mares** is on Zapata between Hidalgo and Guerrero (tel. 3-03-30). Prime location near the docks and popular bars are the most attractive aspects of this joint; otherwise, aggressively average rooms. Not a single guest dares to venture into the questionable poolette. (Singles 66 pesos, doubles 76 pesos. Group rates and long-term discounts.)

Like their fellow shops and hotels, the restaurants in San Lucas have been forced into submission by prevailing *gringo* tastes. Restaurant-bars gang up on tourists along the water, all competing for the prized U.S. dollar. But the cheap spots line Morelos, a safe distance from the million-dollar yachts. **Taquería del Cheef,** Morelos at 20 de Noviembre, a small taco stand, boasts a baseball cap collection of 700 and counting (with no duplicates). Stop by, add a hat to the group and try one of eight varieties of burritos (6 pesos) or a juicy half-pound burger (13 pesos). (Open daily 7:30am-1am.) **The Broken Surfboards,** Hidalgo at Zapata, is an old and repectable taco joint with character. *Quesadillas* 3 pesos, but their pride and joy is breakfast for US$2. (Open daily 6:30am-9pm.) **Mariscos Mocambo,** Morelos at 20 de Noviembre (tel. 3-21-22), across from Taquería del Cheef, is a thatched -roof establishment which offers a refreshing break from the "tourist zone" three blocks away. *Puro* seafood served up fresh daily. Shrimp cocktail 18 pesos, fish and shrimp *empanada* 20 pesos. (Open Mon.-Sat. 9am-9pm.)

Sights and Entertainment All major activity in Cabo San Lucas revolves around the pristine waters surrounding the coast. One of the best beaches in the area, **Playa de Médano,** stretches east on the bay around the corner from the marina. Escape from the blazing sun in one of the beach's restaurants or many *palapas*, which serve up beverages and snacks for parched sun-seekers. The waters of the Playa del Médano are alive with buzzing jet-skis, parasailers, and motorboats full of lobster-red, beer-guzzling vacationers. **Cabo Acuadeportes,** in front of the **Hotel Hacienda** (tel. 3-01-17), offers every watersport desirable, at a price. Explore the busy underwater life with complete snorkeling gear (US$10 per day) or stay above the foamy waves on a catamaran (US$25 per hr.). (Open daily 9am-5pm. Last rental at 3:30pm.) The famous **Arch Rock** of Cabo San Lucas rises only a short boat ride from the marina. To get there, walk through the Plaza Las Glorias hotel, or the big Mexican crafts mart further down Paseo Marina, to the docks, where eager boat captains will be waiting to transport you (US$5 per person). On the same excursion, you'll have the opportunity to disembark and lounge on **La Playa del Amor,** the only beach with access to both the rough, deep blue Pacific and the tranquil Sea of Cortés. Among the many actvities for sale to land-lubbers are horse rentals with guided tours.

The beaches on the Pacific side are farther away than those by the marina, and the ferocious tide makes them unsuitable for swimming. Seclusion-seekers, however, may find them to be just the right thing. To get there, walk out on Marina (or hop a yellow school bus for 1.50 pesos) and turn right across from the Mexican crafts mart. Slip out to the beach between massive condominium complexes right after you pass the Terra Sol Hotel.

The 5-peso bus to San José del Cabo provides access to more beaches. These streches of white sand and glowing blue water are the reason that the Cabos are exploding with tourists, but if you pick the right one you may be able to escape the crowds, even during high season. **El Chileno,** closer to Cabo San Lucas, offers water sports like snorkelling, but **Tulé** boasts nicer surf. Just ask around to find names and descriptions of others, and ask the driver to leave you at the beach of your choice. Buses run to Cabo San Lucas until 8pm, to San Jose until 9pm.

At night, you too can join in the nightly ritual of alcohol-induced gastrointestinal reversal. **El Squid Roe,** Cárdenas and Zaragoza (tel. 3-06-55) serves clients in their singular drive towards inebriation. (Dancing (on any surface) from 11pm-3am. Well drinks 8 pesos. Open daily noon-3am.) A louder, middle-aged crowd at **The Giggling Marlin,** Marina at Matamoros, enjoys a full mug and hanging upside-down like the big catch. (Piña coladas 10 pesos. Happy hour(s) 2-6pm. Open daily 10am-1am.)

Northwest México

SONORA

NOGALES

Nogales has many of the same charms as Tijuana (ease of border crossing, cheap-o curio shops, off-track betting, and cheesy bars), yet fewer Tucsonans visit Nogales than San Diegans do Tijuana. The shorter distance between the San Diego and Tijuana and the maturity level of southern Californians contribute to this disparity. Nogales retains a distinct Mexican flavor and serves as a fine beginning point for those who want to feel like they're in Mexico the instant they cross the border. Its twin city is the smaller and less interesting **Nogales, Arizona.**

Practical Information The **bus terminal** (tel. 3-17-00) and **train station** (tel. 2-00-24) sit directly across from each other on Carretera Internacional, 4.5km from town. **Transportes Norte de Sonora** runs buses to Hermosillo (28 pesos), Tijuana (1 per day, 85 pesos), and Los Mochis (77 pesos). **Tres Estrellas de Oro** has daily departures to the same points, including Mexico City (246 pesos) and Chihuahua (88 pesos). Reserved seating can be purchased one hour before departure. **Greyhound** buses leave for Tucson (US$6.50). The bus station is ½ block from the main border, accessible from the Nogales on the U.S. side of the border every two hours from 6am to 8pm.

Two southbound trains depart daily to Mazatlán and Guadalajara; the *burro* (slow) leaves at 7am and the *estrella* (fast) leaves at 3:30pm. Tickets go on sale one hour before the time of departure, and reservations for the *estrella* can be made at from 8 to 11am. To reach the border and center of town, catch a white school bus market "Centro" (.50 pesos).

Nogales is small enough to navigate on your own. If you usually feel lost without a map, pray that the **tourist office** (tel. 2-64-46) at the border has one in stock. The office is open Mon.-Fri. 8am-5pm, and the staff is friendly but sometimes only Spanish-speaking. In emergencies, call the **Red Cross** (tel. 2-08-10) or **police** (tel. 2-01-04).

It's possible to walk across the border into Mexico without ever talking to a border official. However, if you plan to venture beyond Nogales, obtain a tourist card at the frontier. It's much simpler and cheaper to get the card there than farther south. A grand new border-crossing station *a la* Tijuana is still under construction here, so the immigration and tourism office is not as easy to find as it was once and will be. It's in the other side of the long white buildings that are on the left as you come into Mexico through the temporary crossing.

Most of the curio and craft shops line Obregón, and, just as in Tijuana, you *may* get good deals if you bargain and know something about product quality. Potential turquoise jewelry buyers should ask the vendor to put the rock to "the lighter test." Plastic or synthetic material will quickly melt under a lighter flame. Likewise, when buying silver make sure you see a ".925" stamp on the piece; if it's not there, the goods are bad.

Accommodations and Food A string of budget hotels is situated one block behind the tourist office on Av. Juárez and Obregón. As in most of northern Mexico, rates are steep. **Hotel Imperial,** Obregón 19 (tel. 2-70-62), is a long building with a central spiral staircase and cafeteria on the second floor. Small neat rooms with fan but few windows. (Singles and doubles 60 pesos.) For a bit of class, try **San Carlos Hotel,** Juárez 22 (tel. 2-13-46). Comfy lazy-boys fill the lobby and large rooms with TV and A/C charm the guests. (Singles 72 pesos, doubles 94 pesos.)

There are a fair number of **restaurants** packed in the center of Nogales, and most are overpriced. **La Posada Restaurant,** on Pierson 116 (tel. 2-04-39) off Obregón, jazzes up its walls and ceilings with painted tiles and curious objects. The town's bourgeoisie enjoy fresh foods served on colorful dishes. (*Chimichanga* 6 pesos, steak milanesa 18 pesos, *huevos rancheros* 11 pesos. Open daily 7:30am-10pm.) On Juárez, only half a block from the border, **Restaurant Olga** (tel. 2-16-41) has a TV and dysfunctional counter. (*Comidas corridas* 13 pesos, *chorizo* with eggs US$3. Open daily 6:30am-2am.)

■■■ PUERTO PEÑASCO

Puerto Peñasco partakes of the current of North Americans drifting down toward the prime sun-basking points of mainland Mexico's western coast.

The metaphysical maelstrom of the 20th century has failed to suck in Puerto Peñasco. The business here is sun and fun. Just 65 miles from the border and about three hrs. from Tucson, Arizona, Puerto Peñasco, like northern Baja, attracts hordes of weekenders (albeit with different license plates). It even has an English sobriquet: Rocky Point. If heavily peopled beaches and big hotel discos aren't your thing, 30 mi. north on the road to Sonoita is the **El Pinacate** volcanic area, pockmarked by over 600 craters. Otherwise, the detour off the main road isn't worth it—the beaches farther south are better.

Practical Information The main road, **Blvd. Juárez,** runs into town parallel to the train tracks. From the bus station take a left past the Pemex, and follow Juárez. An orange walking bridge, **Calle Armada Nacional,** goes to the right acros the train tracks to Playa Hermosa. A few blocks farther down Juárez, at the plaza, **Calle Fremont** goes off to the left. Juárez continues through the *centro* to the point.

Puerto Peñasco's **tourist office** (tel. 3-41-29) is in the Jim Bur shopping center on Juárez, next to **Bancomer**. (Open Mon.-Fri. 9am-2pm and 4-7pm, Sat. 9am-2pm.) **Bancomer,** on Juárez and Estrella (tel. 3-24-30), next to the plaza, exchanges currency and traveler's checks Mon.-Fri. 9am-noon. **Chiapas,** 2 blocks east of Juárez on Fremont (tel. 3-23-50), holds the **post office.** (Open Mon.-Fri. 8am-7pm, Sat. 8am-11am. **Postal code:** 83550.) **Buses** depart from Juárez and Calle 24 (tel. 3-35-55). **Transportes Norte de Sonora** has limited service to Mexicali (two per day, 38 pesos) and to Sonoita (daily, 10.50 pesos). Connections south to Hermosillo and Mazatlán can be made on *de paso* buses from Sonoita. The **train station** lies off Constitución, two blocks north of the oblique intersection with Juárez (tel. 3-26-10). Southbound *estrella* (fast) arrives at 1pm (tickets on sale 10am-noon) and the *burro* (slow) at 2am (tickets sold 1-2am). Northbound *estrella* at 5:30pm (tickets 1hr. before) and the *burro* at 3am (tickets 1hr. before). The *estrellas* are often full arriving from both directions, but the *burro's* times are inconvenient. **Lavamática Peñasco,** on Constitución at Morua (tel. 3-22-63), across from Hotel Paraíso del Desierto, will wash or dry clothes for 4 pesos. (Open Mon.-Sat. 9am-7pm.) The **Red Cross,** Fremont at Chiapas (tel. 3-22-66), is open 24 hrs. **Farmacia Don Antonio,** Juárez 89 (tel. 3-21-70) is open Mon.-Sat. 9am-9pm, Sun. 9am-2pm and has a long distance *caseta.* **Hospital Municipal,** Morua and Barrera (tel. 3-33-10), is one block east of Juárez. **Police** wait at Fremont and Juárez (tel. 3-26-26).

Accommodations and Food Budget rooms in Puerto Peñasco are as rare as deserted beaches. Those with proper equipment or a car would do best to stake out a camping spot on the sand. The hotels seemed to have agreed on a US$20 minimum. **Motel El Faro,** Pino Suárez and Armada de Mexico (tel. 3-32-01), is the closest budget hotel to the beach (two blocks). It boasts freshly remodeled rooms covered in piglet pink. Tidy rooms and matching bedspreads charm those Mexican travelers unaccustomed to such coordination. (Singles US$20, doubles US$25. Add US$5 for weekend rates.) **Hotel Villa Granada,** Madero 47 at León de la Barra (tel. 3-27-75), near Las Irresistibles has clay tile roofs hanging over the leafy central courtyard and outdoor restaurant. Screen doors and colored-glass windows give an unusual charm to clean rooms with all the standard features. All-you-can-eat Mexican buffet Sat. US$5. (Singles US$30, each extra person US$5.)

As always, *taquerías* are best for budget grub. The beachside restaurants cater to the North American masses. For typical *gringo* grub, try **Las Irrestibles,** on Constitución (tel. 3-53-47), in front of Hotel Cisar, which is locally famous for its scrumptious donuts and sticky cinnamon buns. Three piece fried chicken US$4, tuna melt US$2.45, pancakes and eggs and bacon US$2. Donuts US$6 per dozen. (Open daily 7am-11pm.) From the minute you sit down at **Asadero Sonora,** on Constitución, in front of the train station, service begins with rows of fresh condiments and ice-cold drinks. Handmade tortillas make the difference here. *Quesadillas* dripping with cheese 2.50 pesos, grilled steak tacos 2.75 pesos. Open daily noon-4am. **Cenaduría Brocheta Crazy,** Juárez and Constitución, is a triangular dining room which barely fits 6 tables and waiters in the stifling heat, but benches outside afford a fresh breeze. Cheap *antojitos* rule. *Sincronizada* 4 pesos, *flautas* with fries 8 pesos.

■■■ HERMOSILLO

If you get an early start and the buses run on time, you can breeze from Tucson to the beaches of Guaymas or Mazatlán in a single day, skipping the lonelier parts of Sonora entirely. But the habitual tardiness of Mexican buses may force you to spend a night in Hermosillo, the Sonoran state capital. Hermosillo is a wealthy, modern city in the heart of a productive agricultural and mining region. Wheat, corn, cotton, pecans, oranges, and grapes all grow in the surrounding countryside, nourished by extensive irrigation and the desert sun.

For the tourist, the most interesting things about Hermosillo are associated with the University of Sonora. The **Museo Regional de Historia** at the university contains many *indígena* artifacts and exhibits on pre-Hispanic and colonial history. It's on Encinas at Rosales on the ground floor of the tall University building. (Open Mon.-Fri. 9am-1pm and 4-6pm., Sat. 9am-1pm.) The tourist office (see Practical Information) has all the information on current exhibits here and at other museums.

Practical Information 277km south of the border, Hermosillo lies on Route 15, the main north-south highway connecting the western U.S. and central Mexico. **Buses** depart from the main terminal on Blvd. Encinas, 2km east of the city center. North and southbound buses depart every hour and with even greater frequency during the afternoon. All service out of Hermosillo is *de paso*; during holidays and weekends you've got to lace up your boxing gloves to win a seat. To get from the bus station to the center of town, cross the street and catch a bus (.80 pesos) marked "Ranchito" or "Mariachi." Taxis will ask 20 pesos for a trip to *el centro*. Pay no more than half this and don't jump in until you agree on a price.

One of the city's most recognizable landmarks is the Hermosillo Flash, a tall structure that flashes the time, temperature, news and brief advertisements day and night. At the junction of Boulevards Luis Encinas (also known as Transversal) and Rosales, the Flash helps the mapless (and those planning to hitch out of town) to orient themselves. The **University of Sonora** is located at this intersection. South on Rosales are the **cathedral** and the **government buildings,** as well as the road to Guaymas. Most of the activity lies inside the square area bordered by Rosales, Juárez, Serdán, and Blvd. Encinas.

The **tourist office** is on Tehuantepec and Comonfort (tel. 17-29-64), 2 blocks west of Rosales on the bottom floor of the Palacio Administrativo. (Open Mon.-Fri.

8am-3pm and 6-9pm, Sat. 9am-1pm.) For **currency exchange,** banks line Encinas and Serdán. **Bancomer,** Serdán and Yáñez (tel. 17-36-81) and all others are open 8:30am-1pm. **Hermex Travel,** Rosales at Monterrey (tel. 17-17-18) serves as the **American Express** office. (Open Mon.-Fri. 8:30am-1pm and 3-6pm, Sat. 9am-1pm.) The **post office,** Serdán and Rosales (tel. 12-00-11) has a *Lista de Correos.* (Open Mon.-Fri. 8am-7pm, Sat. 9am-noon. **Postal code:** 83000.) **Farmacia Margarita,** Morelia and Guerrero (tel. 13-17-73), has *casetas* upstairs in the back for long distance phone calls. Collect calls 3.50 pesos. Open 24 hrs. (**Telephone code:** 62.) Hermosillo even has an **airport,** 10km from town on Transversal toward Kino, served by **Noroeste, Aeroméxico** and **Mexicana** with daily flights to the major cities including Mexico City (544 pesos), and Los Angeles (US$165). **Trains** leave from Estación Pitíc (tel. 17-17-11), north of the city on Rte. 15. Northbound *estrella* (fast) to Nogales and Mexicali leave at 8:50am, and the *burro* (slow) at 4:45pm. Southbound *estrella* to Los Mochis and Guadalajara at 7:50pm, and the *burro* at 12:20pm. Travelers should make reservations for the *estrella* in advance; otherwise, tickets on sale 1hr. before departure at the station or at the **Agencia de Fletes y Pasaje** at Blvd. Transversal and Manuel Gonzaléz. Times subject to change. Take the bus marked "Anapolas" to get to the train station. **Tres Estrellas de Oro** (tel. 13-24-16) dispatches frequent **buses** to: Tijuana, Mexicali, Nogales, Mexico City, and Mazatlán. Buses to Tijuana and Mexico City fill early, so buy tickets at least a day in advance. Buses run to Kino (10 pesos) from the **Transportes de la Costa** bus terminal on Sonora between García and González (tel. 12-05-74). **Lavandería Automatica de Hermosillo,** Yañez and Sonora (tel. 17-55-01), washes or dries clothes for 7 pesos. (Open Mon.-Sat. 8am-8pm, Sun. 8am-2pm.) Medical needs are attended to by the **Red Cross,** Encinas at 14 de Abril (tel. 14-07-69), **Farmacia Margarita,** Morelia at Guerrero (tel. 13-17-73, open 24 hrs.), and **Hospital General del Estado de Sonora,** Transversal at Reyes (tel. 13-25-56). The **police** wait on Periférico Nte. and Noroeste (tel. 18-55-64).

Accommodations and Food Hermosillo offers many budget shelters, but few establishments fall into that comfortable middle bracket. Air conditioning is costly but indispensable, especially in the blistering summer heat. For the truly indigent, five *casas de huéspedes* line Sonora, two blocks west of the park; two more are on Guerrero near Sonora. Prices here are rock-bottom, but the area, which also includes nicer hotels like the Montecarlo, is a red-light district, especially unsafe for lone female travelers. **Hotel Niza,** Elías Calles 66 (tel. 17-20-28), a grandiose hotel of yesteryear, screams art deco with a gigantic colorful globe hanging in the pink atrium. Rooms branching off this marvelous centerpiece have cable TV, A/C and comfortable beds. (Singles 70 pesos, doubles 85 pesos. Traveler's checks accepted.) **Hotel Monte Carlo,** Juárez at Sonora (tel. 12-13-54), features a lobby with ever-blasting TV, and rooms with tile floors and brown furniture. Unfortunate failure of icy A/C downstairs and quiet upstairs to coincide. (Singles 68 pesos. Doubles 74 pesos.) **Hotel Washington,** Dr. Noriega 68 Pte. (tel. 13-11-83), between Matamoros and Guerrero has friendly managment who welcome guests to good-sized rooms with no A/C. (Singles 50 pesos, each additional person 5 pesos.)

A cheap, quick feed can be had at the counters that line the entrances to the public market at Elías calles and Matamoros, and taco and *torta* places cluster around Serdán and Guerrero, serving *taquitos* and *quesadillas* for 3-4 pesos. **Restaurant Jung,** Niños Héroes 75 (tel. 13-28-81), at Encinas, is a vegetarian restaurant dedicated to "health and long life"; every aspect is all-natural, except for the fake silk plants. Connected to a natural products store with funky books. Soybean burgers 10.50 pesos, guacamole 8 pesos, and a big cup of yummy fro-yo 6 pesos. (Open Mon.-Sat. 8am-8pm.) **My Friend,** Elías Calles 105 (tel. 13-10-44), at Yáñez, an air-conditioned fast food joint, whips up the standards: burger with fries and Coke 12 pesos, *torta milanesa* 9 pesos, eggs and ham 10 pesos. (Open Mon.-Sat. 8am-6pm.)

■■■ GUAYMAS

The principal port in Sonora state, and proud home of an extensive shrimping fleet, Guaymas was originally inhabited by the Guaymas and Yaqui tribes. In 1701, Father Kino built the mission of San José 10km north of town. In 1769 the first Spanish settlement was founded. Today, suntanned *norteamericanos* drop by to take a break from the resort life of nearby San Carlos.

Lacking convenient beaches, Guaymas deserves no lengthy stay, but it's the nicest place to break up the trip south to the more alluring resorts at Mazatlán, San Blas, and Puerto Vallarta: its cool ocean breezes give it an advantage over Hermosillo.

The area's beaches are to the north in **Miramar** and **San Carlos.** Yachts hover off San Carlos, but the beaches accessible to the budget crowd are dull and pebbly. In San Carlos the beach gets better past the end of the bus route near Club Med and Howard Johnson's. In Miramar it's better, but small, back along the bus route in front of the big fancy houses.

Nightlife in Guaymas consists of a couple of fairly standard discos. **Casanova,** in the Hotel Armida at the junction of Serdán and the highway (tel. 2-30-50), charges 10 pesos cover and US$2 for a drink (open Wed.-Sun. 9pm-2am); at **Xanadu,** Malecón Malpíca (Av. 11) between 23 and 24 (tel. 2-83-33), the cover is the same and drinks start at 7 pesos,open daily 9pm-2am).

Practical Information Guaymas is six hours south of Nogales by bus and five hours north from Los Mochis. **Buses** and **trains** service inland Mexico, and the **ferry** steams to Santa Rosalía in Baja California. Municipal buses (.60 pesos) run up and down Guaymas's main strip, Avenida Serdán. Buses marked "Miramar" (1 peso) and "San Carlos" (1.50 pesos) reach those beaches north of the city from various points along Serdán. Some travelers at the junction of Serdán and the highway also try thumbing as they wait for bus. Almost everything in Guaymas takes place on Serdán, with the crossing streets running numerically up to the harbor. Women should not walk alone more than two blocks south of Serdán after dark.

Northbound vehicles, including buses, are often stopped by narcotics police. Avoid spending the rest of your vacation in a Mexican prison cell by having your identification ready. Let them search whatever they want: it's better not to assert the right to privacy when dealing with humorless armed *federales*.

The **Tourist Office,** at Serdán at Calle 12 (tel. 2-56-67) on the 2nd floor of the building, is staffed sporadically Mon.-Fri. 9am-2pm and 4-6pm. Banks are located along Serdán for **currency exchange. Bánamex,** Serdán and Calle 20 (tel. 2-00-72), exchanges traveler's checks and greenbacks. (Open Mon.-Fri. 8:30am-midnight.) The **post office,** at Av. 10 between Calle 19 and 20 (tel. 2-07-57), is open Mon.-Fri. 8am-7pm, Sat.-Sun. 8am-noon. **Postal code:** 85400. **Farmacia Santa Martha,** Serdán and Calle 19, has 3 booths for long distance collect calls (5 pesos). (Open Mon.-Sat. 8am-9pm, Sun. 9am-2pm. **Telephone code:** 622.) **Aeroméxico** serves Guaymas with daily **airplane flights** to La Paz (326 pesos), Mexico City (650 pesos), and Tucson (US$103). The Aeroméxico office is located at Serdán and Calle 15. To get to the airport, take the bus marked "San Jose." The **Bus Station,** served by **Tres Estrellas de Oro** and **Transportes Norte de Sonora,** Calle 14 at Rodríguez (tel. 2-12-71), 2 blocks south of Serdán. If you're planning on a northern trip, catch the earliest bus, because the later ones are jammed with chickens and people. Buy tickets 1hr. in advance. Buses leave every hr. to: Hermosillo (15 pesos), Tijuana (120 pesos), Mazatlán (94 pesos), Mexico City (190 pesos), Guadalajara (120 pesos)., and Nogales (8 per day, 49 pesos). Across the street is the **Pacífico** terminal (tel. 2-30-19), which runs to the same destinations at slightly lower prices (Nogales 40 pesos). The old **train** station and current office is located on Serdán at Calle 30 (tel. 2-49-80). Office open Mon.-Fri. 8am-noon and 2-5pm for information or reservations. Trains actually arrive and depart from **Empalme,** 10km south on the International Highway. Buy tickets at Empalme station 1hr. before the train arrives. From

Serdán take the municipal bus marked "Empalme" to the end of the route, then transfer to the other bus marked "Estación." Fast *estrella* train goes south at 9:40pm, north at 6am. To: Hermosillo (15 pesos), Nogales (40 pesos), Mazatlán (75 pesos) and Guadalajara (161 pesos). The slow *burro* train leaves north at 1pm and south at 2:30pm. First class to: Hermosillo (5 pesos), Nogales (13 pesos), Mazatlán (22pesos), and Guadalajara (40 pesos).

The **ferry** ferminal is on Serdán about 1km past. Electricidad (tel. 2-23-24). Boat steams to Santa Rosalía Tues. and Fri. at 8am; tickets are only sold 1 day in advance 8am-2:30pm (*salón* 38 pesos, *turista* 76 pesos). For more detail, see Baja California: Getting Around: By Sea. To get to the ferry terminal, hop an outbound bus and get off at the "Transbordador" sign.

The **Red Cross,** (tel. 4-08-76), is at the northern limit of Guaymas. **Farmacia Sonora,** Serdán at Calle 15 (tel. 4-24-04), is open 24 hrs. **Hospital Municipal:** tel. 2-01-22. **Police** are in Palacio Municipal on Serdán at Calle 22 (tel. 4-01-04).

Accommodations and Food **Casa de Huéspedes Lupita,** Calle 15 #125, (tel. 2-84-09), 2 blocks south of Serdán, is a mammoth "house" with 30 rooms and 12 communal baths, every corner glowingly clean. Iron gates on bedroom doors and 2 fans in every room allow for much-needed ventilation. (Noon check-out. Towel deposit 5 pesos. Singles 23 pesos, with bath 35 pesos. Doubles 33 pesos, with bath 45 pesos.) Look for the "HO EL" sign at **Hotel Rubi,** Serdán at Calle 29 (tel. 2-04-95). Friendly management shows guests to average fare with TV and A/C, and also helps with local questions. Convenient location for those who want work on a shrimp trawler. (Singles 50 pesos. Doubles 60 pesos.) **Hotel Impala,** Calle 21 #40 (tel. 4-09-22), 1 block south of Serdán, displays its antiquity in the black-and-white pictures of Guaymas's past hanging on the walls. Rooms are renovated to present-day glory with matching polyester bedspreads and curtains, A/C and TV. (Key deposit 5 pesos. Singles 70 pesos. Doubles 90 pesos. Triples 120 pesos. Credit cards accepted.)

Seafood is the Guaymas specialty. Local favorites include frog legs, turtle steaks and oysters in a garlic/chile sauce. The **Mercado Municipal,** on Calle 20, one block from Serdán, sells fresh produce as well as clothes, flowers, toys and carved goods. Hot dog vendors line Serdán. **Las 1000 Tortas,** Serdán 188 (tel. 4-30-61), between Calles 17 and 18, has no menu, but the name of this family-run eatery reveals the item of choice: *torta* (6 pesos). Three types of delicious *comidas corridas* (15 pesos) are prepared daily and served noon-4pm. Enchiladas and *gorditas* 12 pesos. (Open daily 8am-11pm.) Red painted picnic tables and funky mirrored walls accompany the weirdo spelling of **Jax Snax,** Serdán at Calle 14 (tel. 2-38-65). Cheap, delicious breakfasts and oven-fresh pizzas are choice. French toast with fresh fruit 8 pesos, yogurt and fruit 8 pesos, mini-pizza 15 pesos. (Open Tues.-Sun. 8am-11pm.)

CHIHUAHUA

■■■ CIUDAD JUÁREZ AND EL PASO, TEXAS

El Paso del Norte was the least difficult way for people, horses, and automobiles to cross the Occidental del Norte and the Sierra Madre into and out of Mexico, and so it nurtured the twin cities of Ciudad Juárez and El Paso. The strategic site, once part of an important *indígena* trading route, was one of the first occupied. Where they merge at the border, El Paso and Juárez are remarkably similar; in fact, if it weren't for the murky Río Grande, it would be impossible to tell the cities apart. Juárez has better wild and seedy border town activity, and while it seems relatively safe during the day, as darkness increases, so does the ratio of the drunk to the sober people wandering the streets. Women should not walk alone or in dark places; everyone should avoid the area more than two blocks west of Juárez's mains street, Juárez.

ORIENTATION

Where to cross the border into Juárez depends on your goal. From downtown El Paso, the **Stanton Bridge** (on Stanton St.) and **Santa Fe Bridge** (on El Paso St.) lead into the heart of **Old Juárez,** also called *el centro*, where markets, restaurants, and bars thrive. Santa Fe Bridge actually becomes **Av. Juárez,** the main drag, while Stanton Bridge turns into **Av. Lerdo.** Two miles east, U.S. 54 crosses the border at the Puente Córdova and becomes **Av. Lincoln:** this road leads to the ProNaf shopping mall and studio complex with resident craftspeople and predictably high prices. The Stanton St. Bridge is restricted to traffic and pedestrians entering Juárez, the Santa Fe to departing vehicles. The **Córdova Bridge** allows two-way traffic. Pedestrians can come and go on the Córdova and Santa Fe bridges.

To cross the border on foot, simply pay the border guard US$.25 per person the way in, US$1.50 on the way out. Cars to Mexico pay US$1, to El Paso US$1.95. To venture farther into Mexico, you must obtain a **tourist card** at the immigration office. You won't need it until you reach the immigration checkpoint 22km into the interior, but if you don't have it then, they'll send you back (see Mexico General Introduction: Documents and Formalities above for more information). The immigration office (Departamento de Población) is located immediately to the right as you cross the Stanton St. Bridge. (Immigration open 24 hrs.) From El Paso airport avoid expensive cabs (US$20) and catch the bus (US$.75) to San Jacinto Park. Walk two blocks up Main St.until you run into the **Tourist Information Center.**

Most of Old Juárez can be covered on foot. Street numbers start in the 600s near the two border bridges and descend to zero at 16 de Septiembre, where Av. Juárez ends. Both Lerdo and Francisco Villa run parallel to Juárez. The ProNaf center can be reached by hopping on the public bus "Ruta 8-A" (.70 pesos) on Malecón between the Departamento de Población and Secretaría de Turismo across the street from bus shelter. Taxis are always available in any part of downtown, but they usually overcharge. Negotiate the price before getting in.

■ El Paso, Texas

Practical Information The **tourist office,** 1 Civic Center Plaza (tel. 544-0062), opposite Greyhound Bus Station at the Santa Fe St. and San Francisco St. intersection, is friendly and well-stocked with brochures, and also sells **El Paso-Juárez Trolley Co.** tickets for day-long tours across the border (Mon.-Fri. US$8, Sat.-Sun. US$10). Open daily 8:30am-5pm; trolleys run daily on the hour, 10am-5pm. **Exchange currency** at **Valuta** (tel. 544-1152), corner of Mesa and Paisano, which has all exchange services, plus a fax. (Open 24 hrs.) The **Greyhound bus station,** 111 San Francisco St. (tel. 532-2365), is sandwiched between Santa Fe St. and El Paso St., in the heart of downtown. Daily service to and from Dallas, Phoenix, New York, Los Angeles, and numerous other U.S. cities. (Storage lockers for US$1. Open 24 hrs.)

Accommodations and Food Staying in El Paso is a better option than facing the dearth of appealing hotels in Juárez. The **Gardner Hotel/Hostel (AYH/HI),** 311 E. Franklin (tel. 532-3661), is 2 blocks up Mesa St. from San Jacinto Park. A friendly group staffs this 75-year-old establishment, which features quiet, clean rooms in the heart of downtown. Weary travelers obtain money-saving advice and maps for both El Paso and Juárez. Reception open 24 hrs. Lockers US$.75 per day, long term, US$.50 per day. Washing machines (US$1.50) and dryers (US$.50). (**Hotel:** TV. Check-out 1pm. Singles US$23, with bath US$35. Doubles US$30, with bath US$40. Add about US$5 to all these prices for tax. **Hostel:** Members only. Spotless kitchen and common room with pool table. Check-out 10am. Bed in 4-person dorm room with sink US$12.) The **Gateway Hotel,** 104 S. Stanton St. (tel. 532-2611), at the corner of S. Stanton St. and San Antonio, features a diner downstairs, clean rooms with bathrooms, and A/C upstairs. A favorite stop for middle-class Mexicans; speak Spanish to get respect and a room. Check-out 4pm. Parking $2 per 24 hrs. (Singles US$21 and up. Doubles US$27 and up.)

El Paso is an American city, and few restaurants other than McDonalds and business-lunch hot dog mills are in the downtown business district. Look for the flashing lights of the **Tap and Bar Restaurant** (tel. 548-9049), at Stanton St. and San Antonio, where the US$3 huevos rancheros or Mexican plate are popular with the locals. Mini-dance floor and disco ball for nighttime use. (Open daily 9am-2am.) **Big Bun** (tel. 533-3926) at 500 N. Stanton serves tacos and burritos as well as big burgers (US$1.10) with salsa on the side. (Open Mon.-Sat. 8am-8pm, Sun. 10am-3pm.)

■ Ciudad Juárez

PRACTICAL INFORMATION

Tourist Office: Secretaría de Turismo, Malecón and Francisco Villa (tel. 14-08-37), in the basement of gray Unidad Administrativa Municipal bldg. on the left of the Santa Fe Bridge. Plenty of brochures, easier if you know Spanish. (Open Mon.-Fri. 8am-8pm, Sat.-Sun. 7am-3pm.)

U.S. Consulate: López Mateos Nte. 924 (tel. 13-40-48). For emergencies dial (915) 525-6060.

Currency Exchange: In Juárez, banks congregate near the bus station and along 16 de Septiembre. Most open Mon.-Fri. 9am-1:30pm. Virtually no *casa de cambio* or bank will accept traveler's checks (a problem throughout northern Mexico, where real greenbacks are the weapon of choice). If you find a place that will take your checks, unload them *pronto*. It is easier and cheaper to exchange in El Paso banks along Stanton, Main, and Mills.

Post Office: Lerdo at Ignacio Peña (tel. 12-02-44). Open Mon.-Fri. 8am-7pm, Sat.-Sun. 9am-1pm. **Postal Code:** 32000.

Telephone: Secrefax, Av. Juárez (tel. 15-15-10), 1 block from Santa Fe Bridge. For an El Paso operator, dial 08; US$1 per minute. Local call 2 pesos for 3 minutes. International calls, fax, and UPS. Open 24 hrs. **Telephone Code:** 16.

Abraham González Airport: (tel. 19-07-57) about 17km out Rte. 45 (Carretera Panorámica). Primary carrier is **Aeroméxico** with flights to Mexico City, Monterrey, and Chihuahua. Catch the crowded school bus marked "Aeropuerto" (.70 pesos).

Train Station: Francisco Villa at Insurgentes (tel. 14-97-17), 12 blocks down Francisco Villa from the Santa Fe Bridge with service to Chihuahua and Mexico City.

Bus Station: Blvd. Oscar Flores 4010 (tel. 13-20-83), just north of the ProNaf center and next to the Río Grande mall; way too far for walking. Take Chihuahuenses from the El Paso terminal to Juárez (US$5) or cram into the school bus "Ruta 1A" at Av. Insurgentes and Francisco Villa. Open 24 hrs. **Chihuahuenses** (tel. 13-06-57) and **Omnibus** offer numerous departures to Mexico City, Monterrey, Guadalajara, and Nuevo Casas Grandes.

Laundromat: Lavasolas, Tlaxcala and 5 de Mayo (tel. 12-54-61).

Red Cross: Henry Durnant in ProNaf center (tel. 16-58-06).

Pharmacy: Farmacia Vibar, 16 de Septiembre (te. 15-61-32), across from the church. Turn right from Juárez. (Open 8am-midnight.)

Hospitals: Hospital Latinoamericano: 250 N. Lopez Mateos (tel. 16-14-67). Supposedly caters to *gringos.* Open 24 hrs.

Emergency: tel. 06.

Police: Oro and 16 de Septiembre (tel. 15-51-51).

FOOD AND ACCOMMODATIONS

In Juárez, hotels that meet only minimal standards are nonetheless some of the most expensive budget accommodations in all of Mexico. The **Hotel Santa Fe,** Lerdo Nte. 673 at Tlaxcala (tel. 14-02-70, fax 12-56-27) houses a helpful, English-speaking staff who are justifiablly proud of their modern conveniences and safety features. Freshly renovated and clean rooms have A/C and TVs with satellite hook-up. (Singles US$29. Doubles US$33. MC, Visa.) Less than a mile from the Santa Fe bridge, the **Hotel San Carlos,** Av. Juárez Nte. 126, (tel. 15-04-19) offers a convenient location for those who want to drink the night away on Av. Juárez. Expect to speak Spanish to obtain a sagging, worn mattress, and baño. (Singles 67 pesos. Doubles 80 pesos. MC, Visa.)

Eateries vary from clean, air-conditioned restaurants catering to tourists to road-side shacks with picnic tables and TV in Spanish. Take your pick; prices vary according to the atmosphere. **Restaurant La Sevillana,** (tel. 12-63-12), ½ block from corner of Juárez and Abraham González, is a relaxed diner with bilingual menus and A/C. Generous servings of filet mignon (28 pesos) and shrimp sautéed in garlic sauce (17 pesos). Serves breakfast, too (9-10 pesos). (Open daily 8am-8pm.) Waiters with bright white shirts and bow ties service **Hotel Santa Fe Restaurant,** Lerdo Nte. 673 (tel. 14-02-70), at Tlaxcala across from the Hotel Impala. This quiet, back street place offers *enchiladas de pollo* (10 pesos) and club sandwiches (10 pesos) served with tortilla chips and salsa. (Open 24 hrs.) **Nuevo Restaurante Martino,** Juárez 643 (tel. 12-33-70), two blocks from the Santa Fe Bridge, is Juárez's attempt at elegance. It boasts more than 100 dishes of all kinds of cuisines and higher than average prices. On weekends, Mexican businessmen give way to tourist families. (Open daily noon to midnight.) Paleteria Michoacanas are everywhere, but the newest, with the widest selection of American thirst quenchers as well as Mexican fruit drinks, is at the corner of M.A. Martinez and Juárez, about halfway from the bridge to the end of the street. Ice cream 2 pesos or US $0.75. (Open daily 10am-5pm.)

SIGHTS

The deforested **Parque Chamizal,** near the Córdova Bridge, is a good place to escape the noise of the city, if not the heat. The **Museo Arqueológico,** Av. Pellicer 1 in mid-park, displays little of interest: one room features plastic facsimiles of pre-Conquest sculptures, and the other wows the crowds with trilobite fossils, rocks, and bones. (Open Mon.-Sat. 9am-2pm, Sun. 1-8pm. Free.) In *el centro* visit the **Aduana Frontensa** where Juárez and 16 de Septiembre cross. Built in 1889 as a trading outpost, it hosts an exhibit of the region's history during the Mexican Revolution. (Open Tues.-Sun. 10am-6pm. Free.) The ProNaf center, distant from the park at Lincoln and 16 de Septiembre, contains the **Museo de Arte** (tel. 13-17-08) with exhibits of Mexican art, past and present. (Open Tues.-Sun. 11am-7pm. Admission 1 peso, students free.) Also at the ProNaf center, the **Centro Artesanal** sells handmade goods at maximum prices; haggle here. The "Ruta 8" bus will take you from *el centro* to ProNaf for .70 pesos; a taxi charges 25 times as much.

ENTERTAINMENT

The *toro* and the *matador* battle in traditional bullfights on occasional evenings during the summer at the **Plaza Monumental de Toros**, República and Huerta (tel. 13-16-56). Seats in the shade cost US$11. Call for dates and times. The **Lienzo de Charro,** on Av. Charro off República, also conducts bullfights and *charreada* (rodeo) on Sunday afternoons during the summer; get the specifics at the tourist office. At the western edge of town, the **Juárez Racetrack** (tel. 17-03-11) rises from Vicente Guerrero. Dogs run Wed.-Sun. at 7:30pm. Sunday matinees during the summer at 2:30pm. Horse racing can be seen only on closed-circuit TV.

Juárez has so many bars that simply counting them can make you dizzy even before you carouse. Many establishments are unsavory, and even some of the savory ones can become dangerous; stick to the glutted strip along Av. Juárez. On weekends, North Americans swarm to Juárez to join their Mexican friends in a 48-hour quest for fun, fights, fiestas, and inexpensive dental work. **Kentucky Club,** Juárez 629 (tel. 14-99-90), was voted Best Bar 1991 by an El Paso paper. Sidle up to the long mahogany bar, backed by intricate woodwork and embossed mirrors so the middle-aged clientele can see and be seen. Must be 21 to be served. (Open 11am-midnight.) **Mr. Fog Bar,** Juárez Nte. 140 (tel. 14-29-48), is also popular. This dimly lit saloon with soft love songs becomes a *romántico* escape from the crazy city. Beer US$1.75. Margaritas US$2.50. (Open Sun.-Thurs. 11am-midnight, Fri.-Sat. 11am-2am.)

■■■ CASAS GRANDES AND NUEVO CASAS GRANDES

Even though the 3½-hour journey south from Juárez through the scenic Chihuahuan Desert is extraordinarily peaceful, arriving at the foothills of the Sierra Madres in the valley of Nuevo Casas Grandes is a cool relief. The valley's claim to fame is the ruins of **Paquimé** (pah-kee-MEH) in Casas Grandes, the most important city in pre-Conquest northern Mexico. Nuevo Casas Grandes may remind you of cities in the North American West. Cowboy hats and enormous brass belt buckles adorn many inhabitants. The absence of tourists lends this slow-paced town an authenticity rare in the North.

ORIENTATION

Nuevo Casas Grandes lies to the southwest of Cd. Juárez and northwest of Chihuahua. The only way to get there is by road. **Omnibus de México** provides the most reliable service with buses to both Cd. Juárez (30 pesos) and Chihuahua (6 per day, 5am-5pm, 36 pesos). The **bus station** is located on Obregón, a half block from 16 de Septiembre.

All of the town's streets are laid out in a nice grid, with the center of town situated between Constitución and Juárez (Obregón runs parallel to these streets) and Minerva and 16 de Septiembre. Go right from the bus terminal two blocks until 5 de Mayo then turn left, go one block, cross the tracks and you are on the main drag **Constitución**.

PRACTICAL INFORMATION

Everything important is within the 10-block downtown area. Exchange currency at the **Casa de Cambio California,** Constitución 207 (open Mon.-Sat. 9am-7pm), or **Banamex,** on 5 de Mayo between Juárez and Constitución (open Mon.-Fri. 9am-2pm and 4-6pm). **Bancomer** at 16 de Septiembre on Constitución has an **ATM** which takes Visa, with 24 hr. access. The **post office,** at 16 de Septiembre and Madero, one block from Obregón, has Lista de Correos (Open Mon.-Fri. 9am-1pm and 3-6pm, Sat. 9am-1pm). The **postal code** is 31700. The **Supermarket: Hiperama,** is located at Juárez and Minerva and is open daily 9am-9pm. **Laundromat, Lavasolas Paquimé** (tel. 4-13-20), stands right behind the Hotel Paquimé on Jesus Urueto. (Open Mon.-Sat. 7:30am-7pm.) **Farmacia Benavides,** at Obregón and 5 de Mayo (tel. 4-55-55) is open daily 8am-10pm. The **police** are on the outskirts of town on Madero. In an **emergency,** dial 4-09-73.

ACCOMMODATIONS

Stock up on water before you hit town because none of these hotels offer *agua purificada*, only *agua potable*. Also, the price of quality hotels has drastically risen here. Check-out time for all listed below is 2pm.

Hotel California, Constitución 209 (tel. 4-08-34), between 5 de Mayo and Minerva. Located on the noisy, central street. The large rooms with tiled floors and wicker furniture are complemented with spotless bathrooms. Rooms in back may be quieter. Old black and white TVs with cable. Mirrors on the ceiling, pink champagne on ice. Check-out: anytime. Singles 80 pesos. Doubles 75 pesos. MC, Visa.

Hotel Juárez, Obregón 110 (tel. 4-02-33), a block from the bus stations. Much English spoken here by the affable owner, Mario, who offers a small dark room with bed and shower to the less affluent traveler. Singles 25 pesos, 39 pesos with two people. Doubles 49 pesos.

Motel Piñón, Juárez Nte. 605 (tel. 4-06-55), 2 blocks down from Minerva. This refurbished motel wrapped around a courtyard boasts a museum with pieces from Paquimé, and free guides to the ruins for groups of five or more. Clean rooms with new carpet and colorful bathrooms also offer cable TV diversion. Singles 85 pesos. Doubles 95 pesos. MC, Visa.

FOOD

The lack of tourists makes dining out with the locals (and the local flies) cheap. The low gringo count, however, means that nightlife is soporific, and the few bars in town do not welcome women.

Restaurante Constantino, Juárez at Minerva (tel. 4-10-05). Convenient to every big hotel. Bilingual menu, but speak Spanish to avoid pointing. *Quesadilla* 12 pesos, big lunch special 17.60 pesos. Bright, clean, large windows give a view of the plaza. Open daily 7am-midnight.

Dinno's Pizza, Minerva and Constitución (tel. 4-02-40). This clean and icily air-conditioned joint features rare English-speaking staff and all-you-can-eat Sunday buffet (20 pesos) including fresh fruit, orange juice and eggs. There's always pizza (small 22 pesos, medium 27 pesos). Open daily 11am-midnight. MC, Visa.

Café de La Esquina, 5 de Mayo at Obregón (tel 4-39-59). Sit down in this simple, worn spot and enjoy a Coke in a frosted mug while the cook prepares fresh tacos (9 pesos) or enchiladas (14 pesos). A/C and breakfast too. Open daily 7am-9pm.

Restaurant Playa Ayul, 16 de Septiembre at Obregon (tel. 4-24-72). Specializing in seafood. A nice, air-conditioned eatery, where you can enjoy a cheap breakfast (5-15 pesos) if you don't mind the smell of fish. Open daily 7am-10pm.

■ Casas Grandes (Paquimé)

Eight km southwest of Nuevo Casas Grandes, the pre-Conquest city of Paquimé lay hidden underground for 600 years. Its architecture suggests that **Casas Grandes** (so named upon excavation) grew out of two different cultures: its many-storied *pueblos* resemble those in the southwestern U.S., but its step pyramids are similar to those in central and southern Mexico. Among the ruins lie a partially-excavated **central market** area as well as a **ball court**. Between 1000 and 1200 AD, Paquimé was the most important agricultural and trading center in northern Mexico. The inhabitants kept parrots and turkeys in adobe pens and built indoor aqueducts and hidden cisterns to supply the *pueblos* in times of siege. Around 1340, Aztec invaders burned the already-abandoned buildings. First exhumed in the early 1970s, Paquimé is now an archaeological zone administered by the Mexican government. Unfortunately, once it had been exposed to the satisfaction of both archaeologists and tourists, its high mud walls began to crumble. Visitors should avoid eroding the thin walls. A plaque commemorates archaeologist Eduardo Contreras, "El Señor de Paquimé," who died in 1986. Restoration efforts continue today.

Paquimé is hidden in the tranquil mountains of Casas Grandes. On summer afternoons, the dry and shadeless ruins can become a blazing inferno with temperatures near 100°F. Be sure to bring sun protection, a broad-brimmed hat (cheap sombreros are available in town) and, most importantly, a gigantic bottle of water to quench your thirst. When traveling from Chihuahua or Juárez, pick up information on the dig ahead of time, because none exists at the site.

To reach Paquimé, take the **yellow municipal bus** at the corner of Constitución and 16 de Septiembre to the central park in Casas Grandes (hourly, 1 peso). Get off the bus at the main plaza, walk toward the back of the bus and continue down that dirt road for about 10 minutes. You will pass through two large dips, turn to the right and then to the left. (Admission to the site Mon.-Sat. 8 pesos, Sun. free. Open daily 10am-5pm.) Some information may be obtained at the tourist center and pottery store at the opposite end of the square, or at the Motel Piñon back in Nuevo Casas Grandes.

■■■ CHIHUAHUA

The capital of Mexico's largest state of the same name was founded in 1709 and quickly grew into a major trading and administrative center, supporting mining operations in the resource-rich western range and cattle enterprises in the surrounding valleys. Today, the lumber industry of the Sierra Madre yields most of the city's income.

Exposed to the sandstorms of Mexico's vast northern desert, Chihuahua may seem little more than an inconveniently located outpost of the civilization to the south. This seclusion convinced Pancho Villa to establish his revolutionary *División del Norte* headquarters here. During the conflict, his eclectic band of cowboys, bandits and vagabonds staged flamboyant attacks against the Porfiriato, streaming down from Chihuahua and assaulting social inequities. The man is a legendary figure to most *Chihuahuenses*, and Quinta Luz, Villa's sprawling colonial home, shines as the city's major attraction.

The peoples who converge on Chihuahua and the surrounding area are as diverse as the land itself. Mennonites came here in flocks from the Pennsylvania Dutch country in the 1920s, attracted by the bountiful pastures. Today they maintain their seclusion and purity in the nearby town of Cuauhtémoc and in other agricultural communities around Chihuahua. Known country wide for their delicious fresh cheese, the Mennonites prosper from beef and dairy cattle ranching. Equally secluded but radically different, the *indígena* Tarahumara people live isolated in the nearby Sierra Madres. They arrive at the city market in the early morning to sell handmade crafts, the men dressed in cowboy attire or baggy shorts and shirts, the women in sandals, shawls and bright skirts.

Chihuahua can become almost charming on a still and sunny day, but beware—the winds that whip across the surrounding desert do not stop for mere budget-traveling mortals. When the gales slice through town—summoning dirt, garbage and rain—the city becomes a river of sorrow.

ORIENTATION

¡Ay! Chihuahua sprawls in every direction, reaching onto the surrounding mountains. Skewered by Route 45 (the Pan American Hwy.), it serves as an important transportation hub for northern Mexico. Trains arrive from the north and south at the **Estación Central de los FFNN,** just north of downtown. Trains to Los Mochis and Creel via the Barrancas del Cobre leave from a different station, south of the city center off Ocampo, three blocks from 20 de Noviembre. To shorten the 20-minute walk to *el centro*, hop on a public bus running up and down Ocampo to Libertad. Pay about 8 pesos for a cab, and set the price before you step in.

Buses arrive at the **Camionera Central** on Blvd. Juan Pablo, far from *el centro*. Go out the other side of the station and across the parking lot to catch a bus to the Cathedral (.90 pesos). Get off when the Cathedral comes into view and walk to the left from Av. Juárez to reach Libertad, which is a pedestrians-only shopping arcade between Independencia and Guerrero. Two other main streets, Victoriá and Juárez, run parallel to Libertad, and Av. Ocampo crosses Juarez one block past the Cathedral. For a good map, get off the bus at Av. Carranza and walk two blocks to the left of the tourist office in the Palacio de Gobierno.

Energetic travelers can easily reach Quinta Luz on foot. Budget hotels and restaurants cluster on the streets behind the cathedral (the boot district). **Avenida Independencia,** which runs in front of the *zócalo*, marks the dividing line for the streets or *calles*. Even-numbered *calles* lie on the south side of Independencia, and those with odd numbers rest on the north side. *Avenidas* running north-south are named.

PRACTICAL INFORMATION

Tourist Office: By 1994 the tourist office will probably have moved from Libertad and Calle 13 to the Palacio de Gobierno (tel. 16-17-42). Friendly information in English and indispensable maps. Open Mon.-Fri. 9am-3pm. **Información y Documentación Turística:** Tecnológica and Padre Infante. Convenient only for motorists arriving in Chihuahua from the highway.

Currency Exchange: Banpaís on Victoira is the first block away from the front of the Cathedral (tel. 16-16-59). Go to the dolares desk. Traveler's checks changed free. Open Mon.-Fri. 9am-1:30pm. For 24-hr. dollar exchange, go across the street to **Hotel San Francisco** (tel. 16-75-50). **ATM: Cajeros Automaticos,** are located near the lobbies of all the tall banks downtown. **Banamex** at Doblado and Carranza accepts the most card types.

American Express: Vincente Guerrero 1207 (tel. 15-58-58), past Allende, right wher Guerrero curves to become Paeo Bolívar. Open Mon.-Fri. 9am-6pm, Sat. 9am-noon.

Post Office: On Libertad, between Vincente Guerrero and Carranza, 1 block from the arcade. Lista de Correos. Open Mon.-Fri. 8am-7pm, Sat. 9am-1pm. **Postal Code:** 31000.

Telephones: In better hotels and scattered among the various parks and plazas. Long distance service available in the plaza in front of the *catedral*. **Telephone Code:** 14.

Telegrams: At the post office with the same hours.

Airport: Blvd. Juan Pablo II (tel. 20-06-16), 14km from town. Served by **Aeroméxico** (tel. 15-63-03) and **Aero Leo López.** To Monterrey, Ciudad Juárez, Mexico City and El Paso. Ground transportation to town available from a booth to your right as you exit the baggage area.

Trains: FFCC Chihuahua al Pacífico, the southern station near Quinta Luz. Walk south on Ocampo and turn right at 20 de Noviembre. Walk to Calle 24 and take a left; you will hit the station after 2 blocks. *Primera* and *segunda* trains through Barrancas del Cobre to Creel (2 per day, about 42 pesos) and Los Mochis (2 per day, about 90 pesos). You must have a ticket to board *primera* trains, and there's a 25% charge to buy a *segunda* ticket on board. Children 5-11 years old are ½ price. *Primera* ticket includes breakfast. Tickets sold Sun.-Fri. 6am-7:30pm, Sat. 6-9am and 3-6pm. (For an explanation of *primera* and *segunda*, see Barrancas del Cobre.) **FFCC Nacionales de México**, the northern station on Av. Tecnologico, has service to and from the north and south.

Bus Station: Huge new structure with restaurants and money changing facilties. Daily service to Acapulco, Mazatlán, Guadalajara, Mexico City, and Creel.

Supermarket: El Fénix, Libertad 505 (tel. 10-26-21), in the shopping arcade. Open daily 9am-9pm.

Laundromat: Lavafácil, Universidad 3500 (tel. 13-82-85).

Red Cross: Calle 24 and Revolución (tel. 11-22-11).

24-hr. Pharmacy: Farmacia Nocturno, Calle Aldama 1510 at Calle 19 (tel. 16-44-14).

Hospital: Hospital Central, Calle 33 and Rosales (tel. 15-90-00), at the end of Colón.

Emergency: Dial 06.

Police: Calle 4 and Ochoa (tel. 10-02-38).

ACCOMMODATIONS

Hotels in Chihuahua are like the city itself—charm is visible through the grit. Half a dozen economical hotels lie between Victoria and Juárez in the area behind the *catedral*.

Nuevo Hotel Reforma, Victoria 809 (tel. 16-24-55). Hotel created from a 2-story Spanish colonial mansion with a central courtyard. Rooms with thin walls can at least boast clean bathrooms and ceiling fans. Check out 2pm. *Agua purificada.* Singles 30 pesos. Doubles 40 pesos.

Hotel Apolo, Juárez 907 (tel. 16-11-00), across from the post office in the noisy center of town, 1 block from the shopping arcade. Clean rooms, comfortable beds and A/C make for a pleasant stay. Check-out 2pm. Singles 80 pesos. Doubles 85 pesos. Credit cards accepted.

Hotel Santa Regina, Calle 3 and Manuel Doblado (tel. 15-38-89, fax 10-1411) Pristine lobby, but small brown rooms with cable TV and central A/C. Check-out 2pm. Singles 87.50 pesos. Doubles 100 pesos. AmEx, MC, Visa. Copies .50 pesos.

Casa de Huespedes Bolívar, Bolívar 309 (tel. 10-09-45), 7 small blocks from Aldama on Calle 5, then look right. Old painted brick house around a sunny little coutyard. Basic bed and bath. Singles 20 pesos. Doubles 40 pesos.

FOOD

Eateries in Chihuahua are not geared toward tourists. Some of the best meals can be found in small *cantinas* with bands (and many drunk, rowdy men).

Mi Café, Victoria at Calle 10 (tel. 10-12-38), across from Hotel San Juan. Put on your sunglasses for this bright, 1950s-style diner with melon-colored vinyl booths, and orange and white checkered ceiling. A 15-peso order of chicken comes as a huge meal, with bread, soup, rice, and poatoes, and dessert. Open daily 7:30am-11pm. Yes to credit cards.

La Parrilla, Victoria 420 (tel. 15-58-56), just south of the *catedral*. Chefs sizzle up fresh meat dishes right before your eyes. Choose the appropriate red wine to accompany your steak and it could be the perfect romantic evening. Juicy T-bone steak 28 pesos. *Quesito con Chorizo*, 13.50 pesos. Open daily noon-midnight. Credit cards accepted.

Dino's Pizza, Manuel Doblado 301 (tel. 16-57-07), across from the Santa Regina. Bakes hot, cheesy pizzas in a comfortable, cool atmosphere. It's a welcome escape from tacos and burritos. Medium pizza with ham 20 pesos, spaghetti 15 pesos. Open daily 8am-midnight. Credit cards: *sí*.

SIGHTS AND ENTERTAINMENT

Heading southwest of the *zócalo* offers an excellent retreat from the grime of downtown. At **Quinta Luz** (the Pancho Villa museum, tel. 16-29-58), visitors can immerse themselves in the turbulence of the revolution through the collection of documents and photographs, paintings of Sr. Villa, his household furnishings, his vast collection of rifles and machine guns (still enough to outfit a small army) and the bullet-ridden Dodge in which he was assassinated. To reach Quinta Luz, head 1.5km south on Ocampo. On the left you will pass a statue of Simón Bolívar, the lively Parque Lerdo, and a monument dedicated to patriot Manuel Ojinaga. A few more blocks down Ocampo bring you to an intersection with a large stone church. This is 20 de Noviembre; turn left and go two blocks to Calle 10, then turn right. Villa's house is two blocks down on the right. (Open daily 9am-1pm and 3-7pm. Admission 1.50 pesos.)

Back in *el centro*, the basement of the *catedral* hides the **Sacred Art Museum,** Libertad and Calle 2 (tel. 10-37-77). Pastoral religious paintings from the 18th century mingle with photos and portraits from the Pope's most recent visit to Chihuahua. (Open Mon.-Fri. 10am-2pm and 4-6pm. Admission 2 pesos adults, 1 peso for children.) For those craving more artistic pleasure, the **Centro Cultural Universitario,** Bolívar and Calle 4 (tel. 16-66-84), hosts a larger exposition of *arte nuevo* from the turn of the century, including the work of many French painters.

Occasional bullfights in the **Plaza de Toros,** Cuauhtémoc and Canal. The **Lienzo Charro,** on Av. Américas west of town, hosts weekend rodeos. Inquire at the tourist office for dates, times and prices. Downtown, Av. Libertad is closed to traffic east of the cathedral and becomes a large, open-air shopping mall on weekends.

Various *cantinas* house themselves in hotel lobbies, offering cheap beer, drunk locals and lively *mariachis* in traditional costumes (women usually not welcome). Relax tired feet at **Bar Los Primos** in the Hotel San Francisco. At the corner of Calle 4 and Paseo Bolívar is the architectural gem **Museo Regional de Chihuahua,** Bolívar 401 (tel. 16-64-84), which houses a collection of elaborate furniture from the early 20th century. There are also exhibits on the Mennonites and the ruins of Paquimé. (Open Tues.-Sun. 10am-2pm and 4-7pm. Admission 3 pesos.)

On Juárez between Guerrero and Carranza, a golden eagle bearing the inscription "Libertad" points to the door of the **prison cell** where Padre Miguel Hidalgo, leader of an early bid for Mexican independence, was held for two months prior to his execution in 1811. Most interesting to Mexican history buffs, the small room displays some of Hidalgo's belongings and letters from early participants in the uprising. (Open Tues.-Fri. 10am-2pm and 4-7pm. Sat.-Sun. 10am-2pm. Admission 1.50 pesos.) Another eagle points to the **Templo de San Francisco** on Libertad and Calle 17, which contains Hidalgo's decaptitated body.

■■■ CREEL

High amid the peaks of the Sierra Madres, the small village of Creel welcomes travelers with a natural beauty and warmth unmatched in northern Mexico. The inhospitable Chihuahuan desert gives way here to spectacular gorges and looming peaks, the land of the Tarahumara people. Easy-going Creel, with its cool mountain climate, is a refreshing oasis from the rest of Chihuahua.

Be forewarned, this mountain retreat is developing rapidly. In the past few years, tourists have journeyed to Creel in increasing numbers, and most hotels have retaliated by expanding and renovating existing structures. The Chihuahuan state government has recently remodeled the *zócalo* and all main streets, planting numerous pine trees throughout town and expanding pavement.

Many Tarahumara come to Creel to sell crafts to curio shops and to pick up supplies. Of Mexico's many *indígena* groups, the Tarahumara have best warded off modern Mexican culture, by still living in isolated caves and wooden houses and resisting all efforts to settle them in villages. The Tarahumara are famous for their non-stop long-distance footraces, which last up to 72 hours. Tarahumara pine-needle baskets, blankets, figurines, ribbons and violins are sold throughout town.

The Tarahumara greatly value their seclusion and tend to shy away from contact with tourists. If you pass Tarahumara cave dwellings, look at the caves from the road, but don't take their obvious accessibility as an invitation to approach more closely or to walk in and have a look-see. Refrain from photographing the Tarahumara at will. If you ask to photograph them, they may agree only out of graciousness and not because they really don't mind. Fortunately, Artesanías Misión (see Practical Information below) sells excellent color prints of the Tarahumara. These photos were taken by the local Jesuit priest, who knows the Tarahumara well enough to do so without offending.

ORIENTATION AND PRACTICAL INFORMATION

The **train station** is located just southwest of the *zócalo*. To reach the *zócalo*, walk 1 block along the tracks in the direction of Los Mochis and turn left. Main street **Mateos** runs parallel to the trains on the opposite side of the *zócalo*.

Tarahumara Information: Artesanías Misión (tel. 6-01-50), on the north side of the *zócalo*. Although not an official tourist office, it is the best source of information on Creel and the surrounding area. Sells books about the Tarahumara, crafts and a map of the region. The mission supports the Tarahumara's cultural development, and the local hospital receives store profits. English-speaking staff. Open Mon.-Sat. 9:30am-1pm and 3-6pm, Sun. 9:30am-1pm. Credit cards and traveler's checks accepted.

Currency Exchange: Banca Serfin (tel. 6-02-50), next door to the Misión. Dollars exchanged 10:30-11:45am. 5% commision for changing traveler's checks. Open Mon.-Fri. 9am-1:30pm.

Post Office: (tel. 6-02-58), on the 1st floor of the Presidencia Municipal bldg. on south side of the *zócalo*. Lista de Correos. Open Mon.-Fri. 9am-1pm and 3-6pm. **Postal Code:** 33200.

Telephones: Long-distance service available at *caseta de larga distancia* in the **Papelería de Todo** on Mateos. Collect calls 2 pesos. Fax. Open daily 9am-8pm. **Telephone Code:** 145.

Train Station: On Av. Tarahumara. Trains leave daily for Chihuahua at 3:15pm (*primera* 43 pesos) and 5:10pm (*segunda* 9 pesos), and for Los Mochis at 12:25pm (*primera*, 51 pesos) and 2pm (*segunda,* 11 pesos). Trains usually run close to schedule. Tickets go on sale at 11:30am for the *primera* to Los Mochis and a half hour before departure time for other trains. Be forewarned that some trains might be "full". In that case, scramble on quickly and aggressively when the train arrives and purchase a ticket on board.

Bus Station: Estrella Blanca (tel. 6-00-73), across the tracks from the *zócalo*. To Chihuahua (8 per day, 26.40 pesos) via Cuauhtémoc (17 pesos).

Market: La Barata de Creel, on Mateos next to Cabañas Bertis. Open daily 9am-8pm.

Laundromat: Lavandería Santa María (tel. 6-00-71), at the Pension Creel on Mateos. Admire the water purification equipment while your clothes spin. Open Mon.-Fri. 9am-2pm and 3-6pm, Sat. 9am-2pm. **Pharmacy: Farmacia Rodríguez,** Mateos 39 (tel. 6-00-52). Open Mon.-Sat. 9am-2pm and 3-8pm, Sun. 9am-1pm.

Police: (tel. 6-00-81), in the Presidencia Municipal bldg. on south side of the *zócalo*.

ACCOMMODATIONS

As Creel flourishes, hotels multiply and prices grow, and the competition for tourist dollars becomes more intense.

Margaritas Casa de Huespedes: Mateos 11 (tel. 16-00-45) is one of the liveliest and cheapest places to stay in all of Mexico. You'll have no trouble finding it—an emissary meets every train to lead you to the house, where you mingle with Margarita's family, friends, and guests. All rooms are freshly renovated, with floor tiles, pine furniture, and heating. Rooms with two single beds and a private bath cost 70 pesos, shared dormitories go for 15-20 pesos per head. To top it off, all prices include two home cooked meals (breakfast at 8am, dinner at 7pm, vegetarians accomodated) and bathroom use. Maragarita's popularity increases with her hectic turnover of guests, but none slip by without some Spanish lessons from the owner herself. Reservations accepted.

Pensión Creel (tel. 6-00-71, fax 6-02-00), at Mateos 61. Bunk or double beds in newly renovated cabins that have well equipped bathrooms and kitchens with microwave. Or opt for the larger hacienda farther from downtown and closer to trails and woods, with shared bathrooms, a fully-equipped kitchen, and a large common room featuring a roaring fireplace and a magazine shelf. Prices range from US$3 if you have your own sleeping bag, through several gradations up to US$10 per person for all features, including breakfast. Group rates. Pesos and credit cards accepted. French and English spoken by those in charge.

Cabañas Bertis, López Mateos 31 (tel. 6-01-08). Log cabin feel with panelled walls, thick wool blankets, and fireplace or wood stove in each abode (wood supplied free). Small private bath included. Rooms with kitchens 150 pesos. Singles 42 pesos. Doubles 65 pesos.

Hotel Korachi (tel. 6-22-07), across the tracks from the train station. A wanna-be hunting lodge where dead animal skins stretch across log-lined walls. Small rooms come without any heat or private bath. Singles 40 pesos. Doubles 60 pesos. Dusty *cabañas* sit under shady trees and include private bath and wood supply. Singles 60 pesos. Doubles 80 pesos.

A campsite can be had for 10 pesos among the boulders and pines around **Lake Arrareco,** 8km down the road where only an occasional port-a-john intrudes upon the scenic views.

FOOD

Creel has yet to spawn gourmet restaurants that cater to the jet set tourists who pass through. The best and cheapest way to dine in Creel is to relish a picnic lunch of fruit and bread on the quiet hillsides outside town. Otherwise, many options exist along Mateos, the main drag. **Restaurant Tío Molcas** attracts many a passerby with fresh pine furniture and woven place mats. Mountain-size serving of steak and fries for 15 pesos, cheese enchiladas for 9 pesos. (Open daily 7am-10:30pm.) **Restaurante Veronica** is a simple joint, popular with the locals, that has unfinished wood floors and mix and match dinner chairs. Sit down to homemade eggs and sausage (8 pesos) and shredded beef *tortas* (7.50 pesos). (Open daily 7am-11pm.)

SIGHTS AND ENTERTAINMENT

The least expensive way to explore the gorges and rivers is to camp or backpack through the region. No extensive supply shop exists in the area for camping needs, but **Pensión Creel** has various gadgets for the outdoors.

Some of the popular sites lie far from the center of Creel. Sympathetic locals gladly offer rides to weary travelers, but the cars in secluded mountain areas may be few and far between (sometimes 1 car per hour), stretching an otherwise reasonable trip into an all-day affair (see Mexico General Introduction: Once There: By Thumb above for more information). *Let's Go* does not recommend hitchhiking. Barrancas del Cobre requires at least a three-hour ride and then quite a hike.

Several outfits in Creel offer **group tours** for those averse to roughing it. **Margarita's** offers some of the cheapest tours in town. A full-day tour runs only US$14 per person, featuring a one hour downhill hike and a warm bath in a winding green stream. Bring plenty of water and food, adequate footwear (no sandals) and a sun hat. Another all-day tour (75 pesos) takes you to **Basaseachic Falls,** a spectacular cascade that plunges 806 ft. into a cool lake. A shorter and cheaper tour (½ day, about US$14) takes you 22km out to the smaller **Cusárare Falls** and the village and mission nearby. Tours require a minimum of four to six people. With the number of visitors at Margarita's, it isn't hard to muster enough takers to venture to Barrancas del Cobre or Cusárare Falls, but assembling a tour to Basaseachic Falls can be a bit tricky. You needn't be staying at Margarita's to take any of these tours.

Pensíon Creel, Hotel Nuevo, and Cabañas Bertis all run similar tours to popular sites. **Motel Parador** (tel. 6-00-75) tours include a bag lunch, and are a little more expensive.

If you really want to experience the Barrancas, consider a trip to **Batopilas,** 140km south of Creel. This involves a 10-hour bus trip over some of the most terrifying roads in existence, and meteorological conditions that can range from suffocating heat to blinding snow in the course of a single voyage. You can jump on the bus in front of the Farmacia Rodríguez on Mateos on Tuesdays, Thursdays and Saturdays at 7am. It returns Mondays, Wednesdays and Fridays at 4am. Remember to take your passport and tourist card; you could be stopped by uptight and heavily armed soldiers. Weary survivors of the voyage can spend the evening at **Casa Bustillos,** across the basketball court as you get off the bus. Fix the room price beforehand to avoid being overcharged. From Batopilas, short daytrips to local villages are easily arranged.

Sticking close to Creel offers many natural delights too. Just ask your hostess to point you in an interesting direction and start walking. The **Valley of Mushroom Rocks** and the **San Ignacio Mission** can be combined into a daytrip, though the government now charges 10 pesos for each site (more if you want to take home photos). To reach the valley and mission, walk down Mateos past the Motel Parador. When the road forks, take the smaller branch to the left, beside the cemetery. A kilometer or so out of town you will pass through the gates of the Tarahumara's *ejidos* (communal lands) containing the caves in which they live. After the cultivated fields, the valley is to the right and the mission at the bottom of the hill. The large **Lake Ararreco** is a cost-free attraction that lies 8km (a half-hour walk) down the highway from Creel. Lazier people hop a ride with one of the passing trucks, but *Let's Go* does not recommend hitching.

At night, the **Motel Parador** and the **Restaurante Tío Molcas** have bars (though officially alcohol may not be served after 8pm). A beer at the more sedate Molcas costs 3 pesos. The Parador rocks late into the night with live guitar and song and many all-too-willing dance partners; it is the job of the *animador* to get women up and dancing with the male patrons.

■■■ BARRANCAS DEL COBRE (COPPER CANYON)

The train daringly careens along canyon walls, plunges into 96 tunnels, and passes briefly along the rim of Barrancas del Cobre, a gorge even deeper than the Grand Canyon. The Barrancas explode with color during the rainy season (July-Sept.) when the plants are in full bloom; they lie sublimely under drifts of snow during the winter months. Any time of year, Copper Canyon is one of Mexico's greatest natural wonders. The **Chihuahua-Pacífico railroad** stretches its tracks from Chihuahua to Los Mochis through the Sierra Madre Occidental and across the Continental Divide. During the 80 years it took to complete, the trans-territorial link was derided by many *gringo* engineers as an impossible task.

Two types of trains make the daily journey. The *primera* is for tourists. Cleaner and equipped with bathrooms and air conditioning, trains run close to schedule. The large, comfortable seats provide amazing leg room. The *segunda* trains carry livestock as well as passengers and have none of the virtues of the *primeras* except that they cost one-third as much and screech along the same tracks. They do, however, have windows that open and an occasional amateur musician.

From the Los Mochis station, the *primera* departs at 6am and the *segunda* at 7am. From Chihuahua, the *primera* leaves at 7am, the *segunda* at 8am. A *primera* ticket from Los Mochis to Chihuahua costs 94 pesos; the *segunda* runs about 20 pesos (see Creel Practical Information above for applicable prices there). The Chihuahua to Creel leg takes six hours by *primera*, while the Creel to Los Mochis track is an eight-hour journey. The *segunda* makes twice as many stops as the *primera*, adding about four hours to any *primera* travel time.

The serious mountain scenery lies between Creel and Río Fuerte, so if you take the *segunda*, you'll zoom by some great views in the dark. For more expansive natural spectacles and less mountain wall out your window, grab seating on the left side of the train traveling towards Los Mochis, and the right side if going toward Chihuahua. Bring food for the trip or you will be forced to rely on either the enchilada saleschildren who run through the train during stops in small towns, or the burrito and *gordita* salespeople at Divisadero. Even worse, you may find yourself at the mercy of the bland, expensive train entrees.

The train ride itself is a spectacular tour of the Sierra Madre mountains, but it can't compare to spending a few days in the region for personal exploration. Between Creel and Chihuahua, the only noteworthy stop is Cuauhtémoc, the center of a community of Mennonites who arrived in the 1920s and are the primary agricultural producers of the region. They maintain the customs and traditions of their Germanic ancestors as well as the language.

At the **Divisadero station,** the jagged mountain edges overlap to create a maze of gorges and rocks at the rim of the Barrancas del Cobre. Seven hours out of Los Mochis on the *primera*, the train stops for 15 minutes of sight-seeing. Everyone on board scrambles out, sprints to the brink, gapes, and sprints back. On the *segunda*, it's more informal. Ask the conductor when the train is going to leave, and be back early. Resist the urge to buy anything from the Tarahumaras, strategically positioned between the train and the canyon, because better examples of their craft are available in Creel at lower prices.

Besides providing a great view, Divisadero is a good point to begin your canyon adventure; guides lounge around outside the expensive hotel. Make no mistake: abundant water, appropriate footwear and a first-aid kit are necessities for even the shortest day trips.

SINALOA

■■■ LOS MOCHIS

The sad truth is that being in Los Mochis is like having to pay to count hunks of dirt. The town is the commercial center of a prosperous agricultural district which exports sugar, cotton, rice, and wheat. Tourists stop here only to catch the train through the Barrancas del Cobre to Creel and Chihuahua, or to catch the ferry to La Paz. The citizens of Los Mochis know that their town is not what you came to Mexico to see; their constant question is, "Where are you going?" But this awareness seems to provoke an eager-to-please attitude in an effort to ease your short stay in their hot and mildly uninteresting city. Though it is possible to disembark the ferry at 6am and catch the second class train that departs an hour later, the prospect of another long ride could keep you in Los Mochis for the day. It's very difficult to get a seat on a northbound bus; you'll have to wait at the station from the crack of dawn to have a fighting chance of boarding. The unlucky souls unable to buy tickets will find themselves stranded in Los Mochis an extra night.

Orientation and Practical Information The ferry to La Paz, Baja California Sur leaves at 9am every day except Sunday from **Topolobampo,** a small fishing hamlet 24km south of Los Mochis. (*Salón*-class tickets only between Topoplobampo and La Paz, 38 pesos). Cars and motorcycles can be brought on the ferry for an additional fee; space is limited. Check prices and times and buy tickets at the Sematur office on Rendón 519 (tel. 5-82-62), open Mon.-Fri. 8am-1pm and 3-7pm, Sun. 9am-1pm. To get to the office, walk nine small blocks out from Juárez on Flores, then turn left on Rendón. You must buy tickets one day in advance before 11am at this office or on the same day on the ferry at Topolobampo.

A **bus** runs to Topolobampo every half hour in the morning starting at 6am (13 pesos); it leaves from a small side street down from the Hotel Santa Anita, between Hidalgo and Obregón. The bus can also be flagged down at Castro and Zaragoza.

When the **Barrancas del Cobre train** stops at Los Mochis, its passengers still have not quite finished the journey to their hotels. The taxis have you captive—they know if you had any other choice you wouldn't be there. In an intriguing phenomenon, bargaining can drive the prices up. All the drivers report in to a price-fixer, dubbed the Godfather by one frustrated backpacker. This situation tempts unscrupulous travelers to bluff their way onto the free bus to the Santa Anita Hotel.

It is hard to find a map of Los Mochis, and the small faded street signs on corner buildings can be hard to read. If you are averse to asking directions from the very friendly *los mochisinos*, it still should not take too long to figure out the simple grid.

Set office hours are the butt of town jokes. The lines at the ever-popular **Bancomer,** (tel. 5-80-81) Leyva and Juárez, may be 30min. long. (Open Mon.-Fri. 8:30am-1pm. Dollars exchanged 9-11am only.) The **post office,** a den of philatelical debauchery, lies at Ordoñez 226 (tel. 2-08-23), lies 2 blocks off Castro, away from Obregon (turn right); 1 block off Prieto. (Open Mon.-Fri. 8am-7pm, Sat. 9am-1pm. **Postal code:** 81200.) **Farmacia Karla,** Obregón at Degollado (tel. 2-81-80), charges 4 pesos to charge other people for international **collect calls.** (Open 24 hrs.) Cheap but noisy collect calls can be placed on public telephones scattered throughout downtown. (**Telephone Code:** 681.) **Tres Estrellas de Oro buses** leave from the station on Obregón just east of Allende (tel. 2-17-57). *De paso* buses run every ½hr., north through Guaymas, Hermosillo and Mexicali to Tijuana and south to Mazatlán. They are often chock-full when they reach Los Mochis; you must wait and see when the bus arrives. Secure seats are easier to obtain on the slower *de local* buses to Guadalajara (2 per day, 102 pesos), to Tijuana (3 per day, 146 pesos) and to Mazatlán (2 per day, 47 pesos). All others are *de paso*, so be on your toes (see Mexico Essentials: Traveling in Mexico). **Norte de Sonora** and **Transportes del Pacífico,** side by side on Morelos between Leyva and Zaragoza, have scrungier buses to the same places for less. Buses to El Fuerte leave from the corner of Independencia and Degollado. For **taxis,** call 2-02-83. For fresh fish, fruit, and vegetables, check the **market** on Obregon between Leyva and Zaragoza, especially on weekends. Los Mochis' hippest threads get washed at **Lavamatic,** Allende 218 just before Juárez, for only 5 pesos, then dry out for 7 more. (Open Mon.-Sat. 7am-7pm, Sun. 7am-1pm.) **Red Cross,** diligent at Tenochtitlán and Prieto (tel. 2-02-92), 1 block off Castro, has ambulance service that never calls it a night. **Farmacia Karla,** Obregon at Degollado (tel. 5-70-07), is open 24 hrs. Hit the **Hospital Fátima,** Blvd. Jiquilpan Pte. 639 (tel. 12-33-12) to check out the local medical scene. **Police** life revolves around Degollado at Cuauhtémoc in the Presidencia Municipal (tel. 2-00-33).

Accommodations and Food Don't waste all night looking for the cozy bed of your childhood dreams. **Hotel Lorena,** Obregón Pte. 186 (tel. 2-02-39), one block from the bus station, is the only place nearly worth its price. Hard-blowing A/C, color cable TV, and comfortable bed provide an oasis of cool in the mid-day sweltering heat. Cafeteria on third floor open 7-11am, 7-11pm for tired early-morning or late-night arrivees. (Singles 75 pesos. Doubles 110 pesos. Traveler's checks and credit cards accepted.) **Hotel Montecarlo,** Flores 322 Sur (tel. 2-18-18), blue building at corner of Independencia. Sizeable, clean, new rooms in well-kept old building with a quiet courtyard; the only old and pretty hotel in Los Mochis. Central A/C. (Singles 75 pesos, with two people 90 pesos. Doubles 110 pesos.) **Hotel Hidalgo,** Hidalgo 260 Pte. (tel. 2-34-56), has deep blue furniture and baby blue walls to cool down rooms with ceiling fan. Open lobby with balcony can become a local hangout if a big game is on TV. (Singles 40 pesos, with A/C 50 pesos. Doubles 50 pesos, with A/C 60 pesos.)

The best and cheapest food is sold in the **public market** between Prieto and Leyva along Castro. One of Los Mochis' few virtues is that the produce for sale is grown nearby, meaning prices are low and quality is high. The *taquerías* and *loncherías* in the market dish out cheap, home-brewed mysteries, many of which pack an excellent punch. The restaurants below are pricier but cleaner than the questionable street-side eateries. Except for the *cantinas* (which women should avoid) and the corner *taquerías,* just about everything in town shuts down at 8pm and alcohol evaporates at 11pm. After that, enter **The Closet,** the bar in the Santa Anita Hotel (on Leyva, between Hidalgo and Obregón), which is as dark and as cramped as its name implies. **El Taquito** is on Leyva between Hidalgo and Independencia (tel. 2-81-19). Sit comfortably in the vinyl booths and bask in cold A/C. Waiters in red jackets serve up fried chicken (10 pesos) and breaded shrimp (30 pesos). Open 24 hrs., **El Terome** at Flores and Independencía under the Hotel Montecarlo (tel. 2-18-18) features high quality seafood , A/C, and TV in a more formal setting. Filet of garlic fish 23 pesos. (Open daily 7am-7pm. Credit cards accepted.)

■■■ MAZATLÁN

Mazatlán means "place of the deer" in Nahuatl. A less appropriate name can hardly be imagined, since there is nothing even remotely pastoral or ruminant about this city. The only wildlife present—genus *Bronzus*, species *norteamericanus*—roams the beaches in large herds.

For centuries Mazatlán has been the youth hostel of history. In 1531, Mazatlán's harbor was chosen as the launching pad for Spanish galleons loaded with gold mined in the Sierra Madres. Three centuries later, the town suffered a U.S. blockade (1847) and then a French bombardment (1864). Mazatlán was also the temporary stomping ground for a group of Confederate Civil War veterans out to preserve their Southern ideals on Mexican soil, and during the Revolution of 1914 the city became only the second in the world to be shelled from the air. A substantial Chinese population once lived here but was summarily expelled 50 years ago.

Despite its eventful past, Mazatlán presents nothing of historical or cultural interest to the traveler. Like other great resorts, the most attractive aspects of Mazatlán are gifts of nature—beautiful sunsets, a glittering ocean and wide golden beaches. Unlike other Mexican resorts which maintain at least a facade of cute *mexicanidad* and cultivate an exotic sheen, Mazatlán couldn't care less. Its tourist zone, spread along a highway, matches its Floridian prototypes gift-shop-for-gift-shop but boasts lower prices and nicer beaches.

ORIENTATION

Mazatlán is a raging cornucopia of transportation, but bus is still the most economical and versatile way to get in and out of the city. The **bus station** lies three blocks behind the **Sands Hotel,** about 2km north of Old Mazatlán. The area around the bus station, with several reasonably priced hotels and restaurants, along with a good beach and the vital "Sábalo" bus line only three blocks away, makes a convenient home base. You can catch the downtown-bound "Insurgentes" bus at the stand one block off the beach across from the chicken barbecuer.

On the far eastern edge of Mazatlán, the **Ferrocarriles del Pacífico** train station opens an hour before departures and closes soon after arrivals. Make your way to a better part of town: the yellow "Insurgentes" bus or the green, beat-up "Cerritos-Juárez" will take you to and from downtown. **Sematur** (tel. 81-70-20) operates ferries Sun.-Fri. to and from La Paz, on Baja California. Their office and dock sit on the southern end of Carnaval, which runs south from Ángel Flores. Meeting the ferry requires a hot 20-min. walk from *el centro*; the "Playa Sur" bus (.70 pesos) makes the trip, and for 10 pesos so will a taxi. Sematur accepts reservations for all classes up to a month in advance during the high season (Dec., July, and Aug.), and recommends that you make them at least two weeks ahead of your scheduled date of departure. In any case, tickets are only sold the day of departure; be sure to reach the office early to procure a spot. (Open daily 8:30am-3pm.)

The Mazatlán **airport** is 30km south of the city. Bus "Atamsa" brings arrivals to their hotels, but no bus returns to the airport; resign yourself to a cab (a whopping 35-40 pesos).

Built on a rocky spur jutting southwest into the Pacific, Old Mazatlán's downtown area surrounds and spills north of the *zócalo*. **Angel Flores,** the southern boundary of the *zócalo*, runs west to **Olas Altas,** a quiet waterfront area that remained Mazatlán's most fashionable district until the tourist onslaught arrived. Both **Juárez,** the eastern boundary of the *zócalo*, and **Serdán,** one block farther east, run north (toward the back of the cathedral) to the cheap hotel district and the area's beach, **Playa del Norte.** From Playa del Norte, the coast arcs to the northeast; the main road tracing the *malecón* starts off as **Olas Altas** south of downtown then becomes **Paseo Clausen** until the tall fisherman's statue where it turns into **Avenida del Mar;** finally it changes once more into **Sábalo** past Valentino's disco emporium. Glitz feeds upon itself through the **Golden Zone,** a colony of exclusive time-share condos, high-rise hotels, overpriced gift shops, and day-glo 7km north of Old Mazatlán, before reaching its apotheosis in the **El Cid Resort**, a world unto itself.

Mazatlán's efficient **bus system** makes getting around the city a breeze. At some point, all the ramshackle municipal buses pass the public market on Juárez, three blocks north of the *zócalo*; if you get lost, you'll eventually return to familiar territory. The most useful bus line is the "Sábalo Centro," serviced by smaller air-conditioned express buses (1 peso) that run from the downtown market to Olas Altas as well as up to Playa Sábalo. The "Cerritos-Juárez" bus (.80 pesos) continues up to Playa Bruja at Puerta Carritos. "Insurgentes" services the bus and train stations, and "Playa Sur" goes to the ferry dock, the lighthouse, and the *Olas Altas* neighborhood. Fare is .60-.80 pesos; buses run every 15min. from 5am-10pm. Feel free to wave down a bus at any point on its route since no set bus stops exist. For late-night disco hopping, you'll have to take a cab or a *pulmonía*, an open vehicle resembling a golf-cart that putters along at 60mph blasting raucous music. Always set the price before you commit yourself to the ride.

Since many of Mazatlán's streets are numbered twice-over, tracking down a particular address can prove difficult.

PRACTICAL INFORMATION

Tourist Office: Olas Altas 1300 (tel. 85-12-20). Walk down Angel Flores past the *zócalo* until you reach the beach, turn left—it's in the tall Bank of Mexico complex. Hands out popular poster ad-maps of the town. Open Mon.-Fri. 8am-3pm.

Consulates: Canada, Loaiza at Bugamblia (tel. 83-73-20), in the Hotel Mazatlán.

Currency Exchange: Banks throughout town exchange Mon.-Fri. 8:30am-11am.

American Express: In the Balboa Plaza Centro Comercial on Camarón Sábalo just before Balboa Towers (tel. 83-06-00). Open Mon.-Fri. 9am-5pm, Sat. 9am-noon.

Post Office: Juárez at Ángel Flores (tel. 81-21-21), across from the *zócalo*. *Lista de Correos* posted. Open Mon.-Fri. 9am-6pm, Sat. 9am-1pm. **Postal code:** 82000.

Telephones: *Caseta* at Serdán 1510. International collect calls 3 pesos for first 3 minutes. Open Mon.-Sat. 7am-8:30pm, Sun. 8am-1pm. Public touch-tone phones are scattered throughout downtown and hotel lobbies. **Telephone Code:** 91.

Telegrams: In the same building as the post office (tel. 81-36-62). Open Mon.-Fri. 8am-8pm, Sat. 8am-12pm.

Airport: 18km south of the city. **Aeroméxico,** Sábalo 310-A (tel. 14-11-11). To Mexico City (5 per day, 580 pesos) and Tijuana (2 per day, 800 pesos). **Mexicana,** Clausen 101-B (tel. 82-77-22). To Guadalajara and Los Angeles.

Train Station: In Col. Esperanza on the east edge of town (tel. 84-67-10). To Guadalajara (*primera* 61 pesos at 11am., *segunda* 18 pesos at 5am) and Mexicali (*primera* 162 pesos at 7am, *segunda* at 11:30pm).

Bus Station: Tres Estrellas de Oro, Transportes del Norte, Estrella Blanca and **Transportes del Pacífico** all serve Mazatlán. Tres Estrellas de Oro has express service to Tijuana (196 pesos) and Los Mochis (44 pesos); regular rides to Nogales (134 pesos) and Guadalajara (50 pesos). Transportes del Norte to Durango (34 pesos), Monterrey, and beyond.

Ferry: Sematur (tel. 81-70-20), port and office located at end of Carnaval, south of *el centro*. To La Paz (at 3pm, 16hrs., *salón* 57 pesos, *turista* 114 pesos, and *cabina* 170 pesos). See "Baja California: Getting Around By Sea" for an explanation of the classes of ferries.

Car Rental: National, Sábalo 7000 (tel. 83-60-00). 85 pesos per day, plus 676 pesos per km. Doesn't include insurance and A/C. Must be 24 years old. **Scooters** available along Malecón for US$15 per day.

Laundromat: Lavafácil, across from the bus station in the same pink building as the Hotel Fiesta. Wash 2 pesos, 10-min. dry 2 pesos. Open Mon.-Sat. 8am-10pm, Sun 9am-2pm.

Red Cross: Obregón 73 (tel. 81-36-90).

24-hr. Pharmacy: Farmacia Parque Zaragoza, Nelson and Morales (tel. 82-83-78). In the pink building at the corner of the park.

Hospital: IMSS, Av. Ejército Mexicano (tel. 83-27-00).

Police: Rafael in Col. Juárez (tel. 81-39-19). **Emergency:** tel. 06.

ACCOMMODATIONS

In the good ol' days, budget hotels in Mazatlán ran about the same as those in other Mexican cities. Of late many seem to have used Mexico's extreme inflation as an excuse to jack up their prices to resort levels. Nonetheless, fine cheap rooms do exist—except on the waterfront, where rates are exorbitant at even the shabbiest places. Budget hotels concentrate around the bus station and in Old Mazatlán along the three avenues east of the main square: Juárez, Serdán, and Azueta. Cheap beds can even be found on Sábalo, near the beaches, for larger groups. Check around.

The busiest seasons in Mazatlán are Christmas and the month following Semana Santa (Easter week). At these times of year, check in early. At other times, prices are negotiable, especially for extended stays. Summer nights in Mazatlán can be very hot and humid; always inspect the cooling system or ventilation in your room before paying. Don't forget: The value of a car rises in direct proportion to its decibel output. If you are looking at a room on the street, keep looking.

Old Mazatlán

This is the noisier part of town and the hotels here are farther from the beach—in Mazatlán that means you can't spit in the ocean from your window—so the rooms are a little cheaper. But if the discos are your scene, cabs will cost more from here than from the hotels west of the bus station. The **Hotel Vialta,** on Azueta (tel. 81-60-27), 3 blocks north of 21 de Marzo, offers a friendly refuge in the leafy courtyard and rooms with a fan and a big shower. (Singles 35 pesos. Doubles 50 pesos.) **Hotel Santa Barbara,** Juárez at 16 de Septiembre (tel. 82-21-20), one block from shore. Has a new pink paint job that makes it stand out like a sore concrete block. Cage yourself in tiny rooms with glowing green showers. (Singles 30 pesos. Doubles 45 pesos. 10 pesos extra for A/C.) No to credit cards, yes to dollars.

Near the Bus Station

Because of greater proximity to sandy beaches and the Golden Zone, hotels in this area put more strain on the wallet. But better rooms can have views of the ocean.

Hotel Club Playa Mar, Av. de Mar 139 (tel. 82-08-33), on the *malecón*. Sip piña coladas while lounging in the tropical landscaped alcove complete with large swimming pool. All rooms offer A/C, TV, private bath, and bar-like area. Parking too. Singles and doubles 66 pesos. Credit cards accepted.

Hotel Emperador, Río Panuco (tel. 82-67-24), across from the bus terminal. 4-story (not 4-star) hotel offers firm beds on concrete slabs and clean bathrooms. Rooms with cable TV and A/C 60 pesos for 1-2 persons; without the luxuries 40 pesos for 1-2 persons, 50 for 3-4 guests. Credit cards accepted.

Hotel Fiesta, Espinoza Ferrusquilla 306 (tel. 81-38-88), also next to the bus terminal. Beds come complete with safety belts so the ceiling fan doesn't blow you away to the land of Oz. Singles and doubles 50 pesos, with A/C 60. Black and white TV costs 5 pesos extra.

Hotel Cabínas, Av. del Mar 123 (tel. 81-57-52), also on the *malecón*. Run down rooms host paintings of Mexican dancers with 11 different signatures. Apartment suites for up to 7 guests with kitchen and ocean view rented on weekly basis (130 pesos per night). Otherwise singles 40 pesos, doubles 50 pesos.

South to Olas Altas

A welcome oasis from the grime and noise of downtown or the frosted hair of the Golden Zone, *Olas Altas* offers tranquility and beauty. Colonial architecture overlooks the beach and crashing sea from which the area took its name.

Back in the 1950s, long before wily developers began constructing multimillion-dollar pleasure palaces along the north shore, Mazatlán's fledgling resort scene clung to *Olas Altas*, a winding 1km road hugging the shore south of town. Today, these old regal hot spots still grace the old strip, but the majority of Mazatlán's tourists bypass their aging displays, choosing instead the flashy young hotels from the north. The majesty and opulence of **Hotel Belmar,** Olas Altas 106 (tel. 85-11-11), is hidden in the hazy marble floors and colorful tiles lining the arches, reminiscent of a resort of yester-year. Monstrous guest rooms with dark wood paneling and bathrooms bigger than some budget bedrooms. Swimming pool, deck and barber shop. Singles with A/C and TV 42 pesos, with ocean view (no A/C) 55 pesos. Doubles with A/C and TV 55 pesos, with ocean view (no A/C) 66 pesos. Credit cards accepted. White-washed building with tropical green trim houses **Hotel La Siesta,** Olas Altas 11 (tel. 81-23-34), with a jungly central courtyard that spills over in the rooms. In case you get bored in Mazatlán, you can play with the A/C, TV, or phone, or just lounge on the balcony overlooking the sea. Singles 60 pesos. Doubles 75 pesos with ocean view. Credit cards accepted.

FOOD

Mazatlán offers a wide variety of culinary tastes from standard *comida corrida* meals to charbroiled T-bone steak, a tourist favorite. Of course, all menus are filled with all-time "Mexican" classics: spicy guacamole, crisp nachos dripping with cheese, and *jalapeño* peppers. All restaurants have adopted the colorful tablecloth as their crowning trademark. What's more, Mazatlán's restaurants are relatively cheap, although, like everything else, food prices escalate as you get sucked north toward the Golden Zone.

Old Mazatlán

The busy **public market,** between Juárez and Serdán, three blocks north of the *zócalo*, serves the cheapest meals in the area. And if you need a headless pig, this is the place. Ample snacking opportunities exist outside in the *fruterías*, *loncherías,* and taco stands.

Restaurant Ostioneria Avenida, Av. Alemán 808 (tel. 82-63-98), south of downtown on the way to the cruise ports. Quite a hike from downtown, but the delectable seafood is well worth it. Mixed platter offers every conceivable item of seafood and more. Tequila and barbecued shrimp 28 pesos, breaded oysters 21 pesos and octopus in garlic sauce 16 pesos. Open daily 8am-8pm.

La Casa de Ana, Consitución 515 (tel. 85-28-39). *Comida vegetariana* on the peaceful Plaza Machado; where the elite meet in Mazatlán. Salads, yogurt, and soyburgers for 4-8 pesos, Sunday buffet 15 pesos. Also beer and breakfast. Open Mon.-Sat. 10am-10pm, Sun. 11am-7pm.

Doney, Escabedo 610 (tel. 81-26-51), right at 5 de Mayo. With a single short name, you know that this place is a few notches up in class—and price. The dark oak doors and huge brick arches lend an ambience that the tourists dig. English menu, naturally. All dishes served with a big basket of nachos. Chicken tacos 9 pesos. *Sincronizadas* 15 pesos. Open daily 11am-10:30pm. Credit cards accepted.

Restaurant Joncol's, Flores 608 Pte. (tel. 81-21-87). Relieve yourself from the midday heat in this air-conditioned restaurant with yellow table cloths and various local awards on the wall. Menu ranges from tostadas (10 pesos) to shrimp in garlic sauce (30 pesos) or fruit salad (10 pesos). Open daily 7am-11pm. Credit cards accepted.

Restaurant Fonda Santa Clara, Olas Altas 106 (tel. 81-64-51). Plastic Corona patio furniture cling together under a shady awning to form a surf-side café. *Quesadillas* 11 pesos, shrimp salad 17 pesos, small nachos 10 pesos. Full bar service.

Restaurant Playa Norte, Paseo Clausen (tel. 85-13-29), next to the fisherman's statue on the beach. Small stone waterfall trickles near the bar as thirsty beach bathers enjoy a tropical drink and *vista del mar* in the shade. Great breakfast special with 2 eggs, beans, potatoes, tortillas and coffee 7.50 pesos. Also fish in garlic butter 22 pesos. Open daily 8am-pm.

North to the Golden Zone

As you move north, prices soar and *norteamericano* culinary influence becomes more pronounced. Look no further if you feel the need for U.S. music, tourists, and Caesar salads.

El Mambo Lonchería, Espinoza Ferrusquilla 204 (tel. 85-04-73), across from the bus station. Mexican pottery, hanging seashells, eclectic art, a macaw, and tasty, large, cheap meals. Beware of the howling buses passing by the entrance. Shrimp in several different styles 16 pesos. *Huevos rancheros* 6.50 pesos. Open daily 7am-7pm.

Restaurant Roca Mar, Av. del Mar at Isla de Los Lobos (tel. 81-00-23). Like most other places along the beach, this offers full bar and an open-air view of the crashing waves, past the rushing traffic. Prices tainted by tourism. Shrimp cocktail 16 pesos. Filet mignon 34 pesos. Grilled fish 25 pesos. Open daily 10am-1am.

SIGHTS AND ACTIVITIES

The alcohol-free **Yate Fiesta** harbor cruises depart daily at 11am for a three-hour tour of Mazatlán by sea. Tickets (35 pesos) are sold at the yacht office (tel. 81-77-00); to get there, take the "Playa Sur" bus to the end of the first dock, past various sport fishing boats near the foot of the lighthouse.

For a 360° "aerial" view of Mazatlán, the sea and the surrounding hills, climb to the top of *el faro* (lighthouse). Once off the Playa Sur bus, walk/hike up the twisting dirt road to the lighthouse at the peak. The walk (about ½hr.) is scorching in the summer sun and the road narrows to a rocky path. Rumor has it that the Mazatlán tower divers practice here.

Mazatlán's tower divers don't quite match the exploits of the cliff divers in Acapulco, but their acrobatic plunges are so extraordinarily dangerous that the discrepancy won't bother you much. Performances take place daily from 10-11am and 4:30-5:30pm, weather permitting. The best viewing angles are just south of the towers; on days when the water is too rough for diving, you can climb the tower to watch the waves break below. Walk to the waterfront on Zaragoza and head south to get to the towers. Though it may seem like it at first, the spectacle is not free—tips are expected.

The **Acuario Mazatlán** (tel. 81-78-15), on Av. de los Deportes, keeps piranhas and 249 other feisty breeds in a slew of cloudy tanks and also has displays on fishing and performing sea lions and birds. The pet pigeons in the aviary are less interesting than the hooded orioles, bar-vented wren, and social flycatchers in the surrounding trees. The Acuario is one block back from the beach and north of the Sands Hotel; the turn-off is marked by a shimmering blue sign. (Open daily 9:30am-7pm. Admission 12 pesos, ages 6-18 6 pesos.)

Mazatlán's greatest asset is its 16km of beach. Just north of Old Mazatlán along Av. del Mar sprawls **Playa Norte,** a decent stretch of sand if you don't mind small waves and the stares of the local *machos* who hang out on the waterfront. Solo women in particular should consider swimming farther north. As you hone in on the Golden Zone, the beach gets cleaner, the waves larger, and the name becomes **Playa Las Gaviotas.** Just past Punta Sábalo, in the lee of the islands, basks **Playa Sábalo** with great waves and manicured golden sand co-opted by crowds of *norteamericanos* and assorted peddlers. Air-conditioned "Sábalo-Centro" buses access all of these beaches.

As Playa Sábalo recedes to the north, crowds thin rapidly and you can frolic on the glorious beaches and in the dramatic surf all by yourself. If you take the yellow "Sábalo bus" (among others) to the last stop and walk left to the beach, you'll be at nearly deserted **Playa Bruja,** with tons of beautiful sand and four- to six-foot waves. Because of its seclusion, it's also the only beach on which you can camp.

William Blake saw the universe in a grain of sand and eternity in an hour. You too may get bored at the beach. Should this befall you, don't abandon Mazatlán. You may simply be in need a brief change of locale. Hop on one of the boats to the **Isla de la Piedra,** where locals go to escape the crowds. Boats leave from the wharf on Av. del Puerto at Gutierrez Najera. To walk there, go out 21 de Marzo from the Cathedral past Serdan to the water, then turn left on Av. del Puerta. (3 pesos round trip.) Boats leave for **Islas Venados,** an island with fine diving and without those annoying fellow-travelers, from **El Cid Resort** in the Golden Zone (5 per day, 15 pesos). Finally, waterpark mania has hit south of the border with the new **Mazagua.** Go crazy in the wave pool or shoot down slippery slides. Located north of the Golden Zone near Puerta Cerritos. (Open daily 10am-6pm. 35 pesos).

ENTERTAINMENT

Hordes of north-of-the-border high schoolers ditch the prom and hit Mazatlán for a reason. Discos and bars clamor for the Golden Zone bucks and the hike (about ½hr. from the bus station) is actually worth it if drunken fiestas are your scene. If not, the thrice-balconied **Teatro Angela Peralta** in the square at Constitución and Carnaval has (sometimes free) plays. As for the clubs:

Bora-Bora, on Sábalo at the southern end of the Golden Zone. You can't miss it—it's in a white stucco version of the haunted Disney mansion on a rocky point. Jammed with touring teenagers clad in neon and dancing on the bars. Cover of 15 pesos includes 2 beers. Open daily 9pm-4am.

Bali Hai, also in Disney mansion. The restaurant-bar offers a small dance floor for those who want to make an exhibition. Popular with the local teens who jam to the Mexican disco/rock. No cover. Open daily noon-4am.

El Caracol, a.k.a. the $6 million disco in the El Cid complex (tel. 83-33-33). The flashing lights, video screens, and fake smoke are almost demolished by the music: New Kids On the Block, C&C Music Factory, and Vanilla Ice, to name just a few. Cover 16 pesos includes 2 drinks. Open 9pm-4am.

Frankie-Oh's, Av. del Mar 1003 (tel. 82-58-00), next to Señor Frog's. Popular with the younger set and often features live Mexican bands with Los Lobos sound. Cover 15 pesos. Open 9pm-4am.

DURANGO

■■■ DURANGO

Durango, a Basque word that means "meadow bathed by a river and surrounded by high mountains beyond the river," was founded in 1563 by Francisco de Ibarra, the man who seems to have colonized half of northern Mexico. Although it lacks the grand colonial architecture of its southern neighbors, the city has a kind of rugged beauty all its own. Buildings adorned with a combination of stone scrollwork, wrought-iron grilles, and glistening blue paint fill the side streets. On top of this, the amazing friendliness of Durango's citizens makes most visits to the city a pleasure; people here pause on the street to give the inquisitive traveler detailed advice and directions and may even deliver visitors to their destinations. Very few residents speak English, but most good-naturedly attempt to understand broken Spanish and crazy gesticulations. Despite the lack of English-speakers, Durango rocks the house with U.S. rap; car stereos and shops pump up the bass and boom. These modern trappings contrast the beautiful mesas on the city's edge that give some idea of the origins of that pithy Basque name and accentuate the town's rough-hewn, frontier feel.

ORIENTATION AND PRACTICAL INFORMATION

The central **bus station** is 3km east of the city center. Getting to the center of town is easy. When you exit the bus terminal, cross the parking lot to the covered benches and take the municipal bus (.50 pesos) marked "Centro" to the **Plaza de Armas** across from the **Catedral**. To return, catch the "Central Camionera" bus from the plaza (.50 pesos). Buses run daily 7am-11pm. If you arrive by **train,** walk a dozen short blocks down Martínez until you reach Durango's main street, **20 de Noviembre.** Turn left and walk a block to the plaza. 20 de Noviembre runs east-west through the plaza with Serdán parallel; Constitución and Zaragoza cross 20 de Noviembre heading north-south. Streets are numbered north and south of Serdán; the *catedral* is on the north side of the Plaza de Armas.

Tourist Office: Hidalgo Sur 408 (tel. 1-21-39), 3 blocks west of the plaza on 20 de Noviembre and left (south) 2 blocks. Good starting point with helpful city maps and advice. Historical literature about Durango on request. Open Mon.-Sat. 10am-3pm and 6-9pm, Sun. 10am-1pm.

Currency Exchange: Bancomer, 20 de Noviembre at Constitución, across from the plaza (tel. 3-20-22). Changes traveler's checks as well as currency. Open Mon.-Fri. 9am-1:30pm. The alternative, **Casa de Cambio** at 20 de Noviembre under the Hotel Roma, stays open Mon.-Fri. 9am-6pm.

American Express: Av. 20 de Noviembre 810 Ote. (tel. 7-00-23, fax 7-01-43).

Post Office: 20 de Noviembre at Laureano Roncal, more than ten blocks east of the *catedral*. Open Mon.-Fri. 8am-5pm, Sat. 8am-1pm. *Lista de Correos* posted around 11:30am. **Postal Code:** 34000.

Telephones: *Caseta* at Martínez Sur 206. Collect calls 4 pesos. Open Mon.-Sat. 8am-9:30pm. Touch-tone public phones found throughout Durango's squares. **Telephone Code:** 181.

Bus Station: On Blvd. Francisco Villa. **Transportes del Norte** (tel. 8-30-81), **Transportes Chihuahuenses** (tel. 8-37-81), **Omnibus de México** (tel. 8-33-61) and **Estrella Blanca** go to most major cities. Prices vary among them, but Estrella Blanca is usually the cheapest. Some destinations: Aguascalientes (29 pesos), Mexico City (66 pesos), Mazatlán (28 pesos), Torreón (17 pesos).

Train Station: Felipe Pescador, at Martínez (tel. 3-34-22). Daily departures north only to Torreón. Connections can be made there. Call for more information.

Red Cross: 5 de Febrero at Libertad (tel. 7-34-44).

24-hr. Pharmacy: Farmacia Pensiones, Constitución at Coronado (tel. 2-99-92).

Hospital: Hospital General, 5 de Febrero at Fuentes (tel. 1-91-15).

Police: Reforma at 5 de Febrero (tel. 754-06).

Emergency: dial 06.

ACCOMMODATIONS

The various old streets in downtown Durango hold plenty of hotels. Many of the cheaper accommodations are centuries-old renovated mansions, complete with courtyard and colonial arches; almost all claim to have housed or hid Pancho Villa for at least a night. Beware the first two weeks of July during the popular Feria Nacional. If you're in town then, grab the first bed you see or prepare to sleep in the bus station.

Hotel Posada Durán, 20 de Noviembre Pte. 506 (tel. 1-24-12), across from the *catedral*. Mahogany-finished French doors open up to a spacious bedroom with desks, four poster beds, and balcony. The interior red-tiled courtyard with trickling fountains comforts the weary traveler with its former colonial grandeur. Singles with bath 44 pesos. Doubles 55 pesos. Reservations, credit cards, and traveler's checks accepted.

Hotel Posada San Jorge, Constitución 102 Sur (tel. 3-32-37). Similar ancient *hacienda* establishment with balcony and courtyard that lacks the refurbishment and charm of the Durán. Large rooms come with mix-and-match '70s furniture and bath. Singles 52 pesos. Doubles 66 pesos. Credit cards accepted.

Hotel Roma. 20 de Noviembre 705 Pte. (tel. 2-01-22). Large hotel tries to supply many of the comforts from home: wall-to-wall carpeting, TV, telephone, bath, even elevator. Small circular windows peep out over random palm trees in the halls. Singles 61 pesos. Doubles 72 pesos. Accepts traveler's checks and credit cards.

FOOD

Durango has slews of little restaurants offering pretty much the same *comida corrida* (7–9 pesos) and *carne asada*. Many cluster along 20 de Noviembre, with some more upscale joints on Constitución Nte.

Al Grano, Negrete 804 at Zaragoza. This small eatery packed with square wooden tables and bright pictures of fruit is popular with the local *vegetarianos*. Breakfast 7 peso or 4-course meal including fruit salad, soup, dish of the day and dessert for 12 pesos. Whole-grain breads and pastries to go. Open Mon.-Sat. 8am-8pm.

Corleone Pizza, Constitución Nte. 114 (tel. 3-31-38). A wide variety of lamps, old movies posters, and fancy drinks make this the ideal setting for a romantic evening. Pizza in flaky pie crusts. Small pizza 11 pesos, spaghetti 6 pesos. Open daily 11:30am-11:30pm.

Far West Steak House Bar and Grill, Florida 1106, at the western end of 20 de Noviembre. The 2-story restaurant has the get-up of an old-West saloon complete with swinging-door entrance, hitching post and gentle piano. This tourist spot lists all the Western films ever shot in Durango and boasts the autographs of celebrities as recent as Kevin Costner. Steak Buffalo Bill 34 pesos. Big Jake Plate 17 pesos. Credit cards accepted. Open daily 1-11pm.

SIGHTS AND ENTERTAINMENT

Few standard tourist attractions in Durango deserve your undivided attention. The **Plaza de Armas,** surrounded by upscale stores, is the city's center of activity and its most interesting sight. Every Thursday and Sunday the state band livens up the area with a wide range of music from the central kiosk. Directly across from the north end of the plaza stands the grandiose 300-year-old **Catedral.** Its construction initiated a period of baroque popularity in the city. The **Palacio del Gobierno,** on 5 de Febrero at Martínez, surrounds a central courtyard with colorful murals depicting the heroic strides toward Mexican independence and democracy. (Open Mon.-Fri. 8am-3pm.)

During the last week of June and first two weeks of July, Durango holds its **Feria Nacional,** which features Mexican singers and bands, cultural demonstrations, bullfights and industrial and agricultural displays. Ask for details at the tourist office (see Practical Information).

A 10km drive north on Route 45 toward Parral will take you to **Villa del Oeste** and **Chupaderos.** These two towns were given makeovers for the filming of westerns, among them John Wayne's *Chisum* and *Big Jake*. While Villa del Oeste is still occasionally used, Chupaderos is a ghost town inhabited by people who act as if it were an ordinary Mexican village. Talk to the tourism office for details and for group bus trips to these and to Los Alamos motion picture village.

Nightlife isn't hopping in Durango. Catch a Mexican flick at **Cinema El Dorado 70,** at 20 de Noviembre and Progreso (6 pesos), or tune in to one of the many radio stations and catch the blend of Mexican, U.S., and even French *música*.

ZACATECAS

■■■ ZACATECAS

The second-to-last thing a traveler expects to find in the prickly desert of Central Mexico is a charming city, yet out of nowhere rises Zacatecas. The arid surroundings augment the colonial beauty of this town, perched between, on, and over mineral-laden hills.

The lifeblood of Zacatecas, like that of Guanajuato, once flowed through veins of silver. A silver trinket, given to early Spanish colonists by an indigenous Cascane in the mid-16th century, triggered the mining bonanza that gave birth to the city. In the 200 years after the Conquest, the hills surrounding Zacatecas were stripped of over US$1 billion worth of silver and other precious metals. Among mining towns, Zacatecas was unusually fortunate: the arts flourished under the patronage of affluent silver barons, and the rows of grand colonial mansions lining the downtown streets speak of generations that displayed their wealth lavishly. In the early 19th century, one devout mine owner paved a walkway from his home to the cathedral with solid silver bars.

The tumultuous history of modern Mexico has left its thumbprint on Zacatecas; in 1914 Francisco "Pancho" Villa's revolutionary forces proved victorious here over Carranza's troops. As revolution atrophied into institution and the mines ran dry, Zacatecas emerged as a hub of sophistication laden with architectural, artistic and natural treasures.

ORIENTATION AND PRACTICAL INFORMATION

At the junction of several major highways, Zacatecas is easily accessible from many cities, including Guadalajara (318km south), Aguascalientes (129km south), and Chihuahua (832km north). All buses arrive and depart from the **central bus terminal** on the outskirts of town. City buses (.30 pesos) await outside: to get to *el centro*, take "Ruta 7"; to return to the bus station, take the "Camionera Central" or "Ruta 8" bus from the east end of Juárez (see below).

Unlike most Mexican cities, Zacatecas has no identifiable center of town. Instead, activity revolves around two main streets: **Juárez,** running roughly northwest, and **Hidalgo,** renamed González Ortega southwest of Juárez. Use the intersection of the two, one block northwest of **Plaza Independencia,** as your point of orientation. Many of the city's colonial monuments lie on or near Hidalgo; if you keep its location vaguely in mind as you try to navigate the twisting, cobblestone streets, you may spend less time bothering people for directions.

Tourist Office: Oficina de Turismo, Hidalgo 61 (tel. 4-05-52), at Callejón del Santero across from the cathedral. The staff is eager to help, and the map is helpful. Open daily 8am-8pm. The Café Acropolis across the street sells more extensive maps for 5 pesos.

Guided Tours: Cantera Tours, Centro Comercial, El Mercado Local A-21 (tel. 2-90-65). Guided 5-hr. tour of the city 60 pesos (children 30 pesos) includes transportation and admission to museums. Office open daily 9am-8pm.

Currency Exchange: Bánamex, Hidalgo 132. Open Mon.-Fri. 9am-5pm. **Bancomer,** Hidalgo at Allende. Open Mon.-Fri. 9am-12:30pm.

Post Office: Allende 111 (tel. 2-01-96), off Hidalgo. *Lista de Correos.* Open Mon.-Fri. 8am-7pm, Sat. 9am-1pm. **Postal code:** 980001.

Telephones: Callejón de Cuevas 111, at the corner of Café Zas, above the bookstore. Collect international calls in the morning only, 5 pesos. Open Mon.-Fri. 8:30am-9:20pm, Sat. 9am-2pm and 4-8pm. Also at Independencia 88-A, across from the Jardín Independencia inside a small mall. International collect calls in the morning only, 2 pesos. Open daily 8am-8:30pm. **Telephone code:** 492.

Telegrams: Hidalgo at Juárez (tel. 2-00-70). Open Mon.-Fri. 9am-8pm, Sat. 9am-noon.

Airport: Accessible by *combi* (every hr., 3 pesos) from the **Mexicana office,** Hidalgo 406. Open Mon.-Fri. 9am-6:30pm, Sat. 9am-5:30pm. They provide the airport's only service to Los Angeles (daily, US$140), Mexico City (daily, 232 pesos), and Tijuana (daily, 425 pesos).

Train Station: Estación de Ferrocarriles (tel. 2-12-04), on González Ortega southeast of *el centro.* A walkable distance from downtown, but all bus routes also pass the station. Southward to: Mexico City (at 8pm, 55 pesos) via Querétaro (36 pesos). Northward toward Ciudad Juárez (at 9:30am, 35 pesos) via Torreón (12 pesos).

Bus Station: Central de Autobuses, Lomas de la Isabélica at Tránsito Pesado (tel. 2-11-12). **Autobuses III Blancos, El Aguila, Autobús de Mexico, Transportes Zacatecos,** and **Camiones Rojos de los Altos** all exist here, but **Estrella Blanca** has the most destinations by far: Monterrey (every hr., 38 pesos); Aguascalientes (every ½hr., 11 pesos); Mexico City (20 per day, 57 pesos); San Luis Potosí (7 per day, 16 pesos) and Guadalajara (hourly, 36 pesos) are among them.

Car Rental: Budget, Mateos 104 (tel. 2-94-58). 2-door Subaru 101 pesos per day, .70 pesos per km.

Laundromat: Rosa Blanca, López Mateos 129, ½ block downhill past the Hotel Colón. 16 pesos for 3kg. Open Mon.-Fri. 8am-7pm, Sat. 8am-5pm.

Red Cross: (tel. 2-30-05) on Héroes de Chapultepec.

Pharmacy: Las Perlas Hidalgo 131, (tel. 2-14-09). Open daily 9am-9:30pm.

Hospital: Hospital General, García Salinas 707 (tel. 3-30-04).

Emergency: tel. 06.

Police: (tel. 2-05-07), on 5 Señores.

ACCOMMODATIONS

Unfortunately, the less expensive hotels in Zacatecas tend to be dingier than budget hotels elsewhere in Mexico. Unless you are able to spend approximately 60 pesos for a single, the youth hostel is the cleanest and least depressing option.

CREA Youth Hostel (HI), Lago La Encantada (tel. 2-11-51), southwest of the city. You'll never find it on foot; fortunately, yellow "Ruta 8" buses run from the Pl. Independencia and from the bus station. Ask drivers for the *Albergues CREA* or get off at the sign for La Encantada. On the city's public land equipped with soccer field, swimming pool and courts for basketball, volleyball and racquetball, the hostel is surrounded by rose bushes and kids. The small, sterile rooms sleep 4 people. Single-sex floors. Clean communal bathroom. 11 pesos per person. Breakfast 9 pesos, lunch and dinner 11.50 pesos each. Open daily 7am-11pm.

Hotel Candesa, Juárez 102 across the street from Pl. Independencia. 3 floors of clean, comfortable modern views. Rooms overlooking Juárez are particularly nice, though almost all have windows. Singles 60 pesos. Doubles 75 pesos.

Hotel El Parque, Gonzalez Ortega 302, near the aqueduct. A longish haul with packs in a quiet area next to a nice park. The rooms are depressingly dark in this modern building, though clean, in a shabby way. Singles 40 pesos. Doubles 50 pesos.

Hotel Zamora, Juárez at Pl. Independencia (tel. 2-12-00). Central location a definite plus. Dirty yellow courtyard leads into somewhat less dirty rooms with less than comfortable beds. Singles 30 pesos. Doubles 40 pesos.

FOOD

Café Acrópolis, on Hidalgo near the cathedral (tel. 2-12-84). Prime location with prices to suit. The brown vinyl booths are filled with middle-aged women and the odd bunch of teenagers gossiping over coffee. Breakfasts 15 pesos. *Quesadillas* on pita bread 13 pesos. Open daily 8am-10:30pm.

La Terraza, in mall right next to cathedral. Although the menu is limited, the atmosphere is pleasant with tables outside on a terrace overlooking the city. Hamburgers 3.50 pesos. Ice cream 3 pesos. Coffee 2.50 pesos. Open daily 10am-9pm.

El Tragadero, Juárez 132. Decorated with New England treescapes, a suit of armor and tasteful hanging lamps. Delicious aromas waft tableward. *Lomito Zacatecas* 7.50 pesos, onion soup 4 pesos. Open daily 8am-10pm.

Café Zas, Hidalgo 201. Lots of couples fill the brown-vinyl booths, eating dessert and listening to the radio. *enchiladas* 6 pesos. Chicken 14 pesos. Coffee 3 pesos. Open daily 8am-10pm.

Los Faroles, Tacuba 129, 2 blocks from the cathedral. Yellow and brown dominate. Tacos in a rainbow of flavors 2 pesos each. Beer 2.50 pesos. Open daily 1pm-midnight.

SIGHTS

Zacatecas's steep winding streets are anointed with colonial churches, monasteries, and plazas. Keep the map in your pocket and you may round a corner and find yourself face-to-face with a soaring red *cantera* stone cathedral, a crumbling convent, or a bustling market.

The towering 18th-century **cathedral,** on Hidalgo four blocks northeast of Juárez, combines three architectural styles. The northern façade is Churrigueresque, the southern is European baroque, while the western facade, a richly carved celebration of the Eucharist, is rumored to be the country's most lavish example of Mexican baroque. St. Gregory's cowboy hat is said to be the signature of the cathedral's unknown Spanish architect. (Open daily 8am-noon and 5-8:30pm.)

The **Palacio de Gobierno,** now the state capitol, stands next to the cathedral. Its centerpiece is the arresting mural which surrounds the interior stairwell. Executed in 1970 by the prominent artist Antonio Pintor Rodríguez, the work traces the history of Zacatecas from the heyday of the Cascanes *indígenas* to today's industrial sophistication. (Open Mon.-Fri. 8am-8pm.)

Across Hidalgo and up the steep Callejón de Veyna, is the **Templo de Santo Domingo.** Built by the Jesuits in 1746, the church contains eight impressive baroque altars of gilded wood and an elaborate 18th-century German pipe organ. (Open daily 10am-2pm and 4-7pm.) Next door, in a building whose past incarnations include a monastery and a jail, is the **Museo de Pedro Coronel,** named after the Zacatecan artist (1922-1985) and containing his tomb, sculptures, and paintings, and one of the best modern art collections in Latin America. Works by Picasso, Braque, Chagall, and Miró jostle for space amidst extensive exhibits of Hogarth's tragicomic drawings and Daumier's caricatures. Mesoamerican and African masks, as well as Japanese, Chinese, Tibetan, Greek, and Roman pieces break the Eurocentric spell. (Open Fri.-Wed. 10am-2pm and 4-7pm, Sun. 10am-5pm. Admission 8 pesos.)

The **Museo Rafael Coronel** is housed amidst the dramatic ruins and plentiful sculpted gardens of the **Ex-Convento de San Francisco.** To get there from the cathedral, follow Hidalgo. At the first fork, bear left; at the second, bear right. The museum's reputation rests on its fabulous collection of masks from around the world, gathered by Rafael Coronel (incidentally the grandson of muralist Diego Rivera). Subsequent galleries boast local "primitive" figurines and Mesoamerican pottery. The final chambers are dedicated to a playful collection of marionettes depicting scenes ranging from hell to a military parade to a village wedding. (Museum open Thurs.-Sat. 10am-2pm and 4-7pm. Admission 5 pesos. Ex-Convent open daily 10am-10pm. Free.)

Southeast of downtown, 39 rose-colored arches mark the end of Zacatecas's famous colonial aqueduct, **El Cubo.** Beside the aqueduct, the verdant **Parque Estrada** borders the former governor's mansion, now the **Museo de Francisco Goitia.** The museum contains a permanent exhibit of the work of Goitia and four other renowned 20th-century Zacatecan artists, including Pedro Coronel and his younger brother Rafael. (Open Tues.-Sun. 10am-2pm and 5-7pm. Admission 5 pesos, student groups free. Sun. free.)

The **Cerro de la Bufa,** named for its resemblance to a Spanish wine-stone, peers down from the city's highest crag. The adjacent **Museo de la Toma de Zacatecas,** erected to commemorate Pancho Villa's decisive victory over Victoriano Huerta's federal troops in the summer of 1914, lays claim to a fascinating array of photographs, cannon, small arms, and other revolutionary memorabilia. (Open Tues.-Sun. 10am-5pm. Admission 5 pesos. Sun. free.) The museum is flanked by a monument to the revolution installed in 1989 to mark the 75th anniversary of the Battle of Zacatecas, and by the early 18th-century **Capilla del Patrocinio,** whose gracefully sculpted *cantera* facade and cloistered courtyards are carved from deep red Zacatecan stone. A short but steep assault on the peak of the hill leads to the **Mausoleo de los Hombres Ilustres de Zacatecas.** The ornate, Moorish structure is worth the hike if only for the view of the city. An even better vista is available from the **Meteorological Observatory,** behind the museum. Also in the vicinity of the museum are a few shops selling arts and crafts, and lodes of geodes for rock jocks. Just below the shops, several small stands serve snacks. Unfortunately, public buses run to La Bufa only on religious holidays, and taxis suck up 5 pesos. The most appealing way to make the trip is by **teleférico** (cable car), which runs between the peak of El Grillo hill and La Bufa every 10 minutes. The imported Swiss cars carry passengers on a seven-and-a-half-minute journey high above Zacatecas. (Open daily 12:30-7:30pm. 8 pesos round-trip. Cable cars run in fine weather only.) Follow Calle Garcia Rojas to its end to the cable car stop.

The **Mina de Edén** (tel. 2-30-02) was one of the region's most productive silver mines during the 19th and early 20th centuries. To get to the mine entrance, follow Juárez northwest (along the *Alameda*, an oblong park lined by some of Zacatecas's grandest colonial mansions), continue along Torreón until it ends, and then turn right—the mine is on that street. About 30 years ago, continual flooding from underground springs made mineral extraction uneconomical. Today a mini-locomotive whisks tourists into the mountain, where they are treated to a guided tour (in Spanish) of the cool subterranean tunnels. A pricy **souvenir shop** down below sells chunks of silver. A **restaurant** and **disco** have crept into one of the mine's larger caverns; on weekends the same locomotive carts partiers who dance to the latest U.S. top-40 hits and buy expensive drinks. (Mine open daily noon-7:30pm. Admission 10 pesos. Disco open Thurs.-Sun. 9pm-3am. Cover 30 pesos.)

Trips to La Bufa and Mina de Edén can easily be combined. At the end of the mine tour, you can either go back the way you came or take an elevator up to El Grillo, where you can catch the *teleférico* to La Bufa. The entire excursion takes about two hours.

■ Near Zacatecas: Guadalupe

The **Museo de Virreinal** (open Tues.-Sun. 10am-5pm; admission 10 pesos) is in the beautiful tiny village of Guadalupe, 7km east of Zacatecas on the highway to Mexico City. A Franciscan convent built in 1707, the museum contains the finest collection of colonial art in the republic. Highlights include a mural by the 18th-century painter Miguel Cabrera, two 16th-century mosaics of St. Peter and St. Francis comprised solely of bird feathers and a 1621 Gutenberg volume on mining. The exhibit is superb. Ask to be shown the choir room where the 30 resident Franciscan monks gather every afternoon for prayer and hymnody. Two people standing in opposite corners of the room can carry on a conversation by whispering into the walls. (Open Tues.-Sun. 10am-4:30pm. Admission 10 pesos, students free.) The collection of antique wagons, carriages, and cars housed next door in the fledgling **Museo Regional** (tel. 3-20-89) is worth a quick peek. (Open Tues.-Sun. 10am-5pm. Free.) "Ruta 13" buses to Guadalupe (.60 pesos) leave from the *Centro Comercial* carpark at the corner of Salazar and López Mateos every 15 minutes.

Northeast México

The cities of northeastern Mexico are often regarded as portals into the country or as pollution-spewing industrial centers; most travelers pass through without appreciating their surroundings. While the area is by no stretch of the imagination the most scenic in the Republic, it is not altogether devoid of charm. Matamoros introduces the traveler to the country's history and to border-town commercialism. Monterrey's wealth has brought a misplaced modicum of cultural sophistication to the city, while Saltillo effortlessly retains a certain unspoiled grace.

COAHUILA

SALTILLO

Unlike its booming neighbor, Saltillo retains the relaxing small-town feel which Monterrey has forsaken in its quest for economic prosperity. Though the population of this state capital of Coahuila has swelled to over 700,000, Saltillo offers a pace of life that is refreshingly slow. Few structures tower more than a few stories, and the scattered government buildings blend easily into the surroundings. The buses slow down and actually stop for pedestrians crossing the street. Saltillo's homey charm, lack of egotistical ambition, and dry climate make it a prime choice for those en route to Mexico City or other more frequented tourist havens.

Saltillo prides itself on its citizens and history. The first inhabitants of the mountainous region were 400 Tlaxcalteca families. These families were craftsmen and weavers by profession and began weaving the brightly colored *sarapes* that are a symbol of Saltillo today. Saltillo's other claim to fame is that it is the birthplace of Venustiano Carranza, the "father of the Mexican Constitution," a general of the Revolution, and Francisco Madero, the first man to seize power from Díaz in 1911. A good time to visit is during the **Feria de Saltillo,** a series of artistic and cultural events from July 18 to August 3.

ORIENTATION

Nestled in a valley surrounded by the jagged Sierra Madre mountains, Saltillo lies 87km southwest of Monterrey, along the desolate Highway 40, which roffers great views of the mountains. Frequent buses plod to and from Monterrey, Guadalajara, San Luis Potosí and Mexico City. Trains are less frequent but chug by en route from Nuevo Laredo to Mexico City and Monterrey to San Luis Potosí.

The **Central de Autobuses** is located about 3km southwest of city center on Blvd. Echeverría Sur. Transport to and from the city center is cheap and easy. After you exit the bus terminal, cross the pedestrian overpass and catch minibus #10 from the small street perpendicular to the boulevard, on the side of Restaurant Jaslo. All buses cost .80 pesos and run daily 6:30am-11pm. Catch a return bus at the corner of **Aldama** and **Hidalgo,** a block down the street from the Cathedral, in front of the entry to the big furniture store.

The train station is much closer to the city center (about 1km) but still a hike if you are laden with baggage. Exit onto Emilio Carranza, turn left, and walk about 400m to **R. Arizpe.** Turn right up to the Alameda. Alternatively, minibus #1B along E. Carranza will take you directly to the center; taxis should charge about 10 pesos.

Although great accommodations can be found near the bus station, most hotels, restaurants, and sights of interest for the budget traveler are located in the center of Saltillo, in or around the two main plazas. The center's streets form a slightly distorted grid not quite aligned with the four cardinal directions. The quiet **Plaza de Armas,** formerly the city's main plaza, contains the cathedral and is bordered by Victoria to the south and Hidalgo to the east. To get to the **Plaza Acuña,** the more commercial of the two, continue past the cathedral down Hidalgo for a block, turn left on Aldama and walk one more block. Plaza Acuña will be on your right.

PRACTICAL INFORMATION

Tourist Office: Acuña and Blvd. Francisco Coss (tel. 12-40-50), about 1.5km north of the center, in the old, red railway station building. Accessible by the same #1B bus from the center and train station. Excellent maps of Saltillo. Open daily 9am-5pm.

Currency Exchange: Unlike many other cities, banks in Saltillo offer the best exchange rates, however, they change dollars only. Most are on Victoria which begins behind the Palacio de Gobierno, across from the cathedral at Plaza de Armas. There are only four *casas de cambio* in the whole city, all offering poor rates—exchange pesos before coming to Saltillo. Closest to the city center is **Casa de Cambio Coin,** Acuña 167 (tel. 14-12-96), across the street from Hotel San Jorge, which changes traveler's checks at miserable rates. Open Mon.-Fri. 9am-1:30pm and 3:30-6pm, Sat. 9am-1pm. **Banamex,** at Allende and Ocampo, behind the Palacio del Gobierno, has a 24-hr. ATM that takes almost anything; AmEx, MC, Visa, Cirrus, and Plus.

Post Office: Victoria 453 (tel. 12-20-90), after Urdiñola. Open for stamps and *Lista de Correos* Mon.-Fri. 9am-5pm, Sat. 9am-1pm. Other branches in the bus station and by the tourist office. Both Mon.-Fri. 8am-3pm. **Postal code:** 25000.

Telephones: Collect calls and direct dial can be made from the pay phones in the post office. Long distance calls paid for directly can be made from Café Victoria, Padre Flores 221. Long distance lines in the bus station as well. **Telephone code:** 84.

Telegrams: Directly next door to the post office on Victoria. Open Mon.-Fri. 9am-5pm, Sat. 9am-noon.

Airport: Aeropuerto Plan de Guadalupe, 20min. northeast of city center off Hwy. 40. The **Saltill-Ramos Arizpe** bus from the bus station or along Acuña in the center can let you off 200m from the airport if you signal the driver on time (until 10:30pm, 1 peso). Taxis in Pl. Acuña charge about 3 pesos to the airport. **Taesa** flies to Mexico City (7am, 260 pesos). Tickets can be purchased at the travel agency in the Hotel San Jorge (tel. 14-95-84). Make reservations 1-2 days in advance.

Trains: E. Carranza, past the Alameda (tel. 14-95-84). The 2 major lines are from Nuevo Laredo to Mexico City and to Piedras Negras. Daily to: Mexico City 1st class (10:15pm, 12hrs., 88 pesos), 2nd class (3am, 20 hrs., 27 pesos), Piedras Negras (8:15am, 12-14hrs., 15 pesos).

Bus Station: Central de Autobuses, Echeverría Sur and Garza, reachable by minibus #10. **Transportes del Norte** (17-07-08), to: Mexico City (8 per day, 92 pesos), Durango (8 per day, 58 pesos), San Luis Potosí (6 per day, 43 pesos), Tampico (6:45, 48 pesos). **Omnibus de México** (tel. 17-03-15) to: Reynosa (12 per day, 32 pesos), Matamoros (9 per day, 42 pesos), Aguascalientes (6 per day, 51 pesos), Mexico City (9 per day, 91 pesos).**Tranportes Frontera** to: Guadalajara (8 per day, 65 pesos), Zacatecas (every hour, 24hrs., 31 pesos), Torreon (every 15mins., 24 hrs., 24 pesos). **Autobuses Blancos** (tel. 17-01-83) to: Tijuana (10pm, 382 pesos), Hermosillo (10pm, 310 pesos), Celaya (7pm, 86 pesos), Moreila (7pm, 102 pesos), Uruapan (7pm, 115 pesos).

Market: De las Fuentes, Treviño 328, between Allende and Acuña also at the bus station, across Blvd. Echverña Sur. Open Mon.-Fri. 9am-8pm, Sat. 9am-9pm, Sun. 9am-3pm. **Soriana,** at Blvd. Francisco Coss. Open Mon.-Sat. 9am-8pm, Sun. 9am-3pm.

Laundry: Laundrymatic, Mutualismo Pte. 310, at Allende, near the tourist office. Self-service 6 pesos to wash and dry. For full service, leave 3 pesos per kg. Open Mon.-Fri. 9am-1pm and 3-8pm.

Red Cross: Cárdenas and Rayón (tel. 14-33-33), northeast of the city center. 24 hrs.

Hospital: Hospital Universitario, Madero 1291 (tel. 12-30-00). 24 hrs.
Police: Treviño and Echeverría Ote. (tel. 15-55-61 and 15-51-62). 24-hr. **emergency phone:** 06.

ACCOMMODATIONS

A few inexpensive and comfortable hotels lie just across the street from the bus station, and there are plenty to be found within a few blocks. Because Saltillo sees relatively few tourists, the few budget accommodations near the center tend not to fill up and offer better conditions for fewer pesos.

Near the center

Hotel Saade, Aldama Pte. 397 (tel. 12-91-20 or 12-91-21), is 1 block west of Pl. Acuña. Professional and well-kept but slightly worn, with bright, airy hallways and clean rooms. (Singles 65 pesos, with TV 75 pesos, doubles 75 pesos, with TV 85 pesos.) **Hotel De Avila,** Padre Flores 211 (tel. 12-59-16). Don't let the huge "Hotel Jardín" sign above fool you. Primo location at the corner of Mercado Juárez, but rooms and floors could use a dusting. Light yellow and baby blue decor will either lull you to sleep or give you inland sea-sickness. An occassional TV. (Singles 40 pesos, doubles 50 pesos.) **Hotel Premier,** at the corner of Allende and Múzquiz (tel. 12-10-50), about 2 blocks down from Pl. Acuña along Allende Similar to Saad, but with even cleaner and fresher room. Phone, TV, and choice bottled water in each. (Singles 75 pesos, doubles 90-100 pesos.)

Across from the bus station

Hotel Central, Echeverría 231 (tel. 17-00-04 or 17-09-03), sits next door to the Hotel Saltillo (below). Lacks the extra touch, but easily compensates with comfort and low price. (Singles 30 pesos, doubles 40 pesos.) **Hotel Saltillo,** Echeverría 249 (tel. 17-22-00), is located directly across from the bus station. Entrepreneurial manager might talk your ear off, but it's worth hearing him out. Spanking new hotel. Untainted rooms have color TV and telephone. Adjoining 24-hr. seafood restaurant. (Singles 75 pesos., doubles with 2 beds 100 pesos.) **Hotel Siesta,** (tel. 17-07-24), to the left of Saltillo. Is almost identical with Central, but has higher prices and stuffier rooms. (Singles 35 pesos, with TV 55 pesos; doubles 50 pesos, with TV 75 pesos.)

FOOD

Saltillo hasn't yet been pegged by the multinational fast-food chains or the mod *cafeterías* that plague Monterrey. Although most eateries are simple family-run cafeterias, there are a few larger restaurants with more varied and distinctive menus.

Boca del Río, Acuña 533 Nte. (tel. 12-41-05), 2 blocks north of Pl. Acuña. Immense restaurant serves only massive portions of sea critters. Anchors and tillers crowd the walls and a giant iron swordfish guards the grill. Octopus in its ink 26 pesos. Fish filet prepared as you like 15-20 pesos. Open daily 9am-10pm.

Taquería Alanís, Padre Flores 231 (tel. 14-09-29). Slightly upscale *taquería* with flower baskets hanging from the ceiling. Sit at the long taco bar to order individual tacos to your belly's content (all kinds only 1.20 pesos a piece).

Café Victoria, Padre Flores 221 (tel. 12-91-31). Clean and efficient cafeteria is well-occupied at all hours. Large *cafés con leche* and baskets of sweet bread popular in the morning. Entrees 6-18 pesos. Open daily 7am-10:30pm.

Restaurant Jalso, Echeverría and Ramón Ruiz (tel. 17-09-75), across the pedestrian overpass from the bus station. Great for a quick breakfast or lunch en route to the city. *Comida corrida* 15 pesos, breakfasts for 12 pesos, entrees 5-19 pesos. Open daily 7am-midnight.

Restaurant El Principal, Allende 702 (tel. 14-33-84), at the corner with Alessio Robles, 4 blocks down Allende from Pl. Acuña. The inevitable window display of freshly roasted baby-goats. Happily orange tablecloths provide nice colorful accents in the stylish brown interior with intimate booths, a small atrium, and hundreds of pictures on the walls. Standard Mexican fare 4-15 pesos. *Cabrito* in a cardboard box for those on the go. Open daily 7am-midnight.

SIGHTS

Although you won't tire from running sight to sight in Saltillo, the few worthy points make for sedate yet satisfying enjoyment. The city offers more beautiful and better-preserved architecture than other northern cities and plenty of pleasant spots to sit outside and enjoy the festive atmosphere. The **Plaza de Armas,** Saltillo's main plaza, differs slightly from the crowded and noisy *zócalos* found in other large Mexican cities. This paved plaza contains neither trees nor benches, but a central fountain gives it a slightly southern European feel. On the east side of the plaza, 200 years of holiness have left the Churrigueresque **Cathedral** in good condition. Try to come in the evening when the bells ring, as families cluster around the fountain and the setting sun highlights the cathedral against the dark mountains behind. On the south side of the plaza is the **Cavie Museum,** which houses exhibits of regional literature, art and culture that change every two to three months. (Open Tues.-Sun. 9am-7pm. Free.) Knock on the door of the adjoining IEBA (Instiuto Estatal de Bellas Artes) if the museum is closed during normal hours.

Plaza Acuña, two blocks northwest of the Plaza de Armas, bustles. Vendors spill out of the **Mercado Juárez,** in the northwest corner of the plaza, while xylophonists hammer away and guitar-players and accordionists rove through the crowds. A typical northern market, it sells mostly souvenir items including hats, rugs, ukeleles and colorful *sarapes.* (Open daily 8:30am-8pm.)

Once you've relaxed in the Pl. de Armas, try relaxing in the **Alameda,** just west of the city center (follow Victoria west from Pl. de Armas), or in the **Church and Park San Francisco,** south of Pl. de Armas. The Alameda is larger and more shaded than others in the north, filled with winding paths frequented by herds of joggers in the wee hours. San Francisco Park is at the corner of Juárez and Cepeda. Plaza Mexico or **El Mirador** (aptly named by the locals), on a hill above the city, offers an astonishing panoramic view of the whole area and the unconquerable mountains around. Take Miguel Hidalgo uphill for a kilometer, turn left on General Cepeda and follow it for another 20-50m, turning onto the winding Gustavo Espinoza to the small plaza with benches and nice old street lamps.

NUEVO LEÓN

■■■ MONTERREY

Unbeknown to most travelers, Monterrey prospers as the base of Mexico's largest industrial complex, a testimonial to the painful potential of development. The downtown *Zona Rosa's* gaudy overexertion cannot sustain itself for more than a few miles from the gleaming epicenter. Although Monterrey lacks baroque churches and ancient ruins, it offers a breath-altering skyline with skyscrapers set against the untouched (if sometimes smoggy) Sierra Madres.

ORIENTATION

As the largest city in northern Mexico, Monterrey is an important transportation hub. All **buses** in and out of the city pass through Monterrey's gargantuan **Central Camionera** at Av. Colón and Villagrán. To reach the center from the bus station, simply take any bus heading south on Pino Suárez. No. 18 stops at Pino Suárez and Colón and will let you off at the southern end of the central Gran Plaza. All local buses run from 6am-11pm. Easier still, hail a **taxi;** you can probably finagle a fare of 20 pesos to the *Zona Rosa.*

The **train station** is at Calzada Victoria, six blocks west of the bus station. To get to the bus station, walk straight ahead on Victoria for two blocks, turn right on Bernardo Reyes, then left on Colón. Bus and train stations are in the northern end of the city, 3km north of the *centro.*

Downtown, **Avenida Constitución** runs west and east along the Río Catarina, a dry 10km-long riverbed that has been converted into athletic fields. From west to east, the largest streets running north-south across Constitución are Gonzalitos, Pino Suárez, Cuauhtémoc, Benito Juárez, Zaragoza and Zua Zua. From north to south, streets running east-west parallel to Constitución are Ocampo, Hidalgo, Padre Mier, Matamoros, 15 de Mayo and Washington. Around Morelos sprawls the *Zona Rosa*, bounded by Padre Mier, Zaragoza, Ocampo and Juárez.

PRACTICAL INFORMATION

Tourist Office: Oficina de Turismo, Zaragoza at Matamoros (tel. 345-08-70 or 345-09-02, also toll free from the U.S. (800) 235-2438 and from Nuevo León 91 800 83-222), in the gray complex of modern buildings on the lower level of the west side of the main plaza. Follow the blue "INFOTUR" signs for English assistance and maps. Open daily 10am-5pm.

Consulates: U.S., Constitución Pte. 411 (tel. 345-21-20), downtown. **U.K.,** PRIV Tamazunchale 104 (tel. 356-91-14). Both are open Mon.-Fri. 8am-5pm.

Currency Exchange: Banks flood the *Zona Rosa* and line Padre Mier in particular, but they don't cash traveler's checks. Most open Mon.-Fri. 9am-1:30pm. **Casa de Cambio Trebol,** Padre Mier Pte. (tel. 42-21-40), across from the Banco Internacional, changes traveler's checks. Open Mon.-Fri. 9am-6pm, Sat. 9am-1pm. Traveler's checks 9am-2pm only, but they may run out of pesos. The best bet for exchanging AmEx checks is at the American Express office (see below).

American Express: Padre Mier Pte. 1424 (tel. 43-09-10), about 1.5km west of the *centro.* Take #4 bus on Padre Mier from the *Zona Rosa*. Open Mon.-Fri. 9am-1pm and 3-6pm, Sat. 9am-1pm.

Post Office: Zaragoza at Washington (tel. 42-40-03), inside the Palacio Federal. Open for stamps Mon.-Fri. 8am-7pm, Sat. 9am-1pm; for registered mail Mon.-Fri. 8am-5pm. **Postal Code:** 64000.

Telephones: Long-distance phones in the pharmacy at the bus station. Long-distance office on 5 de Mayo between Carranza and Galeana. No change for collect calls. Open daily 9am-8pm. Most hotels also offer international services for nominal fees. **Telephone Code:** 83.

Telegrams: Above the post office. Open Mon.-Fri. 9am-8pm, Sat. 9am-1pm.

Airport: 4km northeast of the city center. Taxis charge 27 pesos for the trip, *colectivos* only 11 pesos.

Airlines: Aeroméxico, Cuauhtémoc 818 Sur at Padre Mier (tel. 344-00-87; reservations: 343-55-60), to Mexico City (13 per day, 1½hrs., 454 pesos); Guadalajara (6 per day, 431 pesos); Villahermosa (3 per day, 901 pesos); Hermosillo (2 per day, 654 pesos). **Mexicana,** Hidalgo 922 Pte. (tel. 340-55-11); to Mexico City (6 per day, 500 pesos); Guadalajara (6 daily, 828 pesos); Hermosillo (2 per day, 1347 pesos). **Aerolitoral** (tel. 343-55-60), to Villahermosa (683 pesos); **American Airlines,** Zaragoza 1300 Sur (tel. 340-30-31). **Continental,** Insurgentes 2500 (tel. 33-26-82). All offices open Mon.-Fri. 9am-7pm, Sat. 9am-1pm. Make reservations at least 2-3 days in advance, more for weekend travel.

Train Station: Región Noreste, Calzada Victoria (tel. 375-46-04). The daily train to Mexico City (87 pesos) via Saltillo (10 pesos) is slower and more expensive than the buses.

Bus Station: Colón at Villagrán to Amado Nervo. Center of a bus route universe. **Transportes del Norte,** (tel. 375-42-81) to: Mexico City (14 per day, 12hrs., 100 pesos); Guadalajara (8 per day, 10hrs., 90 pesos); Querétaro (5 per day, 8hrs., 76 pesos), Chihuahua (6 per day, 85 pesos); Aguascalientes (5 per day, 59 pesos); Durango (6 per day, 67 pesos); Mazatlán (4 per day, 100 pesos); Tampico (5 per day, 6hrs., 55 pesos); San Luis (10 per day, 54 pesos); Matamoros (5 per day, 32 pesos); Reynosa (6 per day, 23 pesos); and an hourly service which runs 24hrs. a day to Laredo (28 pesos) and Torreon (38 pesos). **Transportes Frontera,** (tel.

375-09-87) to: Tampico (5 per day, 8hrs., 44 pesos); Tuxpan (4 per day, 10 hrs., 66 pesos); Salamanca (3 per day, 67 pesos); Mexico City (6 per day, 12hrs., 83 pesos). **Autobuses Anahuac,** (tel. 375-64-80) to Morelos (7 per day, 38 pesos). **Estrella Blanca,** (tel. 375-09-87) to Zacatecas (14 per day, 38 pesos). **Rojo de Los Altos,** (tel. 374-72-73) next to Frontiera, by Sala 4 to: Saltillo, every 15min., 24hrs. a day (7.50 pesos). **Futura** and **Turistar** have fewer, more luxurious buses (20-50 pesos more than above prices). The bus station has a 24-hr. pharamacy, an emergency medical help unit in the basement, long distance phone service, and 24-hr. luggage storage in Sala 4 (.80 pesos an hour).

English Bookstore: Sanborn's Department Store, Escombedo just south of Morelos. Open daily 7:30am-11pm. **VIP's,** Hidalgo and Emilio Carranza. Open daily 8am-11pm. **Iztlacihuatl,** Morelos, between Escobedo and Emilio Carranza. Open Mon.-Sat. 10am-8pm.

Market: Gigante, just over the pedestrian overpass from the bus station. Open daily 9am-9pm. **Mercado del Norte,** also known as La Pulga, this huge street market starts about two blocks to your left as you exit the bus station. Anything from cologne to car tires sold daily 7am-10pm.

Medical Emergencies and Assitance: Red Cross, at Alfonso Reyes and Henry (tel. 342-12-12 or 375-12-12), 24hrs. **Cruz Verde,** at Ciudad Madero and Ciudad Victorio (tel. 371-50-50 or 371-52-59), 24hrs.

24-hr. Pharmacy: In the bus station or **Benavides,** at Pino Suárez and 15 de Mayo.

Emergency: Tel. 06.

Police: at Venustanio Carranza and Roberto Matínez, to report theft or loss.

ACCOMMODATIONS

Hotels in Monterrey tend to be overpriced. The unpleasant area around the bus station is home to most of the city's budget hotels, including all those listed below. Many rooms are full by early afternoon. If you are staying in this area alone, take precautions when walking at night, since the streets become deserted around 10pm.

Hotel Conde, Reforma Pte. 427 (tel. 375-71-59 and 372-18-79), off the labryinthine market on your right after heading left (east) down Colón from the bus station. This spotless, modern hotel outshines the others in the area. Sterile rooms have fans, TVs, and phones. Singles or doubles 66 pesos, with A/C 77 pesos.

Hotel Nuevo León, Amado Nervo 1007 (tel. 374-19-00). The best pick of its neighbors on Amado Nervo. Clean and quiet lobby and hallways. Rooms lack spots and some furniture. Hallway phone available. Singles 55 pesos.

Hotel Virreyes, Amado Nervo 902 (tel. 74-66-10). Stalactite-adorned ceilings. The grandmotherly *dueña* may show more concern for you than is necessary. Large rooms a bargain for a big group. Phones. Singles or doubles 50 pesos, with A/C 70 pesos. Room for four with noisy A/C 90 pesos.

Hotel Posada, Amado Nervo 1138 (tel.3 72-39-08). Closest to the bus station means a few pesos more. Small clean rooms with TVs and phones. Adjoining restaurant open 24 hrs. Singles and doubles 66 pesos.

FOOD

Barbecued meats, especially *cabrito* (goat kid), are a specialty of northern Mexico. Charcoal-broiled specimens in restaurant windows lure hungry passersby. Popular dishes include *agujas* (collar bone), *frijoles a la charra* or *borrachos* (beans cooked with pork skin, coriander, tomato, peppers and onions), *machacado con huevos* (scrambled eggs mixed with dried, shredded beef), hot tamales and, for dessert, *piloncillo con nuez* (hardened brown sugar candy with nuts) or *glorias* (candy balls of goat's milk and nuts). Downtown Monterrey is littered with fast-food joints, while the bus station area is filled with cheap, but possibly unhealthy restaurants.

Cafetería y Mariscos Flores, Colón 876, across the street from the bus station. Casual and cheerful. Colorful tablecloths and *piñatas* hanging from the ceiling.

True to its claim, "Always the attention you deserve." Entrees 8-15 pesos. *Comida corrida* 9 pesos, breakfast 5 pesos.

Restaurant Cuatro Milpas, Madero at Julián Villagran (tel. 374-36-03), near the bus station. Ranch-style BBQ smell and atmosphere. The log cabin/ranch house decor takes you away from the concrete jungle. *Machacado* 15 pesos. *Cabrito* filet 35 pesos. Open 24 hrs.

La Puntada, Hidalgo Ote. 123 (tel. 340-69-85), near Juárez in the *Zona Rosa.* Efficient service allows quick turnover of much-coveted tables. Varied menu features piping hot homemade flour tortillas, juices and milkshake-type drinks—pineapple, papaya or melon. Most entrees 6-12 pesos. Open daily 7am-10pm.

Los Pilares, Hidalgo 485 Ote. and Escobedo (tel. 345-36-01), at the Zona Rosa's mini-plaza with the cool fountain. A refrigerated happily pink and green interior offers a peaceful refuge from the bustling heat of the city. All-you-can-eat Mexican and regional fare for 20 pesos daily noon-4pm. All-you-can-eat breakfast for 15 pesos daily 7-11:30am. Entrees range 8-30 pesos. Open daily 7am-midnight.

SIGHTS

Monterrey's disproportionately huge and loud Gran Plaza, also known to many locals as "la Macro" shows the style-less hypocrisy of *nouveau riche* arrogance. La Macro replaced hundreds of old townhouses, as if trying to reject the painful realities of poverty and misery just a few kilometers away. The plaza is bounded by Washington on the north, Constitución on the south, Zaragoza on the west and Zua Zua on the east. The stylish colonial Palacio de Gobierno, which houses the cabinet of the governor of Nuevo Leon state, loiters at its very northern extreme. In front of its southern facade, fountains, waterfalls, and statues of illustrious Mexicans punctuate the **Esplanada de los Héros.** Miguel Hidalgo stands at the northwest corner, Benito Juárez at the northeast, Morelos at the southwest, and Carranza at the southeast. South of the Esplanada is **Parque Hundido** (Sunken Park), a cool and verdant garden gateway for the city's young couples, surrounded by an overlooking complex of tastelessly dark-grey concrete buildings: **Congreso del Estado, Palacio Legislativo,** and **Teatro de La Ciudad.** Further along the Gran Plaza sits **Fuente de La Vida** (Fountain of Life) which douses an immense statue of Neptune with cavorting nymphs and naiads, across the street from the **Monumento al Obrero.** The ultimate addition to the stylistic disjointedness of the whole plaza, however, is the painfully orange needle-like 30m high structure called **Faro del Comercio** (Lighthouse of Business), across Blvd. Zua Zua. from the humble-yet-stately **Catedral.** La Macro's south end is marked by the metal and concrete cube of the **Palacio Municipal**—yet another bow to bureaucracy. The most balanced and tasteful modern buiding in the Plaza is the fascinating **MARCO** (Museo de Arte Contemporaro), Monterrrey's museum of contemporary art, just across the small street from the cathedral. MARCO displays modern Mexican art and major travelling exhibits. (Open Tues. and Thurs.-Sat. 11am-7pm, Wed. and Sun. 11am-9pm. Admission 10 pesos. Students with ID 5 pesos. Free on Wed.)

The **Obispado,** former palace of the bishop of Monterrey, is now a state museum. Constructed in the late 18th century on the side of a hill overlooking the city (ostensibly to employ drought-ravaged *indígenas*), the palace served in the 1860s as a fortress for both the French and Mexican armies. In 1915, Pancho Villa's revolutionary forces stormed the palace and drove the loyalists of Porfirio Díaz out of Monterrey. The museum displays murals, paintings, historic pictures and old weapons, but the view of the city from the site and the decayed exterior are more of a draw than the museum itself. (Open Tues.-Sat. 10am-6pm, Sun. 10am-5pm. Admission 10 pesos.) Take bus #4 from Washington or Juárez crosspoint of Pare Mier and Degollado. Ask the driver to point out the stop.

The Cuauhtémoc Company, for over a century the major producer of beer in Monterrey, has graciously converted one of its old factories into the **Jardines Cuauhtémoc,** two blocks west on Colón and about four blocks north on Universidad from the bus terminal. The "gardens" are a few cement patios surrounded by grass, where visitors sit and drink beer in the shade after visiting the three museums and the **Hall of Fame** (a collection of photographs and documents commemorating Mexico's baseball heroes) located in the old factory.

The **Museo Deportivo,** part of the Hall of Fame, celebrates *charriadas* (rodeos), boxing, soccer and bullfighting. Not surprisingly, the complex also contains a museum devoted to beer—located just to the north of the gate that leads into the gardens, the **Museo de la Cervecería** (tel. 375-22-00) foams over with elegant beer mugs from various countries and other beer culture artifacts. Another gallery, the **Museo de Monterrey,** displays a pedestrian permanent collection of art as well as traveling exhibits; past exhibitions have included work by Robert Mapplethorpe. (Museos Deportivo and Monterrey open Tues.-Sat. 9:30am-9pm, Sun. 9am-5pm. Free.) An appointment must be made to see the Museo de la Cervecería or brewery; check at the other museums for more info. Even without the intellectual and nostalgic stimulation of the museums, the trip is worthwhile if only for the icy bottles of Carta Blanca given away a the stand on the edge of the *museo.* Like nothing else in Monterrey, free beer soothes the weary soul.

Also worth a visit are the **Grutas de García,** 45km northwest of the city. Accesesible by car or bus. Once there, avoid the hard climb of more than 700m by taking the cable railway car (included in the 180 pesos admission). (Open daily 9:30am-5:30pm.) The Grutas are a system of natural chambers; the dozens of sedimentary layers in their walls reveal that 50 or 60 million years ago the caves lay on the ocean floor. Take a **Transportes Monterrey-Saltillo** bus from the terminal; buses only go to the Grutas de García on Sundays, hourly after 9am. The most convenient way to see them is on one of the organized tours by the tourist office every Saturday, beginning at 1:30pm (end 5:30pm back in Monterrey), 25 pesos per person.

TAMAULIPAS

■■■ MATAMOROS AND BROWNSVILLE, TEXAS

In the early 19th century, the recently settled Congregación de Nuestra Señora del Refugio was re-named Villa de Matamoros after a priest slain during Mexico's war for independence. In 1846 Matamoros fell to U.S. general (and later president) Zachary Taylor, who divided the city in two, designating the Río Bravo as the international border.

The unscenic, muddy trickle separating the U.S. and Mexico, mislabeled by Mexicans as the Río Bravo and by *norteamericanos* as the Río Grande, divides two communities which reflect the nations that claim them. Though geographically insignificant, the river marks the transition between two cultures and ways of life.

■ Matamoros

Matamoros offers the inevitably North-Americanized first taste of borderline Mexico, yet due to its distinictive past, remains more authentic than other border cities. The small and chaotically crowded center belies the city's population of 350,000. Locals patiently exploit their proximity to the U.S. and have gladly converted most of the downtown area into a big marketplace. Street vendors can always pull out "something special" that you must need and numerous stands sell tacos, *aguas de frutas* (fruit juices), and *elotes* (corn on the cob; try it with chili and lime). On Sunday evenings residents file into the plaza for their weekly *paseo* (promenade).

ORIENTATION

Matamoros lies 38km west of the Gulf Coast on the Río Bravo. Route 2, which follows the course of the river northwest to Reynosa (100km) and Nuevo Laredo (350km), also passes through the center of Matamoros. Local buses (1.50 pesos) run from the airport to the city center every hour from 5:30am to 8:30pm, dropping off passengers at the corner of Abasolo and Calle 12, 6 blocks northwest of the plaza. Taxis charge 40 pesos for the journey into town. Until 7pm, downtown-bound buses depart regularly from the train station for .80 pesos.

In the center of town, streets form a grid pattern: numbered *calles* run north-south, named *calles* run east-west. The pedestrian mall, where vendors hawk their wares, lies between Calles 6 and 7 on Abasolo. The main plaza lies two blocks east, down Gonzalez. The International Bridge, the only (legal) border crossing, and its immediate area lie in a crook of the Río Grande. Calle Obregón twists from the bridge towards the crossing with Calles 5 and higher, which lead to the market. After crossing the International Bridge, located at the northernmost part of the city, you will pass the customs and tourist offices. To reach the border area from the center of town, take one of the buses or *colectivos* labeled "Puente" (.80 pesos), which let you off in the parking lot of the customs building and tourist office. Taxi drivers in the market area will try to charge exorbitant prices to the border, but the persistent should be able to whittle them down to 5 pesos.

CROSSING THE BORDER

Due to prohibitive increases in insurance rates, few buses and taxis have crossed the border since 1989. Currently, the two best options are by foot or by private car whose entire documentation is with you (see Mexico General Introduction: Planning Your Trip: Vehicle Permits).

A 100m-long bridge joins Matamoros and Brownsville. Pedestrians pay 25¢ or .80 pesos to leave either country. Crossing by foot is as easy as inserting a quarter and passing through a turnstile. Autos pay US$1 or 32 pesos, but be sure you have checked your insurance before you cross—most U.S. insurance is null and void in Mexico.

To get a six-month permit (the only kind available) at the border, you must have your Social Security number, documentation showing ownership of the car and license plate identification and registration. The fee is determined on the spot according to the value of the car (you may unexpectedly find that you are driving a treasure chest), and can be paid in cash or with any major credit card. If you're going to Matamoros just for the day, it may may be a much better idea to park on the U.S. side and walk.

U.S. citizens need to obtain a tourist card (FMT) for travel beyond Matamoros. An FMT can be obtained in the immigration office to the right directly after the International bridge or in the Matamoros bus station. The immigration desk is the first one immediately to your left as you enter the door closest to the to the International Bridge, and is supposedly open 24 hrs. Look for the green uniformed officers; there are no signs. If the officer marks only 30 days on your card, ask for more, now rather than later. There are checkpoints at all roads leading out of Matamoros into Mexico, considerably further from the U.S. border.

Finding transportation on either side of the border is no problem; taxis and *peseras* (public buses, all cost .80 pesos) circle the area in buzzard-like search of prospective passengers.

PRACTICAL INFORMATION

Because of U.S. daylight savings time, Matamoros clocks run one hour behind of those in Brownsville from April to October.

Tourist Offices: Delegación Turismo. Get your Matamoros maps in Brownsville at the Brownsville Chamber of Commerce, only two blocks from the border.

About 50m beond the border, the proudly amanteurish "Tourist Information an Guides" service is run by local English-speaking taxi drivers. Open roughly between 8am and 10pm daily. **Informacíon Turism,** in a small building across the street from the **Gran Hotel Residencial,** where Obreón turns into Hidalgo. Photocopied maps and touristy hotel and restaurant listings (tel. 3-82-41; open Mon.-Fri. 9am-2pm and 3-7pm). Try upscale hotels for English information.

U.S. Consulate: 232 Calle 1 (tel. 6-72-70 or 6-72-72), at Azaleas. Open Mon.-Fri. 8am-10am and 1-4pm.

Currency Exchange: Banks line Calle 6 and the new central Plaza Hidalgo. Open for exchange 9am-1:30pm. Both **Bancomer** at Matamoros and Calle 6, across from **Hotel Colonial** and **Serfín,** on Plaza Hidalgo, at Calle 6 and Gonzalez, have 24-hr. ATMs for advances on Visa and Diner's Club, while **Multibanco Comermex,** 2 blocks into the center of Matamoros from the **Gran Hotel Residencial,** along Obregón, offers a 24-hr. Cirrus ATM. Better rates at the *casas de cambio* near the plaza, on Calle 6, and on Abasolo (the pedestrian mall). Open (approx.) Mon.-Fri. 9am-6pm, Sat. 10am-1pm.

Post Office: In the bus station. Open Mon.-Fri. 8am-5pm. **Postal Code:** 87300.

Telephones: Try the small, nondescript *casa de larga distancia* at Morelos and Calle 8. Open daily 8am-1pm and 3-6pm. **Telephone Code:** 891.

Airport: Servando Canales Aeropuerto, on Rte. 101, the highway to Ciudad Victoria, 5km south of town. **Aeroméxico,** Obregón 21 (tel. 3-07-02), has service to Mexico City (6pm, 555 pesos). Open Mon.-Sat. 10am-5pm.

Train Station: Ferrocarriles Nacionales de México (tel. 6-67-06), on Hidalgo between Calles 9 and 10. Slow daily service to Reynosa (18 pesos) and Monterrey (38 pesos) beginning at 9:20am. Buy a ticket ahead of time and arrive early for boarding. Crowds of vendors hop on at every stop to sell everything from tacos to ten-pound slabs of freshly butchered raw meat.

Bus Station: Central de Autobuses, Canales at Aguiles. Take any bus or *pesera* (minibus) marked "Central"; taxis line up outside. Like a supermarket—pick your favorite brand of bus line: first or second class. Luggage lockers available in the 24-hr. restaurant for 6 pesos per day or 3 pesos for 2 hr. **Omnibus de México** (tel. 3-76-93) to Monterrey (5 per day, 5 hr., 33 pesos), Laredo, and Durango. **ADO** (tel. 2-01-81), to Veracruz via Tampico and Tuxpan (3 per day, 45 pesos). **Monterrey Codereyta Reynosa Transporte** (tel. 3-57-68) offers the cheapest and most frequent buses to Monterrey (15 per day, 28.50 pesos). Buy a *directo* ticket to avoid endless local stops. **Autobuses de Norte** (tel. 2-27-77) to Monterrey (videobus, 5 per day, 5 hr.,33 pesos), to Mexico City (2 per day, *ejecutivo* with a snack bar, 205 pesos, 4 per day; *primera* and video, 150 pesos).

Market: Gigante, directly across from the bus station, with a big red "G." Supermarket, general store, pharmacy, and cafeteria. Open daily 9am-9pm .

Laundromat: 313 Calle 1, 3 doors north of Ocampo. Exit the bus station and go right immediately; 1 short block down Canales, at Calle 1, go right 2½ blocks. On your left as you head toward city center. Self-service wash and dry 3 pesos each. Open daily 8:30am-9pm.

Red Cross: Caballero at García (tel. 2-00-44). 24 hrs. For emergency medical aid also try the **clinica** along Canales, 3 blocks from the Central towards the center of the city along Calles 4 and 5. Open 24 hrs.

24-hr. Pharmacy: Farmacia Aristos del Golfo. On Calle 1 between Gonzalez and Morelos. Joined to the hospital—large beige building with blue writing on the sides. Many pharmacies in market area are open during the day.

Police: Tel. 2-03-22 or 2-00-08. Friendly and helpful, but little English spoken. Open 24 hrs.

ACCOMMODATIONS

Budget travelers will be able to find plenty of low-cost accommodations in the market area. Though less comfortable and grubbier, these hotels cost at least half as much as those in Brownsville.

Hotel Majestic, Abasolo 89 (tel. 3-36-80), between Calles 8 and 9 on the pedestrian mall. Feels homiest of all, with colorful curtains and bedspreads in the darkish rooms; some even have TVs. Excellent location outweighs lack of toilet seats and peeling paint. Singles 30 pesos. Doubles 35 pesos.

Hotel México, Abasolo 87 (tel. 2-08-56), next door to the Majestic. Yellow-and-red-tiled decor. Shabby but clean rooms, toilets without seats, but a great location. Some rooms have balconies over the pedestrian mall. Singles 30 pesos. Doubles 40 pesos.

Hotel Colonial, Matamoros 601 (tel. 6-64-18), at Matamoros and Calle 6, 3 blocks east of the market. Large white building with brown trim, across from Bancomer. Lobby lies below three floors of clean red-tiled rooms with fans. Bathrooms lack toilet seats, showers lack curtains. Suspicious-looking drinking water available. Adjoining cafeteria. Singles 30 pesos. Doubles 35 pesos.

Hotel Araujo, Abasolo 401 (tel. 2-22-66), between Calles 4 and 5. Similar room conditions but less convenient than the hotels farther up on Abasolo. Two stories of rooms open onto a small, dingy central courtyard. Attentive family keeps rooms and sheets clean (though both have seen better days) and the noisy, sporadic A/C running. Singles and doubles 32 pesos.

FOOD

Select from family-run cafeterias or predictably-inflated tourist joints.

Café y Restaurant Frontera, Calle 6 between N. Bravo and Matamoros (tel. 3-24-40). Yellow building with red heart hanging outside. A popular weekend hangout for drinking and winding down. Two floors of booths and a jukebox. A wide range of seafood, steaks, and salads, all under 12 pesos. Open daily 7am-10pm.

Cafetería 1916, 191 Calle 6, (tel. 3-07-27), between Matamoros and Abasolo. A cool and quiet refuge from the bustle. Try *sincronizadas 1916* (flour tortilla with ham, chicken and avocado) for 9.50 pesos, or other Mexican specialties for 7.50-9.50 pesos. Open daily 10am-10pm.

Café de Mexico, on Gonzalez between Calle 6 and Calle 7. Huge central TV allows you to keep up with the soaps while you eat. Everything 12 pesos or less. *Fajitas con frijoles* or *chiles rellenos* 11 pesos. Open daily 7:30am-11pm.

Krystá l, Matamoros between Calle 6 and Calle 7 acros the unavoidable Hotel Ritz (big neon R); (tel. 2-11-90 will connect you to the Ritz, ask for a transfer to Krystál). Modern and hip eatery by Matamoros standards. Green booths are surrounded by mirrored walls. *Plato de frutas* 7 pesos, *quesadillas* with french fries and guacamole 9 pesos. All entrees 8.50-12.50 pesos. Open daily 7am-11pm.

SIGHTS AND ENTERTAINMENT

Matamoros's indoor market spreads for several blocks and spills out into the street. It is divided into the old market, or **Pasaje Juárez,** and the new market, **Mercado Juárez.** Entrances to Pasaje Juárez are on both Matamoros and Bravo between Calles 8 and 9 under a sign that says "Old Market." The new market's entrance is on Abasolo between Calles 9 and 10. Both markets cater largely to "spring-breakers" and the tourist trade, selling such souvenirs as jewelry, hammocks, hats, T-shirts, and hard liquor (each person of age can carry 1 quart back to the U.S.). Shop proprietors will flog their wares with gusto, but consider making major purchases farther south, where souvenirs like piñatas and blankets are cheaper. (Markets open daily : "Old" 7am-7pm, "New" 7am-8pm).

The city's central plaza, the **Plaza Hidalgo**, is a shady, pleasant place to sit, a fact well-known to young *matamorense* couples who relax there in the afternoon shade. Statues of Miguel Hidalgo and Benito Juárez stand on the west side along Calle 6. **City Hall** is the large white building with murals on its facade, also on Calle 6. Across the plaza lies the cathedral.

Mexican history buffs should visit the **Casa Mata Museum,** at the corner of Guatemala and Santos Degollados. Here you can look at revolutionary photographs, artifacts, and picayunes, as well as figurines and pottery from southern *indígena* groups. From the bus station, take the first right out the entrance and walk seven blocks on Guatemala or take the *pesera* to the hospital and walk down Calle 1 to Santos Degollados and turn left. (Open Tues.-Sun. 9:30am-5:30pm. Free.)

For a refreshing break from souvenir-hunting, join hordes of bar-hoppers and sink into the the ventilated out-of-this-dirty-hot-world atmosphere of **Las dos Republicás** on Calle 9, between Matamoros and Abasolo (tel. 2-97-50; open daily 8am-8pm). Huge 18-oz. frozen Maragritas (US$6) are served in glasses that could almost hold a basketball, and *piña de la casa* is served in a real pineapple. You keep the pineapple, they keep US$7. For something more authentically Mexican, try the **Bar Los Toros,** two doors down from Las Dos Repúblicas, where rowdy groups of men swig Coronas (3 pesos). Although permitted inside, females may not feel at ease.

■ Brownsville, Texas

At first, Brownsville may seem to be just another Mexican town which happens to lie within U.S. borders. However, a trip across the bridge reveals that, despite a common language and historical ties, Matamoros' crowded markets and packed *colectivos* (with their destinations shoe-polished on the windows) have a vastly different flavor and feel. Brownsville residents enjoy a more peaceful pace of life in surroundings where public hygiene still has meaning. Brownsville provides travelers from either direction with a wide range of services and a relatively uncrowded border crossing. While both directions remain fast and easy on foot, automobile crossing can become congested. The influence of Mexican language and culture fades away as the miles from the border increase.

ORIENTATION

Brownsville's streets are laid out in a grid, by a large bend in the Río Grande near the International Bridge. Texas Rte.4 from the northeast (International Blvd.) and Texas Rte.415 from the northwest (Elizabeth St.) converge at the tip of this bend. North-south Highways 83 and 77 cut through the middle of the city. Boca Chica (Hwy. 281 and 48) swoops from the mid-west to Brownsville and South Padre international airport at the eastern extreme of the city. Elizabeth St., lined mostly with clothing and shoe stores, is Brownsville's main commercial district and a good point of reference.

Local buses, which can be confusing, run 6am-7pm (fare US$.75). Buses to all areas of the city leave from city hall, which is on E. Washington St. between E. 11th and E. 12th. Pick up schedules at the desk inside the building or call 548-6050 for route and schedule information.

PRACTICAL INFORMATION

Chamber of Commerce: 1600 E. Elizabeth (tel. 542-4341). Brimming over with maps and brochures but not a great source of tourist information. Open Mon.-Fri. 8am-5pm.

Brownsville Information Center: Farm Rd. 802 (tel. (800) 626-2639 or 541-8455), at Central Blvd. adjacent to Motel 6. Friendly and knowledgeable staff. Maps and brochures like there's no tomorrow. Get your Matamoros maps here. From City Hall, take the "Jefferson Central" or *Los Ebanos* bus. Get off right before the highway at the pyramid-shaped tan building. The stop is after the Sunrise mall. Open Mon.-Sat. 8am-5pm, Sun. 9am-4pm.

Currency Exchange: *Casas de cambio* litter International Blvd. **Interex Money Exchange,** 801 International Blvd. (tel. 548-0303), exchanges traveler's checks. Open daily 10am-6pm.

Telephone area code: 210

Telegrams: Western Union, 2814 International Blvd. (tel. 542-8695). Send or receive telegrams, messages and money orders. Open daily 7:30am-8pm. Two other locally reputable companies provide the same services. **Valley Check Cashiers** at 1401 E. Washington St. (tel. 546-6634) and 2921 Boca Chica Blvd.

(541-7700) as well as H.E. Butt Grocery 2250 Boca Chica Blvd. (541-1251) and 1628 Central Blvd. (541-4816).

Airport: The most convenient airport is **Valley International Airport** (tel. 430-8600), in Harlingen, Texas, 25mi. (42km) northwest of Brownsville. From Brownsville, a taxi to the airport costs US$40-45. The bus charges US$24 for the lonesome cowpoke plus $12 a head for company. Some get free rides from the airport to Brownsville on one of the vans to the expensive hotels. **Brownsville and South Padre International Airport,** at 700 S. Minnesota (tel. 542-4373) currently offers four flights a day to Houston. They are all served by Continental (tel. (800) 231-0856).

Bus Stations: Greyhound, 1134 E. Charles St. (tel. 546-7171). Luggage locker US$1 per day. Service to McAllen (8 per day, US$7.50), and Laredo (2 per day, US$32). Also serves Houston, Dallas, and San Antonio (4 per day). Schedule changes frequently; call to confirm. Reservations can be made up to 1 day in advance. **Valley Transit Company,** 1305 E. Adams (tel. 546-2264), at 13th St. Lockers available for 75¢ per day. To: Laredo (at 8:15am and 2:15pm, US$32); McAllen (at 6:45am, 7:00am, 10:30am, 2:45pm, 4:30pm, 10pm, US $7.50); Del Río (2 per day, US$55).

Market: H.E.B. #1 food and drug stores. Across the street from the post office on Elizabeth. Open Mon.-Sat. 7am-9pm. and Sun. 8am-9pm.

Laundromat: Holiday Laundry, Elizabeth and West 6th. About ½ mi. (1km) NW from the International Bridge. Self service wash US$.75 per load, US$.25 per dry.

Emergency: Tel. 911, 24 hrs.

Police: 600 E. Jackson (tel. 911 or 548-7000), 24 hrs.

ACCOMMODATIONS

Brownsville hotels look and feel like the Ritz for those coming from Mexico, but the prices can't compare to Mexican bargains. The downtown area near the International Bridge offers the best bargains and convenience, but is less safe at night than the distant area along the North Expressway.

Hotel Colonial, 1147 E. Levee St. (tel. 541-9176). Refrigerated *hacienda*-style lobby leads to ample, clean rooms with phone and TV. US$40 for singles or doubles, $5 for each additional person over 16 years old. Turn on the A/C yourself and endure the heat for 1hr.

Cameron Motor Hotel, 912 E. Washington (tel. 542-3551). Unblemished lobby/lounge with an affable staff. Sparkling rooms with fan, A/C, TV and phone. Singles US$23, with bath $34. Doubles with bath $40.

Motel 6, 2255 North Expressway (tel. 546-4699), off Hwys. 77 and 802. Large, clean rooms with the works (TV with movies, A/C, phone), but miles from the city center. Take the "Jefferson Central" or *Los Ebanos* bus (last bus leaves at 7pm). US$30.50, additional adults $7, kids under 18 free in parents' room.

FOOD

Brownsville restaurants serve a border blend of Mexican and U.S. cuisine in casual cafés. The downtown area (near the International Bridge) hosts a plethora of affordable restaurants.

Texas Café, in Market Square, adjoining City Hall (tel. 542-5772). Murals of Brownsville circa 1890 give it a historical feel, and the location makes it perfect for a quick bite while waiting for the bus. Simple grill food for about US$3, dine in or take out. Open 24 hrs.

Lucio's Café, 1041 E.Washington (tel. 542-0907). Bright café packed with regulars at all hours for good reason. Multiple ceiling fans and colorful Mexican fabrics cloak the walls, making the atmosphere cool, pleasant, and relaxed. Jukebox in the corner plays Spanish soft rock favorites. Monstrous portions at low prices. Try the roast pork with rice or French fries, beans, and salad (US$4.50). Open 24 hrs.

Mr. Amigo Café, 1141 E. Levee, off 12th St. Small and simple (tel. 541-1231). Decor must have been a low priority. Great for breakfast—huge stack of pancakes (US$2) and homemade hot biscuits with jelly ($.50). Open Mon.-Sat. 7am-4pm.

Oasis Café, 1417 E. Adams, 1 block down from the Valley Transit bus station. Crowded with locals eating full meals even early in the morning. *Carne guisada* goes for US$3.25. Lengthy list of burgers. Open Mon.-Sat. 6am-5pm.

■■■ TAMPICO

If you've ever seen John Huston's *The Treasure of the Sierra Madre*, you might remember Tampico as the hot, dirty, unfriendly oil town that every foreigner was itching to skip. Tampico may be more friendly today, but otherwise Huston's portrayal holds true: a kidney stone of a city. Ironic geographic fate has made Tampico a necessary transport pit stop in the race south to more beautiful locales. Enough amenities have cropped up here to make a brief stay tolerable, but hold your breath and remember that the shorter your stay, the happier you will be. A relaxing nearby beach, **Playa Miramar,** is accessible on bus "Playa" or "Escollera" (1 peso from the corner of López de Lara and Madero).

Orientation and Practical Information To get the the city center from the bus stop, take the yellow taxis (10-12 pesos), the minibuses (1 peso), or the *colectivos* (shared taxis, .70 pesos, 1.40 with luggage). Like most routes, these stop on López de Lara at the intersection with Madero. The town is centered around the nearby **Plaza de Armas** and the **Plaza de la Libertad.**

The **tourist office,** Olmos Sur 101 (tel. 12-00-07), on the 2nd floor, in the orange and white building on the northeast corner of Pl. de Armas, dispenses photocopied city maps and useless brochures. (Open Mon.-Fri. 9am-2pm and 3-7pm.) The **U.S. Consulate agency** is located at Ejército Mexicano 503, Suite 203, in the northern colonia Guadalupe (tel. 13-22-17). (Open Mon.-Fri. 10am-1pm.) Exchange currency or AmEx traveler's cheques at **Banorte** (tel. 12-47-91) at the Pl. de Armas, corner of Oolmos and Mirón. (Open: Mon.-Fri. 10am-1pm). **Post Office:** Madero 309 OTE at Juárez (tel. 12-19-27), on Pl. de la Libertad. (Open for *Lista de Correos,* stamps, and registered mail Mon.-Fri. 8am-7pm, Sat. 9am-1pm.) Another branch is in 2nd-class bus terminal. (Open Mon.-Fri. 9am-3pm.) **Postal Code:** 89000. Collect calls can be placed at pay **phones** in both plazas and the 24-hr. long-distance *caseta* at the bus station. **Phone code:** 12.

Trains leave from the small station located in small park at corner of Héroes de Nacozári and Aduana (tel. 12-11-79), 3 blocks south of Pl. de Armas. Trains to Monterrey (7:45am, 16 pesos) and San Luis Potosí (8am, 13.50 pesos). Tickets available daily 5:30-8am. The **bus station,** on Zapotal, north of the city, has adjoining 1st- and 2nd-class terminals. Carriers **ADO** (tel. 13-41-82), **Omnibus Oriente** (tel. 13-37-18), and **Blancos** (tel. 13-48-67) run almost continuously to Poza Rica (25-30 pesos), Mexico City (75-90 pesos) and Veracruz (80 pesos), with fairly frequent service to Tuxpan, Reynosa, Villahermosa, Pachuca, San Luis Potosí, and Matamoros. For other destinations, investigate other carriers.

In an emergency, dial 06. The **Red Cross** (15-03-38 or 16-50-79; 15-40-47 in Ciudad Madero) has 24-hr. ambulance service. Some doctors speak English at the **Hospital General de Tampico** (tel. 15-22-20, 15-30-30, 13-09-32, or 13-20-35), Ejército Nacional 1403 near the bus station. The **police** (tel. 12-11-57 or 12-10-32; 15-03-22 in Ciudad Madero) are located on Tamulipas at Sor Juana de la Cruz.

Accommodations and Food Clean and secure budget accommodations are rare in Tampico. In the city center, near the plaza, try the **Hotel Capri,** Juárez 202 Nte. (tel. 12-26-80). Spartan rooms, bare walls, clean sheets, fans and nicely tiled baths and floors are an excellent deal at 35 pesos for both singles and doubles. Close to the bus station, **Hotel Allende,** Allende 122 (tel. 13-82-57), the newish-looking gray building, has simple, almost clean rooms with noisy and wobbly fans. To get there, exit the bus station to the right, take the first right, and walk ½ block. (Singles and doubles 33 pesos.) **Hotel La Central,** Bustamante 224 (tel. 17-09-18), is directly across from the bus station. Cool fish logo and funky swan chairs, but the hotel itself is really nothing special. Slightly more worn-out than the Allende. Fans in rooms, which are survivable for a short stay. (Singles 33 pesos, doubles 39 pesos.)

For its size, Tampico does not have an especially wide variety of restaurants. It does, however, support countless replicas of standard seafood cafeterias. **Café Mundo,** López de Lara y Díaz Mirón (tel. 14-18-31) is a good value and nice atmosphere relative to the other options; sit at the mile-long counter under the massive clock. All menus (15-17 pesos) come with beans, fresh bread and coffee. (Open 24 hrs.) The 25 tables of the **Cafetería Emir,** Olmos Sur 107 (tel. 12-51-39) are always filled with people drinking coffee, eating fresh bread from the adjoining bakery and people watching in a relaxed atmosphere. Their old-fashioned coffee machine makes delicious *café con leche*, and chicken *tamales* (2.60 pesos) are a specialty. (Open daily 6am-midnight.)

Central México

NAYARIT

TEPIC

The border between the states of Sinaloa and Nayarit is a geographical as well as a political watershed—volcanic highlands and a tropical coastline erupt where the northern desert comes to an end. Home of the Cora and Huichol peoples, Nayarit entered the world's consciousness via Carlos Castaneda's book *Journey to Ixtlán*, which was inspired by the hallucinogens of a small town halfway between Tepic and Guadalajara. Nayarit, the greatest exporter of fruit among the Mexican states, reputedly produces the lion's share of the nation's marijuana crop. Tepic, the capital of Nayarit, is an important crossroads because of its proximity to San Blas (70km northwest), Puerto Vallarta (169km south), Mazatlán (278km north), and Guadalajara (240km southeast).

Located just a holler away from the intersection of Routes 15 (running from Mexico City through Guadalajara to Nogales) and 200 (which runs from Guatemala along the Pacific coast), Tepic is something of a transport hub, and not much more.

The **bus station** is served by **Norte de Sonora, Tres Estrellas de Oro, Omnibus de México, Transportes del Pacífico, Estrella Blanca,** and **Transportes Frontera.** Norte de Sonora runs the most buses, with service to every major destination save Puerto Vallarta, including Mexico City (4 per day, 12hrs., 74 pesos), Guadalajara (13 per day, 4hrs., 22 pesos); Nogales (also through Mazatlán, 2 per day, 24hrs., 140 pesos) and San Blas (7 per day, 1¾hrs., 65 pesos). Transportes del Pacífico has the most frequent service to Puerto Vallarta (27 per day, 3½hrs., 17.50 pesos), but the last bus leaves at 8pm. Activity at the station is so frenetic that turn-around time need not exceed one hour unless a bus is canceled or completely full.

As you leave the **bus station,** *el centro* is down the highway to the left; cross the street and catch one of the orange buses (.25 pesos) at the *parada*. The **train station,** on Allende at Juárez has a train daily to Guadalajara, at noon (8 pesos). To get there, hop on a "Ferrocarril" bus at the bus station or downtown at the corner of México Sur and Hidalgo.

If, for whatever reason, you should wind up spending a night in Tepic, two hotels corner the market on cheap and easy layovers. The **Hotel Tepic,** Martínez 438 (tel. 3-13-77), has halls that summon up visions of cheap, shabby hospitals. Painters ran out of blue before getting to the rooms, which are bare but for a thin-mattressed bed and a warped desk. (Singles 30 pesos. Doubles 35 pesos for one bed, 47 pesos for 2 beds.) Next door at Martínez 430, the **Hotel Nayar** (tel. 3-23-22), has slightly larger rooms and bathrooms and makes some effort at decoration in the form of fluorescent plastic flower arrangements. (Singles 25 pesos. Doubles 32 pesos for 1 bed, 40 pesos for 2 beds.) In both hotels, rooms looking away from the bus station are much quieter, although you'll pass up the charming view of the dark satanic sugar mill. To find these budget waystations, take a left leaving the bus station, another left on the first street, and they'll be on your right after a block. If you want to stay downtown, **Hotel Serita** has clean rooms with large windows and a pleasant lobby. (Singles 35 pesos. Doubles 45 pesos.)

Economical food can be found at **Altamirano,** México Sur 109, which serves a scrumptious plate of *enchiladas con pollo y crema* for 10 pesos (open daily 7am-11pm) and **Parroquia,** Amado Nervo 18, 2nd floor, overlooking the main plaza.

Three monstrous *quesadillas* go for 7 pesos, a generous orange juice for 3.50 pesos. (Open daily 9am-9pm.)

The **regional tourist office,** México Sur 34, files its brochures under a thick layer of dust for that hip-yet-elusive casual look. Nonetheless the staff is friendly and helpful, but has no maps. (Open Mon.-Fri. 9am-7pm.) Bundles of **banks** and *casas de cambio* along México Sur make this the best area to change money. The former operate Monday through Friday, 9am-noon. The latter have variable hours, but Monday through Saturday 9am-7pm is a common schedule.

The bus station holds a **post office** and a **telegram office** (both open Mon.-Fri. 9am-1pm). The bus station has **LADATEL** phones and **telephone service** every day from 6am to 10pm. Credit card calls can be made from the public telephone on the east side of the station. The desperate can surrender a mean 6 pesos to the *Larga Distancia* on México Nte. 286, across from the cathedral. Tepic's **telephone code** is 321.

If you are in need of a hospital try **Hospital General de Tepic** (tel. 3-41-27), on Pasco de la Loma. To make the 20-minute walk from the bus station, take a left as you leave the building and another left at the intersection with Arenide México. After three blocks, take the right-hand fork at the rotary, and two blocks later the hospital is on your left. A cab is 4.50 pesos. The **police station** (tel. 2-01-63) is at the intersection of Avenidas Mina and Oaxaca, but it's too far to walk from the center, and no buses go there; take a cab for 5 pesos.

Avenida México, running north-south, is downtown Tepic's main drag. At its northern terminus, the fountainous **Plaza Principal** is incessantly active, dominated on one end by the cathedral and on the other by the **Palacio Municipal.** South of the plaza lie the **Museo Regional de Nayarit** (open Mon.-Fri. 10am-3pm; free), at México Nte. 91, and the **state capitol,** a gracefully domed structure dating from the 1870s, at México and Abasolo. At Av. México's southern end, turn west (uphill) on Insurgentes and you'll come to the huge and enchanting park known as **La Loma.** A miniature train encircles the park, running Tues.-Sat. 10am-4pm (1.50 pesos).

■ Near Tepic: Beaches and Ixtlán

Puerto Vallarta and San Blas are the most compelling lures for beach-o-philes passing through Tepic, but southern Nayarit has a number of little-known beaches which sacrifice social life for the greater goal of unpopulated sand. Chief among these is the beautiful, undeveloped **Chacala,** which lies on a dirt road out of **Las Varas;** also **Rincón de Guayabitos,** 16km farther south, with limited accommodations, and **Punta de Mita,** close enough to Puerto Vallarta for nightlife and far enough away for peaceful sleep.

Fifty km south of Tepic spreads the deep and clear **Laguna de Santa María del Oro,** a lovely 3km-wide lagoon which reaches into the depths of an extinct volcano. A second-class **México y Victoria** bus departs every hour from the Tepic bus terminal for the town of Santa María. From there you can hitch the remaining 8km to the lagoon. The lake's banana tree-lined rim is riddled with scenic camping sites, though facilities are sparse and the water features the usual gang of amoebas.

Another 50km south toward Guadalajara is the town of **Ixtlán,** of Carlos Castaneda fame. Only the **Toltec ruins** 1km south of town make Ixtlán worth mentioning. Though inferior in size and importance to sites farther south and east, they may be your only taste of Mexico's pre-Conquest days if you're not going beyond Guadalajara. Of particular interest is the **Temple of Quetzalcóatl,** the largest structure on the site, replete with sacrificial altars.

JALISCO

■■■ GUADALAJARA

The state of Jalisco revolves around the dipole of Puerto Vallarta, a vacuous seaside resort, and Guadalajara, a metropolis of considerable sophistication. *Tapatíos*, as Guadalajarans call themselves, have parlayed their geographically marginal position into a tremendous expansive force. When violent revolutionary unrest shook the streets of Mexico City during the early 19th century, many Spanish colonists were forced to flee northwest to then-remote Guadalajara. Here, the frontier of civilization gave birth to the cultural icons of the fledgling republic: tequila, *mariachi*, and the hat dance.

Alas, history has given way to urbanization and devleopment; Guadalajaran cultural innovations have slipped into stereotype. Still, the four large central plazas, stately Spanish architecture, and numerous museums and theatres of the city's downtown guard the vestiges of Guadalajara's past. Appreciation of the city requires more effort than appreciation of the gorgeous coast to the east and the postcard-perfect cities of the Bajío. Summer heat waves and the infinity of unspectacular one-story houses away from the central plazas occlude the *Tapatío* charm.

ORIENTATION

Guadalajara lies 650km west-northwest of Mexico City. Hourly buses in all directions, several trains per day and daily planes to all points in Mexico and many U.S. cities ensure that Guadalajara remains readily accessible.

Buses run from Guadalajara's **airport,** Aeropuerto International Miguel Hidalgo, every hour to the *antigua* **bus station** in the south of town (1.50 pesos). From there any "Centro" bus will take you into the center of town. A *combi* will drop you anywhere downtown for 7-20 pesos, depending upon how full it is, but beware—some drivers have commission arrangements with downtown hotels. *Combis* run from town to the airport from the Mexicana office (Díaz de Leon 951, via minibus #625 along Avenida Juárez) every hour. A taxi costs up to 45 pesos, depending on the time of day; be sure to settle the fare before getting taken for a ride.

A new bus station, the well-organized, clean and efficient **Nueva Central Camionera,** has arisen in the town of **Tlaquepaque,** southeast of Guadalajara on the highway to Mexico City. Each of seven terminals has been conveniently outfitted with a hotel and tourist information booth near the exit. The people who staff these kiosks are startlingly well-informed. If you tell them the name of a hotel, even a dirt cheap one, they'll tell you how much it costs, which bus to catch and how to get there from the bus stop. Buses (.70 pesos), *combis* (.70-1 peso), and taxis (18 pesos) all head downtown from directly in front of any terminal. To reach the station from downtown, catch a bus on Av. Revolución, or Av. de Septiembre across from the cathedral. Both the red bus #275 (or 275A) and a green bus marked "Nueva Central" will take you there. In a taxi, be sure to specify the *new* bus station, since some drivers may zip you to the old station and then make you pay extra to go to Tlaquepaque.

The **train station** lies at the foot of Independencia Sur. To get from the station to the heart of Guadalajara, at the intersection of **Independencia** and **Juárez,** take a taxi (12 pesos) or bus #60 or #62. You can also walk to Independencia, only a block from the station, and take bus #45 north to the intersection with Juárez.

A plethora of street signs makes Guadalajara easy to navigate. Intersections in the compact downtown district are clearly marked, and only a few streets run at rebellious angles. Finding your way around outside the *centro* is more difficult because the streets change names at the borders between Guadalajara's four sectors. Guadalajara's **shopping district** centers around the intersection of Av. Juárez and Avenida Alcalde/16 de Septiembre.

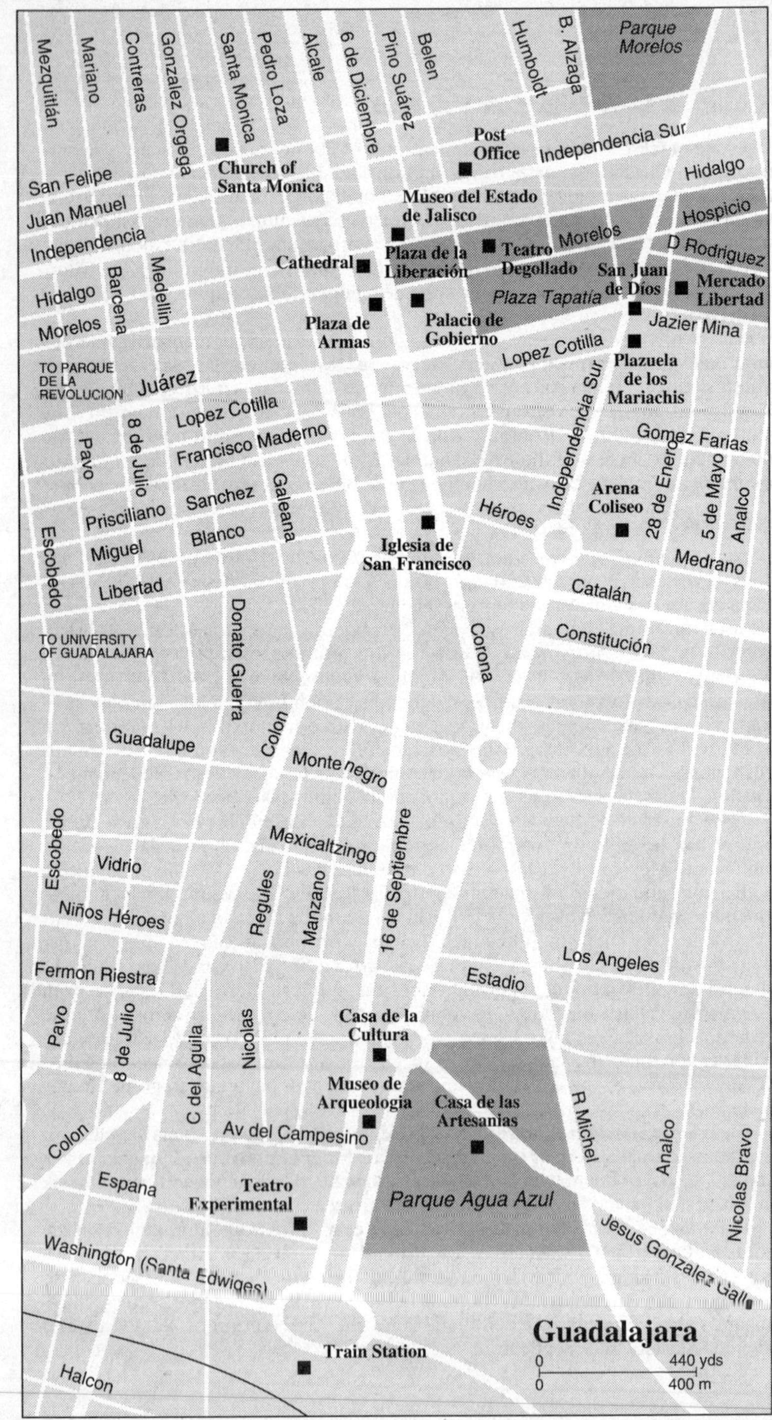
Parque Morelos
Mezquitlán
Mariano
Contreras
Gonzalez Orgega
Santa Monica
Pedro Loza
Alcale
6 de Diciembre
Pino Suárez
Belen
Humboldt
B. Alzaga
Post Office
Independencia Sur
Hidalgo
Church of Santa Monica
San Felipe
Juan Manuel
Museo del Estado de Jalisco
Hospicio
Independencia
Morelos
Teatro Degollado
D Rodriguez
Cathedral
Plaza de la Liberación
San Juan de Díos
Mercado Libertad
Hidalgo
Barcena
Medellin
Plaza Tapatía
Morelos
Plaza de Armas
Palacio de Gobierno
Jazier Mina
Lopez Cotilla
TO PARQUE DE LA REVOLUCION
Juárez
Plazuela de los Mariachis
Lopez Cotilla
Independencia Sur
Pavo
8 de Julio
Francisco Maderno
Gomez Farias
Prisciliano
Sanchez
Galeana
Héroes
Arena Coliseo
28 de Enero
5 de Mayo
Analco
Escobedo
Miguel
Blanco
Iglesia de San Francisco
Medrano
Libertad
Catalán
Donato Guerra
Corona
Constitución
TO UNIVERSITY OF GUADALAJARA
Guadalupe
Colon
Montenegro
Escobedo
Mexicaltzingo
16 de Septiembre
Vidrio
Regules
Manzano
Niños Héroes
Los Angeles
Fermon Riestra
Estadio
Pavo
8 de Julio
C del Aguila
Nicolas
Casa de la Cultura
Museo de Arqueologia
Casa de las Artesanias
R Michel
Av del Campesino
Colon
Analco
Nicolas Bravo
Espana
Teatro Experimental
Parque Agua Azul
Jesus Gonzalez Gallo
Washington (Santa Edwiges)
Guadalajara
Train Station
0
440 yds
0
400 m
Halcon

The **Plaza Tapatía** is an oblong area which contains the **cathedral**, the **Teatro Degollado,** many churches and museums, broad open spaces, and countless stores. With many of the most expensive hotels and restaurants, as well as the university and the U.S. Consulate, the area west of Pl. Tapatía is the most prosperous part of town.

The poorer *colonias* (suburbs) could be dangerous at any time of day. Check with the tourist office before exploring. Throughout Guadalajara, it is wise to stick to lit streets after dark and to take taxis after 11pm. Solo women travelers should avoid Av. Independencia after this hour as well. Independencia has a magnetic field which attracts raucous, drunken men. A massive sewage explosion in 1992 has also brought a resurgence of cholera to the city, though mainly confined to poorer districts. Visitors should be vaccinated against the infection.

The city's extensive **bus system** runs far, wide and often. Though somewhat rough around the edges (usually crowded, always noisy, and sometimes uncomfortable), buses (.70 pesos to any destination) are an excellent way to get just about anywhere in the city. Buses #60 and #62 run the length of Calzada Independencia, from the train station to the *Parque Mirador*. The "Par Vial" bus used to run down Javier Mina and Juárez, but due to subway construction on those roads it now goes down Independencia, then turns onto Vallarta and travels west, turning just short of López Mateos. Coming back eastward it cruises Hidalgo, three blocks north of Juárez. Bus #258 from San Felipe, three blocks north of Hidalgo, runs from near the Pl. Tapatía down López Mateos to the **Plaza del Sol,** the grand central station of nightlife, surrounded by *discotecas* and more expensive nightspots and shopping centers. Bus #24 goes the length of López Mateos, from Zapopan to beyond the Pl. del Sol, in both directions. Buses run between 6am and 10:30pm. Guadalajara recently opened the first part of its subway system. Of little use to travelers, the lone route lies beneath the pavement of Av. Federalismo, a north-south city bisector. Your cards rightly played, a taxi anywhere within the city limits should not cost more than 25 pesos. Haggle 'til it hurts.

PRACTICAL INFORMATION

Tourist Offices: State Office, Morelos 102 (tel. 658-22-22), in the Pl. de la Liberación, next to the Pl. Tapatía. A native English speaker, others who are more or less fluent, and a cornucopia of helpful information. They hand out "*centro*" maps (a better city map in the free tourist paper, *Guadalajara Weekly*). The magazine *Very Oir* lists cultural events for the month. Also complete listing of hotels, restaurants, and emergency hotlines. Open Mon.-Fri. 9am-8pm, Sat.-Sun. 9am-1pm. **Federal Tourist Office,** Degollado 50 (tel. 614-83-71), around the corner from the state tourist office. Sketchy material on Guadalajara, but they have free information on every Mexican state. Open Mon.-Fri. 8am-3pm.

Tours: Panoramex, Federalismo 948-305 (tel. 610-51-09). A wide range of trips, including to Ajijic, Chapala, Tlaquepaque, and Tonalá, for budgets of all sizes, beginning at 50 pesos for a city tour, plus Tlaquepaque, lasting 4 hrs. Open Mon.-Fri. 9am-2:30pm and 4:30-7pm, Sat. 9am-1pm. More information available at the state tourist office (above).

Consulates: U.S., Progreso 175 (tel. 625-27-00; emergencies 626-55-53). Open Mon.-Fri. 8am-2pm. **U.K.,** Paulino Navarro 1165 (tel. 611-16-78). Open Mon.-Fri. 9am-2pm and 4-7pm. **Canada,** Fiesta Americana Hotel, Local 30 on the Minerva traffic circle (tel. 15-86-65, ext. 3005). Open Mon.-Fri. 10am-1pm. For other countries, try the **Oficina de la Asociación Consular** (tel. 15-55-55), or the state tourist office (above) which has complete listings.

Currency Exchange: Banks have higher rates for traveler's checks, but *casas de cambio* offer better rates for cash. **Bancomer,** Corona 140, between Juárez and López Cotilla, open Mon.-Fri. 9am-1:30pm. **Bánamex,** Juárez at Corona, same hours. **Casa de Cambio Escobedo,** López Cotilla 221, offers a particularly good rate on dollars, a few pesos above other exchange houses. Open Mon.-Fri. 9am-6pm, Sat. 9am-2pm.

American Express: Vallarta 2440 (tel. 630-02-00), at Plaza los Arcos. Take the "Par Vial" bus and look for the office on your right after about 15 blocks. Full financial services and travel agency. Open Mon.-Fri. 9am-2:30pm and 4-5pm, Sat. 9am-noon.

Post Office: On Carranza, between Juan Manuel and Calle de Independencia (not Independencia Sur), 1 block north of the Teatro Degollado. Open Mon.-Fri. 8am-7pm, Sat.-Sun. 9am-1pm. City mailboxes rumored to be unreliable. **Postal code:** 44100 or 44101 for surrounding area.

Telephones: Long distance office, Donato Guerra 72, between Moreno and Juarez. No charge for collect calls. Open daily 7am-8:30pm. Orange public phones are for local calls and take 50- or 100-peso coins. Blue phones are for long distance and take 1000-peso coins. **Telephone code:** 36.

Telegrams: Palacio Federal, Alcalde and Juan Álvarez (tel. 613-99-16); and at the airport. Open Mon.-Sat. 9am-3pm.

Airport: 17km south of town on the road to Chapala. Don't pay more than 40 pesos for a cab. Served by: **Aeroméxico** (tel. 689-02-57), **Mexicana** (tel. 649-22-22), **American** (tel. 689-03-04), and **Delta** (tel. 630-35-30).

Train Station: At the foot of Independencia Sur, just before the tunnel, south of the *centro* (tel. 650-08-26, 650-04-44 for a Spanish recording). Prices vary widely depending on train and class of ticket. Southbound to: Mexico City (7:30pm, 12hrs., 11-61 pesos) via Querétaro (10 pesos); Manzanillo (8hrs., 18 pesos); and Colima (5hrs., 20 pesos). Northbound to: Mazatlán (17 pesos), Mexicali (200pesos), and Los Mochis (43-83 pesos). Buy tickets at least a week in advance. In the station, desk to the left as you enter is far more helpful than the recalcitrant ticket-window staff. Open for ticket sales daily 8am-8:30pm. (See Orientation for info on bus and taxi rides to and from station.)

Bus Station: In Tlaquepaque (see Orientation above). 30-odd carriers insure easy access to the northern half of the Republic. **Terminal 1: Servicios Coordinados** is the most frequent to Mexico City (22 per day, 8hrs., 44 pesos). **Autobuses la Piedad** to Celaya (transport hub of the Bajío, every ½hr., 6hrs., 30 pesos). **Terminal 2: Autobuses del Occidente** to Lázaro Cárdenas (5 per day, 11hrs., 45 pesos). **Terminal 3: Transportes del Pacífico** to Tijuana (16 per day, 36hrs., 190 pesos). **Tres Estrellas de Oro** to Puerto Vallarta (14 per day, 6hrs., 38 pesos) and Mazatlán (3 per day, 8hrs., 35 pesos; some Tijuana-bound buses also stop in Mazatlán). **Terminal 4: Autocamiones del Pacífico** to Manzanillo (15 per day, 8hrs., 30 pesos). **Terminal 6: Estrella Blanca** to Zacatecas (17 per day, 6½hrs., 35 pesos) and Fresnillo (12 per day, 7hrs., 38 pesos). **Terminal 7: Omnibus de México** to Tepic (8 per day, 4 hrs., 23 pesos) and Laredo (2 per day, 15hrs., 94 pesos).

Car Rental: Most places are on Niños Héroes or at the airport. **Budget,** Niños Héroes 934 (tel. 613-00-27); **Avis,** Niños Héroes 9 (tel. 613-90-11); **National,** Niños Héroes 961c (tel. 614-71-75), or **Hertz** (tel. 614-61-39). U.S. citizens need U.S. driver's license, major credit card, and 21 years under their belt. Prices around 75 pesos per day plus .60 pesos per km and 35 pesos per day insurance.

English Bookstores: Sandi Bookstore, Tepeyac 718 (tel. 621-08-63), in Colonia Chapalita. Take bus #50 from Garibaldi. Extensive selection of new books and North American newspapers. Open Mon.-Fri. 9:30am-2:30pm and 3:30-7pm, Sat. 9:30am-2pm. The Hyatt carries day-old copies of the *New York Times,* while the Sanborn department store at Juárez and Corona carries a mind-boggling range of magazines.

Cultural and Arts Information: Departamento de Bellas Artes (tel. 614-16-14), Jesus Garcia 720. Publishes a seasonal calendar of events. Open Mon. Fri. 8am-3pm, Sat. 8am-1pm.

Laundromat: Lavandería San Antonio, López Cotilla 1234. Wash and dry 8 pesos; soap 1.50 pesos. Open Mon.-Sat. 8:30am-7:30pm, Sun. 8:30am-1:30pm.

Red Cross: Accqui and Juan Manuel (tel. 614-27-07), near the Pl. Morelos.

Green Cross Hospital: Tel. 614-52-52.

Pharmacies: Farmacia de Descuento, Pedro Moreno 518, open 8am-10pm; **Farmacia Guadalajara,** Javier Mina 221 (tel. 617-85-55). Open 24 hrs.

Hospitals: Hospital del Carmen, Tarascos 3435 (tel. 647-48-82). **Nuevo Hospital Civil,** Salvador Quevedo y Zubieta 750 (tel. 618-93-62). If your *turista* shackles you to the toilet, most hotel managers know a doctor who speaks English.
Police: Independencia Nte. 840 (tel. 617-60-60 or 618-02-60).

ACCOMMODATIONS

Although Guadalajara is a major city with numerous five-star hotels, there are some good finds available for the budget traveler as well, many of which offer special rates for stays of one week.

A good alternative to budget hotels is the *posada*. *Posadas* are small, family-run establishments that, for a few extra pesos, provide large and better-furnished rooms, better security, and frequently include meals as well. The drawbacks are less privacy and less freedom to stay out late. Check at the tourist office for a list.

Outside of the *posadas*, reservations are only neccessary in February, when the city plays host to a large cultural festival.

Near the Plaza Tapatía

With room prices more or less consistent (and prices often based as much on haggling ability as quality), bedding down in the convenient *centro* isn't a bad idea. It's probably safer, though noisier, than other options, and convenience is a definite plus.

Posada San Pablo, Madero 218 (tel. 613-33-12). Not only the nicest, but also the cheapest place in town. Large clean rooms with ceilings over 15ft. high, some with balconies. Lovely green tinted covered courtyards and canaries in this gracious family's house. Singles 35 pesos. Doubles 45 pesos.

Hotel Las Américas, Hidalgo 76 (tel. 613-96-22). Unimaginative but comfortable. Wall-to-wall carpets, curtains and gleaming hallways. *Agua* galore. Traffic noise is the sole drawback to this hotel's great location: right down the street from Pl. Tapatía. Singles 50 pesos. Doubles with 1 bed 55 pesos, with 2 beds 60 pesos.

Hotel Sevilla, Sánchez 413 (tel. 614-90-37). Modern and basic, but clean. Phones and TVs. Singles 40 pesos. Doubles with 1 bed 60 pesos, with 2 beds 70 pesos.

Posada Regis, Corona 171 (tel. 613-30-26). Large clean rooms with very tall ceilings off of large, dark courtyard with an ancient movie projector that shows movies each day. Deals for multi-night stays. Singles 80 pesos. Doubles 100 pesos.

Hotel Universo, López Cotilla 161 (tel. 613-28-15). A bargain which offers a lot for the dough. TVs and phones in every room. Suites available for extra *dinero*. Singles 88 pesos. Doubles 99 pesos.

Hotel Hamilton, Madero 381 (tel. 614-67-26). This hotel is dark for a number of reasons: its dark side-street location, the scarcity of lightbulbs, the dark maroon bedspreads, and the dust. But the dark can be almost cozy in a away, and its not too expensive. Singles 35 pesos. Doubles with 1 bed 40 pesos, with 2 beds 45 pesos.

Hotel Maya, López Cotilla 39 (tel. 614-54-54). Walls, showers, bedspreads, restaurant are all basic, all concrete, all dizzying sky blue—the rooms feel like large, underwater prison cells. Singles 40 pesos. Doubles 50 pesos.

East on Javier Mina

Nicer hotels are closer to Plaza Tapatia, where the neighborhood is not only more central, but also safer. Javier Mina and especially the dark side streets off of it can become dangerous at night. If the cheaper options above don't work out (or if you just want to be closer to Plaza de los Mariachis) these hotels are basic, modern, and clean.

Hotel Ana Isabel, Javier Mina 164 (tel. 617-79-20). Like a cruise ship (not that any budget traveler would know) with a thin narrow hall, small rooms with small windows, tiny TVs, and tiny sinks with rings (to hold onto or hang a towel). Also clean. Singles 45 pesos. Doubles 55 pesos.

Hotel Imperio, Javier Mina 180 (tel. 617-50-42). A yellow color scheme and remarkably polite staff brighten the central courtyard. The bathrooms show their age but continue to function. The traffic below might as well be routed through the rooms. Singles 40 pesos. Doubles 45 pesos.

Hotel Azteca, Javier Mina 311 (tel. 617-74-66). Lobby a bit snazzier than the others in the neighborhood; an elevator whisks you upward. Plenty of furniture, fans and linoleum-esque floors. Pistachio-green bathrooms want to be loved. Singles 40 pesos. Doubles 45 pesos.

Hotel México 70, Javier Mina 230 (tel. 617-99-78). Clean large rooms with blue walls and blue bathrooms. Rooms overlooking the street have balconies. Singles 35 pesos. Doubles 45 pesos.

West to University

Strange as it may seem, the university campus located eight long blocks west of Pl. Tapatía is considerably more peaceful than the rest of the *centro*. Because most university-related action ends by nightfall you gain nothing but tranquility by staying in this area. **Posada de la Plata,** López Cotilla 619 (tel. 614-91-46). A large clean rooms around a comfortable courtyard with red tile and a large lazy dog. The place remains popular with travelers. (Singles 35 pesos. Doubles 55 pesos.) **Hotel La Paz,** La Paz 1091 (tel. 614-29-10), near Donato Guerra. Clean, basic and in the boonies, but the rooms do have TVs. (Singles 40 pesos. Doubles 50 pesos.)

South to Train Station

Before opting to bed down in this industrial wasteland, it would be wise to remember that there is nothing to do in this area except sleep. Better hotels await you in Guadalajara's lively *centro*. **Hotel Estación,** Independencia Sur 1297 (tel. 619-00-51), is—unfortunately—just to the left as you leave the station. Rooms have as much charm as a baggage compartment, though the lobby and bathrooms appear uncontaminated by dirt. (Singles 39 pesos. Doubles 49 pesos.) Six long blocks from the station is **Hotel Flamingos,** Independencia Sur 725 (tel. 619-99-21). Catch the #60 bus and get off at Los Angeles if you have bags. It is small, noisy, and dark, but very cheap with a pleasant cafeteria in lobby. (Singles 25 pesos. Doubles with 1 bed 30 pesos.)

FOOD

There is a Guadalajaran restaurant for almost any budget. Those to whom money is no object will find that Guadalajara is packed with high-class French, Italian and Japanese restaurants.

All sorts of bacteria cavort in the food and water in Guadalajara; even locals have to reckon with the microscopic creatures. A program has been launched by the state of Jalisco to improve the hygiene in food establishments, and many insist that the food quality has improved. Restaurants and cafeterias should be relatively safe, but avoid sidewalk stalls and the food in *Mercado Libertad*, and drink only when you can see the cooler whence the fluid came.

Near Plaza Tapatía

Hidalgo 112, at Hidalgo 112. A glorified juice bar with pine tables and traditional blue glass. Read the paper and chat with the locals after the lunchtime rush. Fantastically cheap. Large good fruit yogurt with granola served in a huge martini glass (3 pesos), as well as juices and sandwiches (from 3 pesos). Open daily 8am-9pm.

Restaurante La Alemana, on Blanco at 16 de Septiembre. Live Germanesque music nightly, great cheap food and free-flowing beers from the huge wooden bar. Huge plate of *enchiladas con pollo* 6 pesos, ½ chicken 16 pesos. Open daily noon-1am.

El Farol, Moreno 466, 2nd floor. Decent food at low prices. 2 prized tables overlook the street in this tiled restaurant with vinyl chairs. Friendly owner. Complementary *buñuelos*, dripping with sugary syrup, for dessert. Entrees 10-16 pesos. Plate of enchiladas 12 pesos. Open daily 10am-2am.

La Chata, Corona 126 (tel. 613-05-88). Colorful checked tablecloths and dark wooden chairs. Unfortunately, the open kitchen makes this restaurant hot Entrees around 20 pesos. *Huevos* 10 pesos. Open daily 9am-10:30pm.

Restaurant Aquarius, Sánchez 416, across from Hotel Sevilla. New Age Mexi-style. Wear your finest peasant shirt and brandish your cosmic consciousness. Freshly squeezed orange juice 3 pesos. Vegetarian *comida corriente* 18.40 pesos.

Café Madrid, Juárez 262 (tel. 614-95-04). Looks like a small-town bus depot lunch spot in front, the men watching TV et al. In back more formal tables and a large mural on the wall. Steak 18 pesos. *Commida corrida* 18 pesos. Open daily 8am-10pm.

Las Yardas Bar, Juárez 37. A fun, music-filled bar with a few simple dishes. Eclectic decor. During happy hour (Mon.-Thurs. 7-9pm) enjoy the 2-for-1 beer (45 pesos) special. Open daily noon-11pm.

Sandy's Restaurant, Alcalde 130. Gray carpeting, booths, and balconies overlooking Pl. de los Mártires. Suit-clad men and elegant women hit this place during power lunch breaks. Breakfasts 10 pesos. Mexican dishes 16-22 pesos. Open daily 7am-8pm.

East to Javier Mina

Restaurants near Javier Mina will fill your stomach, but not in any particularly refined way. **Restaurant del Pacífico,** Pl. de los Mariachis (tel. 621-91-88). Surprisingly, the *carne asada* (12 pesos) here beats that of many more expensive places, and it'll fill you up with no trouble. Lots of beer drinking transpires here till the cows come home. Brew 3.50 pesos. (Open daily 8am-1am.) **Restaurant Flamboyen,** Independencia Sur 164 (tel. 613-00-76), in the Hotel de los Reyes. Denny's just might be able to win a copyright infringement suit, except this place gets surreal around midnight, when other places close. A serious late-night hang out, the bar stocks all sorts of crazy drinks. *Huevos a la mexicana* 10 pesos. Beer 5.60 pesos. (Open 24 hrs.) **Restaurant Nuevo Faro,** López Cotilla 24. Quick and filling. Good breakfast dishes: *omeleta mexicana* 7.50 pesos. Entrees 7-12 pesos. *Comida corriente* 11 pesos. (Open daily 8am-10pm.)

West from Chapultepec to López Mateos

Here, a few extra pesos buy superior quality and elegant atmosphere. Most places below cluster near the intersection of Vallarta and Chapultepec, on the "Par Vial" bus route. It's worth the trip.

Los Itacates Fonda, Chapultepec Nte. 110 (tel. 625-11-06). Fancy *típico* restaurant with an extensive menu of many Mexican delicacies. Blessed by better and cheaper food than most other restaurants in any district. Full of middle- and upper-class Mexican families. Mexican ceramic plates and crafts on the stucco walls and large blue painted wooden chairs. Great breakfast buffet 15 pesos. *Pollo molle* 15 pesos. Tacos 5 pesos. Open Mon.-Sat 8am-11pm, Sun. 8am-6:30pm.

Café Don Luis, Chapultepec 209 at Libertad (tel. 625-65-99). Coffees and desserts. A great place to revive your sleepy bones after a *siesta*; the Angel's Kiss (Kahlúa, coffee and eggnog) will add some zip for 5 pesos. Open daily 10am-2pm and 5-10pm.

Recco, Libertad 1973 (tel. 625-07-24), just off Chapultepec. White tablecloths, metal plates, and old block and white photos on the walls. Those in T-shirts or shorts will feel underdressed. *Fettucine alfredo* 17 pesos. The friendly owner speaks almost fluent English. Filet mignon 35 pesos. Mon.-Sat. 1pm-midnight, Sun. 1-10pm.

La Trattoria, Niños Héroes 305 (tel. 622-18-17), 1 block east of López Mateos. Call for reservations or face the prospect of a long wait. Italian food in a large, sterile room. Fettucini alfredo 17 pesos. Most meat dishes 27 pesos. Large portions. Open Mon.-Sat. 1pm-midnight, Sun. 1-8pm.

Las Margaritas, López Cotilla 1477 (tel. 16-89-06), just west of Chapultepec. Inventive (and expensive) vegetarian food. Yellow and green middle-eastern motif and tunes by the Mamas and the Papas. Menu in English and Spanish. Open Mon.-Sat. 8:30am-9pm, Sun. 8:30am-6pm.

La Hacienda de Jazo, Justo Sierra 2022, just off Chapultepec Nte. In a courtyard so quiet you'll forget you're in a city. Live piano daily 3-6pm; at all other times, Lionel Richie, et al. are piped in. Meat and fish entrees 12-18 pesos. Open Mon.-Sat. 1-8pm.

SIGHTS

Guadalajara's museums are the best introduction to Mexican culture and history outside Mexico City.

Downtown

The four plazas in downtown Guadalajara provide a wide-open refuge from the otherwise packed streets. Most corners are punctuated by horse-drawn carriages that offer hour-long tours for about 35 pesos. The spacious **Plaza de la Liberación,** with its large, bubbling fountain, is surrounded by the **cathedral, Museo Regional, Palacio de Gobierno** and **Teatro Degollado.** A modern sculpture depicts Hidalgo breaking the chains of slavery in commemoration of his 1810 decree, signed in Guadalajara, to abolish the trade.

The **Palacio de Gobierno,** built in 1774 on the plaza's south side, is a Churrigueresque and neoclassical building graced by yet another mural by Orozco; the sight of Hidalgo's feverish eyes looking down from the wall strikes fear in the heart of many an unsuspecting visitor. A second Orozco mural covers the ceiling in the **Sala de Congreso.** This one depicts *indígenas* in slavery and the heroic Miguel Hidalgo and Benito Juárez. (Open Mon.-Sat. 9am-3pm and 6-9pm; *Sala de Congreso* open 9am-6pm when the legislature is not in session.)

The imposing **cathedral** faces the Teatro Degollado across Pl. de la Liberación. Begun in 1558 and completed 60 years later, this edifice is a whirl of architectural styles. An 1848 earthquake destroyed the original towers, and ambitious architects replaced them with much taller ones. Fernando VII of Spain donated the 11 richly ornamented altars in appreciation of Guadalajara's help during the Napoleonic Wars. One of the remaining original altars is dedicated to Our Lady of the Roses; it is this altar, and not the botanical beauties, that gave Guadalajara its nickname, "City of Roses."

The doors to the sacristy are usually shut, but one of the attendants may let you in. Required proper dress is a show of respect. Inside the sacristy rests the *Assumption of the Virgin*, by famed 17th-century painter Bertolemé Murillo. The towers, known as the *cornucopias*, can be climbed with the permission of the cathedral's administrators, who hole up in the rear of the building to the right of the altar. Enter the cathedral from the back. The 60m jaunt affords the best view in town. (Church open Mon.-Sat. 8am-8pm; tourists unwelcome on Sunday.) On the cathedral's west side lies the arboreal **Plaza de los Laureles;** on the north, the **Plaza de los Mártires** commemorates *tapatíos* who died in various wars.

A building constructed in 1696 on the north side of the Pl. de la Liberación houses the **Museo Regional de Guadalajara.** Also known as the Museo del Estado de Jalisco, Liceo e Hidalgo, this museum chronicles the history of western Mexico, beginning with the Big Bang. The first floor is devoted to the country's pre-Hispanic development and includes meteorites, woolly mammoth bones, metalwork, jewels, and some Aztec art lamenting the Spanish Conquest. Maps of human migratory routes and patterns of settlement and disquisitions on various indigenous peoples give an excellent sense of the continuity of the country's development before the arrival of the Spanish. Collections of colonial art, modern paintings, and an exhibit on the history of the revolution occupy the second floor. (Open Tues.-Sun.

9am-3:45pm. Admission 10 pesos, students free. Free to all on Sundays. Movies, plays and lectures in the museum auditorium. Call tel. 614-99-57 for information.)

Attend the Ballet Folklórico at 10am on Sunday mornings to get a good look at the **Teatro Degollado,** a neoclassical structure on the Pl. de la Liberación's east end. The interior features gold-and-red balconies, a sculpted allegory of the seven muses on the pediment, and Gerardo Suárez's depiction of Dante's *Divine Comedy* on the ceiling. You can visit any time when there is no performance scheduled (tel. 613-11-15). Tickets available at the theater box office (see Entertainment below).

The **Plazuela de los Mariachis** lies on the south side of San Juan de Dios, the church with the blue neon cross at Independencia and Javier Mina. The *plazuela* is really a glorified alley, lined with bars and budget restaurants where flashy *mariachis* hustle soused *gringos*. Immediately after sitting down, roving musicians will attmempt to separate you and your pesos at the rate of 8 pesos a song, post-haggling. The daily festivities peak at lunch time, again at dinner and continue late into the night.

From the Pl. Tapatía, you can see the dome of the 190-year-old **Hospicio Cabañas** at the corner of Hospicio and Cabañas, 3 blocks east of Independencia. It was here that Padre Hidalgo signed his proclamation against slavery in 1811; the building has since served as an orphanage and an art school. In the main chapel, Orozco painted a series of murals in 1938-39, which some regard as his best work; the dome holds Orozco's nightmarish rendition of the Four Riders of the Apocalypse. *Espejos* (mirrors) are available free for those who don't want to strain their necks, or you can lie down on one of the many benches set up for reclined viewing. The *hospicio* also houses a collection of Orozco drawings and lithographs recently moved from his home in west Guadalajara, as well as other rotating exhibits. (Open Tues.-Sat. 10:15am-6pm. Admission 5 pesos, 3 pesos with student ID.)

If you've heard the promotional hoopla for the **Mercado Libertad,** at Javier Mina and Independencia, reality may disappoint. Mexico's largest daily market offers three floors of schlock and cheap food. The prices here are much lower and the shopkeepers less frenzied, however, making it possible to browse in relative tranquility. Most of the food has been sitting out all day and may not be clean. (Open daily 9am-8pm, but some merchants do not open on Sun.) A more authentic and fascinating market is **El Baratillo** on Javier Mina, approximately 15 blocks east of *Mercado Libertad*. El Baratillo lasts all day Sunday and sometimes stretches for 30 or 40 blocks. Everything imaginable is peddled here, from hot tamales to houses. From *Mercado Libertad*, walk two blocks to Gigantes and catch bus #37 or #38 heading east.

South

Almost everything inside the **Casa de las Artesanías de Jalisco** on González Gallo (the street which bisects *Parque Agua Azul*) is for sale. Pottery, jewelry, furniture, and clothing, all of it from Tlaquepaque and Tonalá (see Near Guadalajara below), cost more here than they do in those two villages, but the quality is extraordinary. For those who don't have the time and the energy to do the legwork involved in trips from the city, the *casa* will show you the best of what you're missing. (Open Mon.-Fri. 10am-7pm, Sat. 10am-4pm, Sun. 10am-2pm.)

A large, fenced-in tract of woods and gardens with numerous fountains and statues, **Parque Agua Azul** provides a haven for those tired of the noise of south Guadalajara. (Open daily 10am-6pm. Admission 3 pesos.)

West

Guadalajara's **Zona Rosa,** the upper-class shopping district, centers on Chapultepec, west of the university. Cultural activity in the city's wealthier areas focuses on the **Plaza del Arte,** one block south on Chapultepec from its intersection with Niños Héroes. Local artists bare their souls on a rotating basis in the plaza's **Centro de Arte Moderno.** (Open daily 8am-2pm and 4-7pm.) The **Galería Municipal,** on the Pl. del Arte, also showcases local painters. Stand-up comedy and performance art periodically enliven the premises. Watch for notices on the blackboard at the Departamento de Bellas Artes, at García 720 (tel. 614-16-14).

The **Tequila Sauza Bottling Plant,** Vallarta 3273 (tel. 647-66-74), on the outskirts of Guadalajara, is a shrine for serious tequila fans. Pay homage here to the golden elixir of life. (Free tours Mon.-Fri. 10am-noon.) Take the "Par Vial" bus west to the end of the line then catch *combi* #130 in front of the Hotel Fiesta Americana. The plant is just before the overpass. Bus #45 will take you back into town.

ENTERTAINMENT

Although there is no lack of things to do at night in Guadalajara, the streets usually become deserted at night fall and are often dangerous.

The **Ballet Folklórico** has toured the world, entertaining audiences with stage antics and the famed Mexican hat dance. There are two troupes in Guadalajara, one affiliated with the University of Guadalajara and the other with the state of Jalisco. The former, reputedly better, performs in the Teatro Degollado on Sunday at 10am (followed by the **State Philharmonic Orchestra** at noon). Tickets (10-50 pesos) are sold the day before the show at the Teatro Degollado ticket office (open daily 9:30am-5:30pm). Spend the extra pesos for a front seat and arrive a half-hour before the show because seats are not reserved within sections, and performances nearly always sell out. The state troupe performs Wednesdays at 8:30pm in the theater of the Hospicio Cabañas (tickets 15 pesos). Call tel. 617-44-40, ext. 22, for more information.

University facilities, scattered throughout the city, have created a market for high culture on a low budget. The **Departamento de Bellas Artes** coordinates activities at a large number of stages, auditoriums, and movie screens across the city. The best source of information on cultural events is the blackboard in their lobby at García 720 (see Sights above) which lists each day's attractions. The two principal dramatic stages are the **Teatro de Guadalajara** (tel. 619-58-23) and the **Teatro Experimental** (tel. 619-37-70), across the street from each other at Pl. Juárez, on the west side of *Parque Agua Azul.* While the works at the Experimental are recommended only for those proficient in Spanish, the program at the Teatro de Guadalajara includes more easily understood comic and popular works.

The **Instituto Cultural Cabañas** presents live music on an open-air stage in the Hospicio Cabañas at least once a week (tickets 15 pesos, students 12 pesos). Drop by the Hospicio Cabañas ticket counter (see Sights above), or look for flyers with the Cabañas insignia (a building with pillars) for current schedules. Each October, Guadalajara hosts a month-long festival of cultural and sporting events with fireworks and special displays representing each state in the republic.

For Luis Buñuel retrospectives and other vintage screenings, head to the cinema at Bellas Artes. The **Cine Cinematógrafo,** at Vallarta 1102 (tel. 25-05-14), just west of the university, is a repertory film house that changes its show weekly (tickets 3 pesos).

For live jazz, try the **Copenhagen,** at Américas and López Mateos near the statue of Columbus, or **La Hosta,** at México and Rubén Darío. Nightlife in this hopping town centers on the Pl. del Sol, near the southern end of López Mateos. **Osiris** (20 pesos), at Jardines de los Arcos on Lázaro Cárdenas, receives rave reviews from locals. It's private, but if you convince the bouncers of your foreign origin (it shouldn't be hard), they'll let you in. **Ciros,** on the Pl. del Sol, is another popular disco. Again, members only, but foreigners accepted. They may even let you in wearing sneakers, but don't count on it (cover 25 pesos). **Oz,** next door, is the ultimate in glam. Far away from Kansas. Couples only, preferably with expensive clothing. Non-Mexican non-members admitted, but the bouncers have fun making people wait. (Cover 30 pesos per couple.) A younger, hipper crowd (guys with long hair) inhabits the kinder, gentler **Iceburg** (tel. 622-77-78) in the Hyatt Hotel complex on López Mateos, two blocks from the Pl. del Sol. People here are actually friendly, and if you rap with the bouncer long enough, he may give you free passes. Otherwise, cover 25 pesos. (All of the above places are open Thurs.-Sun. 10pm-2 or 3am.) **Terraza del Oasis,** Hidalgo 436, occasionally has live bands.

Gay clubs support more nightlife here than in any other city outside the Federal District. The upscale *Zona Rosa* along Chapultepec is a favorite gathering place. The best-known gay disco is **Unicornio,** López Mateos. Other hangouts include **S.O.S.,** La Paz 1413 at Escoza (closed Sun.), which has incredibly vibrant drag shows, and **Monica's,** Alvaro Obregón 1713, popular with the young crowd. (Open Wed.-Sun. 11pm-4am.) The **Jesse James,** Ramos Millán 955, is a honky tonk complete with country-and-western music. A mixed gay and straight crowd also frequents **Chivas López Cotilla** and **Degollado.**

Sports

Bullfights take place in the Pl. de Toros, at Nuevo Progreso on the northern end of Independencia, almost every Sunday from October to April. Posters throughout the city broadcast each contest. Take bus #62 north. The ticket and information office is at Morelos 229 (tel. 613-55-58). Guadalajara also features *charreadas* (rodeos), held in Parque Agua Azul every Sunday.

Soccer games draw the biggest crowds in this city. The *Chivas,* the local professional team, is the crowd's favorite and a powerful contender for the national championship each season. Don't even think about uttering the name of the team's arch-rival from Mexico City, the *Pumas*. Matches are held from September through May in **Jalisco Stadium,** at the University of Guadalajara and at the Universidad Autónoma. The ticket office (tel. 642-18-40) is on Colomos Pte. 2339 at López Mateos. Tickets can also be purchased at the stadium box office on the day of the game.

Ice-skating, of all things, is possible year-round at the Hyatt Regency on Pl. del Sol (tel. 622-59-32). You can rent skates for around 12 pesos. (Open Mon.-Thurs. 5-7pm and 7:30-9pm, Fri.-Sun. 4:15-6:15pm and 8:15-9:45pm.)

Public **swimming pools** in Guadalajara are filthy. If you've got to get wet, try one of the private sports clubs (at least 10 pesos), but many no longer permit non-members. People have been known to sneak into the Hyatt's pool. The easiest option may be an extended shower at your hotel.

■ Near Guadalajara

Excursions from Guadalajara are prime opportunities for souvenir-hunting. East of the city, **Tlaquepaque** and **Tonalá** peddle high-priced artisanry; to the north **Zapopan** craft work sells at the Casa de Artesanías de los Huichol; on the shores of Laguna Chapala, 40km to the south, the villages of Chapala, Ajijic, and Jopotlán welcome tourist excursions and an ever-expanding population of North American retirees.

Northwest of the city is the town of **Zapopan,** site of the **Basílica de la Virgen de Zapopan,** a giant edifice erected in the 16th century to commemorate a peasant's vision. The walls of the church are hung with many decades' worth of *ex-votos*, small paintings on sheet metal honoring the Virgin's aid in diseases and accidents. Pope John Paul II visited the shrine in 1979, and a statue of him holding hands with a beaming *campesino* boy now stands in the courtyard in front of the church. The **Casa de Artesanías de los Huichol,** a museum and crafts market for Huichol handwork, remains Zapopan's chief point of interest. Clothing, *ojos de dios* (eyes of god) and *makrames*, colorful designs of yarn on wood, are sold at bargain prices. To get there, catch the #275 bus northbound on the Av. 16 de Septiembre and de-bus at the big church. (Open Mon.-Fri. 10am-1:30pm and 3:30-6pm. Free.)

The "village" of **Tlaquepaque,** on the #275 (or 275A) bus route a few stops before the Nueva Central, is a pleasant tourist trap. High class shops set in old colonial mansions line Independencia, the main drag, selling silver, handicrafts, leather and ceramics. Cheaper goods of lesser quality can be found in the *mercado* just off the main square. The **Museo Regional de las Cerámicas y los Artes Populares de Jalisco** has an interesting collection of antique regional crafts, as well as newer pieces for sale. Another fun if touristy spot is **La Roja de Cristal,** Independencia 232, where artisans blow glass by hand Mon.-Fri. 9:30am-2:30pm, Sat. 9:30am-12:30pm. Their goods are then sold Mon.-Sat. from 10am to 7pm. Just don't visit on a Sunday when virtually all the shops are closed.

It is best to go to Tlaquepaque on a daytrip from Guadalajara. There are only two hotels in the town. The clean, dark, mildew-smelling rooms at **Posada en el Parían,** Independencia 74 (tel. 35-21-89) go for 40 pesos for singles and 55 pesos for doubles. Reserve in advance or arrive early. The **Hotel Tlaquepaque,** Juárez 36 (tel. 35-00-87) features very turquoise and not-so-clean rooms. (Singles 35 pesos, Doubles 40 pesos.) The central block of restaurants, along Independencia, boasts a number of more or less identical establishments. Of these restaurants, **Paco's** seems to avail itself of slightly better people-watching potential. *Mole poblano* (at the neighboring places too) 15 pesos, *quesadillas* 10 pesos. If Paco's doesn't suit you, try **Salón Imperial, Monterrey,** or **Beto's.** *Mariachi* groups strut their stuff there, too. Bands will perform at your table for a hefty 25 pesos. When you want to return downtown, hop on a #275 bus at the corner of Niños and Independencia.

Had it with shopping? Head to **Parque Mirador,** at the northern end of Independencia. The park's main attraction is its proximity to the 670m gorge of the Río Santiago, where waterfalls cascade over the cliffs during the rainy season. (Open daily 9am-7:30pm. Admission .60 pesos. Take bus #60 north along Independencia.) Also on Independencia is the modern, lush **Guadalajara Zoo.** There's nary a cage to be seen inside, and the place has more of the feel of a theme park with train rides, dolphin shows, fun fair, and hordes of awe-struck children. (Open daily 10am-6pm. Admission 10 pesos, children 8-16 5 pesos.)

Tonalá is a scaled-down version of Tlaquepaque, mainly because it's harder to reach. Visit Tonalá on Thursday or Sunday, when the town briefly awakens from its near-perpetual *siesta*. Tonalá specializes in inexpensive, conservatively decorated ceramics. While Tlaquepaque offers greater variety, Tonalá has made fewer concessions to the tourist industry and retains more of its natural charm. You can still find women weaving beautiful, multi-colored rugs and sewing dolls. Patient ceramics merchants paint personalized messages onto their products. In Tonalá, you get the soft sell as people take the time to converse with you without making you feel obligated to purchase something.

Tonalá has the added benefit of letting you visit a near-rural village with the safety of a long *combi* lifeline back to the more comfortably urban Guadalajara. Buses #103 and #104, which run through downtown Guadalajara along Moreno, are the best way to reach Tonalá (.50 pesos).

Forty km south of Guadalajara lies **Lago de Chapala,** Mexico's second largest lake. The towns of **Chapala, Ajijic,** and **Jocotepec** along the northern shore of the lake present a peaceable mix of Mexican tourists, North American retirees, artists, and would-be artists from around the world. While living in Ajijic in the 1940s, before the plague of industrial development rendered swimming in the lake impossible, D.H. Lawrence wrote *The Plumed Serpent*. Stark mountains still haunt the lake's opposite shore, keeping the setting beautiful. English-speakers will feel at home in Chapala and Ajijic: there are so many expatriates here that half of the signs are in English and the other half are bilingual.

You can get to Chapala from the *antigua* bus station (every ½hr., 45min., 4.50 pesos). There are two acceptable options for anyone wishing to stay near the lake. A haunt for Mexico's wealthy, staying near the lake can be expensive, though you do get a lot for your pesos. In Chapala, the **Hotel Nino,** Madero 202 (tel. 5-21-16) once played host to dictator Díaz's weekend soirées. Now considerably more sedate, the airy hotel has clean, simple rooms with floral stencils set around a pretty courtyard with restaurant and pool. (Singles 40 pesos, doubles 60 pesos. *Menú del día* 24 pesos, breakfasts 8-12 pesos.)

Just down the road lies the prettier village of **Ajijic** (catch the bus—1.20 pesos—from the corner of Madero and de Velasco in Chapala). The **Posada Las Calandrias,** on the Carretera Chapala (tel. 5-28-19), has clean singles for 50 pesos and doubles for 75 pesos, set around a gleaming pool popular with local wedding parties. Next door, Brady Bunch-style bungalows go for 80 pesos with all the amenities, including kitchens. Have the area to yourself during the week; the crowds from Guadalajara hit Chapala mostly on the weekends. Tours are also available; call Panoramex (tel. 10-51-09).

For food try **Beto's**, right next to the Hotel Nino. The food is generally decent, and the pace relaxed: entrees 8-14 pesos. Beer is by far the most popular item on the menu, but the chilly margaritas go down easy. For a great lunch in Ajijic, try **Danny's,** located just off the highway. Gorgeous burgers, lunches and sandwiches run 4-7 pesos. (Open Mon.-Sat. 8am-5pm, Sun. 8am-1pm.) For those who feel like a splurge, try the lunchtime buffet in **Hotel Nueva Posada**, Donato Guerra 9 (tel. 5-33-95). Sumptuous Italianate interior and sculpted gardens leading down to the lake just might make the feast worth 34 pesos.

■■■ PUERTO VALLARTA

In 1956 tabloid headlines were touting Puerto Vallarta as an unspoiled paradise. Richard Burton and Elizabeth Taylor's torrid affair while on location shooting *Night of the Iguana* helped paint Puerto Vallarta as the world headquarters of sensuality. Back then, neither highway nor telephone wire hitched it to the outside world; since that time, Puerto Vallarta has undergone a radical facelift. Thirty-five years and millions of dollars later, Puerto Vallarta is a world-class resort with stunningly groomed beaches, luxurious hotels and gorgeous mansions. What brought people here in the first place—the clear water and beautiful beaches—though more crowded now, still remain beautiful.

While all of Puerto Vallarta revolves around tourism, the form it takes varies greatly; the city naturally divides itself into different areas. In the south end of town, where the best swimming beach is and where the more reasonable hotels are located, there is a certain, if somewhat artificial charm: white stucco buildings, red-tiled roofs, and cobbled streets. On the north side of the river, larger nightclubs, and more expensive clothing stores find a home, while still further north international resorts line the highway.

ORIENTATION

Running west to the shore, the **Río Cuale** bisects Puerto Vallarta before emptying into the ocean. The southern half of town maintains a more authentic Mexican identity and contains virtually all the cheap hotels, best beaches, budget restaurants, and frantic dance clubs. The glitzy area north of the river could be mistaken for a stateside beach resort and it houses nearly all of the city's tourist services.

The main streets in the southern half are **Insurgentes** and **Vallarta,** which run north-south two blocks apart, and **Lázaro Cárdenas,** which runs east-west. A park two blocks south of the western end of Lázaro Cárdenas serves as a **bus** and **combi terminal;** you'll find it at the northern end of Olas Altas and Playa de los Muertos, the waterfront area. Route 200 from Manzanillo runs into town south of the river, becoming Insurgentes. It and Vallarta run north from Lázaro Cárdenas to the two bridges that link the south and north sections.

The main streets in the north are **Morelos,** the continuation of Vallarta, and **Juárez,** one block east. Four blocks north of the Vallarta bridge is the **Plaza Mayor,** whose cathedral, with its crown of open metalwork, serves as a landmark. The ritzy waterfront between Pl. Mayor and 31 de Octubre, called the **Malecón,** contains overpriced restaurants and cheesy t-shirt shops. North of the Malecón, Morelos becomes **Perú** and runs through a working-class neighborhood before joining the coastal highway. North along the highway lie the **airport,** the **marina**, and the **ferry terminal.**

Taxis charge about 10 pesos to travel between the **Playa de los Muertos** and the entrance to the highway. The municipal **buses,** which operate daily from 6am to 10:30pm, cost only .80-1.20 pesos (*combis* .80-1.50 pesos). All northbound buses and *combis* originate at the park on Olas Altas and run up Lázaro Cárdenas to Insurgentes, across the Insurgentes Bridge, west on Libertad a few blocks, north on Juárez, and onto the highway. In the opposite direction, buses enter the city on México, which turns into Díaz Ordaz and then runs into Morelos, crossing the Vallarta bridge before heading back to the party.

PRACTICAL INFORMATION

Tourist Office: In the Presidencia Municipal (tel. 2-02-42), on the northern side of the Pl. Mayor; enter on Juárez. Centrally located and loaded with maps and other information. Excellent English spoken. Open Mon.-Fri. 9am-9pm, Sat. 9am-1pm.

U.S. Consulate: Miramar at Libertad (tel. 2-00-69), just north of the Río Cuale. Open Mon.-Fri. 9am-9pm.

Currency Exchange: Several large banks around the Pl. Mayor change currency, but many only 9am-1pm. **Banca Promex,** Juárez 386, changes money Mon.-Fri. 9:30am-12:30pm. *Casas de cambio* have lower rates and are open longer, typically Mon.-Sat. 9am-2pm and 4-8pm.

American Express: Centro Comercial Villa Vallarta (tel. 2-68-77), a few blocks north of the Sheraton via buses marked "Pitillal," "Juntas," or "Ixtapa." English is spoken. Open Mon.-Fri. 9am-2:30pm and 4-6pm, Sat. 9am-1pm.

Post Office: Morelos 444 (tel. 2-37-02), at Mina, 2 blocks north of the Pl. Mayor. *Lista de Correos.* Open Mon.-Fri. 8am-7pm, Sat.-Sun. 9am-1pm. **Postal code:** 48300.

Telephones: LADATEL phones can be found on every corner. **Telephone code:** 322.

Airport: 8km north of town via the coastal highway. Buses labeled "Ixtapa" or "Juntas" pass the airport; you can catch them on Lázaro Cárdenas or Insurgentes. If you're coming from the airport, there is a bus stop on the same side of the highway, 30m to your right as you leave the airport area. Buses run 5am-11pm and cost .90 pesos. *Combis* to and from the airport cost 17 pesos per person to and from south of the river, 5 pesos per person to and from north of the river. Taxi fare is 16 pesos to the Plaza Mayor. **Aeroméxico,** at the airport (tel. 1-18-97), **Mexicana,** Juárez 152 (tel. 2-50-00), and other airlines have frequent flights to: Guadalajara (190 pesos one-way), Mexico City (320 pesos one-way), Los Angeles (US$229 one-way) and New York (US$426 one-way).

Bus Station: No central bus station. Each bus line operates its own office-*cum*-depot in the south side of the city. Destinations, frequency of service, and prices all vary by company. **Tres Estrellas de Oro,** Carranza 322 (tel. 2-62-82), has the most frequent service to Guadalajara (6hrs., 45 pesos), and Tijuana (1 per day, 190 pesos); **Transportes Cihuatlan,** at Madero and Constitución, operates more buses south to Manzanillo (6hrs., 30 pesos); **Transportes del Pacífico,** Insurgentes 282 (tel. 2-10-15), sends buses to Tepic (every ½hr., 18 pesos); **Transportes Norte de Sonora,** Madero 343 (tel. 2-16-50), serves Guadalajara (6hrs., 42 pesos), Mexico City (16hrs., 98 pesos), and Tepic (3hrs., 17 pesos).

Ferry: Terminal Marítima (tel. 2-04-76), 4½km north of town off the coastal highway.

Car Rental: There's a slew of options at the airport, or try **Hertz** in the Hotel Camino Real on Carranza (tel. 3-01-23 ext. 310), **Budget** in the Sheraton (tel. 2-67-66) or **Del Alba,** Centro Matamoros 179 (tel. 2-29-59). Most firms require drivers be 25 yrs. of age and have a valid credit card.

English Bookstore: Super Mercado Gutiérrez Rizo (known as "GR"), at Constitución and Serdán, has a selection analogous to that of U.S. supermarkets—trashy romances and adventure novels. No James Joyce. Books 20-30 pesos. Open daily

6:30am-10pm. **A Page in the Sun,** Olas Altas at Rodriguez. Sells used English books. Open daily 9am-10pm.

Laundromats: Lavandería Automática, Madero 407. Wash for 10 pesos per 3kg. Open daily 3am-8pm.

Pharmacy: Farmacia CMQ, Basilio Badillo 367, ½ block inland from Insurgentes (tel. 2-29-41). Open 24 hrs.

Hospital: CMQ Hospital, Basilio Badillo 365 (tel. 3-00-11 or 3-19-19). English spoken. Open 24 hrs.

Police: Iturbide at Morelos (tel. 3-25-00).

ACCOMMODATIONS AND CAMPING

Puerto Vallarta's sleeping options conveniently queue up in ascending socio-economic order, from the beach south of town (free) to the Sheraton in the north. The best cheap hotels are south of the Río Cuale, on or near Madero. Make sure the fan works before whipping out your wallet.

In general, hotels do not accept unpaid reservations. Go room-hunting as early as possible; 1pm is a common check-out time, but most hotels know what's available before then and fill up early in the day. Larger hotels don't mind storing even the grungiest of backpacks for the day, usually free of charge, and most of the cheaper places will do the same if they're full when you show up. The first price listed applies for June, the least expensive month of the year. December tends to be the most expensive. Prices vary in other months.

Officially, Puerto Vallarta frowns on shiftless beach bums, but most travelers encounter no problems. Even many of the local dogs are friendly. Some beachfront clubs have night guards who may keep an eye on those who request their permission before bedding down. Many people dig into the sand behind the Hotel Los Arcos or the Castle Pelícanos, which is government property, or into the open space between the John Newcombe tennis courts and the Sheraton.

Hotel Yasmin, Basilio Badillo 168 (tel. 2-00-87), 1 block from the beach. By far the nicest place for the money. A verdant courtyard with tables and chairs leads to clean, airy rooms with fans, floral stencils, desks, and spotless bathrooms. Singles 45 pesos. Doubles 50 pesos.

Hotel La Misión, Lázaro Cárdenas 207 (tel. 2-05-52). Dwarfed by its ritzier neighbors and just 1½ blocks from the beach. Small rooms have fans, clean bathrooms and a view of the pool. Singles 45 pesos. Doubles 60 pesos. Dec. singles 50 pesos. Doubles 70 pesos.

Hotel Villa del Mar, Madero 440 (tel. 2-07-85), 2 blocks east of Insurgentes. Best of the rest with tacky sea-faring motif. Clean but dark rooms cooled by strong fans and bathrooms in this large brick building. Singles 34 pesos. Doubles 42 pesos.

Hotel Azetca, Madero 473 (tel. 2-27-50). Clean, if small, rooms off of a motel-like brick courtyard. Singles 26 pesos. Doubles 32 pesos. December singles 31 pesos. Doubles 37 pesos.

Hospedaje Hortencia, Madero 339 (tel. 2-24-84). Basic, somewhat tattererd rooms, off a dilapidated open-air courtyard. Singles 35 pesos. Doubles 40 pesos.

Posada El Real, Madero 285 (tel. 2-05-87). Narrow peach concrete courtyard and small basic rooms. Friendly owner. Singles 30 pesos. Doubles 40 pesos.

Hotel Bernal, Madero 423 (tel. 2-36-05).Peewee sized rooms with basic amenities off of a closed courtyard. Singles 26 pesos. Doubles 32 pesos.

FOOD

Puerto Vallarta's Malecón specializes in tourist traps with North American cuisine. Cheaper, down-home places are numerous on the south side, especially on Madero near Insurgentes, and in the market on the north side, where Insurgentes crosses Río Cuale. The **market** is open Monday through Saturday from 8am to 8pm. **Super Mercado Gutiérrez Rico (GR),** at Constitución and Serdán, provides a huge array of foodstuffs (open daily 6:30am-10pm). Many taco and *quesadilla* stands prosper south of the river, near the cheap hotels.

South

Cafe de Olla, Basillo Badillo 168, next to Hotel Yasmin. Good Mexican and American fare in a friendly atmosphere. Great smelling grilled food and iced tea (with purified ice!). Grilled chicken 20 pesos. Lime-meringue pie 5 pesos.

La Fonda China Poblana, 222 Insurgentes (tel. 2-04-49). A pleasant surprise. Plain dark ground floor gives way to an airy 2nd floor, devoid of decor, with a balcony. Stuff yourself for 20 pesos, drinks included. Tasty and enormous order of enchiladas 13 pesos. Guacamole to match, 8 pesos. Open 24 hrs.

El Galieto-The Corner Bar, Vallarta 264, serves tiny tacos with gourmet ingredients, or normal-sized steamed tacos (6 pesos). *Quesadillas*? Choose from chicken, beef, eggplant and mushroom (12 pesos). 8 sauces to choose from, but unfortunately a bar atmosphere and a lot of *gringos.* Open daily noon-1am.

Restaurant Gilmar, Madero 418. Red chairs under red and white arches. A local favorite for the breakfast special (7 pesos), which includes juice, coffee, and 2 eggs any style with beans and tortillas. Complete dinner 15 pesos. Open Mon.-Sat. 7:30am-11pm.

North

Me Gusta, Domínguez 128, just east of Díaz Ordaz (tel. 2-41-31). A generally nifty if expensive, open-air spot. Beer (4 pesos) comes in enormous ceramic mugs and the burgers are juicy ½-pounders. Bacon burger 20 pesos. Order of 3 enchiladas 38 pesos. Sweeping view of the pelicans swooping over the ocean. Open daily 3-11pm.

Frutilandia, Díaz Ordaz 520, on the waterfront, but look hard—it's dwarfed by chintzier places. Giant plastic bananas and mangoes hang from the ceiling. Epic mango shakes 5 pesos, fruit salad with yogurt and granola 8 pesos. Open daily 8am-10pm.

El Pollo Vagabundo, México 1295, a few blocks south of the Sheraton (tel. 2-43-99). In a more Mexican neighborhood, a real Mexican restaurant—small, unpretentious with maps of Puerto Vallarta on the walls; breakfast special 11 pesos. Roasted ½-chicken 13 pesos. Open daily 8am-10pm.

SIGHTS

To get the most out of Puerto Vallarta, cultivate a taste for its 40km coastline. Some of the least crowded and most gorgeous beachfronts stretch along the coast south of town on the road to **Mismaloya** (see Near Puerto Vallarta). The best beach in Puerto Vallarta itself, **Playa de los Muertos,** extends south from Muelle de los Muertos in the southern part of town near the budget hotels. Named for the victims of a conflict between pirates and *indígenas*, the beach has withstood attempts to dub it the cheerier *Playa del Sol*. To get there, walk all the way west on Lázaro Cárdenas and then south along the poorly-named **Playa de Olas Altas** (Big Waves Beach). If you spend much time here, watch out or you may buy something—hawkers of everything imaginable prowl about aggressively, preying on tourists.

Various water sports generate a lot of activity during the morning hours but trickle off by mid-afternoon. **Parasailing** (US$20-$30 a shot) is particularly popular; parachutes are scattered on the beach across from the square where the *combis* leave, and their owners will descend upon you if you look even remotely interested. **Aquamarina,** Rodríguez 125, charges 17 pesos per day for snorkel, mask and fins. (Open Mon.-Sat. 11am-3pm.)

On the northern beach, around the Sheraton, the currency of choice is the U.S. dollar—in bulk. Parasailing is even more popular in this area (US$30 per ride), and **waterskiing** is also possible (US$20 per hr.). The patio of the Sheraton bar is only a few steps from the pool.

Municipal efforts to render the **Río Cuale** a cosmopolitan waterway meet with mixed success for about ¼mi. inland and fail completely thereafter. Walk inland along the riverbank to get an idea of the town's layout. Anyone alone (particularly and predictably women) should be careful when walking this stretch of the river and should avoid doing so altogether after dark. **Isla Río Cuale,** between the two bridges, supports small stores selling simple baubles, bangles, and *botanas*. The **Museo del Cuale,** at the seaward end of the island, divides its single room between contemporary works by local artists and a small collection of pre-Aztec figurines from Jalisco and Nayant. (Open daily 9am-3pm. Donation requested.)

The river can also be reached from the north via Zaragoza, which merits a casual meander. Stairs lead up the mini-mountain beginning behind the Church of Guadalupe, breaking out amid bougainvillea and hibiscus into the wealthy **Zaragoza** neighborhood, known locally as **Gringo Gulch.** The prominent bridge spanning the apex of the street connects Elizabeth Taylor's humble *pied-à-terre* with Richard Burton's. Other ritzy cliff dwellings accompany Zaragoza on its descent to the river.

In the square from which *combis* leave, three-hour **horse rentals** go for 55 pesos; bargaining may work here.

ENTERTAINMENT

Puerto Vallarta proffers something for everyone, whether it's a cocktail in the moonlight or a dance across a crowded room. Most of the upscale action is along Díaz Ordaz on the northern waterfront, where clubs and restaurants cater to suntanned professionals holding pricey rum drinks and bopping to "American Top-40" dance tracks. Down south, and at **Carlos O'Brian's,** the crowds of young teeny-boppers are aware of the latest New Kids hit but not much else. Discos cater to those who can spring a 20- to 30-peso cover charge in high season and pay 6 pesos per beer. Puerto Vallarta is home to a thriving, if small, gay scene, and gay men are generally accepted here. Lesbians, however—as in most of Mexico—meet with a less understanding reception. Two bars in Vallarta are frequented primarily by gay men: **Los Balcones** and the **Piano Bar.** Save a small fortune by obtaining free passes (which may not be honored during peak tourist season) from the condo hawkers who lurk around the Malecón. Most discos aren't worth visiting until 11pm or midnight; the time is well-spent drinking in cheaper bars.

Los Balcones, Juárez 182 at Libertad (tel. 2-46-71). The best club in town. International crowd lazes on the many balconies overlooking Juárez and Libertad and gets busy on the dance floor to house music and older dance faves. Many gay couples and a few lesbian couples hang out here. Beer and soda 6 pesos, mixed drinks 8 pesos, margaritas and piña coladas 9 pesos. Starts hopping at 11:30pm. Open daily noon-3am.

Carlos O'Brian's Bar & Grill & Pawnshop, Díaz Ordaz at Pipila (tel. 2-14-44). Pawning is not the main event. O'Brian's attempts successfully to be the biggest party in town—block-long lines wrap around the building all night, waiting to enter the 3 bars, 2 dining rooms, and 1 large dance floor. There's nothing Mexican about this place except the Corona served up in buckets; by the 8-oz. bottle it costs 4.50 pesos. Cover 20 pesos, includes 2 drinks. Open noon-1:30am.

Andale, Olas Altas 425 (tel. 2-15-04). Video bar caters to a teeming crowd of *norteamericanos* and Mexicans of all ages who down shots to collective shouts of *¡ándale!* Margaritas 6 pesos, beer 3 pesos. Open daily 10am-3am; most crowded 7pm-2am.

Franzi, on Isla Río Cuale, at the foot of the Vallarta Bridge. Find a table on the shady patio, order a margarita and listen to the jazz. Entertainment gets no mellower than this. Promotes itself as a "twilight" spot. Frequented by a professional Mexican crowd and lots of *nuevo-wavo gringo* couples. Entrees 20-45 pesos, mixed drinks 8 pesos. Live music Wed. and Fri.-Sun. 8-11pm. Open daily 6pm-1am.

■ Near Puerto Vallarta

Puerto Vallarta's best beaches start a few km south of town. The first two or three you come across are monopolized by resorts and condos, and though they're nicer and quieter than the ones back in town access to them is usually only through the hotels. Farther down the coast lies **Los Arcos,** a group of pretty rock islands hollowed out in places by pounding waves. Similar rocks litter much of Mexico's

Pacific coast, but the waves of Bahía de Banderas render these formations most impressive. The coastline here lacks sand, but it still serves as a platform from which to start the 150m swim to the islands. Bring a mask or goggles or risk missing the tropical fish that flit through the underwater reefscape. Flippers avail against the heavy currents, and be careful where you step as the coral is sharp enough to draw blood. To get there take the bus to Mismaloya and ask the driver to stop at Los Arcos or Hotel de los Arcos. It's not only cheaper to go by yourself (and not on the cruises that are advertised everywhere) you also get to spend more time enjoying the fish.

The beautiful crescent beach of **Mismaloya** lies just around the bend to the south. Best known as the setting of *Night of the Iguana* and Schwarzenegger's *Predator*, Mismaloya has recently been encircled by large hotels and is only slightly less crowded than the beaches in town. The area still harbors both sets; the former is now a series of crumbling castle-like houses, overlooking the southern end of the beach. All that remains of the latter, 40 minutes by foot down the dirt road through town, is a burned out helicopter hull displayed proudly by the locals.

The road veers away from the coast just beyond the **Boca de Tomatlán.** This narrow cove contains only a small beach but offers a breather from the touristy hubbub of the northern coastline. A couple of small **restaurants** cater to the *gringos* who pass through. Don't come here trying to find cheaper passage to beaches farther south—boats from the Boca are more expensive than the cheapest cruises from Vallarta, unless you have a party of eight.

The last place to check out on the southern road is **Chico's Paradise,** 5km inland from the Boca de Tomatlán. Take in a gorgeous view of the **Tomatlán Falls** while having a drink at Chico's huge and airy *palapas*. You'll have to take a **taxi** (25 pesos from Mismaloya) or a long-distance Transportes de Cihuatlan bus (see Practical Information) to get there unless you have your own vehicle.

Further south along the coast lie the beaches of **Las Ánimas, Quimixto,** and **Yelapa,** all of which are accessible only from the ocean. Las Ánimas and Quimixto are twins—long stretches of unoccupied sand backed by small villages and a few *palapas* offering seafood to tourists. Quimixto also proffers a small waterfall to those who tire of the beach. The trip can be made in an hour by foot from the beach, or in a half hour by rented mule.

The popular boat ride to **Yelapa** is, in a way, a bit of a fake. Yelapa is supposed to be a secluded peasant fishing village but its seemingly simple *palapa* huts were designed by a *norteamericano* architect whose definition of rustic included interior plumbing and hot water. Many of these are occupied for only part of the year, and short- and long-term rentals can be arranged easily for widely varying and sometimes surprisingly low prices. Many travelers opt to slough off their packs for a time and join the sizeable expatriate community that exists here. The beach fills with hawkers and parasailers during the day, but the town, a 15-minute walk from the beach, remains *tranquilo*—with waterfalls and nude bathing upstream and poetry readings downstream, nobody's ready to leave. Don't miss the secluded swimming hole at the top of the stream that runs through town; follow the path uphill along the stream, and just before the restaurant, duck under the water pipes to the right of the trail and head up the track. About 50 ft. before it rejoins the stream bed, an inconspicuous trail leads off to the left to a deep pool which overlooks the bay.

The cheapest way to get to the boats-only beaches is via the **Autobús Acuático** water shuttle. It leaves twice a day (10am and 1pm) from the Muelle de los Muertos and stops at Mismaloya, Las Ánimas, and Yelapa. It's cheaper to take bus #2 or an **Autotransportes del Pacífico Camioneta** from the municipal bus station by Muelle de los Muertos to Mismaloya or La Boca and catch the water shuttle from there. It cruises by about 20 minutes after it leaves Los Muertos. Passage from Mismaloya to Yelapa costs 15 pesos. Boats return at noon and 4pm, but don't miss the last one or you will be stranded.

If you prefer something more organized, **cruises** to points south of Vallarta leave the marina every day from 8am on. The cheapest cruise to Yelapa is 40 pesos, but most are more of a splurge. Tops is 130 pesos, including food and drink. Information about the dazzling variety of tours available can be found in the tourist office, at any large hotel, or in the marina. If you are over 25 (in some cases 23), gainfully employed, and have a major credit card, you can save money on all of the activities listed above, or on a 24 hr. jeep rental (US$5-15). Lots of new developments, condos and resort facilities offer freebies to potential buyers; the most common deal is an invitation to eat a free breakfast or lunch at the resort, spend a few hours enjoying its facilities and then buy tickets (usually at half-price) to any or all of a list of popular tours and cruises. The catch is that you have to listen to their ultra-high-pressure sales pitch which can verge on coercion. Don't under any circumstances relinquish your credit card. Remember, you are under no obligation to do anything whatsoever. If by some fluke the salespeople overlook you, you can find them in booths on the *Malecón*. While you're at it, try to scrounge a few free disco passes off these rather unsavory characters.

■■■ JALISCO COAST

North of the Bahía de Navidad, the highway swings toward the sea to reach the **Bahía Tenacatita,** fringed with idyllic beaches. The sparse settlements are the kinds of villages where the locals stop sipping their early morning sodas to stare as you get off the bus (they are just curious and usually incredibly helpful). The larger villages of **Tenacatita** and **La Manzanilla** offer a stray hotel or two, but most visitors prefer camping on the beach. Even farther north, on the **Costa Careyes,** budget travelers are as rare a species as the *careyes* (turtles) for which the area is named. Steep cliffs and rocky shoals render most of the "Turtle Coast" inaccessible, and what little isn't might as well be. The infamous Club Med in one secluded cove and a newly spawned hotel-and-condo complex in the next are both prohibitively expensive. If you wish to exercise (discreetly) your right to public beach, share the sand in front of the **Hotel Careyes** with its well-to-do Mexican clientele. A tame pelican and a beautiful pool should satisfy even the fussiest of moochers. Buses travel all along this coast—just tell the driver where you want to hop off, then cross your fingers and ask lots of directions to catch the bus out.

The beaches here are some of the coast's finest. Gradually sloping white sand meets waves whose irregular patterns result from the offshore islands. Flying fish taunt cruising pelicans, and the diving birds provide entertainment until the sunset takes over that role. Well-marked access roads lead from the highway to the local favorites **Playa Pérula, Playa La Fortuna,** and **Playa Chamela.**

The **Bahía Chamela** has been completely overlooked by the tourist circuit. The village itself is more a cartographical expression than a true community. A few ramshackle stores and a couple of restaurants cluster on the inland side of the highway near San Mateo in the middle of Chamela. The lack of development is no fluke; ruthless resort magnates have met their match in the Mexican armed forces, who control most of the beach and have squelched almost all plans for development in the area. Many, however, are still not deterred. The beaches of the Bahía are largely deserted, and many find them a perfect place to pitch your tent and soak up the sun. Large, forbidding signs label army property "off-limits," and travelers should certainly get permission from local soldiers before pounding any stakes. The number of army personnel on the beaches swells in February, March, May and June, so you may want to give this adventure a miss.

Three villages in the area offer the visitor rudimentary supplies and services. **Pérula** is the largest of these, sporting two hotels and a number of restaurants, most of which fill up in the afternoon but close down for dinner. The cheapest accommodation besides the beach goes for 65 pesos for two, but rumor has it that a cheaper place will soon be hosting visitors. In addition, haggling may well work, especially in low season. Pérula can be reached from the highway via a 2.5km stretch of dirt road, which begins immediately south of the road to **Ejido La Fortuna,** directly across from where the bus stops.

Under no circumstances should a single traveler attempt to get to the beaches. Several local people have disappeared from this area; women should go in groups of no less than three.

San Mateo is on the highway, but don't blink or you'll miss it. There's one **hotel** in town run by Señor Pío Nogales, known locally as Don Pío. The rooms aren't exactly luxurious, but they do have their own dusty bathrooms and the view of the bay is stunning. Don Pío's house is two blocks up the dirt road from the bus station on the inland side of the highway; look on the left for the gray, breeze-block domicile. (Singles 20 pesos, 2-bed rooms 30 pesos, 3-bed rooms 35 pesos.) Chances of a vacancy are pretty good, but the house has no phone so a trip to San Mateo should hold some suspense.

Restaurant Los Pelícanos serves good food but has no fixed menu or prices (haggling is feasible). Alternatively, head north down the road 2km to **Villa Polenesia** for reliable chow at good prices. They also have official camping spaces and room for a handful of RVs, should you so require.

Many find hitching conditions along the highway to be excellent during the day, but hitching is not a recommended practice. Those hitching to a specific beach travel with the flow of people (beachward at dawn, homeward at dusk). Otherwise the beaches lie about one hour by **bus** from Melaque (7 pesos) and four-and-a-half hours from Puerta Vallarta (28 pesos). Buses pass about every half hour, connecting the villages (2 pesos).

■■■ BAHÍA DE NAVIDAD

Completing Jalisco's "Tourist Trangle," this placid haven juxtaposes the *gringo*-trodden Guadalajara and Puerto Vallarta. Poised on the north and east banks of the Bahía de Navidad, a sheltered cove of talcum sand and shimmering water, the towns of **Melaque** and **Barra de Navidad** are only are a few kilometers apart. Both towns remain largely unmarred by tourist activity. Barra retains the authenticity of a charming small Mexican town—so small, in fact, that it has neither bank nor *panadería*—while at the same time it has sufficient facilitites to absorb substantial numbers of tourists. Melaque is larger, busier, and less charming than Barra. Made up almost exclusively of one-story concrete buildings, its streets are wider and dirtier than Barra's narrow the tree-lined ones, its restaurants less homey, its beachfront more developed, and its waves less exciting. Nevertheless, both beaches are spectacular, their picturesque sunsets framed between the two spits of the cove.

Melaque and Barra de Navidad are 55km northwest of Manzanillo on Rte. 200, or 240km southwest of Guadalajara on Rte. 54. The towns themselves lie a few km apart: two if by sea, five if by highway. Northbound buses hit Barra first and southbound ones do the reverse.

Municipal buses or **combis** (1.50 pesos) connect the two towns every 15 minutes or so. But it is faster to take one of the larger buses heading to Manzanillo that leave on the hour from both towns' bus stations. These cost the same, but are faster and more comfortable. Of course, the 30- to 40-minute walk along the beach between the towns is the true hard-core budget option; don't go alone and take a cab after dark (15 pesos); as some women have been harassed along this stretch,.

■■■ MELAQUE

Practical Information Melaque's new bus station sits at the intersection of **Carranza Gómez Farías,** the main drag, which runs parallel to the beach. From the bus station, turn left on Gómez Farías and walk two blocks to reach **López Mateos.** Another left turn takes you to the town plaza, a few blocks inland. López

Mateos and **Hidalgo,** one block beyond it and parallel to it, are the main cross streets towards the ocean.

Despite its size and swank bus station, Melaque has no bank; nor does Barra de Navidad. A **casa de cambio** across from the bus station changes dollars at a poor rate. (Open Mon.-Fri. 9am-1pm and 3-6pm.) The **post office,** Morelos 44 (tel. 7-02-30), on the plaza at López Mateos, has *Lista de Correos*. (Open Mon.-Fri. 9am-1pm and 3pm-6pm, Sat. 9am-1pm. **Postal code:** 48980.) The **phone office,** on Morelos 52 (tel. 7-00-23), charges 5 pesos for collect calls. (Open Mon.-Sat. 7am-2pm and 4-9pm, Sun. 8am-2pm and 5-9pm.) LADATELs are by the bus station. **Telephone code:** 333. **Buses** leave from the bus station (see above) to Puerto Vallarta (5hrs., 25 pesos), Guadalajara (6½hrs., 34 pesos), and Manzanillo (1½hrs., 8 pesos). **Red Cross,** (tel. 8-23-00), is 15km away in Cihuatlán. **Farmacia Plaza,** López Mateos 43 on the Plaza (tel. 7-00-67), is south of the plaza. (Open Mon.-Sat. 8am-2pm and 4-9:30pm, Sun. 8am-2pm and 6-8pm.) The **hospital,** or **Centro de Salud,** Cordiano Guzmán, between Corona and Gómez Farías,)on the right going toward the beach), is open 24 hrs. The **police,** (tel. 7-00-80), on López Mateos, north of the plaza, are available 9am-3pm.

Accommodations and Camping Melaque is larger than Barra de Navidad and has more hotels, but some are beyond the budget range. **Bungalows Villamar,** Hidalgo 1 (tel. 7-00-05), just off the beach, merit staying in Melaque on their own. Large, well-scrubbed beachside bungalows with two bedrooms, each with two double beds and a large living-dining room area with fully equipped kitchen. Well-kept flowery grounds and a deck with spectacular view of the ocean. (2 people 65 pesos. 4 people 95 pesos. 8 people 140 pesos. 5 bungalows. Call in advance to reserve.) **Hotel Hidalgo,** Hidalgo 7 (tel. 7-00-45), halfway between the plaza and the beach, is a family affair, with an especially friendly English-speaking proprietor. 14 clean and small rooms (with chests of drawers and spotless but microscopic bathrooms) surround the schizophrenic courtyard, living room, and kitchen (which also serves as the family's laundry room). Ask the management to turn on the fan, since there are no switches in the room. (Singles 35 pesos. Doubles 45 pesos. Winter singles 58 pesos. Doubles 74 pesos.) Pleasant **Hotel San Nicolás,** Gómez Farías (tel. 7-00-66), ½ block west of López Mateos, has somewhat decrepit rooms, some with small balconies above the street, bay views, and sliding glass doors bathrooms that could be in better shape. (Singles 40 pesos. Doubles 50 pesos. More expensive in winter.) **Playa Trailer Park,** marring the beach at Gómez Farías and López Mateos (tel. 7-00-65). 45 lots with electricity, water, sewer hook-ups and access to bathrooms (.50 pesos) and showers (2 pesos). Two-person trailer or camping site 35 pesos. Each additional person 5 pesos. Six-person bungalows 120 pesos.

Many people park trailers or pitch tents at the far western end of Melaque, between the sandy beach and rock formations. The site is flat but strewn with litter and rocks, not to mention vehicles and tents. If you only need room for one tent, a far better spot lies along the shore past this rentable parking lot, just before the rocky beach. Otherwise, hunt for more creative sites between the two towns. A small, land-locked lagoon separates the beach and jungle; people pitch tents on the oceanside or crash among the crabs between Melaque and the lagoon. But look before you sleep; at least one landowner has posted a "no camping" sign. As always, clean up after yourself.

Food During the summer, restaurants ship in shrimp from the north, but in high season local fishing boats catch everything that is served on the waterfront. Lobster here is trapped illegally, so help the persecuted crustacean's cause by ordering oysters instead. Beachfront restaurants exude tropical ambience, with an appropriate price tag attached. More authentic (and less expensive) Mexican places lie around the central plaza. Cheaper still are the nameless, dirt-floored eateries in the *mercado* and near the bus station or the sidewalk food stands that materialize after the sun sets and the plaza awakes from its heat-induced slumber. Watch out for the amoebas that hang out in *mercados*.

Los Pelícanos, lies in the row of *palapas* on the beach 50m beyond Hotel Melaque. The proprietor, New Yorker Philomena "Phil" García, considers herself the fairy godmother of the wayworn *gringo* and is a fixture of the local expatriate scene. Breakfast (around 8 pesos) and great seafood (19 pesos) will cure most cases of homesickness. (Open daily 8am-11pm, off-season daily 11am-7pm.) **El Buen Gusto,** Lopes Mateos 18, is a family run restaurant located in a shed with a metal roof. Eat on card tables with white tablecloths and enjoy the tasty inexpensive food. *Huevos* 6 pesos. (Open daily 8am-11pm.) **Restaurante Bar el Dorado,** a *palapa* connected to the Hotel Club Náutico at the western end of Gómez Farías, sets the mood with pink tablecloths and napkins and a full bar that's even open for breakfast. *Huevos rancheros* 9 pesos, pancakes 9 pesos, shrimp 32 pesos. (Open daily 8am-10:30pm.)

Sights and Entertainment In Melaque the beach gets more crowded towards its western end, and the waves get smaller. Restaurants and aqua-activities, such as **jet-ski rental** (US$30 per hr.) also increase in density towards this end of the beach.

Melaque's most famous attraction is its **Fiesta de San Patricio** (March 8-17), which has achieved a near-mythic stature in the surrounding area for its raucous intensity. After filling yourself with Jalisco's finest tequila, dancing to *salsa* until your legs feel like *mermelada*, and watching fireworks while riding the bucking bronco, try not to pass out until after you've attended the blessing of the fleet and the all-day procession. Philomena García's bash the night before, rumor has it, keeps the residents across the bay awake with its commotion. Drop by her restaurant, **Los Pelícanos** (see Food), to get in on it.

Although probably very few people actually come to Melaque for the nightlife there, few refuse it when it's thrust upon them. **Disco Tango,** where Gómez Farías runs into Vallarta, monopolizes the chic action and is home after hours to Melaque's under-30 tourist crowd. (Cover 10-15 pesos, beer 5 pesos.) Melaque's other dance floors are comparatively modest and relatively interchangeable: **Discotheque Albatros** is a half-block inland from the *zócalo*; **Discotheque Hollywood,** on Ramón Corona, lies two blocks east of Hidalgo. (Cover 5-15 pesos.)

■■■ BARRA DE NAVIDAD

Practical Information Barra de Navidad's bus stop is at Veracruz 226, on the corner of Nayarit. Veracruz runs roughly parallel to **Legazpi,** the main street that hugs the beach. Turn left on Veracruz from the bus station to get to *el centro*. Depending on who is working at the **tourist office,** Sonora 15 (tel. 7-02-37), English may or may not be spoken, and their information is better for other places than for Barra itself. (Open Mon.-Fri. 9am-7pm, Sat. 9am-1pm.) **Agencia de Viajes Viacosta,** Veracruz 204 (tel. 7-06-65), arranges plane tickets only. (Open Mon.-Fri. 9am-8pm, Sat. 9am-6pm, Sun. 10am-noon.) Barra has neither bank nor *casa de cambio;* the closest *casa de cambio* is in Melaque (see above), or try the small general store on **Legazpi,** a block from the police station. The **post office,** Guanajuato 100, is 1½ blocks inland from Veracruz on the south side of the maritime monument, near the bus station. *Lista de Correos* is posted around 10:30am. (Open Mon.-Fri. 8am-3pm. **Postal code:** 48987.) The **telegram office** is at Veracruz 69, on the corner by the plaza. (Open Mon.-Fri. 9am-3pm.) **Farmacia Zurich,** Legazpi 156 (tel. 7-07-31), is open daily 8am-10pm. For medical attention, the **Centro de Salud,** on Puerto Navidad (no phone), is down Veracruz out of town, make a right just after the signs for El Marquez, and just before Veracruz becomes a highway. The Centro is the second building on the right. **Police** wait at Veracruz 179 (tel. 7-03-99).

Accommodations and Food Barra has a deceptive dearth of budget accommodations. The best spot to camp or park your trailer is the extreme south end of town, on the sandbar near the breakwater. Use the toilet (.50 pesos) and the shower (2 pesos) in one of the nearby sand-floored eateries; look for the hand-lettered signs that read "Sanitario/Regadera." **Posada Pacífico,** Mazatlán 160 (tel. 7-03-59), features comfortable, white rooms, a pleasant courtyard, clean, shower curtains and killer fans. The friendly *dueña* lets guests park in the driveway if there's room. (Singles 40 pesos. Doubles 50 pesos. In winter singles 60 pesos. Doubles 80 pesos.) Immaculate rooms with large bathrooms at **Hotel Delfín,** Morelos 23 (tel. 7-00-68), have access to a dreamy terrace overlooking the leafy courtyard, pool and lagoon. Worth the extra pesos. (Singles 65 pesos. Doubles 75 pesos. In winter singles 90 pesos, double 100 pesos.) **Bungalows Karelia,** on Legazpi (tel. 7-01-87), at the beach next to the Hotel Bogavante, are a good deal for 3 or more. Airy suites house refrigerator, table, chairs, stove and fan but lack the crucial screens and kitchen utensils. (Doubles 75 pesos. Each additional person 15 pesos.)

Restaurants line the south end of the beach with beautiful views, and on Veracruz, many families open their living rooms as informal restaurants. For basic Mexican food in a pleasant atmosphere—checkered tablecloths and wooden chairs—try **Restaurant Paty,** on the north corner of Veracruz and Jalisco, across from restaurant Chela. It is popular with locals for its delicious, inexpensive food. Grilled *pollo* 10 pesos. Three *quesadillas* 6 pesos. (Open daily 8:30am-11pm.) The beachside tables at **Restaurant Pacífico,** Legazpi 206, offer great sunset viewing and a stirring vista which inspires the 2-for-1 happy hour (4-7pm). Breakfast special is a bargain at 8 pesos. Fish 16 pesos. (Open daily 8am-10:30pm.) **Crepes y Café,** Veracruz 101, is 50% vegetarian. The French proprietor whips up delicious sweet and non-sweet crepes. Healthy alternatives include *pan integral* and yogurt. Their boast of "best coffee in town" may be true. Complete breakfast with crepe, yogurt, and fruit 17 pesos. Unfortunately, dinner tends to be on the expensive side. Basic ham and cheese crepe 16 pesos. (Open Fri.-Wed. 8am-noon and 5-10pm.) **Restaurant Eloy,** Yucatán 47, jutting out into the lagoon, is small and cheesy with colorful flowers and pleasant owners. Fish 15 pesos. *Huevos* 8 pesos. (Open daily 8am-9:30pm.) Dine outdoors on the tree-lined sidewalk or indoors amidst potted plants at **Restaurant y Cenaduría Chela,** Veracruz 102. Very popular locally at dinnertime. Order of four tacos, 6 pesos. Fish fillet 12 pesos. (Open daily 8am-midnight.)

Sights and Entertainment The slightly larger waves of Barra de Navidad are seldom big enough for surfing, but the crowd here tries admirably. During the rainy season, however, the waves between Barra and Melanque are sometimes close to perfect. **Mariner,** Legazpi 154, across the street from the church, rents surfboards, boogie boards and skindiving equipment (each 5 pesos per hr. plus deposit of passport or credit card), as well as **bicycles** (16 pesos per day; open daily 9am-10pm).

While the short trip across the lagoon to the village of **Colimilla** makes a pleasant diversion, the steep price for small groups is considerably less than pleasant. For 30 pesos round-trip, a *lancha* will deposit up to eight passengers amid Colimilla's palms, pigs, cows, and open-air restaurants, or at the far end of the lagoon. A 1km stroll from here is the deserted **Playa de los Cocos,** which has larger breakers than those in Barra. If you don't want to swim back, remember to fix a time to be picked up. For 50 pesos per hour, zoom off in the same *lancha* full of equipment for tuna, sailfish, or marlin fishing. Big catches are most common June through December; operators have formed a cooperative, so the prices are fixed. Their office and docks lie at the very end of Veracruz.

A source of sinful pride for Barra is the **Iglesia de San Antonio,** on the corner of Jalisco and Veracruz, four blocks south of the bus station. The church, a modern structure, holds a different attraction for visitors than the stately colonial architecture prevalent in Mexico's touristed places of worship. Inside hangs *El Cristo del Ciclón* (Christ of the Hurricane). Its arms, instead of being extended to form the traditional crucifix, are bent and, still attached to the body, droop earthward as if in a shrug. Legend has it that when Hurricane Lilly furiously struck the bay at dawn on September 10, 1971, a young girl burst into the church begging the icon for help, causing Christ's arms to detach from the crucifix in order to hold the hurricane back and save the town from destruction. (Church open daily 7am-8pm.)

The only game down the strand in Barra de Navidad is **El Gaeón/Aladino's** (cover 10 pesos). The all-age clientele throbs as one, as everyone out past midnight is here. (Beer 3.50 pesos, mixed drinks 6 pesos.) A number of 2-1 happy hours along Legazpi make the giddy trip towards inebriation that much cheaper.

COLIMA

■■■ MANZANILLO

Residents of Colima state proudly point to Manzanillo as the home of its finest beaches and the brightest hope of its economic future. In their delirious efforts to transform Manzanillo into the next Cancún, however, these worshippers of the tourist god have overlooked the undeniable fact that a working port can never become a world-class resort. The workhorse of Mexico's Pacific coast, Manzanillo attracts ships from as far away as Russia. A navy repair station faces the city's main plaza, and *el centro* is a sweaty, workaday place unappealing to the beachgoing tourist.

Most tourists, therefore, avoid central Manzanillo altogether, and stay at glossy resorts on Manzanillo's two bays of golden-brown sand to the north and west of town. Life in these areas is good thanks to the fortuitous combination of currents and latitude, keeping Manzanillo cooler in summer than Acapulco and Puerto Vallarta. The reasonably priced hotels of Manzanillo, however, all lie in the midst of the loud and brazen port action. A 20-minute bus trip (1 peso) or a 12-peso taxi ride separates *el centro* from the beaches. If all you seek is sand and surf, you'd do better to repair to some secluded village, such as Cuyutlán or Barra de Navidad, where there is no metropolis between your hotel and the Pacific. Even the smaller town outside of Manzanillo proper tends to be grimier than most Mexican beach towns; the resorts themselves bad imitations of Club Meds that look out onto the highway, the beaches black from the nearby volcanoes, with litter occasionally strewn about.

Practical Information Manzanillo lies 96km west of Colima and 355km south of Guadalajara. The main **bus station** lies on the outskirts of town between Laguna Cuyutlán and the ocean. The local bus labeled "Centro" runs from the station to the corner of 21 de Marzo and Hidalgo (.50 pesos). From there, a right turn onto Allende and another one onto México will lead you to the *zócalo*. A **taxi** (tel. 3-23-20) from the bus station to the center of town costs 4 pesos.

The **Jardín Obregón,** Manzanillo's plaza, is the most useful orientation point in town. The plaza faces north onto the harbor, but boxcars often obstruct the glorious view of PEMEX tankers. **Morelos** runs along the north (waterfront) edge of the plaza, **Juárez** along the south. **Avenida México,** Manzanillo's main street, runs south from the plaza. Most hotels and services are nearby. The **tourist office** has basic information in the Palacio Municipal on the *Jardín*. (Open Mon.-Fri. 9am-11pm.) **Bancomer,** México 220 (tel. 2-26-90), exchanges currency Mon.-Fri. 8:30am-noon. Many banks line México. The **post office** is on 5 de Mayo between Juárez and Morelos (tel. 2-00-32), 1 block east of the *Jardín*. (Open Mon.-Fri. 8am-7pm, Sat. 9am-1pm.) **Computel,** Madero 72, ½ block off the *zócalo*, charges 5 pesos for collect calls. (Open daily 6:45am-10pm.) **LADATELs** lie two blocks from the *Jardín* on México and on the *Jardín* itself. Manzanillo's **airport** is actually in Playa de Oro, on the highway between Manzanillo and Barra de Navidad, about one

Name

Address

City State Zip Code

Place Stamp Here

Centro Mexicano Internacional
14542 Brookhollow, Suite 279
San Antonio, TX 78232

hour from Manzanillo. **Combis** (tel. 3-21-80) to the airport (20 pesos) leave every hr. from the hotel Fiesta Mexicana (tel. 3-21-80), on the Miramar bus route 2.5km out of the city on the left. **Mexicana,** Mexico 382 (tel. 2-17-01), is open Mon.-Fri. 9am-2pm and 2:45-6pm, and **Aeroméxico,** (tel. 2-17-11) in the Centro Comercial, Carrillo Puerto 107 (tel. 2-12-67), is open Mon.-Sat. 9am-7pm. Flights to: Mexico City (350 pesos), Guadalajara (200 pesos), and Los Angeles (US$300). More importantly, the **bus station,** on Hidalgo, about 1km east of downtown, features **Soc. Coop. de Autotransportes** (tel. 2-04-32), with buses every 15min. to Armería (2.50 pesos), Tecomán (3 pesos), and Colima (5 pesos). **Autobuses de la Costa** (tel. 2-10-03) serves Puerto Vallarta (4½-6½ hrs., 20 pesos), and Guadalajara (17 per day, 8hrs., 45 pesos). **Tres Estrellas de Oro** (tel. 2-01-35) serves Mexico City (15hrs., 121 pesos). The **train station,** on Niños Héroes, near Morelos east of the plaza, has one second-class train per day at 6am, to Colima (1½hrs., 4 pesos), Guzmán (6hrs., 7 pesos), Guadalajara (9hrs., 15 pesos), and 49 other stops en route. Tickets can only be purchased the same day, starting at 5am. The **Red Cross** (tel. 2-00-96) is 10 de Mayo and Bocanegra. **Farmacia Manzanillo,** Juárez 10, faces the plaza. (Open daily 9am-10pm.) **Hospital Civil,** is on the San Pedrito circle (tel. 2-10-03 or 2-09-03). **Police** are in the Presidencia Municipal (tel. 2-10-04).

Accommodations and Food It's slim pickings; Manzanillo does not cater to the tourist of any stripe. Hotels in the center of town are better than those near the bus station, a rough nighborhood that is dangerous at night. **Camping** on Playa Miramar is also feasible, and restaurants may allow you do it. Many of the houses on the beach are deserted for part of the year. As far as safety is concerned, it's generally a good idea to situate yourself near an occupied house, hotel or restaurant, unless you are traveling with a large body of retainers.

Hotel Flamingo, Madero 72 (tel. 2-10-37), is one block south of the *zócalo*. No flamingos here, but still the best bet for your money. Clean, basic rooms, if a bit musty. Bathrooms clean with shower curtains. (Singles 40 pesos. Doubles 50 pesos. Reservations recommended.) **Hotel Emperador,** Dávalos 69 (tel. 2-23-74), one block west of the plaza's southwest corner, is above a restaurant whose aromas make the mouth water; this may be its only virtue. No hot water but clean bathrooms. The barren rooms, some without windows, are a claustrophobe's nightmare. (Singles 40 pesos. Doubles 45 pesos.) Psychedelic staircases lead to large rooms at **Hotel Miramar,** Juárez 122 (tel. 2-10-08), probably untouched since the birth of rock-and-roll. You could fit a small roller rink on any of the vast, checkered balconies. (Singles 40 pesos. Doubles 45 pesos. Reservations recommended.) The cell-like rooms at **Casa de Huéspedes Petrita,** Allende 20 (tel. 2-01-87), feature odd bar/screens over the windows and a clunky, functional communal bathroom. (Singles 25 pesos. Doubles 30 pesos.)

Manzanillo is sprinkled with a few good restaurants, but because tourists mostly put up closer to the beach, the market is strictly local and the food downtown comes with few frills. **Restaurante Chantilly,** on the plaza at Juárez and Moreno, provides the usual Mexican staples to crowds of newspaper-reading professionals. Though the food is nothing to write home about, the view of the *zócalo* makes it a good spot for people-watching. (Waffles 7 pesos. Shrimp 19 pesos. Open Sun.-Fri. 7am-10pm.) Below the hotel of the same name, **Restaurant Emperador,** Dávalos 69 (tel. 2-23-74), has blank walls and fluorescent lights that aren't nearly as pleasing as the food. (Enchiladas 5 pesos. Open daily 9am-10:30pm.) Look hard for **Los Narangos,** México 366; there's not even a sign outside. If there's a table available here at lunchtime, however, you're lucky: it's an institution with locals. Breakfast is not quite so popular. (*Huevos a la mexicana* 6 pesos. *Caldo de pollo* 7 pesos. Generous juices 3.50 pesos.)

Sights Two nearby, bays, **Bahía Manzanillo** and **Bahía Santiago,** serve Manzanillo's beach needs. The former has more expensive hotels and cleaner golden sand than its neighbor's, but its beach slopes more steeply, creating a strong undertow. The beaches at Bahía Santiago, though twice as far from *el centro*, are more popular among *aficionados*, though the noisy highway lies just behind them.

The closest good beach on Bahía Manzanillo, **Playa Las Brisas,** has a few secluded spots, but parts of the beach are crowded with luxurious hotels and bungalows. To get to Las Brisas from downtown Manzanillo, take a **taxi** (12 pesos) or the "Las Brisas" **bus** (1 peso). Catch the bus on México or on the highway going toward the airport and Barra de Navidad. Alternatively, catch the "Miramar" bus and ask the driver to let you off at the *crucero*. From the crossroads, turn left toward populated shores or stake out a private section of beach right at the junction.

The "Miramar" bus continues west of Peninsula Santiago, gear-grinding toward other excellent beaches on Bahía Santiago. The bay here is not used for shipping, and thus the water is cleaner than at Las Brisas. The "Miramar" buses (1.40 pesos to the Bahía) leave every 15 minutes from the train station, three blocks east of the plaza on Niños Héroes. The best place to get off is where everyone else does—at **Miramar Beach,** where a footbridge crosses the highway. This is the most crowded section of the beach, but it has the best beachfront restaurants where you can rent boogie boards and surfboards (5 pesos per hr.). Crowds disappear 20m east or west of the beach club that owns this stretch of sand. The waves are adequate for boogie boarding and bodysurfing, but if you can figure out a way to use a surfboard here, you should move to Waikiki and give lessons. For tranquility, head for **La Avedencía,** a calm cove on the west side of the peninsula, or get the bus to stop just before it turns away from the coast after the footbridge.

■ Near Manzanillo: Paraíso and Cuyutlán

Paraíso may soon be destroyed by the gods for its hubris, but while it exists it outclasses its unsightly brother city, nearby **Armería.** A well-paved road connects the two towns, cutting through 7km of banana and coconut plantations before it dead-ends into the black sands that surround Paraíso's thatched, beachfront restaurants. A few weathered fishing boats litter the tranquil shoreline, holding back the emerald green surf.

Just before the main road becomes the beach, you'll see Paraíso's only other street, the lushly named **Calle Adán y Eva,** which runs along the back of the beachfront restaurants. A left turn here will take you to the village's only hotel, the **Hotel Paraíso** (tel. 2-47-87), with big well-maintained rooms, spotless showers and a pool. (Singles and doubles 60 pesos.) The extensive beach makes perfect terrain for bootleg campers, and owners of some of the *enramadas* may let you shack up under their thatched roofs if you're worried about rain. The Hotel Paraíso offers showers (2 pesos) and bathrooms (.50 pesos) to anyone who should care to use them. In high season (especially Dec. and April) there may be rooms available in private Paraíso houses, so ask around.

Restaurants run the slim gamut from rustic *enramadas* to dirt-floored *comedores*. Predictably, locally caught seafood dominates menus, which barely differ from place to place in either offerings or prices. **Restaurant Paraíso,** in the Hotel Paraíso (see above), is reliable and has snazzy service. The tasty *shrimp a la diable* even come without their shells for 19 pesos. (Open daily 8am-6pm.)

Buses (1.50 pesos) run to and from the vestibule in Armería, a last resort place to pass the night, every 45 minutes from 6am to 7:30pm. There is also a **long distance telephone** in the *tienda rural* across the street from the bus stop (tel. 4-29-10). They charge using the "give me whatever you think is appropriate" scale. (Open Mon.-Sat. 9am-9pm, Sun. 9am-6pm.)

If you're a budding Thoreauvian hungry for peace and silence, then **Cuyutlán** is a wonderful place to visit (pop. sub-1000), especially in the off season when shut-up buildings and empty streets give it a ghost-town feel. Local residents of this sleepy town choose not to perform concerts, instead they leave entertainment to the natural attractions. In fact, the *zócalo* is usually as deserted as the beaches, where, after a quick stroll away from deserted umbrellas, you have the sand all to yourself. However, within the high season (Dec.-May), lifeguards and a well-planned *malecón* make the dark-brown sands even more attractive for the domestic tourists who come in droves. During the summer months, the wild blue waves pound the shore's dark sand without an audience.

Cuyutlán's most unusual distinction is the renowned **green wave,** a phenomenon that occurs regularly in April or May. Quirky currents and phosphorescent marine life combine to produce 10m swells that glow an unearthly green.

The road from Armería, 15km to the northeast, becomes **Yavaros,** running east to west, parallel to the coastline, as it enters town. It intersects **Hidalgo,** which runs north-south, along the east side of the town square, and a left at this intersection takes you to the beach. Buses coming from Armería (2 pesos) make a right here onto Hidalgo, off Yavaros and away from the beach before they stop at the *parada* (bus stop) which serves as a bus station on Hidalgo. **Veracruz,** Cuyutlán's other mighty boulevard, is parallel to Yavaros, one block off the beach and three blocks from Yavaros.

Most of Cuyutlán's municipal services are within one block of the *zócalo*. The owner of the Hotel Morelos will **change money** if they have the cash. **Telephones** are at Hidalgo 47 (tel. 4-18-10), one block north of the *zócalo*. (Collect calls 2 pesos. Open Mon.-Sat. 9am-1pm and 4-8pm, Sun. 9am-1pm.) **Farmacia del Carmen** is at Hidalgo 121. (Open Mon.-Fri. 4-8pm, Sat.-Sun. 9am-2pm and 4-8pm.) A **Centro de Salud** is one block west of the *zócalo* on Yavaros at Madero. The **police** reside at Hidalgo 143 (tel. 1-00-13), one block south of the *zócalo*. **Buses** leave from the *parada* for Armería every 40 minutes from 6:30am to 7:30pm (2 pesos). There is no public transportation to Paraíso from Cuyultlán, or vice versa.

Waves, green or regular, lap at the doorsteps of most of the budget hotels. The **Hotel Morelos,** Hidalgo 185 (tel. 17), at Veracruz, sports incredibly plush, spacious rooms with fans and hot water, not to mention the privilege of dwelling amongst all the flowers in Cuyutlán. All this can be yours for 30 pesos per person. In the **Hotel Fénix,** Hidalgo 201 (tel. 147), at Veracruz, the rooms may be taller than they are wide, but there's a fan in each one, and the bathrooms are tidy enough to use. (20 pesos per person.) If you arrive in Cuyutlán during a crunch period (e.g. Christmas or *Semana Santa*) you may have to try one of the inland hotels, such as **Posada San Antonio,** Hidalgo 139, one block seaward from the plaza. It is only open during Mexican vacations. If you'd rather **camp,** a trek 200m to the right of Cuyutlán's hotels will lead to a private patch of black sand. Or string up a hammock in one of the *palapas* to the left of the hotels—most of them are vacant in summer. Campers and daytrippers can use the toilets (1 peso) and showers (1.50 pesos) at Hotel Morelos.

Even if you do like seafood, you may get sick of it—the lack of variety boggles the mind. Below the hotel, the **Restaurant Fénix,** Hidalgo 201, grows decorative flowers. Somehow, the Fénix also stays pretty well-stocked—you might be able to get *tostadas*. (Shrimp any style 22 pesos. Orange juice 3 pesos. Open daily 8am-10pm.)

■■■ COLIMA

The capital of Colima state is hardly a tiny village (pop. 100,000), but nonetheless manages to maintain a certain small-town benevolence—men and women sit around and chat all afternoon on the benches of the *zócalo*, and locals smile as they give directions to tourists. The central plazas are as picturesque now as they were when the city was founded in 1523, but modern civilization has not left Colima unmarked; serenades in the *zócalo* on Sunday afternoons must now contend with cruising automobiles blaring Vanilla Ice's greatest hits. This under-visited city rewards those few who stray from the well-trodden coastal route. Visitors are welcomed with a gratifying change of scenery and a good place to shake the sand from the shoes, and visit its great little museums and theaters.

ORIENTATION

A string of plazas runs east to west across downtown Colima. The arcaded **Plaza Principal,** flanked by the cathedral and the Palacio de Gobierno, is the business center of town. On the other side of the cathedral and *palacio* is the smaller, quieter **Jardín Quintero.** Three blocks farther east on Madero is the large, lush **Jardín Núñez,** the other significant reference point in town. Many tourist services are on **Hidalgo,** which parallels **Madero** one block to the south.

The main **bus station** is 2km out of town, but mini-buses zip by incessantly. Buses #4 and 5 pass through the center a few blocks from the *zócalo*. Buses run by **Soc. Coop. Colima Manzanillo** (from Tecomán and Manzanillo) have their own depot, just north of the suburban stop and downhill from the *centro* on Degollado.

PRACTICAL INFORMATION

Tourist Office: Hidalgo 75 (tel. 2-40-60), 1 block west of Pl. Principal. Staffed by young'uns who try to be helpful. Maps that won't quit. English spoken. Open Mon.-Fri. 9am-3pm and 5-9pm, Sat. 9am-1pm.

Currency Exchange: Bánamex, on Hidalgo 188, 1 block east of Pl. Principal. No commission and a good rate, but hell might freeze over as you wait in line. Money exchange in the basement. Open Mon.-Fri. 9am-noon. **Casa de Cambio** on the corner of Morelos and Juárez on Park Nuñez. Open Mon.-Fri. 9am-2pm and 4:30-6:30pm, Sat. 9am-2pm.

Post Office: Madero 247 at Revolución, on the northeast corner of the *Jardín Núñez. Lista de Correos*. Open Mon.-Fri. 8am-6pm, Sat. 8am-noon.

Telephones: Computel, Morelos 234 on the south side of the *Jardín Núñez*. Collect calls 5 pesos. Open daily 7am-10pm. Also **Farmacia Colima** (see below). Collect calls 2 pesos for 3min. Open daily 7am-10pm. There is also a multitude of blue international phones. **LADATELs** on both plazas. **Telephone code:** 331.

Telegrams: Madero 243, at the post office. Open Mon.-Sat. 9am-8pm.

Bus Stations: Colima has 3. The well-mopped and airport-like **Central de Autobuses,** is 2km out of town on bus #4 or #5 (.50 pesos). **La Linea** operates the most buses to Guadalajara (3hrs., 20.50 pesos) and also serves Uruapan (1 per day at 10:30pm, 6hrs., 30 pesos). **Tres Estrellas de Oro** has 1st class service to Tijuana via the coast (1 per day, 220 pesos) and Mexico City direct (70 pesos), plus other northern points. **Omnibús de México,** your best bet to the east, goes to Monterrey (1 per day, 14hrs., 110 pesos) and Aguascalientes (1 per day, 6hrs., 37 pesos). Until the station on Nicolás Bravo reopens, **Soc. Coop. Colima** operates from a makeshift station 3 blocks south on Degaldo from Pl. Principal. They have buses to Manzanillo (1¼hrs., 7 pesos) that also stop in Tecomán (4.50 pesos). Suburban buses, with destinations like San Antonio (see near Colima), Agua Caliente, Comala and La Becerrera come and go irregularly from a parking lot 2 blocks further south on Degaldo, next to the *Parque Regional*.

Train Station: At the southern edge of town (tel. 2-92-50). Taxi fare 4 pesos. To Guadalajara (1st class 9 pesos, 2nd 5 pesos) at 3pm, and Manzanillo (1st class 3 pesos, 2nd 2 pesos) at 1:30pm. Offices open daily noon-3pm.

Laundromat: Lavandería Automática Jando, Juárez 70. 3 pesos per kg. Open Mon.-Sat. 9am-9pm.

Red Cross: Aldama at Obregón (tel. 2-14-51).

Pharmacy: Farmacia Colima, Madero 1, at the northeast corner of the Pl. Principal (tel. 2-00-31). Open Mon.-Sat. 9am-9pm.

Hospitals: Hospital Civil, San Fernando at Ignacio Zandoval (tel. 2-02-27). **Centro de Salud,** Juárez at 20 de Noviembre (tel. 2-00-64 or 2-32-38).

Police: Juárez at 20 dc Noviembre (tel. 2-18-01 or 2-64-00).

ACCOMMODATIONS

Hotel San Lorenzo, Calle Cuauhtemoc 149, from Pl. Principal go west 2 blocks to Calle Cuauhtemoc and walk left 3 blocks. Basic, large, clean rooms for a good price with professional service. Singles 35 pesos. Doubles 45 pesos.

Hotel Ceballos, Portal Medellín 12 (tel. 2-44-49), on the north side of the Pl. Principal with large French doors. Elegant columned halls with high ceilings sweep towards your spacious room some with desks and A/C. One of the nicest hotels you will find for this amount of money. Singles 65 pesos. Doubles 71 pesos.

Casa de Huéspedes, Morelos 265 (tel. 2-34-67), just off the southeast corner of *Jardín Núñez*. Somewhat decrepit rooms in a very friendly family's house with flowery entrance-way and chickens filling the courtyard. Singles 20 pesos, with bath 25 pesos. Doubles 30 pesos, with bath 35 pesos.

Hotel Flamingos, Rey Colíman 18 (tel. 2-25-25), 1 block south of Park Nuñez. Cool, clean, 70's-style rooms, some with balconies. Modern building without much personal charm. Singles 50 pesos. Doubles 60 pesos.

FOOD

Most of Colima's pleasant restaurants and cafes cluster around the Pl. Principal.

Samadhi, on Mequina, near Guerrero opposite the church. Delicious vegetarian food served in a leafy courtyard with pink portals and comfortable chairs. Free newspapers and classical music promise to extend lunch until twilight. Yogurt with fruit 4 pesos. *Quesadillas* with mushrooms 5.50 pesos. Open Fri.-Wed. 8am-10pm, Thurs. 8am-5pm.

Los Naranjos, Barreda 34. *Periódico*-perusing *señores* sip coffee between mellow lilac and beige walls. Eggs start at 6.50 pesos, *filet mignon au champiñones* 32 pesos. Open daily 8am-11pm.

Restaurant Típico Los Portales, Serdán 15, in Comala, on the south side of the *zócalo*. Basic Mexican fare on a terrace overlooking the Plaza. Very popular with locals for food and drinks. Coronas 3 pesos. Chicken 17 pesos. Open daily 9am-1am.

La Arábica, Guerrero 162. A treat for caffeine fiends. Fed up with instant Nescafé? Take a seat in the verdant courtyard among poetry-reading types and enjoy your cappuccino (4.50 pesos) and homemade grenadine (4 pesos). Mostly drinks. Open daily 8am-11pm.

SIGHTS

In Colima's well-maintained **Plaza Principal,** white park benches surround a gazebo and several decorative fountains. The double arcade around the plaza encompasses the **Museo de Historia,** the Hotel Ceballos and a handful of stores and sandwich shops. The commercial establishments continue along the pedestrian malls, which radiate from the plaza's corners.

On the east side of the plaza, much of the state government is housed in the **Palacio de Gobierno.** An inviting building with breezy courtyards, the *palacio* also contains a four-wall **mural,** completed in 1954 by Jorge Chávez Carrillo in honor of the bicentennial of Hidalgo's birth. The intricate mural, covering the walls of the staircase closest to the Pl. Principal, moves counterclockwise through Mexico's tumultuous history. The staff the **information booth** at the foot of the stairs doesn't speak much English, but the free lecture on the mural (about 15min.) is thorough and interesting. Anglophones get an abbreviated version (booth staffed Mon.-Fri. 9am-3pm).

Adjoining Colima's municipal complex is the renovated colonial **Santa Iglesia Cathedral.** The Spanish first built a church on this spot in 1527, but an earthquake destroyed the original structure of wood and palm, and fire consumed its replacement. They had the gall to build another one. To this day the paintings of the evangelists bear scars from the earthquakes and volcanic eruptions of 1900, 1932, and 1941. The cathedral is still the most striking building in Colima, and the fading paint of its dome and towers does little to decrease its grandeur. The Neoclassical interior glitters with gilt paint, chandeliers and polished marble. In the pulpit designed by Othón Bustos rests a statue of San Felipe de Jesús, the city's patron saint. (Open daily 8am-9pm. Avoid visiting during services.)

Colima's **Museo de Las Culturas de Occidente** (tel. 2-31-55), is an excellent museum devoted to pre-Columbian art from the area. Rarely seen outside the state, the Colima ceramic figurines are among the most playful and captivating artifacts in Mexico. To get there take the bus towards University of Colima from Av. Rey Colimán. Open Tues.-Sun. 7am-9pm.

Colima's newest museum, the **Museo de Historia,** is at 16 de Septiembre and Reforma on the south side of the Pl. Principal, and houses a small collection of pre-Columbian ceramics, in addition to a gallery devoted to contemporary works by local artists. (Open Mon.-Sat. 10am-2pm and 4-8pm, Sun. 5-8pm. Free.) Colima's **Museo Universitario de Culturas Populares,** at Manuel Gallardo and 27 de Septiembre, has a very small informal museum and gift shop with handmade reproductions of local ceramics. (Open Mon.-Sat. 9am-2pm and 4-7pm.) A far more extensive collection of pre-Columbian artifacts from the region are displayed at the **Museo de Cultura y Arte Popular,** part of the Universidad de Bellas Artes (tel. 2-29-90) at 27 de Septiembre and Gallard Azmoro. The collection is dominated by figurines recovered from nearby tombs, and, if you can read Spanish and dig archaeology, the descriptions of the pre-Aztec western coast serves as a useful complement to the pieces. (Open daily 9am-7:30pm. Free.) Catch the "Nte." bus (.60 pesos) from the Gran Flamingo and get off on the corner of 27 de Septiembre and San Fernando. Mural fanatics also may wish to investigate two other wall pieces at the University of Colima's **Rectoría.** The first is at the Rectoría bus stop (route "Sur" or "Norte," .50 pesos), completed in 1989 entirely with naturally colored pebbles. The second is inside the Rectoría itself.

The church of **San Francisco** (on bus #5 route), with its brick, circular nave and simple interior, sits amidst the ruins of the first church erected in Colima by the Spanish and a host of *primavera* trees that bloom a vibrant yellow in March. (Open daily 10-11:30am and 5-8pm.) Also of note are the churches of **San José,** on Quintero just a short walk up Madero from the Pl. Principal, which is the focus of a scenic well-to-do colonial neighborhood; and **El Sagrado Corazón,** on the corner of 27 de Septiembre and Aldama, known for its beautiful interior and stained glass. (Open 9am-2pm and 4-8pm.)

Beyond the city to the southeast (also visible from the top of the cathedral) rises **Colina La Cumbre.** The chapel on its summit is open to "the entire brotherhood of man" (women included)—but only on the eighth day of each month. The chapel and its grounds are a popular site for picnics. Seek access to the hill via any bus to Pihuamo or Tepames from the suburban bus stop (1 peso; see Orientation); just ask for La Cumbre. Remember to bring your own drinking water.

■ Near Colima

In Nahuatl, Colima means "place where the old god is dominant." The old god is **El Volcán de Fuego** (3820m). Recorded eruptions date back to the pre-Conquest era, and today El Fuego emits frequent puffs of smoke and steam to assert its status as the only active volcano in Mexico. **El Nevado de Colima** (4240m), stands taller than its neighbor but is dormant and not much fun at parties. Guadalajara-bound *locales* (from the new bus station) pass through the town of **Atenquique,** 57km away. From here a 27km unimproved dirt road runs to the summit of El Fuego. The trip is only recommended for four-wheel-drive vehicles, though logging trucks based at the factory in Atenquique make trips up this road to spots near the summit. Almost at the top of El Fuego is the **Joya Cabin,** which lacks all amenities except a roof. Because of the frequency of volcanic activity, the park is only open sporadically; if you're planning a trip to the top, call the **police** ahead of time (tel. 2-18-01 or 2-64-00). The twin peak, **El Nevado,** can also be climbed. Buses from **Guzmán** (83km away) limp up to **Joya,** whence you can make your epic assault on the summit.

If you don't mind a few insects and just have to get away from it all, think about going to **Laguna Carrizalillo,** 12km north of Comala. Visitors come to sit in the pervading peace. **Bungalows** with kitchens and fire-places are available (quads 7 pesos). **Laguna La María** is larger, closer to the volcanoes and more visited, so options for accommodations are diverse. (*Cabañas* for 6 with a full kitchen 96 pesos; no kitchen, 21 pesos.) **Buses** (2.50 pesos) marked "La Becerrera" for La María leave Colima's suburban bus station daily at 7am, 1pm and 5pm, but the schedule is not strictly adhered to, especially returning to Colima (official times 7:30am, 2pm and 4:30pm). To make accommodations reservations at Carrizalillo or La María, ask at the Colima **tourist office** (tel. 2-40-60).

If your hotel rooms lack hot water, find some at **El Hervidero,** 35km to the east. The thermal waters there (77°F) are said to have medicinal properties. Closer to town, the spring at **Agua Caliente** (17km east) bubbles away, but the swimming doesn't rival El Hervidero's. To get to either pool, catch the "Pihuamo" bus from the suburban station (4 per day, returning 2hrs. later). At the *crucero* of Agua Caliente (2.50 pesos from town), a dirt road leads through 2km of ranch land before reaching the yellow waters. Follow it straight ahead (there are a number of forks and intersections) despite your best instincts (ignore the cows). El Hervidero is 6km from **Puerto de Anzar,** the closest point to the spring on the bus route (4 pesos to this hamlet). From there a nice hike separates you from soothing heat. It is best, at any time of year, to ask a local whether it is possible to reach these springs before setting off.

A small colony of *indígena* artisans thrives 9km north of Colima in **Comala** where the *tianguis* (*indígena* market) sells bamboo baskets, clocks and wooden furniture on Mondays from 8am to 3pm. The town's **church,** at Degollado and Madero on the *zócalo*, supports a thriving population of bats who have free run of the nave. There is a row of popular restaurants on the south side of the *zócalo;* a nice place to enjoy the afternoons. Buses to Comala leave Colima's suburban bus station (every 15min. 6am-10pm, 1.20 pesos).

AGUASCALIENTES

■■■ AGUASCALIENTES

The capital city of Aguascalientes lies in the center of the state of the same name. Rich soil and abundant spring water (much of which is naturally hot, giving the area its composite name, meaning "hot waters") make this area ideal for agriculture. Little has disrupted Aguascalientes over its 400-year history. The signing of the Convention of Aguascalientes, which united Villa and Zapata in their ill-fated alliance against Carranza during the revolution, was the city's cameo in the drama of history. Today, Aguascalientes is a huge, sleepy industrial and agricultural town, relatively uninteresting to the casual visitor.

The most worthwhile stop in town is the **Museo de Guadalupe Posada.** Its namesake, an engraver and cartoonist, helped turn public opinion against Porfirio Díaz at the end of the dictator's reign. The museum, which exhibits Posada's engravings and caricatures of Díaz, sits on León next to the Templo del Encino, 4 blocks south of López Mateos. (Open Tues.-Sun. 10am-2pm and 4-8pm. Free.) The charming **Basílica de la Asunción de las Aguascalientes** (open daily 6am-9pm) and the **Palacio de Gobierno** (open Mon.-Fri. 8am-9pm), on the Pl. de la Patria, will satisfy desperate colonial history buffs wandering up from the Bajío. Inside the Palacio courtyard is a mural painted in 1961 by Osvaido Barra Cunighan, part of which portrays the atrocious condition of *indígena* miners at La Mina de Edén. From March 10 to April 15, visitors pour into Aguascalientes to witness the annual **Feria de San Marcos.** Make hotel reservations at least a month in advance.

Though Aguascalientes has the full range of hotels, **accommodations** are inexplicably expensive near the bus station, especially since there is nothing there but *torta* stands and concrete. An exception to this rule is the **Hotel Continental** (tel. 15-55-48) on Brasil (the side street on the left directly as you leave the station) at the corner with Guatemala. The simple rooms have TVs and closets, and the bathrooms gush hot water. The restaurant dishes up huge quantities of burritos for a mere 5 pesos. (Singles 38 pesos. Doubles 45 pesos.) Closer to the *centro* there are a few affordable options. **Hotel Senioral,** Colon 104 (tel. 15-16-30) has clean pleasant rooms, those overlooking the Plaza de Patria with door-size windows. (Singles 40 pesos. Doubles 52 pesos.) On the other side of the plaza, across the street from cathedral, is **Hotel Rosales,** Guadalupe Victoria 108 (tel. 15-21-65). The plants in the old, dark courtyard areas are as dusty as the rooms and the bathrooms could be cleaner. (Singles 40 pesos. Doubles 50 pesos.)

Aguascalientes does not offer great variety in the way of **food**. Small stands line the pedestrian walkways —especially Juárez— and fresh produce can be bought of at the **mercado** on 5 de Mayo. For the hungry, the **Pizza Palace,** López Mateos 207, has an all-you-can-scarf buffet of pizza, spaghetti, burgers, and salad daily noon-5pm (13 pesos). Pizzas start at 9 pesos. (Open daily 11am-1am.) Near the plaza, at Madero 220, is **Mitla.** Management encompasses three generations of the same family. Wood paneling and waiters in white jackets. *Huevo* for 7.50 pesos, enchiladas at 13 pesos.

Shake it all night long with the locals at **Disco El Cabus,** Blvd. Zacateca at Campestre (tel. 8-28-80), in the Hotel Las Trojes. (Beer 6 pesos. Cover 35 pesos. Open Thurs.-Sun. 9pm-2am.) Check out the raucous laser light at **Fantasy,** Ayuntamiento 117-201 (tel. 6-82-02). Mixed drinks will set you back about 8 pesos. (Cover about 20 pesos. Open Thurs.-Sat. 9pm-2am.) Both spots are 18 and over, and men must wear pants.

Aguascalientes is 168km west of San Luis Potosí, 128km south of Zacatecas and 252km northeast of Guadalajara. **Avenida Circunvalación** encircles the city; **Avenida López Mateos** cuts through town on an east-west slant. The **bus station** is a few blocks west on Av. Circunvalación from the north-south Av. José María Chávez. "Centro" buses (.70 pesos) run from outside the bus station to the Mercado Morelos, two blocks north (on Morelos) of the central **Plaza de Patria.** To get back, "Central Camionera" buses traverse the length of Rivero y Gutiérrez (parallel to and 1 block north of Madero). Taxis cost about 5 pesos to the center.

The **tourist office** is located at Pl. Patria 141 (tel. 15-11-55), in the first floor of the *zócalo* de Gobierno. Comprehensive maps of the city and English brochures covering just about every state. Open Mon.-Fri. 8am-3pm and 5-8pm, Sat. 10am-1pm. **Currency Exchange:** Bánamex, 5 de Mayo, at the Pl. de la Patria. Open Mon.-Fri. 9am-1:30pm. The **post office** is at Hospitalidad 108 (tel. 5-21-18), 1 block east of the plaza on Madero, then left on Morelos and right on Hospitalidad. Open for stamps and *Lista de Correos* Mon.-Fri. 8am-5pm, Sat.-Sun. 9am-1pm. **Police**: López Mateos at Héroes de Nacozari (tel. 15-41-75), or tel. 06 for emergencies.

SAN LUIS POTOSÍ

■■■ SAN LUIS POTOSÍ

A sprawling, urban capital of 80,000 people, San Luis Potosí advertises itself as "The City of Plazas" and indeed it does have three splendid central plazas. Unfortunately, the charm and colonial architecture of these quiet plazas is not reflected in the rest of city. Elsewhere the streets are lined with modern buildings, bargain department stores, and street vendors selling mostly plastic goods.

Founded in 1592, San Luis Potosí was named to honor Louis, King of France. After the Spaniards learned from the Huachichiles of the rich mines in the region, the word "Potosí" was appended because the city's mineral wealth was comparable to that of Potosí in Bolivia. Gold and silver helped make San Luis Potosí one of the three most important cities in Mexico during the 17th century, when it had jurisdiction over most of northern Mexico, including Texas and Louisiana.

ORIENTATION AND PRACTICAL INFORMATION

San Luis Potosí is at the approximate center of a triangle of Mexico's largest cities—Monterrey, Guadalajara and Mexico City. Five main highways (Rtes. 57, 85, 70, 49, and 80) lead into San Luis Potosí.

To get downtown from the bus station catch an "Alameda" or "Centro" **bus** (.50 pesos) and get off at **Parque Alameda**, the first big stretch of green after the railway tracks. Always confirm the destination because drivers are sometimes fail to change their windshield signs and your bus could be headed for Timbuktu even if it says "Centro." **Taxis** to *el centro* cost 7 pesos.

San Luis' main drag is **Avenida Carranza,** which runs east-west and passes the north side of the **Plaza de Armas,** the city's historic center, east of which it answers to **Los Bravos. Madero,** parallel to Carranza/Los Bravos and one block south, is another important thoroughfare. It touches the Plaza de Armas's south side, east of which it goes by **Othón.** Two blocks east of the plaza on this street lies the **Plaza del Carmen.** One block further east lies the *Alameda*, where the bus from the station leaves visitors. The train station is on Othón opposite the *Alameda*.

Tourist Office: Carranza 325 (tel. 12-30-68), to the right of the Hotel Panorama. Just about the swankiest tourist office in Mexico. Helpful staff abound with excellent maps and info. Open Mon.-Sat. 8am-9pm.

U.S. Consulate: Carranza 1430 (tel. 12-15-28), via the "Morelos" bus. Open Mon.-Fri. 9am-noon, but can be reached in the afternoons as well. The police (see below) and the tourist office have consulate employees' home numbers in case of emergency.

Currency Exchange: Many banks around the Pl. de Armas open Mon.-Fri. 9am-noon, including **Banco Mexicano Somex,** Allende at Arista, 2 blocks north of the plaza's northwest corner. **Bancomer,** at Allende and Los Reyes, 3 blocks north of the plaza, open 9am-1:30pm. The *casa de cambio* at Obregón 407 is open Mon.-Fri. 9am-2pm and 4-8pm, Sat. 9am-2pm.

Post Office: Morelos 235 (tel. 2-27-40), between Salazar and Insurgentes, 1 block east and 4 blocks north of Pl. de Armas. *Lista de Correos* posted Mon.-Fri. 8am-2pm. Open Mon.-Fri. 9am-7pm, Sat. 9am-noon. **Postal code:** 78000.

Telephones: Computel, Carranza 360, opposite the Hotel Panorama. International collect calls 2 pesos. Open Mon.-Sat. 7am-10pm. Also try at Los Bravo 423, ½ block west of Constitución. International collect calls 5 pesos per 5 min. Open Mon.-Sat. 9am-8pm. **Telephone code:** 48.

Telegrams: Escobedo 200 (tel. 12-33-18), at the south end of Pl. del Carmen. Open Mon.-Fri. 9am-8pm, Sat. 9am-noon.

Airport: (tel. 2-00-95), Served by **Mexicana,** Madero at Uresti. Flights to: Mexico City, Monterrey, Chicago. Office open Mon.-Fri. 9am-6pm.

Train Station: On Othón near the middle of the north side of the *Alameda*. To: Mexico City (5:30pm and 10:30am, 6hrs., 45 pesos); Monterrey (5:35am and midnight, 8hrs., 43 pesos); Aguascalientes (noon, 6hrs., 7 pesos).

Bus Station: Central Camionera Plan de San Luis (tel. 12-74-11), 2 blocks south of the Glorieta Benito Juárez, several kms east of the city center along Av. Universidad. 12-odd different bus companies, each serving 15-40 cities. From here you can easily get anywhere in the northern half of the republic. **Transportes Vecedor** goes to Tampico (6 per day, 54 pesos). **ETN** sends first-class buses to Mexico City (about every hr., 70 pesos) and Guadalajara (8 per day, 55 pesos). **Flecha Amarilla** provides second-class service to: Mexico City (8 per day, 36 pesos), Dolores Hidalgo (11 per day, 12.50 pesos), Guanajuato (7 per day, 19 pesos), San Miguel de Allende (5 per day, 16 pesos), and Gogorrón (every 15min., 4.50 pesos). **Estrella Blanca** to Zacatecas (7 per day, 11.50 pesos),

Monterrey (hourly, 45 pesos), and Matamoros (3 per day, 79 pesos). **Autobuses Rojos** head for Santa María del Río (every hr., 6:30am-11:30pm, 3.80 pesos).

Taxis: tel. 12-21-22.

Car Rental: Budget, Carranza 885A (tel. 14-50-59).

Car Trouble: Ángeles Verdes Auxilio Turístico, Jardín Guerrero 14 (tel. 14-09-06).

Laundromat: Lavandería La Burbuja, Nicolás Zapata 535. 4kg load costs 14 pesos and takes 2hrs. Open Mon.-Sat. 9am-7pm.

Red Cross: Juárez at Díaz Gutiérrez (tel. 15-33-22 or 15-36-35).

Pharmacy: Farmacia Impina, Carranza 326 (tel.12-77-75). Open daily 8am-10pm.

Hospital: Hospital Central, Carranza 2395 (tel. 13-03-43 or 13-43-95), several km west of *el centro* along Carranza, on the west side of the city.

Police: Palacio Municipal (tel. 12-28-04 or 12-54-76).

ACCOMMODATIONS

Try to avoid all lodgings near the bus station: the neighborhood is sleazy and you'll get better deals closer to the center of the city. But if proximity to the bus station is a priority, stay at **CREA Youth Hostel (HI)** (tel. 12-66-03 or 2-11-51), on Diagonal Sur in front of Glorieta Benito Juárez, 2 blocks straight ahead as you exit the bus station. Tiny 4-person rooms with uncomfortable beds and unbearable mosquitoes, but everything is clean, including the communal bathrooms. Separate women's and men's areas. Access to sports complex with basketball courts, soccer fields, swimming pool, and track. (11pm curfew. 11 pesos per person, 1 peso discount with CREA, HI, or AYH card. Blankets, sheets, pillowcase, towel and locker included. Breakfast an additional 9 pesos, lunch and dinner 11.50 pesos.)

Hotel de Gante, 5 de Mayo 140 (tel. 12-14-93). By far the nicest hotel for the money. Impeccable rooms with phones, TVs and the occasional bathtub or view of the plaza. Singles 54 pesos. Doubles 64 pesos.

Hotel Plaza, Jardín Hidalgo (tel. 12-46-31), on the south side of the Pl. de Armas, next to Sears. Respectful and helpful older staff. Rooms have a certain faded charm. Rooms with plaza views a clear cut above the rest. Singles 45 pesos. Doubles 55 pesos.

Hotel Principal, Juan Sarabía 145 (tel. 12-07-84), ½ block from Pl. San Juan. Near Juan Sarabía and Plaza del Carmen. Don't be put off by the uninviting exterior. The rooms are clean and basic, management elderly and poetic. Singles 30 pesos. Doubles 40 pesos.

FOOD

For some reason all the restaurants in this town look like they belong in airports or bus depots, with prices to match. There are several dishes that are particular to San Luis Potosí. *Taquitos dorados* are thin slices of chicken or beef rolled in corn tortillas and deep-fried; *tacos potosinos* are stuffed with cheese and vegetables. *Enchiladas potosinas* are filled with cheese, red chiles and onions, sometimes smothered in more cheese. Delicious *nopalitos* are tiny pieces of cactus cooked in a tomato, oregano and onion sauce. *Cabuches* are small, yellow cactus fruit, served in a *ranchero* sauce. As unusual as it sounds, *chongos coronados* (curdled milk in sweet maple water) is a popular dessert.

La Conicute, Carranza 700 (tel. 12-93-04). High ceilings, heavy wooden tables, Mexican tiles, hanging plants, and colored ceramic plates. Great Mexican and *potosino* dishes for around 28 pesos. *Comida corriente* 15 pesos. Open daily 8am-midnight.

Restaurante Posada del Virrey-Cafetería, Jardín Hidalgo 3 (tel. 12-70-55), on the north side of Pl. de Armas. This popular restaurant in the plaza is housed in a building that was once the home of Mexico's only female viceroy. 7 kinds of beer in huge, frosty mugs 3.50 pesos each. Breakfasts 15-20 pesos. Spanish chicken 17 pesos. Open daily 8am-11pm.

Mac's (tel. 14-18-63), across the street from the Cathedral. Mock wooden tables but real wood chairs with leather seats, orange stucco partitions, and waitresses in pink diner outfits. Buffet breakfast of coffee and 4 different *platillos* 13 pesos, banana split 9 pesos. Open daily 8am-10:30pm.

Torteria Nueva, Allende 220 (tel. 12-77-80). Your basic sandwich plate but bigger, always crowded, and slightly classier. *Tortas* 5 pesos. Enchiladas 9 pesos. Makes deliveries. Open Mon.-Sat. 8am-9pm. For slightly longer hours and Sunday service try the somewhat more expensive Las Tortas on the corner.

Rendez Vous, Carranza 315 (tel. 12-17-77). This square, airport-style restaurant (two walls filled with pictures of Paris) attracts an older professional crowd discussing the nuances of life in San Luis. Somewhat less expensive than many of its look-alikes. *Menú del día* 16 pesos, breakfast 7-15 pesos, cappuccino 2.50 pesos. Open daily 7am-10:30pm.

Restaurante La Parroquia, Carranza 301 (tel. 12-66-81), on the south side of Pl. de los Fundadores. An interior reminiscent of a bus terminal cafeteria—the lunchtime traffic is about as heavy. Booths have great people-watching potential. Breakfasts 10-20 pesos, *tacos de pollo* 12 pesos. Open daily 8:30am-10pm.

SIGHTS AND ENTERTAINMENT

Often called the "City of Plazas," San Luis Potosí has three main plazas, the most central of which is the **Plaza de Armas** (also known as **Jardín Hidalgo**). At the beginning of the 17th century, residents watched bullfights in the dusty plaza from the balconies of the surrounding buildings. Now you can watch a red sandstone gazebo, completed in 1848, that bears the names of famous Mexican musicians.

From the **Palacio de Gobierno,** on the west side of the Pl. de Armas, Benito Juárez dispatched assassins to murder Emperor Maximilian. Maximilian, Miramón, and Mejí were eventually executed on June 19, 1867, near Querétaro, the imperial stronghold established after General Bazaine abandoned the country. On the second floor, in the **Sala Juárez,** is a diorama of the dramatic meeting between Juárez and Princess Salm Salm, who begged Juárez for Maximilian's life on the night before the execution. Plastic figures of the unmoved Juárez and the beautiful princess are positioned in front of the table at which Juárez signed Maximilian's sentence. The *sala* also contains a mask and a portrait of the President. As you enter the palace, go upstairs and turn left at the top of the staircase—the Sala Juárez is the first room on your left. (No fixed hours, but usually open Mon.-Fri. 9:30am-3pm.)

Opposite the Palacio de Gobierno stands the **cathedral,** its two towers crowned at night by blue neon crosses. The cathedral was completed in 1710, but in 1855, when San Luis became a diocese, the building was "upgraded." Miners are said to have donated gold and silver to beautify the interior, and marble statues of the apostles (small copies of those at the Basilica of San Juan de Letrán in Rome) were placed in the niches between the Solomonic columns of the baroque facade. The northern gray sandstone tower was built at the beginning of this century to commemorate the centennial of Mexico's independence. (Open daily 8am-7pm. The religious community of San Luis is particularly concerned that tourists not visit on Sundays or during mass.)

The **Palacio Municipal,** on the northeast corner of the plaza, was rebuilt after local citizens torched the original structure to protest Carlos III's expulsion of the Jesuits from the Americas. It boasts a traditional red stone courtyard with painted stairwell and simple mosaic steps. One block west of the southwest corner of the Pl. de Armas is the **Antigua Real Caja** (Old Royal Treasury), the city's only existing secular baroque building. With its truncated corner facade, the building belongs now to the Universidad Autónoma de San Luis Potosí.

East of the Pl. de Armas on Othón is the modest **Casa Othón,** home of the illustrious *poeta potosino* Manuel José Othón (1858-1906). The house has been restored to its original state and contains a collection of original works, photographs and documents relating to the poet. (Open Tues.-Fri. 8am-2pm and 4-6pm, Sat.-Sun.

10am-2pm. Free.) One block further east on Othón is the **Plaza de Carmen,** with its elaborate fountain supported by bronze fish.

Nicolás Fernando de Torres, a rich *Sevillano* of the early 18th century, made his fortune in San Luis Potosí. After his death, his estate was used to found a church and convent of the ascetic Carmelite order. The complex encompassed a large area, but today only the **Iglesia del Carmen** remains on the northwest corner of the plaza of the same name. In the opinion of many *potosinos*, the church is the most beautiful religious building in the city. Affixed to the facade are statues of San Eliseo, San Elías and, at the very top, the Madonna. The main altar was reconstructed with sandstone by architect Tresguerras after the original was destroyed in 1827. (Open daily 7:30am-1:30pm and 4-9pm. Again, avoid visiting during religious ceremonies.)

The colorful **Museo Nacional de la Máscara,** Villerías 2 (tel. 230-25), is in the Palacio Federal, ½ block south of the Pl. del Carmen along Villerías. This beautiful building of pink sandstone contains hundreds of masks from every Mexican region. An eloquent diatribe against cultural Eurocentrism opens this remarkable exhibit. (Open Tues.-Fri. 10am-2pm and 4-6pm, Sat.-Sun. 10am-2pm. Free.)

Two blocks south and one block west from the Pl. de Armas's southwest corner is the **Plaza de San Francisco,** with its own bronze fountain, quaint cobblestone street and red sandstone buildings. Eight years after the city's founding, construction began on the **Iglesia de San Francisco,** on the west side of the plaza. Less ornate than its local counterparts, the orange stucco facade boasts a Sevillian clock (1785) and statues of St. Francis. Inside, the doorway to the Salón de Profundis depicts St. Frailón washing the sacred cuts of St. Francis. A wonderful Churrigueresque fountain dominates this room where Franciscans are said to have chanted the *De Profundis* each morning. (Open daily 8am-7pm.) The **Plaza de Aranzazu** (or western Pl. de San Francisco) is a simple plaza that sits at the end of cobbled Universidad.

The **Museo Regional Potosino,** Galeana 450 (tel. 12-51-85), along the street on San Francisco's southern side, occupies the former Franciscan convent grounds. The government seized the land in 1950 and converted part of it into the museum. Inside on the museum's first floor is the marvelous **Capilla a la Virgen de Aranzazu.** *Aranzazu* means "from within the thorns"—a shepherd found the altar's image of the Virgin in a prickly thicket. The *ex-votos* along the walls are a tradition among Mexico's faithful; each depicts a miracle that a parishioner has experienced. They are often painted anonymously and hung in the church near an image of the Virgin Mary. A huge 18th-century hymnal stands to the right of the altar and next to the bishop's sedan chair. (Museum open Tues.-Fri. 8am-2pm and 4-6pm, Sat.-Sun. 10am-2pm.)

Archaeological exhibits on the first floor consist of artifacts from different parts of the country: two *yogos*, large stone rings placed around people's heads for burial; the dress of modern *indígenas*; and artifacts from San Luis Potosí's colonial past–boxes, locks, irons, spears, branding irons, daggers and 12th-century chain mail. (Museum open Tues.-Sat. 10am-6pm, Sun. 10am-2pm. Free.) Three blocks east along Manuel Othón from the Pl. de Armas is the expansive **Alameda Juan Sarabía** with its trees, benches, statues, and artificial ponds, but beware: the area is dangerous at night. A San Luis Potosí anomaly erupts on park's south side. The **Centro de Difusión Cultural** of the Instituto Potosino de Bellas Artes, Av. Universidad and Negrete (tel. 2-43-33), is not a graceful colonial edifice but a modern structure of bold curves and concrete. The museum devotes four large halls to contemporary artists, while caretakers provide New Age music to complete the mood. (Open Tues.-Sat. 10am-2pm and 5-8pm, Sun 10am-2pm and 6-8pm.)

The **Parque Tangamanga** has it all: three lakes for paddle-boating and fishing; a baseball field; motor-cross, auto-cross, and bike-cross grounds; a running path; and a playground complete with electric cars. Other park facilities include a planetarium, an observatory, and the open-air **Teatro de la Ciudad,** which hosts frequent cultural and artistic events (information at tourist office). To get to the park, catch a yellow and blue Perimetral bus (.80 pesos) on Constitución across the *Alameda*. Get off at the Monumento a la Revolución. (Open daily 9am-6pm. Free.)

Chic *potosinos* insist that **Arushal,** Muñoz 195 (tel. 17-42-30), is the best club in town. The decor almost matches its namesake, a city in Tanzania. A gigantic elephant's head (fake), some stuffed animals (real), and incredible lights and sound create quite a *selva* (jungle) mood. (Cover 25 pesos, drinks 7 pesos, and the usual dress required–no shorts, sandals, or sneakers. Open Thurs.-Sat. 9pm-3am.) **Oasis,** on the highway to Mexico City, is somewhat more intimate and also much beloved. (Cover 25 pesos. Open Thurs.-Sat. 8pm-2am.) Taxis after dark to either place cost 10 pesos.

The last two weeks of August mark the **Fiesta Nacional Potosina.** Concerts, cock and bullfights, fireworks, and a parade guarantee a swell time for all.

■ Near San Luis Potosí

Santa María del Río, 45 minutes south of San Luis, is the state's renowned *rebozo* (shawl) capital. The **Escuela de Artesanías** here has a wide selection, but the best of the best are made in private homes. Ask one of the instructors or administrators in the school to direct you to private craftspeople. (See San Luis Potosí: Bus Station above for transport details.)

Also south of San Luis is the state-run and reasonably priced resort of **Gogorrón.** Make reservations at the office of Centro Vacacional Gogorrón in the Edificio San Rafael, Othón and Zaragoza, 4th floor (tel. 14-66-55 or 12-36-36). Guests enjoy the waters of the hot spring, even hotter Roman baths, and swimming pools. Staying the night in this facility is an expensive but restorative way to end an extended low-budget stay in Mexico. (*Cabañas chicas* 124 pesos, 34 pesos per additional person; 3 meals and bath included.) For daytrippers, the Roman baths cost 8 pesos per hour. Use of the other facilities costs only 6 pesos per day, including access to the pool and shower. **Flecha Amarilla** buses (3 pesos) leave for Gogorrón every ½ hour from San Luis Potosí bus station. If you're driving, take the highway to Querétaro, go right at the sign that says Villa de Reyes and proceed 19km to Gogorrón. All reservations and arrangements should be made at the San Luis office.

There are also mineral springs at **Ojo Caliente,** 40km south of San Luis Potosí on Hwy. 57 to Querétaro and at Lourdes, 64km from San Luis Potosí on Hwy 57. Agua de Lourdes supposedly cures all ills, especially gastric and intestinal ones, and is sold in take-home bottles in case the baths fail to heal you on the spot. A small hotel here serves meals. (For reservations call (48) 17-14-04 from San Luis Potosí or go in person to the Lourdes office at Francisco Zarco 389.)

El Bajío

A vast, bowl-shaped plateau of fertile soil, rolling farms and verdant hillsides stands slightly below central Mexico's volcanic range. However, it was the rich underground that has brought prosperity to the region since the 16th century: silver. For nearly four centuries, the mineral wealth of the Bajío has determined the course of its history. The area's richest mines—Real de Santa Fe, Real de Rayas, and Real de San Bernabé—had been discovered by the local aristocracy by 1550, but it was not until 1750, when the silver trade was rerouted to Mexico City, that Bajío's cities rose to be among the wealthiest and most influential in Mexico. As the city of Guanajuato began to supply most of the country's minting silver, it became the commercial and banking center of this thriving region, trading manufactured goods for crops from the nearby agricultural towns of Salamanca, Irapuato, León, San Miguel and Celaya.

The Bajío has long been a favorite destination for questing U.S. expatriates because of its vibrant social life and distinguished history.

GUANAJUATO

GUANAJUATO

Guanajuato's history has been molded by economic success and historical tragedy. In 1558, incredible veins of silver were discovered in the area; veins which, over the next 200 years, would produce much of the world's silver supply and make Guanajuato one of Mexico's richest and most important cities.

After amassing its wealth under Spanish domination, however, Guanajuato led the way in the fight for independence. When King Carlos III raised taxes in 1765 and cut the landowners' and miners' share of silver profits, Guanajuato protested. When he banished the Jesuits from Latin America in 1767, Guanajuato, where the Jesuits had just completed their Templo de la Compañía, was outraged. During Hidalgo's stop here in 1810, sons of both the wealthy *guanajuatense* landowners and poor mine workers helped him overrun the Spaniards' stronghold at Alhóndiga de Granaditas. The loyalist Colonel Calleja then marched from Mexico City to make an example of Guanajuato. Calleja reclaimed the city from the rebels, ordered scaffolds built in all the plazas and began a gruesome "lottery of death," in which names were randomly drawn from a sombrero and citizens hanged as a lesson to those who dared to rise against the Spanish Empire.

The colonial silver barons also left behind a less political legacy—Guanajuato overflows with beautiful monuments to their ostentation. Guanajuato is also the birthplace of muralist Diego Rivera, whose earliest works are infused with impressions of the city. Today, the city supports five outstanding museums, several film clubs and four theaters. During the **Festival Internacional Cervantino,** held in October in honor of the author of *Don Quijote*, Guanajuato sponsors performances of drama, classical music, and ballet in an atmosphere of Dionysian debauchery. Guanajuato's university students and numerous musicians provide an animated and youthful social life, which keeps even older folks awake.

ORIENTATION

The city of Guanajuato is in the center of Guanajuato state, 54km southwest of Dolores Hidalgo and 44km north of Irapuato. The shortest way from Mexico City is via that wonderful burg Celaya on Rte. 57/45. León and Irapuato have become the state's main crossroads, with many bus connections to Guanajuato from either of these cities. Guanajuato's **bus station** is about 3km west of town. From the bus station catch the "El Centro" bus (.80 pesos) or take a taxi for considerably more money (8 pesos).

In Guanajuato, accurate maps are almost impossible to find, few streets are open to traffic, and still fewer follow a linear path. The best map on record can be purchased at the offices of INEGI, on the third floor in the same white building as the Agora Restaurant, on Allende near the **Jardín Unión** (though it is expensive). At the center of the city are the **Plaza de la Paz** and the imposing **basilica. Avenida Juárez** zigzags in a westerly direction from here to the market, the tourist office and the bus station; to the east of the plaza, it is called **Avenida Sopeña.** Roughly following the path of Juárez/Sopeña, the **Subterránea** is an underground avenue constructed between 1963 and 1966 beneath the former bed of the Río Guanajuato, which now flows in an adjacent concrete channel. On the surface, innumerable alleys branch off Juárez/Sopeña. When you become lost (a fact, not a possibility), remember that the avenue is always downhill from where you are. Because of the topography, only one or two streets with automobile traffic run north-south for more than a couple of blocks. Buses (.80 pesos) cross the city both on the surface and underground; service terminates at 10pm. To get to destinations that buses don't reach, taxis run for 4-8 pesos.

PRACTICAL INFORMATION

Tourist Office: Dirección General de Turismo, Juárez at Pl. de la Paz (tel. 2-00-86). A poor map and useless brochures, but some helpful verbal information. They sell better literature for 4-5 pesos. Open Mon.-Fri. 8am-7:30pm, Sat.-Sun. 10am-2pm.

Currency Exchange: Banks line Juárez and the Pl. de la Paz, but many exchange currency only Mon.-Fri. 9:30am-12:30pm. The best hours are at **Banco Mexicano Somex,** Sopeña 18, 1 block east of the Teatro Juárez. Open for exchange Mon.-Fri. 9am-1:30pm. There are no *casas de cambio*, but some restaurants and hotels change U.S. dollars.

Post Office: Ayuntamiento (tel. 2-03-85), down the street from the Universidad de Guanajuato. Open for stamps and *Lista de Correos* Mon.-Fri. 8am-8pm, Sat. 9am-1pm; for registered mail Mon.-Fri. 9am-6pm, Sat. 9-11:30am. **Postal code:** 37700.

Telephones: Lonchería y Caseta de Larga Distancia Pípila, Alonso 14 (tel. 2-09-83), down the street from Casa Kloster. International collect calls 3000 pesos. Open Mon.-Sat. 9:30am-9:30pm, Sun. no fixed hours. Another *caseta de larga distancia* on 28 de Septiembre, near the Museo de la Alhóndiga. Collect calls 5 pesos. Open 9am-9:30pm. **Telephone code:** 473.

Telegrams: Sopeña 1 (tel. 2-04-29), to the left of the Teatro Juárez. Open Mon.-Sat. 9am-8pm.

Bus Station: Central de Autobuses, west of the *centro*. **Flecha Amarilla** to San Miguel de Allende (9 per day, 6.50 pesos), Morelia (every hr. 6:30am-7:40pm, 14.50 pesos), San Luis Potosí (5 per day, 10.50 pesos), Aguascalientes (6 per day, 15 pesos), Dolores Hidalgo (every 20min., 3.50 pesos), Mexico City (3 per day, 42 pesos), and to the Monumento a Cristo Rey (5 per day, 4 pesos). **Estrella Blanca.** 1st class to Monterrey (2 per day, 60 pesos) and Guadalajara (3 per day, 23 pesos). Other carriers: **Servicios Coordinados, Tres Estrellas de Oro,** and **Omnibus de México.**

Laundromat: Lavandería Automática, Manuel Doblado 28 (tel. 2-67-18). Wash 5 pesos. Dry 5 pesos. Open 8am-8:15pm.

Red Cross: (Tel. 2-04-87), on Juárez west of the market.

Pharmacy: Farmacia La Perla de Guanajuato, Juárez 146 (tel. 2-11-75). Makes deliveries. Open daily 9am-9pm.

Hospital: Moving near bus station in summer of 1993, contact police or tourist office for number.

Police: Alhóndiga 8 (tel. 2-02-66 or 2-27-17), 1 block from Juárez.

ACCOMMODATIONS

The neighborhood around the *basílica* is the quietest and also the prettiest. If you're coming for the Festival Cervantino, it is best to make reservations in advance.

Casa Kloster, Alonso 32 (tel. 2-00-88). From the *basílica* take a right just after the tourist office, then another right on Alonso. The best deal in town. Modern, spotless, tiled communal bathrooms. Rooms surround an open courtyard filled with flowers, plants and birds. Ebullient guests. Very popular with longer-term travelers. 25 pesos per person.

Hotel Posada San Francisco, Juárez at Gavira (tel. 2-20-84), next to the market. Dark and narrow lobby, proudly sporting letters of appreciation from government officials, gives way to dark, but clean bedrooms with wood beds, some with balconies. The 2nd floor lounging area offers TV and a suit of armor for your enjoyment. Singles 50 pesos. Doubles 60 pesos.

Hotel Posada La Condesa, Pl. de la Paz 60 (tel. 2-14-62), a block from the *basílica*. The lobby is a wild and crazy mix of neon, a shrine to the Madonna, and rusty suits of armor. The rooms, in need of a paint job, smell like mildew. Singles 30 pesos. Doubles 40 pesos for 1 bed, 70 pesos for 2 beds.

Hotel Central, Juárez 103 (tel. 2-04-60), across the street, 1 block from the market. Clean but small rooms surround a narrow covered courtyard. Many without windows. Singles 50 pesos. Doubles 60 pesos.

FOOD

Although prices tend to rise near the Jardín Unión—due to the high density of *gringos* in the area—there are a number of pleasant, inexpensive restaurants in Guanajuato's numerous plazas and on the streets close to the *basílica*. For cheaper food, try the Mercado Hidalgo with its numerous fruit and taco stands.

Truco No. 7, at (hey!) Truco 7 (tel. 2-83-74), 1st left beyond the *basílica*. High ceilings, local art, fine pottery, jazz, and the long-term *gringo* crowd. Extremely reasonable *comida corrida* (9 pesos) and *huevos* (3-6 pesos), though entrees are more like 20 pesos. Cappuccino 3 pesos. Open daily 8am-11:30pm.

Cafetería y Restaurante Pinguin, *Jardín Unión* (tel. 2-14-14). Excellent central location and extremely low prices make it a great breakfast place, with espresso machine and a bulletin board advertising local cultural events. Clientele a mix of university students and *norteamericanos*. Eggs 3-4 pesos, juices 3 pesos. Open daily 8am-9:30pm.

La Flor Allegre, Pl. San Fernando (upstairs from Pl. de la Paz). This small north american-run restaurant has only a few tables outside. Inside, classical music plays, and on the bright blue walls is a wild collection of posters and a shelf with English language books. *Comida corrida* 8 pesos. Open Fri. and Mon. 2-10pm, Sat.-Sun. 10am-10pm, though somewhat erratic hours.

Café El Retiro, Sopeña 12 (tel. 2-06-22), across from Teatro Juárez. Dark, "romantic" lighting, round tables, round-backed chairs, and incongruously loud music. Primarily a bar, but also serves reasonably-priced food. Big tacos 6.5-10 pesos. *Tortas* 4.5-5.5 pesos. *Comida corrida* 14 pesos. Kitchen open daily 8am-11pm. Bar open until 2am.

La Carreta, Juárez 96 (tel. 2-43-58). Chicken rotisserie outside, wagon wheels, picnic tables, and faded black-and-whites of older Guanajuato inside. If it's too crowded, share a table with other diners. ¼ chicken 7 pesos, brew 3-5 pesos. Open daily 8am-9:30pm.

SIGHTS

Nestled deep in a ravine, Guanajuato's colonial center is a maze of narrow streets, massive stone bridges, and ex-aqueduct walkways. Columns of *cantera verde*—greenish layered stones—mark many of Guanajuato's colonial structures (including the interior of the Alhóndiga de Granaditas and the porch of the Pl. de Roque). At night, guitarists roam the streets, folk groups play in plazas, and bars resound with oldies.

Signs spread throughout the city denote self-guided walking tours. The most popular is "Ruta 2," between Pl. de los Ángeles and the Templo de San Diego. This route takes in the most famous alley in the city, the **Callejón del Beso** (Alley of the Kiss), which at some points is narrower than one meter. Tradition has it that two lovers who lived on opposite sides of the alley were kept apart by their families but could still kiss each other from their balconies.

Museums in Guanajuato explore the historical, the artistic, the monumental and the macabre. Qualifying for the last is the **Museo de las Momias,** next to the city cemetery. The minerals and salty water of Guanajuato's soil naturally mummified the 100-odd corpses now on display in the museum. Exhumation began a century ago when the state government decreed that those in city cemeteries whose relatives did not begin paying crypt rights within two years would have to be disinterred. Somebody decided to put them on exhibit, and before long a lucrative business reared its ugly head. A guide points out the purplish, inflated body of a drowning victim; a woman buried alive, frozen in her attempt to scratch her way out of the coffin; a Chinese woman; two fashionable Frenchmen; a man who died by hanging and another who was stabbed. Some buried babies still wear the colorful attire of saints—they were dressed like St. Martin and St. Joseph to ensure divine intercession on their ride to heaven. The mummies are the most popular sight in Guanajuato, drawing a larger crowd than the unghastly museums downtown. At the exit, vendors hawk morose candy figurines of the most memorable mummies. The museum is west of town; to get there, catch a "Momias" bus (.40 pesos) in front of the Cine or Mercado. (Open daily 9am-6pm. Admission 5 pesos. For those fun vacation slide shows, photo permits cost 3 pesos.)

The **Museo y Casa de Diego Rivera,** Pocitos 47 (tel. 2-11-97), chronicles the life of Guanajuato's most famous native son. While the first floor recreates the Rivera home at the time of Diego's birth, the upper floors are devoted to his paintings and sketches. Arranged chronologically, early works show the influence of Parisian friends like Picasso and Mondigliani, as Spanish landscapes give way to Cubist sketches and elongated nudes. Yet by 1920 and *Paisaje zapatista* ("Zapata Countryside"), the bright colors and simple tones of Rivera's own Mayan-influenced style are evident. Don't miss his outstanding watercolor illustrations for the *Popol Vuh* (sacred book of the Maya), in which he imitates Mayan iconography, and a sketch for a section of the mural commissioned in 1933 by New York's Rockefeller Center (it was destroyed after a portrait of Lenin was discovered in it). A second version now hangs in the Palacio de Bellas Artes in Mexico City. This sketch, which portrays a woman enslaved by a machine with the head of Adolf Hitler, was not incorporated into the final mural. (Open Tues.-Sat. 10am-1:30pm and 4-6:30pm, Sun. 10am-2:30pm. Admission 5 pesos.)

The **Museo de la Alhóndiga de Granaditas,** on Calarza at the west end of Pocitos (tel. 2-11-12), is more conventional. Constructed as a granary between 1797 and 1809, this building witnessed some of the most crucial and bloody battles in the fight for Mexican independence. In 1810, the supporters of Spanish rule locked themselves inside to defend the building against rebels led by the priest Don Miguel Hidalgo y Costilla. The rebels won the battle after an *indígena* mine worker known as Pípila (whose historic importance the giant statue above the city commemorates) strapped a huge slab of stone to his back, rendering him impervious to loyalist musket balls, and set the building's wooden door ablaze. Later that same year, the leaders of the independence movement, among them Hidalgo, Juan Aldama and Ignacio Allende, were captured and decapitated; their heads were strung up from the four corners of the Alhóndiga. Now the Alhóndiga is an ethnographic, archaeological, and historical museum. A chamber on the first floor charts the course of Mexico's nationhood. Other exhibits display *indígena* artisanry of the Bajío region: toys, masks, firecrackers, engraved machetes, tapestries, clay *indígena* deities and odd little candy dolls and sculptures of horse skeletons, to be consumed on *El Día de los Muertos* (Day of the Dead). The hall, containing huge busts of the heroes of independence is stunning, but the museum's finest exhibit—and one of the best historical accounts in any Mexican museum—traces the social history of Guanajuato from the Conquest through the Revolution with texts, illustrations, and local artifacts. Another gallery shows Romualdo García's photographs of Mexican people just before the Revolution of 1910. (Open Tues.-Sat. 10am-2pm and 4-6pm, Sun. 10am-4pm. Admission 10 pesos, free Sun. Photo permit 2 pesos.)

The **Museo del Pueblo de Guanajuato,** Pocitos 7 (tel. 2-29-90), next to the Universidad de Guanajuato, was inaugurated in 1979. It features rotating exhibits of local artwork, 18th-century religious oils, one gallery of colorful pre-Conquest ceramics, and samples of the Bajío's best pottery. Two rooms are dedicated to the work of recent local artists Olga Costa and José Chávez Morado. Chávez Morado has recently finished a new mural in what served as the baroque chapel of this ancient building. The hall, which hosts chamber music concerts, is also decorated by stained glass, murals with *indígena* motifs, and Mexican poetry. (Open Tues.-Sat. 9am-1pm and 4-6:30pm, Sun. 10am-3pm. Admission 5 pesos.)

The new, fascinating, and most single-minded museum in Guanajuato is the **Museo Iconográfico del Quijote,** Manuel Doblado 1 (tel. 2-67-21), east of the *Jardín Unión*. Housed in a gorgeous colonial mansion, its ten big galleries contain over 600 works of art inspired by Cervantes's *Don Quijote*: paintings and sculptures, stained-glass windows, candlesticks, and clocks. Artists like Dalí, Picasso, Daumier and Pedro Coronel have all interpreted Quijote; so have scores of lesser-knowns. (Open Tues.-Sat. 10am-1:30pm and 4-6:30pm, Sun. 10am-2:30pm. Free.)

The **Jardín Unión,** in the heart of the city, one block east of the basilica, is the town's social center. This triangular plaza has shops, cafés, and enough guitar-strumming locals to appease the tourist and student hordes. Looking down on the *Jardín* from the nearby hill is the **Monumento a Pípila,** which commemorates the miner who torched the Alhóndiga's front door. The angry, titanic effigy of Pípila looks most impressive at night, when it is illuminated by spotlights. The patio in front of the statue commands an outstanding view of the city. To reach the statue, follow Sopeña to the east and take the steep Callejón del Calvario to your right across the street from Lavandería El Centro (a 10-min. climb), or hop a bus marked "Pípila" from Pl. de la Paz.

The **Teatro Juárez** (tel. 2-01-83) faces one corner of *Jardín Unión*. After designing the theater to suit his tastes, Porfirio Díaz inaugurated the building in 1903 for a Verdi opera. The Romanesque facade is unabashedly gaudy, consisting of 12 columns, 10 lampposts with multiple branching lights, nine statues of muses standing loftily on the cornices, and two bronze lions. The auditorium betrays its Moorish design: half-circles, Arabesques, and endlessly weaving frescoed flowers in green, red, yellow, and brown make the interior look like a gigantic Arabian carpet. Imported materials, such as embellished metal and textiles from France and stained glass from Italy, abound in the smoking rooms, bar, and corridors. On one stairway, a rich painting depicts the old emblem of Guanajuato—a blindfolded virgin who stands for unconditional faith. The blindfold was removed by revolutionaries to signify that the Porfiriato could no longer deceive the people with illusions of fortune and progress. The Teatro Juárez still hosts plays, governmental offices, and the main events of the Festival Cervantino. (Open Tues.-Sun. 9:15am-1:45pm and 5-7:45pm. Admission 3 pesos. Camera permit 1.50 pesos.)

Another self-aggrandizing Porfirian edifice is the **Palacio Legislativo de la Paz,** the state capital, across from the Posada de la Condesa near the basilica. Christened by Díaz in 1900, the building is an adaptation of the Greek Parthenon. Italian marble, wall and floor mosaics, and a decorative zinc ceiling ornament the interior. (Open for viewing Mon.-Fri. 10am-5pm, extended and weekend hours for special events. Free.)

Outdoors, the many parks, plazas and lakes of the city provide unpretentious pleasure. Perhaps most beautiful of Guanajuato's many natural attractions is the **Ex-Hacienda de San Gabriel de Barrera** (tel. 2-06-19). Seventeen glorious gardens in different styles (Italian, Arab, English, etc.) cover about three acres of territory. Cobbled paths, well-groomed flora of all sorts, and abundant whistling birds make this place a stroller's dream. The *ex-hacienda* itself, a 16th-century structure, abuts the gardens. The rooms contain furniture, silverware, and paintings of the epoch. The most interesting chamber is the medieval-looking dining/living area, spanned by a wide, low, brick archway. Strangely violent sacred paintings suggest the return of Catholicism's repressed barbarism under the influence of the New World. To get there, take a bus from Juárez for the *Central*, and tell the driver you're headed to San Gabriel de Barrera. (Open daily 9am-7pm.)

The white Moorish towers known as **El Faro,** high in the mountains to the right of the reservoirs, make a good climb. From here you can admire the peculiar jutting stone mounds that have inspired many *guanajuatense* painters. To get to this part of town, take an eastbound "Presa" bus (.60 pesos), which stops at the underground stop by the *mercado*. (Open daily 9am-6pm. Admission 5 pesos. Camera permit 2 pesos.)

Dozens of candelabra in the lush Doric interior of the **Basílica de Nuestra Señora de Guanajuato,** looming over the Pl. de la Paz, illuminate fine ornamental frescoes, relics and three paintings of the Madonna by Miguel Cabrera. The wooden image of the city's protector, Nuestra Señora de Guanajuato, rests on a pure silver base and is believed to be the oldest piece of Christian art in Mexico. Next to the university and one block north of the basilica is the more interesting Jesuit **Templo de la Compañía.** The temple was finished in 1765, but shut down two years later when the Jesuits were expelled from Latin America. Characterized by eccentric *estípite* pilasters, the facade shows off Guanajuato's Churrigueresque architecture at its best. (Open daily 7am-8pm.)

Mercado Hidalgo, one block east of the tourist office, went up in 1910 with a monumental neoclassical arch as an entrance. Inside, both the seafood *cocteleríás* and the vendors who sell musical instruments are trustworthy. Guanajuato's famed ceramic mugs have declined in quality, but the woolen items are quite cheap and the wide variety of sombreros will satisfy any head. (Most vendors open daily 9am-9pm.)

Finally, about 3km north of Guanajuato stands the Templo de San Cayetano, better known as **La Valenciana.** The church was finished in 1788 with three magnificent altars, carved from wood and covered with a sheet of 24-karat gold to inflame the covetous. To get to the church, take the "Valenciana" bus, which leaves approximately every hour from the street immediately downhill from the Alhóndiga de Granaditas. (Open daily 9am-6pm.)

ENTERTAINMENT

Each year, for two or three weeks in late October, Guanajuato stages the **Festival Internacional Cervantino,** also known by its old name, the **Entremeses Cervantinos.** The city invites repertory groups from all over the world to participate with the *estudiantinas*, strolling student minstrels of the Universidad de Guanajuato. The festival takes place mostly at local theaters. Guanajuatans put on the bulk of the always sold-out dramatic productions, while foreigners contribute films, folk dances and music ranging from classical and opera to jazz and rock. Make hotel reservations early.

From June 22 to 26, Guanajuato celebrates the **Feria de San Juan** at the Presa de la Olla with cultural events, fireworks, sports, and much more. Similar but shorter celebrations occur on **Día de la Cueva** (July 1), on May 31 and on August 9 (commemorating the arrival of the Virgin of Guanajuato to the city). The religious celebrations in December include the famous *posadas*, which re-create Mary and

Joseph's search for budget accommodations in Bethlehem without the *Let's Go: Israel and Egypt* guide.

Throughout the rest of the year, theater, dance and music are performed regularly if less frequently; check the tourist office for information, or consult the posters around town. Student groups present films almost every day of the week. Call the **Teatro Principal** (tel. 2-15-26), the **Teatro Cervantes** (tel. 2-11-69), or the **Teatro Juárez** (tel. 2-01-83) for specifics. (Tickets 5-10 pesos.)

The bars and cafés in the immediate vicinity of the *Jardín Unión* are friendly and comfortable, even for single women; **La Perla,** right on the *Jardín*, is probably the classiest of the bunch (beer 5 pesos). If things slow down on the *Jardín*, it's because they're picking up in the **Guanajuato Grill,** at Alonso 20. When school's in, the grill fills nightly with Guanajuato's friendly and thirsty students (beers 6 pesos). Couples only, but these pairs can easily be arranged spontaneously at the door—no cover. (Open nightly 8pm-2am.) As night wears on, many of them move on to **Donde** at Sopeña 19, source of some of Guanajuato's cheapest beer. Buckets of Corona (6 normal-sized bottles) go for 15 pesos, but there's no dancing (open Tues.-Sun. 8pm-2am, no cover). The trendy **Galería,** in the Hotel Parador San Javier, is the best-known spot for the seriously dance-minded. Look sharp (slacks, no sandals) or risk not getting in. (Cover 25 pesos.)

The most offbeat and entertaining club in town is **El Rincón del Beso** (a.k.a. Peña Bohemia), on Alonso east of Casa Kloster. The nightly sing-alongs and riotous poetry interpretations get going around 11pm (no cover). (Open Thurs.-Sat. 9pm-2am.)

Other popular discos include **Sancho's,** Pl. de Cata (tel. 2-19-76, cover averages 20 pesos); The plush **El Cantador,** Nejayote 17 (tel. 2-14-60), in the luxurious Hotel Real d'Minas, features live groups doing romantic Mexican numbers. **De los Santos,** on Guillermo Valle near the music school (tel. 2-07-09), impersonates the interior of a mine, with high stone walls and large wooden beams across the ceiling. The dark, romantic atmosphere and tranquil music call for candlelight.

■ Near Guanajuato

About 20km from Guanajuato, on top of a mountain 2850m above sea level, is the **Monumento a Cristo Rey,** completed in 1956. The mountain, called the **Cerro del Cubilete,** is considered the geographical center of Mexico. The dark bronze statue of Jesus is over 16m tall and weighs more than 80 tons. Although the statue is striking, you may spend more time observing the surrounding landscape; miles of wavy green and blue hills are visible from the top, and on rainy days you may be above the clouds. Take the "Cristo Rey" bus from the bus station (4 pesos, 1hr.).

■■■ DOLORES HIDALGO

The mild-mannered Don Miguel Hidalgo y Costilla, resident priest in the town of Dolores, was calmly plotting to sever Mexico's relations with the Spanish crown when he discovered that the government of New Spain had learned of his plans. He took decisive action. On Sunday, September 16, 1810, the people of Dolores were woken at 5am by the tolling of the parish church bell. In response, they gathered at the church, where they heard Hidalgo proclaim Mexico's independence from Spain. Hidalgo rallied an army to march on the capitol, but he didn't live to see the birth of the Republic.

Though Dolores witnessed these great events, not much of historical significance has happened here since. Late in 1947, the Mexican government declared Dolores Hidalgo the "Cradle of Independence." Today, the only things cradled in this sleepy town are a handful of museums and the communal memory of the glorious struggle. The best way to see Dolores is on a daytrip from San Miguel or Guanajuato

ORIENTATION AND PRACTICAL INFORMATION

Dolores Hidalgo sits in the middle of the state of Guanajuato, about 50km northeast of the state capital and about 42km away from San Miguel de Allende. To get downtown from the **bus station** at Hidalgo and Chiapas, walk straight out the door, take a left on Hidalgo and go three blocks. This brings you to the **Jardín**, the **tourist office, Plaza Principal**, and the **Parroquia**. The **Río Dolores** runs east-west through the city; streets are arranged in a grid parallel and perpendicular to the river. A city map is useful since streets have different names on opposite sides of the city.

Tourist Office: Delegación de Turismo (tel. 2-08-01), on Pl. Principal in the arcade to the left of the *Parroquia*. The staff is enthusiastic when they are there. Official hours Mon.-Fri. 9am-6pm, Sat.-Sun. 10am-2pm, if door happens to be unlocked.

Currency Exchange: Banco del Centro, Guerrero and Jalisco (tel. 2-07-55), on the southeast corner of the Pl. Principal. Open for currency exchange Mon.-Fri. 9am-2pm. **Bancomer** (tel. 2-05-90), on the west side of the plaza. Open Mon.-Fri. 10am-1:30pm.

Post Office: Puebla 22 (tel. 2-08-07). Open Mon.-Fri. 8am-7pm, Sat. 8am-noon. **Postal code:** 37800.

Telephones: Restaurante Plaza (tel. 2-01-59), on the south side of the plaza. International collect calls 5 pesos. Open Mon.-Sat. 9am-2pm and 4-8pm. The **Hotel Caudillo** provides 24-hr. service for guests. International collect calls free for guests. **Telephone code:** 468.

Telegrams: Puebla 22 (tel. 2-04-63), in the post office. Open Mon.-Fri. 9am-1pm and 3-6pm, Sat. 9am-noon.

Bus Station: Hidalgo at Chiapas. **Flecha Amarilla** is the lone carrier. To: Mexico City (1 per hr., 5hrs., 30 pesos); San Luis Potosí (every ½hr. 5:40am-7pm, 12 pesos); León (about 1 per hr., 10 pesos); Guanajuato (every ½hr., 6 pesos); and San Miguel de Allende (every 15min., 7am-8pm, 3.5 pesos).

Pharmacy: Farmacia Dolores, Pl. Principal 21 (tel. 2-09-48). Open daily 9am-6pm.

Hospital: Hospital Ignacio Allende, Hidalgo 12 (tel. 2-00-13).

Police: In the Cárcel Municipal (tel. 2-00-21), on San Luis Potosí 1 block north of Pl. Principal.

ACCOMMODATIONS

Most of the lodgings in this village are posh for the sake of urban tourists visiting their national shrine. Nonetheless, they are reasonably priced, especially compared to those in San Miguel. Even so, you might wish to stay in San Miguel or Guanajuato because unless you enjoy browsing in ceramic shops, there isn't much to keep you occupied here.

Hotel Posada Cocomacán, Querétaro at Guanajuato (tel. 2-00-18), on the *Jardín*. Wood floors, tiled walls and romantic lighting in rooms off a central courtyard. Clean bathrooms. Singles 60 pesos. Doubles 70 pesos.

Hotel Caudillo, Querétaro 8 (tel. 2-01-98), across the street from the *Parroquia*. Clean rooms with TVs and that rustic motel something—unfortunately, including that smell. Local tiles everywhere, including the ceilings. Singles 45 pesos. Doubles 49 pesos.

Posada Dolores, Yucatán 8 (tel. 2-06-42), 1 block west of the Pl. Principal. Very small but clean, stark cell-like rooms. Every corner and, perhaps, closet forms a room in this friendly establishment. Passable communal bathroom. Singles 20 pesos. Doubles 25 pesos, with bath 35 pesos.

FOOD

Dolores Hidalgo offers nothing remarkable in the way of food, and one restaurant is pretty much like the rest.

Alborada Restaurante, Zacatecas 9 (tel. 2-09-51), across from the Museo Independencia. A sunny-courtyard restaurant decorated with plants, flowers, and umbrellas over each table. *Huevos al gusto* 6 pesos. *Quesadilla* 2 pesos. *Comida corrida* 16 pesos. Open daily 8am-8pm.

D'Jardín, Pl. Principal 30, on the Jardín. Tile resembles 1970s high-fashion linoleum. Colorful simulated hanging plastic plants put on the finishing touches. *Comida corrida* 15 pesos, tacos 7 pesos. Open daily 8am-7pm.

Restaurant El Delfin, Guerrero at Veracruz (tel. 2-22-09). Don't be fooled by the demure-looking bottle of picante sauce on the table, but if you do slip up, they stock 6 types of beer (3.50 pesos) to cool your tongue. Mostly seafood dishes. Shrimp 27 pesos. Meat 10 pesos. Open daily 9am-7pm.

SIGHTS AND ENTERTAINMENT

Mexico's "Cradle of Independence" is a small, minimally interesting community. In the four blocks between the bus station and Museo Independencia you've just about seen it all. That said, the beautiful **Parroquia,** where the *Grito de Dolores* was sounded, still stands. Constructed between 1712 and 1778, the church, with its large and intricately worked facade and twin towers of pink stone, dominates the Pl. Principal. Although the interior is dusty and somewhat deteriorated, the two side altars are magnificent examples of baroque art. It's not unusual for Mexico's presidents to return to the *Parroquia* on the anniversary of Hidalgo's proclamation to repeat it verbatim. (Open daily 7am-2pm and 4-7pm.)

The **Museo Casa Hidalgo,** at Morelos and Hidalgo, one block from the Pl. Principal, was Hidalgo's home from 1804 until 1810. Many of his belongings, including fine Mexican and European furniture and ceramics, are on display. Documents and works of art relating to the independence movement, as well as diverse lottery cards and a fabulous Mutepec **Tree of Life** (with Hidalgo at its center), fill rooms off a central scenic courtyard. (Open Tues.-Sat. 10am-6pm, Sun. and holidays 10am-5pm. Admission 13 pesos, free Sun. and for students with ID.)

The **Museo Independencia,** Zacatecas 6, lies less than one block northwest of the *Parroquia*. Here the exigencies of Spanish rule, the onset of independence, and the life and works of Miguel Hidalgo are presented in melodramatic murals and modern dioramas. Grisly paintings depict *conquistador* brutality in disturbing realism. (Open Mon.-Fri. 9am-2pm and 4-7pm, Sat.-Sun. 9am-3pm. Admission 2 pesos. Free for students with IDs.)

Dolores Hidalgo is heralded as Mexico's foremost **pottery** center, and ceramic shops abound. Though quality work may certainly be found, especially on smaller streets, don't hold your breath, as three-foot mass-produced frogs were the current fashion in summer 1993.

The **Cine Telocali,** on Guanajuato just off the square, shows the latest Mexican greats for 5 pesos. Otherwise, you might have to wait for the **Fiestas Patrias,** celebrated September 1-17, for official entertainment. Most of the cultural activities (folk dancing and singing), athletic tournaments (basketball, baseball, soccer), and fireworks take place during the final week.

■■■ SAN MIGUEL DE ALLENDE

Juan de San Miguel, a Franciscan friar accompanied by a group of Tarasco and Otoní *indígena* converts, founded San Miguel el Viejo in 1542. The first years of the village's existence were ill-starred; in the heart of Chichimec territory, the *pueblo* almost perished from their attacks. In 1555, however, when silver was discovered in Zacatecas, the *virrey* (viceroy) of New Spain saw the need to secure the lines of communication between his office in Mexico City and the ore. San Miguel falls on a straight line between those two points, and by the end of the 16th century the silver trade had re-christened the town San Miguel el Grande.

San Miguel's fifteen minutes of fame came in 1810. On September 16, Hidalgo arrived in the city with a rebel army. The question of San Miguel's allegiance was soon resolved by Ignacio Allende, who convinced the population of the righteousness of Hidalgo's mission. The army stayed three days in San Miguel, reorganizing and assimilating new recruits, before pushing on toward the capital. In 1826, the infant republic commemorated Allende's deeds by renaming the town after him.

Today San Miguel attracts flocks of foreign tourists (especially *gringos*) and has become a center of expatriate life. It was here that Neal Cassady, the prototype of Kerouac's hero in *On the Road*, died, hit by a train while walking the tracks to Celaya. While hip young Americans still visit or study here, many older American retirees have settled here as well and middle-aged vacationers fill the five-starred hotels. Here it is no feat to find a Reuben sandwich or Haagen Daz ice cream. Mexican life does continue amidst the American activity, especially in the *mercado,* and many of the natives are particularly friendly toward Americans, eager to practice their English or help you with your Spanish.

Renowned for its artisanry and academics, San Miguel has another resource that prospective visitors often overlook—a mild climate. The town is almost never oppressively hot, thanks to its 2000m elevation. Beware the ides of June and July, however. Cold afternoon drizzle or drenching all-day downpours can turn the streets into gushing streams.

ORIENTATION AND PRACTICAL INFORMATION

San Miguel lies midway between Guanajuato and Querétaro, 428km northwest of Mexico City. From the **bus station** to the center (known as the **Jardín** or **Plaza de Allende**), take the bus (.80 pesos) or a taxi (5 pesos). On foot, turn right (east) as you exit the station and walk 1km on Calzada de la Estación, which turns into San Francisco before coming upon the *Jardín*. The **train station** lies another km west of the bus station on the same road.

Most attractions are within walking distance of the *Jardín*. Getting lost here is no easy feat. The small size of the town and the near-grid of its streets facilitate navigation. Streets south of the *Jardín* that run east-west change their names every few blocks. A good source of current information on the town is the weekly newspaper *Atención*, available at the tourist office next to the *Jardín*.

San Miguel has a small and tolerated gay and lesbian population, mostly *gringo* expatriates. Furthermore, San Miguel has a reputation as a place for men and women to meet each other. To avoid desperate Don Juans, women should not walk alone at night. Crime, though, is virtually nonexistent.

Tourist Office: Dirección General de Turismo (tel. 2-17-47), on the Pl. de Allende next to the *Parroquia* and Restaurante La Terraza. Knowledgeable and helpful staff speaks English and distributes handy maps. Open Mon.-Fri. 10am-2:45pm and 5-7pm, Sat. 10am-1pm, Sun. 10am-noon.

U.S. Consular Representative: Macías 72 (tel. 2-23-57), opposite Bellas Artes. Office hours Mon. and Wed. 9am-1pm and 4-7pm, Tues. and Thurs. 4-7pm, or by appointment. In case of emergency dial 2-00-68 or 2-09-80.

Currency Exchange: Bánamex, on the west side of the *Jardín*, changes money 9am-noon and 4-6pm. Most other banks exchange 9am-noon. *Casas de cambio* give slightly lower rates: **Allen W. Lloyd y Asociados,** Jardín at Hidalgo (open Mon.-Fri. 9am-5pm), and **Deal,** Correos 15 (open Mon.-Fri. 9am-2pm and 4-6pm, Sat. 9am-2pm).

American Express, Hidalgo 1 (tel. 2-18-56). Full financial and travel services and cardholders' mail. Employs a few English speakers but won't exchange checks. Open daily 9am-2pm and 4-6:30pm.

Post Office: Appropriately at Correos 16 (tel. 2-00-89), 1 block east of the *Jardín*. *Lista de Correos*. Open for registered mail Mon.-Fri. 9am-6pm; for all other services Mon.-Fri. 8am-7pm, Sat. 9am-1pm.

Telephones: El Toro Lonchería, Macías 52, across from the Hotel Sautto. International collect calls 2 pesos. Open Mon.-Sat. 9am-1:30pm and 3-8pm, Sun. 10am-2pm.

Telegrams: (Tel. 2-00-81), adjacent to the post office. Open Mon.-Fri. 9am-1pm and 3-6pm, Sat. 9am-noon.

Train Station: Ferrocarriles Nacionales de México (tel. 2-00-07), located 2km west of town.

Bus Station: (Tel. 2-22-06), on Calzada de la Estación, 1km west of the center. **Herradura de Plata** to Mexico City (every 2hrs. 5am-7pm, 29 pesos) and Querétaro (every ½hr., 6 pesos). **Flecha Amarilla** to Guanajuato (every 2hrs., 7 pesos), Aguascalientes (3 per day, 23 pesos), San Luis Potosí (every 2hrs., last at 5:40pm, 16 pesos), and Dolores Hidalgo (every ½hr., 305 pesos). **Omnibus de México, Tres Estrellas de Oro,** and **Servicios Coordinados** also have less frequent service to and from San Miguel.

Taxis: Sitios de Taxis (tel. 2-01-92), or on the Jardín.

Car Rental: Gama Rent-a-Car, Hidalgo 3 (tel. 2-08-15). 68 pesos per day and extra per km. Special weekly rates. Open Mon.-Sat. 9am-2pm and 4-7pm.

English Bookstore: El Colibrí, Sollano 30 (tel. 2-07-57). Superb, if expensive, selection of classics, science fiction, history and current best sellers. After 25 years, staff knows just about all there is to know about San Miguel. Open Mon.-Sat. 10am-2pm and 4-7pm. Also, the public library (see below) evacuates old paperbacks by selling them for about 2 pesos each.

Public Library: Insurgentes 25 (tel. 2-02-93), next to La Española. An important feature of expatriate social life. Free language exchange. Open Mon.-Fri. 9am-2pm and 4-7pm, Sat. 10am-1pm.

Laundromat: Lavamágico, Pila Seca 5 (tel. 2-08-99). Will pick up and deliver a 4kg load for a mere 12 pesos. Open Mon.-Sat. 8am-8pm.

Red Cross: (Tel. 2-16-16), km1 on Carretera Celaya.

Pharmacy: Farmacia Allende, San Francisco 3 (tel. 2-00-74), ½ block from the *Jardín*. Open daily 9am-9pm.

Hospital: Clínica la Salud, Hidalgo 28 (tel. 2-04-30). Open 24 hrs. for emergencies. English-speaking physician.

Police: (Tel. 2-00-22), in the Presidencia Municipal.

ACCOMMODATIONS

The invisible hand of supply and demand is at work here. Plenty of room-hungry, dollar-toting *gringos* and relatively few hotels have sent prices skyward—accommodations here are dearer (and nicer) than in most other spots in Mexico. May and June you may want to make a reservation several days in advance to play it safe. If you're planning an extended stay, check for notices of rooms for rent on the bulletin board at the Instituto Allende, Ancha de San Antonio 20, southwest of the *Jardín*, and in popular *norteamericano* cafés and hotels.

The San Miguel International Hostel, Organos 34 (2-06-74), 1 block west of Jardín on Canal, right on Macias, 3 blocks to Organos, left on Organos another block and a half. This friendly American-run establishment makes you feel right at home. A sitting room equipped with English books, music and a piano, chairs arranged outside in the courtyard, kitchen use (3 pesos per day for the privilege), and optional Spanish lessons (5 pesos) in the afternoon. Clean single-sex dorms (4-10 people per room) and bathrooms. (15 pesos, continental breakfast included.) 2 private single rooms and 1 private double, as well (35 pesos each; reserve several days in advance to play it safe).

Casa de Huéspedes, Mesones 23 (tel. 2-13-78). Serene, flower-filled courtyard complete with lounge chairs and *New Yorker* magazines. Immaculate rooms, some with kitchens, and wonderfully friendly staff. Singles 40 pesos. Doubles 60 pesos. Better rates for extended stays.

Hotel Posada de Allende, Cuna de Allende (tel. 2-06-89), around the corner from the Parroquia. Large, wallpapered rooms off of a small courtyard, 1 wall of which is the Parroquia. Run by 2 elderly women who make candy on the side. Singles 40-50 pesos. Doubles 60 pesos.

Hotel Quinta Loreto, Loreto 13 (tel. 2-00-42), 3 blocks north and 1 block east of the *Jardín*, down a cobbled driveway. Popular place with *norteamericanos.*

Great large rooms with tiled bathrooms, a flower-filled garden, tennis courts, and a pool. Singles 70 pesos. Doubles 85 pesos.

Hotel Posada de las Monjas, Canal 37 (tel. 2-01-71), 3 blocks west of the *Jardín*. A good deal: elegant lobby comes complete with rug, prints, flowers, TV and goldfish. A maze of plant-filled courtyards with fountains. Dirt-free carpeted rooms with desks and stone-floored bathrooms. Restaurant and bar. Singles 70 or 150 pesos (2 sizes). Doubles 90 or 180 pesos.

FOOD

The sweet aroma of international cuisine wafts through the cobbled streets of San Miguel and fine restaurants grace almost every corner. Unfortunately, their prices are as *norteamericano* as their clientele. As a general rule, American and European fare tends to be expensive, and not quite the home cooking you miss. Taco stalls and inexpensive *loncherías* hide in and around the *mercado* on Colegio. *Elotes* and *tortas* can be found in the tiny square on Insurgentes between Macías and Hidalgo.

El Correo Restaurante, Correo 23 (tel. 2-01-51), 1 block from La Parroquia and across from, yes, the Casa de Correos. Luxurious appearance pleasantly belies reasonable prices. Loaded: stencilled walls, flowered placemats, a sophisticated crowd, and its own bird. Waffles 7 pesos. Quesadillas 6 pesos. *Spaghetti bolognese* 14 pesos. Open Thurs.-Tues. 9am-9:30pm.

Restaurant "El Infiernito," Mesones 23 (tel. 2-23-55). Ceramic bulldogs, stuffed iguanas, pictures of Jesus and psychedelic art adorn the dining area. The specialty is *pollo rostizado* (10 pesos). *Huevos al gusto* 7 pesos. *Menú del día* 13 pesos. Open daily 9am-midnight.

Mama Mía, Umarán 8 (tel. 2-20-63), west of the *Jardín*'s southwest corner. Eat your dinner to live mariachi music under paper lanterns hung from the trees overhead. It's a *norteamericano* crowd here eating this Italian food (although the cooks and waiters are native). Pasta 16-25 pesos. Meat 29-48 pesos. Open 8am-1am.

La Colima, El Reloj 21, north of the *Jardín*. A great little bakery with constantly warm sesame rolls. Cheapest breakfast in town. *Bolilos* (Mexican breads) .50 pesos. *Conches* 1 peso. Rolls .20 pesos. Open Mon. 8:30am-2pm, Tues.-Sat. 6am-2pm and 5:30-9pm, Sun. 6-9am.

SIGHTS

Magnificent churches, colonial homes, an art gallery and artisans' boutiques populate the cobbled streets around the *Jardín*. The only way to experience San Miguel is on your own two feet. The public library gives guided **home and garden tours** of the city in English most days at noon (25 pesos). Alternatively, just wander off on a random tangent from the *Jardín*; almost every street has an interesting shop, and San Miguel's small size makes it hard for even the klutziest to get lost.

La Parroquia, next to the *Jardín*, is one of the most distinctive churches in Mexico. Its facade and tower were designed and realized by the *indígena* mason Zeferino Gutiérrez, who is said to have learned the Gothic style from postcards of French cathedrals. The size and beauty of the church make it a landmark for miles around. (Open daily 8am-9pm.)

The **Museo Histórico de San Miguel de Allende,** on the corner of Canal and Cuna de Allende, just west of *La Parroquia*, resides in the home where Allende, a leader of the anti-colonial putsch, once lived. Don Ignacio's status is obvious from his magnificent, partly Baroque mansion. The eclectic museum combines tributes to Allende with unrelated exhibits on astronomy and paleobiology. (Open Tues.-Sun. 10am-4pm. Free.)

At the corner of Canal and Macías, two blocks west of the *Jardín*, stands the enormous **Iglesia de la Concepción.** Distinguished by its splendid two-story dome crowned with a representation of the Immaculate Conception, the church was finished in 1891. Pairs of Corinthian columns adorn the lower level. Inside are polychrome sculptures of St. Joseph and the Immaculate Conception, and an interesting juxtaposition of paintings and graves. (Open daily 8am-8:30pm.)

Founded in 1712, the **Templo del Oratorio de San Felipe Neri** lies at the corner of Insurgentes and Loreto, two blocks east of the library. Its engraved baroque facade shows *indígena* influence, and its interior is mainly Neoclassical, but the styles collide, as the church has been rebuilt many times. On the west side of the church, the towers and the dome belong to the **Santa Casa de Loreto,** a reproduction of the building of the same name in Italy (enter on the right side of the altar in San Felipe Neri). The floors and the lower wall friezes are covered with glazed tiles from China, Spain and Puebla. (Open daily 7-8pm.)

One block east of the *Jardín* at Juárez and San Francisco, the **Iglesia de San Francisco** includes a tall, dark red neoclassical tower attributed to the architect Tresguerras. Finished in 1799, the church's Churrigueresque facade honors many saints. Several small paintings in the interior are so elevated and enveloped in darkness that you'd have to be a bat to appreciate them. To the right as you face San Francisco is the **Iglesia del Tercer Orden,** one of the oldest and most decayed churches in San Miguel, constructed by the Franciscan order between 1606 and 1638. The main facade contains an image of St. Francis and symbols of the Franciscan order. (Both open daily 8am-8pm.)

The two contemporary cultural centers of San Miguel are the **Bellas Artes** and **Instituto Allende**. Set in a converted 18th-century convent, the Bellas Artes (a.k.a. Centro Cultural Ignacio Ramírez El Nigromante, on Macías next to the Iglesia de la Concepción, tel. 2-02-89) boasts a traditional courtyard that overflows with cappuccino-sipping artists. Shifting exhibits by both contemporary Mexican and foreign artists fill the main three halls. The upper floor sports studios for current art students and smaller galleries for local craftspeople. (Open daily 10am-1pm and 4:30-6pm.) Built as a church in 1735, the **Instituto Allende**, Ancha de San Antonio 20, in the southwestern part of the city, received its present incarnation as an art school in 1985. Affiliated with the University of Guanajuato, its two galleries show and sell the works of current students. (Open daily 9am-noon and 3-6:30pm.)

The **Parque Juárez,** three blocks south of the *Jardín* on Aldama and then Carranza, is the greenest, but unfortunately, also the smelliest (because of its stagnant stream) of San Miguel, reverberating with the calls of tropical birds. Die-hard cagers can often join a pick-up basketball game involving both *gringos* and locals. Some of the most elegant houses in San Miguel surround this park.

Tres Cruces is a hill east of town with three crosses on it. San Miguel, the surrounding valley and the faraway mountains are magnificently visible from the hill. Walk three blocks east on San Francisco from the *Jardín*, turn right (south) on Real (you'll pass a PEMEX station) and walk until you see the crosses on the right. This part of the walk takes about 15 minutes and passes through some picturesque alleys along the way. Three blocks before reaching the official *mirador* (lookout), you can turn right and ascend to the hilltop (another 15min.).

The mild climate of San Miguel rarely demands aquatic relief, but should the mercury rise to swim level, head to the *balneario* at **Taboada,** 6km down the road to Dolores Hidalgo. The facilities here include two pools, a bar/restaurant and playing fields. Before you can immerse, you must catch the bus marked "Taboada" at the municipal bus stop. To get to the stop, head east along Mesones toward the market. Turn left on Colegio and, after one block, turn right onto a small plaza. Buses (3 pesos) leave here for Taboada at 9am, 11am, 1pm and 3pm, and return to San Miguel 15 minutes after the above hours. (*Balneario* open Wed.-Mon. 7am-5pm. Admission 6 pesos.)

ENTERTAINMENT

San Miguel's cultural calendar is full. The magazine *Atención,* on sale at the public library, has details of most events. In addition, both the Bellas Artes and Instituto Allende have bulletin boards crammed with information on upcoming jazz, classical guitar, dance and folk song concerts, as well as theatrical productions and lectures by both locals and *gringos*. Concerts and theater usually cost a few pesos and are held at either site—double check there for details. The **Biblioteca Pública** (public library), Insurgentes 25, arranges informal evenings of conversation in Spanish and English (Thurs. 7-9pm, Sat. 5-7pm), providing a relaxed atmosphere in which to meet Mexican students and other travelers, as well as near-complimentary cookies. (Sometimes held at **Casa Luna,** Cuadrantes 2; check at the library or in *Atención*.)

San Miguel has a deserved reputation as a town with a real nightlife. On Wednesdays, many popular clubs dispense with the normal cover charge, and the whole town turns out. **Pancho and Lefty's,** is on Mesones between Macías and Hidalgo. At night, the mostly *gringo* crowd gets busy to live rock'n'roll. (Open Wed.-Sat. 7pm-2:30am. Fri.-Sat. cover for men 20 pesos. Wed. 2-for-1. Beer 7 pesos. Mixed drinks 11 pesos.) **Mama Mía** in front of the restaurant (see Food) has a huge TV screen in a small dark room. (Drinks 7 pesos. Open daily 7pm-3am.) **Laberintos,** Ancha de San Antonio 7, is distantly related to a wine cellar. Vintage disco and *salsa* tunes permeate the dance floor. (No cover Thurs; Fri. cover 6-10 pesos; Sat. cover 15 pesos; Sun. cover 5 pesos. Open Thurs.-Sun. 8pm-3am.) **El Ring,** Hidalgo 25, the best dance floor in town, heats up around 11:30pm when the tireless from other hot-spots come like moths to the flame.Play the latest dance tracks from the U.S. and Latin America. (Cover Thurs.-Sun. 30 pesos, drinks 7-11 pesos. No shorts or sandals allowed for males. Open Wed.-Sun., 10pm until everyone leaves, usually around 5am.)

San Miguel is reputed to have more festivals than any other town in Mexico. Most nights the gazebo in front of the cathedral plays host to some musical extravaganza. Beyond national and religious holidays, San Miguel celebrates the birthday of Ignacio Allende on January 21; the Fiesta de la Candelaria on February 2, marking the start of spring and the birthday of El Padre de Miguel; and the festival of San Miguel's guardian saint (third weekend in Sept.), when bulls run free through the center of the city in imitation of the *encierro* in Pamplona, Spain.

ACADEMIC INSTITUTIONS

Many visitors to San Miguel study at one of its schools for foreign students. Starting dates, intensity of instruction, and hiring policies vary, though many foreigners arrange classes and a homestay (approximately US$450 a month) upon arrival. The **Bellas Artes** (tel. 2-02-89) conducts a number of four-week courses throughout the year in fine arts and language at a cost of about US$70 per month. For information, write to Señora Carmen Masip de Hawkins, Macías 75. During the year the **Academia Hispano-Americana** (tel. 2-03-49) runs two-, four-, eight- and twelve-week sessions in Spanish language, literature, history, psychology, current events and Mexican folklore. Two weeks cost US$200. For information write to the Registrar, Academia Hispano-Americana, Mesones 4. **Inter Idiomas** (tel. 2-21-77) organizes language programs of two hours per day at US$45 per week or US$160 per month, plus a one-time US$15 registration fee. Address inquiries to Mesones 15.

QUERÉTARO

■■■ QUERÉTARO

On June 19, 1867, on Querétaro's Cerro de las Campanas (Hill of Bells), after handing each of the assembled soldiers a gold coin, Emperor Maximilian uttered his famous last words: "Mexicans, I am going to die for a just cause: the liberty and the independence of Mexico. May my blood be the last shed for the happiness of my new country. *¡Viva México!*" Fifty years later, at the end of a bloody revolution, the victorious leader Carranza chose this spot for the drafting of the constitution that governs the Republic to this day. Querétaro has also been the site of less noble events. It was here that the peace treaty after the Mexican-American War of 1848 was signed, in which Mexico was forced to cede much of its northern territories, the present U.S. states of California, Arizona, New Mexico, Colorado and Nevada.

Today, Querétaro has the feel of a European city: elegant 18th- and 19th-century architecture, wide brick streets, traffic jams, chic clothing stores, couples strolling on the pedestrian promenades, and flocks of pigeons—the emblem of all real cities—in its numerous fountain-centered squares.

ORIENTATION AND PRACTICAL INFORMATION

Querétaro is on two of the country's most heavily traveled highways—Rte. 120 and Rte. 57. Its streets form a grid, and nearly all important sites are within walking distance of the **Jardín Obregón,** the four streets Corregidora, Madero, Juárez, and 16 de Septiembre on each of its sides. The **bus station** is on Carretera Panamericana, across the street from the **Alameda Hidalgo,** a wild park. To reach the Jardín, turn left (west) upon leaving the station, walk one block to Corregidora, then turn right (north) and walk four blocks. The **train station** is a good distance from the Jardín, about two blocks beyond the end of Corregidora in the northernmost part of the city. To get to the train station from downtown, catch a "Ruta 13" *taxibus* (.70 pesos) and get off at the railroad tracks. Take a right on the tracks and walk two blocks.

Tourist Office: State Tourist Office, Pasteur Sur 17 (tel. 14-56-23), in the Pl. de Independencia. Friendly English-speaking staff hands out helpful maps and listings of cultural events around the city. Free city tours in Spanish daily at 10:30am. Open Mon.-Fri. 9am-2pm and 5-8pm, Sat.-Sun. 10am-1pm. **Federal Tourist Office,** Constitución 10020 (tel. 13-85-11).

Currency Exchange: Banks near the Jardín Obregón are open Mon.-Fri. 9am-12:30pm, but some exchange currency only until noon. **Casa de Cambio de Querétaro,** Madero 6, in the mall on the Jardín Obregón's south side, is open Mon.-Fri. 9am-3pm. At other times, try the jewelry stores near the Gran Hotel, but expect unfavorable rates.

Post Office: Arteaga Pte. 7 (tel. 12-01-12), 2 blocks south of the Jardín Obregón, between Juárez and Allende. Open Mon.-Fri. 8am-7pm, Sat. 9am-noon.

Telephones: Long-distance *caseta* at the bus station. No collect calls. Open 24 hrs. Efficient *caseta* at 5 de Mayo 33. International collect calls 12 pesos. Open Mon.-Sat. 9:30am-2pm and 4:30-9pm. **Telephone code:** 463.

Telegrams: Allende Nte. 4 (tel. 12-01-63), 1 block west of the Jardín Obregón. Open Mon.-Fri. 9am-8pm, Sat. 9am-1pm.

Train Station: Allende (tel. 12-17-03), in the northern part of the city. To: San Miguel de Allende (12:45pm, 10.8 pesos); Mexico City (5:30am, 26 pesos); San Luis Potosí (12:45pm, 21 pesos); Guadalajara (midnight, 11 pesos).

Bus Station: (Tel. 12-17-30), on Carretera Panamericana, 4 blocks south and 1 block east of the Jardín. Station contains a 24-hr. long-distance telephone booth, a cafeteria and a squadron of food booths and shops. Frequent service, but almost all buses are *de paso.* **Flecha Amarilla** sends the most buses to: Irapuato (from there a change of buses to Guanajuato, every 15min., 9 pesos); Aguascalientes (4 per day, 25 pesos), Guadalajara (hourly, 34 pesos), and Dolores Hidalgo (hourly, 4.5 pesos). **Tres Estrellas de Oro** sends buses to Mexico City (hourly, 22.5 pesos) and **Herradura de Plata** to San Miguel de Allende (every ½hr., 6 pesos). 10 or so other carriers also operate from Querétaro.

Taxis: (Tel. 12-36-66 or 12-31-43), but they're cheaper if flagged down.

Laundromat: Lavandería Automática La Cascada, Loc 18 Commercial Mexicana (tel. 16-56-96). 3kg for 15 pesos. Open Mon.-Fri. 9am-2pm and 4-8pm, Sat. 9am-2pm.

Red Cross: Hidalgo Pte. 93 (tel. 12-17-06).

Pharmacies: Farmacia Central, Madero 10 (tel. 2-11-29), on the Jardín's south side. Open Mon.-Sat. 9am-8pm. **Farmacia El Fénix,** Juárez Nte. 73 (tel. 2-01-79), 1½ blocks north of the Jardín Obregón. Open daily 8am-10pm.
Hospital: Hospital Civil, Reforma 21 (tel. 16-20-36).
Police: Constituyentes Pte. 20 (tel. 12-15-07).

ACCOMMODATIONS

Resist the urge to curl up at the hotels near the bus station. Cheaper and considerably more charming places abound a few blocks away, around the Jardín Obregón. Because Querétaro is such a large city, the finest hotels are outside the budget traveler's range while the cheapest lack that small-town family charm.

Hotel Hidalgo, Madero Pte. 11 (tel. 12-00-81), 1 block west of the Jardín. Pleasant colonial architecture and central location. Rooms with terraces are considerably nicer than their hot and claustrophobic counterparts without. Singles 40 pesos. Doubles 55 pesos.

Hotel San Agustín, Pino Suárez 12 (tel. 2-39-19), between Allende and Juárez. This modern building has no charm, but the rooms and bathrooms are clean and cool and the staff friendly. Rooms overlooking the street lack the cell-like ambiance of the others. Singles 45 pesos. Doubles 60 pesos.

Hotel San Francisco, Corregidora Sur 144 (tel. 2-08-58), 3 blocks south of the Jardín Obregón, near the bus station. Functional, clean rooms with bright blue walls. Most rooms have windows to the outside and are, therefore, cooler than many other Querétaro hotels. Singles 40 pesos. Doubles 50 pesos.

Hotel del Márquez, Juárez Nte. 104 (tel. 2-04-14), 3 long blocks north of the Jardín Obregón. The beautiful newly tiled bathrooms are an anomaly in this hotel. One wonders whether the bedrooms have been touched—or the windows opened—since the 1950s. Orange and brown ratty material clothes these furnace-like rooms. Singles 40 pesos. Doubles 50 pesos.

FOOD

Several inexpensive restaurants face the Jardín Obregón. Charming but expensive *loncherías* and outdoor cafés rim the nearby Pl. Corregidora, while taco, *torta,* and other fast-food stands line 5 de Mayo. Beware, most restaurants stop serving their *menú del día* at 5 or 6pm.

Restaurante de la Rosa (tel. 14-47-22), on Juárez at Peralta, across from the Teatro República. Basic Mexican food served in a friendly atmosphere by a woman who will eagerly encourage you to "practice your Spanish." Eat beneath hanging plants and lanterns in your straight-back wooden chair. Buffet breakfast, *menú del día* (until 5pm at 10-12 pesos), *carne a la carta* (usually 15 pesos). Open Mon.-Sat. 9am-9pm.

Restaurante Manolo's, Madero 6 (tel. 14-05-50), on the south side of the Jardín Obregón. Some tables sit outside the restaurant in the corridor of a quiet mall. Tranquil, relaxed restaurant with white and yellow walls and wooden chairs. The white-tiled kitchen is open to show the cooks at work. Specialty is *paella. Menú del día* 15/21 pesos. Open daily 8am-9pm.

Café del Fondo, Jardín Corregidora 12. Small coffee establishment ideal for cracking that new novel. Pink staircase, pine tables and local art enhance the tranquility. Breakfasts from 5-8 pesos. Fancy coffees 3.2-9.7 pesos. *Comida corriente* 8.4 pesos. Open daily 8am-10pm.

Ibis Natura Vegetana, Juárez Nte. 272, ½ block north of the Jardín Obregón (tel. 4-22-12). Restaurant in a health-food store set up fountain-shop style. Long narrow room with wooden counter and reflecting stainless-steel ceiling. Yogurt 4.5 pesos. Soyburger 5.5-7.5 pesos. Open Sun.-Fri. 9:30am-9:30pm.

SIGHTS

Querétaro draws crowds with its rich historical and religious past. The city abounds not only in beautiful architecture, but also in intriguing legends and patriotic memories. Many sights are within easy walking distance of the Jardín Obregón.

Most intriguing of all is the **Convento de la Santa Cruz,** south of the Jardín. Follow Corregidora to Independencia and turn left; after walking a few blocks, you'll reach the convent on a plaza dedicated to the founders of the city. Nearly everything inside Santa Cruz is original, including the furnishings of the room in which Emperor Maximilian awaited his execution. In one courtyard, trees grow thorns in the form of crucifixes. Legend has it that the thorns began growing in this manner after one of the original friars accidently left his cane stuck in the ground near the trees. They are reportedly the only trees of their kind in the world, and attempts to plant seedlings in other locations have failed. (Guided tours daily 10am-6pm. Some donation expected and a few English guides available. Open Mon.-Fri. 9am-2pm and 4-6pm, Sat.-Sun. 11am-6pm.)

Northeast of the Alameda, along Calzada de los Arcos at the end of Independencia, rises the **Acueducto,** now an emblem of the city of Querétaro. The aqueduct, with its 74 arches of quarry stone, was constructed between 1726 and 1738 as a gift from the Marqués del Villas del Águila to a perpetually dry community.

Up 5 de Mayo to the east of the Jardín is the **Plaza de la Independencia,** a monument to Don Juán Antonio Urrutia y Aranda, that quenching *marqués*. Four stone dogs around his statue drool respectfully into a fountain. The plaza is bordered by beautiful colonial buildings, the most notable being the **Casa de la Corregidora,** home of Doña Josefa Ortíz de Domínguez, heroine of the 1810 Independence movement. The *casa* is now the seat of the state's government, so only the courtyard may be viewed. (Open Mon.-Fri. 8am-9pm, Sat. 9am-2pm.)

The colorful **Templo de la Congregación,** one block north of the Casa de la Corregidora at Pasteur and 16 de Septiembre, has two white towers and a central dome. The frescoes and stained glass are splendid and the pipe organ is one of the most elaborate in Mexico. (Open Mon.-Sun. 7:30am-9pm.)

Teatro de la República (tel. 102-58), at Ángela Peralta and Juárez. Many an historic event has transpired here: in 1867, the final decision on Emperor Maximilian's fate; in 1917, the drafting of the constitution; and in 1929, the formation of the Partido Nacional de la Revolución (PNR), the precursor of today's ruling Partido Revolucionario Institucional (PRI). (Open Mon.-Fri. 9am-8pm, Sat. 9am-1pm.)

The **Museo Regional** is located in the **Ex-Convento de San Francisco,** at Corregidora and Madero (tel. 12-20-36), to the east of the Jardín Obregón. Rebuilt in the 17th century's idea of the Renaissance style, the former convent possesses a cloister with two stories of colonnades. The museum displays many of the artifacts associated with the events that have taken place in Querétaro, and it even played a gloomy part in that history as the sentencing site of the leaders of the 1810 movement for independence. Exhibits include various artifacts culled from the dustbin of history, such as the table upon which the unjust 1848 peace treaty with the U.S. was signed. Temporary exhibits of contemporary art greet you at the entrance, and the entire upstairs area is devoted to 17th- and 18th-century religious paintings. (Open Wed.-Sat. 10am-6pm, Sun.-Tues. 10am-3:30pm. 10 pesos. Free for students with ID.)

Overshadowing the Museo Regional is the newer **Museo de Arte de Querétaro,** Allende 14 (tel. 12-23-57), across the Jardín Obregón at Pino Suárez. The original edifice, an 18th-century Augustinian monastery, was reconstructed in 1889 during the Porfiriato. Richly decorated arches and sculpted columns punctuate the patio. An exhibit on *querétana* architecture supplements an entire floor of Baroque paintings. Galleries of European painting, 19th- and 20th-century Mexican art and work of the 20th-century *queretareano* Abelarto Ávila complete the collection. (Open Tues.-Sun. 11am-7pm. Admission 5 pesos, students free.)

The **Cerro de las Campanas,** where Maximilian surrendered his sword to General Escobedo in 1867, is a half-hour walk from *el centro*. To reach the monument, walk a few blocks north of the Jardín Obregón on Corregidora and turn left onto General Escobedo. Proceed on Escobedo until the street ends at Tecnológico, then take a right, and you will come to the monument. To the left of the Cerro de las Campanas and up a low hill, Maximilian's family built a small chapel over the ground where the emperor and two of his generals were shot. Three small white memorials inside designate the places where each took his last breath. The man at the entrance to the chapel will gladly provide further historical detail. Up the stairs to the left of the chapel stands a large stone sculpture of Benito Juárez, the man responsible for Maximilian's execution. (Open Tues.-Sun. 6am-6pm. Free.)

ENTERTAINMENT

Local entertainment, like most everything else in Querétaro, revolves around the Jardín Obregón. Open-air brass band concerts are given in the gazebo Sunday evenings from 6 to 8pm, and myriads of jugglers, *mariachis,* and magicians perform there less regularly. *Mariachi* goes strong in the Jardín de los Platitos, where Juárez meets Av. Universidad north of the *zócalo*. Things start to heat up at about 11pm on Fridays and Saturdays when people head for the Jardín, request a song or two, and sing and dance along.

Call the **Academía de Bellas Artes,** Juárez Sur at Independencia (tel. 6-36-01), to find out what the students of the Universidad Autónoma de Querétaro have in store for the public (ballets, piano recitals, theatrical events and, less frequently, folk dance presentations). The annual **Feria de Querétaro** takes place during the second week of December.

The Querétaro student body spends its money at a number of discos. The classiest spot in town is **Discoteca Misiones,** on the highway to Mexico City in 5-star Hotel Ex-Hacienda Jurica. More convenient to the center of town are **JR's,** at Zaragoza and Tecnológico, and **Tiffani's,** at Zaragoza Pte. 67. The local twentysomething crowd does its thing at **JBJ,** Blvd. Zona Dorada 109 (tel. 14-32-32).. Club-goers tend to stay home during the week, so you may find establishments shut then.

MICHOACÁN DE OCAMPO

The Aztecs dubbed the lands surrounding Lake Pátzcuaro Michoacán, or "country of fishermen," because nearly all of the region's indigenous Purépeche subsisted by the rod and net. The Purépeche empire, which at one point controlled most of western Mexico, was one of the few civilizations to successfully resist Aztec expansionism. In fact, the Purépeche diverge from other Mesoamericans in more than just their fighting prowess: their language, culture, and even their terraced agricultural plots have led archaeologists to believe that they originally emigrated from what is now Peru—and are thus culturally closer to the Incas than to any of their neighbors in Mexico.

Purépeche hegemony lasted from around 800 AD, when they first settled Michoacán, until the Spanish expedition arrived in 1522. The conquistadors enslaved the Purépeches and forced their conversion to Christianity, but some cultural traditions persisted. Purépeche music, dances (such as *la danza de los viejitos)* and art were insuppressible. Their language, which you may hear spoken in Janitzio and the smaller villages around Lake Pátzcuaro, also survives intact. Locals refer to themselves as *Tarascos,* and thousands of stories exist to explain how they came to be known by this name. The most plausible claims that the last Purépeche lord, cowardly Tangaxhuán II, turned over the whole empire to ruthless and gold-hungry conquistador Nuño de Guzmán in 1530. The Purépeche lord also gave his four daughters to Nuño and the other Spanish officers. Some witty Purépeches started calling the Spaniards *tarascues* (sons-in-law), and conquistadors in turn used the term when addressing the Purépeches.

Michoacán de Ocampo

Michoacán's fierce tradition of independence has spawned three separate revolts or conspiracies, José Mariá Morelos's being the most significant. Though the state played a small role in the 1910 Revolution, its inhabitants are nonetheless proud of their history of rebeling against injustice. The state's official name, Michoacán de Ocampo, honors Melchor Ocampo, a leader in the wars for independence.

Since the colonial period, Michoacán's mild weather, fertile soil, and abundant water has made the state one of Mexico's leading agricultural centers. The surrounding forest-covered mountain ranges also attract hunters and wildlife enthusiasts. Large parts of the state still maintain their pristine natural character, untouched by modern civilization. But Michoacán is by no means simply mile after mile of *maíz* and cattle; the state also offers bustling, densly populated towns.

■■■ MORELIA

Morelia remains largely unmarred by the 20th century: rose-colored stone arcades surround the *zócalo,* government buildings with high ceilings and open courts line **Avenida Madero,** and outside the center, whitewashed houses wear parapeted roofs and windows as big as doors. Despite its charm, Morelia has escaped becoming a tourist trap. Here one can see a busy and habitable city at work. Rural life and urban sophistication coexist here with women from the surrounding countryside selling fruit to the students who crowd the theatres and discos at night.

ORIENTATION

Situated 287km west of Mexico City via Rte. 15, Morelia is the largest city on the southerly route from the capital to Guadalajara, another 312km to the northwest. The streets in Morelia form a large grid, and walking in the city is pleasant and relatively uncomplicated. Most sights are well within walking distance of the **zócalo** and the adjacent **cathedral** which are on **Avenida Madero,** Morelia's central boulevard. North-south street names change at Madero, and east-west street names change every other block; Madero never forsakes its name. Where there are two street names on a corner, the newest looking placard is usually correct.

The "Ruta Verde" *combi* (8.50 pesos) connects the **train station** to **Plaza Carrillo,** four blocks south and two blocks west of the *zócalo*. Coming from the train station, cross the street and wait at the *parada* (stop). To get downtown from the **bus station,** go left (east) as you leave the building, take your first right onto Valentín Gómez Farías, walk two blocks, and then make a left on Av. Madero—the *zócalo* is three blocks ahead. For longer trips, public transit in Morelia is adequate (see Morelia Practical Information: Public Transportation below). If you're in need of a cab, head for the bus station, where taxis are prolific 'round the clock.

PRACTICAL INFORMATION

Tourist Offices: State Tourist Office, Nigromante 79 (tel. 13-26-54), on Nigromante at Madero Pte. in the Palacio Clavijero, 2 blocks west of the *zócalo*. From the bus station, walk two blocks south on Valentín Gómez Farías to Av. Madera Pte. and turn left—it is on the far corner of that block. Very clear, though somewhat distorted, map of the center of town and more sketchy ones of the areas outside a 5-block radius are distributed by a helpful and friendly young staff. Walking tours arranged here. Open Mon.-Fri. 9am-2:30pm and 4-8pm, Sat.-Sun. 10am-8pm.

Currency Exchange: Banks are scattered throughout the center of the city and there is a particularly high concentration on Av. Madero east of the cathedral. Most are open for exchange Mon.-Fri. 9am-1pm, but will only change dollars until noon; the sole exception is **Bancomer,** which changes until closing time. Two **casas de cambio** near the *zócalo* are Ocampo 178 (tel. 2-84-48) at Zaragoza, which doesn't have great rates but is open Mon.-Fri. 9am-2pm and 4-6:30pm, Sat. 9am-2pm; and Valladolid 38, which has an English-speaking staff and is open Mon.-Fri. 9am-6pm, Sat. 9am-1pm.

American Express: On the east side of town several miles from the center. Servicentro Las Américas L-27, Artilleros Del 471520, postal code 5820 (tel. 14-19-50). Open Mon.-Fri. 9am-2pm and 4-7pm, Sat. 10am-2pm.

Post Office: Av. Madero Ote. 369 (tel. 12-05-17), 5 blocks east of the cathedral. Open for Lista de Correos and stamps Mon.-Fri. 8am-7pm, Sat.-Sun. 9am-1pm. **Postal Code:** 58000.

Telephones: 24 hr. long-distance service in the bus station. **Casas de larga distancia** dot the city (usually around 8 pesos per minute to the U.S). Fax machine on Madero opposite the *zócalo,* but no collect calls. For international collect calls, try the phones at the post office (free). **Telephone Code:** 451.

Telegrams: Av. Madero Ote. 371 (tel. 12-06-81), next to the post office. Open Mon.-Fri. 9am-8pm, Sat. 9am-1pm.

Airport: Aeropuerto Francisco J. Múgica (tel. 3-67-80), on Carretera Morelia-Cinapécuaro at km27. Has Aeroméxico and Mexicana information. Destinations include Mexico City (around 297 pesos) and Guadalajara (around 207 pesos).

Train Station: (tel. 16-16-97), on Av. del Periodismo. To Mexico City (1 per day at 10:55pm, 8hrs., sleeper 40 pesos), and Uruapan (1 per day at 5:25am, 3hrs., 10 pesos).

Bus Station: Ruíz, at V. Gómez Farías (tel. 2-56-64). **Herradura de Plata** to Mexico City (more than 1 per hr., 4½hrs., 33 pesos). **Flecha Amarilla** goes most frequently to Guadalajara (17 per day, 5hrs., 16 pesos); Guanajuato (10 per day, 4hrs., 9.10 pesos); and San Luis Potosí (via Querétaro, 4 per day, 7hrs., 28 pesos). **Ruta Praíso/Galeana** goes to Cárdenas (15 per day, 8hrs., 20.50 pesos); frequent departures to Pátzcuaro and Uruapan. **Tres Estrellas de Oro,** longer-distance to Mazatlán (1 per day, 15hrs., 51.50 pesos) and Monterrey (1 per day, 13hrs., 63 pesos).

Public Transportation: Buses (.50 pesos) and *combis* (.70 pesos) serve the city well (6am-10pm), but during rush hour they inevitably overflow with passengers and move slowly through horrendous traffic. *Rutas* 2 and 4 ply Av. Madero regularly in both directions, and are useful for getting to and from the Parque Cuauhtémoc and the aqueduct.

Laundromat: There are numerous *lavenderías* throughout the city. One is: **Lavandería Automática Ivon** (tel. 14-31-58), on the Circuito de Campestro. 7 pesos per kg. Open Mon.-Fri. 9am-8:30pm, Sat. 9am-7:30pm.

Red Cross: Ventura 27 (tel. 14-51-51), at the end of Banuet, next to the Parque Cuauhtémoc.

Pharmacy: Farmacia Moderna, Corregidora 566 (tel. 12-91-99). Open daily 9am-10pm.

Emergency: Call the police at tel. 12-22-22.

Police and Transit Police: (tel. 12-30-24), on 20 de Noviembre, 1 block northwest of the Fuente de las Tarascas at the end of the aqueduct.

ACCOMMODATIONS

Despite a multitude of budget hotels south of Av. Madero and just west of the cathedral, rooms can be hard to find during the university summer session (July-Aug.). At other times, something is sure to be available. None of the hotels are outstanding bargains, but all budgets and tastes are covered.

CREA Youth Hostel (HI), Chiapas 180 (tel.13-31-77), at Oaxaca. Take a taxi or walk west on Madero Pte. and turn left on Cuautla. Continue south on Cuautla for 7 blocks, then turn right on Oaxaca and continue 3 blocks to Chiapas. A good deal if you don't mind sacrificing a little privacy. Cleaner than most CREAs, with a ping-pong table and swimming pool to boot. Beds 11 pesos, breakfast 6 pesos, lunch and dinner 7.50 pesos.

Hotel Colonial, 20 de Noviembre (tel.12-18-97). Cozy courtyard graced by stone arches and pillars. Glows a deep yellow. High ceilings, large windows, and a friendly staff. All rooms with bath and TV. Singles 35 pesos. Doubles 50 pesos.

Hotel El Carmen, Ruíz 63 (tel. 12-17-25), 3 blocks north of Av. Madero between Juárez and Morelos. Melon-colored tiled lobby with stone pillars. Small but clean rooms, some without windows, but those with look out onto a beautiful, quiet plaza. All rooms with bath. 30 pesos single, 40 pesos double, an extra 10 pesos for a room with TV.

Posada Don Vasco, Vasco de Quiroga 232 (tel. 12-14-84), 3 blocks east and 2 blocks south of the cathedral, adjacent to La Hostería del Laurel restaurant. Open courtyard with green plants, brown walls. Dark rooms with peeling paint, but high ceilings and clean bathrooms. Singles 45 pesos. Doubles 57 pesos. *Cuartos economicos* (smaller, sparser, and darker): singles 25 pesos, doubles 30 pesos.

Hotel Mintzicuri, Vasco de Quiroga 227 (tel. 12-06-64), across from the Posada Don Vasco (above). Origin of the intriguing name is unknown, but the mural spanning the walls of the lobby may provide a clue. Small, uniform, clean rooms overlooking a courtyard with cars parked below. Sparkling clean bathrooms. Singles 52 pesos. Doubles 66 pesos.

Posada Lourdes, 340 Av. Morelos Nte. (tel. 12-56-03), across from the Casa de Cultura. True to its name's religious motif. If all you want is a clean bed for a few dollars, then disregard the narrow foreboding stairs. Singles 25 pesos. Doubles 30 pesos.

FOOD

Good inexpensive food can be found throughout the city. Almost every street has at least one family-run restaurant that opens onto the street with a few tables, makeshift chairs and *comida corrida* (usually around 7 pesos). The restaurants on the *zócalo* tend to be more expensive, but are reasonable and pleasant for breakfast.

Numerous taco and tortilla stands can be found around **Plaza Agustín** and in front of the bus station.

Cafe Lefiance, Pino Suarez 567. 1 block north of Madero. A real restaurant: uniform carved wood chairs, tablecloths, romantic lighting and all, with prices that match the smaller, more informal restaurants. *Comida corrida* 8 pesos.

La Hostería del Laurel, Quiroga 232, adjacent to Posada Don Vasco. You may have to share a table. Lively crowd, including families, chows down 'neath the arched ceiling with exposed beams. *Comida corriente* 6.50 pesos.

Restaurant-Bar La Huacana, Aldama 116 (tel. 12-53-12), at Obeso. The gargantuan oil painting behind the stage makes a nice backdrop for the large cafeteria-like dining area. Stone walls provide great acoustics for the *mariachis* who play Mon.-Sat. 3-5pm and 9-10pm. *Comida corrida* 15 pesos. Enchiladas 12-17 pesos. Open Mon.-Sat. 9am-11pm, Sun. 9am-5pm.

Pizza Real, Muñiz 158-B (tel. 13-34-89). Big, tasty pies smothered in sauce served by friendly, talkative folk. Individual pizza 14 pesos, double 18 pesos and group-sized 27 pesos. Open daily noon-11pm.

Super Pollos, Av. Madero Ote. at Silva (tel. 12-11-14), 2 blocks east of the post office. Cheap oil paintings and an even cheaper wine-bottle clock are the only things to look at here. Great *pollo placero con enchilada* 12 pesos. Breakfast from 5 pesos. Open daily 8am-9pm.

SIGHTS

On its 100th anniversary in 1986, the **Museo Michoacano,** Allende 305 (tel. 12-04-07), one block west of the *zócalo* at Abasolo, underwent a complete renovation. Museum exhibits are now divided into five categories: ecology, archaeology, the colonial period, the struggle for freedom and independent Mexico. Among the most important exhibits is a huge, anonymous painting completed in 1738, *La Procesión del Traslado de las Monjas.* Notes by Diego Rivera call the canvas a ground-breaking work of profound realism in an era when religious themes still dominated art. It depicts colonial society with encyclopedic attention to each social group and its relative importance. Oils on religious themes by Miguel Cabrera and his students are also worth a look, as are those by a trio of indigenous 19th-century artists—Manuel Ocaraza, Felix Parra and Jesús Torres. On the stairway, a powerful mural by Alfredo Zalce portrays those who have shaped Mexico's history and criticizes Mexicans' blind admiration of U.S. mass culture. (Open Tues.-Sat. 9am-7pm, Sun. 9am-2pm. Admission 17 pesos. Free for those under 13 and over 60, for students with ID, and for everyone on Sundays.)

Construction of the **cathedral** overlooking the *zócalo* continued for almost a century (1660-1745) and the drama of its construction can be traced through the different styles of the final product. The massive structure combines the neoclassical idiom with earlier baroque and *Herreriano* (named for the architect of El Escorial, outside Madrid) styles. In the 19th century, a bishop removed the elaborate baroque filigree from the altarpieces and frescoes, and renovated the church's interior in the symmetric and sober Doric neoclassical style. *Indígenas* sculpted the *Señor de la Sacristía,* the oldest treasure of the church, out of dry corn cobs and orchid nectar. In the 16th century, Felipe II of Spain donated a gold crown to top off the masterpiece. (Open 9am-8:30pm.)

Morelos's former residence now contains the **Museo de Morelos,** Morelos 232 (tel. 13-26-51), one block east and two blocks south of the cathedral. The museum displays *El Caudillo's* sable, religious vestments, military ornaments and uniform, as well as other mementos of the surge for independence. Plaques (in Spanish) describe the phases of the war and maps illustrate the campaigns and troop movements. (Open daily 9am-7pm. Admission 1 peso. Free on Sun.) More of a civic building than a museum, the **Casa Natal de Morelos** (Birthplace of Morelos) stands at Corregidora 113, one block south of the cathedral. Glass cases preserve his war cartography, communiqués, letters and additional paraphernalia. Both areas are emblazoned with murals by Alfredo Zalce. Outside there is a beautiful and, yes, shady, courtyard watched over by the martyr's stein bust. Great for an afternoon read. (Open Mon.-Fri. 9am-2pm and 4-8pm, Sat. 9am-2pm. Free.)

The **Casa de Cultura**, Morelos Nte. 485, 3½ blocks north of Madero (13-13-20), is a gathering place for artists and musicians, students and the artistic American traveler. This elegant peach colored stone building houses a bookstore, numerous art galleries, a theater, and a lovely shady cafe. Dance, voice, and silkscreen classes are also offered here as well as a complete listing of the cultural events around the city.

The **Museo de Artesanías,** at Humbolt and Juan de San Miguel, is a huge craft museum and retail store. Actual examples of the crafts are organized by the town of their origin; on display are colorful macramé *huipiles,* straw airplanes, and guitars. Other crafts include geometrically decorated pottery from workshops in Patambán, painstakingly carved white wood furniture, and clay biblical vignettes. The *museo* is impressive, but better prices await you in Pátzcuaro. (Open daily 9am-8pm. Free.) Outside, on the **Plaza Valladolid,** many similar crafts are sold in the market. This plaza marks the site of the 1541 founding of the city of Valladolid. But don't be fooled; despite its colonial appearances, the plaza was built in 1968.

The city's aqueduct, built in 1788, sides a pleasant pedestrian avenue perfect for evening strolls in the western part of the city. Nearby, the well-lit **Plaza de Morelos** is marked by an equestrian monument to José Maria Morelos commissioned by the Diaz dictatorship and ironically inaugurated by the revolutionary forces that toppled him. The **Fuente de las Tarascas** completes the city's romantic center, a copy of the original whose fate remains the subject of imaginative local lore. At night, the area is expertly illuminated to highlight its relaxing splendor.

ENTERTAINMENT

Lisitngs of events can be found at the Casa de Cultura (see Sights above). The **Casa Natal de Morelos** (see Sights above) projects excellent international art and history movies during the week at different times in the early evening (call tel. 13-26-51 for more information). The Cine-Club, sponsor of the films, alternates movies weekly and organizes Eastern European and contemporary Mexican film festivals. Admission is free so seats are rare. **Cinema Victoria,** at Madero Pte. 944-C (tel. 12-43-10), two blocks west of the Hotel San Jorge, features Hollywood's latest interspersed with slice-and-dice and Bruce Lee flicks (admission 4 pesos). For older North American movies, check out **Sala Eréndira** (tel. 12-12-87) on Santiago Tapia behind the Palacio Clavijero.

See plays at 8pm on Wednesday night in the **ISSTE Morelos theater** (tel. 12-92-36), on Av. Madero in the western part of the city. The theater's university and amateur groups perform picaresque plays, pantomime, and—hold on to your black garters!—a Spanish version of *The Rocky Horror Picture Show.*

For a wilder night out, try the **Disco Molino Rojo,** in front of the Plaza Las Américas shopping center in the far eastern reaches of town. At the **Baron Rouge,** in the Plaza Rebullones's basement, next to Parque Cuauhtémoc, the young rowdies are more interested in drinking than dancing. (Both open Thurs.-Sun. 8pm-1am, Fri.-Sat. 8pm-2am.)The college kids flock to **Club XO,** at Calzada Capistre and Acueducto. (Open Thurs.-Sun. 9pm-2am.) Also popular but a smidgen more sedate is **Bambalina's,** Escutín 225 at Lázaro Cárdenas. (Open Thurs.-Sun. 9pm-2am.) Cover about 10 pesos; domestic drink prices about 5 pesos.

Drag the kids off to the zoo in the **Parque Benito Juárez.** To get there, take the "Guenda" *combi* from the corner of Allende and Galeano. (Open daily 11am-6pm. Admission 2 pesos.)

■■■ PÁTZCUARO

Ordained priest and bishop in 1540 at the age of 75, Vasco de Quiroga established his episcopate in the former Purépeche capital, Pátzcuaro. He had been sent to supersede Núñex de Guzmán, the avowed enemy of Cortés and a man with "a reputation for cruelty and extortion, unrivalled even in the annals of the New World." Four years later, Pátzcuaro was selected as the capital of the Michoacán region. Inspired by the humanitarian ideals of Thomas More, Bishop Quiroga defended the Purépeche people from landowners and mining magnates. He taught the residents of each Purépeche village around the Lago de Pátzcuaro a different craft, thereby stimulating community trade and economic health.

Pátzcuaro, with its well-planned colonial architecture, locally crafted woolen goods, and proximity to the island of Janitzo, attracts numerous tourists; its two main squares, **Plaza Bocanegra** and **Plaza Quiroga,** are lined with hotels. Each square has its own atmosphere, reflected in its hotels. The first, near the market, is so busy as to make walking difficult at any time of day, while the second, with its central fountain and well-shaded and rosebush-lined paths, is elegant and quiet. Despite the tourists and surprisingly large population of 40,000, Pátzcuaro retains the atmosphere and authenticity of a peaceful, friendly small town.

ORIENTATION

Route 14 leads into the city of Pátzcuaro from Morelia (70km) and Mexico City, first crossing Quiroga and Tzintzuntzán to the north and nearby Tzurumútaro to the east, and then continuing on to Uruapan, 67km to the southwest.

The quickest way to reach the center from the **bus station** is by *combi* (.75 pesos) or city bus (.50 pesos). Make sure the vehicle you're using is in fact going to the center—many drivers neglect to change their signs when they change routes.

The city of Pátzcuaro encompasses two distinct areas. **Downtown** perches on a hill about 5km south of the mainly residential lakefront. To reach the **lake** from downtown, jump on a public bus labeled "Lago," "San Pedro," or "Sta. Ana," which passes by the east side of Pl. Gertrudis Bocanegra, Portal Regules and Portal Juárez about every five minutes (.50 pesos). These buses rattle down the hill along Av. de las Américas and will brake long enough to drop you off at the restaurant-lined docks, from which *lanchas* (boats) depart for the island of Janitzio and other points around the lake.

PRACTICAL INFORMATION

Tourist Office: Ibarra 1 at Mendoza (tel. 2-12-14), ironically placed in a sanatorium. Office is the 3rd door on the right in the courtyard. Helpful staff. Good map. Mon.-Sat. 9am-2pm and 4-7pm, Sun. 9am-2pm.

Currency Exchange: Banco Serfín, Portal Morelos 54 (tel. 2-15-16), on the north side of Pl. Quiroga. Open Mon.-Fri. 9am-1:30pm.

Post Office: Obregón 13 (tel. 2-01-28), ½ block north of Pl. Bocanegra. Open Mon.-Fri. 8am-7pm, Sat. 9am-1pm. **Postal code:** 61600.

Telephones: Hotel San Agustín, Portal Juárez 29, on Pl. Bocanegra. International collect calls 5 pesos. Open Mon.-Fri. 8am-10pm, Sat. 2-4pm. **Telephone code:** 454.

Telegrams: Títere 15 (tel. 2-00-10), 1 block east and 1 block south of the library. Open Mon.-Fri. 9am-6pm, Sat. 9am-noon.

Train Station: (Tel. 2-08-03), at the bottom of Av. de las Américas near the lakefront. 1st class to Mexico daily at 9:30pm, 2nd class 9am. 1st and 2nd class to Uruapan daily at 7am.

Bus Station: Off of Circunvalación, south of town. **Herradura de Plata** to Mexico City (6hrs., 40 pesos). **Flecha Amarilla** to Guadalajara (11:30pm, 5hrs., 27 pesos). **Galeana,** frequent service to Morelia (every 15min., 5.5 pesos), Uruapan (every 15min., 5.5 pesos), Quiroga (every 10min., 3.5 pesos), and Santa Clara del Cobre (every ½hr., 2 pesos).

Laundromat: Lavandería Automática, Terán 14 (tel. 2-18-22), 2 blocks west of the Pl. Quiroga. 4 pesos per kg, wash and dry. Takes 3-5 hrs. Open Mon.-Sat. 9am-2pm and 4-8pm.

Pharmacy: Principal, Portal Juárez 33 (tel. 2-06-97, after hours 2-26-50). Open daily 9am-9pm.

Hospital: Romero 10 (tel. 2-02-85). **Clínica del Centro,** Portal Hidalgo, on Pl. Quiroga (tel. 2-19-28). 24-hr. service.

Emergency: Cuerpo de Rescate, Pl. Quiroga, booth 79 (tel. 2-18-89). 24-hr. service.

Police: Hidalgo 1 (tel. 2-18-89), on the western edge of the Pl. Quiroga.

ACCOMMODATIONS

Pátzcuaro has hotels to suit all budgets, including those on the tighter budget. Hotels away from the busy Plaza Bocanegra are usually quieter.

Posada de la Salud, Serrato 9 (tel. 2-00-58), 3 blocks east of either plaza, ½ block past the basilica on its right. Beautiful courtyard, gorgeous carved furniture from Cuanajo, cloud-soft mattresses, and clean bathrooms. Hot water 24 hrs. Singles 35 pesos. Doubles 55 pesos.

Hotel Valmen, Lloreda 34 (tel. 2-11-61), 1 block east of the Pl. Bocanegra. Aztec tile and squawking birds fill the courtyards. Well-lit rooms, some with balconies, though the plumbing is a bit erratic. Singles 25 pesos. Doubles 40 pesos.

Hotel San Agustín, Portal Juárez 27 (tel. 2-04-42), on the western side of Pl. Bocanegra. Don't be turned away by the dark narrow hallway. The rooms are large, bathrooms clean, and staff friendly. Rooms on the right side of the hall are significantly nicer, their door-size windows overlooking the roof of Pátzcuaro.

Posada de la Rosa, Portal Juárez 30 (tel. 2-08-11), on the west side of Pl. Bocanegra. Red tiles and lots of sunlight. Rooms with a view onto the plaza are the nicest. Communal bathroom is functional. 20 pesos, 30 pesos with bath for singles and doubles.

FOOD

Fish from the nearby lake can be found in restaurants throughout the city. *Pescado blanco* is far and away the most plentiful and popular dish. *Charales* (smelts), served in the restaurants along Pátzcuaro's lakefront and on Janitzio, are small sardine-like fish fried in oil and eaten whole by the fistful. Their popularity is proving an environmental nightmare (they are consistently overfished), so if you can resist their attractive appearance, do so. *Caldos de pescado* (fish broth) bubble in large clay vats outside open-air restaurants, particularly on Janitzio. These spicy soups, loaded with fish and sometimes shrimp, crab, and squid, are a meal in themselves.

Most of the small restaurants by the docks close daily at 7pm. *Pescado blanco* usually goes for 25 pesos and fish soup for 10 pesos. More traditional Mexican food, as well as seafood, can be found in town. More formal restaurants with tablecloths, locally crafted furniture, and sometimes tables outside under the arcades, ring Plaza Quiroga. Less formal, and also less expensive, restaurants tend to be closer to Plaza Bocanegra and the market area where good street food is sold as well.

Restaurant El Patio, Pl. Quiroga 19 (tel. 2-04-84), on the south side of the plaza. The quality food and pleasant atmosphere explain the somewhat lofty prices. The sophisticated decor blends still-lifes, empty wine bottles and pillars of rough stone. Read your menu by the light of locally crafted hanging lamps. Complete breakfasts 10-20 pesos. *Menú del día* 18 pesos. Fish 25 pesos. Open daily 8am-10pm.

Fonda del Santuario, Codallos 44 (tel. 2-01-29), 1 block from El Santuario in the market on the left. Cheery courtyard with hanging plants and great lunchtime *menú del día* for a mere 10 pesos. Open Sun.-Fri. 9am-4pm.

Restaurant y Cafetería La Casona, Quiroga 30 (tel. 2-11-79), on the north side of Pl. Quiroga. White walls, wooden beams, and black metal chandeliers create a classy minimalist look. Complete breakfasts 7-8 pesos, fish 28 pesos. Open daily 8am-9pm.

SIGHTS

Pátzcuaro's unique handcrafts—hairy Tócuaro masks, elegant Zirahuén dinnerware, and thick wool textiles—are sold in the Pl. Bocanegra's **market** and in small shops along the passage next to Biblioteca Gertrudis Bocanegra. Bargaining is easier when you buy more than one item, but don't expect a deal on the arrestingly handsome wool articles, which include thick sweaters, brilliantly colored *saltillos* and *ruanas* (stylized ponchos), rainbow-colored *sarapes*, and dark shawls. Retailers stubbornly stick to their prices, however beseechingly you may plead. Still, these items are far from expensive. Sweaters usually sell for the equivalent of US$12-20. Naturally dyed articles generally cost more than brightly colored chemically dyed ones. The haphazard piles of woolens in the market may conceal more treasures than the boutique displays, so nosing around before buying may be productive.

When Vasco de Quiroga came to Pátzcuaro, he initiated not only social change, but bold architectural projects as well. Quiroga conceived the **Basílica de Nuestra Señora de la Salud,** at Lerín and Serrato, as a colossal structure with five naves arranged like the fingers of an extended hand. Each finger was to represent one of Michoacán's cultures and races, with the hand's palm as the central altar representing the Catholic religion. Although construction began in 1554, civil opposition to the ostentation of the building and repeated earthquakes prevented all but the first nave from being opened until 1805. Later, two more earthquakes and a fire forced the church to shut down and undergo reconstruction several times. (Open daily 7am-8pm.)

Today the basilica features a grandiose Romanesque altar. Intricate parallel stripes of frescoed arabesques cross the high, concave ceiling of the church, forming impressive vaults. An enormous glass booth with gilded Corinthian columns and a dome protects the Virgen de la Salud sculpture; when Vasco de Quiroga asked a few Tarascans to design an image of the Virgin in 1546, they complied by shaping her out of *tatzingue* paste made from corn cobs and orchid honey. On the eighth day of May and December, pilgrims from all over Mexico crawl from the plaza to the basilica on their knees to beg the Madonna to perform miracles.

Down the street from the basilica, on Lerín near Navarette, is the **Casa de Artesanías.** Originally a convent for Dominican nuns, also called the **Casa de los Once Patios,** this complex now contains non-clerical craft shops, a small gallery of modern Mexican art and a mural depicting Vasco de Quiroga's accomplishments. The Casa de Artesanías sells superb musical instruments (guitars, flutes and *güiros*) and cotton textiles. For woolens, the market is still your best bet. (Open daily 9am-2pm and 4-7pm.)

The **Museo Regional de Artes Populares,** on the corner of Lerín and Alcanterillas, one block south of the basilica, was once the Colegio de San Nicolás Obispo, a college founded by Vasco in 1540. This fantastic museum displays pottery, copperware and textiles produced in the region. Particularly appealing are the *maque* and *laca* ceramics collections. (Open Mon.-Sat. 9am-7pm, Sun. 9am-3pm. Admission 12 pesos, free Sun.)

Statues of Pátzcuaro's two most honored citizens stand vigil over the town's two principal plazas. The ceremonious, banner-bearing Vasco de Quiroga inhabits the plaza that bears his name. Vast and well-forested, the Pl. Quiroga feels more like a city park than a *zócalo*. The massive, Amazonian, bare-breasted Gertrudis Bocanegra looks out from the center of **Plaza Gertrudis Bocanegra.** A martyr for Mexican independence, Bocanegra was executed by a Spanish squadron in the Pl. Quiroga in October 1817. People say bullet holes still mark the ash tree to which she was tied. Calle Zaragoza spans the two blocks that separate the plazas.

Biblioteca Gertrudis Bocanegra, on the plaza of the same name, occupies the former site of a temple to St. Augustine. The library's multicolored mural by Juan O'Gorman illustrates the history of the Purépeche civilization from pre-Conquest times to the Revolution of 1910. (Open Mon.-Fri. 9am-7pm.) When the next-door **Teatro Caltzontzín,** once part of the Augustinian convent, became a theater in

1936, an as-yet-unfulfilled prophecy was uttered: one Holy Thursday, the theater will crumble as punishment for the sin of projecting movies in a sacred place. You can peek at it in the afternoons, Monday through Saturday. If you dare to test the prophecy, catch a flick (from Mexico and the U.S., 5 pesos); check the posted schedule.

Three km east of the city, at the end of Av. Benigno Serrato, is **El Humilladero** (Place of Humiliation), where the cowardly king Tanganhuán II surrendered his crown, dominions and daughter to the sanguinary Cristóbal de Olid and his Spanish troops. Two peculiar features distinguish this chapel: on its altar stands a rare monolithic cross, undoubtedly older than the date inscribed on its base (1553); on the facade are images of gods which represent the sun and the moon—used to lure Purépeches to Catholicism.

ENTERTAINMENT

At night, the life shifts to the **Disco El Padian,** in the shopping center of the same name (cover 5-10 pesos; take a taxi for about 5 pesos from the square) and the bar **El Padierna,** on Av. de las Américas, between the two Glonettas, which has live music most nights for after-hours fun. But on the whole, such urban eccentricities are not tolerated here. The **Pátzcuaro Cine Club** shows films Tuesdays at 7:30pm in the Escuela Vasco de Quiroga (next to the Museo de Artes Populares). Inquire at the tourist office (see Practical Information) for details.

The town hosts several fiestas during the year. An animated post-Christmas tradition in Pátzcuaro is the pair of **pastorelas,** celebrated on January 6 to commemorate the Adoration of the Magi, and on January 17 to honor St. Anthony of Abad. On both occasions, the citizens dress their domestic animals in bizarre costumes, ribbons and floral crowns. Pátzcuaro's *Semana Santa* attracts people from all across Mexico. Particularly moving is the **Procesión del Silencio** on Good Friday, when a crowd marches around town mourning Jesus' death in silence. The biggest celebration is the **Feria Artesanal y Agrícola,** held at the beginning of December to honor the Virgen de la Salud. This festival includes craft contests, plant sales and fireworks shows. **Noche de Muertos** (Nov. 1-2) holds special importance for the Tarascan community; candle-clad fishing boats row out to Janitzio on the first night, heralding the start of a two-night vigil in the graveyard. The first night commemorates lost children; the second remembers adults.

■ Near Pátzcuaro

The tiny island of **Janitzio,** inhabited exclusively by Tarascan *indígenas* who speak the Purépeche dialect, subsists solely on its tourist trade, another example of the economic marginalization of the *indígenas* in modern Mexico. The very steep main street is lined with stores selling woolen goods, hard-carved wooden chess sets, masks, and kick-knacks. (Unfortunately, both the quality and the prices tend to be geared towards the tourist.) Between the shops are numerous restaurants that all sell the same thing: *pescado blanco* and *charales* (the restaurants towards the top of the island tend to be nicer, with views overlooking the lake). At the summit of the island towers the monumental **statue of Morelos,** the father of Mexican independence. Once inside this statue that is so big it can be seen clearly from Pátzcuaro, a mural tracing the principle events in Morelos's life and the independence struggle follows a winding staircase into the shoulder of the statue. From there, the stairs continue into the cuff of Morelos's sleeve, where openings in the statue permit a spectacular view of the lake. (Admission 1 peso.)

To get to the island, first hop on a **bus** labeled "Lago," "San Pedro," or "Sta. Ana" at the corner of Portal Regules and Portal Juárez at the Pl. Bocanegra. The bus (.60 pesos) rambles to the docks, where you'll stand in a long but fast-moving line to get a **ferry** ticket (round-trip 8 pesos). Ferries leave when they fill up (about every 30 min., 9am-5pm, ½hr.). Check the time of the last boat, since Janitzio does not accommodate the stranded. From the boats, the serene towns of Jarácuaro,

Nayízaro, Puácuaro and Ihuatzio are visible along the verdant lake shore. Before docking, the boats are inundated by Janitzio's fishing people, who paddle out in canoes and briefly demonstrate the use of their butterfly-shaped nets for picture-takers in hopes of earning a small contribution. To reach the other towns around the lake, take a second-class **Flecha Amarilla** bus. (See Practical Information.)

Santa Clara del Cobre, 16km south of Pátzcuaro, was a copper-mining town in its heyday. After the mines closed down, the village devoted itself exclusively to crafting copperware. Every single store sells copper plates, pans, bowls and bells. Prices here are only slightly better than elsewhere in Mexico, but the quality and variety are vastly superior. For a quick look at some of the more exotic pieces, step into the **Museo de Cobre,** close to the plaza. There is little to see in Santa Clara beyond *artesanías*; this side trip requires only a couple of hours. Galeana **buses** leave for Santa Clara every 30min. (2 pesos, 20min.) from the bus station in Pátzcuaro.

The lake at **Zirahuén** makes for another scenic daytrip as well as a good spot for camping. Not as large as Lago de Pátzcuaro, Zirahuén (Where Smoke Rose) is more open, unobstructed by marshes and islands and considerably cleaner (many people actually swim in it). If you want to **camp,** hike up one of the ridges that border the lake and set up in any one of the numerous spots that overlook the water; the landowner—if there is one—may ask you to pay a few pesos. Heavy afternoon rains during June and July can turn summer camping into a soggy experience.

The colonial town itself, with its woodwork shops, also merits a visit. To get there, take the **bus** from the second class station in Pátzcuaro (3 per day, 20min., 2 pesos). If you have wheels, take the road to Uruapan and look for signs to Zirahuén. From Santa Clara del Cobre you can hike about 11km along a dirt road that traverses the wooded slopes to Zirahuén, or catch a ride with people headed to Uruapan from Pátzcuaro. Hitching is not recommended, however.

Tzintzuntzán (Place of the Hummingbirds) was the last great city of the Tarascan empire. In the middle of the 15th century, the great Purépeche lord, Tariácori, on his deathbed, divided his empire among his three sons. When, some years later, Tzitzipandácuari reunited the empire, he chose Tzintzuntzán as the capital; the old capital, Pátzcuaro, became a dependency. It's former glory relegated to history, Tzintzuntzán is but a tiny town now famed for its delicate multi-colored ceramics displayed on tables along Calle Principal.

A peculiar pre-Conquest temple, the **Yácatas,** sits on a hill just outside the city. The base of each *yácata*—all that remains today—is a standard rectangular pyramid. The missing parts of the *yácatas*, however, are what made them unique; each was originally crowned with an unusual elliptical pyramid constructed of shingles and volcanic rock. The pyramids are situated along the long edge of an artificial terrace 425m long and 250m wide. Each building represents a bird. This vantage point commands a view of the **Lago de Pátzcuaro.** (Open daily 10am-5pm. Admission 10 pesos.) Also of interest is the 16th-century Franciscan **convent** closer to town. The olive shrubs that now smother the extensive, tree-filled atrium were originally planted by Vasco de Quiroga.

Tzintzuntzán perches on the northeastern edge of the Lago de Pátzcuaro, on the road to Quiroga and Morelia about 15km from Pátzcuaro. Bring a sweater; Tzintzuntzán can be chilly and damp.

Wooden toys are among the specialties of **Quiroga,** 8km north of Tzintzuntzán near the highway to Morelia. Quiroga's excellent daily **market** sells crafts from most of the region. Intricately carved and painted wooden masks are produced in **Tócuaro,** west of Pátzcuaro on the road around the lake to Erongícuaro. Masks here cost half of what they do in Morelia or Mexico City. To get to Tócuaro, walk down toward the Pátzcuaro pier, cross the railroad tracks, and follow signs to Erongícuaro to the left. You can take the **Flecha Amarilla** bus, too; watch for people waiting by the side of the street.

■■■ URUAPAN

A checker on a checkerboard of ex-*encomienda* farmland, Uruapan offers a convenient base for exploring the nearby waterfall, national park and Parcutín Volcano. About 175km west of Morelia and 320km southeast of Guadalajara, Uruapan can be a stopover on the way to or from Playa Azul (260km to the south) and other Pacific coast resorts, or a side trip from Morelia or Pátzcuaro. Everything in town is within easy walking distance of the *zócalo*, a good orientation point. The statue in the center faces south, looking down **Cupatitzio, Carranza** runs into the southwest corner of the square from the west, and **Obregón** is its continuation on the eastern side of the plaza. The east and south sides of the square are lined with various **portales,** and **Ocampo** runs along its western edge. The **train station** (tel. 4-09-81) is located on Lázaro Cárdenas in the eastern part of town, accessable by the "Zapata," "Zapata Revolución," or "Foviste" buses. Trains to Mexico City (1st class 7:15pm, 12hrs., 18 pesos, sleeper 65 pesos; 2nd class 6:35am, 14 hrs., 15.30 pesos); office open daily 7:30am-7:30pm. **Buses** leave from Benito Juárez (Rte. 15 to Pátzcuaro), in the northeast corner of town. To reach the station from the zócalo, take bus "Central Camionera" or simply "Central" (8 pesos). **Galeana** serves Morelia (2hrs., 11 pesos) and Pátzcuaro (1hr., 5.50 pesos). **Flecha Amarilla** (tel. 3-18-70) has buses to: Querétaro (6hrs., 26 pesos), Mexico City (7hrs., 48 pesos), San Luis Potosí (10hrs., 44 pesos), Manzanillo (10hrs., 34 pesos) and Zamora (50min., 10 pesos). **La Linea** is a good bet for Guadalajara (5hrs., 34 pesos). To get to *el centro* from the bus station, jump a bus marked accordingly (.60 pesos). Cabs also do the trick. The 2.5km trek to the center is a bit much with luggage.

Practical Information The **tourist office,** 5 de Febrero 17 (towards the back of the shopping mall, ½ block south of the eastern end of the *zócalo*, tel. 4-06-33) is open Mon.-Fri. 9am-2pm and 4-7pm, Sat. 9am-2pm. To change money, try **Centro Cambiario**, at Portal Matamoros 19; open Mon.-Fri. 9am-2pm and 4-7pm. Sat. 9am-1pm. The **post office,** Reforma 13 (3 blocks south from *zócalo* on Copitizio and left one block, tel. 3-56-30), is open Mon.-Fri. 8am-7pm, Sat-Sun. 8am-1pm. **Long distance** services at the High Life Perfumery, 5 de Febrero, across the street from the tourist office, and open daily 9am-8pm, or the bus station (open 24 hrs.) **Telephone Code:** 452. A **laundromat** on Carranza 47 at García, 4 blocks west of the *zócalo* (tel. 3-26-69) washes 3kg for 14 pesos. (Open Mon.-Sat. 9am-2pm and 4-8pm.) **Farmacia Fénix,** Carranza 1 at Ocampo (tel. 4-16-40) is open daily 8am-9pm. For medical needs, try the **Red Cross** (tel. 4-03-00) or the **Hospital Civil** on San Miguel (tel. 3-46-60), 7 blocks west of the northern edge of the *zócalo*. The **police** can be found at Eucalyptos at Naranjo (tel. 4-06-20).

Accommodations Cultivating a taste for the "good ol' days" may help you relate better to Uruapan's hotel selection. The nicest joint in town, **Hotel Villa de Flores,** Carranza 15 (1½ blocks from the *zócalo*, tel. 4-28-00), features spotless, post-independence bathrooms, large tasteful cool rooms, a beautiful flower-filled courtyard that invites hummingbirds, and lounging in its comfortable, shady lounge areas. The hotel has its own restaurant and bar and TVs in all rooms. (Singles 55 pesos, doubles 65 pesos.) An evening of melodramatic Victorian prints, narrow stairways and an occasional view of the zócalo costs only 25 pesos for both singles and doubles at the **Hotel Moderna,** Portal S. Degollado 7 (on the eastern edge of the zócalo, tel. 4-02-12). The peeling blue and brown rooms of the **Hotel Capri,** Portal Santo Degollado 10, are tolerable because of the hotel's location (right on the zócalo) and low prices. (One bed, for 1 or 2 people, 25 pesos; 2 beds 35 pesos.)

Food Residing in an agricultural region of fruit and avocados, food is cheap and tasty in Uruapan. Fresh fruit abounds, and the marketplace (½ block north of the *zócalo* on Constitución) dedicated to *antojitos típicos* does a booming business.

Good food is sold by many vendors around the *zócalo*; you can even get pancakes in the morning for 1 peso. Between **Constitución** and **Patzcuaro y Quiroqa** (walk ½ block down Constitución to a small store stairway on the left and up the stairs) is an outdoor square where, for very little money (7 pesos for most dishes) you can get a great dinner, lunch, or snack. Try the **Café Tradicional de Uruapan,** Carranza 5-B, for coffee (3-5 pesos) and cake, or breakfast (7-17 pesos). Though the prices are steep, this cafe with large carved wood chairs offers a place to relax, talk, or read for a while, escaping the bustle of the city. (Open daily 8:30am-2pm and 4-10pm.) To mix with PRI *politicos,* head to the **Restaurant La Pérgola,** Portal Carrillo 4 (tel. 3-50-87). Opening onto the south side of the *zócalo*, this smoky, stately restaurant is a nice place for drinks underneath the wood arches and murals, but too pricey for dinner. (Open daily 8am-11:30pm.)

Sights A few lesser sights may fill the lingering moments in Uruapan. Crafts of Michoacán state are displayed at the **Museo Regional de Arte Popular** (tel. 4-21-38) on the *zócalo*. The building which now houses the museum was the first hospital in the Americas, and today it is home to a smattering of ceramic dining equipment and a small but interesting collection of masks. (Open Tues.-Sun. 9:30am-1:30pm and 3:30-6pm. Free.) If you haven't the time to catch the natural wonders surrounding Uruapan, the **Parque Nacional Barranca del Cupatitzio** at the western end of Independencia is a little bit of jungle on the edge of town. (Open daily 8am-6pm. Admission 1 peso.)

■ Near Uruapan

Further afield sits the town of **Angahuan**, precariously perched near the still active **Paricutín Volcano.** In 1943, the volcano erupted and gushed lava for eight straight years, consuming entire towns and leaving a 700m mountain in its wake. The surrounding land mass is pure, porous, hardened lava. In one area, the lava covered an entire village except for the church steeple, which now sticks out of a field of cold, black stone. You can rent horses and a guide to ascend the volcano (about 15-30 pesos, but haggle hard), or go down into the valley to take a closer look at the church. Both trips take about three to four hours unless you are feeling manic. There are **bungalows** on the outskirts of the village, near the track to the church, that rent big, basic six-bed rooms for 90 pesos (ask the tourist office to make reservations). **Buses** run to Paricutín and Angahuan from the bus station (every ½hr. 7am-8pm, 45min., 4 pesos).

The waterfalls at **Tzaráracua** (sah-RA-ra-kwa), 10km from Uruapan on the road to Playa Azul, cascade 20m into small pools. The first waterfall, called Tzaráracua, is about 1km from the small parking lot—you can walk or ride a horse there (round-trip 15 pesos). The path goes down a flight of cobbled stairs, and hoofing it yourself should take about five to ten minutes, but getting back uphill takes at least twice as long. Another 1.5km beyond the large pool is the **Tzarárecuita,** actually two smaller pools that are free of pollution, perfect for swimming and well worth the extra hike. For an extra 15 pesos you can get there with horses and a guide. Skinny-dipping is popular in the chill water, but watch out for peepers and keep an eye on your clothes. Buses marked "Tzaráracua" leave the south side of the *zócalo* every hour but without a precise schedule (2 pesos). Buses mainly run in the morning, so be sure to to find out what time the last bus back to Uruapan leaves, or you might be stranded at the waterfall.

If guitars are on your Mexican shopping list, go to **Paracho,** 30km north of Uruapan. Carefully crafted six-strings pack just about every store. Fantastic bargains are available; top-of-the-line guitars go for the equivalent of US$130; some are as cheap as US$15. Even if you're not buying, the trip should still prove interesting for the beauty of the scenery and the chance to watch the skillful artisans at work. In the first week of August the town holds an internationally renowned **guitar festi**[illegible] Musicians and craftspeople partake in a musical orgy that includes classical co[illegible] in the *zócalo's* church, fireworks, dancing and guitar-making competitions. If you decide to stay over in the town, the **Hotel Oriental,** behind the market across the *zócalo*, has clean rooms with baths. (Singles 20 pesos. Doubles 25 pesos.) To get to Paracho, hop a bus bound for Zamora (3 pesos) from the Central Camionera.

■■■ PLAYA AZUL

A mere 30km from the border with Guerrero, Playa Azul maintains an easygoing and tolerant posture, attracting people from an array of geographic locations and tax brackets. A pretty (albeit slightly rocky) beach and sunset boost Playa Azul's appeal. Waves break far from shore, and at any given moment at least three lines of white water face the potential surfer or swimmer. The gap between the first and second is calmest and suitable for children; swimmers of average ability should feel comfortable between the second and third.

Practical Information To get to Playa Azul, you'll probably have to go through Lázaro Cárdenas, 24km away. Most bus lines, regardless of what their representatives tell you, stop only at the crossroads 1.5km outside Playa Azul. Buses and *combis* in Lázaro Cárdenas run from 5am to 9pm, leaving from the PEMEX station on the western end of Cárdenas and dropping you off at another PEMEX station on the western edge of Playa Azul. The trip costs 2.50 pesos and takes anywhere from 25 to 45 minutes, depending on how many stops are made along the way. Departures are very frequent at both ends of the ride.

Admirers of orderly city planning will be distressed by the breezy informality of Playa Azul. Although all streets theoretically have names, no one seems to know or care what they are. This can be a bit disconcerting if you arrive at night without a clue as to your current location. (Bring a flashlight—the lack of street lights makes it really dark.) By day, however, the town is easy to navigate. The PEMEX station, where buses stop, is on **Cárdenas,** which runs south to the sea on the western edge of town. If you walk two blocks seaward, you'll reach the stretch of tarmac called **Carranza** that serves as Playa Azul's main street, running parallel to and one block from the beach. Turn left and walk east a few blocks to reach the would-be center of town, marked by the Hotel Playa Azul and a cross street on which you'll find restaurants, taco stands and *fondas.* A dirt and/or mud road, parallel to the main street but closer to the sea, runs past most of the *enramadas* (thatched-roof restaurants) that line the beach. Two blocks inland from the main street is another paved east-west road called **Independencia,** where you'll find most of Playa Azul's pharmacies, *papelerías* and other stores.

The **post office** is more or less across the street from Hotel Pacífico, about a 20-min. walk from the PEMEX station. From the center of town, walk on Carranza with the ocean on your right and turn left when you reach the park; it's the building on your right at the first dirt road you come to. (Open Mon.-Fri. 9am-1pm and 3-6pm. **Postal code:** 60982.) **Telephones** are on Independencia, 2 blocks north of the Hotel Playa Azul; collect calls cost 4 pesos and up. (Open Mon.-Sat. 8am-9pm, Sun. 9am-1pm. **Telephone code:** 753.) **Telegrams** (tel. 6-01-06), are next door to the post office. (Open Mon.-Fri. 9am-3pm.) **Public Bathrooms and Showers** are inland of Pala[illegible]caiboon Cárdenas, 2 blocks south of PEMEX station. **Farmacia Eva** [illegible]árdenas next to the PEMEX station, is open daily 8am-9pm. For medi-[illegible] 24-hour emergency care, go to the **Centro de Salud,** next door to [illegible] **[illegible]olice** are at the east end of Carranza (no phone).

[illegible]tions and Food Some doze in sleeping bags directly on the [illegible]he free hammocks slung in the *enramadas,* whose owners usu-[illegible]t you use the space as long as you eat there beforehand. If you [illegible]taurant's hammock, make sure the proprietors are aware of that [illegible] otherwise you may be discomfited when all unoccupied hammocks are taken down at night. Bear in mind that a tent or elaborate foreign equipment could tempt the otherwise harmless passerby. When camping on the beach, stay within sight of an inhabited *enramada* and inform the occupants of your presence, especially if you plan to leave your belongings in one place for an extended period of time.

If you must have the luxury of a bed, Playa Azul offers adequate albeit somewhat overpriced lodgings. **Hotel del Pacífico,** on Carranza (tel. 6-01-06), a couple of blocks east of Hotel Playa Azul, is the best buy. Rooms are large, clean and comfortable. More importantly, they're only 15 yards from the beach. (Singles 25 pesos. Doubles 45 pesos. May be negotiable.) **Bungalows de la Curva** (tel. 6-00-58), which sits one block south of the PEMEX station, is a small step up in both quality and price. The small pool is a welcome addition to the basic, clean rooms and *agua purificada*. (Singles 40 pesos. Doubles 60 pesos. Bungalow with kitchen for 1-2 people 80 pesos.) **Hotel Costa de Oro,** on Zapata (tel. 6-00-86), is four blocks east of the PEMEX station. Rooms are clean though overwhelmingly brown. Bathrooms are fitted with those ever-elusive toilet seats. (Singles 30 pesos. Doubles 40 pesos.) Prices go up in high-season (Dec.-May).

Don't worry about finding the cheapest *enramada* in Playa Azul—they all charge the same prices for meals. *Ceviche* costs 1 peso, fish entrees 15-20 pesos, eggs *al gusto* 6 pesos. Baby Coronas are 2 pesos, Modelos 3.50 pesos and all *refrescos* 1.50 pesos. Shrimp *al gusto* 25 pesos. If you can't face an *enramada* early in the morning, the best breakfasts in town emanate from the **Hotel Playa Azul.** Try the fantastic hotcakes (6 pesos) and freshly squeezed (or however it's done) papaya juice (2 pesos). Eat by the hotel's beautiful pool and after breakfast take a few laps—better yet, stay for the day and get the most out of the 10 pesos it will cost you, as a non-guest, to use the pool.

HIDALGO

Many of Hidalgo's cities are easily explored on a daytrip from Mexico City, but although the state has been economically important to Mexico since Aztec rule, few areas are of interest to the foreign visitor. Hidalgo has spent history under the influence of the mighty cities of Mexican history: El Tajín, built by the Totonacs, the mysterious Teotihuacán, and Tula, the Toltec city built by the god-king Quetzalcóatl. In latter days, the dull exigencies of production have made Hidalgo less of a prize. Hidalgan cuisine is delicious and exotic. If you do venture into Hidalgo, visit the capital city, Pachuca, and the archaeological ruins of Tula.

■■■ TULA

The signs on the road leading into Tula admonish visitors and residents alike to keep the town clean because of its historical significance. That significance, however, could be easily overlooked—the quiet *zócalo*, bustling market and plentiful taco stands do little to distinguish Tula from other Mexican towns. It doesn't even feel old. The city is in easy daytrip range from Mexico City (80km along Rte. 57 and 85) and from Pachuca (75km); it's also a nice stop for those traveling to or from the Bajío.

Once the Toltec's greatest city, ancient Tula was constructed at the foot of a hill in a region of brooding volcanic mountains. In the final years of Teotihuacán, a band of Chichimecs and Toltecs, led by Mixcoatl-Camaxtli, wandered through the Valley of Mexico before deciding to conquer the Otomí area between present-day Tula and Jilotepec. Supposedly Mixcoatl-Camaxtli then led his people to what is now the state of Morelos, where he married, had a son and subsequently lost his throne. When the son, Ce Acatl Topitzin, grew up, he is thought to have recovered the throne and moved the capital to the foot of the mountain called Xicuco, where he founded Tula.

Ce Acatl Topitzin (a.k.a Quetzalcóatl) is the most venerated king in *indígena* history and mythology. After he founded Tula, he fled (in 884 AD) to the Gulf coast because of strife with neighbors who did not agree with his peaceful ways and who rejected the god he worshiped (for whom he was named). In the years following, several kings expanded Tula into the center of the mighty Toltec empire.

The Toltecs, meaning "builders" in Nahuatl, relied on irrigation for their agricultural success and modeled their architecture after the Teotihuacán style, although the buildings at Tula are of poorer quality than those at Teotihuacán. During the 200-year-long Toltec heyday, the kingdom abandoned its once passivist stance for the violent and bloody sacrificial scene for which it is now notorious. Crop failures and droughts may have weakened the Toltec capital in 1116, and the Chichimecs saw their chance and destroyed Tula, leaving the ruins that exist today at the foot of Xicuco.

Despite its historical significance, the archaeological site at Tula–part of a **national park** (tel. 9-17-73) dedicated to preserving the plants and animals of this semi-desert–is relatively unimpressive. The first structures you see as youreach the main plaza are ballcourt #1, on the north side of the plaza, and Pyramid B, the **Temple of the Atlantes** (sculptured columns), on your left. Dangerously steep steps go up the temple's south face. The roof of this temple was held up by the four monolithic statues known as the *atlantes*. These 4.6m-high statues represent the warrior priests who led the worship of the warlike Tezcatlipoca.

The wall at Pyramid B's northern side, termed the **Coatepantli,** is a facade with reliefs of jaguars in procession, a deity in headdress and heart-devouring eagles. Reliefs of serpents feasting on live humans beautify the adjacent wall.

To the west of Pyramid B is a plaza filled with remains of many columns. This area is called the **Palacio Quemado,** or burnt palace; it is thought to have been either an administrative center in ancient Tula, or the city market. Even without its gaping mouth you can recognize a familiar Chac-Mool. On the east side of the plaza, to your left as you descend Pyramid B, is **Pyramid C.** This building, still not entirely excavated, is sometimes called the Main Building. In front of the ballcourt is a wall called the **Tzompantli,** or place of skulls, thought to have been built by the Aztecs. Early excavations found skulls and teeth on this wall.

The only other excavated structure of interest in the area is **El Corral,** 1.5km north of the main plaza. Because this building is rounded, it is thought to have been dedicated to the god of wind. A dirt path leads north to his shrine from the northern border of the main plaza. The **Museo Jorge R. Acosta,** at the entrance to the ruins, concerns itself with Toltec religion, crafts, leisure-time activity and socioeconomic hierarchy. Although the explanatory information is in Spanish, the museum is definitely worth a visit even for English-speakers.

A written guide is sold for 10 pesos. The museum complex also includes a cafeteria, bathrooms and an information desk where you can request a free guided tour and brochures. (Site open daily 9:30am-4:30pm. Admission 13 pesos. Free Sun. and holidays. Museum free with site ticket.) The town-to-ruins walk is long but manageable: from the plaza, turn left on Zaragoza (the first street toward the bus station). When you reach Ocampo, a sign points to the "Parque Nacional Tula";turn right, and head towards the highway. One street before the main highway, turn left on the road marked by the stone statue. The park lies about 1km up, off the road to the left. For those not up to the hike, **taxis** will take you to the site from town for 5 pesos. Taxis aren't available at the site itself for the return, but hailing one on the highway usually poses no problem

Because Tula is a small town and most people book through just to see the ruins, the budget accommodation is a rare animal. A few cheap and clean hotels do exist Not the most luxurious place in town, but probably the best deal, **Auto Hotel Cuéllar,** 5 de Mayo 23 (tel. 2-04-42), is well-furnished with a bureau and wardrobe in each room. (Singles 40 pesos, with TV 50 pesos. Doubles 50 pesos, with TV 62 pesos.) Hard to miss in the cream-colored building with red trim, bright orange lettering and the sign advertising TV and 24-hr. hot water, is **Hotel Cathedral,** Zaragoza 106 (tel. 2-08-13), right off the plaza. It has small bathrooms, but it's a centrally located and comfortable crash pad. (Singles 49 pesos. Doubles 55 pesos.) Eating establishments are sparse too. Typical *taqueterías* can be found on 5 de Mayo and Zaragoza. Though you may be lonely dining out in Tula, **Restaurant Casa Blanca,** at Hidalgo and Zaragoza, offers a slightly more refined atmosphere in which to sit alone. (5-course *comida corrida* 15 pesos, chicken entrees 15 pesos. Open 8am-10pm.) **Restaurant El Ranchito,** Zaragoza near Hidalgo, is a casual and unembellished family-run restaurant. The place looks tiny when you first enter, but don't worry, there's another room in back. No official menu, but the nice family will cook whatever you feel like eating for unbelievably low prices (5-12 pesos). (Open daily 9am-8pm.)

Downtown Tula consists of a few commercial streets surrounding a central *zócalo.* To reach the *zócalo* from the bus station, turn right down Xicotencatl and then left at Ocampo. Follow the signs to the centro, turning left down Zaragoza. There is no **tourist office,** but the town is small and friendly enough that people on the street will probably be willing and able to answer any question. **Change money** at Bánamex, Leandro Valle 21, down Juárez from the *zócalo.* (Open Mon.-Fri. 9am-noon.) The **post office** is on Av. Ferrocarril. (Open Mon.-Fri. 8am-7pm, Sat. 9am-1pm.) Make **calls** at Teléfonos de Mexico, Av. 5 de Mayo 3, near Mina. (Open Mon.-Sat. 8am-10pm, Sun. 8am-3pm.) **Telegrams** (tel. 2-00-37) are behind the market, in a construction zone. The small gray building is behind the white Loconsa building. (Open Mon.-Fri. 9am-9pm, Sat. 9am-noon.) The **IMSS Clínica Hospital,** Ocampo at Xicotencatl (tel. 2-10-46) in the large brown building, is open for emergencies 24 hrs. The **pharmacy** there is open Mon.-Fri. 24 hrs. The police are on 5 de Mayo 408 (tel. 2-01-85).

NORTHERN VERACRUZ

The northern half of Veracruz generally receives little attention from budget travelers, which is surprising, considering its indisputable attractions. Tuxpan's miles of white sand beaches and shoreside solitude are unavailable to the same extent anywhere else in Mexico. Papantla is an open-air museum dedicated to the culture of the Totonacs, while ruins of their ancient past lie nearby in El Tajín. Jalapa, the state capital, is blessed with all the graces of an inland colonial city—comfortable, cool, cultured, and cosmopolitan.

■■■ TUXPAN (TUXPAM), VERACRUZ

For those descending from the north, Tuxpan and its nearby beaches are a peaceful though provincial relief. For those traveling from the south or west, they may be a disappointment. The friendly family atmosphere, evident in the narrow streets filled with cycling kids and the shaded outdoor cafés in the *zócalo*, marks a departure from the industrial north and its grimy cities. The beach, only 12km away, fills with families every weekend as both kids and parents splash in the clear blue-green water and dig in the fine sand. The town, whose name derives from the Totonac word Tochpan meaning "Place of Wildly Hopping Rabbits" hosts the streams of shoppers and fruit vendors who flow freely along the city's riverfront, where boats incessantly load and unload fish, mangos and bananas.

Orientation And Practical Information Route 180 connects Tuxpan and Papantla and continues north to Tampico, three to five hours away depending on the route taken. Route 180 requires a ferry ride from Tampico; alternatively, Route 127 curves west from Route 180 in Potrero del Llano. Veracruz is 347km southeast, and Mexico City 328km southwest via Route 130. Tuxpan spreads along the northern bank of Río Tuxpan. Two small city gardens, ambitiously called parks, and what lies between constitute the center of town. Parque Reforma is one block inland from the river on Humboldt, west of the central commercial center. Parque Rodríguez Cano lies on the waterfront, just south of the busiest part of town. To reach these parks from the ADO bus station, turn left from the exit and head to the water. Rodríguez Cano is three blocks to your right (west). Continue three more blocks along the river to reach Parque Reforma, one block inland from the river on Humboldt. To get to the beach, take the "Playa" bus east from the riverfront road. Catch the bus at the lone tree along the boardwalk, two blocks west of the ADO station (every 10 min., 6am-8:30pm, 2 pesos).

When making local calls, it may be necessary to dial a 1 before the five-digit numbers listed here. The **tourist office,** run by the Delegación de Turismo (tel. 4-01-77), on Garizurieta 2 #302 along the western edge of Parque Rodríguez Cano (enter building under DELMAR doorway and climb to the 3rd floor), employs a youthful staff with bad maps. (Open Mon.-Sat. 8am-3pm and 4-7pm.) Currency exchange is difficult; an outbreak of counterfeiting has induced local paranoia. Try **Bancomer,** Juárez at Zapata. (Open Mon.-Fri. 9am-1:30pm. Changes currency and checks Mon.-Fri. 9:30am-noon. Rates are mediocre.) Checks may be easier to cash at **Banco Internacional,** along Juárez, about 1½ blocks west from Parque Reforma (Mon.-Fri. 10am-12:30pm), or **Banamex,** at the side street off the northern part of Parque Reforma, for a 24-hr. ATM. The **post office,** on Morelos 12 (tel. 4-00-88), 2 blocks east of Parque Reforma, is open for stamps, *Lista de Correos*, and packages Mon.-Fri. 8am-8pm, Sat. 9am-1pm; for registered mail Mon.-Fri. 8am-6:30pm, Sat. 9-11am. **Postal Code:** 92800. Make collect calls from the special long distance **phones** on the side of Parque Reforma, on the back of the Hotel Riveria. (Open Mon.-Fri. 8:30am-1:30pm.) A credit card phone in the telegram office takes MC, Visa, and AmEx. **Telegram office,** Ortega 20 (tel. 4-01-67), just beyond "Pollo Feliz" sign on left-hand side of the street, is open for telegrams Mon.-Fri. 9am-8pm, Sat. 9am-5pm; for money orders Mon.-Fri. 9am-5pm, Sat. 9am-1pm.

Tuxpan has several **bus stations. ADO** Rodríguez 1 (tel. 4-01-02), has first-class service to: Tampico (29 pesos), Mexico City (38 pesos), Poza Rica (60 pesos) (where buses leave to Papantla every 10 mins., 6am-11:30pm, 1.50 pesos), Papantla (58 pesos), Veracruz, Puebla, and Jalapa. **Blancos,** Constitución 18 (tel. 4-20-40), 2 blocks past the bridge, has second-class service to many of ADO's destinations, without the cleanliness or comfort. Many buses run off schedule; call or stop by to confirm departure times. **Omnibus de México,** (tel. 4-11-47), at the bridge and waterfront is a small first-class station with only a few destinations; to Mexico City (2 per day, 36 pesos), Guadalajara (2 per day, 91 pesos), Tampico (2 per day, 26 pesos), Queretaro (3 per day, 48 pesos), and Poza Rica (10 per day, 6 pesos).

For medical attention, contact the **Red Cross,** Galeana 40 (tel. 4-01-58), 8 blocks west of the center along the river, right on Galeana and 4 blocks north, next to the police station. They provide 24-hr. emergency and ambulance service to any medical facility. **Farmacia Independencia,** (tel. 4-03-12) Independencia 4, on the riverfront side of the market. The **Hospital Civil,** Obregón 13 (tel. 4-01-99), 1 block west of the bridge, then 1½ blocks inland and up the inclined driveway on the right, provides 24-hr. emergency service.The **police** can be found at Galeana 38 (tel. 4-02-52 or 4-37-23), 8 blocks west of the center along the river, next door to the Red Cross. (Open 24 hrs.)

Accommodations and Food Budget hotels lie between Parque Reforma and Parque Rodríguez Cano. **Hotel El Huasteco**, Morelos 41 (tel. 4-18-59), diagonally across the street from Lonchería Mérida (below) at Parque Reforma, is the best budget option despite its tiny and dark rooms. The noisy A/C is a life-saver in the unbreatheable hot and humid Tuxpan nights. (Singles 40 pesos, doubles 46 pesos.) **Hotel Parroquia,** at the sidstreet to the left of the Cathedral on Parque Rodríguez Cano (tel. 4-16-30). Light rooms with strong neon lamps, fans, almost comfortable beds, shower curtains and toilet seats. Tender white lizards will guard you in your sleep from evil mosquitoes and other bugs. The rooms up front are far breezier and noisier. (Singles 44 pesos, doubles 55 pesos.) **Hotel del Parque,** Humboldt 11 (tel. 4-08-12), on the east side of *Parque Reforma*, puts you right in the thick of things if you can deal with a little noise (the hotel is right above a gym/Tae Kwan Do studio). Uncomfortable beds and worn showers, but the rooms are large and clean. Terrace overlooks the *Parque Reforma*. (Singles and doubles 44 pesos.)

Soulless hotel cafeterias permeate Tuxpan. The majority serve mostly *antojitos mexicanos* and lots of seafood. **Barra de Mariscos del Puerto,** at Juárez and Humboldt (tel. 4-46-01), across from the southeast corner of Parque Reforma is decorated with a sea motif to set the mood. *Parrillada de Mariscos* (a veritable seafood menagerie) can feed two for 30 pesos. (Open daily 8am-11pm.) **Lonchería Mérida**, Humboldt and Morelos (tel. 5-74-24), on the northeast corner at the *Parque Reformaserves* authentic fare to locals and Tuxpan's sporadic tourist alike. *Plátanos fritos* and *tamales* for 2 pesos each, everything else 6-8 pesos. Take-out available. (Open daily 7am-2pm and 5-11:30pm.) **Cafetería El Mante,** Rodríguez 11, two doors up from ADO station (away from waterfront), is busier and livelier than any of the hotel cafés. Strictly Mexican and reasonably priced (10-15 pesos) entrees are served round the clock in an open atmosphere decorated with a poster of Seattle.

Sights and Entertainment Although Tuxpan can boast neither grand cathedrals nor museums of world renown, the city's sights are like a draft of local vintage—pleasant and soothing. Near the simple white cathedral lie several parks ideal for a good book, a quiet meal or a fine afternoon watching the world-as-movie. On the west side of the Parque Reforma lies the **Museo Regional de Antropología e Historia** (open Mon.-Sat. 10am-2pm and 4-6pm, Sun. 10am-1pm. Free), which is inside the **Casa de la Cultura** and has a smattering of Huastec pottery. The Mercado Rodríguez Cano sells mostly food, clothing and practical goods. The main entrance is at Rodríguez and the waterfront, near the ADO station.

A true find rests on the other side of the river. Accessible by blue ferry for .50 pesos (1 peso for foreigners) the **Casa de la Amistad México Cuba** (a.k.a. La Casa de Fidel Castro) chronicles Mexican-Cuban connections over the past three centuries. The helpful caretaker will make sure you appreciate the exhibits and will add personal commentary. The first part of the museum is in an old warehouse and consists mostly of photographs of Havana before and after the revolution. *Sala #1* of the second building revisits the days of piracy and Spanish imperialism in the Caribbean. *Sala #2* is the main event, containing pictures of a slim Fidel and a young Ché Guevara practicing their marksmanship. In addition, it houses Castro's uniform, a map of Castro's route from Tuxpan to Cuba in 1956 and various pictures of the young revolutionaries flexing their muscles on a beach near Tuxpan. The final building is the actual bedroom and bath Castro used for the three years he stayed in Tuxpan. Pictures like *Castro in the Mountains of Cuba* and *Castro with Mexican President Cárdenas* (who nationalized the petroleum industry in 1938) line the walls. The exhibit ends with a farewell letter from Ché to Castro and a replica of the *Granma*, the ship which carried the soon-to-be victorious revolutionary fighters to Cuba. To get to the museum, after you disembark the ferry, walk to the right along the river on the wide sidewalk and continue straight up the dirt road. It's parallel to the northern part of Tuxpan, beyond even Galeana. (Open Mon.-Sun. 7am-5pm. Free, of course.)

Tuxpan's greatest asset is its 2km of very merry riverfront. The *malecón* (pier) is a lively place, with Spanish rap tunes drifting through the squads of people walking to and from town. Palm trees and benches line the boardwalk, which parallels the water and offers views of the fishing people hauling in their catch. They sell their haul up and down the waterfront and congregate in the greatest numbers under the bridge, where piles of pineapples, bananas, shrimp, and fish can be had for a bare minimum.

Twelve km east of Tuxpan's city center, the river flows to the gulf, and the beach used to extend 20km in either direction. Near the bus stop the beach can be crowded and slightly dirty, especially in season, but the wide expanse of fine sand continues far enough for you to stake a private claim somewhere down the line. The water is relatively clean and safe for swimming, though coagulated oil from a nearby refinery sometimes washes ashore. Seafood cocktails from the quintillions of cheap seafood stands cost 8-12 pesos. Buses (2 pesos) marked "Playa" leave Tuxpan for the beach every 15 minutes from 6am to 10pm; the last bus returns at 8:30pm. Though there are a number of bars in the center, the best nightlife begins a few blocks down the river after the crowds in the *Parque Reforma* thin out. Just past Allende on Reyes Heroles, facing the river, sits **La Puesta del Sol,** which serves food, beer and mixed drinks to quiet customers enjoying the live music, tropical and salsa (tel.4-73-66). Just a block down is **Charlôt** (tel. 4-40-28; open Tue.-Sun. noon-midnight), which serves appetizers or drinks outdoors or inside its classy establishment. Turn right on Pérez to find **La Bamba,** a high-tech sunken video bar accentuated by its glowing neon entrance and large-screen musical entertainment. A professional crowd drinks cocktails and beers served by the bucket.

■■■ PAPANTLA, VERACRUZ

The Totonacs dominated the top half of what is now the state of Veracruz for hundreds of years, until Aztec conquest circa 1450. In turn, Cortés, with assistance from the Totonacs, crushed the Aztec Empire in the 16th century. Ultimately the Totonacs fared no better than any other indigenous group under the Spanish, but in Papantla (pop. 125,000) Totonac culture persists, beautifully and accessibly. The ancient ritual flight of the *voladores* is justly famous, thrilling observers with commercial regularity in the *zócalo*. Papantla is the best base to explore El Tajín, the Totonac capital city ruins and one of the most impressive archeological sites in Mexico. Crawling up the green foothills of the Sierra Madre Oriental, Papantla looks out onto the gorgeous plains of Northern Veracruz. The *zócalo* is crowded with friendly locals, while *indígenas* continue to don traditional dress: the men in wide white bloomers, the women in lacy white skirts and embroidered blouses with shawls. The city is exceptionally proud of its indigenous history; when Totonac rebels rose up in 1836, Papantla was their stronghold. Though their struggle was politically unsuccessful, in Papantla the *indígena* culture prevailed.

Orientation and Practical Information Papantla lies 250km northwest of Veracruz and 21km southeast of Poza Rica along Route 180. The ruins of El Tajín lie 12km south of the city. The *centro* is marked by the plaza (formally known as **Parque Téllez**), the cathedral to the south, Enríquez on the plaza's downhill northern edge, Juárez perpendicular to the left, and 20 de Noviembre perpendicular to the right as you face the cathedral. To get from the first-class bus station to the *centro*, turn left onto Juárez out of the station and veer left at the fork. Taxis (8 pesos to the *centro*) pass frequently along Juárez. If you arrive at the second-class bus station (on a microbus from Poza Rica, 1.50 pesos), turn left outside the station and ascend 20 de Noviembre three steep but short blocks to the northwest corner of the plaza.

The tourist office (tel. 2-01-23), in the yellow building at the base of the **Monumento al Volador,** dispenses Spanish brochures, a joke map and vanilla-scented souvenirs. (Open Mon.-Fri. 9am-1pm and 3-6pm, Sat. 9am-2pm.) Exchange currency at any of the three banks on Enríquez. **Banamex,** Enríquez 102, may be the most helpful, and has a 24-hr. ATM for MC, Visa, Cirrus, and Plus. (All banks open for exchange Mon.-Fri. 9am-1pm.) The **post office,** at Azueta 198 (tel. 2-00-73), on the second floor, is open for stamps and *Lista de Correos* Mon.-Fri. 9am-1pm and 4-7pm, Sat. 9am-noon; for registered mail Mon.-Fri. 9am-1pm and 3-5pm. (**Postal Code:** 93400.) Make international collect calls at local hotels or at the pharmacy on the eastern side of the plaza (7 pesos; open daily 9am-10pm). **Hotel Tájin,** Nuñez y Domínguez 104, charges 15 pesos for collect calls, and is open 24 hrs. (**Telephone Code:** 784.) The **telegram office** is located at Enríquez 404 (tel. 2-05-84), about 5 blocks east of the *zócalo.* (Open for telegrams Mon.-Fri. 9am-8pm, Sat. 9am-noon; for money orders Mon.-Fri. 9am-1pm and 3-5pm, Sat. 9am-noon.)

Papantla has two bus stations. The first-class **ADO** station, on Juárez 207 serves Poza Rica (10 daily, 3 pesos), Jalapa (7 daily, 30 pesos), Veracruz (daily, 39 pesos), Mexico City (4 daily, 32 pesos), Tuxpam (3 daily, 9 pesos), Puebla (8 daily, 38 pesos), and Tampico (7 daily, 33 pesos). The **second class terminal,** known better as *Transportes Papantla*, 20 de Noviembre 200, is best for its frequent service (approximately every 10-15min. 6am-11:30pm) to Poza Rica (35min., 1.50 pesos). All buses leave as they fill up, pay after you board. **Poza Rica** (21km northwest) is a much more convenient bus transfer spot. Their **ADO** terminal (tel.2-04-29 or 2-00-85) serves Mexico City (21 daily, 33 pesos), Tampico (21 daily, 33 pesos), Papantla (15 daily, 2.50 pesos), Veracruz (13 daily, 45 pesos), Villhermosa (12 daily, 88 pesos), Jalapa (11 daily, 32 pesos), Tuxpan (9 daily, 7 pesos), Puebla (5 daily, 32 pesos). The **Red Cross** on Pino Suárez, at Juárez (tel. 2-01-26), responds to emergencies and minor accidents, with ambulances or appropriate specialists. (Open 24 hrs.) **Farmacia Aparicio,** Enríquez 103, on northern border of the plaza, is open daily 7am-10pm. For **emergency medical assistance,** try the Clínica IMSS, 20 de Noviembre at Lázaro Cárdenas (tel. 2-01-94), in a big beige building. From the ADO station, take a right and walk 2 blocks to Cárdenas (no sign except "Clínica IMSS"), then turn left. IMSS is ½ block up on your right. (Open 24 hrs.) **Police** can be reached at 2-00-75 or 2-01-50, or in the Palacio Municipal 24 hrs.

Accommodations and Food Few accommodations of any variety are available in Papantla; try nearby Poza Rica, 21 km from Papantla, easily accessible by bus. **Hotel Pulido,** Enríquez 205 (tel. 2-00-36), 1½ blocks down Enríquez, has dark rooms and crusty bathrooms with fans, flowery sheets and amusing curtains. Beware of the basement "restaurant," a bar where it's often drunk amateur night on the piano until all hours. (Singles 40 pesos, doubles 60 pesos.) **Hotel Tajín,** Nuñez y Domínguez 104 (tel. 2-01-21), ½ block to the left as you face the cathedral, is a light-blue building with rounded terraces overlooking the valley. Spotless rooms with TV and phone, with A/C or fan. (Singles with fan 60 pesos, with A/C 86 pesos; doubles with fan 73 pesos, with A/C 100 pesos.) Attractive murals in the lobby and hallways belie the worn rooms in **Hotel Totanacapán,** 20 de Noviembre and Olivo (tel. 2-12-24 or 2-12-18), 4 blocks down from the plaza. TV, fans, and nice bathrooms do manage to compensate, however. (Singles with fan 52 pesos, with A/C 75 pesos; doubles with fan 75 pesos, with A/C 90 pesos.)

Papantla's few restaurants serve regional delicacies to tourists looking for the real thing. Most restaurants stick to very reasonably priced *antojitos mexicanos* ("little cravings"); try some pork tamales wrapped in banana leaves. **Restaurante Los Costales,** Obisbo de las Casas 105, lies 4-5 short blocks down Lázaro Muño, and right 1½ blocks uphill. This authentic and enchanting family-run restaurant is decorated with artifacts and *costales* (regional tough cloth bedsheets). Excellent menus *del día* all cost 8 pesos, including soup and a huge main dish. (Open Mon.-Sat. 9am-11pm.) **Restaurante Enrique,** Enríquez 103, attached to the Hotel Premier is somewhat expensive, but worth it. Great ale, bright blue tablecloths and porthole fish tanks add to the surreal effect. *Fillete relleno* is a richly-garnished filled and breaded fillet (25 pesos) while *casuela de mariscos* is just as tempting, but prepared in a clay pot (25 pesos). (Open daily 8am-7pm.) **Restaurante Terraza,** Reforma 100, on the second floor, southwest corner of the *zócalo,* isn't fancy, but a pleasant spot where you can sit outside and survey plaza activity below. All dishes, including *cecina* (dried meat), cost less than 15-20 pesos. (Open daily 7:30am-midnight.)

Sights and Entertainment Most of the sights in town are on or adjacent to the park, and relate to the city's Totonac heritage. South of the plaza but slightly farther uphill is the **Catedral Señora de la Asunción,** remarkable not so much for its interior but for the 50m-long, 5m-high stone mural carved into its northern wall. The mural, called Homenaje a la Cultura Totonaca, was created by Teodoro Cano to honor local Totonac heroes and folkloric figures. The focus is on the plumed serpent Quetzalcóatl whose image runs along the full length of the carving. At the far left of the mural is a representation of the Dios del Trueno (god of thunder), who announces the coming of the rains. From left to right, the mural follows a rough chronological outline, moving from the mythical first family to the discovery of maize, which ended the nomadic lifestyle and established Totonac agricultural civilization. The mural moves on to depict the Pyramid of the Niches, the focal point of El Tajín, flanked by characteristic male and female faces with typical round cheeks, smallish noses and smiles. Next, the ballplayers from the courts of El Tajín vie for the right to ritualistic death but deified mortality. Modern products, oil and the vanilla bean, lie to the right, and the mural ends with the head of Quetzalcóatl. Five faces belonging to local figures important in the history of Papantla are carved near the open jaw.

The cathedral's spacious courtyard on the hill commands a view of the *zócalo.* The courtyard, christened the **Plaza de los Voladores,** is the site of the ceremony in which five male *voladores* acrobatically entreat the rain god Tlaloc to water the year's crops. The performance begins with five elaborately costumed men climbing a stationary pole to a platform about 20m above the plaza. Having consumed courage-enhancing fluids, four of the hardy five start to "fly"—hanging by their feet from ropes wound around the pole. They spin through the air and slowly descend. All this to the music of the fifth man, who plays a flute and dances on the pin-head of the pole. Originally, the four fliers corresponded to the four cardinal directions, and the different positions assumed during descent were related to requests for specific weather conditions. With the rise in tourism, however, the performance has lost its meteorological significance and gone the way of much *indígena* religion, subjugated to commercial exigencies. Instead of once every 52 years , the *voladores* now fly as often as the tourist is able to pay them. If you visit during the ten-day Festival of Corpus Christi, held in mid-June, you might see the *voladores* perform as often as thrice a day. Papantla comes alive with games, typical food stands, artistic expositions, fireworks, traditional dances and cockfights.

Papantla's latest effort to enshrine its *voladores* is the **Monumento al Volador,** a gigantic flute-wielding *indígena* statue erected in 1988 atop a hill, visible from all over town. To get to the monument, where you can read explanatory plaques and see Papantla in its entirety, walk up Reforma along the right side of the cathedral; bear left and walk uphill. At night the monument is marked by a small red light, which looks oddly like the tip of a burning cigarette.

A mural decorates the inside of the *zócalo*'s centerpiece, a domed kiosk. Painted by Arturo Cano in the 1960s, the mural represents the indigenous conception of creation. The four cardinal points are personified as warriors, each representing different natural calamities that have befallen Mesoamericans. The *zócalo* is also furnished with a set of mosaic benches framing small paintings of the Totonacs, in a style typical of northern Veracruz.

The town's two markets lie next to the central plaza. Mercado Juárez, at Reforma and 16 de Septiembre, off the southwest corner of the *zócalo*, specializes in poultry and veggies but is neither particularly colorful nor low-priced. Mercado Hidalgo, on 20 de Noviembre, off the *zócalo*'s northwest corner on a small triangular block, vends many of the same items as Mercado Juárez. In addition Hidalgo offers a large collection of traditional handmade clothing amidst its supply of machine-made outfits. The men's garb consists of striking white sailor shirts and baggy white pants. Unlike *indígenas* from other regions of Mexico, the Totonacs have no qualms about women wearing clothing designed for men, and often gather in amused groups to watch fitting sessions.

■ Near Papantla: El Tajín

The Totonacs' most important city and religious center, El Tajín lies in ruins a half-hour bus ride south of Papantla. Named after the Totonac god of thunder, the site has revealed Aztec, Mixtec/Zapotec and Mayan influence, but it has otherwise shed little light on the origins of Totonac culture. The well-preserved buildings contain enough alluring carvings and artwork to require a visit. June through August *voladores* perform here daily. The rest of the year, they perform only on Saturday and Sunday. The exhibition lasts about 15 minutes, and starts when enough spectators assemble at the pole inside the entrance booth. A seated man in costume requests a donation of a few pesos.

A **museum** near the entrance shows pottery and carvings discoveries of El Tajín, but lacks explanatory plaques for most of the objects. The exhibit of local poisonous beasties should dissuade you from wandering off the clearly marked paths.

Beyond these buildings, at the entrance to the site, a detailed map stand greets visitors. From there, a path leads to the central area among four large symmetrical and well reconstructed pyramids. Due to the recent completion of their restoration, explanatory signs may not exist for every site. Those that do are written in Spanish, English, French, German, and Totananco. The next area is El Tajín's main plaza. The first temples to the left enclose the most interesting of Tajín's ballcourts. Three pairs of wall carvings, two at each end and one in the center of each wall, all in excellent condition, give tips for fans of the ubiquitous pre-conquest ball game, *pok-ta-pok.* The grassy ballcourt is in between the two long walls directly to your left. Returning to the main cluster of ruins, you will see buildings labeled #1, 3, 4 and 5 on the map. Directly in front lies building 4, to the right building 3, and diagonally to the left building 1, the famous Pyramid of the Niches.

The **Pyramid of the Niches** is a unique piece of calendrical architecture: seven levels with a total of 365 niches corresponding to the days of the year—they were once done up in red and blue paint. Some archaeologists believe that the temple guarded the Totonac llama (flame), a symbol of life and prosperity. The Totonacs marked time in 52-year epochs, during which a single flame was kept continuously burning. At the end of each epoch, the carefully nurtured flame was used to ritually torch many of the settlement's buildings. Each new epoch of rebuilding and regeneration was inaugurated by the lighting of the new flame.

Building 5, to the left of the Pyramid of the Niches, is notable for the well preserved statue of a Totonac god. Visitors may pay their respects by bowing their heads.

The **main plaza** near the Pyramid of the Niches is known simply as Tajín; the area beyond these structures, set on a series of hills and terraces, is called Tajín Chico. Archeologists hypothesize that this was the residential and administrative center of El Tajín. Some buildings here are in good condition, but most have not been excavated, reconstructed or even carefully preserved. As a result, park officials don't mind if visitors scamper up the higher buildings to get a view of the site and surrounding rolling hills.

To get to Tajín Chico, head north to a long flat building; to the right is a small, recently excavated ballcourt, with another series of wall carvings, smaller and more faded than the first set. To the left of the ballcourt is a tiny sign pointing the way to Tajín Chico. Turn left at this sign and ascend the stairs of the building all the way at the western border of the site. Turn right at the top of the stairs to see structures "B" and "C" ahead.

Nothing in Tajín Chico is clearly marked. The first building at the far end is worth visiting for its interior. This building has a Mayan-influenced primitive arch (*cor-*

beled). If you ascend the steep staircase, you can walk all the way around the square and view the surrounding hills from each direction. The building farthest to the north is the building of the columns, not much to look at itself, but offering the best view of the whole complex. It is barely reachable by a tiny winding path among rich vegetation.

The entrance to the entire El Tajín site is 300m down the access road off Route 180 beside the "Archaeological Zone" billboard. (Site open daily 9am-5pm. Admission 13 pesos, free for Mexican students—try your foreign ID anyway, Sun. and holidays free.) Be equipped with an adventurous spirit and plenty of water to battle the dry, hot sun of Tajín Chico. There is no guidebook available at the site, but one may be purchased at the **Museo Nacional de Antropología** in Mexico City.

El Tajín is accessible from the **Transportes Papantla** second-class terminal. Board any bus headed for the tiny village El Chote (6 pesos); from there, pick up the bus bound for Poza Rica (1 peso). This bus stops at the very entrance of the site. To return to Papantla, take the "San Andrés," "Coyutla," or "Coxquihui" bus to El Chote and change there for Papantla. If lucky, you might be able to catch one of the minibuses that runs directly between Papantla and El Tajín. These buses run every hour to hour and a half (schedule not dependable) and leave from the southwest corner of the park (2 pesos).

■■■ JALAPA (XALAPA)

Sitting high on a mountain slope, Jalapa (or sometimes Xalapa) will surprise visitors with its decrepit colonial beauty, cultural legitimacy, and strapping heavy atmosphere. The capital of the state of Veracruz, Jalapa is home to the University of Veracruz, a world-class museum of anthropology and a handful of beautiful parks and gardens.

Downtown Jalapa is a busy, giddy place; from there the city ripples outward. Take time to kick up and down the cobblestone streets that cling to ravines, cliffs, and even a small extinct volcano. Every avenue offers a magnificent vista of the craggy peaks surrounding the city, and most streets cut through a park at some point.

ORIENTATION

Jalapa lies 104km northwest of Veracruz along Route 140 and 308km east of Mexico City. Trains and first- and second-class buses stop in Jalapa; buses offer the most frequent service and most varied destinations. The train station is at the extreme northeastern edge of the city, a good 40-minute walk or about a 6-peso taxi ride from the center.

The first class ADO and the second class AU bus terminals are both housed at 20 de Noviembre 571, east of the city center. They share a brand-new, state-of-the-art building. Upon arrival, you'll have to fight the urge to spend a few days in the bus station. Not only is it clean and efficient, it seems a sparkling emporium, offering long-distance phone service, baggage check, and a wide selection of food and drink, as well as the requisite complement of eager taxi drivers (4 pesos to the *zócalo*). To catch a bus to the *zócalo* (1 peso), first exit the station complex by descending the long, terraced steps to street level. From there buses marked Centro or, inexplicably, Terminal head downtown.

Jalapa is initially quite confusing. Many streets follow no discernible pattern and change names every few blocks. El Parque Juárez functions as the whole *zócalo* and approximate center of the city. Enriquez, the main east-west thoroughfare, fronts the park on its north side. One block south of Enríquez, Zaragoza runs (roughly) parallel to both of them. Clavijero, at the west of the park, and Revolución, at the east end, ascends north, perpendicular to Enríquez.

Orienting yourself in the park is not difficult. Facing north, the Palacio Munipal will be directly in front of you, across Enríquez. The huge Palacio del Gobierno will be to your right. The Cathedral is just off the northeast corner of the park. Two blocks east of the park, Enríquez splits in two: Zamora continues east while Xalapeños veers up to the northeast.

PRACTICAL INFORMATION

State Tourist Office: Camacho 191 (tel. 8-72-02), a 20min. walk from the *zócalo*. Any yellow minibus heading west on Enríquez will get you there (1 peso). The office will be on your left. Relatively unhelpful. Good maps (5 pesos) and a slew of free brochures. No English spoken. Open Mon.-Fri. 8am-3pm and 6-9pm, Sat. 9am-1pm.

Currency Exchange: None of the banks in downtown Jalapa will exchange traveler's checks. Try the American Express office or the *casa de cambio* at Zamora 36. (Open Mon.-Thurs. 9am-1:30pm and 4-6pm, Fri. 9am-1pm and 4-6pm.)

American Express: Carrillo 28, 3 blocks east of the *zócalo* off Enríquez (tel. 7-41-14). Helpful staff will change money or traveler's checks, but only when the office has the cash. They will also hold mail for card members. (Office open Mon.-Fri. 9am-8pm. Cashier open Mon.-Fri. 9am-2pm and 4-7pm.)

Post Office: In the Palacio Federal, at Zamora and Diego Leño. Open Mon.-Fri. 8am-8pm, Sat. 9am-1pm. Open for Lista de Correos Mon.-Sat. 8am-1pm. Postal code: 91001.

Telephones: Many *casetas* hide in the cafés along Zamora, but the best bet is the southwest corner of the Parque Juárez at Guerrero 9. International collect calls 4 pesos. Open daily 8am-10pm.

Telegrams: Around the corner from the post office at Zamora 70. Open Mon.-Fri. 9am-8pm, Sat. 9am-1pm.

Buses: from CAXA (Central de Autobuses de Xalapa), first class ADO buses run to Puebla (20 pesos, 5am, 6am, 7am, 8am, 10:45am, 12:30pm, 3pm, 7pm, 8:30pm), Mexico City (38.50 pesos, 6am, 7am, 8am, 9am, 10am, 11am, 1pm, 3pm, 7pm, 9:30pm, midnight) and to Veracruz (13.50 pesos, about every 20 min.) From the same terminal, AU buses go to Puebla (17.50 pesos, every hr.), Mexico City (31 pesos, every hr.) and Veracruz (10 pesos, every ½-hr.)

English Language Bookstore: Books-R-Us, Diego Leño 30 (tel. 8-45-40), around the corner and 3 blocks south of the post office. Full selection of American comics and magazines. Also used paperbacks (5 pesos) and current bestsellers (25 pesos). Will trade books as well. Open Mon.-Sat. 10am-2pm, 4-8pm.

Library: Biblioteca de la Ciudad, Juárez 2. Open Mon.-Fri. 8am-10pm, Sat. 8am-9pm, Sun. 8am-8pm.

Market: Revolución at Altamirano, 2 blocks north of the Parque Juárez. Open daily 8am-sunset, but for the freshest, cheapest food in town come at night when the trucks unload their cargo. **Chedraui,** in the mall, Plaza Crystal, on the corner of Independencia and Lázaro Cárdenas. The biggest (and only) supermarket in town. Open daily 8am-9pm.

Laundromat: Lavandería Los Lagos, Diche 25 (tel. 7-93-38), right around the corner from Casa de Artesanías. 3.5kg washed and dried for 14.80 pesos. Open Mon.-Sat. 9am-8pm.

Red Cross: Clavijero 13 (tel. 7-81-58 or 7-34-31), 1 block north of the Parque Juárez. 24-hr. ambulance service.

Pharmacies: Farmacia del Dr. Rancón, on the corner of Saraga and Revolución (tel. 8-09-35). Open 24 hrs. Many other pharmacies nearby on Revolución.

Police: Officially at the Cuartel San José, at the corner of Arteaga and Aldama (tel. 8-18-10), but lots of heavily armed cops hang out at the at the Palacio de Gobierno, across the street from the cathedral.

ACCOMMODATIONS

Jalapa is full of comfortable, economical, and convenient accommodations. On warm nights the mosquitoes may get to you. On cool nights ask for extra blankets. Many budget hotels are conveniently grouped on Revolución, close to the *zócalo*, the parks, and the market.

Hotel Limón, Revolución 8 (tel. 7-22-07). Probably the best deal in the city. Some of the rooms are tiny, but without exception spotlessly clean. The tall courtyard is covered with pretty multicolored tiles, but the turquoise-blue paint lends the interiors an unfortunate swimming-pool feel. Singles 28 pesos. Doubles 32 pesos, with two beds 40 pesos.

Hotel Citlalli, Clavijero 43 (tel. 8-34-58). Plain concrete rooms with dark wood accents. This newly built hotel has all the amenities (TV, *agua purificada*, huge sparkling bathrooms), even if it's a bit short on character. For busy executives, the hotel has four fax lines. Singles 40 pesos. Doubles 55 pesos. Triples 67 pesos.

Hotel Continental, Zamora 4 (tel. 7-35-30). Musty rooms with ancient bathrooms, but a great location and cheap restaurant in hotel's tall inner courtyard. (*Comida corrida* 8 pesos.) Check out 5pm. Singles 30 pesos. Doubles 35 pesos.

FOOD

For those tired of beans and tortillas, Jalapa will provide happy relief; many eateries prepare excellent, imaginative meals at low cost. Particularly inexpensive cuisine can be found in the market and at the many stands around it.

La Sopa, Callejon del Diamante 3-A (tel. 7-80-69). Hip, happening, and filling, this hang-out can't be beat. When it's crowded (as it usually is), join an occupied table and make a friend. First-rate *comida corrida* for 6.50 pesos. Two block east of the *zócalo*, off Enríquez. Open daily 1-5pm, 7pm-midnight.

Restaurant Terraza Jardín, Enríquez, on the Parque Juárez (tel. 8-97-13). Inside it's just a big room with tables; relax there with a newspaper, or grab a space at one of the many outdoor tables to watch the crowds in the park go by. Crazy bronze sculpture entertains on the west wall. Full breakfast of corn flakes, toast, juice, and coffee 6 pesos. Eggs start at 5 pesos. No English. No credit cards. Open Mon.-Sat. 8am-11pm.

Café de la Parroquia, Zaragoza 18, right next door to the Beaterio. Much more casual than its neighbor, but similarly fine fare. Steak and fries 11 pesos. Lemonade with mineral water 2.10 pesos. Open daily 7:30am-10:30pm.

Casona del Beaterio, Zaragoza 20, near the Palacio de Gobierno. Among the best Jalapa has to offer, at great prices. Open courtyard features small bar. As popular for drinks and coffee as for dinner. Entrees 7-30 pesos. The Italian food can be heavy. Crepes are rich and soupy. Visa/MC accepted. Open daily 8am-10pm.

SIGHTS

Jalapa's beautiful, brand-new **Museo de Antropología** (tel. 5-09-20) displays an excellent collection approaching that of the all-encompassing Museo Nacional de Antropología in Mexico City. The museum is extremely well-organized and takes visitors through the ages of ancient civilizations in Mexico, region by region. All exhibits (including maps, timelines and photos) are in Spanish. The museum sits on a large open lawn that makes for excellent sunning on a clear day. (Open Tues.-Sun. 10am-5pm.) Admission 8 pesos. Video camera 35 pesos extra. Wheelchair-accessible and wheelchairs available on-site. To reach the museum from the *zócalo*, walk north on Revolución, turn left at the first busy intersection (Juárez) and follow to Acueducto; the museum is on the left. The walk takes approximately 45 minutes—or catch one of the yellow buses on Enríquez (1 peso), all of which pass the museum. You may choke on exhaust fumes before one of the yellow buses is empty enough to let you on; the surest method is to compromise—walk part-way to escape the *zócalo* crowds and ride the rest. Taxis cost about 4 pesos. Photography buffs will enjoy the **Centro Recreativo Xalapeño,** Xalapeño 31, which houses excellent and diverse exhibits by international artists. (Open Mon.-Sat. 11am-8pm, Sun. 11am-6pm. Free.)

Jalapa's two main public parks merit visits. The **Parque Ecológico Macuitepetl** is essentially a preserve for the flora and fauna indigenous to the Jalapa area. Neat brick paths wind up the side of an extinct volcano through thick vegetation that hides flocks of screeching birds. The summit, the highest point in the area at 1586m above sea level, affords a sublime view. (Open Tues.-Sun. 6am-5pm. Free.) To get to the park, catch one of the buses marked "Mercado/Corona" at the corner of Revolución and Altamirano. Two blocks south of the *zócalo* on Diche lies the second park, the **Paseo de los Lagos,** which consists of a large lake and beautiful lawns and gardens. The **Casa de Artesanías,** at the north end of the lake, is a state-run handicrafts store. (Open Mon.- Sat. 9am-3pm.)

The **zócalo** itself is of some interest to the sightseer. Across Enríquez from the plaza stands the **Palacio de Gobierno,** notable largely for its interesting French design. The Convento de San Francisco once stood on the site of Parque Juárez. It was built in 1534 (three years after the arrival of the *conquistadores*) and razed in 1886. Today the park is a busy spot with terrific views of Jalapa and the surrounding mountains. Also on the *zócalo*, the colonial cathedral contains a body of religious paintings and a huge bronze bell which was shipped from London in 1778.

ENTERTAINMENT

El Ágora de la Ciudad, beneath the Parque Juárez downtown (enter through the stairwell in the southwest corner of the park), serves as the city's cultural center. Its theater shows many foreign films; paintings and sculptures fill the corridors. A sophisticated crowd mills about. Fine books and musical recordings for sale. (Open daily 8:30am-9pm.) **El Teatro del Estado,** at Ignacio de la Llave and Rubén Bouchez (tel. 7-31-10), holds enticing performances—the Orquesta Sinfónica de Jalapa and the Ballet Folklórico de la Universidad Veracruzana appear regularly. The tourist office has posters for some events; contact the theater directly for schedules and ticket prices. From the *zócalo*, walk left on Enríquez and then left on Llave.

Jalapa also boasts a few moderately busy discos, including **Ya'x** at the **Plaza Crystal** (tel. 5-65-00) on the corner of Lázaro Cardenas. (Open daily from 10pm; 15 peso cover Sat. and Sun. nights only.) **Mama Mia** has live rock 'n roll, jazz, and other species of music on Wednesdays and Thursdays; look for prominently posted notices in town.

■■■ VERACRUZ

Upon reaching the east coast of New Spain in 1519, Hernán Cortés constructed a base from which he would launch one of the most effective military episodes in history. After the Spanish Conquest, his coastal headquarters grew into Veracruz, the principal city and main port in the state.

An English fleet took a Spanish beating here in 1567, but, unfortunately for the Spanish, Sir Francis Drake was among the few who escaped. Then, in 1683, 600 pirates, rowdy and French, held and looted the city. During the "Pastry War," President Santa Anna fled Veracruz but would soon return to expel the French invaders. Winfield Scott's 10,000 American troops took the city in 1847 after a week-long siege. Napoleon III had designs on all of Mexico, and used Veracruz as his toe-hold, installing Maximilian as ruler in 1864. Veracruz saw more action in the Revolution of 1910 and again in 1914, when American troops returned, this time to keep German guns from reaching Victoriano Huerta, the conservative dictator.

The crumbling fortresses along the coast bear witness to the extensive destruction, but these days their seaward-pointed cannon see no action save what the beachside revelers provide.

Music and dancing are higher priorities in Veracruz than in other Mexican cities. The number of marimba bands squeezed into the *zócalo* boggles the mind, and many restaurants and bars feature nightly music. In the evening, brassy military and civic bands blare through the plaza as the flag of the Republic is lowered. After the sun sets, the volume of the marimba bands and soulful crooners is elevated even further still.

As Mexico's major port on the Gulf Coast, Veracruz hosts sailors and merchants from around the world. A strong Caribbean accent lilts in the speech of some of the locals, while others have a European inflection, and any number of regional Mexican accents will test the limits of your Spanish. Other cultures influence not just the city's voices but also its architecture, a graceful hybrid of the colonial and the modern. Although Veracruz offers a few standard tourist sights, the *zócalo* remains the biggest draw. Here, wandering vendors sell everything: t-shirts bearing random English slogans, mass-produced handicrafts, and even your name written on a grain of sand. Veracruz is quite popular with vacationing Mexicans; it is a busy port town, almost devoid of peace and quiet. Come here to dance and drink deep of a somewhat debauched marrow.

ORIENTATION

Veracruz lies on the southwestern shore of the Gulf of Mexico. Tampico is 421km to the north via Route 180; Jalapa, the state capital, sits 140km inland via Route 140; Puebla and Mexico City are due west on Route 150, 304km and 421km respectively; and Oaxaca is 421km to the south.

Veracruz's **Central de Autobuses** houses both the first- and second-class bus stations. First-class ADO lies directly on Díaz Mirón, the city's major cross-town street. Second-class AU opens onto La Fragua, one block to the east. About 14 blocks north of the Central de Autobuses (to the right when leaving the building) the *Parque Zamora* interrupts Mirón. Seven blocks on Independencia beyond the park, buildings give way to the *zócalo*. Buses labeled "Díaz Mirón" travel along Díaz Mirón to *Parque Zamora* and points farther downtown (.70 pesos). Taxis will take you downtown for 5 pesos.

The **train station** is at the north end of the Pl. de la República. To reach the *zócalo* from the station, turn right from the exit, walk diagonally across the plaza and turn right on Lerdo at the far end of the plaza; the *zócalo* is one block ahead. Taxis from the Central de Autobuses to the train station cost about 6 pesos. The city's **airport** is 4km south of town on Route 150. Taxis to the *zócalo* cost about 35 pesos.

Downtown Veracruz is laid out grid-style with streets either parallel or perpendicular to the coast. **Díaz Mirón** runs north-south and converges with **Avenida 20 de Noviembre** south of downtown at the **Parque Zamora.** Here, the two streets become **Independencia,** the main downtown drag.

Independencia forms the western boundary of the **zócalo,** also called the **Plaza de Armas** or **Plaza de la Constitución.** The northern boundary, **Lerdo,** runs east and becomes the southern limit of the **Plaza de la República,** home of the train station and post office, and drop-off point for many municipal bus routes. **Insurgentes,** one block south of the *zócalo* behind the cathedral, runs east into **Camacho;** the two streets serve as Veracruz's waterfront promenade.

Women may find themselves the object of more male attention in Veracruz than in smaller towns. The attention usually amounts to no more than invitations to discos and city tours from waiters, bank tellers, and random men on the street. Women may want to exercise caution when going out at night, however—a firm and polite refusal will be grudgingly accepted during the day, but at night it may well be taken as a challenge to overcome.

PRACTICAL INFORMATION

Most services are conveniently located downtown, either near the *zócalo*, on Independencia, or in the Pl. de la República.

Tourist Office: Dirección de Turismo. In the Palacio Municipal (tel. 32-19-99), on the *zócalo*. Helpful staff speaks some English and distributes reams of excellent maps and pamphlets. The photocopied map of downtown is especially useful. Open daily 9am-9pm.

U.S. Consulate: Víctimas del 25 Junio 388 (tel. 31-01-42). On the corner with Gómez Farias, several blocks south of the *zócalo*. Open Mon.-Fri. 9am-1:30pm.

The addresses and phone numbers of several other consulates in Veracruz are readily available at the tourist office.

Currency Exchange: Bancomer and **Bánamex** both have branches at the intersection of Independencia and Juárez, one block from the *zócalo*. **Bancomer** (tel. 31-07-07) is open for exchange Mon.-Fri. 9:30am-1:30pm. **Bánamex** (tel. 36-05-80) is open for exchange Mon.-Fri. 9am-1pm, and also has an automated teller that accepts Cirrus, MC, and Visa. **La Amistad Casa de Cambio,** Juárez 112 (tel. 31-24-50), just east of Independencia, offers slightly lower rates but is open Mon.-Fri. 9am-5pm. Front desks of the big hotels will change cash all hours, but it is difficult to impossible to change traveler's checks on weekends.

American Express, Camacho 222 (tel. 31-45-77), across from Villa del Mar beach. Catch the "Villa del Mar" bus from the corner of Serdán and Zaragoza; office is on the right—their blue and white sign is clearly visible. They won't cash traveler's checks, but will hold client mail. Open Mon.-Fri. 9am-1pm and 4-6pm, Sat. 9am-noon.

Post Office: Pl. de la República 213 (tel.32-20-38), several blocks north of the *zócalo*. Facing the Palacio Municipal, walk east on Lerdo for 2 blocks to Aduana, turn left and walk 2 blocks to Pl. de la República; it's the large white colonnaded building on the right. Open for stamps and *Lista de Correos* Mon.-Fri. 8am-8pm, Sat. 9am-1pm. **Postal code:** 91700.

Telephones: Long distance *caseta* at 5 de Mayo 1243, in between Molina and Serdán. Surcharge for collect calls is a whopping 20 pesos. Open Mon.-Sat. 9am-8pm, Sun. 9am-1pm. **Telephone code:** 29.

Telegrams: (tel. 32-25-08) on the Pl. de la República next to the post office. Open for telegrams Mon.-Fri. 9am-5pm, Sat. 9am-noon. For money orders Mon.-Fri. 9am-5pm, Sat 9am-noon.

Airport: (tel. 34-00-08) on the highway to Mexico City, 4km south of downtown Veracruz. Both **Aeroméxico** and **Mexicana** are represented by **Viajes Carmi,** Independencia 837 (tel. 31-27-23), north of the *zócalo*. Open Mon.-Fri. 9am-1pm and 3:30-7:30pm, Sat. 9am-1pm. **Mexicana** also has a separate office at the corner of 5 de Mayo and Serdán, north-east of the *zócalo* (tel. 32-22-42). Open Mon.-Fri. 9am-1:30pm and 3:45pm-7:30pm. Office at the airport (tel. 38-00-08). Open Mon.-Fri. 6am-11pm. 4 flights per day to Mexico City (50min., .30 pesos).

Train Station: Ferrocarriles Nacionales de México (tel. 32-25-69), on the Pl. de la República in a large, white bldg. near the water at the northern extreme of the plaza. Baggage check available. (Open 7am-noon and 6-9:30pm. 3 pesos per suitcase per day.) Slow, cheap trains leave for Mexico City and Jalapa every morning. Buy tickets the same day as the train. Ticket office opens at 6am.

Bus Station: Díaz Mirón 1698 (tel. 37-57-49), about 20 blocks south of the *zócalo*. **ADO** 1st class to: Mexico City (51.50 pesos, 1am, 6am., 4pm), to Jalapa (13.50 pesos, about every half hour), to Puebla (37 pesos 6:15am, 8:15am, 10:15am, 11:30am, 1:30pm, 3:15pm, 6pm, 11:30pm), to Santiago Tuxtla (14.50 pesos, aprox. every half hour), to José Cardel (5 pesos, about every half hour). 2nd class **AU** terminal sits behind the ADO terminal on La Fragua, 1 block east of Díaz Mirón.

Taxis: Taxis Por Teléfono de Veracruz (tel. 34-62-99) will send you a taxi at a slightly higher price than if you flag one down yourself. Veracruz is divided into zones, with set fares for taxi travel between the zones, which should be posted in the taxi. Fares outside these zones are negotiable.

Car Rentals: Fast Auto Rental, Lerdo 241 (tel. 31-83-29), between 5 de Mayo and Independencia. Open Mon.-Sat. 9am-2pm and 4-7pm, Sun. 9-11am. Small VWs for 137.50 pesos (includes insurance) plus .83 pesos per km. **Jomar,** in the Hotel Colonial (tel. 31-63-79). Small VWs for 80 pesos per day plus 35 pesos insurance and .605 pesos per km. Open Mon.-Sat. 9am-9pm, Sun. 9am-2pm.

Supermarket: Chedraui, Díaz Mirón 440 (tel. 31-42-75), 4 blocks south of *Parque Zamora* on the way to the ADO station. Open 8am-9pm.

Laundromat: Lavandería Automática Mar y Sol, Madero 572, between Arista and Serdán. 3kg washed and dried for 12 pesos for same day service, 9.70 pesos for next day pick-up. Open Mon.-Fri. 9am-2pm and 4-8pm, Sat. 9am-5pm.

Red Cross: On Díaz Mirón between Orizaba and L. Abascal (tel. 37-55-00) , 1 block south of the Central de Autobuses. No English spoken. 24-hr. emergency service and ambulance on call.

Pharmacy: Farmacias El Mercado, Independencia 1197 (tel. 32-08-83), next to the Gran Café de la Parroquia. Open daily 7am-2am.

Police: On Allende between Cortés and Canal (tel. 32-37-61 or 32-28-33). From the *zócalo*, walk (with the Palacio Municipal behind you) 7 blocks on Zamora and turn left on Allende for 5½ blocks. Little English spoken. Open 24 hrs.

ACCOMMODATIONS

Veracruz is full of hotels. You're looking for a ceiling fan or at least a big window. Many hotels offer air-conditioned rooms. If you're going to be in town anytime around the Carnaval (see Entertainment) book ahead or arrive early, as the city is jam-packed. Otherwise, reservations are unnecessary.

Downtown Area

These hotels are either on the *zócalo* or around the corner to the northeast, on Morelos.

Hotel Sevilla, Morelos 359 (tel. 32-42-46), on Pl. de la República. Just around the corner from the *zócalo*. Rooms to be happy in—high ceilings, color TV, clean bathrooms and quiet ceiling fans. Ask for a corner room to get a cross breeze (and cross-marimba). Singles 50 pesos. Doubles 60 pesos. Triples 70 pesos.

Casa de Huéspedes La Tabasqueña, Morelos 325 (no telephone) 100m north of Hotel Sevilla, this small operation rents cozy rooms, some with no windows, all with working fans and thin walls. Singles 30 pesos. Doubles 45 pesos.

Hotel Concha Dorada, Lerdo 77 (tel. 31-29-96), on the *zócalo*. Hey, Man! Groovy '70s spreads! 100% poly, right? Nice rooms. Dreary hallways. Terrifying elevator. Notable primarily for its air-conditioning and prime (read: musical revellers yards from your pillow) location. Many singles have no A.C., making them of questionable value. Singles 60 pesos. Doubles 100 pesos.

Parque Zamora and Bus Station

Hotel Avenida, Uribe 1300 (tel. 32-44-92), at Mirón, about halfway between *Parque Zamora* and the bus stations. These rooms lose their sunlight-enhanced charm at night. Clean and neat. Location fairly inconvenient, despite proximity to Díaz Mirón. Singles 30 pesos. Doubles 40 pesos. Triples 50 pesos.

Hotel Acapulco, Uribe 1327 (tel. 31-88-97), down the street from Hotel Avenida. Slightly more expensive and slightly nicer than its neighbor. Clean, functional. Singles 39 pesos. Doubles 48 pesos. Anytime the city is crowded prices rise to Singles 60 pesos. Doubles 75 pesos.

Hotel Central, Díaz Mirón 1612 (tel. 32-22-22), next to the ADO station. Large, modern building with marble lobby and leatherette easy chairs. Rooms and bathrooms likewise: modern and sanitary. Watch cars race by on Díaz Mirón from rooms with a balcony. All rooms have fans, phones; most have a TV. Singles 50 pesos. Doubles 70 pesos, with 2 beds 90 pesos.

Hotel Rosa Mar, La Fragua 1100 (tel. 37-07-47), behind the ADO station and across the street from AU station. The location is nothing to holler about unless you're just passing through Veracruz, in which case it's very convenient. Small, but spotlessly clean, swimming-pool green rooms. Communal TV in lobby. Singles 35 pesos. Doubles 55 pesos.

FOOD

It's that coastal thing—all the menus in Veracruz are stuffed with seafood. Shrimp, octopus, *dorada*, red snapper, and a host of other sea beasts are hauled in daily from the Gulf. The cheapest way to enjoy these delicacies is to head for the **fish market** on Landero y Coss between Arista and Zaragoza. A healthy portion of *ceviche*, the regional specialty, runs about 3.50 pesos. Other local favorites include *paella* (whatever happens to be on hand, mixed with saffron rice) and fish served *a la veracruzano* (in an olive, onion, tomato and caper sauce). The greatest concentrations of restaurants are on and around the *zócalo* and in the area east of Zaragoza. Cheaper *antojitos* and *torta* restaurants are located further south of the *zócalo*.

Gran Café de la Parroquia, Independencia 105, on the southwest corner of the *zócalo*. Drink its famous *café con leche*, in a large open hall filled with the sound of clinking glasses (the preferred method of getting more hot milk for your coffee). *Marimba* bands serenade the patrons from the outside. Large coffee 3 pesos. Big plate of papaya 3 pesos. Open daily 6am-1am. Less crowded with consequently better and friendlier service at the 2nd location, Insurgentes at 16 de Septiembre. Open daily 8am-2am.

Cocina Veracruz, on the corner of Madero and Zamora. A pearl of a place. Escape the inflated prices of the *zócalo* and the waterfront. Great food and a fully local crowd. Soup with vegetables 2 pesos. Delicious *comida corrida* 4.50 pesos. Eggs to taste 3.50 pesos. Newsprint for napkins. Open daily 7am-11pm.

Pizzería Piro Piro Da Antonio, Arista 692 (tel. 31-61-44), between Independencia and Zaragoza. Excellent pizza with thick floury crust and hundreds of pictures of Italy all over the walls. Also pasta and beer by the yard. (Very) small cheese pizza 10 pesos. Large cheese pizza 36 pesos.Open daily 9am-1am. Buffet served 11am-5pm.

El Tiburón, Landero y Coss 167 (tel. 31-47-40), at Serdán. Lots of tables with mess-proof vinyl tablecloths in a big room clearly devoted to the art of eating without distractions. Filet of fish and salad 16 pesos. Most meat dishes under 23 pesos. Open daily 6am-7pm.

SIGHTS

Most of the spiritual energy in Veracruz concentrates on the *zócalo*, and the most energy you must expend here to stay entertained involves moving from café to café around the plaza. A colonial cathedral takes up the south side of the *zócalo*, and under its high-domed mosaic ceiling, the clinking of glasses at the nearby *Parroquia* is barely audible.

For one take on the city's history, visit the **Museo Histórico de la Revolución Carranza** by a small park near the waterfront, on Insurgentes between Hernández and Xicoléncatl. The museum, also called Museo Constitucionalista, is upstairs and to the left in a yellow colonial lighthouse which also houses offices of the Mexican Navy. When entering the building, do not approach the armed sailor at the door. Stay to your right, and polite Navy personnel will direct you upstairs. One room contains Carranza's bed, desk and furniture, replicating the room in which ideas for reform laws and the Constitution germinated and grew. Another room traces Carranza's life from baptism to his term as governor of Coahuila state. A third room marks his presidency and participation in writing the Constitution of 1917, three years before his death. The sailor at the museum's front desk can provide you with a written guide explaining (in English) many of the exhibits. (Open Tues.-Sun. 9am-1pm and 4-6pm. Free.) For a deeper glimpse into the past, visit the **Baluarte de Santiago,** on 16 de Septiembre between Canal and Rayón. This 17th-century bulwark protected inhabitants from swashbuckling pirates like Francis Drake. It is the last fort still standing along the old city wall. The tiny museum inside the fort displays a beautiful collection of pre-Hispanic gold ornaments. (Museum open Tues.-Sun. 10am-4:30pm.)

The **Museo Cultural de la Ciudad,** Zaragoza 397 (tel. 31-84-10) at Morales, is a funky museum set in an old orphanage. Check out the displays of Latin American and African anthropology, photos of the city, and scenes from daily life. (Open Mon.-Sat. 9am-4pm. Admission 3 pesos.)

Around the corner from the Museo Cultural de la Ciudad lurks the **Instituto Veracruzano de Cultura** (IVEC), ensconced in a huge purple building on the corner of Canal and Zaragoza (tel. 31-69-67). Temporary exhibits feature work from accomplished art students throughout Mexico. (Open Mon.-Fri. 9am-9pm, Sat. 9am-7pm, Sun. 10am-noon. Free.)

El Castillo de San Juan de Ulúa, begun in 1582, is another reminder of the city's former military importance. There isn't much to see inside the fort, but its architecture is intriguing, and the view across the harbor to the city is superb. To reach the fort, take the bus of the same name (.70 pesos) from the east side of the Pl. de la República, in front of the Aduana building. (Open Tues.-Sun. 9am-5pm (no one admitted after 4:30). Admission 13 pesos. Free Sun.)

Once upon a time, bathing was possible directly off the golden shores of the city. Today, however, the bay is a case study of the toxic impact of big oil on big cities. Locals still swim in the water, but, considering the health risk, the short trip south to **Playa Villa del Mar** is a better idea. The beach is fairly clean and reasonably uncrowded. Restaurants, juice-bars, and some expensive hotels line **Blvd. Camacho** across the street from the beach. Playa Villa del Mar is a fairly pleasant hour-long walk from the *zócalo* along the waterfront, or catch one of the frequent buses from the corner of Serdán and Zaragoza (.90 pesos for the big rickety buses, 1.20 pesos for the smaller, more modern vans; both have either "Villa del Mar" or "Boca del Mar" plainly visible on the front). Beyond **Villa del Mar, Boca del Río, Antón,** and **Linzaro** offer increasingly acceptable swimming conditions. The brand-new aquarium, billed as the largest in Latin America can be reached on the bus; ask to be let off at *El Acuario* or *Playón de Hornas.*

ENTERTAINMENT

The city's best entertainment is free in the *zócalo*, at least in December and in the summer months when musicians, dancers and clowns entertain every night except Monday. Performances begin at 8pm, but the audience begins to gather at 7pm.

Discotheque La Capilla, Independencia 1064, in the Hotel Prendes between Lerdo and Juárez, plays top-40 spiced with some local *mariachi* pieces. (Open Thurs.-Sat. 10pm-3:30am. There is no cover per se, but a 20 peso drink minimum instead.) The **Disco Morruchos,** in the Hotel Emporio at Insurgentes and Xicoléncatl on the water (tel. 31-38-20), is a bit more chic but plays the same tunes. (Open Thurs.-Sat. 11pm-4am. Cover 10 pesos.) The hippest disco is also the most expensive: **Ocean,** Ruiz Cortines y Callo 8 (tel. 37-63-27), in Playa del Mar charges a 40 peso cover. Cough up the pesos and boogy amidst elaborate fountains, pulsing lights, and lush greenery.

Bars are ubiquitous in Veracruz. The entire north side of the *zócalo* is a series of indistinguishable bars serenaded by *marimba* bands and solicited by Chiclets-pushers (beers 4 pesos). For cheaper, tuneless fare, try one of the many indoor bars located on and near Landero y Coss, east of the *zócalo*.

If a dark, cold room full of strangers suddenly appeals to you, Veracruz has several **cinemas.** For English language films, check out **Plaza Cinema,** Arista 708, next to Pizzería Piro Piro Da Antonio (tel. 31-37-87). At Díaz Mirón 941, between Iturbide and Mina, is **Cinema Gemelos Veracruz** (tel. 32-59-70). Admission for all cinemas 8 pesos.

Billares Maupome, at the intersection of Landero y Coss and Serdán, charges 8 pesos per hour for one of their ten well-maintained pool tables. If you ask nicely, they'll even tune the TV set to cable-delivered CNN (Open daily 9am-midnight.)

Veracruz's **Carnaval**—a nationally renowned, week-long festival of parades, concerts and costumes—takes place in late February or early March (during the week before Ash Wednesday). For further information on *Carnaval*, contact the offices of the organizers, in the Palacio Municipal on the *zócalo* (tel. 36-10-88, ext. 149 or 32-99-62), right next door to the tourist office. (Open Mon.-Fri. 10am-2pm and 6:30-8:30pm.) Make reservations early.

■ Near Veracruz: Zempoala Ruins and José Cardel

One of the most impressive archaeological sites in the state of Veracruz, the ruins at Zempoala (or just as often, Cempoala) lie 40 kilometers north of Veracruz, just off Route 180. Buses from Veracruz run frequently to nearby José Cardel, making the ruins an easy and edifying excursion.

Zempoala was one of the largest southern Totonac cities, part of a federation that covered much of Veracruz in pre-Hispanic times. In 1469, Zempoala was subdued by the Aztecs and reluctantly joined their federation. Thus, when Cortés arrived in 1519, the Totonacs and their chief, Chicomacatl (famous, primarily, for having been enormously fat), welcomed the Spaniard and lent him soldiers for his campaign against Moctezuma at Tenochtitlan in 1521. It was at Zempoala that Cortés defeated (and imprisoned) Panfilo de Narváez, who had been sent by Diego de Velázquez, the governor of Cuba, to teach the cocky *conquistador* some respect for his higher-ups.

To reach Zempoala from Veracruz, you must first take a bus to José Cardel; a trip of 45 minutes. From its Central on Díaz Mirón, ADO runs first-class buses to José Cardel (about every half hour, 5.50 pesos). From the second-class bus station on La Fragua, Autotransportes Teziutecos makes the same trip (every 10 minutes, 5am-9:30pm. 2.60 pesos). In José Cardel, ADO buses stop on Independencia, two blocks from the southeast corder of the *zócalo*. The second-class bus station lives on the south side of the *zócalo*.

To reach Zempoala from José Cardel, catch a *colectivo* (1 peso) one block east and one block north of the northeast corner of the *zócalo*, ask the driver to let you out at *las ruinas*. The trip takes about 10 minutes. In Zempoala, you will be dropped off at the intersection of Av. Prof. José Ruiz and Av. Fco. del Paso y Troncoso Norte. Walk 100m on Fco. del Paso y Troncoso Norte, where a small ticket booth marks the entrance to the site. If driving from Verazcruz, follow Route 180 past the city of José Cardel until you come to the Zempoala city turn-off. Follow it until a half-hidden sign for the ruins appears on the right (about 1km before town; the sign has a Coca Cola insignia on top and "Sitio Arqueológico" on the bottom). A microscopic museum, to your left as you enter, displays a small collection of pottery and figurines unearthed here, and sells a much-needed English mini-guide to the ruins (3 pesos).

The large structure at the north end of the site is the Main Temple, with a wide staircase ascending its front. Just south and to the right of the Main Temple is a structure known as Las Chimeneas, wherein was found a Mayan-like clay figure. In front of the Main Temple and Las Chimeneas are two somewhat mysterious "Round Structures."

The Great Pyramid, probably a monument to the Sun God, and the smaller Temple of the Wind God are at the western boundary of the site, off to your left (beyond the museum) as you enter. (Site open daily 9am-6pm, 10 pesos. Free for students and teachers with I.D. Free Sun.) catch a *colectivo* back to José Cardel across the street from where you were dropped off. If you can't stand the heat, get out of the kitchen or catch a cab (about 20 pesos back to José Cardel). Buses run all afternoon and into the evening.

Because of Cardel's proximity to Veracruz, there is really no reason to stay the night. Should the need arise, however, **José Cardel** has all the amenities. Most services cluster either around the *zócalo* or by the first class ADO bus station. On the southeast corner of the *zócalo*, **Farmacia Santiago** (2-04-31) is open daily from 7am-10pm. Across the street is **Supermarket Mi Super** (Open Mon-Sat. 7am-8pm. Sun. 7am-2pm.) The **police** station (2-03-52) is in the Palacio Municipal, on the north side of the *zócalo*. The **Red Cross** (tel. 2-02-26. 24 hr. ambulance service) is four blocks west of the *zócalo* on Emiliano Zapata, the street leading into town from Route 180. **Bancomer,** on the south side of the *zócalo*, is open for exchange Mon.-

Fri. 9am-noon. Small **restaurants,** *refresco* stands and a movie theater round out the *zócalo*. **Hotel Plaza** (tel. 2-02-88) sits across from the ADO bus station and offers huge, frilly, pastel rooms, each with A/C and color TV. (Singles 50 pesos, doubles 70 pesos.) The restaurant in the lobby is open daily 7am-11pm.

SOUTHERN VERACRUZ

The polluted ports of Coatzacoalcos and Veracruz flank the most enticing stretch of Mexico's Gulf Coast. The verdant, rolling volcanic hills beckon to visitors in vain—the area remains virtually untouristed (and cool) even in summer. Only Laguna Catemaco draws a heavy (domestic) crowd to its shores in season. Catemaco monopolizes the area's fun-in-the-sun business because of its proximity both to fine beaches on the lake and to some of Mexico's best Gulf Coast beaches. Nearby San Andrés Tuxtla, the region's largest city and unofficial capital, offers a healthy range of hotels and restaurants and swanky Mexican cigars. San Andrés also has excellent bus connections to Catemaco, Santiago Tuxtla, the Tres Zapotes ruin site and larger cities such as Veracruz and Mexico City. Horseback riding and hiking are popular outside San Andrés. In Santiago Tuxtla, the only other town of note in the Dos Tuxtlas, life is even slower than in Catemaco. With only two hotels and a small museum, the fastest moves in town are made at the *zócalo*'s foosball tables.

Route 180 is the main artery of the Dos Tuxtlas area. From Acayucán in the south, it passes north to Catemaco, San Andrés and Santiago Tuxtla before continuing along the coast to Veracruz. All sights outside these three cities lie on secondary dirt roads served by local buses.

■■■ CATEMACO

Catemaco rests beside a large lake on the green volcanic slopes of the Tuxtlas range. The town is tremendously popular with Mexican tourists during *Semana Santa*, Christmas and the summer holidays. On the first Friday in March, Catemaco hosts an annual gathering of shaman, medicine men, and witches from all over Mexico—hence the profusion of *brujos* (sorcerers) in business establishment names. For disbelievers, swimming and scenic lake-isles, bars and dance clubs, suffice to entertain.

Practical Information Although Catemaco lies along Route 180, few first class **ADO buses** stop here on journeys north or south to major cities; you usually have to change in San Andrés and catch another bus to Catemaco. Buses run frequently from Catemaco to major cities like Mexico, Veracruz and Jalapa, as well as to San Andrés Tuxtla and Santiago Tuxtla. Streets in Catemaco are poorly marked, but the basilica on the *zócalo* is usually visible. **Carranza** runs along the west side of the *zócalo*, while **Aldama** runs parallel on the east side (closer to the lake). They are both unlabeled, but between the *zócalo*, with its landmark basilica, and the road that follows the lake (called either Playa or Malecón), it's difficult to lose your way. The entire town can be covered on foot in 10 minutes, and all services crowd around the *zócalo*. The **ADO** station sits on Aldama north of the *zócalo*, one block behind the basilica. **Autotransportes Los Tuxtlas** stops two blocks south of the *zócalo*, on Cuahtemoc, which runs parallel to, and one block north of, Aldama.

Las Brisas Hotel, Carranza 3 (tel. 3-00-57), provides **tourist information.** Sr. Moreno is the official "State Tourist Coordinator" for Catemaco and the coastal areas. He speaks no English but will gladly show you a map of the region. **Multibanco Comermex** (tel. 3-01-15), on the *zócalo* exchanges traveler's checks only Mon.-Fri. 10am-noon. **Post office,** Mantilla, in between the lake and Hotel Los Arcos. (Open Mon.-Fri. 9am-1pm and 3-6pm, Sat. 9am-1pm. Usually open all afternoon, contrary to official hours. **Postal Code:** 95870.) Official **telephone** *caseta* does not allow